FEB 1 0 1998

DISCARI

D1417591

THE
BROWN BOOK
OF BRASS LOCOMOTIVES

THE
BROWN BOOK
OF BRASS LOCOMOTIVES
THIRD EDITION

JOHN GLAAB

CHILTON BOOK COMPANY
Radnor, Pennsylvania

PHOTO CREDITS

All photographs in this book are by Carl Neustrand, except as noted beow.

Photos by Gregory E. Dixon: page 29, 32, 34, 42, 43, 72 (bottom), 84 (both), 88 (bottom), 94, 106 (top), 108 (top), 117 (both), 122, 124 (both), 125, 128, 134, 144, 145, 153, 154 (top), 183, 198, 211, 221 (bottom)

Photos by Kenneth Prince: pages 49, 66 (top)

Photos by Ron Salwasser: page 39 (top)

Photos by G. T. Darwin: pages 93, 96 (bottom)

Photos by OMI/Mardan Photos: pages 131, 148–152, 165, 182, 188, 194, 200, 201 (bottom), 204, 209, 210, 218 (top), 223

Photos by Key Imports: pages 133, 170, 177

Photo by Pacific Fast Mail: page 139

Photos by MTS Imports: pages 236 (bottom), 237, 238

Copyright © 1994 by John Glaab
Copyright © 1982, 1980 by R. A. Brown
Third Edition All Rights Reserved

Published in Radnor, Pennsylvania 19089, by Chilton Book Company

Designed by Anthony Jacobson
Manufactured in the United States of America

Library of Congress Cataloging in Publication Data

Glaab, John.
    The Brown book of brass locomotives / John Glaab. — 3rd ed.
        p.   cm.
    Includes bibliographical references and index.
    ISBN 0-8019-8395-9
    1. Locomotives—Models. I. Title.
TJ630.G58   1994
625.1'9'075—dc20   92-54706
                                                         CIP

1 2 3 4 5 6 7 8 9 0   3 2 1 9 8 7 6 5 4

Contents

Preface

Collecting brass model trains is a fairly recent hobby, compared to the traditional collecting hobbies such as stamps, coins, and books. It probably began with the American GIs stationed in Japan after World War II who had craftsmen on the Ginza build brass models from drawings and pictures published in the American modeling magazines. However, mass-produced models were not imported into this country until the 1950s, and these models were really not intended to be collector's items. Rather, they were priced to appeal to the average model railroader who wanted something with better details than the available die-cast models.

As time passed, the Japanese builders became proficient in producing models that pushed the state of the art in detail and performance. This began to attract a new class of modeler who was more concerned with accuracy and detail. The hobby of collecting brass models began to emerge in an organized fashion.

Today a vast array of brass models are available from several importers and manufacturers. A collector now has the ability to tailor his or her collection to a specific railroad, period of history, type of locomotive, or even to find an accurate model of the locomotive his or her father or grandfather worked on.

Acknowledgments

Christine Glaab, my wife, who organized the diesel section, constructed the bibliography, and persevered through weekends and evenings when I was submerged in the database.

Barbara Anoskey, my mother-in-law, who proofed *everything* and brought order to the notes.

Tom Marsh, Overland Models, for providing virtually unlimited access to production data and photos.

Joel Lovitch and Andy DePuzzo, MTS Imports, for suggesting that the traction section be broken into four parts—electric locos, MU & Subway, Interurban, and City Cars—and for reviewing all of the traction data for accuracy.

Fred Hill, Original Whistle Stop, Pasadena, Ca., for reviewing all of the prices and data.

Deane Mellander, for reviewing the entire manuscript and correcting my errors of style and pricing of the EBT equipment.

Brian Sappington, for providing expert notes on PFM ''Crowns,'' Limited Production Models, and handbuilts.

Gerry Zogaric, for editing the Logging and Geared sections and providing data on some of the earliest handbuilts.

Dave DaVita, Key Imports, for providing photos and production data on models imported by Key.

Bob Hess, for reviewing the pricing and production data for errors.

Mort Mann, Sunset Models, for providing production data and dates on models imported by Sunset.

Jack LaRussa, NJ International, for addressing the subject of PFM ''Crowns'' in a logical manner and convincing me that ''it isn't a 'Crown' unless PFM said it is.'' Also special thanks for creating *Brass Modeler and Collector,* a magazine that provided invaluable data on early importers and builders.

Dave Simon, Nickel Plate Products, for providing production data on his models.

Howard Zane, Great Scale Train Show, Timonium, Md., for allowing me to photograph many models from his excellent collection.

Tom Evans, for proofing the Pennsy section and correcting several omissions.

Dr. Arnold Herskovic, for allowing me to photograph his excellent collection of HO-scale steam locomotives.

Introduction

Early brass models were very crude by comparison with today's models. Turnings and stampings were used, instead of the now more familiar lost-wax castings and photo etchings. Motors and drive mechanisms often failed to operate satisfactorily. Even some of the most expensive models of this time incorporated drives that were very noisy.

But the Japanese builders were constantly looking to improve their product. The availability of better photos, drawings, and other data combined with the use of American-made lost-wax castings, initiated an era of models that displayed excellent accuracy and craftsmanship. Mechanisms were improved, but still incorporated open-frame motors and gearboxes that were less than precise. By the mid-60s, the Japanese models had reached a point where a model could be taken out of the box, lubricated, couplers installed, and set to run on the layout. The models were truly ready-to-run. And run they did, reliably and consistently.

With the Japanese economy steadily improving against the American dollar, it was inevitable that the Japanese models would increase in price. In some cases the increase in price was over 50% in one year. This fact, combined with the Japanese desire to continue to rerun the same prototype again and again caused sales to fall. Importers began looking for other builders, and inevitably other countries, where brass models could be made.

It is fairly certain that the Japanese were involved in educating the Koreans and may have purchased subassemblies from Korea that were incorporated into Japanese models. However, as the Korean builders became more proficient, it was inevitable that they would want to build entire models for export. Northwest Shortline was the first American company to begin importing Korean brass models. As might be expected, the Koreans didn't begin by building locomotives. They started with simpler projects—freight cars, cabooses, simple line side structures (signal bridges, water tanks, etc.), but as time passed the Koreans acquired the skills to start building steam locomotives.

The early attempts of these builders were fraught with problems. Soldering and assembly skills were still being learned and quite frequently models couldn't be removed from the box without some small detail part falling off. Models exhibited erratic running qualities. One model would run superbly while another from the same lot wouldn't run at all. Entire runs of models were made with motors wired backwards, or with gearboxes that disintegrated in 4-5 hours, or even worse with dimensional or technical flaws that ruined the appearance and accuracy of the model. If this sounds like harsh criticism of the Korean builders, it isn't intended to be so. Considering the cultural, language, and distance barriers, the Koreans did a remarkable job of learning what was needed to successfully build a saleable brass model.

The Koreans had two favorable things going for them—price and variety. While the Japanese were pursuing the European and Japanese markets with the more expensive models, the Koreans chose to produce fairly large runs (up to 1,000 pieces) and hold the price down. Combined with this was the willingness of the Korean builders to quickly build a wide variety of models that had never before been produced. Whereas the Japanese were willing to produce a generic model that represented a particular class of locomotive, the Koreans would often produce several versions of the prototype representing specific locomotives.

This production philosophy prevailed for a few years but began to falter as the market became flooded with Korean models. It was exacerbated by different importers simultaneously producing exactly the same model. Several of the smaller Korean builders ceased to exist while a few prevailed to capture the bulk of the market. These survivors were innovative and aggressive. Factory painted models became the norm rather than the exception. Motors and gearboxes reached a degree of perfection undreamed of in the 60s and specialized lost-wax castings were being used that displayed a new level of detail.

A Brief History of *The Brown Book*

While all of this was going on, there was little or no information available to the collector about current prices, dates of manufacture, quantities produced, availability, and so on. In 1980 Ray Brown authored the first edition of *The Brown Book* and set forth to clarify some of these questions. For the first time, the hobby of collecting brass model trains was treated to a rigorous and organized tabulation of data that would be very useful to the collector. The first edition was followed by a second edition in 1982. Several new models were added, prices adjusted, and errors corrected. I had the opportunity to correspond with Ray while he was working on the second edition and offered assistance in pricing C&O and other eastern models.

In 1985 Ray passed away while working on a third edition. I was fortunate to pick up his manuscript and data and continue the effort. In taking on the task of developing the third edition I became very familiar with Ray's research. It is apparent that Ray rigorously scanned ads in every modeling periodical for dates and prices, an effort that can only be described as herculean. Unfortunately, advertisements from that era were often optimistic. Ads were often placed months before the model was expected and therefore prices and dates of availability are questionable. In a few instances importers advertised models, complete with dates and prices, that were never actually produced. For the third edition every existing importer was contacted and asked for data. I am pleased to state that I have received excellent cooperation from almost all of the major importers.

This data has produced some very interesting observations. Several models thought to be rather common appear to be very rare (for example, the late Gem USRA engines) and others have lingered in the importers' inventories for several years. Both of these factors relate directly to the collectability and market price of the models. Data from the major importers shows an explosion in the production of Korean-built brass locomotives between 1973 and 1979. The majority of this increase has been in the production of steam locomotives. Beginning in 1980 the production of diesel models began to rise until in 1989 there were over 450 different diesel models made. Comparing this to the period from 1954 to 1979 shows a significant increase in the market for diesels. One possible explanation for this increased interest is the changing demographics of the collectors. However, despite the larger number of young people and the market for diesel models, diesels have not reached the collectability status of steam locomotives. While some steam locomotives have increased in value by as much as 6,000%, diesel values have remained rather constant or increased only modestly. There are of course, notable exceptions and these are noted in the diesel section of the book.

Whereas the information from the importers has been essential in determining the basic production quantities, the data from dealers and collectors regarding current pricing has been a revelation. During the period from 1982–1987 *The Brown Book* was an excellent indicator of the state of the market. But after 1987 prices began to change radically, especially for the premium Japanese models. Limited production models produced by Tenshodo, Goto, Toby, Fujiyama, United, Nakamura, and a few others began to rise sharply in price. The driving force behind this price rise was the increased number of Japanese collectors. Large numbers of the better Japanese models continue to find their way into the hands of Japanese collectors who were willing to pay premium prices. The result was a sudden scarcity of these models and a tendency for dealers and collectors alike to treat these models as investment commodities. This trend is now beginning to show up in higher prices for the Japanese production models from these same builders.

As the hobby of collecting brass models has become more organized, a variety of other activities have taken place which assist the collector in the pursuit of brass models. Kumata, one of the early builders in Japan, published an outstanding two-volume set of books entitled, *The Art of Brass in Model Railroading*. These books provide an excellent photo reference for a large number of models produced by almost all of the Japanese builders. Train shows, once the exclusive domain of toy train collectors, have broadened to include the sellers of brass models. Several importers have produced high quality books and catalogs that serve as excellent references on their models. In addition, several woodworkers now specialize in the manufacture of display cases for these models, and custom painters and model restorers are constantly busy improving the appearance of the locomotives.

Using the Third Edition

Readers familiar with the previous editions of *The Brown Book* should be aware of some differences in the method of presenting the data in this edition. Ray's original format has withstood the test of time and has been preserved. Only where new data could be provided or where information could be clarified have changes in the format been made. The major change is in the presentation of the data on electrics. This has now been broken into four separate sections: electric locomotives, city cars, MU and subway cars, and interurbans. This makes a neater presentation that allows faster reference.

The second change deals primarily with the presentation of data regarding the PFM models. Models are no longer listed as CR–1 (Crown #1), CR–2, etc. PFM never labeled their Crowns as such and the prevailing practice of listing Crown models in numerical sequence unfortunately included models that PFM did not consider Crowns. The sixth edition PFM catalog explains that there are three categories of non-production models. Crowns, reportedly produced in the largest quantities, Limited Production models, produced in smaller runs, and Handbuilts, which are the rarest. To lump all of these together as Crowns is inconsistent with the stated PFM practices and treats the very rare and the semi-production models (Crowns) with the same degree of recognition. Therefore, I have chosen to use the PFM descriptors (H for Handbuilt; LP for Limited Production; CR for Crown; S for Silver Plated; and P for Production) in the space normally provided for the importer's model number. You will note in the listing that no prices are provided for the Silver Plated models. I have never seen one of these models offered for sale, so I have declined to speculate on the price.

A significant change in the format of listing diesel locomotives is the addition of a column identifying the specific railroad. In previous years most diesel models were generic. Since 1983 there has been an explosion in the production of diesel models that are detailed and/or painted for specific railroads. Rather than include this in the notes section a column has been added to the listing for roadname. Again, this is intended to provide faster reference.

One problem that defies a strictly "correct" answer is whether to include American made brass locomotives. My inclination was to omit them. There are several reasons for this: most production models, if not all, were only offered as kits and production data is almost impossible to find; data on models from the American custom-builders (Jerry White, Joe Dorazzio, Bill Lenoir, etc.) is similarly difficult to find; and last, but not least, is that most collectors are more interested in the models from Japan and Korea.

Collecting HO Brass Models

Record Keeping

Probably the most important aspect of caring for a collection, any collection, is knowing what you have and where it is. Good record keeping is a must if the collection is to maintain its value. With the advent of the home computer this has become a much more manageable exercise. The choice of the computer and the software is a matter of personal preference, there is no one perfect answer. But whatever you use you will need some sort of database or spreadsheet program. These two types of software perform similar functions, at least from the standpoint of inventory management. If you want to make lengthy comments as part of your records I would suggest a database program. But if your comments are short, dates, prices, condition, road number, etc. then a spreadsheet program is quite acceptable.

Table #1 is a sample of what I use for recording my collection. It is a simple spreadsheet that allows me to locate a model, and I can also sort the data in a variety of ways. Note that each model has an inventory control number. This number is also on a sticker attached to the box. It is NOT engraved on the model. Although some collectors like to engrave their social security number and other data on the model for identification purposes in the case of a theft, I personally feel that this devalues the model. If you feel you must uniquely identify each model for insurance purposes, mark the model inside the boiler and tender. This can be done with stick on labels quite easily by removing the boiler and tender tank and then placing the labels inside. Most thieves are not sophisticated enough, or are in too big a hurry, to look for labels inside the models.

Displaying Your Collection

Most collectors, unfortunately, do not display their models—most models spend their existence in their original box. This is, at best, a mixed blessing. It is unfortunate that the model is not on display to be appreciated, but the good news is that the model kept in the box is extremely well preserved, in most cases.

Keeping the model in the box can present some problems, however. Much of the early foam rubber packing was made from a fairly unstable compound that will deteriorate and crumble, no longer providing any protection for the model. Even worse is the red foam, which, as it deteriorates, bleeds its color onto the brass model. I have seen painted models totally ruined by this substance, and even unpainted models have been stained by red residue to the point where the natural brass has been discolored. My advice is to keep your boxed models wrapped in a non-clinging plastic wrap (some cling wraps leave a shiny residue) and check the foam packing every few months to assure that it is still in good condition.

One of the newer services being offered by custom painters and brass craftsmen is model restoration. In most cases this consists of restoring the finish, but on some models it is possible to replace broken castings with identical replacements. The finish is, however, the more common problem. Many of the earlier brass imports were delivered in a natural brass finish with a clear overspray. These early oversprays were porous and allowed the brass to oxidize. This, unfortunately, dulls the finish, and ruins the appearance of the model. Today restorers use a variety of techniques to restore the original finish; abrasive blasting and non-etching chemical solutions are the favorites. Using these techniques, it is possible to restore the original appearance with a minimum of trouble and expense.

Specialized Collections

As this hobby of collecting brass has come of age there has been a tendency toward specialization. In the early days the variety of models was extremely limited. Importers produced what they preferred with little attention to the desires of the market. This is not so difficult to understand when you consider that virtually all of the importers were model railroaders and had their own preferences. If you didn't happen to be a fan of the particular railroad for which models were being produced, you bought the available model and lettered it for your favorite railroad. At one time about the only 2–8–0 you could buy was the ubiquitous Santa Fe 1950 Class 2–8–0 from Pacific Fast Mail. I have seen these models painted an lettered for almost every railroad in the U.S. and several fictitious railroads as well. In recent years the variety of available models has increased to the point where you can not only buy, for example, a 2–8–0 for your favorite road, but you may have the choice of three or four variations.

Such variety has led to collectors specializing in several possible areas. The most common collecting practice is collecting the models unique to a particular railroad. Another popular practice is collecting by wheel arrangement, e.g., 4–8–4's, 2–8–8–2's, etc., and even other collectors focus on

Table 1
Steam Loco Listing

Inv. Date	Item #	Whyte Class	Road	Road Class	Scale	Importer/mfgr.	Paint	Value	Comments
11/21/87	1	0-4-0	B&O		HO	Varney		$xxx.xx	No Motor, original metal version, CV Valve Gear
11/21/87	2	0-6-0	CSTPM&O		HO	PFM	cp.	$xxx.xx	"Omaha," mid-run
11/26/87	3	0-6-0	UP		HO	Balboa	cp. #25	$xxx.xx	by Gascoyne, ptd. C&O, not correct
11/26/87	4	0-8-0	C&O	C-14	HO	Akane	cp. #102	$xxx.xx	USRA CB&Q version, cp. by McFarland
11/26/87	5	0-8-0	C&O	C-14	HO	Akane		$xxx.xx	modified USRA, new tender, redetailed by me
11/26/87	6	0-8-0	CB&Q		HO	Akane		$xxx.xx	CB&Q Version, Xmas present, Christine
11/24/87	7	0-8-0	C&O	C-15a	HO	PFM	cp. #110	$xxx.xx	modified C-16 by Gascoyne, 2 pgs. in MR
11/26/87	8	0-8-0	C&O	C-15a	HO	Lambert	cp. #119	$xxx.xx	"Platinum" Version
11/26/87	9	0-8-0	C&O	C-15a	HO	Soho/Lambert		$xxx.xx	"Silver" Version
11/26/87	10	0-8-0	C&O	C-16	HO	PFM	cp. #276	$xxx.xx	"Crown" C&O/N&W version, cp. by Gascoyne
11/26/87	11	0-8-0	C&O	C-16	HO	PFM		$xxx.xx	"Crown," corrected to C&O,w/Canon CN-22 & NWSL gearbox
11/26/87	12	0-10-0	C&O	C-12	HO	Cust. Brass	cp. #136	$xxx.xx	reworked mech., work by Stone
11/26/87	13	0-10-0	C&O	C-12	HO	Cust. Brass		$xxx.xx	w/Gascoyne scratch tender
11/26/87	14	2-6-0	C&O	E-5	HO	PFM	cp. #428	$xxx.xx	built from V&T 4-6-0 by Gascoyne
11/26/87	15	2-8-0	SF		HO	PFM		$xxx.xx	SF 1950 version, no tender
11/26/87	16	2-8-0	C&O	G-9	HO	Overland	cp. #1023	$xxx.xx	"Sport" Cab. new details, redetailed & Ptd. by me
11/21/87	17	2-8-0	C&O	G-9	HO	Overland	cp. #1045	$xxx.xx	Big Cab w/9RE tender, cp. by Zane
07/16/88	18	3 Tk.Shay	"B"		HO	PFM	Class "B"	$xxx.xx	Arch Bar tks, wood cab., unsuperheated
11/26/87	19	2-8-0	C&O	G-9	HO	Overland		$xxx.xx	Big cab, w/12VC tender
11/26/87	20	2-8-2	C&O	K-2	HO	Mantua/Cary	cp. #1174	$xxx.xx	kitbash award in RMC June 73
11/21/87	21	2-8-2	C&O	K-2	HO	Hallmark	cp. #1192	$xxx.xx	
11/26/87	22	2-8-2	C&O	K-2	HO	Scratch	cp. #1205	$xxx.xx	built by Gascoyne from Penn Line
11/22/87	23	2-8-2	C&O	K-3	HO	PFM	cp. #1210	$xxx.xx	"Crown" w/rect. tender, from NY auction
12/25/87	24	2-8-2	C&O	K-3	HO	PFM	cp. #1217	$xxx.xx	"Crown" w/16VC tender
11/22/87	25	2-8-2	C&O	K-3a	HO	PFM	cp. #2342	$xxx.xx	w/Worthington & Rect. tender
11/22/87	26	2-8-2	C&O	K-3a	HO	Key	fp. #2338	$xxx.xx	"Custom Series #35." w/Elesco FWH & 16VC tender
01/28/88	27	2-8-2	C&O	K-3a	HO	Key		$xxx.xx	w/Worthington & Rect. tender
09/15/89	28	2-8-2	C&O	K-3	HO	Key	fp. #1233	$xxx.xx	"Custom Series #35." w/Elesco FWH & Rect. Tender
11/26/87	29	2-8-2	USRA	Light	HO	Akane		$xxx.xx	some tarnish
11/26/87	30	2-8-2	USRA	Heavy	HO	Akane	cp. #3204	$xxx.xx	tender lettered GN, weathered
11/25/87	31	2-8-4	C&O	K-4	HO	LMB		$xxx.xx	crude, incorrect
08/24/88	32	0-8-0	C&O	C-16	HO	W&R	fp. #248	$xxx.xx	finished by R. Hunter
11/26/87	33	2-8-4	C&O	K-4	HO	PFM	cp. #2718	$xxx.xx	
11/26/87	34	2-8-4	C&O	K-4	HO	PFM	cp. #2783	$xxx.xx	white decals
11/22/87	35	2-8-4	C&O	K-4	HO	PFM	cp. #2727	$xxx.xx	modified to early version by me
12/25/87	36	2-8-4	C&O	K-4	HO	PFM	cp. #2730	$xxx.xx	"Hy-Grade" version, last run
11/22/87	37	2-8-4	C&O	K-4	HO	Key		$xxx.xx	late version
11/26/87	38	2-8-4	C&O	K-4	HO	Key	cp. #2716	$xxx.xx	2716 version, not Southern version
11/27/87	39	2-8-4	C&O	N-1	HO	PFM	cp. #2699	$xxx.xx	NKP Berk. modified to C&O by Gascoyne
11/26/87	40	2-8-4	AM		HO	PFM	cp. #2733	$xxx.xx	NKP Berk. mod. to Alleghany Mid. for T. Koester

unique types, e.g. streamlined locos, Shays, logging, etc. The result of this specialization has led to some spectacular collections that are definitely of museum quality.

One new trend that has begun to emerge is the collecting of the very early, often handbuilt, models. In years past these early models were virtually ignored. Modelers and collectors were primarily interested in obtaining the finest, most accurate scale model of a particular locomotive. These early handbuilt models often lacked lost-wax castings and other fine detail parts, which made them somewhat less desirable than the newer models. But as time passed, collectors began to see these early handbuilts as having a historic interest—they were examples of the work of the best craftsmen at that time. Each model was, for all intents and purposes, custom built. An individual Japanese craftsman might produce only five or six per year. Thus their rarity added to the mystique of collecting these models.

Data on these early handbuilts is almost non-existent. Only PFM has kept good records and published the quantities and dates. The PFM quantities reflect what they imported but are not a good measure of what was made or even brought into this country. In the '50s some of the smaller importers would go to Japan and buy models from Japanese hobby shops for resale in the U.S. And since some of these models came from the Tenshodo hobby shop, they were the same models being sold by PFM. Thus when the listing on one of these rare handbuilts states for example, ten produced, that number is only relevant to the particular importer. Other models may have found their way into the marketplace via the "informal" importers I've just described.

Modified Models

From the beginning, when brass models first began to be imported in quantity, until sometime in the mid-70s there was a significant "hobby-within-a-hobby" where talented individuals would take a brass model and redetail it for a specific railroad's locomotive or perhaps modify it to resemble a locomotive from another railroad. This phenomenon was most frequent when an importer brought in a model for a particular railroad that may have had a strong resemblance to a locomotive of another railroad. If the facts be known, prototype steam loco builders didn't custom build every loco, many were stock designs and railroads would order these locomotives with various modifications and changes in appliances. The modeler in many instances, was just doing what the prototype locomotive builder did. Thus an importer may bring in a Frisco "Russian" 2–10–0 and a modeler might change it into a Western Maryland I–1 2–10–0. Probably the most frequent modifications took place on USRA engines. These stock designs were reproduced time and time again on the prototype and modelers would take these engines and change appliances to better resemble a particular engine on a specific railroad.

The craftsmanship and accuracy of the modification play an extremely large role in determining the final value of the modified model. Good research combined with quality craftsmanship when modifying a production model will usually result in a unique model that demands a higher price, but the contrary can be just as true when the model is very rare. A modified PFM Crown, for example, rarely brings as much as a pristine version. Why? Collectors prefer Crowns and other limited production models in their original condition.

Importer Variations

The hobby of modifying brass locomotives has declined somewhat due to the increased research being done by the importers. It should be no surprise that if an importer brings in several variations of a model, it will sell better. If the variations are specific to one road, a collector of that road may have to have all the versions. If the model is authentic to several roads, the market is even broader. Overland, Precision Scale, and Key have all had great success bringing in versions of models that started on the Korean builder's workbench much the same; but with changed cylinders, cabs, and detail parts, they significantly differ in final appearances. The importers have done what the modeler had done for himself in the past.

This is not to say that every variation of every locomotive type has been built. Many variations are still possible that have never been modeled. But several of the modelers who did modification work in the past have found that it is often easier to present their research data to the importer, who will then have a run of models produced with several variations. An excellent example of the success of this practice is the C&O G-9 2-8-0, which was originally produced by Rok-Am for Overland Models. When this model was first imported in 1979, it was done in the older version with a large steel cab. Several modelers, knowing of the existence of commercial etched brass cabs for the later version, changed this cab and detail parts to make a model that was not available from the importer. In 1991, when Overland had Ajin remake the C&O G-9, three versions were presented—two different versions with short cabs, and one with the larger, older style cab.

Pennsy fans will remember that several builders have made PRR J-1 and J-1a 2-10-4 models over the years. Yet the C&O fans couldn't get any importer to bring in a C&O T-1 2-10-4. (The engines are the same, with the exception of cosmetic details). Custom builders and modelers, over the years, made dozens of conversions. Only in later years have Westside, Key, and Sunset exploited the similarities to make PRR and C&O versions of these engines available to the collector.

Painting

There really only seem to be two schools of thought when it comes to painting brass models: Never do it, always do it. The arguments for either of these positions are based on personal preference and aesthetics. Both positions are equally valid. But regardless of your position, you will sooner or later wind up dealing with a painter. Unpainted models, or more correctly, natural brass models with a clear overspray, will eventually tarnish and lose their luster. A restorer and painter will be needed.

For restoration work the process is relatively simple. The restorer performs the finish restoration and oversprays the model with a clear lacquer. But the situation is much more complicated when you wish to have a locomotive custom painted. Since each custom painter is an artist, each has a distinct style. It is the combination of their style and your tastes that must be accommodated. Some painters prefer to weather a model to make it look like the actual working prototype. If you prefer your models to look like museum displays you will not be comfortable with this painter's work. A good paint job certainly does add value to the model. Factory paint jobs sell for more than the unpainted models, so it is logical to expect a paint job of professional quality to add similarly to the value. However not every custom paint job is factory quality. Accuracy and authenticity play a major role in determining if the paint job will add to or subtract from the final value of the model. If the paint job is incorrect, wrong colors, wrong decals, etc. it will devalue the model. And if the model is painted for a freelance model railroad the paint job will almost always reduce the value of the locomotive, regardless of the quality of the work.

The actual process of painting a brass locomotive varies from painter to painter. Some do not fully disassemble the model but paint the sub-assemblies and clean the mechanism of excess overspray. Other custom painters prefer to fully disassemble the model, paint each part separately, and reassemble the model. This is the preferred method for sound equipped engines. It produces a cleaner mechanism, eliminating all of the fine paint overspray that can cause sound equipped engines to sound scratchy and distorted. As you might imagine this method takes more time and costs considerably more to perform. If you prefer your models weathered it is unnecessary to go the route of full disassembly. Since the weathering must be applied to the fully assembled model, it is inevitable that some overspray will get into working parts. Thus the model will require a final cleanup anyway.

Original Boxes

Many of the brass locomotives now on the market, even those which are commonly available, were built on a "one-run-only" production schedule, and therefore determining the age of the model is relatively easy. However, many models, especially those imported by Pacific Fast Mail, were made in productions runs over a period of several years. Frequently, modification or refinements were made from run to run that uniquely identify the particular model. And although the model may or may not display some differences from run to run, the box may tell more about the particular model than the model itself. In the past, modelers and collectors have often paid little attention to the box. This can be a serious mistake. The wrong model in the wrong box can lead to serious errors in determining the correct price for the model. I know of one outstanding collection which had no boxes. When the owner got a new model he gave the box to his dog to play with. It would be hard to calculate how many thousands of dollars worth of cardboard that dog shredded.

Very early brass locomotives from Japanese builders such as Tenshodo and International were packed in mahogany boxes with hinged or sliding covers. The 1955 Tenshodo NYC 4–6–4 unpainted kit was packed in a cigar-box shaped wooden box with brown painting and a white label, a hinged cover and internal partitions. The 1955 International factory-painted GN GP–9 screwdriver kit was packed a wooden box with sliding cover. Models from Tetsudo were typically packed in cardboard boxes with yellow coverings with the words "Tetsudo-Mokeshi" printed diagonally several times across the top and on the sides. By 1957 the wooden boxes had been replaced with light brown mottled paper-covered cardboard boxes. Packing was shredded clear cellophane. The very early "flywheel" Shays, the 90 Ton Shay and some of the other early United models were packed in silver-blue boxes with a candy-box type of lid that extended about one-third of the way down the side. The edges of the box and the lettering were done in gold foil. These boxes, in good shape, are very hard to find.

Early United models, such as the Crown AT&SF #3776 4–8–4s of 1955, were packed in heavy corrugated cardboard boxes which were painted blue and measured about 7″ by 10″ by 4″. Cardboard partitions divided the box into two long compartments, filled with excelsior into which the locomotive and tender, each in a plastic bag, were placed. A plain white paper label with "United" and the identifying information typed on it, was glued to one end. In the late '50s United models were packed similarly in boxes measuring 12″ by 6″ by 3 1/2″, which were covered with dark green paper. The interior wrapping changed from excelsior to a padded paper wrapping which was wrapped in corrugated paper. The model was enclosed in a plastic bag as before. The wrapped engine and tender were then taped to thin boards running the full length of the box. This helped to prevent damage to the pilot or cab in the event of impact on the end of the boxes. The 1959–1960 Atlas-Toby C&O Greenbriers and the N&W Y–6b 2–8–8–2 models were packed in such boxes with the Gold United Crown emblem printed on the end, and measuring 10 1/4 by 5 1/2 by 3 1/4 inches. These boxes were used as late as 1963 on the Toby built AT&SF 4000 series 2–8–2s.

The early AT&SF 4101 Class Berkshires, imported in 1960 and earlier, were packed in green boxes measuring 10 3/4 by 6 by 3 1/4 inches, whereas the models starting in 1961 and the newly introduced AT&SF 2–10–2 models were shipped in boxes with a blue, cloth textured covering, measuring 10 1/2 by 5 by 3 1/4 inches. This was the beginning of what has come to be called the PFM "denim" box. Packing was changed to eliminate the thin wooden boards and the plastic locomotive bag now bore the blue United logo. The D&RGW L–131 2–8–8–2s (box was marked L–125) and the N&W Class A 2–6–6–4s were sold in similar boxes (13 3/8 by 5 3/8 by 3 3/8 inches) during this period. Small yellow labels on the box ends proclaiming that the models were powered by Pittman DC–70 or DC–71B motors were common.

The USRA Light Pacifics imported during the early and middle '60s were shipped in blue boxes covered with a cloth textured paper. The corrugated wrappings were replaced by a blue-green foam liner. The models were wrapped in clear plastic sheets imprinted with a blue United logo. The packing and boxes for the USRA 2–8–2's made from 1962 to 1966 were identical except that the box tops were covered with smooth silver paper imprinted with variable shading of fine blue lines with "United" and "HO Scale Model Locomotive" printed on the top and one end. "USRA Light Mikado 2–8–2" was printed on a yellow label on the same end. Rumor was that this box style was developed for Tenshodo, rejected , and used by United for this locomotive.

By 1963 United had standardized non-corrugated 2 3/8 by 6 3/4-inch boxes. The AT&SF 3776 Series 4–8–4s imported in 1963–64 were packed in such boxes measuring 13 3/8 inches long with

"Santa Fe" in red and the United logo in gold on the box ends. The lid wrapper was dark blue textured paper and the bottom was white with black paper covered sides. During this era most narrow gauge models such as the RGS #20 came in two-inch deep boxes with textured blue lids, lettered in gold on the ends only.

The first of DM&IR 0–10–2s in 1965 was sold in 10 1/8 inch long boxes with "DM&IR 0–10–2" and the United logo all printed in gold on the end of standard dark blue cloth textured lids. The box bottoms were covered with this paper. Rubberized horsehair pads were placed above and below the gray foam surrounding the model. In 1967, the box dimensions were changed to 2 1/2 by 6 5/8 by 10 3/4 inch, and covered with smooth medium-blue paper printed in gold with 'DM&IR 0–10–2," the United logo, PFM logo, and "Mf'd by Atlas Industries, Inc., Kawaguchi, Japan, exclusively for Pacific Fast Mail." The 1966 vintage B&O 1–2 0–8–0, E–27ca 2–8–0, and C&NW e–2b models were all imported in this type box with only the dimensions varying.

United geared locos imported from 1965 to 1966 were in dark blue boxes measuring 2 3/8 by 6 7/8 by 8 1/4 inches, with the cloth textured paper covering. They were packed completely in gray foam, except the Climax, Heisler, and three-truck "B" Shay, which had rubberized horsehair layers above and below the model. The 50-ton Vulcan Duplex had a box of the same width and length but 1/4-inch deeper and covered with the uniform medium blue paper. All lettering was in gold. The Pacific Coast Shay came in gray foam, the same box as the Duplex, but with silver lettering.

From 1967 to 1977 box lids were smooth blue-grey covered about 2 1/2 inches deep with silver printing on the top and ends. Grey foam plastic was used as the main insert as well as top and bottom sheets. In addition to model designation, ends were lettered 'Mf'd by Atlas Industries, Inc., Kawaguchi, Japan exclusively for Pacific Fast Mail." Sometime in 1977 PFM reverted to the textured blue and silver box lids, but other specifications remained the same.

From about 1964 the Tenshodo production models were wrapped in clear plastic sheets or bags, packed in yellow foam with the locomotive usually above the tender in a single silver-top, black-bottomed box. Labels were printed in blue on a white background. Most of the Crown models were packed similarly except that in most cases the labels were printed in gold on a black background and included the PFM winged logo with the word "Crown" in the lower right corner. The 1950 to 1970 Tenshodo UP Big Boy 4–8–8–4s and the 1962 and 1963 UP Challenger models had the locomotive and tenders packed in separate boxes. By the early 1970s, the Tenshodo large articulateds were packed with the loco and tender in a single large silver/black box with the gold on black Crown labels.

Models from Fujiyama and Toby were typically packed in dark green boxes with a white or black bottom. In later years, silver-foil labels were used by Fujiyama. Later Crown models from Fujiyama incorporated the PFM winged logo as well as the single word "Crown" in the lower right corner of the label.

Gem models produced by Olympia were typically packed in boxes with a felt textured exterior. Most of the production models were packed in boxes with dark green top and ends. An occasional blue box can be found. Most of the "Ruby Signature" models were packed in boxes of the same size but with a red felt exterior. Some of the Ruby Signature PRR S–1 steam turbines were packed in green felt textured boxes.

Identifying Models

Several of the builders and importers have taken special pains to uniquely identify their premier models. Small photo engraved plaques located on the driver retainer plate are the preferred method of marking. PFM models from United typically designated Crowns with the PFM winged logo. Crowns from Fujiyama did not use the logo but bore the word "Crown" and the serial number and signature of S. Fuyara. CB Royale Models from NJ Custom Brass carry a small photo-engraved plate mounted on the driver retainer plate with the CB Royale logo the serial number and the year of manufacture. The Gem Ruby Signature models have the markings engraved directly into the driver retainer plate. They are marked with an identification number, the word Olympia, the signature of H. Tagaya, and the year produced.

Very early handbuilts were often marked with a number stamped into the frame. On articulateds this number is often found on the front engine top plate behind the cylinders. Almost impossible to spot on a painted locomotive, it is even difficult to find without a magnifying glass or without removing the front engine from the model. Late PFM handbuilts often bore the serial number on the left side of the frame under the cab.

Pricing

The primary function of *The Brown Book* is, of course, to provide pricing information, and this is a difficult process. Regional differences in pricing (for example, Santa Fe models sell better in the Southwest than in the Northeast), lack of good data (it can't be priced if it doesn't get traded), and latent problems with some models (poor motors/gearboxes, etc), can cause the price of a model to change radically in a short time. Ray's determined prices by rigorously scrutinizing dealers lists. On some models, Ray would have as many as twenty recorded prices. He then used the highest price as the "Mint" price and an average of the remaining prices to determine the "Average" price. My own experience is that the average price is of marginal value. The mint price is the starting point for all pricing decisions and this price is normally the most current price for that model. Just as with automobiles, a "cream puff" may bring more than the recorded mint value. Demand and availability also play a part in this process. Models in less than perfect condition will also cause the price to be less. But the prices of the rarer models defy more than a snapshot of the current market.

What does the future hold? I think its fair to say that the production of brass models for the American market will continue indefinitely. As prices rise, importers will seek new builders and new countries to produce models. Even now, some importers have begun exploring the possibilities of producing models in what was the Soviet Union. The major builders in Korea have, for some time, been producing excellent models. I expect this trend to continue with more innovations in detail and performance to appear on future models. Painted models will continue to be the popular choice of collectors. Some modelers and collectors are hoping that one of the major importers will team up with one of the producers of carrier control systems and offer models ready to run with the chosen control system.

PART I

STEAM LOCOMOTIVES

Akron, Canton & Youngstown Railroad

Whyte Class	Owner Class & Type	Model Production					List Price	Resale		Remarks
		Importer	Builder	Cat #	Quan.	Yrs.		Mint	Avg.	
2-8-2	#407 Mikado	Key	Samh		50	81	350	370		See Note #1

Alton & Southern Railroad

Whyte Class	Owner Class & Type	Model Production					List Price	Resale		Remarks
		Importer	Builder	Cat #	Quan.	Yrs.		Mint	Avg.	
0-6-0	Switcher	MBA				58	26	170		Working Headlight

Arkansas & Louisiana Missouri Railway (A&LM)

Whyte Class	Owner Class & Type	Model Production					List Price	Resale		Remarks
		Importer	Builder	Cat #	Quan.	Yrs.		Mint	Avg.	
4-6-0	Ten Wheeler	PFM	Tensh	H	1	61				See Note #113
4-6-0	Ten Wheeler	PFM	Fujiyama	P	440	67	40	260		See Note #1
4-6-0	Ten Wheeler	PFM	Fujiyama	P	980	71	60	260		See Note #3
4-6-0	Ten Wheeler	PFM	Fujiyama	P	600	77	175	300		See Note #594

The A&LM 4–6–0 by Fujiyama, imported by PFM, is a fine model from one of Japan's premier builders. Although the prototype belonged to an obscure southern railroad, the model has wide appeal for its aesthetic balance and good running qualities. A favorite among modelers with small layouts, it lends itself well to private roadnames and other southern short lines which owned very similar engines.

Atchison, Topeka & Santa Fe Railway (AT&SF)

Whyte Class	Owner Class & Type	Model Production					List Price	Resale		Remarks
		Importer	Builder	Cat #	Quan.	Yrs.		Mint	Avg.	
0-4-0T	Shop Switcher	Key	Samh		150	85	272	430	400	#2298, Crane on Stack
0-6-0T	2299 Switcher	WMC	Samh		300	79	215	360	300	Fireless Cooker
0-6-0	9000 Switcher	Bal	KTM			67-68	50	300	225	See Note #500-501
0-6-0	9000 Switcher	Bal	KTM			69-71	60	300	225	See Note #501
0-6-0	2100 Switcher	Hall	DongJ		600	77	150	230	180	See Note #502
0-8-0	825 Switcher	Sun	Samh	HSF201	400	76	128	190	145	See Note #503
2-8-0	C-9 Consol	Sun	ThaWai	HO-33A		90	200			
2-6-0	2526 Mogul	Hall		H50220						ex. KCM&O 130 Series
2-6-2	#1000 Prairie	Key	Samh		400	77	140	230		See Note #1000
2-6-2	#1050 Prairie	Key	Samh		1000	75	130	220		See Note #1001
2-6-2	1800 Prairie	Bal	KMT/KTM		420	67	60	290		
2-6-2	1800 Prairie	CustB	KMT	ST-208	525	75	190	275		

Atchison, Topeka & Santa Fe Railway (cont'd)

Whyte Class	Owner Class & Type	Model Production					List Price	Resale		Remarks
		Importer	Builder	Cat #	Quan.	Yrs.		Mint	Avg.	
2-8-0	789 Consol	Sun	Samh	HSF101	500	75	129	200		789-823, Canon Motor
2-8-0	825 Consol	Sun	Samh		500	77	135	210		825-864, Canon Motor
2-8-0	1900 Consol	Sun	ThaWai	HO107	200	89	185	230		low cost series
2-8-0	1950 Consol	PFM	Atlas/Asahi	P	399	56	40	200		Kit
2-8-0	1950 Consol	PFM	Atlas/Asahi	P	460	56	40	200		See Note #505
2-8-0	1950 Consol	PFM	Atlas/Asahi	P	1	56				See Note #504
2-8-0	1950 Consol	PFM	Atlas/Asahi	P	862	57	40	200		Turned Details
2-8-0	1950 Consol	PFM	Atlas/Asahi	P	670	58	40	200		
2-8-0	1950 Consol	PFM	Atlas/Asahi	P	1050	59	40	200		See Note #4
2-8-0	1950 Consol	PFM	Atlas/Asahi	P	400	60	40	200		See Note #5
2-8-0	1950 Consol	PFM	Atlas/Asahi	P	765	61	40	200		See Note #6
2-8-0	1950 Consol	PFM	Atlas/Asahi	S	1	62				See Note #7
2-8-0	1950 Consol	PFM	Atlas/Asahi	P	275	62	40	200		
2-8-0	1950 Consol	PFM	Atlas/Asahi	P	335	63	40	200		See Note #8
2-8-0	1950 Consol	PFM	Atlas/Asahi	P	300	64	40	200		See Note #9
2-8-0	1950 Consol	PFM	Atlas/Asahi	P	285	65	40	200		See Note #10
2-8-0	1950 Consol	PFM	Atlas/Asahi	P	300	66	48	200		Brake Shoes added
2-8-0	1950 Consol	PFM	Atlas/Asahi	P	265	67	48	200		See Note #11
2-8-0	1950 Consol	PFM	Atlas/Asahi	P	380	68	58	200		
2-8-0	1950 Consol	PFM	Atlas/Asahi	P	500	70	80	200		
2-8-0	1950 Consol	PFM	Atlas/Asahi	P	500	72	88	230		See Note #12
2-8-0	1950 Consol	PFM	Atlas/Asahi	P	700	75	175	230		See Note #13
2-8-0	1950 Consol	Sun	ThaWai	HO106	400	89	185	230		low cost series
2-8-0	"2341" Class Consol	PFM	Unknown	P	1	56				See Note #1920
2-8-0	2507 Consol	Hall	Goto		750	73	135	265		See Note #14
2-8-0	2507 Consol	Hall	Goto		250	75	225	265		See Note #14
2-8-2	Mikado	AHM	Mizuno			78		125	100	some die cast parts
2-8-2	Mikado	Sun	Samh	HO109APD	100	92	299	250		fp., See Note #1002
2-8-2	Mikado	Sun	Samh	HO108D	100	92	250	210		See Note #1003
2-8-2	Mikado	Sun	Samh	HO108APD	100	92	299	250		fp., See Note #1004
2-8-2	Mikado	Sun	Samh	HO109AD	100	92	250	210		See Note #1005
2-8-2	Mikado	Sun	Samh	HO108P	100	92	299	250		fp, See Note #1006
2-8-2	Mikado	Sun	Samh	HO108PD	100	92	299	250		
2-8-2	Mikado	Sun	Samh	HO109D	100	92	250	210		See Note #1008
2-8-2	Mikado	Sun	Samh	HO109BPD	100	92	299	250		fp.,See Note #1009

The ubiquitous Santa Fe 1950 Class 2–8–0 built by Atlas/Asahi for PFM has been one of the all-time best-selling brass steam locomotives ever made. With over 8,500 made from 1956–1975 this model is an excellent example of the history of the art of building brass models. From turnings and punched rivets to fine castings and photoengravings, this model displays the state-of-the-art of its time.

Atchison, Topeka & Santa Fe Railway (cont'd)

Santa Fe's efforts at streamlining generally met with mixed responses. While better than some other color combinations, the use of powder blue used over a darker blue could never be kept clean. Number 3460 was the only streamlined Hudson the Santa Fe owned. Five sister engines escaped the streamlining treatment. PFM imported this Tenshodo-built engine in 1975.

Whyte Class	Owner Class & Type	Model Production					List Price	Resale		Remarks
		Importer	Builder	Cat #	Quan.	Yrs.		Mint	Avg.	
2-8-2	Mikado	Sun	Samh	HO108AD	100	92	250	210		See Note #1010
2-8-2	Mikado	Sun	Samh	HO109BD	100	92	250	210		See Note #1003
2-8-2	Mikado	Sun	Samh	HO109PD	100	92	299	250		fp., See Note #1011
2-8-2	Mikado	Sun	Samh	HO108	100	92	250	210		See Note #1012
2-8-2	#3100 Mikado	Hall	DongJ	HS0003		82	290	325	300	See Note #17
2-8-2	#3129 Mikado	Hall	DongJ	HS0004		82	292	380	300	See Note #18
2-8-2	#3160 Mikado	H4W			100	59	50	290	245	See Note #506
2-8-2	#3160 Mikado	AHM	Mizuno			78	200	120	100	See Note #19
2-8-2	#3160 Mikado	Intl	Takara			56	35	200	150	See Note #15
2-8-2	#3160 Mikado	MBA	Mizuno		20	58	48			
2-8-2	#3160 Mikado	PFM	Unknown	H	1	50's				
2-8-2	#3160 Mikado	PFM	Atlas/Naka	H	12	61	144	4500	4000	See Note #507
2-8-2	#3160 Mikado	Sun	Samh	HO55	400	78	195	290		See Note #1013
2-8-2	#3160 Mikado	Sun	Samh		400	78	195	290	230	See Note #16
2-8-2	#3187 Mikado	Key	Samh			88	558	670		fp., 15,000 gal. Oil Tender
2-8-2	#3192 Mikado	Sun	Samh		200	78	195	290	220	See Note #508
2-8-2	#3192 Mikado	Sun	Samh	HO55A	400	78	195	230		See Note #508
2-8-2	#3256 Mikado	Key	Samh			89	558	670		12,000 gal Oil Tender
2-8-2	#3258/3287 Mikado	Key	Samh		30	89	558	670		12,000 gal Coal Tender
2-8-2	#4000 Mikado	PFM	Toby	P	500	63	50	705	550	See Note #509
2-8-2	#4000 Mikado	PFM	Toby	P	300	62	50	705	550	See Note #509
2-8-2	#4000 Mikado	PFM	Toby	S	1	62				See Note #7
2-8-2	#4000 Mikado	Sun	Samh	HO14	300	77	158	190		See Note #510
2-8-2	#4000 Mikado	Sun	Samh		500	77	158	275	250	fp.,See Note #510
2-8-2	#4027 Mikado	Key	Samh			89	558	570		12,000 gal Oil Tender
2-8-4	Berkshire	WMC		MO-91		82	399	500	410	
2-8-4	#4100 Berkshire	PFM	Atlas/Asahi	P	200	64	50	250	195	See Note #21
2-8-4	#4100 Berkshire	PFM	Atlas/Asahi	P	225	62	50	260	210	See Note #21
2-8-4	#4100 Berkshire	PFM	Atlas/Asahi	P	290	61	50	235	185	See Note #21
2-8-4	#4100 Berkshire	PFM	Atlas/Asahi	P	400	70	75	265	240	See Note #21
2-8-4	#4100 Berkshire	PFM	Atlas/Asahi	P	165	65	55	250	200	See Note #21, w/bk shoes.
2-8-4	#4100 Berkshire	PFM	Atlas/Asahi	P	200	60	50	220	170	See Note #5
2-8-4	#4100 Berkshire	PFM	Atlas/Asahi	P	500	72	115	280	225	See Note #22
2-8-4	#4100 Berkshire	PFM	Atlas/Asahi	S	1	62				See Note #7
2-8-4	#4100 Berkshire	PFM	Atlas/Asahi	P	400	57	50	260	210	See Note #511
2-8-4	#4100 Berkshire	PFM	Atlas/Asahi	P	770	59	50	260	210	See Note #20
2-8-4	#4100 Berkshire	PFM	Atlas/Asahi	P	860	58	50	290	225	See Note #511
2-8-4	#4100 Berkshire	PFM	Atlas/Asahi	P	220	67	60	260	205	See Note #21

Atchison, Topeka & Santa Fe Railway (cont'd)

Santa Fe steam always had a compact, purposeful appearance. The 4000 Class Mikados illustrate this very well. Built by Baldwin from 1921–26, they were the last class of Mikados on the AT&SF. The total roster numbered 101 engines, and they went through many shoppings and changes in their lifetime. Most were oil burners, except for #4070–4085, which were coal burners. This distinctive engine with two sand domes is faithfully reproduced for PFM by Toby models.

Whyte Class	Owner Class & Type	Model Production					List Price	Resale		Remarks
		Importer	Builder	Cat #	Quan.	Yrs.		Mint	Avg.	
2-8-4	#4193 Berkshire	WMC	Nakamura	MO-114	320	78	340	450	350	See Note #512
2-8-4	#4197 Berkshire	PSC		15516						ex. B&M
2-8-4	#4199 Berkshire	WMC	Nakamura	MO-106	100	77	330	380	310	See Note #513
2-10-0	#2565 Decapod	Hall	DongJ	HS0002		86-87	299	290	240	
2-10-2	#900/1600 Santa Fe	Hall	DongJ		600	77	163	235	180	See Note #514
2-10-2	#1600 Santa Fe	PSC	KTM	MO-63		82	339	440	345	See Note #515
2-10-2	#1600 Santa Fe	WMC	KTM	MO-63	150	79	300	440	350	See Note #515
2-10-2	#3010 Santa Fe	WMC	KTM	MO-63	1149	75-77	190	410	320	See Note #515
2-10-2	#3010 Santa Fe	WMC	KTM	MO-63		82	339	450	345	
2-10-2	#3800 Santa Fe	Key	Samh		300	79	280	440	350	See Note #24
2-10-2	#3800 Santa Fe	NWSL	Toby		200	61-65	70	300	225	See Note #517
2-10-2	#3800 Santa Fe	PFM	Atlas/Asahi	P	500	72	115	300	240	See Note #23
2-10-2	#3800 Santa Fe	PFM	Atlas/Asahi	P	400	70	75	290	230	See Note #23
2-10-2	#3800 Santa Fe	PFM	Atlas/Asahi	S	1	62				See Note #7
2-10-2	#3800 Santa Fe	PFM	Atlas/Asahi	P	220	64	55	260	200	See Note #23
2-10-2	#3800 Santa Fe	PFM	Atlas/Asahi	P	220	67	60	280	220	See Note #23
2-10-2	#3800 Santa Fe	PFM	Atlas/Asahi	P	190	65	60	270	210	See Note #23, w/bk. shoes
2-10-2	#3800 Santa Fe	PFM	Atlas/Asahi	P	485	62	55	320	220	See Note #518
2-10-2	#3800 Santa Fe	PFM	Atlas/Asahi	P	280	61	55	235	175	See Note #518
2-10-2	#3820 Santa Fe	Key								See Note #1014
2-10-2	#3829 Santa Fe	Key								See Note #1015
2-10-2	#3842 Santa Fe	Key								See Note #1016
2-10-2	#3870-75 Santa Fe	Key								See Note #1017
2-10-4	Texas	PFM	Tensh #113	H	7	55	90	2200		See Note #1951
2-10-4	Texas	PFM	Tensh #113	H	6	56	106	2200		See Note #25
2-10-4	Texas	PFM	Tensh #113	H	20	57	106	2200		See Note #25
2-10-4	Texas	PFM	Tensh #113	H	15	58	106	2200		See Note #25
2-10-4	Texas	PFM	Tensh #113	H	8	59	130	2200		See Note #25
2-10-4	Texas	PFM	Tensh #113	H	35	60	130	2200		See Note #25
2-10-4	Texas	PFM	Tensh #113	H	49	65	158	2600		See Note #25 & 26
2-10-4	#5000 Texas	Hall	DongJ		750	76-77	220	320	255	See Note #29
2-10-4	#5001 Texas	WMC	Samh	MO-125	400	78	650	700		See Note #520
2-10-4	#5011 Texas	PFM	Atlas/Asahi	P	501	74	250	350	275	See Note #28
2-10-4	#5011 Texas	PFM	Atlas/Asahi	P	1	75	250			
2-10-4	#5011 Texas	PFM	Atlas/Asahi	P	500	73	198	350	260	NMRA Review 4/71
2-10-4	#5011 Texas	PFM	Atlas/Asahi	P	500	70	100	350	275	See Note #27
2-10-4	#5011 Texas	PFM	Atlas/Asahi	P	500	72	120	380	275	Blind Main Drivers
2-10-4	#5011 Texas	PFM	Atlas/Asahi	S	1	70				See Note #7
2-10-4	#5011 Texas	PFM	Atlas/Asahi		150	82	808	1100	900	See Note #525
2-10-10-2	#3000 Articulated	WMC	KTM	MO-65	1110	76-	290	650	525	See Note #526

Atchison, Topeka & Santa Fe Railway (cont'd)

Whyte Class	Owner Class & Type	Importer	Builder	Cat #	Quan.	Yrs.	List Price	Mint	Avg.	Remarks
4-4-2	#1400 Atlantic	Key	Samh		65	87	414	450		fp.
4-4-2	#1400 Atlantic	Key	Samh		10	87	320	350		
4-4-2	#1452 Atlantic	Key	Samh		10	87	320	410		
4-4-2	#1452 Atlantic	Key	Samh		65	87	414	450		fp.
4-4-2	#1480 Atlantic	Bal	KMT	SF-1	332	64	50	260	200	See Note #30
4-4-2	#1480 Atlantic	Bal	KMT	SF-1	110	66	53	235	175	
4-4-2	#1480 Atlantic	Bal	KMT	SF-1		71	98	235	160	fp.
4-4-2	#1480 Atlantic	Bal	KMT	SF-1	{500}	71	94	210	150	
4-6-0	#468 Ten Wheeler	CustB	KMT	ST-209			189			See Note #31
4-6-0	#468 Ten Wheeler	Hall	DongJ	HS0005		85	275	320		
4-6-2	#1226 Pacific	Key	Samh		800	77	157	230	175	See Note #528
4-6-2	#1337 Pacific	Hall	DongJ		200	78	230	270		See Note #531
4-6-2	#1337 Pacific	PFM	Fujiyama	P	500	72	120	380	300	See Note #529
4-6-2	#1337 Pacific	PFM	Fujiyama	P	500	76	225	380	300	See Note #530
4-6-2	#1369 Pacific	Hall	DongJ		350	78	250	290		See Note #34
4-6-2	#3400 Pacific	AHM	Mizuno			74	140	110	85	See Note #535
4-6-2	#3400 Pacific	Bal	KTM			68	70	320	240	See Note #534
4-6-2	#3400 Pacific	Key	Samh		600	78	180	220	160	See Note #33
4-6-2	#3400 Pacific	Key	Samh		500	78	170	290		See Note #32
4-6-2	#3400 Pacific	MGray	KTM			62	55	320	240	See Note #533
4-6-2	#3400 Pacific	PFM	Atlas/Naka	H	12	61	132	4500		See Note #532
4-6-2	#3500 Pacific	Hall	Ajin		350	81	236	260	190	See Note #536
4-6-4	Hudson	PFM	Atlas/Kawai	H	9	57	125	4500		See Note #539
4-6-4	#3450 Hudson	Key	Samh		600	77	170	260	210	See Note #36
4-6-4	#3450 Hudson	Key	Samh		600	77	170	260	210	See Note #37
4-6-4	#3450 Hudson	Key	Samh		300	78	180	260	210	See Note #537
4-6-4	#3460 Hudson	PFM	Tensh #139	P	750	60	48	260		See Note #540
4-6-4	#3460 Hudson	PFM	Tensh #239	P	50	60	45	235		Kit
4-6-4	#3460 Hudson	PFM	Tensh #139	P	250	61	48	270		See Note #540
4-6-4	#3460 Hudson	PFM	Tensh #239	P	50	61	45	250		Kit
4-6-4	#3460 Hudson	PFM	Tensh #139	P	250	62	55	280	210	See Note #540
4-6-4	#3460 Hudson	PFM	Tensh #239	P	50	63	50	260		Kit
4-6-4	#3460 Hudson	PFM	Tensh #139	P	350	63	55	290	220	See Note #540
4-6-4	#3460 Hudson	PFM	Tensh #139	P	175	64	55	300	230	See Note #540
4-6-4	#3460 Hudson	PFM	Tensh #139	P	375	65	65	320	240	See Note #540
4-6-4	#3460 Hudson	PFM	Tensh #139	P	295	67	65	330	250	See Note #540
4-6-4	#3460 Hudson	PFM	Tensh #139	P	100	71	125	350	275	See Note #541

Santa Fe's method of classifying locos was different than most. The class was numbered by the first engine in the class. Thus, loco #3131 was in the #3129 class. Built by Baldwin 1n 1916, she served until late 1949 when she was scrapped. Santa Fe was one of the first big roads to move from the Consolidation to the Mikado as its primary freight power. The first Santa Fe Mikes arrived in 1903 and the roster finally totaled 308 in all. This model was imported by the 'House of Four Winds' and is easily identified by its somewhat thicker than normal driver tires.

Atchison, Topeka & Santa Fe Railway (cont'd)

| Whyte Class | Owner Class & Type | Model Production | | | | | List Price | Resale | | Remarks |
		Importer	Builder	Cat #	Quan.	Yrs.		Mint	Avg.	
4-6-4	#3460 Hudson	PFM	Tensh		150	80	575	530	500	See Note #35
4-6-4	#3460 Hudson	TMS	Tetsudo							See Note #538
4-6-4	#3460 Hudson	WSM	Samh	MO-125	400	78	245	290		See Note #542
4-6-4	#3460 "Blue Goose"	PFM	Tensh #163	P	250	68	125	650		See Note #35
4-6-4	#3460 "Blue Goose"	PFM	Tensh #163	P	350	71	135	650		See Note #35
4-6-4	#3460 "Blue Goose"	PFM	Tensh #163	P	300	75	340	700	650	See Note #35 & 542
4-6-4	#3462 Hudson	Direct	Fomras		6	85	1790	1800		Handbuilt
4-6-4	#3462 Hudson	Intl	Akane		100	59	40	200	160	See Note #38
4-8-2	Mountain	Sun	Samh	HO110BP	100	91	299	290		fp., See Note #1018
4-8-2	Mountain	Sun	Samh	HO110B	100	91	250	250		See Note #1018
4-8-2	Mountain	Sun	Samh	HO110CP	100	91	299	290		fp., See Note #1019
4-8-2	Mountain	Sun	Samh	HO110AP	100	91	299	290		fp., Single Dome, coal
4-8-2	Mountain	Sun	Samh	HO110A	100	91	250	250		Single Dome
4-8-2	Mountain	Sun	Samh	HO110C	100	91	250	250		See Note #1019
4-8-2	Mountain	Sun	Samh	HO110AE	100	91	250	250		1 Dome early buy (?)
4-8-2	#3700 Mountain	Bal	KMT		413	65	70	350	225	See Note #39
4-8-2	#3702 Mountain	Sun	Samh	HO-21A						Hodges Trailing Truck
4-8-2	#3700 Mountain	Sun	Samh	HSF1001	950	76	160	280	220	See Note #40
4-8-4	#2900 Northern	TMS	Tetsudo							See Note #544
4-8-4	#2900 Northern	WMC	Samh	MO-125	400	78	650/3	280	220	See Note #543
4-8-4	#3751 Northern	Key	Samh		50	81	357	370	285	fp., Note #546
4-8-4	#3751 Northern	Key	Samh		1000	76	160	260	195	See Note #44
4-8-4	#3751 Northern	Key	Samh							final Rebuild
4-8-4	#3751 Northern	Key	Samh		400	78	257	290	220	Classic Series
4-8-4	#3765 Northern	Key	Samh		400	78	257	290	230	See Note #45
4-8-4	#3776 Northern	PFM	Atlas/Asahi	P	380	69	80	330	255	See Note #42
4-8-4	#3776 Northern	PFM	Atlas/Asahi	P	500	72	130	350	275	See Note #549
4-8-4	#3776 Northern	PFM	Atlas/Naka	H	8	55	125	4500		See Note #548
4-8-4	#3776 Northern	PFM	Atlas/Asahi	P	340	68	80	320	250	See Note #549
4-8-4	#3776 Northern	PFM	Atlas/Asahi	P	300	64	60	300	230	See Note #549
4-8-4	#3776 Northern	PFM	Atlas/Asahi	P	280	65	60	300	235	See Note #549
4-8-4	#3776 Northern	PFM	United		75	82	808	760	525	See Note #46 & 549
4-8-4	#3776 Northern	PFM	Atlas/Asahi	P	620	63	60	290	225	See Note #583
4-8-4	#3776 Northern	PFM	Atlas/Asahi	S	1	62				See Note #7
4-8-4	#3776 Northern	PFM	Atlas/Asahi	P	450	71	100	340	265	See Note #549
4-8-4	#3776 Northern	PFM	Atlas/Asahi	P	405	66	60	310	240	See Note #549

The early #3751 Class 4–8–4's of the Santa Fe weren't the handsomest 4–8–4's on the roster, with their double sand domes and high mounted Elesco feedwater heater, but they were good performers. A total of 14 engines were built by Baldwin between 1927 and 1929. The Key model depicts the engine after conversion from coal to oil and the addition of 80-inch drivers.

Atchison, Topeka & Santa Fe Railway (cont'd)

Whyte Class	Owner Class & Type	Model Production					List Price	Resale		Remarks
		Importer	Builder	Cat #	Quan.	Yrs.		Mint	Avg.	
4-8-4	#3776 Northern	PFM	Atlas/Asahi	P	335	67	70	320	245	See Note #549
4-8-4	#3784 Northern	PFM	United		75	82	808	760	545	See Note #47
4-8-4	#3784 Northern	PFM	Atlas/Asahi	P	600	75	250	410	300	See Note #43
4-8-4	#3784 Northern	PFM	Atlas/Asahi	P	930	62	55	320	250	See Note #41
4-4-6-2	#1398 Articulated	WSM	Samh	MO-149	300	79	385	620	480	See Note #527

Atlanta & West Point Railroad

Whyte Class	Owner Class & Type	Model Production					List Price	Resale		Remarks
		Importer	Builder	Cat #	Quan.	Yrs.		Mint	Avg.	
4-6-2	#290 Pacific	Key	Samh		50	82	350	395	370	See Note #2

Atlantic Coast Line Railroad (ACL)

Whyte Class	Owner Class & Type	Model Production					List Price	Resale		Remarks
		Importer	Builder	Cat #	Quan.	Yrs.		Mint	Avg.	
0-6-0	Switcher	Intl	Takara			57	20	150		Kit
0-6-0	Switcher	Intl	Takara			57	25	150	105	
4-6-2	P-5 Pacific	Key	Samh			75	79	266	320	250	Light USRA
4-8-2	Mountain	Key								Light USRA
4-8-4	R-1 Northern	OMI	DongJ	1402	425	77	190	350	275	80" Drivers
4-8-4	R-1 Northern	OMI	DongJ	1402.1	25	78	244	400	300	fp., two-tone gray

In 1938, Baldwin delivered twelve class R–1 4–8–4 Northerns to the ACL. They were not immediately successful, but after rebalancing, they proved to be excellent heavy passenger power with the ability to reach speeds in excess of 90 mph. Normally assigned to trains between Richmond, Va., and Jacksonville, Fl., they could make the run with 20 heavyweight cars in 14 hours and 5 minutes. Overland imported this Dong Jin-built model in 1977. The paint is a striking two–tone gray scheme.

Baltimore & Ohio Railroad (B&O)

Whyte Class	Owner Class & Type	Model Production					List Price	Resale		Remarks
		Importer	Builder	Cat #	Quan.	Yrs.		Mint	Avg.	
0-4-0T	C-16 Switcher	Gem	Samh	SH-119	1000	73	75-100	160	120	Dockside
0-4-0T	C-16 Switcher	PFM	Sakura/Ko	P	550	66	15	180	125	Dockside, Zamac
0-4-0T	C-16 Switcher	PFM	Sakura/Ko	P	500	63	14	180	125	Dockside, Zamac
0-4-0T	C-16 Switcher	PFM	Sakura/Ko	P	500	65	14	180	125	Dockside, Zamac
0-4-0T	C-16 Switcher	PFM	Sakura/Ko	P	1000	62	14	180	125	Dockside, Zamac
0-4-0T	C-16 Switcher	PFM	Sakura/Ko	P	700	64	14	180	125	Dockside, Zamac
0-4-0	Switcher	AHM						110		"Mother Hubbard"
0-4-0	C-16a Switcher	Gem	KMT-Samh	SH-118	932	72	75-120	150	100	Slope-Back Tender

Baltimore & Ohio Railroad (cont'd)

Whyte Class	Owner Class & Type	Model Production					List Price	Resale		Remarks
		Importer	Builder	Cat #	Quan.	Yrs.		Mint	Avg.	
0-4-0	C-16a Switcher	Intl	Takara			54	15	80	50	Kit
0-4-0	C-16a Switcher	Intl	Takara			59	19	90	65	
0-4-0	C-16a Switcher	KenK						110		
0-4-0	C-16a Switcher	MBA				59	17	110		fp.
0-4-0	C-16 Switcher	MBA				57		80		
0-6-0	D-30 Switcher	Akane	Akane			62	33	130	85	See Note #48 & 450
0-6-0	D-30 Switcher	Imp								
0-8-0	Switcher	Akane	Akane			63	48	190	150	USRA
0-8-0	L-1 Switcher	Sun		HO130DP	100		300			fp.
0-8-0	L-1 Switcher	Sun		HO130D	100		250			
0-8-0	L-2 Switcher	PFM	Atlas/Asahi	P	270	67	60	260	210	See Note #85
0-8-0	L-2 Switcher	PFM	Atlas/Asahi	P	475	66	48	260	210	See Note #85
0-8-0	L-2 Switcher	PFM	Atlas/Asahi	P	600	75	180	320	250	See Note #85
0-8-0	L-2 Switcher	PFM	Atlas/Asahi	S	1	65				See Note #7
0-8-0	L-2 Switcher	PFM	Atlas/Asahi	P	400	71	80	290	220	See Note #85
0-8-0	L-2 Switcher	PFM	Atlas/Asahi	S	1	66				See Note #7
0-10-0	U-1b Switcher	WMC	Samh	MO-96	700	77	180	310	240	G-File #96
2-8-0	E-24a Consol	Lam	CAB	901	500	74	190	380	300	See Note #49
2-8-0	E-27ca Consol	PFM	Atlas/Asahi	P	601	75	180	330	260	See Note #85
2-8-0	E-27ca Consol	PFM	Atlas/Asahi	S	1	65				See Note #7
2-8-0	E-27ca Consol	PFM	Atlas/Asahi	P	400	71	85	330	260	See Note #85
2-8-0	E-27ca Consol	PFM	Atlas/Asahi	P	380	69	65	260	200	See Note #85
2-8-0	E-27ca Consol	PFM	Atlas/Asahi	P	460	66	50	260	200	See Note #85
2-8-0	E-27ca Consol	PFM	Atlas/Asahi	S	1	66				See Note #7
2-8-0	E-27ca Consol	PFM	Atlas/Asahi	P	760	67	55	260	200	See Note #85
2-8-0	#3100 Consol	PFM	Atlas	H?	1	55				
2-8-0	E-60 Consol	SunDanc	Daeki			200	88	324	380	
2-8-0	E-60 Consol	SunDanc	Daeki			88				cp. See Note #1020
2-8-2	Q-1aa Mikado	Ortl	DaiYng	0404		84		440		
2-8-2	Q-1c Mikado	PSC	FM	16534		91	311			
2-8-2	Q-1c Mikado	PSC	FM	16534-1		91	355			fp.
2-8-2	Q-3 Mikado	PFM	United		440	62	50	300	240	See Note #455
2-8-2	Q-3 Mikado	PFM	United		500	63	50	300	240	See Note #455 & 570
2-8-2	Q-3 Mikado	PFM	United		155	64	50	300	240	See Note #455 & 570
2-8-2	Q-3 Mikado	PFM	United		230	66	55	300	240	See Note #455 & 570
2-8-2	Q-3 Mikado	WMC	Samh	MO-90	401	77	150	380	300	See Note #1021
2-8-2	Q-4 Mikado	PSC	FM	16536-1		91	355			fp.

Most of the steam engines on the B&O had a profile that somehow made them look like "family." You rarely confused them with another road's engines. Not so with the KB1 & KB1a. Purchased surplus from the Seaboard Air Line, they soon became favorites with the crews for their good ride and easy steaming. This model was built by Dong Jin and imported by Sunset Models.

Baltimore & Ohio Railroad (cont'd)

B&O inherited many of their locos from other roads via merger and acquisition. The P–8 Class 4–6–2 was such an engine, coming from the Cincinnati, Indianapolis and Western. Despite its foreign road heritage, it has the look of a B&O engine, with its high headlight and round number board mounted in the center of the boiler front. The model was made as a short semi-production run by modifying an OMI Monon K–5 Pacific. Dimensionally, the B&O and Monon are quite similar. With the addition of a different tender, the replication is very credible. Modifications of this type often allow the model to capture the look of a prototype that has not been produced by an importer. Two versions of this model were produced by ESCMRA in 1990 and 1991.

In the early 1940s the B&O needed faster freight power. Rather than build a new class of engines, Q–4b Mikado #4482 was refitted with a semi-water tube boiler, larger cylinders, 70-inch drivers and a 15,000-gallon Vanderbilt tender. B&O was impressed with the performance, and converted three aging Q–1c Mikados into this new class Q–4d. The later three engines were mechanically identical to #4482 but had 12,000-gallon Vanderbilt tenders. Westside Model Company imported this Samhongsa-built model in 1978.

Whyte Class	Owner Class & Type	Model Production					List Price	Resale		Remarks
		Importer	Builder	Cat #	Quan.	Yrs.		Mint	Avg.	
2-8-2	Q-4 Mikado	PSC	FM	16536		91	311			
2-8-2	Q-4b Mikado	Akane	Akane	400F		59	29	130	90	
2-8-2	Q-4b Mikado	Akane	Akane			60	35	140	100	Unsprung Drivers
2-8-2	Q-4b Mikado	Gem	Akane	AK-104	6	62	40	320	245	See Note #1022
2-8-2	Q-4b Mikado	Gem	Akane	AK-104	9	63	40	320	245	See Note #1022
2-8-2	Q-4b Mikado	Gem	Akane	AK-104	214	64	35	140	100	Unsprung Drivers
2-8-2	Q-4b Mikado	Gem	Akane	FM-104	200	64		320	245	See Note #1022
2-8-2	Q-4b Mikado	Gem	FuMod	FM-104	20	67	60	320	245	Sprung Drivers
2-8-2	Q-4b Mikado	Intl	Akane			59	30	130	100	Kit
2-8-2	Q-4b Mikado	Intl	Akane			59		150		Unsprung Drivers

Baltimore & Ohio Railroad (cont'd)

Whyte Class	Owner Class & Type	Importer	Builder	Cat #	Quan.	Yrs.	List Price	Mint	Avg.	Remarks
2-8-2	Q-4b Mikado	PSC	FM	16538-1		91	355			fp. See Note #1023
2-8-2	Q-4b Mikado	PSC	FM	16538		91	311			See Note #1023
2-8-2	Q-4b Mikado	WMC	Samh	MO-66	1210	76	140	250	180	See Note #574
2-8-2	Q-4b Mikado	WMC	Samh	MO-66A	500	76	150	280	210	See Note #575
2-8-2	Q-4b Mikado Tender	Gem	Akane	FT-104	100	64		60	55	
2-8-2	Q-4d Mikado	WMC	Samh	MO-110	500	78	170	310	240	See Note #51
2-8-2	Q-7f Mikado	PSC	FM	16532		91	311			
2-8-2	Q-7f Mikado	PSC	FM	16532-1		91	355			fp.
2-10-2	S-1 Santa Fe	LMB	KMT	K1008	600	66	80	320	250	See Note #1024
2-10-2	S-1 Santa Fe	LMB	KMT	K1008	800	62	80	320	250	See Note #1024
2-10-2	S-1 Santa Fe	OMI	Ajin	1496.1	10	89	807	760		6-Wheel tender, fp.
2-10-2	S-1 Santa Fe	OMI	Ajin	1496	80	89	714	705		6-Wheel tender
2-10-2	S-1 Santa Fe	PFM	Atlas/Nakayama	H	5	59	160	4500		Handbuilt
2-10-2	S-1a Santa Fe	OMI	Ajin	1498	50	89	714	670		4-Wheel tender
2-10-2	S-1a Santa Fe	OMI	Ajin	1498.1	10	89	807	760		4-Wheel tender, fp.
2-10-2	S-1a Santa Fe	OMI	Ajin	1497.1	26	89	807	650		6-Wheel tender, fp.
2-10-2	S-1a Santa Fe	OMI	Ajin	1497	130	89	714	670		6-Wheel tender
2-10-2	S-1a Santa Fe	WMC	Samh	MO-81	801	77	170	280	220	6100 class
2-6-6-2	KK-4b Articulated	Key	Samh		75	82	570	880	650	
2-6-6-4	KB-1 Articulated	Sun	DongJ	HO37	85	82	629	720		See Note #1025
2-6-6-4	KB-1a Articulated	Sun	DongJ	HO37A	85	82	629	720		See Note #1026
2-8-8-0	EL-3a Articulated	Sun	DongJ	HO36	179	82	629	750	525	See Note #52
2-8-8-4	EM-1 Articulated	Akane	Akane	800F		59	77	400	300	See Note #1027
2-8-8-4	EM-1 Articulated	Aristo	Akane			59	98	350	250	See Note #1027
2-8-8-4	EM-1 Articulated	Gem	Akane	800	25	63	115	450	300	
2-8-8-4	EM-1 Articulated	Gem	Akane	IM-108	10	62	115	400	300	Unsprung
2-8-8-4	EM-1 Articulated	Intl	Akane			59	98	350	275	See Note #1027
2-8-8-4	EM-1 Articulated	Key	Samh		75	83	800	975	900	#7620
2-8-8-4	EM-1 Articulated	Key	Samh		75	83	800	975	900	#7600
2-8-8-4	EM-1 Articulated	Takara	Akane			61	80	250	225	Blum's 1961 Sale
2-8-8-4	EM-1 Articulated	WMC	Samh			79	457	670	525	
4-4-2	A-2 Atlantic	CustB	KSM	ST-240	75	82	361	350	260	
4-4-4	J-1 Jubilee	CustB	KSM	ST-238	300	77	164	200	160	See Note #54
4-4-4-4	N-1 Duplex	WMC/PSC	Samh	MO-147		79-83	313-385	560	450	See Note #58
4-6-0	B-18 Ten Wheeler	GHC	KTM			59-61		200	125	fp.
4-6-0	B-18 Ten Wheeler	HOT	KTM					220	140	
4-6-0	B-18ca Ten Wheeler	Sun	Samh	HO35		80	213	235	170	#2024, Improved version
4-6-0	B-18ca Ten Wheeler	Sun	Samh	HO35		80	193	235	160	steam line missing left side

The design of the T–3b Mountain was heavily influenced by B&O experiments with upgrading aging Mikados into faster, more powerful Q–4d class engines. Taking this process one step further, several old Pacifics and Mikados were converted into the T–3 Class Mountains. With extended boilers, new frames, and a wide variety of mechanical changes, the T–3b proved to be an excellent dual-service locomotive. Westside Models imported this Samhongsa-built model in 1976.

Baltimore & Ohio Railroad (cont'd)

| Whyte Class | Owner Class & Type | Model Production | | | | | List Price | Resale | | Remarks |
		Importer	Builder	Cat #	Quan.	Yrs.		Mint	Avg.	
4-6-2	P-1d Pacific	OMI	DongJ	1403	500	77	180	325	240	
4-6-2	P-1d Pacific	Ortl	Samh	0438		84	375	375		
4-6-2	P-5 Pacific	Key	Samh		150	79	240	320	240	USRA Light
4-6-2	P-7 Pacific	Aristo	Akane			58	38	140	100	See Note #56
4-6-2	P-7 Pacific	Gem	Akane	AK-103	209	64		225		sprung
4-6-2	P-7 Pacific	Gem	Akane	AK-103	10	62	33-40	225	125	
4-6-2	P-7 Pacific	Gem	Akane	FM-103	200	64		250		sprung
4-6-2	P-7 Pacific	Gem	Akane	AK-103	11	63	33-40	225	125	See Note #56
4-6-2	P-7 Pacific	Gem	FuMod	FM-103	68	67	60	250	140	Sprung Drivers
4-6-2	P-7 Pacific	Intl	Akane			59	29	150	110	See Note #56

The first B&O Pacifics showed up on the property in 1906. In 1927, the first P–7 class engine arrived resplendent from Baldwin in an olive green paint scheme with red and gold striping. Carrying the names of 20 of the first 21 presidents (you couldn't have two ''President Adams'' on the roster), they were intended to pull the B&O varnish. The model pictured is a GEM ''Fuji'' version imported in 1967. It is basically the Akane engine with several mechanical and detailing improvements. Sprung drivers, better castings, brake shoes, and improved rivet detail made this a significant improvement over its Akane predecessor.

B&O's largest motive power was the 2–8–8–4, EM–1. Built late in the steam era (1944–1945), these Baldwin-built engines were equipped with the latest technology. With roller bearings on every axle, superheaters, thermic syphons and more, the B&O spared no innovation. Even so, they were gone by 1960. The Key model pictured represents the engines #7600–7619 as built in 1944. Samhongsa, the largest builder in Korea-produced this model in 1983. It is an excellent example of the fine quality of models that can now be expected from the major Korean builders.

Baltimore & Ohio Railroad (cont'd)

| Whyte Class | Owner Class & Type | Model Production | | | | | List Price | Resale | | Remarks |
		Importer	Builder	Cat #	Quan.	Yrs.		Mint	Avg.	
4-6-2	P-7 Pacific	Intl	Akane			60		150		Kit, unsprung drivers
4-6-2	P-7 Pacific "Presidents"	Key	Samh		40	89	557	705		See Note #1028
4-6-2	P-7 Pacific "Presidents"	Key	Samh		50	89	643	850		fp., See Note #1029
4-6-2	P-7 Pacific	Key	Samh		50	84	485	650		President, 1935 version
4-6-2	P-7 Pacific	Key	Samh		75	84	514	620		fp.
4-6-2	P-7 Pacific "Presidents"	Key	Samh		70	89	557	705		See Note #1030
4-6-2	P-7 Pacific "Presidents"	Key	Samh		65	84	485	650		President, as delivered
4-6-2	P-7c Pacific	Key	Samh		15	85		560		
4-6-2	P-7c Pacific	Key	Samh		45	85	514	620		fp.
4-6-2	P-7d Pacific	Key	Samh		100	84	515	650	475	See Note #55
4-6-2	P-7d Pacific	Key	Samh		45	85			430	"Cincinnatian" #5301, fp.
4-6-2	P-7d Pacific	Key	Samh		75	84				'Cincinnatian', #5303
4-6-2	P-7d Pacific	Key	Samh	#22				650		See Note #1031
4-6-2	P-7d Pacific	Key	Samh		15	85			430	'Cincinnatian', #5303, fp.
4-6-2	P-7e Pacific	Key	Samh		100	84	515	650		#5314
4-6-2	P-8 Pacific	ESCMRA	Ajin		45	90	439			cp., See Note #1032
4-6-2	P-8 Pacific	ESCMRA	Ajin		27	91	489			cp., See Note #1033
4-6-4	V-2 Hudson	CustB	KSM	ST-204	200	78	215	235	180	"Lord Baltimore"
4-8-2	T-3b Mountain	WMC	Samh	MO-74	1000	76	150	375		Rectangular Tender
4-8-2	T-3t Mountain	WMC	Samh	MO-119	400	78	190	430		See Note #57 & 672
4-8-2	T-4 Mountain	Key	Samh		60	89	564	760		
4-8-2	T-4 Mountain	Key	Samh		65	87	650	850		fp.
4-8-2	T-4 Mountain	Key	Samh		10	87	443	560		
4-8-2	T-4a Mountain	Key	Samh		65	87	650	850		fp.
4-8-2	T-4a Mountain	Key	Samh		10	87	564	760		

Bessemer & Lake Erie Railroad

| Whyte Class | Owner Class & Type | Model Production | | | | | List Price | Resale | | Remarks |
		Importer	Builder	Cat #	Quan.	Yrs.		Mint	Avg.	
2-10-4	Texas	Key								square sand dome
2-10-4	Texas	NPP	KMT			74	209	325		square sand dome, fp.

Boston & Albany Railroad (B&A)

| Whyte Class | Owner Class & Type | Model Production | | | | | List Price | Resale | | Remarks |
		Importer	Builder	Cat #	Quan.	Yrs.		Mint	Avg.	
2-8-2	#1200 Class Mikado	Key				91	950	840		fp.
2-8-2	#1200 Class Mikado	Key				91	790	790		
2-8-4	A-1a Berkshire	Cont						410	325	6-wheel tender
2-8-4	A-1a Berkshire	LMB				64	65	320	225	6-wheel tender
2-8-4	A-1a Berkshire	LMB				59	60	310		Boston & Albany
2-8-4	A-1a Berkshire	LMB				59	60	310		6-wheel tender
2-8-4	A-1b Berkshire	NPP	KMT			77	323	320	240	See Note #269
2-8-4	A-1b Berkshire	NPP	KMT		325	77	280	290	200	MR Review 11/77
2-8-4	A-1b Berkshire	NPP	KMT			77	280	290	200	See Note #268
2-8-4	A-1b Berkshire	NPP	KMT		170	77	323	350	240	fp.
2-8-4	A-2a Berkshire	Alco	KMT			75	268	380	300	See Note #268
2-10-2	Z-1a Santa Fe	Key	Samh		100	78	210	430		See Note #270
4-6-6T	D-1a Suburban	CustB	Rok-Am	ST-250	500	77	158	325	160	See Note #59
4-6-6T	D-1a Suburban	Intl				56	35	190	110	See Note #59
4-6-4	J-2 Hudson	Key	Mizuno			75	84			
4-6-4	J-2c Hudson	Key	Mizuno			75	84			round sand dome

Boston & Albany Railroad (cont'd)

The Boston and Albany's A–1 2–8–4 ushered in the era of "Super Power." Almost a direct descendent of the New York Central's H–10 class, these were the first freight engines to incorporate a four-wheel trailing truck. This allowed for a larger firebox and thus greater steaming capacity. After completing trials on the B&A in the summer of 1925, the A–1 began a sales tour for Lima that included a trip to the C&O's Alleghany Division. The C&O management was so impressed that they ultimately placed orders for 2–8–4's, 4–8–4's, 2–10–4's, and 2–6–6–6's, from Lima, all based on the "Super Power" concept initiated by the A–1. The original A–1 utilized a large rectangular tender with 6-wheel trucks. When B&A ordered their first 25 engines, they opted for a smaller tender with 4-wheel trucks. In all, B&A acquired 55 A–1 Class engines (#1400–1454) between 1925 and 1930. This model of the A–1b class (#1425–1444) was built by Kumata for Nickel Plate Products.

Boston & Maine Railroad (B&M)

Whyte Class	Owner Class & Type	Model Production					List Price	Resale		Remarks
		Importer	Builder	Cat #	Quan.	Yrs.		Mint	Avg.	
2-6-0	B-15B Mogul	OMI	MSM	1516	50	90	537	500		w/snowplow pilot
2-6-0	B-15B Mogul	OMI	MSM	1515	100	90	501	470		w/switching pilot
2-6-0	B-15C Mogul	OMI	MSM	1514	100	90	501	470		w/road pilot
2-6-0	B-15c Mogul	PFM	Samh	P	750	75	150	280	200	Snow Plow included
2-8-0	K-7a Consol	NERS	Samh			85	320	380		See Note #1034
2-8-0	K-7a Consol	NERS	Samh			85	365	430		See Note #1035
2-8-0	K-7b Consol	NERS	Samh			85	365	430		See Note #1036
2-8-0	K-7b Consol	NERS	Samh			85	320	380		See Note #1037
2-8-0	K-8b Consol	Sun	Samh		250	79	238	300	230	Elesco FWH
2-8-4	Berkshire	PSC		15508						See Note #1038
2-8-0	K-8b Consol	Sun	Samh		250	79	234	290	225	Worthington FWH
2-8-4	T-1a Berkshire	PSC		15510						See Note #1039
2-8-4	T-1a Berkshire	WMC	Nakamura	MO-114	320	78	330	560	450	See Note #60 & 61
2-8-4	T-1b Berkshire	LMB	Tetsudo			63	70	290	175	See Note #61
2-8-4	T-1b Berkshire	PSC		15512						See Note#1040
2-10-2	S1B Santa Fe	CustB	DaiYoung	ST-895E	150	81	407	570	450	See Note #1041
2-10-2	S1B Santa Fe	CustB	DaiYoung	ST-895C	150	81	407	570	450	See Note #1042
4-4-0	A-41 American	PFM	SKI	P	200	79	245	380	300	fp.
4-4-2	J-1 Atlantic	NERS	Samh			88				Rectangular Cab Windows
4-4-2	J-1 Atlantic	NERS	Samh			88				Arch Cab Windows
4-4-2	J-1 Atlantic	NERS	Samh			88				fp., Rect Cab Windows
4-4-2	J-1 Atlantic	NERS	Samh			88				fp., Arch Cab Windows
4-6-2	P-2b Pacific	OMI	JPMod	1451	150	84	323	390		See Note #62
4-6-2	P-2d Pacific	OMI	Ajin	1456	100	84	323	390		See Note #1043
4-6-2	P-4b Pacific	???	Sakura							See Note #1044
4-8-2	R-1A Mountain	Key	Samh		50	87	650	610		fp.
4-8-2	R-1B Mountain	Key	Samh		50	87	650	610		fp.
4-8-2	R-1C Mountain	Key	Samh		50	87	650	610		fp.
4-8-2	R-1d Mountain	AHM	Olympia		400	73		320		
4-8-2	R-1d Mountain	AHM	Olympia			73	180	250	225	fp.

Boston & Maine Railroad (cont'd)

The Boston & Maine Railroad is often thought of as having very little large power. Considered by most steam fans as primarily a commuter railroad, few photos were taken of the larger freight power. The S1b 2–10–2 exemplifies the look of a highly modernized 2–10–2, with Coffin feedwater heater, double air pumps, and all-weather cab. Custom Brass imported two versions of this Dai Young-built model in 1981.

Whyte Class	Owner Class & Type	Importer	Builder	Cat #	Quan.	Yrs.	List Price	Mint	Avg.	Remarks
4-8-2	R-1d Mountain	Gem	Olympia	EH-131P	100	69	135	375	350	fp.; See Note #1045
4-8-2	R-1d Mountain	Gem	Olympia	EH-131	300	69	120	325	300	See Note #1045
4-8-2	R-1d Mountain	Gem	Olympia	EH-131	300	70	120	325	300	See Note #1045

Canadian National Railways (CN)

Whyte Class	Owner Class & Type	Importer	Builder	Cat #	Quan.	Yrs.	List Price	Mint	Avg.	Remarks
0-6-0	O-18a Switcher	LMB	KMT			67	40	150	110	
0-6-0	O-18a Switcher	PFM	Samh	P	350	76	143	230		See Note #1047
0-6-0	O-18a Switcher	Pike/F&G		80RU		64-66	50	180	125	
0-6-0	O-18a Switcher	Van	Samh		350	76	143	230	170	MR Review 11/76
2-6-0	"424" Mogul	PFM	Unknown	H	1	56				
2-6-0	D-5c Mogul	PFM	Toby	P	150	69				See Note #65
2-6-0	"411" Class	PFM	Unknown	H	1	56				
2-6-0	D-5c Mogul	PFM	Toby	P	100	62		220	165	See Note #64
2-6-0	Mogul	PFM		H	1	58	116			See Note #63
2-6-0	E-10a Mogul	PFM	Samh	P	250	74	120			See Note #1047
2-6-0	E-10a Mogul	Van	Samh		250	74	120	190	130	See Note #66
2-8-0	N-5d Consolidation	PFM	Samh	P	300	74	140			See Note #1047
2-8-0	N-5d Consol	Van	Samh		300	74	140	230	170	See Note #67
2-8-0	M-3p Consol	Van	Samh							
2-8-0	N-1a,b Consol	Van	Samh			84	443	380		Elesco FWH
2-8-2	S-2 Mikado	PFM	Samh	P	300	76	175			See Note #1049
2-8-2	S-2 Mikado	Van	Samh		300	76	175	235	175	See Note #68
2-8-2	S-2a Mikado	Van	Samh			80	435	290	300	See Note #69
2-10-2	T-2a Santa Fe	Van	Samh			79	390	460	350	See Note #71
4-6-0	H-6g Ten Wheeler	PFM	Samh	P	150	77	165			See Note #1047
4-6-0	H-6g Ten Wheeler	Van	Samh		150	77	165	190	150	See Note #72
4-6-2	K-3g Pacific	OMI	Ajin	1459	125	87	414	410		#5612-5626 w/Elesco FWH
4-6-2	K-3b Pacific	OMI	Ajin	1467	100	86	407	400		#5578-5596
4-6-2	J-4e Pacific	PFM	Samh	P	300	75	155			See Note #1050
4-6-2	J-4e Pacific	Van	Samh		300	75	155	190	140	See Note #73
4-6-4	K-5a Hudson	PFM	Samh	P	150	78	225			See Note #1047
4-6-4	K-5a Hudson	Van	Samh		150	78	255	300	225	See Note #74

Canadian National Railways (cont'd)

Canadian National had 1,000 Class O 0–6–0's on its roster, most of which were acquired from mergers and purchases of other roads. This excellent example of the class was developed and imported into Canada by Van Hobbies. Pacific Fast Mail imported a number of the same model into the U.S. in cooperation with Van Hobbies.

In 1944, Canadian National received its last new steam locomotives from Montreal Locomotive Works. The U–1f 4–8–2's (#6060–6079) made a handsome appearance with their bullet nose, green and gold paint scheme, and streamlined side skirting. Known as "Bullet-Nosed Betties" on the CN, some engines later lost their bullet noses, which gave them an appearance quite similar to the CN Hudsons. Samhongsa built this excellent replica for Van Hobbies in 1976.

Whyte Class	Owner Class & Type	Model Production					List Price	Resale		Remarks
		Importer	Builder	Cat #	Quan.	Yrs.		Mint	Avg.	
4-8-2	U-1f Mountain	PFM	Samh	P	350	76	198			See Note #1051
4-8-2	U-1f Mountain	Van	Samh		350	76	198	280	200	See Note #76
4-8-2	U-1d Mountain	Van	Samh			81	385		300	See Note #75
4-8-4	U-4a Northern	MODX				85	139			
4-8-4	U-4a Northern	NPP	Park		200	77	242	290	225	
4-8-4	U-2g Northern	PFM	Toby	LP	150	76	330	750	450	See Note #78
4-8-4	U-2g Northern	PFM	Toby	LP	250	72	158	700	400	See Note #77
4-8-4	U-2e Northern	Van								#6167 Class
4-8-4	U-4a Northern	Van	Samh		75	82	465		315	See Note #81

Canadian Pacific Railway (CP)

Whyte Class	Owner Class & Type	Importer	Builder	Cat #	Quan.	Yrs.	List Price	Mint	Avg.	Remarks
0-6-0	U-3e Switcher	PFM	Samh	P	375	75	140			See Note #1047
0-6-0	U-3e Switcher	Van	Samh		375	75	140	200	160	
0-8-0	V-5a Switcher	Van				82	385	410	295	#6600 Class
2-8-0	N-2 Consol	PFM	Toby	P	150	64	48	235	175	See Note #87
2-8-0	N-2 Consol	PFM	Samh	P	250	73	120			See Note #1052
2-8-0	N-2a Consol	F&G		61RU		66	60	170	120	#3617 Open Cab
2-8-0	N-2a Consol	Pike/F&G		61RU	300	64	55	170	120	#3617 Open Cab
2-8-0	N-2b Consol	Van	Samh		250	73	120	200	150	See Note #88
2-8-0	M-4 Consol	Van	Samh			84				
2-8-2	P-1d/e Mikado	Van	Samh			79	391	410	325	See Note #92
2-8-2	P-2 Mikado	PFM	Samh	P	300	74	145			See Note #1047
2-8-2	P-2 Mikado	PFM	Toby	P	100	66	50	440	350	See Note #90
2-8-2	P-2a Mikado	Van	Samh		250	81	391	410	270	See Note #89
2-8-2	P-2j Mikado	Van	Samh		300	74	145	220	170	See Note #91
2-10-0	R-3a Decapod	Van	Samh			80	425	410	300	See Note #93
2-10-2	S-2a Santa Fe	Van	Samh			81	435	440	330	fp.; See Note #1053
2-10-2	S-2a Santa Fe	Van	Samh			79	430	430	310	See Note #94
2-10-4	T-1a Selkirk	PFM	Samh	P	300	75	250			See Note #1047
2-10-4	T-1a Selkirk	Van	Samh		300	75	250	410	300	See Note #96
2-10-4	T-1b Selkirk	Northern	Samh			83	462	490	385	
2-10-4	T-1c Selkirk	F&G				61-64	80	235	175	See Note #95
2-10-4	T-1c Selkirk	PFM	Samh	P	350	76	198			See Note #1047
2-10-4	T-1c Selkirk	Van	Samh		350	76	198	350	265	See Note #97
2-10-4	T-4a Selkirk	Northern	Totem			82	460	490	370	See Note #98
4-4-4	F-1a Jubilee	Van	Samh			74	145	220	165	See Note #99
4-4-4	F-2a Jubilee	Nrthn/Totem	WYang			83	352	330	250	See Note #86
4-4-4	F-2a Jubilee	PFM	Samh	P	250	74	145			See Note #1047
4-6-0	D-4g Ten Wheeler	F&G		62RU		67	60			
4-6-0	D-4g Ten Wheeler	Gem	Olympia	OC-104	149	67	50			See Note #1047
4-6-0	D-4g Ten Wheeler	Northern	Totem			81	290		240	#417-492; 62' drivers
4-6-0	D-10 Ten-Wheeler	PFM	Atlas/KTM	P	50	58	35	235	175	See Note #100
4-6-0	D-10 Ten-Wheeler	PFM	Atlas/KTM	P	110	62	38	250	190	See Note #100
4-6-0	D-10 Ten-Wheeler	PFM	Kawai	H	1	55				
4-6-0	D-10 Ten-Wheeler	PFM	Samh	P	300	73	90			See Note #1047
4-6-0	D-10 Ten-Wheeler	PFM	Atlas/KTM	P	200	59	38	240	180	See Note #100
4-6-0	D-10 Ten-Wheeler	Van	Samh		300	73	90	200	150	See Note #100
4-6-2	G-2 Pacific	PFM	Toby	P	50	67	55	350	275	See Note #102
4-6-2	G-2 Pacific	PFM	Toby	P	200	62	50	320	250	See Note #102
4-6-2	G-2 Pacific	Van	Samh			84				
4-6-2	G-3 Pacific	PFM	Samh	P	300	74	145			
4-6-2	G-3 Pacific	PFM	Toby	P	400	66				See Note #1047

In 1929, Canadian Pacific received twenty Class T–1a 2–10–4's from the Montreal Locomotive Works. Light by North American standards, these slim-looking engines were known as "Selkirks" on the CP. By 1938, the railroad had decided on a streamlined look for its motive power, and these engines received a rather tasteful repaint and streamlining that enhanced their appearance. The photo shows a Van Hobbies T–1a as it appeared before streamlining.

Canadian Pacific Railway (cont'd)

Whyte Class	Owner Class & Type	Model Production					List Price	Resale		Remarks
		Importer	Builder	Cat #	Quan.	Yrs.		Mint	Avg.	
4-6-2	G-3 Pacific	Van	Samh		300	74	145	230	170	See Note #103
4-6-2	G-3a Pacific	Van	Samh			82	415	430	400	See Note #104
4-6-2	G-3d Pacific	PFM	Samh	P		81	415	430	400	
4-6-2	G-3g Pacific	Van	Toby	S-74		66	55	410	380	See Note #101
4-6-2	G-4a,b Pacific	Van	Samh			83	465	490	450	#2700 Class
4-6-2	G-5b,c Pacific	Van	Samh							#1202-1271
4-6-4	H-1a/b Hudson	PFM	Samh	P	150	77	180			See Note #1047
4-6-4	H-1a/b Hudson	Van	Samh			77	180	260	180	See Note #107
4-6-4	H-1c Hudson	Van	Samh			79		290	200	See Note #108
4-6-4	H-1d Hudson	PFM	Samh			93	1390			fp., See Note #1558
4-6-4	H-1e Hudson	PFM	Samh			93	1350			fp., See Note #1558
4-6-4	H-1e Hudson	PFM	Tensh #166	P		80-81	745	705	550	See Note #106
4-6-4	H-1e Hudson	PFM	Tensh #166	P	1	69				
4-6-4	H-1e Hudson	PFM	Tensh #166	P	20	71	160	650	500	See Note #105
4-6-4	H-1e Hudson	PFM	Tensh #166	P	299	70	160	590	450	See Note #105
4-8-2	I-1a Mountain	Van	Samh			82	450	440	315	#2900-2901
4-8-4	K-1 Northern	Van	Samh		150	77	210	350	250	See Note #109
4-8-4	K-1a Northern	PFM	Samh	P	150	77	210			See Note #1047

Central Pacific - Union Pacific

Whyte Class	Owner Class & Type	Model Production					List Price	Resale		Remarks
		Importer	Builder	Cat #	Quan.	Yrs.		Mint	Avg.	
4-4-0	#60 & #119 American	Balboa	KTM					550	500	fp., See Note #1054
4-4-0	#60 & #119 American	PFM	Atlas/Asahi	S	1	68				See Note #7
4-4-0	#60 & #119 American	PFM	Atlas/Asahi	P	500	71	100	450	375	See Note #384
4-4-0	#60 & #119 American	PFM	Atlas/Asahi	P	879	69	90	450	375	See Note #384
4-4-0	#60 & #119 American	PFM	Atlas/Asahi	P	290	68	90	450	375	See Note #384

Two of the most recognizable locomotives in American railroading aren't distinguished by any particular oddities or examples of great design. Rather, they were simply in the right place at the right time. The Central Pacific ''Jupiter'' and the Union Pacific #119 were both stock models of the ''American,'' or 4–4–0 wheel arrangement. They met at Promontory, Utah, on May 10, 1869, signifying the completion of America's first transcontinental railroad. The models shown are the PFM ''Centennial Set,'' made by Atlas/Asahi.

Central of Georgia Railway

Whyte Class	Owner Class & Type	Model Production					List Price	Resale		Remarks
		Importer	Builder	Cat #	Quan.	Yrs.		Mint	Avg.	
4-8-4	K Northern	OMI	JPMod	1440	100	82	396	420	320	#451-458

Central Railroad of New Jersey

Whyte Class	Owner Class & Type	Model Production					List Price	Resale		Remarks
		Importer	Builder	Cat #	Quan.	Yrs.		Mint	Avg.	
0-6-0	B-2 Switcher	OMI	MSM	1502	40	89	419	410		#50-100
0-6-0	B-3 Switcher	OMI	MSM	1499	40	89	419	410		#1-8
0-6-0	B-3a Switcher	OMI	MSM	1500	40	89	419	410		#9-23
0-6-0	B-3b, B-4 Switcher	OMI	MSM	1501	80	89	419	410		#24-33, B-4
2-8-2	M2as Mikado	OMI	Ajin	1475	55	87	484	550		See Note #1055
2-8-2	M3as Mikado	OMI	Ajin	1477	75	87	500	550		See Note #1056
2-8-2	M3as Mikado	OMI	Ajin	1478	70	87	500	550		See Note #1057
2-8-2	M3s Mikado	OMI	Ajin	1476	100	87	514	575		See Note #1058
4-2-4T	Inspection Engine	Fomras	Fomras			86	299			Inspection Engine "Star"
4-2-4T	Inspection Engine	Fomras	Fomras			85	269			Inspection Engine "Star"
4-6-0	L-6s Ten-Wheeler	Red	Toho		1400	71	75	235	175	See Note #110
4-6-0	Ten-Wheeler	Intl				54	25	180	125	Camelback
4-6-0	T-38 Ten Wheeler	Key								Camelback
4-6-0	T-40 Ten Wheeler	Key								Camelback
4-6-4T	H-1s Suburban	Hunt	KMT			68	55	190	125	See Note #1059
4-6-4T	H-1s Suburban	ModW	KMT			71	45	190	145	See Note #1060
4-6-4T	H-1s Suburban	PFM	Atlas/Asahi	P	475	69	70	350	225	
4-8-0	K-1 Twelve Wheeler	CustB	DaiYng	ST-210	175	85	465	320	250	Camelback
4-8-0	K-1as Camelback	PSC	D&D	16106		90	482			
4-8-0	K-1as Camelback	PSC	D&D	16106-1		90	544	510		fp., CRR of NJ
4-8-0	K-1as Camelback	PSC	D&D	16106-2		90	544	510		fp. Jersey Central
4-8-0	K-1s Camelback	PSC	D&D	16050-1		90	544	510		fp., CRR of NJ
4-8-0	K-1s Camelback	PSC	D&D	16050-2		90	544	510		fp. Jersey Central
4-8-0	K-1s Camelback	PSC	D&D	16050		90	482			
4-8-0	K-1s Camelback	PSC	D&D	16050		90	459	430		

"Camelbacks" were popular on many eastern roads because they could accommodate the large fireboxes needed to burn the anthracite coal common to the area. They were not, however, so popular with the crews. They were hot for the engineer, cold for the firemen, and dangerous for both. This fine replica of the Jersey Central's 4–6–0 was imported by Red Ball.

Central Vermont Railway

Whyte Class	Owner Class & Type	Model Production					List Price	Resale		Remarks
		Importer	Builder	Cat #	Quan.	Yrs.		Mint	Avg.	
2-8-0	M-3a Consol	CustB	DaiYng	ST-933E	50	85	482	410		w/Elesco FWH
2-8-0	M-3a Consol	CustB	DaiYng	ST-933C	125	85	482	410		w/Coffin FWH
2-8-0	N-5a Consol	NERS	Samh							w/Elesco FWH

Central Vermont Railway (cont'd)

| Whyte Class | Owner Class & Type | Model Production | | | | | List Price | Resale | | Remarks |
		Importer	Builder	Cat #	Quan.	Yrs.		Mint	Avg.	
2-10-4	T-3a Texas	PFM	Samh	P		78	265	330	250	See Note #111
4-8-2	U-1a Mountain	OMI	Ajin	1452	110	85	394	410		#601 & 602
4-8-2	U-1a Mountain	OMI	Ajin	1458	140	85	394	410		#603 w/Smokelifters

Chesapeake & Ohio Railway (C&O)

| Whyte Class | Owner Class & Type | Model Production | | | | | List Price | Resale | | Remarks |
		Importer	Builder	Cat #	Quan.	Yrs.		Mint	Avg.	
0-8-0	C-15 Switcher	PSC	Nakamura	15270		82	399			w/sound & lights
0-8-0	C-15a Switcher	Lam	CAB	9040	500	77-76	342	300	290	See Note #114
0-8-0	C-15a Switcher	Lam	CAB	9050	400	77	440	400		See Note #576
0-8-0	C-15a Switcher	Soho	CAB	0641	100	78	120	270	235	See Note # 115
0-8-0	C-16 Switcher	PFM	Tensh #145	LP	136	64	80	275		See Note #1061
0-8-0	C-16 Switcher	PFM	Tensh #145	LP	115	66	80	300	275	See Note #1061
0-8-0	C-16 Switcher	PFM	Tensh #145	LP	30	67	85	350	300	See Note #112
0-8-0	C-16 Switcher	PFM	Tensh #145	LP	200	63	80	250	225	See Note #1061
0-8-0	C-16 Switcher	PFM	Tensh #145	LP	230	70	115	390	350	See Note #1198
0-8-0	C-16 Switcher	PSC	D&D	16136-1		90	557	450		fp. #255-284
0-8-0	C-16 Switcher	PSC	D&D	16136		90	470			#255-284
0-8-0	C-16 Switcher	PSC	D&D	16136-1		90	557	449		#255-284, fp.
0-8-0	C-16 Switcher	PSC	D&D	16136		90	470	390		#255-284
0-8-0	C-16 Switcher	W&R	Samh		37	88	421	530		#240-254; also VGN.
0-8-0	C-16 Switcher	W&R	Samh		59	88	492	575		fp. #240-254; also VGN.
0-10-0	C-12 Switcher	Austin ?	Tetsudo?			50's		220		See Note #1062
0-10-0	C-12 Switcher	CustB	KSM	ST-284	500	77	165	290	190	See Note #1063
2-8-0	G-9 Consol	OMI	Rok-Am	1414	450	79	214	260	230	See Note #116
2-8-0	G-9 Consol	OMI	Rok-Am	1433	50	80	243	300	280	See Note #117
2-8-0	G-9 Consol	OMI	Ajin			91	635	600		See Note #1065
2-8-0	G-9 Consol	OMI	Ajin			91	635	600		See Note #1064
2-8-0	G-9 Consol	OMI	Ajin			91	635	600		See Note #1066
2-8-2	K-2 Mikado	Hall	DongJ		500	76	210	260	230	See Note #118
2-8-2	K-3 Mikado	Key	Samh		42	85	471	580	530	21RA w/Elesco
2-8-2	K-3 Mikado	Key	Samh		13	85	529	630	580	21RA w/Elesco, fp.

Most train buffs think of big steam when C&O is mentioned. With much of the main line crossing the Alleghenies of West Virginia there certainly was need for big engines. But before 1900, C&O's roster was much like every other road's. 4–4–0's, 2–6–0's, and big power in the 2–8–0. Engine #428 is a Class E–5 2–6–0 built by Baldwin in 1908 and obtained in the merger of the Virginia Air Line in 1912. This exquisite little model was built from a PFM V&T 4–6–0 by John Gascoyne. Modifying existing prototypes to closely resemble a particular engine or a locomotive from another road is one of the highest forms of craftsmanship in the hobby of model railroading.

Chesapeake & Ohio Railway (cont'd)

Much of the C&O's lighter branch line work was done by 2–8–0's, Classes G–7 and G–9. These engines began life in the early 1900s and served up to almost the end of steam. As with most steam engines that were solidly designed, they went through a variety of changes in their lifetime. The OMI model shown here depicts the Class G–9 2–8–0 as it might have appeared in the early '50s, with "Sports Cab," flying numberboards, and Walschaerts valve gear.

C&O used big switchers. Most were 0–8–0's but a few 0–10–0's were used, primarily in the long, flat yard at Peach Creek, W.V. The model shown is an early example of the craftsmanship from Japan. Probably built in the early 1950s, it displays no brass castings but is fully sprung. No manufacturer can be identified. It may have been built for an American GI stationed in Japan by one of the many builders who occupied the Ginza district.

| Whyte Class | Owner Class & Type | Model Production | | | | | List Price | Resale | | Remarks |
		Importer	Builder	Cat #	Quan.	Yrs.		Mint	Avg.	
2-8-2	K-3 Mikado	PFM	Atlas/Asahi	CR	350	78	550	730	650	See Note #120
2-8-2	K-3 Mikado	PFM	Atlas/Asahi	CR	350	78	495	730	590	See Note #119
2-8-2	K-3a Mikado	Key	Samh		12	85	471	580	530	16VC w/Elesco
2-8-2	K-3a Mikado	Key	Samh		17	85	529	630	580	21RA W/Worthington, fp.
2-8-2	K-3a Mikado	Key	Samh		20	85	471	580	530	21RA w/Elesco
2-8-2	K-3a Mikado	Key	Samh		18	85	471	580	530	16VC W/Worthington
2-8-2	K-3a Mikado	Key	Samh		20	85	529	630	580	16VC W/Worthington, fp.
2-8-2	K-3a Mikado	Key	Samh		18	85	529	680	620	16VC w/Elesco, fp.
2-8-2	K-3a Mikado	Key	Samh		33	85	471	580	530	21RA W/Worthington
2-8-2	K-3a Mikado	Key	Samh		12	85	529	630	580	21RA w/Elesco, fp.
2-8-2	K-3a Mikado	PFM	Atlas/Asahi		250	80-88	698	530	470	See Note #578
2-8-4	K-4 Kanawha	Direct	United-minari			89	1170	1200		See Note #1067
2-8-4	K-4 Kanawha	Direct	United-minari			89	1170	1200		See Note #1068
2-8-4	K-4 Kanawha	Direct	United-minari			90	1170	1200		See Note #1628

Chesapeake & Ohio Railway (cont'd)

| Whyte Class | Owner Class & Type | Model Production | | | | | List Price | Resale | | Remarks |
		Importer	Builder	Cat #	Quan.	Yrs.		Mint	Avg.	
2-8-4	K-4 Kanawha	Key				92	995	850		See Note #1069
2-8-4	K-4 Kanawha	Key				93	1070			fp., See Note #1070
2-8-4	K-4 Kanawha	Key	Samh		50	83	415	420		See Note #1071
2-8-4	K-4 Kanawha	Key	Samh		4	83	400	400		See Note #1072
2-8-4	K-4 Kanawha	Key	Samh		75	83	400	400		See Note #1073
2-8-4	K-4 Kanawha	Key				94	1070			fp., See Note #1074
2-8-4	K-4 Kanawha	Key				94	1070			fp., See Note #1075
2-8-4	N-3 Kanawha	Key				94	1070			fp., See Note #1076
2-8-4	K-4 Kanawha	Key				94	1070			fp., See Note #1077
2-8-4	K-4 Kanawha	Key				94	1070			fp., See Note #1078
2-8-4	K-4 Kanawha	LMB				60	48	130	110	
2-8-4	K-4 Kanawha	LMB				61	60	150	125	sprung drivers
2-8-4	K-4 Kanawha	PFM	Atlas		1	56	125			Handbuilt
2-8-4	K-4 Kanawha	PFM	Atlas/Asahi	P	450	77	275	320	250	See Note #123
2-8-4	K-4 Kanawha	PFM	Atlas/Asahi	P	500	72	120	260	200	
2-8-4	K-4 Kanawha	PFM	Atlas/Asahi	P	500	71	95	235	175	
2-8-4	K-4 Kanawha	PFM	Atlas/Asahi	P	502	74	210	290	225	
2-8-4	K-4 Kanawha	PFM	Atlas/ Nakayama	H	5	60		5000	4500	See Note #121
2-10-2	B-1 Santa Fe	CustB	DaiYng	ST-279B	40	84	523	470	360	See Note #125
2-10-2	B-1 Santa Fe	CustB	DaiYng	ST-279A	70	84	523	470	370	See Note #124
2-10-2	B-1 Santa Fe	CustB	DaiYng	ST-279C	40	84	523	470	360	See Note #126
2-10-2	B-3 Santa Fe	Sun	Samh		400	77	169	235	170	See Note #127
2-10-4	T-1 Texas	CustB	DaiYng	ST-275	500	77	232	350	260	See Note #128
2-10-4	T-1 Texas	Key	Samh		60	85	585	750	600	fp., lighted.
2-10-4	T-1 Texas	Key	Samh			92	1000	850		
2-10-4	T-1 Texas	Key	Samh			92	1075	900		fp.
2-10-4	T-1 Texas	Key	Samh		40	85	528	650	550	
2-10-4	T-1 Texas	Sun		HO133		90	275	225		Sparce detail
2-10-4	T-1 Texas	WMC	KTM	MO-130	250	78	357	350	285	See Note #129
2-6-6-2	H-4 Articulated	CustB	DaiYng	ST-871	200	80	498	450	410	See Note #117
2-6-6-2	H-4 Articulated	Key	Samh		20	85	757	850	610	12VC tender. fp.
2-6-6-2	H-4 Articulated	Key	Samh		15	85	686	775	555	12VC tender
2-6-6-2	H-5 Articulated	Gem	FuMod	FM-215	10	67	100	415	350	See Note #1917
2-6-6-2	H-5 Articulated	Key	Samh		75	81	557	480	445	See Note #131
2-6-6-2	H-6 Articulated	Key	Samh		25	85	686	775	560	12VC tender
2-6-6-2	H-6 Articulated	Key	Samh		40	85	700	800	570	16VC tender
2-6-6-2	H-6 Articulated	Key	Samh		15	85	770	900	615	16VC tender, fp.
2-6-6-2	H-6 Articulated	Key	Samh		35	85	700	775	630	21RA tender
2-6-6-2	H-6 Articulated	Key	Samh		15	85	770	900	730	21RA tender, fp.

Even with all of the huge steam on the C&O roster, the bulk of the work was done by 2–8–2's and 2–8–4's. The K3 class 2–8–2's were the workhorses of the C&O stable from 1924 through the early 1940s. The 2–8–2 is a Class K–3 PFM Crown built in 1978.

Chesapeake & Ohio Railway (cont'd)

In 1943, C&O ordered their first 2–8–4 from Alco. Based on the design of the NKP Berkshire, C&O had a winner. The 2–8–4 or "Kanawha" was built by United-Minari in 1989 and was never advertised in this country. This version incorporates the external air tanks, a version that had not been previously modeled.

Whyte Class	Owner Class & Type	Model Production					List Price	Resale		Remarks
		Importer	Builder	Cat #	Quan.	Yrs.		Mint	Avg.	
2-6-6-2	H-6 Articulated	Key	Samh		20	85	757	850	620	12VC tender. fp.
2-6-6-2	H-6 Articulated	PFM	Atlas/Asahi	P	235	66	85	400		See Note #577
2-6-6-2	H-6 Articulated	PFM	Atlas/Asahi	P	325	65	80	400		See Note #577
2-6-6-2	H-6 Articulated	PFM	Atlas/Asahi	P	380	69	100	450		See Note #577
2-6-6-2	H-6 Articulated	PFM	Atlas/Asahi	P	500	74	285	480		See Note #133
2-6-6-2	H-6 Articulated	PFM	Atlas/Asahi	S	1	64				See Note #7
2-6-6-2	H-6 Articulated	PFM	Atlas/Asahi	S	1	63				See Note #7
2-6-6-2	H-6 Articulated	PFM	Atlas/Asahi	P	260	68	85	480		See Note #577
2-6-6-2	H-6 Articulated	PFM	Atlas/Asahi	P	475	64	80	480		See Note #577
2-8-8-2	H-7 Chesapeake	CustB	Goto	ST-296	100	83	940	1300	1100	See Note #1079
2-8-8-2	H-7a Chesapeake	CustB	Goto	ST-265	350	77	698	1150	950	See Note #139
2-6-6-6	H-8 Alleghany	Akane	Akane	900F		59	110	450	350	See Note #134
2-6-6-6	H-8 Alleghany	Austin	Tetsudo			55-56		1600	1400	
2-6-6-6	H-8 Alleghany	Gem	Akane	IM-102	64	62	160	400	350	Unsprung, no brake shoes
2-6-6-6	H-8 Alleghany	Gem	Akane	IM-102	100	64	150	550	450	sprung, brake shoes
2-6-6-6	H-8 Alleghany	Gem	Akane	900	15	63	160	400	350	
2-6-6-6	H-8 Alleghany	Intl	Takara		1	59	139	350		See Note #135
2-6-6-6	H-8 Alleghany	Key	Samh		20	86	965	1050		early vers. mod., fp.#1600
2-6-6-6	H-8 Alleghany	Key	Samh		200	81	685	850		intermediate version
2-6-6-6	H-8 Alleghany	Key	Samh		100	81	685	850		See Note #136
2-6-6-6	H-8 Alleghany	Key	Samh		100	81	685	850		See Note #138
2-6-6-6	H-8 Alleghany	Key	Samh		30	86		1025		early version, fp.#1600
2-6-6-6	H-8 Alleghany	Key	Samh		60	86		1025		late version, fp. #1645
2-6-6-6	H-8 Alleghany	Key	Samh		20	86		1025		early vers. mod.,#1600
2-6-6-6	H-8 Alleghany	Key	Samh		60	86	879	975		late version, #1645
2-6-6-6	H-8 Alleghany	PFM	Fujiyama		110	83	1325	1600		CROWN; fp., good runner
2-6-6-6	H-8 Alleghany	PFM	Fujiyama	CR	90	79	1283	1200		See Note #137
2-6-6-6	H-8 Alleghany	PFM	Tensh #124	H	9	56	154	3500		fp., See Note #1297
2-6-6-6	H-8 Alleghany	PFM	Tensh #124	H	30	62	188	3500		fp., See Note #1952
2-6-6-6	H-8 Alleghany	PFM	Tensh #124	H	1	55	123	3500		fp., Handbuilt
2-6-6-6	H-8 Alleghany	PFM	Tetsudo	H	4	56	80	2500		Handbuilt
2-6-6-6	H-8 Alleghany	PFM	Tetsudo	H	1	55	75	2500		Handbuilt
2-6-6-6	H-8 Alleghany	PFM	Fujiyama	CR	24	80	1400	1600		See Note #1081

Chesapeake & Ohio Railway (cont'd)

Lima built five different orders of Alleghanies for the C&O. Train buffs tend to divide these into three broad categories: the early (without number boards), the mid (with flying number boards and five over-fire jets), and the late (with the number boards and nine over-fire jets). The photo shows the recent OMI model of the late version. This model is an excellent example of the craftsmanship that can now be obtained from Korea. This is Ajin's first articulated.

The C&O "Alleghany" is generally regarded as the "Big Boy" of the East. Rail fans will argue endlessly which was bigger, or was more powerful, all to no avail. With the great popularity, it is no wonder that models of the Alleghany abound. Records show more than 1,000 models have been imported into this country, but there are probably far more than that if the number of models built for the Japanese market is considered. The model pictured represents one of the earliest mass-produced models of the Alleghany. This model was received in an M.B. Austin box and was probably built by Tetsudo. The author has two models of this engine and each has slight detail differences. This is typical of handbuilt models since each one was the work of a particular craftsman. The incorporation of detail differences may have been an attempt to make each handbuilt model unique. Tetsudo was not the only builder to make slight changes from model to model—this can also be seen in early Toby handbuilts.

Whyte Class	Owner Class & Type	Model Production					List Price	Resale		Remarks
		Importer	Builder	Cat #	Quan.	Yrs.		Mint	Avg.	
2-D-2+ 2-D-2	M-1 Turbine	CustB	Orion	ST-129X	45	82	598	800		unpainted
2-D-2+ 2-D-2	M-1 Turbine	CustB	Orion	ST-129	200	80	650	950		fp., See Note #151
4-4-2	A-16 Atlantic	OMI	JPMod	1435	200	81	271	380	300	#286 w/9RA tender
4-6-0	F-11 Ten Wheeler	Ortl	DaiYng	0040	250	80	240	320	260	MR 10/80
4-6-0	F-11 Ten Wheeler	Ortl	DaiYng	0092	12	81	272	375	300	fp.
4-6-2	F-15 Pacific	OMI	JPMod	1445	25	83	315	330	300	12VC Tender
4-6-2	F-15 Pacific	OMI	JPMod	1447	75	83	315	310	225	Rectangular Tender
4-6-2	F-17 Pacific	Key	SKI		50	90	856	800		fp.
4-6-2	F-17 Pacific	Key	SKI		11	90	856	800		See Note #1092
4-6-2	F-17 Pacific	PFM	United	CR	250	79	731	950		See Note #140
4-6-2	F-18 Pacific	Key	SKI		9	90				

Chesapeake & Ohio Railway (cont'd)

The middle series of Alleghanies (#1610–1644) have never received the photographic or press coverage of the very early or late engines. Mechanical differences were slight, the most obvious was the five over-fire jets in a straight line, whereas the later engines had nine arranged in a staggered fashion. Samhongsa built this fine replica of ''Lima's Finest'' for Key Imports in 1981.

Before the Alleghany, C&O had need for a large engine to move coal over the Alleghenies. The H–7 and H–7a 2–8–8–2's were the answer. Built by Schenectady and Baldwin in 1924–26 they spent their life in coal-drag service. They weren't fast or clean, but they did reduce the double heading that had plagued C&O operations for several years on the steep grades. This model of the H–7 was imported by NJ Custom Brass and was built by Goto, one of the premier Japanese builders.

C&O had three distinctively different-looking groups of Northerns. The first group, #600–604, bore the names of Virginia statesmen on the side of the sand dome. These engines were used on the C&O's famous passenger trains, the ''George Washington,'' the ''FFV,'' and the ''Sportsman.'' The model shown is an early PFM Crown built by Atlas/Toby in the 1959–60 time frame. Toby, one of the premier builders in Japan, also built some fine O-gauge models.

Chesapeake & Ohio Railway (cont'd)

Whyte Class	Owner Class & Type	Model Production					List Price	Resale		Remarks
		Importer	Builder	Cat #	Quan.	Yrs.		Mint	Avg.	
4-6-2	F-18 Pacific	Key	SKI		45	90	856	725		fp. See Note #1083
4-6-2	F-19 Pacific	Key	SKI		65	90	856	725		fp.
4-6-2	F-19 Pacific	Key	SKI		8	90				
4-6-2	F-19 Pacific	PFM	United	CR	225	79	731	950		See Note #141
4-6-4	L-1 Hudson	CustB	DaiYng	ST-880	175	83	548	550		See Note #142
4-6-4	L-1 Hudson	PSC	D&D	15890-1		88	549	442		fp. orange, See Note #142
4-6-4	L-1 Hudson	PSC	D&D	15890-2		88	549	442		fp. yellow, See Note #142
4-6-4	L-1 Hudson	PSC	D&D	15890		88	499	402		See Note #142
4-6-4	L-2 Hudson	AMBr	Fomras		10	81	3500	2700	2500	See Note #145
4-6-4	L-2 Hudson	CustB	DongJ	ST-270	600	77	193	200	175	See Note #146
4-6-4	L-2 Hudson	Direct	Fomras		]10	85	3500	2700	2500	Handbuilt
4-6-4	L-2 Hudson	Gem	Olympia	DH-109	5	65		350		
4-6-4	L-2 Hudson	Gem	Olympia	DH-109	624	62	80	350	170	See Note #144
4-6-4	L-2 Hudson	Gem	Olympia	DH-109	109	64		350		See Note #144
4-6-4	L-2 Hudson	PFM	Fujiyama	CR	16	89	1500	2200	2000	See Note #1084
4-6-4	L-2a Hudson	AmBr	Fomras		5	81	3500	2700	2500	See Note #145 & 579
4-6-4	L-2a Hudson	CustB	DaiYng	ST-269	400	79	385	280	200	
4-6-4	L-2a Hudson	Direct	Fomras		-5	81-83	3500	2700	2500	Handbuilt
4-6-4	L-2a Hudson	OMI	Ajin	1493	100	88	657	620		See Note #579
4-6-4	L-2a Hudson	OMI	Ajin	1493.1	200	88	713	670		fp., See Note #579
4-6-4	L-2a Hudson	PFM	Fujiyama	CR	26	87-88	1470	2000	1800	See Note #1085
4-6-4	L-2a Hudson	PFM	Atlas/Nakayama	H	11	61	135	8000		See Note #143
4-8-2	J-2 Mountain	Akane	Akane			64	62	235	160	USRA Version as received
4-8-2	J-2 Mountain	CustB	DaiYng	ST-803	500	78	234	290	225	#543-549
4-8-2	J-2 Mountain	Gem	Olympia	DH-112	300	64	90	380	275	See Note #464
4-8-2	J-2 Mountain	Gem	Olympia	RS-112	50	68	125	940	700	See Note #147
4-8-2	J-2 Mountain tender	Gem	Olympia	OT-112	50	64		80		
4-8-2	J-2 Mountain	Gem	Olympia	RS-112	50	64		940	700	See Note #147 & 464
4-8-2	J-2 Mountain	Gem	Olympia	DH-112	12	65				See Note #464
4-8-4	J-3 Greenbrier	CustB	DongJ	ST-802		80	363	300	225	See Note #581
4-8-4	J-3 Greenbrier	Key	Samh		15	84	614		525	fp., See Note #1086
4-8-4	J-3 Greenbrier	Key	Samh		15	84	614		495	fp., See Note #1087
4-8-4	J-3 Greenbrier	OMI	DongJ	1405	500	78	245	290	230	#605-606
4-8-4	J-3 Greenbrier	PFM	Atlas/Toby	CR	25	60	125	3200		See Note #150
4-8-4	J-3 Greenbrier	PFM	Atlas/Toby	CR	25	59	125	3200		See Note #1940
4-8-4	J-3a Greenbrier	Akane	Akane		N/A	N/A	N/A			See Note #1088
4-8-4	J-3a Greenbrier	AmBr	Fomras		10	85	3500	2600		Handbuilt
4-8-4	J-3a Greenbrier	Gem	Olympia	DH-103	269	68	100	375	325	See Note #582

In 1941, the C&O needed new passenger power and went to Baldwin for what was to become the heaviest 4–6–4 ever built. Equipped with all the latest appliances, including Franklin Type B rotary poppet valves, these engines soon established themselves as not only big, but powerful. The model pictured is one of 12 imported by PFM in 1961 and built by Nakiyama, one of the finest brass craftsmen in Japan. Nakiyama specialized in small runs of highly detailed models. The accuracy and workmanship of this model far exceeded the vast majority of models being built in 1962 and compares favorably with some of the finest models being built today.

Chesapeake & Ohio Railway (cont'd)

A 2–10–4 is a big engine with a limited purpose—heavy mainline freight power. Never built to be fast enough for hotshot freights or passenger work, most "Texas" types spent their lives pulling long, heavily loaded trains. Simpler to maintain than articulateds they were often favored where the curves were broad and the grades were steady. The C&O T–1 "Texas" was, in fact, an enlargement of the very successful Erie S–3 Berkshires. The styling was a departure from C&O practice. The flying pumps were gone and the headlight remained centered on the boiler face. Nonetheless, the styling was distinctively late Lima, and that was synonymous with C&O. So successful was the design that Pennsy copied it for their famous J–1's. Samhongsa produced this fine model for Key Imports in 1985.

Whyte Class	Owner Class & Type	Model Production					List Price	Resale		Remarks
		Importer	Builder	Cat #	Quan.	Yrs.		Mint	Avg.	
4-8-4	J-3a Greenbrier	Gem	Olympia	DH-103P	75	68	110	435	375	fp., See Note #147 & 582
4-8-4	J-3a Greenbrier	Gem	Olympia	DH-103	68	64	90	375	300	See Note #582
4-8-4	J-3a Greenbrier	Key	Samh		60	84	614	725	575	#613 w/Elephant Ears. fp.
4-8-4	J-3a Greenbrier	Key	Samh		15	84	614	725	560	#610, fp.
4-8-4	J-3a Greenbrier	Key	Samh		60	84	557	448	455	#613 w/Elephant Ears
4-8-4	J-3a Greenbrier	Key	Samh		60	84	557	650		#614 excursion engine, fp.
4-8-4	J-3a Greenbrier	PFM	United		250	81	881	900		See Note #1089
4-8-4	J-3a Greenbrier	PFM	Atlas/Toby	CR	50	60	125	3300		See Note #149
4-8-4	J-3a Greenbrier	PFM	Atlas		1	56	125			See Note #148
4-Tk Shay	C-12 Shay	PSC	Nakamura	15238		82	569	675	650	See Note #642

Chicago, Burlington & Quincy Railroad (CB&Q)

Whyte Class	Owner Class & Type	Model Production					List Price	Resale		Remarks
		Importer	Builder	Cat #	Quan.	Yrs.		Mint	Avg.	
0-6-0	G-8 Switcher	Ortl		P596		87	379	370		See Note #1090
0-6-0	G-8 Switcher	Ortl		0896		87	321	320		w/single air pump
0-6-0	G-8 Switcher	Ortl		P896		87	379	370		See Note #1091
0-6-0	G-8 Switcher	Ortl		0596		87	321	320		See Note #1092
0-8-0	F-2 Switcher	OMI	Ajin	1470	150	86	357	350		tilting coal bunker
0-8-0	Switcher	Akane	Akane	Ak-20		63	48	200	160	See Note #1093
0-8-0	Switcher	Gem	FuMod	FM-203	1	67	50	220	175	See Note#1093
2-6-2	R-1 Prairie	MODX	NKP		100	84	140	120		fp., can motor
2-8-0	Consol	Aristo				58	25	150	110	fp C&S
2-8-2	O-1a Mikado	LMB				81	395			See Note #152
2-8-2	O-1a Mikado	LMB				81	295			See Note #154
2-8-2	O-1a Mikado	LMB	KMT			81	360	320	260	See Note #153
2-8-2	O-1a Mikado	LMB	KMT		200	66	65	180	130	See Note #1094
2-8-2	O-1a Mikado	LMB	KMT		200	66	65	180	130	See Note #1095
2-8-2	O-1a Mikado	Ortl		P080		82	272			See Note #550
2-8-2	O-1a Mikado	Ortl		0080		81	250		195	See Note #155
2-8-2	O-1a Mikado	Ortl	DaiYng	0081	50	81	250		205	See Note #156
2-8-2	O-1a Mikado	Ortl	DaiYng	0015	300	79	243	260	205	See Note #1096
2-8-2	O-1a Mikado	Ortl	DaiYng	0016	200	80	247	280	225	Elesco FWH
2-8-2	O-4 Mikado	OMI	TaeHwa	1427	200	81	296	290	225	See Note #157
2-10-2	E-5b Santa Fe	Key	Samh		150	78	170	260	200	See Note #158
2-10-2	M-2a Santa Fe	OMI	TaeHwa	1432	100	81	353		280	Elesco FWH

Chicago, Burlington & Quincy Railroad (cont'd)

The C&S/CB&Q Class M–3 2–10–2's #6300–6309 were a USRA design of 1919. These engines spent most of their life on the C&S tracks in heavy freight service. Similar in design to the CB&Q's O–4 Mikados, they differed by using Southern valve gear. Two of the ten engines, #6303 and #6308, used Elesco feedwater heaters, while the remainder of the class used Worthington BL heaters. They performed notably for over 30 years. Key Imports produced this Samhongsa-built model in 1978.

Burlington's big O–5 Northerns were exceptionally fine locomotives, with performance rivaling that of contemporary diesel-electrics. A total of 36 engines comprised the O–5 and O–5a classes. The original order of O–5s (#5600–5607) were built by Baldwin and used the cylindrical Elesco feedwater heater mounted forward of the stack. Subsequent O–5as used Worthington feedwater heaters, which added to their massive appearance. Three O–5s survive, one each at Sheridan and Douglas, Wyoming, and a third in the Colorado railroad museum at Golden. Custom Brass produced the O–5 in both coal and oil versions in 1978.

Whyte Class	Owner Class & Type	Model Production					List Price	Resale		Remarks
		Importer	Builder	Cat #	Quan.	Yrs.		Mint	Avg.	
2-10-2	M-2a Santa Fe	OMI	TaeHwa	1434	100	82	353		275	Worthington FWH
2-10-4	M-4a Colorado	LMB	KMT		160	64	90	210	150	running boards not level
2-10-4	M-4a Colorado	LMB	KMT		150	67-78	95	235	160	running boards not level
2-10-4	M-4a Colorado	NPP	KMT		100	75	340	420	225	See Note #551
2-10-4	M-4a Colorado	NPP	KMT		400	75	260	320	245	fp., See Note #551
2-6-6-2	T-1 Articulated	Trains					75			shown in catalog
4-6-0	K-2 Ten-Wheeler	NPP			1000	74	150	180	130	MR Review 6/75

Chicago, Burlington & Quincy Railroad (cont'd)

Whyte Class	Owner Class & Type	Model Production					List Price	Resale		Remarks
		Importer	Builder	Cat #	Quan.	Yrs.		Mint	Avg.	
4-6-2	S-2 Pacific	LMB	KMT		562	67	65	190	135	#2900-2949
4-6-2	S-2 Pacific	PFM			5	60				
4-6-4	S-4 Hudson	Sun	Samh		300	80	275	275	250	3 Versions in box
4-6-4	#3000 Hudson	NPP	Daeki		20	84	294	300		See Note #1097
4-6-4	#4000 Hudson	NPP	Daeki		100	84	363	380		Streamlined, AELOUS
4-6-4	#4000 Hudson	NPP	Daeki		25	84	330			Vestibule cab
4-6-4	#4001 Hudson	NPP	Daeki		50	84	330			roller bearing
4-8-2	B-1a Mountain	OMI	Rok-Am	1406	500	78	193	230	175	MR Review 12/78
4-8-4	O-5 Northern	OMI	JPMod	1438	200	82	379		205	See Note #162
4-8-4	O-5 Northern	Ortl		0724		87	508	480		#5600-07, w/Elesco FWH
4-8-4	O-5 Northern	Ortl		0725		87	508	480		#5608-20, w/Worth. FWH
4-8-4	O-5 Northern	Ortl		0726C		87	508	480		#5621-35, coal version
4-8-4	O-5 Northern	Ortl		0726O		87	508	480		#5621-35, oil version
4-8-4	O-5 Northern	Ortl		P726O		87	580	660		#5621-35, oil version, fp.
4-8-4	O-5 Northern	Ortl		P724		87	580	660		fp., See Note #1098
4-8-4	O-5 Northern	Ortl		P725		87	580	566		fp., See Note #1099
4-8-4	O-5 Northern	Ortl		P726C		87	580	660		#5621-35, oil version
4-8-4	O-5 Northern	PFM	Toby	CR	25	58	125	2600		See Note #1938
4-8-4	O-5 Northern	PFM	Toby	CR	100	61	125	2600		See Note #161
4-8-4	O-5a Northern	CustB	DiaYng	ST-220	250	78	298	350	300	Vestibule cab, oil tender
4-8-4	O-5a Northern	PFM	Toby	CR	100	63	125	2600		See Note #160
4-8-4	O-5a Northern	PFM	Toby	CR	100	69	150	2600		See Note #159
4-8-4	O-5a Northern	PFM	Toby	CR	100	65	125	2600		See Note #1100
4-8-4	O-5b Northern	CustB	DiaYng	ST-220C	250	78	298	350	300	Vestibule cab, coal tender

Chicago & North Western Railway (C&NW)

Whyte Class	Owner Class & Type	Model Production					List Price	Resale		Remarks
		Importer	Builder	Cat #	Quan.	Yrs.		Mint	Avg.	
0-6-0	#23 Switcher	PFM	Atlas/Asahi	P	475	63	38	230		See Note #1101
0-6-0	#23 Switcher	PFM	Atlas/Asahi	S	1	63				See Note #7 & #1101
0-6-0	#23 Switcher	PFM	Atlas/Asahi	P	290	64	38	230		See Note #1101
0-6-0	#23 Switcher	PFM	Atlas/Asahi	P	230	65	40	230		See Note #1101

Designed primarily for the Chicago-Omaha mainline, C&NW's Class H 4–8–4's were huge; only three roads had larger engines of this type. High horsepower for sustained periods of high-speed running was what C&NW had in mind, and that's what they got. The H's weren't perfect; however, they were modern for 1929. Earlier engines had proved to be a maintenance problem with cracking in the firebox area. They were later shopped and received new cast steel engine beds. Further improvements included roller bearings on all axles and alloy side and main rods. PFM imported two "Crown" versions of this locomotive in 1963, '65, and '66. The first version was built by Sakura (Tokino) and the later engines by Fujiyama. This was a very unusual practice for importers at that time, because Japanese builders did not commonly duplicate other builder's models. The versions were different, however. The Sakura model depicts the rebuilt version, while the Fujiyama model shown above depicts the engine as built. Both are superior models.

Chicago & North Western Railway (cont'd)

Whyte Class	Owner Class & Type	Model Production					List Price	Resale		Remarks
		Importer	Builder	Cat #	Quan.	Yrs.		Mint	Avg.	
0-6-0	#23 Switcher	PFM	Atlas/Asahi	P	240	66	40	230		See Note #1101
0-6-0	#23 Switcher	PFM	Atlas/Asahi	P	300	67	43	230		See Note #1101
0-6-0	#23 Switcher	PFM	Atlas/Asahi	P	500	70	55	230		See Note #1101
0-6-0	#23 Switcher	PFM	Atlas/Asahi	P	500	73	100	290	210	See Note #1101
0-6-0	M-2 Switcher	Trains	KMT		400	67	45	230		
0-8-0	Switcher	PFM	Kawai	H	3	57	95	2400		
2-8-0	Z Consol	NPP	Daeki		100	83	351			cp.; See Note #1102
2-8-0	Z Consol	NPP	Daeki		100	83	299			See Note #1102
2-8-2	J-2a Mikado	OMI	KookJ	1407	250	78	190	300	240	poor solder work
2-8-4	J-4 Berkshire	NPP	Sato		120	80	337	380		MR Review 7/80
2-8-4	J-4 Berkshire	NPP	Sato		250	83	299	400		
2-8-4	J-4 Berkshire	NPP	Sato		50	83	360	400		fp.
2-8-4	J-4 Berkshire	OMI	KookJ	1422	200	80	157	290		
4-4-2	D Atlantic	MBA			20	58	30	180	130	working headlight
4-4-2	D Atlantic	MBA			60	58	32	180	135	
4-4-2	D Atlantic	OMI	Ajin	1469	125	86	357	350		w/straight cylinders
4-4-2	D Atlantic	OMI	Ajin	1468	125	86	357	350		w/slanted cylinders
4-4-2	D Atlantic	PFM	Tensh #111	P	1	54				
4-4-2	D Atlantic	PFM	Tensh #111	P	58	55	30	140	100	
4-4-2	D Atlantic	PFM	Tensh #211	P	76	55	30	130	90	Kit
4-4-2	D Atlantic	PFM	Tensh #111	P	93	56	37	150	105	
4-4-2	D Atlantic	PFM	Tensh #211	P	45	56	30	130	95	Kit
4-4-2	D Atlantic	PFM	Tensh #111	P	176	57	34	150	110	
4-4-2	D Atlantic	PFM	Tensh #211	P	90	57	30	140	120	Kit
4-4-2	D Atlantic	PFM	Tensh #211	P	75	58	30	150	120	Kit
4-4-2	D Atlantic	PFM	Tensh #111	P	220	58	34	160	130	
4-4-2	D Atlantic	PFM	Tensh #111	P	105	59	34	160	140	
4-4-2	D Atlantic	PFM	Tensh #111	P	300	59	38	180	160	See Note #172
4-4-2	D Atlantic	PFM	Tensh #111	P	300	60	38	180	160	See Note #172
4-4-2	D Atlantic	PFM	Tensh #211	P	50	60	33	170	150	Kit
4-4-2	D Atlantic	PFM	Tensh #211	P	25	61	33	180	160	Kit
4-4-2	D Atlantic	PFM	Tensh #111	P	100	61	38	190	170	See Note #172
4-4-2	D Atlantic	PFM	Tensh #111	P	300	62	38	190	180	See Note #172
4-4-2	D Atlantic	PFM	Tensh #211	P	25	62	33	180	160	Kit
4-4-2	D Atlantic	PFM	Tensh #111	P	100	64	38	200	180	See Note #172
4-4-2	D Atlantic	PFM	Tensh #111	P	200	65	38	200	190	See Note #172
4-4-2	D Atlantic	PFM	Tensh #111	P	140	66	45	210	190	See Note #172
4-6-0	R-1 Ten-Wheeler	Hall	DongJ		250	80	250	320	280	
4-6-2	E Pacific	NPP	Tae Hwa		25	83	360	420		fp.
4-6-2	E Pacific	NPP	Tae Hwa		75	83	303	350		
4-6-2	E-2A Pacific	OMI	MSM	1491	225	89	554			
4-6-2	E-2b Pacific	PFM	Atlas/Asahi	S	1	66				See Note #7
4-6-2	E-2b Pacific	PFM	Atlas/Asahi	P	440	66	55	280		
4-6-2	E-2b Pacific	PFM	Atlas/Asahi	S	1	67				See Note #7
4-6-2	E-2b Pacific	PFM	Atlas/Asahi	S	450	68	60			
4-6-2	E-2b Pacific	PFM	Atlas/Asahi	S	400	70	90	280	180	
4-6-4	E-4 Hudson	NPP	KMT		180	75	190	280	280	See Note #173
4-6-4	E-4 Hudson	NPP	KMT		150	76	243	350		fp., see Note #173
4-8-4	H Northern	CustB	DaiYng	ST-827	200	79	330	440		See Note #176
4-8-4	H-1 Northern	CustB	DaiYng	ST-287H1	200	79	330	410		See Note #177
4-8-4	H Northern	PFM	Sakura/Takeno	CR	100	63	125	2800		See Note #174
4-8-4	H Northern	PFM	Fujiyama	CR	144	65	135	2200		See Note #1939
4-8-4	H Northern	PFM	Fujiyama	CR	150	66	135	2200		See Note #175

Chicago Great Western Railway

Whyte Class	Owner Class & Type	Model Production					List Price	Resale		Remarks
		Importer	Builder	Cat #	Quan.	Yrs.		Mint	Avg.	
4-6-0	Ten-Wheeler	Cont	Tetsudo			58	25	90	60	Kit
2-8-2	#750 Mikado	Key	Samh		50	81	340	315	270	
4-6-0	Ten-Wheeler	MBA				59				

Chicago, Milwaukee, St. Paul & Pacific RR

| Whyte Class | Owner Class & Type | Model Production | | | | | List Price | Resale | | Remarks |
		Importer	Builder	Cat #	Quan.	Yrs.		Mint	Avg.	
2-6-2	K-1 Prairie	Intl				55	25-32	140	95	
2-6-2	K-1 Prairie	Intl				55	28-30	100	70	Kit
2-6-2	K-1 Prairie	MBA				60	41	160	120	See Note #164
2-6-2	K-1 Prairie	MBA			150	57-59	28-30	100	70	Brass Kit
2-6-2	K-1 Prairie	NWSL	Rok-Am	56-1	400	76	150	190	140	See Note #167
2-6-2	K-1 Prairie	NWSL	Rok-Am	46-1		80	185		150	See Note #166
2-6-2	K-1 Prairie	NWSL	Rok-Am	46-1	400	76	150	190	140	See Note #165
2-6-2	K-1 Prairie	PFM	Atlas	H	10	56	50	700		See Note #163
2-6-2	K-1 Prairie	PFM	Atlas/KTM	P		58	42			See Note #1103
2-6-2	K-1 Prairie	PFM	Atlas/KTM	P	1	56				
2-6-2	K-1 Prairie	PFM	Atlas	H	10	55	50	700		See Note #163
2-6-2	K-1 Prairie	PFM	Atlas/KTM		1	57				Black Plate Finish
2-6-2	K-1 Prairie	PFM	Atlas/KTM	P	1	54	28			Kit
2-6-2	K-1 Prairie	PFM	Atlas/KTM	P	320	57	38	150	110	
2-6-2	K-1 Prairie	PFM	Atlas/KTM	P	62	55	28	110	75	Kit
2-6-2	K-1 Prairie	PFM	Atlas/KTM	P	11	56	28	120	80	Kit
2-8-2	L-2 #676	NPP	NKP			50	86	426	420	See Note #132
2-8-2	L-2a #507	NPP	NKP			25	86	426	358	w/angle front cab
2-8-2	L-2a #565	NPP	NKP			25	86	426	358	w/square cab
2-8-2	L-2b #415	NPP	NKP			25	86	426	358	round headlight
2-8-2	L-2b #425	NPP	NKP			25	86	426	358	w/angle front cab
2-8-2	L-2b #485	NPP	NKP			50	86	426	358	st. cab, reg. pilot
2-8-2	L-3 Mikado	MBA				60	50	170	150	Heavy USRA
2-8-2	L-3 Mikado	MBA				50s				See Note #168
2-8-2	L-3 Mikado	OMI	JPMod	1420	150	80	286	310	235	See Note #169
4-4-2	A Atlantic	NPP	KMT		850	72	117	160	130	See Note #1104
4-4-2	A Atlantic	NPP	KMT		150	71	100	230	170	See Note #170
4-4-2	Atlantic	OMI	Ajin	1463	100	87	393			"A" Modernized
4-4-2	Atlantic	OMI	Ajin	1462	100	87	393			"A" Original
4-6-0	Ten-Wheeler	NPP	WYang		125	83	365			fp,;See Note #1105
4-6-0	Ten-Wheeler	NPP	WYang		125	83	280			See Note #1105
4-6-0	Ten-Wheeler	OMI	Ajin	1446.1	100	89	623			fp.
4-6-0	Ten-Wheeler	OMI	Ajin	1446	200	89	554			#GBPS
4-6-2	F-1 Pacific	OMI	Ajin	1441	110	85	414			See Note #262
4-6-2	F-3 Pacific	OMI	Ajin	1439	80	85	394	331		#6160 semi-streamlined
4-6-2	F-3 Pacific	OMI	Ajin	1437	110	85	386			#163 standard
4-6-4	F-6 Baltic	PFM			H	6	56	63	4500		

In 1937, Baldwin built 30 Class S–2 Northerns for the Milwaukee Road and followed them up in 1940 with ten more. Built primarily for fast freight service, they were occasionally used to pull the "Olympian" when tourist business was heavy. With 26-inch by 32-inch cylinders, 74-inch drivers, and a tractive effort of 70,800 lbs., they were among the largest 4–8–4's of the time. Similar in appearance to the D&RGW M–68 class 4–8–4's, the S–2s were built by Baldwin just one year earlier than the M–68s. Fujiyama produced this fine model for Pacific Fast Mail in 1981 and later in 1986. Interestingly, Fujiyama produced the same prototype for Northwest Short Line in 1967.

Chicago, Milwaukee, St. Paul & Pacific RR (cont'd)

The Class K–1 Prairies of the Milwaukee Road were built with large fireboxes to burn lignite. In 1907, the Brooks works delivered 50 engines, which went into immediate service. Less powerful than contemporary 2–8–0's, their virtue was the ability to burn cheap coal that other engines couldn't tolerate. By 1909, the Milwaukee Road had 150 Prairies on their roster. These engines were originally intended as prairie power but soon found their way onto all of the western divisions. Notoriously dirty to operate due to the use of ''Roundup'' or ''Rosebud'' coal, they were not loved by the crews. Some engines were later converted to oil, to no one's objection. Rok-Am produced this model of the K–1 Prairie for Northwest Short Line in 1976.

Whyte Class	Owner Class & Type	Model Production					List Price	Resale		Remarks
		Importer	Builder	Cat #	Quan.	Yrs.		Mint	Avg.	
4-6-4	F-6a Baltic	AHM	KMT	405		67	100	285	160	See Note #171
4-6-4	F-6a Baltic	PFM	United	S	1	67				See Note #7
4-6-4	F-6a Baltic	PFM	United	P	450	71	90	290	225	
4-6-4	F-6a Baltic	PFM	Atlas/Asahi	P	405	67	60	270	200	
4-6-4	F-6a Baltic	PFM	United	P	490	68	70	280	210	
4-6-4	F-7 Baltic	NPP	KMT			500	75	195	290	200	See Note #1106
4-6-4	F-7 Baltic	OMI	Ajin	1483	100	89	571			Modernized
4-6-4	F-7 Hudson	OMI	Ajin	1482	100	89	571			Original
4-8-4	S-2 Northern	NWSL	Fujiyama			300	67	105	940	700	See Note #332
4-8-4	S-2 Northern	PFM	Fujiyama			86				fp.
4-8-4	S-2 Northern	PFM	Fujiyama			81	995	870	640	
4-8-4	S-2 Northern	PFM	Tetsudo	H	8	56	123	4500		
4-8-4	S-3 Northern	Direct	Fomras			6		3500		Custom Built
4-8-4	S-3 Northern	OMI	DongJ	1411	300	79	235	235	160	1950 Version
4-8-4	S-3 Northern	OMI	DongJ	1410	300	79	235	235	160	1944 Version

Chicago, Rock Island & Pacific Railroad (CRIP)

| Whyte Class | Owner Class & Type | Model Production | | | | | List Price | Resale | | Remarks |
		Importer	Builder	Cat #	Quan.	Yrs.		Mint	Avg.	
0-8-0	S-57 Switcher	PFM	Tensh #144	P	200	62	45	290		See Note #1107
0-8-0	S-57 Switcher	PFM	Tensh #144	P	150	64	45	290		See Note #1107
0-8-0	S-57 Switcher	PFM	Tensh #144	P	300	63	45	220		See Note #1107
4-6-0	#9 Ten-Wheeler	Trains				67	40	180	125	See Note #178
4-6-2	P-42 Pacific	OMI	Ajin	1465	200	86	407	400		#950-#979
4-8-2	M-50 Mountain	Hall	Ajin		150	81	300	300		
4-8-4	R-67 Northern	Hall	Goto	HS0047	450	78	560	400		See Note #179

Rock Island received its first R-67 Northern from Alco in 1929, and by 1930 had the largest fleet of 4-8-4's in the country. Originally designed for freight service, they proved fast enough for passenger service. Later rebuilds increased the driver diameter from 69 to 73 inches further increasing their speed. The R-67 heavily influenced the design of NYC "Niagaras" and the Milwaukee Road's S-3 class. About as handsome as a 4-8-4 could get, Hallmark imported this beautifully made Goto model in 1978.

Colorado Midland Railway

| Whyte Class | Owner Class & Type | Model Production | | | | | List Price | Resale | | Remarks |
		Importer	Builder	Cat #	Quan.	Yrs.		Mint	Avg.	
0-6-0	Switcher Ser 91	MEW			500	66	50	225	175	#100-102
2-8-0	Consol Series 115	Hall	KyongD		300	77	135	200	130	#1-10
2-8-0	Consol Series 281	Hall				88	283	280		Modernized
2-8-0	Consol Series 159	Hall	DongJ		300	80	198	220	165	See Note #180
2-8-0	Consol Series 159	Hall	DongJ			83	242	260		modernized; See Note #180
2-8-0	Consol Series 175	Hall	DongJ		200	83	242	260		#301-306
2-8-0	Consol Series 136	MEW	KTM		500	65	45	260	170	#49-53
4-6-0	Ten Wheeler	PFM	Unknown	H	1	50's				See Note #1108
4-6-0	Ten-Wheeler 93	MEW			500	64	45	150	175	See Note #930
4-6-0	Ten-Wheeler 102	Hall	KyongD		500	77	135	200	130	See Note #931

Colorado & Southern Railway

| Whyte Class | Owner Class & Type | Model Production | | | | | List Price | Resale | | Remarks |
		Importer	Builder	Cat #	Quan.	Yrs.		Mint	Avg.	
2-8-0	Consol	Aristo				58	25	150	110	fp.
2-10-2	#909 Santa Fe	Key	Samh		100	78	170	290	225	See Note #466
2-6-6-2	Mallet Articulated	Sunset				80				Sampson
2-6-6-2	Mallet Articulated	Sunset				80				Trojan

Colorado Springs & Cripple Creek District

Whyte Class	Owner Class & Type	Model Production					List Price	Resale		Remarks
		Importer	Builder	Cat #	Quan.	Yrs.		Mint	Avg.	
2-6-2	Prairie	Hall	Ajin		250	81	225	235	160	

Delaware & Hudson Railroad (D&H)

Whyte Class	Owner Class & Type	Model Production					List Price	Resale		Remarks
		Importer	Builder	Cat #	Quan.	Yrs.		Mint	Avg.	
4-6-0	Ten-Wheeler	PFM	Atlas		1	55				
4-8-4	K-62 Northern	NPP	NAP		600	75	225	250	225	
4-6-6-4	J Challenger	Key	Samh		25	84	786	920	725	
4-6-6-4	J Challenger	Key	Samh		50	84	857	1000	775	fp.

Delaware, Lackawanna & Western Railroad (DL&W)

Whyte Class	Owner Class & Type	Model Production					List Price	Resale		Remarks
		Importer	Builder	Cat #	Quan.	Yrs.		Mint	Avg.	
2-8-2	#2100 Mikado	NPP	WYang		75	87	389	380		w/foot board pilot
2-8-2	#2100 Mikado	NPP	WYang		75	87	389	380		w/road pilot
4-6-2	N-6 Pacific	NPP	WYang		100	84	330	320		#1100 series; 79″ drivers
4-6-2	N-6 Pacific	NPP	WYang		100	84	330	320		See Note #1109
4-6-2	N-9 Pacific	OMI	Ajin	1536		93	795	670		
4-6-2	N-9 Pacific	OMI	Ajin	1536.1		93	999	850		fp. #1123 multi-color
4-6-2	N-12 Pacific	OMI	Ajin	1537		93	795	670		
4-6-2	N-12 Pacific	OMI	Ajin	1537.1		93	999	850		fp. #1136 black & chrome
4-6-4	M-1 Hudson	NPP	KMT		75	77	295	180	130	See Note #181
4-6-4	M-1 Hudson	NPP	KMT		75	77	329	200	150	See Note #184
4-6-4	M-1 Hudson	NPP	KMT		250	83	226	235	170	See Note #183

DL&W management had always been considered rather conservative in advertising and public relations, so it was with no little surprise that when streamlining came into vogue the DL&W made a radical departure into what they called "streamstyling". The application of wings to passenger engines wasn't as fanciful as it may first appear. The wings did not completely cover appliances as many other roads' streamlining did, and so DL&W got a combination of eye-catching style and practicality. While other roads were paying industrial designers to decorate their locomotives with the latest in art deco styling, DL&W simply yielded to the suggestion of its superintendent of motive power, Charles J. Scudder, who designed the wings. It should come as no surprise that Mr. Scudder was a bird fancier. Mr. Scudder's wings were so successful that they were applied to 4–6–2's, 4–6–0's and one 4–4–0, the only 4–4–0 in America to ever be streamlined. Only one locomotive, Pacific #1123, ever received the green and red trim. The two models shown above are classes N–9 and N–12, built by Ajin Precision for Overland Models. The excellent workmanship, accuracy, and striking paint scheme are representative of the high quality of models now being produced in Korea.

Delaware, Lackawanna & Western Railroad (cont'd)

Whyte Class	Owner Class & Type	Importer	Builder	Cat #	Quan.	Yrs.	List Price	Mint	Avg.	Remarks
				Model Production				Resale		
4-6-4	M-1 Hudson	NPP	KMT		75	77	329	200	150	See Note #182
4-6-4	M-1 Hudson	NPP	KMT		250	83	256	260	200	See Note #184
4-6-4	M-1 Hudson	NPP	KMT		75	77	285	180	130	See Note #183
4-8-2	P-1 Mountain	OMI	Ajin	1430	200	87	442	420		#1401-1405
4-8-4	Q-4 Pocono	NPP	KMT		500	75		220	190	See Note #186
4-8-4	Q-4 Pocono	NPP	KMT		500	75		235	200	See Note #185
4-8-4	Q-4 Pocono	NPP	KMT		500	75		235		See Note #187

Denver & Rio Grande Western Railroad (D&RGW)

Whyte Class	Owner Class & Type	Importer	Builder	Cat #	Quan.	Yrs.	List Price	Mint	Avg.	Remarks
				Model Production				Resale		
0-6-0	S-33 Switcher	PSC	KSM	PK-30		80	149	180	125	Kit
0-6-0	S-33 Switcher	PSC	KSM	15021	175	79	241	270	200	#60-62
2-6-0	Mogul	ACI				54-55	20	70	40	See Note #188
2-6-0	Mogul	Intl	Takara			54	23	70	45	Kit
2-6-0	Mogul	Intl	Takara			59	28	100	65	Diamond Stack
2-6-0	Mogul	MBA				60-61	25-37	150	90	fp. Diamond Stack
2-6-0	Mogul	MBA				59-60	25-35	120	75	Diamond Stack
2-6-0	Mogul	PFM	Atlas		2	55				See Note #189
2-6-0	Mogul	PFM	Atlas		3	56		20		Kit
2-6-0	Mogul	PFM	Atlas		2	54				See Note #189
2-6-0	Mogul	WAS	Kawai			57		100		"Old Timer" kit
2-8-0	Consol	WAS				57				"Old Timer" kit
2-8-0	Consol	Sun		HO66						
2-8-0	#583 Consol	Key	Samh		1000	77	120	200	140	See Note #190
2-8-0	C-48 Consol	Key	SKI		65	89	700	660		fp., Herald', See Note #1110
2-8-0	C-48 Consol	Intl				60				
2-8-0	C-48 Consol	Key	SKI		85	89	700	660		fp., See Note #1111
2-8-0	C-48 Consol	Trains			450	68	55	200	130	fp.
2-8-0	C-48 Consol	Key	SKI					560		See Note #1110
2-8-0	C-48 Consol	NPP	KMT		480	74	147	160	120	fp.
2-8-0	C-48 Consol	Key	SKI					560		See Note #1112
2-8-2	K-59 Mikado	Key	Samh		1000	76	140	190	140	open frame motor; 63" drivers
2-8-2	K-62 Mikado	Sun	Samh		400	76	144	220	160	D&SL Coffin FWH

In 1929 the D&RGW received the first of the M–64 class Northerns. Longer passenger trains and tighter schedules made them the obvious replacement for the M–75 Mountains. In all, fourteen engines (#1700–1713) were purchased. They provided excellent service on one of the most mountainous railroads in the U.S. PFM imported four runs of this engine between 1959 and 1973. All were built by Atlas/Toby, and all carry the ''Crown'' label. Toby ''Crowns'' are noted for their rock-solid construction, good mechanisms, and accurate proportions.

Denver & Rio Grande Western Railroad (cont'd)

Whyte Class	Owner Class & Type	Importer	Builder	Cat #	Quan.	Yrs.	List Price	Mint	Avg.	Remarks
2-8-2	K-62 Mikado	Sun	Samh	HLSD801	200	76	139	200	170	D&SL
2-10-2	F-81 Santa Fe	PFM	United			78	821	730	650	See Note #192
2-10-2	F-81 Santa Fe	PFM	United			78	821	620	550	See Note #191
2-6-6-2	L-96/Z-1a Articulated	CustB	DaiYng	ST-839	300	79	350	450	325	See Note #193
2-6-6-2	L-62 Articulated	Ortl	Samh	P597						
2-6-6-2	L-62 Articulated	Ortl	Samh	0597						
2-8-8-2	L-109 Articulated	CustB	Goto	ST-857	100	80	830	705	650	Royale, ex N&W Y-2
2-8-8-2	L-95 Articulated	Key	Samh		150	83	686			fp. #3404 & 3407
2-8-8-2	L-95 Articulated	Key	Samh		200	79	470	520	490	See Note #197
2-8-8-2	L-96 Articulated	Key	Samh		100	83	686			fp. #3401
2-8-8-2	L-96 Articulated	Key	Samh		200	79	470	530	500	See Note #198
2-8-8-2	L125 Articulated	PFM	Atlas/Kawai	H	6	59		440	400	Sheet Steel Pilot
2-8-8-2	L131 Articulated	PFM	Atlas/Asahi	P	580	61	100	470	425	See Note #194
2-8-8-2	L131 Articulated	PFM	Atlas/Asahi	P	1	73	275			#3600-3609
2-8-8-2	L131 Articulated	PFM	Atlas/Asahi	P	140	64	100	530	470	See Note #195
2-8-8-2	L131 Articulated	PFM	Atlas/Asahi	P	500	72	275	560	500	See Note #196
2-8-8-2	L125 Articulated	PFM	Atlas/Kawai	H	1	60				Sheet Steel Pilot
2-8-8-2	L125 Articulated	PFM	Atlas/Kawai	H	1	58				Sheet Steel Pilot
2-8-8-2	L131 Articulated	PFM	Atlas/Asahi	P	95	63	100	500	375	See Note #195
2-8-8-2	L131 Articulated	PFM	Atlas/Asahi	P	450	77	495	620	500	
2-8-8-2	L131 Articulated	PFM	Atlas/Asahi	P		81	865	890	550	can motor
2-8-8-2	L-107 Articulated	W&R	Samh		42	86	850	800		fp.
2-8-8-2	L-107 Articulated	W&R	Samh		20	86	850	800		fp., See Note #1113
2-8-8-2	L-107 Articulated	W&R	Samh		13	86	800	760		
4-6-0	T-29 Ten-Wheeler	PFM	Tensh/Adachi	P	550	71	75	200	150	See Note #200
4-6-2	P-44 Pacific	PFM	Samh	P	790	77	198	220	160	See Note #1114
4-8-2	M-69 Mountain	Sun	Samh	HDRG701	200	76	142	190	140	See Note #205
4-8-2	M-75 Mountain	PFM	Tensh #169	CR	300	76	625	820	625	See Note #201
4-8-2	M-75 Mountain	Key	Samh		200	79	300	320	250	See Note #202
4-8-2	M-75 Mountain	Key	Samh		250	79	300	330	260	See Note #1115
4-8-2	M-75 Mountain	Key	Samh		25	80	357	390	300	See Note #203
4-8-2	M-75 Mountain	Key	Samh		25	80	357	400	300	See Note #204
4-8-2	M-78 Mountain	CustB	DaiYng	ST-298	500	78	253	270	175	NMRA Review 1/79
4-8-4	M-64 Northern	Key	Samh		700	77	230	280	200	Classic Series
4-8-4	M-64 Northern	Key	Samh		700	78	257	290	230	
4-8-4	M-64 Northern	PFM	Atlas/Toby	CR	25	59	125	2600		See Note #1117
4-8-4	M-64 Northern	PFM	Atlas/Toby	CR	100	62	125	2600		See Note #1942
4-8-4	M-64 Northern	PFM	Atlas/Toby	CR	100	71	185	1400		See Note #206
4-8-4	M-64 Northern	PFM	Atlas/Toby	CR	100	73	325	1400		See Note #1941
4-8-4	M-68 Northern	PFM	Toby	CR	100	67	130	2700		See Note #1116

By 1938, the D&RGW needed additional heavy passenger power, and a new class of 4–8–4's were ordered from Baldwin bearing the designation M–68. D&RGW purchased only five (#1800–1804), but these engines served well and became the prototype for the MoPac's #2000 class engines. Key Imports delivered this Samhongsa-built model in 1978.

Denver & Rio Grande Western Railroad (cont'd)

Definitely not the most handsome articulated on the D&RGW roster, the L–95 2–8–8–2's, nonetheless, lasted well into the diesel era. Built by Alco in 1913, they were renumbered from 1060–1075 to 3000–3415 in 1924. Samhongsa produced this unusual model for Key Imports as it appeared in 1913 with the original slide-valve front cylinders.

Whyte Class	Owner Class & Type	Model Production					List Price	Resale		Remarks
		Importer	Builder	Cat #	Quan.	Yrs.		Mint	Avg.	
4-8-4	M-68 Northern	PFM	Toby	CR	100	68	145	2700		See Note #1943
4-8-4	M-68 Northern	Key	Samh		700	78	257	325		
4-6-6-4	L-97 Challenger	Key	Samh		35	89	1195			fp., #3800
4-6-6-4	L-97 Challenger	Key	Samh			93	1520			unpainted
4-6-6-4	L-97 Challenger	Key	Samh			93	1630			fp., See Note #1118
4-6-6-4	L-97 Challenger	Key	Samh		50	82	713	600		
4-6-6-4	L-97s Challenger	PFM	Tensh #114	CR	35	73	425	720		See Note #199
4-6-6-4	L-105 Challenger	Key	Samh		25	84	843			w/Elesco FWH
4-6-6-4	L-105 Challenger	Key	Samh		25	84	843	800		w/Worthington FWH
4-6-6-4	L-105 Challenger	Key	Samh		50	84	914			fp., w/Elesco FWH
4-6-6-4	L-105 Challenger	Key	Samh		50	84	914			fp.,w/Worthington FWH
4-6-6-4	L-105 Challenger	MGray	KTM			62	110	500	375	See Note #1119
4-6-6-4	L-105 Challenger	PSC		15168		84	650			w/Worthington FWH
4-6-6-4	L-105 Challenger	PSC		15352		84	650			w/Elesco FWH
4-6-6-4	L-105 Challenger	WMC	KTM			77	425	530	400	
4-6-6-4	L-105 Challenger	WMC	KTM	MO-28	970	71-72	170-187	470	375	Westside G-File #28

Denver & Salt Lake Railroad (D&SL)

Whyte Class	Owner Class & Type	Model Production					List Price	Resale		Remarks
		Importer	Builder	Cat #	Quan.	Yrs.		Mint	Avg.	
2-8-2	Mikado	Sun	Samh		400	76	144	220	185	See Note #207
2-8-2	Mikado	Sun	Samh	HDSL801	200	76	139	200	150	
2-6-6-0	Articulated	PFM	Atlas/Asahi	P	480	69	90	350	250	Became D&RGW
2-6-6-0	Articulated	PFM	Atlas/Asahi	P	450	78	475	500	350	Became D&RGW
2-6-6-0	Articulated	PFM	Atlas/Asahi	P	701	75	250	440	300	Became D&RGW
2-6-6-0	Articulated	PFM	Atlas/Asahi	P	500	71	110	380	260	Became D&RGW
2-6-6-0	Articulated	PFM	Atlas/Asahi	P	501	74	215	410	275	Became D&RGW

Detroit & Toledo Shore Line Railroad

Whyte Class	Owner Class & Type	Model Production					List Price	Resale		Remarks
		Importer	Builder	Cat #	Quan.	Yrs.		Mint	Avg.	
2-8-2	#22 Mikado	Key	Samh		50	81	340		270	Light USRA

Duluth, Missabe & Iron Range Railway (DM&IR)

Whyte Class	Owner Class & Type	Model Production					List Price	Resale		Remarks
		Importer	Builder	Cat #	Quan.	Yrs.		Mint	Avg.	
0-10-2	S-7 Switcher	PFM	Atlas/Asahi	S	1	65				See Note #7
0-10-2	S-7 Switcher	PFM	Atlas/Asahi	P	170	67	70	410	300	See Note #209
0-10-2	S-7 Switcher	PFM	Atlas/Asahi	P	460	65	70	380	275	See Note #208
2-8-2	N-2 Mikado	NWSL	Fujiyama		400	71	70	330	260	Elesco FWH, D&IR
2-8-2	N-3 Mikado	NWSL	Fujiyama		500	69	74	380	300	See Note #210
2-10-2	E-1 Santa Fe	Key	Samh		100	78	210	250	190	USRA Elesco FWH
2-10-4	#700 Texas	Key								
2-10-4	E-4 Texas	LMB	KMT		162	64	90	235	170	See Note #1120
2-10-4	E-4 Texas	LMB	KMT		150	67	99	250	175	See Note #1120
2-10-4	E-4 Texas	NPP	KMT		500	74	209	235	170	See Note #1121
2-8-8-4	M-4 Yellowstone	Akane	Akane	700F		59	75	400	300	
2-8-8-4	M-4 Yellowstone	Aristo				59	98	350	250	
2-8-8-4	M-4 Yellowstone	Gem	Akane	AK-107	4	62	110	440	350	Unsprung Drivers
2-8-8-4	M-4 Yellowstone	Gem	Akane	IM-107	100	64		440		
2-8-8-4	M-4 Yellowstone	Gem	Akane	AK-107	4	67		440		
2-8-8-4	M-4 Yellowstone	Gem	Akane	IM-107	4	64		440		
2-8-8-4	M-4 Yellowstone	Gem	Akane	AK-107	11	63	110	440	350	Unsprung Drivers
2-8-8-4	M-4 Yellowstone	Intl	Akane			59-60	98	375	275	Unsprung Drivers
2-8-8-4	M-4 Yellowstone	PFM	Tensh			83	1765	1800		
2-8-8-4	M-4 Yellowstone	PFM	Atlas/Toby	CR	25	60	188	3500	3200	
2-8-8-4	M-4 Yellowstone	PFM	Atlas/Toby	CR	25	59	188	3500	3200	See Note #211
2-8-8-4	M-4 Yellowstone	WMC	Samh			80	570	670	525	See Note #1122
2-8-8-4	M-4 Yellowstone	WMC	Samh			80	570	670	525	See Note #212

In 1919, Alco delivered ten USRA light 2–10–2's to the Duluth, Missabe & Northern Railroad. They retained their original numbers, 506–515, when the DM&N merged with the Duluth & Iron Range Railroad. Loaded with appliances, double air pumps, Elesco feedwater heater, high mounted air tanks, and doghouse on the tender, this engine looks like it is ready to move some iron ore. Over the years, these engines were modified and modified again, until no two looked alike. Samhongsa produced this version of the E–1 class with the original cab for Key Imports in 1978.

Erie Railroad

Whyte Class	Owner Class & Type	Model Production					List Price	Resale		Remarks
		Importer	Builder	Cat #	Quan.	Yrs.		Mint	Avg.	
0-8-8-0	L-1 Articulated	CustB	DaiYng	ST-222	120	84	780	1450		
2-8-2	N-1 Mikado	NPP	Dauki		25	84	334	350	265	See Note #1123
2-8-2	N-1 Mikado	NPP	Dauki		25	84	334	350	265	See Note #1124
2-8-2	N-1 Mikado	NPP	Dauki		25	84	334	350	265	See Note #1125
2-8-2	N-1 Mikado	NPP	Dauki		25	84	334	350	265	See Note #1126
2-8-4	S-1 Berkshire	CustB	KSM	ST-227	250	81	368	300	230	
2-8-4	S-2 Berkshire	CustB	KSM	ST-816	80	81	378	450	345	
2-8-4	S-3 Berkshire	Ortl	Jonan	0054	105	83	393	375		w/2 Boxpox drivers, fp.
2-8-4	S-3 Berkshire	Ortl	Jonan	P568		85	393	375		w/2 Boxpox drivers, fp.
2-8-4	S-3 Berkshire	Ortl	Jonan							check sale price

Erie Railroad (cont'd)

From the very beginning, Erie was different. When other roads were building to 4-foot 8 1/2-inch gauge, Erie was building to 6-foot gauge. When it came to big engines, Erie had some of the largest and strangest. Number 2601 was the only Camelback Mallet ever built. She must have been a nightmare for the firemen. N.J. Custom Brass imported this model.

The ''Matt Shay'' triplex was a huge failure. It never could maintain steam. LMB imported this impressive model in 1961.

Whyte Class	Owner Class & Type	Model Production					List Price	Resale		Remarks
		Importer	Builder	Cat #	Quan.	Yrs.		Mint	Avg.	
2-8-4	S-4 Berkshire	PFM	Fujiyama	P	445	66	55	440	325	
2-8-4	S-4 Berkshire	PFM	Fujiyama	P	295	68	70	470	350	fp. black/Silver
2-10-0	Decapod	Sun	SMI	HO121P	100	91	250			
2-10-0	Decapod	Sun	SMI	HO121	100	91	300			fp.
2-10-2	R-1 Santa Fe	Alco	Kobra	S-124	300	77	175	310		
2-8-8-8-2	Triplex	Key	Samh		65	85	829	1350		fp. #5014; See Note #587
2-8-8-8-2	Triplex	Key	Samh		85	85	829	1350		fp. #5016: See Note #587
2-8-8-8-2	Triplex	Key	Samh		125	80	642	1100		See Note #587
2-8-8-8-2	Triplex	Key	Samh		75	80	642	1100		See Note #586
2-8-8-8-2	Triplex	LMB			100	61	198	530	400	See Note #213

Erie Railroad (cont'd)

Whyte Class	Owner Class & Type	Model Production					List Price	Resale		Remarks
		Importer	Builder	Cat #	Quan.	Yrs.		Mint	Avg.	
2-8-8-8-2	Triplex	LMB				71	250	670	525	See Note #214
2-8-8-8-2	Triplex	LMB				69	225	620	475	See Note #214
4-6-0	G-15b Ten Wheeler	NPP	WYang		50	84	314	300		See Note #1127
4-6-0	G-15a Ten Wheeler	NPP	WYang		50	84	314	300		See Note #1128
4-6-2	K-1 Pacific	NPP	TaeHwa		50	84	314	300		See Note #1127
4-6-2	K-1 Pacific	NPP	TaeHwa		50	84	314	300		See Note #1128
4-6-2	K-5 Pacific	Key	Samh		100	80	315	450		See Note #215
4-6-2	K-5 Pacific	Key	Samh		60	87	429	670		fp. #2915, Coasting Drive
4-6-2	K-5 Pacific	MGray	KTM			62	58	500		
4-6-2	K-5a Pacific	Key	Samh		100	80	325	500		See Note #216
4-6-2	K-5a Pacific	Key	Samh		50	81	371	520		See Note #217
4-6-2	K-5a Pacific	Key	Samh		100	82	335	500		See Note #218
4-6-2	K-5a Pacific	Key	Samh			88	430	530		#2915, Coasting Drive
4-6-2	Pacific	Key	Samh		90	85	336	470		1940 Version
4-6-2	Pacific	Key	Samh		60	85	407	560		#2938-40, 1941 era ,fp.

Florida East Coast Railway

Whyte Class	Owner Class & Type	Model Production					List Price	Resale		Remarks
		Importer	Builder	Cat #	Quan.	Yrs.		Mint	Avg.	
4-8-2	Mountain	OMI	Ajin	1455	50	85	423			See Note #219

Grand Trunk Western Railroad (GTW)

Whyte Class	Owner Class & Type	Model Production					List Price	Resale		Remarks
		Importer	Builder	Cat #	Quan.	Yrs.		Mint	Avg.	
2-8-2	S-3a Mikado	Key	Samh		150	77	160	220	170	See Note #70
4-6-2	J-3a Pacific	OMI	Ajin	1464	75	86	407	375		
4-8-2	U-1e Mountain	OMI	Ajin	1505	165	90	718			
4-8-2	U-1e Mountain	OMI	Ajin	1506	60	90	723			w/smoke shield
4-8-4	U-3a Northern	Ortl	Samh	0049	125	82	379		300	See Note #79
4-8-4	U-3b Northern	Ortl	Samh	0050	175	82	390		310	See Note #80
4-8-4	U-4b Northern	Van	Samh		75	82	465		315	fp.,See Note #83
4-8-4	U-4b Northern	NPP	Park		200	77	242	300	240	See Note #84
4-8-4	U-4b Northern	NPP	Kimura		100	83	290			fp.

Great Northern Railway (GN)

Whyte Class	Owner Class & Type	Model Production					List Price	Resale		Remarks
		Importer	Builder	Cat #	Quan.	Yrs.		Mint	Avg.	
0-6-0	A-9 Switcher	WMC	Tsubomi	MO-73	1000	76-77	160	200	150	See Note #220
0-8-0	C-4 Switcher	Ortl	DaiYng	0024	350	80	220	260	180	Converted from F-8
0-8-0	C-1 Switcher	PFM	Tensh #157	H	3	54-55				See Note #1129
0-8-0	C-1 Switcher	PFM	Tensh #157			85			500	See Note #1130
0-8-0	C-1 Switcher	PFM	Tensh #157	LP	300	68	80	320	225	fp.
0-8-0	C-1 Switcher	PFM	Tensh #157	LP	500	65	50	290	200	See Note #1131
0-8-0	C-1 Switcher	PFM	Tensh #157	LP	275	71	98	350	250	fp.
0-8-0	C-1 Switcher	PFM	Unknown		1	56				See Note #1132
2-6-0	D-5 Mogul	Sun	TaeHwa	HO-25	250	81	242	260	200	See Note #588
2-6-2	J-1 Prairie	Ortl	Samh	P650		87	422	410		fp. Glacier Park
2-6-2	J-1 Prairie	Ortl	Samh	0650		87	354	350		
2-8-0	F-8 Consol	Key								
2-8-0	F-8 Consol	PFM	Tensh #158	P	500	66	65	290	200	fp., See Note #552
2-8-0	F-8 Consol	PFM	Tensh #158	P	350	68	100	350	250	fp. Glacier Park
2-8-0	F-8 Consol	PFM	Tensh #158	P	10	67	65	320	225	
2-8-0	F-8 Consol	PFM	Tensh #158	P	150	77	375	460	350	See Note #222
2-8-0	F-8 Consol	PFM	Tensh #158	P	400	71	113	380	275	See Note #221
2-8-0	F-8 Consol	PFM	Tensh #158	P	300	75	255	410	300	See Note #221

Great Northern Railway (cont'd)

On a road where big steam was the order of the day, Atlantics just didn't seem to fit in. Great Northern didn't have many and they didn't last long into the '40s, even with the shortages of motive power caused by WWII. The Class K–1 4–4–2's with their Belpaire firebox, high domes, and above-center-mounted headlight had the typical Great Northern look. It may be an Atlantic with a Belpaire firebox, but it would never be mistaken for a Pennsy Atlantic. Custom Brass imported 400 of these KSM-built engines in 1978.

Whyte Class	Owner Class & Type	Model Production					List Price	Resale		Remarks
		Importer	Builder	Cat #	Quan.	Yrs.		Mint	Avg.	
2-8-0	F-1 Consol	Sun	Samh	HO15A	600	77	135	180	125	See Note #223
2-8-2	O-1 Mikado	PFM	Tensh	H	3	54-55				See Note #1135
2-8-2	O-1 Mikado	PFM	SKI	P		83	482		320	See Note #1136
2-8-2	O-1 Mikado	PFM	SKI	P		83	482		320	See Note #1134
2-8-2	O-1 Mikado	Sun	Samh	HGN100	900	75	160	200	150	See Note #229
2-8-2	O-3 Mikado	OMI	Rok-Am	1419	280	79	300	290	200	See Note #1133
2-8-2	O-3 Mikado	OMI	Rok-Am	1419	20	80	414	350	275	See Note #231
2-8-2	O-4 Mikado	Sun	Samh	HO24	400	77	160	200	150	See Note #230
2-8-2	O-7 Mikado	PSC				87	497	470		
2-8-2	O-7 Mikado	PSC		15364		88	497			See Note #1139
2-8-2	O-7 Mikado	PSC		15364-3		88	549			w/Open Cab, fp.
2-8-2	O-7 Mikado	PSC		15488		88				See Note #1138
2-8-2	O-7 Mikado	PSC		15364-2		88	497			w/Open Cab
2-8-2	O-7 Mikado	PSC		15364-1		88	549			w/Vestibule Cab, fp.
2-8-2	O-8 Mikado	PFM	Tensh	H	3	54-55				See Note #1137
2-8-2	O-8 Mikado	PFM	Tensh	P	5	55	60			See Note #224
2-8-2	O-8 Mikado	PFM	Tensh	P	75	57	45	160	120	Kit
2-8-2	O-8 Mikado	PFM	Tensh	P	433	57	50	180	125	See Note #225
2-8-2	O-8 Mikado	PFM	Tensh	P	150	58	45	170	125	Kit
2-8-2	O-8 Mikado	PFM	Tensh	P	320	58	50	180	130	Sand Cast Pumps
2-8-2	O-8 Mikado	PFM	Tensh	P	200	59	50	190	135	
2-8-2	O-8 Mikado	PFM	Tensh	P	300	60	50	190	140	
2-8-2	O-8 Mikado	PFM	Tensh	P	25	60	45	180	135	Kit
2-8-2	O-8 Mikado	PFM	Tensh	P	25	61	45	190	130	Kit
2-8-2	O-8 Mikado	PFM	Tensh	P	25	62	45	190	145	Kit
2-8-2	O-8 Mikado	PFM	Tensh	P	200	62	50	210	160	See Note #226
2-8-2	O-8 Mikado	PFM	Tensh	P	100	63	50	220	170	fp.
2-8-2	O-8 Mikado	PFM	Tensh	P	100	64	50	235	180	fp. Glacier Park
2-8-2	O-8 Mikado	PFM	Tensh	P	75	82	1125			fp.
2-8-2	O-8 Mikado	Sun	Samh	HO11	300	76	159	220	170	See Note #228
2-8-2	O-8 Mikado	Sun	Samh		300	76	156	210	160	See Note #227
2-10-2	Q-1 Santa Fe	Ortl	DaiYng	0131	100	82	365	410	295	See Note #232
2-10-2	Q-1 Santa Fe	Ortl	DaiYng	P130		82	450			cp., See Note #554
2-10-2	Q-1 Santa Fe	Ortl	DaiYng	0130	150	82	365	410	295	See Note #554

Great Northern Railway (cont'd)

Whyte Class	Owner Class & Type	Model Production					List Price	Resale		Remarks
		Importer	Builder	Cat #	Quan.	Yrs.		Mint	Avg.	
2-10-2	Q-1 Santa Fe	PFM	Tensh #155	LP	300	72	175	500	460	See Note #233
2-10-2	Q-1 Santa Fe	PFM	Tensh			84				Worthington FWH
2-10-2	Q-1 Santa Fe	PFM	Tensh #155	LP	100	69	125	470	375	fp.
2-10-2	Q-1 Santa Fe	PFM	Tensh #155	LP	100	65	90	410	340	fp.
2-10-2	Q-1 Santa Fe	PFM	Tensh #155	LP	512	64	90	410	340	unpainted
2-10-2	Q-1 Santa Fe	PFM	Tensh #155	LP	160	67	110	410	340	fp.
2-10-2	Q-1 Santa Fe	Sun	Samh		800	79	233	260	200	See Note #234
2-6-6-2	Articulated	Intl				58	55	290	200	
2-6-6-2	L-1 Articulated	PFM	Tensh	CR	200	78	950	1400	1200	See Note #1140
2-6-6-2	L-1 Articulated	PFM	Tensh	CR	300	79	995	1400	1200	Crown, fp. Green
2-6-6-2	L-2 Articulated	LMB				60	55	320	225	
2-6-6-2	L-2 Articulated	MBA				60	54		265	fp., catalogued
2-6-6-2	L-2 Articulated	PFM	Atlas/KTM	H	1	55				
2-6-6-2	L-2 Articulated	PFM	Atlas/KTM	H	128	57	60	1300	1200	See Note #1141
2-6-8-0	M-2 Articulated	Ortl	Samh		4	84				fp., See Note #1142
2-6-8-0	M-2 Articulated	Ortl	Samh	0051-2	100	84	664		535	See Note #1143
2-6-8-0	M-2 Articulated	Ortl	Samh	0051-1	60	84	664		535	See Note #1142
2-6-8-0	M-2 Articulated	PFM	Tensh #156	LP	300	73	325	820	750	fp. Glacier Park
2-6-8-0	M-2 Articulated	PFM	Tensh #156	LP	100	66	125	650	600	fp.
2-6-8-0	M-2 Articulated	PFM	Tensh #156	LP	190	65	125	650	600	fp.
2-6-8-0	M-2 Articulated	PFM	Tensh #156	LP	189	64	125	650	600	See Note #1958
2-6-8-0	M-2 Articulated	PFM	Tensh #156	LP	202	70	170	650	600	fp. Glacier Park
2-6-8-0	M-2 Articulated	PFM	Tensh #156	LP		78		940	870	fp. Glacier Park
2-8-8-0	N-3 Articulated	PFM	Tensh #161	LP		82		950	870	fp.
2-8-8-0	N-3 Articulated	PFM	Tensh #161	LP	300	76	595	900	850	See Note #235
2-8-8-0	N-3 Articulated	PFM	Tensh #161	LP	90	68	225	850	750	
2-8-8-0	N-3 Articulated	PFM	Tensh #161	LP	300	67	225	850	750	See Note #1152
2-8-8-0	N-3 Articulated	PFM	Tensh #161	LP	300	73	335	850	820	
2-8-8-0	N-3 Articulated	PSC		15272		84	589			fp.
2-8-8-0	N-3 Articulated	WMC		MO-167		80	559	590	440	
2-8-8-2	R-1 Articulated	Ortl	Samh	0424	25	85	786	800		open cab
2-8-8-2	R-1 Articulated	Ortl	Samh	P425		85	836	850		fp. black, open cab
2-8-8-2	R-1 Articulated	Ortl	Samh	P426		85	886	900		fp. Glacier Park, open cab
2-8-8-2	R-1 Articulated	Ortl	Samh	0427	25	85	786	800		closed cab
2-8-8-2	R-1 Articulated	Ortl	Samh	P428	25	85	836	850		fp. black, closed cab
2-8-8-2	R-1 Articulated	Ortl	Samh	P429	25	85	886	900		fp. Glacier Park, closed cab
2-8-8-2	R-1 Articulated	PFM	Tensh	H	1	56				See Note #1150
2-8-8-2	R-2 Articulated	Key	Samh			89				Closed Cab

Great Northern owned two classes of 2–10–2's, the Q–1, and Q–2. Looking very much like a 2–8–2 with an additional set of drivers, the Q–2 sported the GN traditional Belpaire firebox, huge cab, and Vanderbilt tender. With 63-inch drivers and a tractive force of 87,130 lbs., it was definitely built to handle heavy freight. These huge engines were not well-liked by the road foremen or the crews, for they were poorly balanced and, aside from being rough riders, did considerable damage to the rails. Oriental imported this fine replica of the Q–1 in 1982.

Great Northern Railway (cont'd)

Great Northern's S–1 Class 4–8–4's followed typical GN design practice with a huge Belpaire firebox and likewise large Vanderbilt tender. The six Baldwin-built engines of this class had 73-inch drivers and 68,466 lbs. of tractive effort. Built in 1929, they were clearly intended for dual-service use. From the early '50s through the late '70s, Pacific Fast Mail imported over 4,220 models of this engine. Builders included Tetsudo, Atlas, and Tenshodo, who made, by far, the greatest number of engines. The model shown was built by Tenshodo in the late 1960s.

Whyte Class	Owner Class & Type	Importer	Builder	Cat #	Quan.	Yrs.	List Price	Resale Mint	Resale Avg.	Remarks
2-8-8-2	R-2 Articulated	Key	Samh			89		1175		fp., See Note #1145
2-8-8-2	R-2 Articulated	Key	Samh			89				Original Cab
2-8-8-2	R-2 Articulated	Key	Samh			89				fp., See Note #1146
2-8-8-2	R-2 Articulated	Key	Samh			89		1175		fp., See Note #1147
2-8-8-2	R-2 Articulated	PFM	Tensh #160	H	3	54-55				See Note #1148
2-8-8-2	R-2 Articulated	PFM	Tensh #160	LP		79	1095	1400		fp. Glacier Park
2-8-8-2	R-2 Articulated	PFM	Tensh #160	LP	300	74	495	1200		See Note #1149
2-8-8-2	R-2 Articulated	PFM	Tensh #160	LP	400	66	178	1000		unpainted
2-8-8-2	R-2 Articulated	PFM	Tensh #160	LP	150	69	198	1000		See Note #1151
4-4-0	American	Gem	KMT	SH-103	950	74	150	180	135	See Note #237
4-4-2	K-1 Atlantic	CustB	KSM	ST-228	400	78	190	200	150	
4-4-2	K-1 Atlantic	Ortl	Samh							
4-4-2	K-1 Atlantic	Ortl	Samh							fp. Glacier Park
4-4-2	K-1 Atlantic	Ortl	Samh	0652		87	342	340		
4-6-0	E-15 Ten-Wheeler	OMI	Rok-Am	1400	500	77	135	160	125	
4-6-0	E-8 Ten-Wheeler	Ortl		0454		85	357	350		circa 1915
4-6-0	E-8 Ten-Wheeler	Ortl		0455		85	357	350		Modernized
4-6-0	E-6 Ten-Wheeler	PFM	Atlas/Asahi	P	700	76	210	290	200	Coal Tender
4-6-0	E-6 Ten-Wheeler	PFM	Atlas/Nakayama	P	1	60				See Note #1153
4-6-2	H-5 Pacific	LMB				64	50	200	145	added detail from '61 model
4-6-2	H-5 Pacific	LMB				61	40	200	140	
4-6-2	H-6 Pacific	Ortl		0651		87	372	370		69" drivers
4-6-2	H-6 Pacific	Ortl		P651		87	439	410		fp. Glacier Park
4-6-2	H-5 Pacific	PFM	Atlas/Asahi	P	501	73	150	235	180	See Note #518
4-6-2	H-5 Pacific	PFM	Atlas/Asahi	P	750	72	110	210	160	See Note #518
4-6-2	H-5 Pacific	PFM	Atlas/Asahi	P	600	76	210	260	210	See Note #518
4-6-2	H-4 Pacific	PFM	Tensh		3	54-55				
4-6-2	Pacific	PFM	Atlas	H	1	58				
4-6-2	H-4 Pacific	WMC	Nish	MO-34	1500	73-74	120	200	155	See Note #1154
4-6-2	H-7 Pacific	WMC	Samh	MO-93		77	160	190	140	See Note #239
4-8-0	G-1 Twelve Wheeler	PFM	Atlas/Toby	CR	100	60	50	1060	650	See Note #1155
4-8-0	G-3 Twelve Wheeler	PFM	Samh	P	500	78	213	250	190	#720-769
4-8-2	P-2 Mountain	PFM	Tensh #162	LP	300	72	168	500	450	See Note #241
4-8-2	P-2 Mountain	PFM	Tensh #162	LP	300	75	325	590	450	See Note #240
4-8-2	P-2 Mountain	PFM	Tensh #162	LP	250	68	100	440	400	See Note #240
4-8-2	P-2 Mountain	PFM	Tensh #162	LP	250	67	98	410	375	See Note #240
4-8-2	P-2 Mountain	WMC		MO-142		79	279	290	230	See Note #242
4-8-4	S-1 Northern	PFM	Tensh #137	P	400	61	55	290	220	fp.

Great Northern Railway (cont'd)

By any criteria, the Great Northern's R-2 Class 2-8-8-2's were among the most impressive articulated steam locomotives ever built. Constructed by the road's own Hillyard shops, this type, in its final form, exerted 151,000 lbs. of tractive effort and could handle freights unassisted over the longest grades. It must have been quite a sight to watch an R-2 thundering up Marias Pass with a mile of freight cars trailing behind. Between 1966 and 1979, Tenshodo produced over 850 of these ''Limited Production'' models for Pacific Fast Mail. Prized for their excellent craftsmanship and superior paint work, the Tenshodo R-2 is an excellent model.

Whyte Class	Owner Class & Type	Model Production					List Price	Resale		Remarks
		Importer	Builder	Cat #	Quan.	Yrs.		Mint	Avg.	
4-8-4	S-1 Northern	PFM	Tensh #137	P	400	64	55	330	250	fp.
4-8-4	S-1 Northern	PFM	Tensh #137	P	220	65	65	340	260	fp.
4-8-4	S-1 Northern	PFM	Tensh	P	25	60	50	260	200	Kit
4-8-4	S-1 Northern	PFM	Tensh #164	LP	300	74	340	590	520	fp., See Note #590
4-8-4	S-1 Northern	PFM	Tensh	P	50	61	50	280	210	Kit
4-8-4	S-1 Northern	PFM	Tensh #137	P	250	62	55	300	230	fp.
4-8-4	S-1 Northern	PFM	Tensh			79	925	1060	700	See Note #244
4-8-4	S-1 Northern	PFM	Tensh #137	P	250	68	90	410	325	fp., See Note #590
4-8-4	S-1 Northern	PFM	Tensh #137	P	350	70	125	470	350	fp., See Note #590
4-8-4	S-1 Northern	PFM	Tetsudo	H	1	50's				See Note #1157
4-8-4	S-1 Northern	PFM	Tensh #137	P	895	59	55	270	200	fp.
4-8-4	S-1 Northern	PFM	Tensh #137	P	250	63	55	320	240	fp.
4-8-4	S-1 Northern	PFM	Tensh #137	P	75	58	55	260	190	fp., See Note #243
4-8-4	S-1 Northern	PFM	Tensh	P	150	59	50	250	190	Kit
4-8-4	S-1 Northern	PFM	Tensh #137	P	200	66	75	350	275	fp.
4-8-4	S-1 Northern	PFM	Atlas	H	4	59	153	4500	4000	
4-8-4	S-1 Northern	PFM	Tensh #137	P	400	60	55	280	210	fp.
4-8-4	S-2 Northern	Ortl		0360		85	486	460		open cab
4-8-4	S-2 Northern	Ortl		0361		85	486	460		Vestibule Cab
4-8-4	S-2 Northern	Ortl		P361		85	557	530		See Note #1156
4-8-4	S-2 Northern	Ortl		P360		85	557	530		open cab, fp.
4-8-4	S-2 Northern	PFM	Tensh #143	LP	50	65	125	450	350	fp. Glacier Park
4-8-4	S-2 Northern	PFM	Tensh #143	LP	310	77	450	550	500	See Note #245
4-8-4	S-2 Northern	PFM	Tensh #143	LP	75	63	125	550	500	fp. Glacier Park
4-8-4	S-2 Northern	PFM	Tensh #143	LP	50	66	125	400	360	fp. Glacier Park
4-8-4	S-2 Northern	PFM	Tensh	H	1	54				See Note #1158
4-8-4	S-2 Northern	PFM	Tensh #143	LP	16	59	125	500	475	See Note #1957
4-8-4	S-2 Northern	PFM	Tensh #143	LP	300	71	185	550	520	fp. Glacier Park
4-8-4	S-2 Northern	PFM	Tensh #143	LP	200	68	130	470	450	fp. Glacier Park
4-8-4	S-2 Northern	PFM	Tensh #143	LP	90	61	125	400	375	fp. Glacier Park
4-8-4	S-2 Northern	PFM	Tensh #143	LP	25	62	125	375	320	fp. Glacier Park
4-8-4	S-2 Northern	PFM	Tensh #143	LP	50	64	125	430	390	fp. Glacier Park
4-8-4	S-2 Northern	WMC	Samh	MO-120	400	78	200	320	225	
4-6-6-4	Z-6 Challenger	PFM	Tensh #165	LP	300	71	285	850	800	fp.
4-6-6-4	Z-6 Challenger	PFM	Tensh #165	LP	250	75	525	900	850	See Note #236
4-6-6-4	Z-6 Challenger	PFM	Tensh #165	LP	100	76	525	900	850	See Note #236
4-6-6-4	Z-6 Challenger	PFM	Tensh #165	LP	230	69	245	800	750	unpainted

Great Western Railway

| Whyte Class | Owner Class & Type | Model Production | | | | | List Price | Resale | | Remarks |
		Importer	Builder	Cat #	Quan.	Yrs.		Mint	Avg.	
2-10-0	Decapod	Emp				79	225	200	150	#90 Strasburg

Illinois Central Railroad (IC)

| Whyte Class | Owner Class & Type | Model Production | | | | | List Price | Resale | | Remarks |
		Importer	Builder	Cat #	Quan.	Yrs.		Mint	Avg.	
0-8-0	Switcher	W&R	Samh							
2-4-4T	Suburban	Gem	Sankyo	ST-101	400	66	40	175		Forney Suburban
2-8-0	#900 Consol	Hall	DongJ		800	75	135	150	100	Modern
2-8-2	Mikado	Alco	Rok-Am		300	81	332	250	190	
2-8-4	#7000	PFM				88	484	460		
2-8-4	#8000	PFM				88	556	520		fp.
2-8-4	#7000	PFM				88	556	520		fp.
2-8-4	#8000	PFM				88	484	460		
2-10-2	Santa Fe	Sun		HO921	100	88	243	240		"Prestige Series"
4-6-0	Ten-Wheeler	Aristo				58	30	150	100	"Casey Jones"
4-6-0	Ten-Wheeler	Red			300	62	40	160	115	"Casey Jones"
4-8-2	#2500 Mountain	Hall	DongJ		500	76	190	220	175	MR Review 10/76

The increasing emphasis on faster freight schedules caused the Illinois Central Paducah shops to rebuild 56 early 1920s-vintage heavy 2–10–2's into heavy 4–8–2s with 70-inch Box-pok drivers. These very successful #2500 series freight Mountains featured squared-off sand boxes and unshielded air compressors on the deck. Dong Jin built this model for Hallmark Models in 1976.

Indiana Harbor Belt Railroad

| Whyte Class | Owner Class & Type | Model Production | | | | | List Price | Resale | | Remarks |
		Importer	Builder	Cat #	Quan.	Yrs.		Mint	Avg.	
0-8-0	Switcher	PFM	Atlas/Kawai	H	5	58	125	1800	1700	See Note #246

Indianapolis Union Railway

Whyte Class	Owner Class & Type	Model Production					List Price	Resale		Remarks
		Importer	Builder	Cat #	Quan.	Yrs.		Mint	Avg.	
0-8-0	Switcher	MBA				60	35	150	100	See Note #1159

Kansas City Southern Railway

Whyte Class	Owner Class & Type	Model Production					List Price	Resale		Remarks
		Importer	Builder	Cat #	Quan.	Yrs.		Mint	Avg.	
2-8-0	Consol	Hall						190		
2-10-4	J Texas	PFM	Atlas/Nakayama	H	12	63	169	6500		See Note #247
2-10-4	J Texas	PFM	Atlas/Nakayama	H	1	63	169	7000		See Note #248
2-10-4	J Texas	Hall	Ajin		200	81	344	440	270	

Kansas City Southern owned a total of ten huge Class J 2–10–4's. These 1937 Lima-built behemoths were exceeded in size only by Santa Fe's huge 2–10–4's. Modern in every respect, with all-weather cabs, Worthington feedwater heaters, dual front, mounted air pumps, and cast integral air tanks, these engines were as powerful as they looked. Built to relieve an aging fleet of Mallets, their performance exceeded expectations. Engines #900–904 were built as coal burners, while #905–909 were oil burners. Hallmark imported 200 of the beauties from Ajin Precision in 1981.

Lake Shore & Michigan Southern Railway

Whyte Class	Owner Class & Type	Model Production					List Price	Resale		Remarks
		Importer	Builder	Cat #	Quan.	Yrs.		Mint	Avg.	
4-6-0	Ten Wheeler	LMB	KMT		500	61	30	160	115	
4-6-0	Ten Wheeler	LMB	KMT		500	61	27	120	80	
4-6-0	Ten Wheeler	Prec				61	30	150	105	
4-6-0	F-51 Ten Wheeler	KenK		3512		59-68	30-40	190	130	See Note #604
4-6-0	F-51 Ten Wheeler	KenK		3512K		63	27	130	85	Kit; See Note #604

Lehigh & Hudson River Railway (L&HR)

Whyte Class	Owner Class & Type	Model Production					List Price	Resale		Remarks
		Importer	Builder	Cat #	Quan.	Yrs.		Mint	Avg.	
2-8-2	#80 Mikado	Key	Samh		50	82	350	380	285	#80, Light USRA

Lehigh Valley Railroad (LV)

Whyte Class	Owner Class & Type	Model Production					List Price	Resale		Remarks
		Importer	Builder	Cat #	Quan.	Yrs.		Mint	Avg.	
2-8-2	N-1 Mikado	CustB	KSM	ST-885	250	80	298	475	450	Camelback
4-2-4T	Inspection Loco	Red	Kumata		200	64	38	200	150	See Note #496
4-6-2	K5BS Pacific	OMI	Ajin	1488.1	150	90	894			cp, "John Wilkes"
4-6-2	K5BS Pacific	OMI	Ajin	1488	75	90	680			"John Wilkes"
4-8-4	T-2 Wyoming	CustB	DaiYng	ST-248W	100	81	388	350	250	Worthington FWH
4-8-4	T-2 Wyoming	CustB	DaiYng	ST-248E	200	81	388	370	270	Elesco FWH
4-8-4	T-2b Wyoming	CustB	DaiYng	ST-248		81	388	370	270	

Extensive tests with the "Four Aces" Timkin demonstrator persuaded the Lehigh Valley Railroad to order 4–8–4 "Wyomings" with 70-inch drivers for fast freight service. In 1931 T-1A engines, numbered 5100–5110, and T-2a engines, numbers 5200–5210, were delivered from Alco. The T-2 pictured is a Custom Brass import.

Long Island Railroad (LI)

Whyte Class	Owner Class & Type	Model Production					List Price	Resale		Remarks
		Importer	Builder	Cat #	Quan.	Yrs.		Mint	Avg.	
2-8-0	Consol	Imp	Akane			60	33	150	110	See Note #249
2-8-0	Consol	MBA				59	35			Camelback
2-8-0	H-51a Consol	Intl	Takara			61	35	150	110	Camelback
4-6-0	G-53sd Ten-Wheeler	CustB	KMT	ST-200	825	74	130	265		NMRA Review 5/75
4-6-0	G-5s Ten Wheeler	Alco	Samh	S-138	50	83	349	320	250	#25
4-6-0	G-5s Ten Wheeler	Alco	Samh	S-139	50	83	349	320	250	#39
4-6-0	G-5s Ten Wheeler	WMC	KTM	MO-72	527	76	140	190	140	PRR K-4 Tender
4-6-0	G-5s Ten Wheeler	WMC	KTM	MO-72	527	76	140	160	120	WMC G-File #72

Louisiana & Arkansas Railway

Whyte Class	Owner Class & Type	Model Production					List Price	Resale		Remarks
		Importer	Builder	Cat #	Quan.	Yrs.		Mint	Avg.	
4-6-0	D-22 Ten-Wheeler	PFM	Samh	P	750	76	160	220	165	"Hustler"

Louisiana & Arkansas Railway (cont'd)

The Louisiana & Arkansas 4–6–0 started life as a 1913 Baldwin-built stock model. Baldwin produced a large number of very similar engines, which were purchased by short-line railroads thoughout the country. They seemed to be especially popular with roads in the deep south. In the mid-'30s, the 63-inch drivers were replaced with 69-inch ones for better speed on the "Hustler," the overnight train from New Orleans to Shreveport. Pacific Fast Mail imported this Samhongsa-built model in 1976.

Louisville & Nashville Railroad (L&N)

Whyte Class	Owner Class & Type	Model Production					List Price	Resale		Remarks
		Importer	Builder	Cat #	Quan.	Yrs.		Mint	Avg.	
2-8-0	H-29a Consol	PFM				85			330	
2-8-0	H-28a Consol	PFM				85			330	
2-8-2	J-3 Mikado	Key	Samh		50	82	350	380	285	USRA Light #1500
2-8-2	J-4 Mikado	OMI	JPMod	1424	95	80	296	280	220	See Note #250
2-8-4	M-1 Berkshire	Gem	Katsumi	DH-102	300	61	60	350	250	See Note #468
2-8-4	M-1 Berkshire	Key				93	995			See Note #1160
2-8-4	M-1 Berkshire	Key				93	1070			fp., See Note #1161
2-8-4	M-1 Berkshire	Key				93	1070			fp., See Note #1162
2-8-4	M-1 Berkshire	Key				93	995			See Note #1163
2-8-4	M-1 Berkshire	WMC	KTM	MO-25	285	71	90	380	275	See Note #468
2-8-4	M-1 Berkshire tender	Gem	Katsumi	KT-102	100	62		90		
4-8-2	L-1 Mountain	Key	Samh		50	81	350	380	275	USRA Light

Maryland & Pennsylvania Railroad (Ma & Pa)

Whyte Class	Owner Class & Type	Model Production					List Price	Resale		Remarks
		Importer	Builder	Cat #	Quan.	Yrs.		Mint	Avg.	
0-6-0	#30 Switcher	WMC	Samh	MO-101	400	77	167	220	190	See Note #252
0-6-0	#29 Switcher	WMC	Samh	MO-100	300	77	160	220	190	See Note #251
2-8-0	Consol	Akane	Akane	200K		59	20	100		Kit, See Note #1164
2-8-0	Consol	Akane	Akane			62	33	160	130	See Note #1164
2-8-0	Consol	Intl	Akane			59	29	140	120	See Note #1164
2-8-0	Consol	Gem	Akane	200	20	63	23	150	130	
2-8-0	Consol	Gem	Akane	200	37	64		160		See Note #1164
2-8-0	Consol	Gem	Akane	FM-102	4	65	50	180	150	See Note #1164
2-8-0	Consol	Aristo				57	25	130	100	fp., See Note #1164
2-8-0	Consol	Intl	Akane			59	25	100	60	Kit, See Note #1164
2-8-0	#23-26 Consol	PFM	Atlas/Asahi	P	1	56				See Note #1165
2-8-0	#23-26 Consol	PFM	Atlas/Asahi	P	121	56	38	150	130	See Note #253
2-8-0	#23-26 Consol	PFM	Atlas/Asahi	P	195	56	38			Kit

Maryland & Pennsylvania Railroad (cont'd)

The Ma & Pa's light consolidations were an excellent example of the pre-WWI Baldwin design that was used by many short-line railroads in the U.S. Slide valves, Stephenson valve gear, spoked pilot wheels, wooden cabs, round domes, and low tenders were the design features that gave Baldwin engines their distinctive look. Ma & Pa had four of these engines, #23–26, and they served the line for many years. From 1956 through 1974, PFM imported over 4,700 of these Atlas/Asahi-built engines. Atlas/Asahi (United) has produced some of the most durable, well-proportioned models ever made. These engines are very popular with modelers who have limited space for their model railroads, for the engines will negotiate 18-inch radius curves and can still be purchased at reasonable prices.

| Whyte Class | Owner Class & Type | Model Production | | | | | List Price | Resale | | Remarks |
		Importer	Builder	Cat #	Quan.	Yrs.		Mint	Avg.	
2-8-0	#23-26 Consol	PFM	Atlas/Asahi	P	370	57	38	150	130	
2-8-0	#23-26 Consol	PFM	Atlas/Asahi	P	300	58	38	160	130	
2-8-0	#23-26 Consol	PFM	Atlas/Asahi	P	350	59	38	160	140	
2-8-0	#23-26 Consol	PFM	Atlas/Asahi	P	230	60	38	160	140	
2-8-0	#23-26 Consol	PFM	Atlas/Asahi	P	390	61	38	160	140	
2-8-0	#23-26 Consol	PFM	Atlas/Asahi	S	1	62				See Note #7
2-8-0	#23-26 Consol	PFM	Atlas/Asahi	P	190	62	38	170	150	
2-8-0	#23-26 Consol	PFM	Atlas/Asahi	P	270	64	38	170	150	
2-8-0	#23-26 Consol	PFM	Atlas/Asahi	P	375	65	40	180	160	
2-8-0	#23-26 Consol	PFM	Atlas/Asahi	P	280	66	40	180	160	
2-8-0	#23-26 Consol	PFM	Atlas/Asahi	P	265	67	43	190	170	
2-8-0	#23-26 Consol	PFM	Atlas/Asahi	P	385	69	50	190	180	
2-8-0	#23-26 Consol	PFM	Atlas/Asahi	P	500	70	63	200	180	
2-8-0	#23-26 Consol	PFM	Atlas/Asahi	P	502	74	140	220	190	
2-8-0	#41 Consol	OMI	MSM	1507	60	89	515	490		w/o Elesco FWH
2-8-0	#42 Consol	OMI	MSM	1508	100	89	526	350		
2-8-0	#43 Consol	PFM	Atlas/Asahi	P	600	71	85	220	190	See Note#1166
2-8-0	#43 Consol	PFM	Atlas/Asahi	P	500	73	135	235	200	See Note#1166
2-8-0	#43 Consol	OMI	MSM	1513	100	89	526	350		See Note#1167
4-4-0	American	Alco	Rok-Am		300	78	189	200	180	#6; RM review 1/79.
4-6-0	Ten Wheeler	Gem	Olympia	GN-108	35	64				
4-6-0	Ten Wheeler	OLEX				60	32	130	90	See Note #254
4-6-0	Ten Wheeler	Gem	Olympia	GN-108	15	65				
4-6-0	Ten Wheeler	Gem	Olympia	GN-108	236	61				
4-6-0	Ten Wheeler	Gem	Olympia	GN-108	252	62	50	160	130	

Midland Valley Railroad

Whyte Class	Owner Class & Type	Model Production					List Price	Resale		Remarks
		Importer	Builder	Cat #	Quan.	Yrs.		Mint	Avg.	
2-8-2	#601 Mikado	Hall	Mizuno		500	70	85	210	190	See Note #255

Missouri-Kansas-Texas Railroad (Katy)

Whyte Class	Owner Class & Type	Model Production					List Price	Resale		Remarks
		Importer	Builder	Cat #	Quan.	Yrs.		Mint	Avg.	
0-8-0	C-2a Switcher	Hall	Ajin		350	79	202	210	190	See Note #238
0-8-0	Switcher	MBA				60	28	140	90	fp., unlettered
0-8-0	C-2a Switcher	Intl				56	30	130	80	See Note #256
0-8-0	C-2a Switcher	Intl				56	25	130		Kit
2-6-0	J-5 Mogul	Hall	Ajin		350	79	187	210	190	RM Review 11/79
2-8-0	K-8 Consol	Hall	Goto		600	74	200	235	200	41% Consolidation
2-8-2	L-2d Mikado	Hall	DongJ		500	76	180	200	180	#881-920
4-6-2	H-3a Pacific	Hall	Fujiyama		500	69	125	320	235	See Note #257

Missouri Pacific Railroad (MoPac)

Whyte Class	Owner Class & Type	Model Production					List Price	Resale		Remarks
		Importer	Builder	Cat #	Quan.	Yrs.		Mint	Avg.	
0-8-0	Switcher	W&R	Samh							USRA
2-8-0	#100 Consol	Hall	DongJ		650	76	140	160	140	
2-8-2	#1310 Mikado	Key	Samh		50	81	380	390	350	See Note #258
2-8-2	#1310 Mikado	Key	Samh		75	85	420	420		fp.
2-8-2	#1400 Mikado	Hall	DongJ		500	77	180	210	180	
2-8-4	Berkshire	OMI	Ajin	1442	25	87	521	650		See Note #1168
2-8-4	BK-63 Berkshire	OMI	Ajin	1461	100	87	460	430		#1901-1925
2-10-2	#1715 Santa Fe	Sun	Samh	HO-21	200	77	169	220	200	See Note #259
2-8-8-2	#4000 Articulated	Hall		HS0099	100	83	597	650	590	See Note #260
4-6-2	P-73 Pacific	PFM	Samh	P	750	76	185	220	190	Worthington BL FWH

The MoPacs #2200 series Northerns were copies of the very successful D&RGW M–68 Class. Cabs and appliances differed, but under the skin they were brothers, if not twins. The D&RGW engines had been built to haul passenger trains in the mountains, but the design suited itself to MoPac's flatter terrain. Weighing in at 496,000 lbs., with a tractive effort of 67,200 lbs., these 1943 Baldwin-built Northerns provided excellent service in freight and passenger assignments. With front-mounted pumps, Worthington feedwater heater, and properly centered headlight, the MoPac #2200s looked every part the culmination of the 4–8–4 design. Fujiyama produced 600 of these fine "Crown" models for PFM between 1972 and 1977.

Missouri Pacific Railroad (cont'd)

Whyte Class	Owner Class & Type	Model Production					List Price	Resale		Remarks
		Importer	Builder	Cat #	Quan.	Yrs.		Mint	Avg.	
4-6-2	#6600 Pacific	Hall	Ajin		500	78-81	214	200	180	Elesco FWH
4-8-2	MT-69 Mountain	Key	Samh		50	81	335	350	320	See Note #261
4-8-2	5300 Class	Key	Samh		75	85	336	330		
4-8-2	MT-69 Mountain	Key	Samh		50	81	393		380	fp.,See Note #261
4-8-4	#2200 Northern	PFM	Fujiyama	CR	300	72	225	750	675	Crown
4-8-4	#2200 Northern	PFM	Fujiyama	CR	300	77	560	850	775	See Note #263
4-8-4	Northern	OMI	Ajin	1460	175	87	517	490		#2101-2125

Monon Railroad

Whyte Class	Owner Class & Type	Model Production					List Price	Resale		Remarks
		Importer	Builder	Cat #	Quan.	Yrs.		Mint	Avg.	
2-8-2	J-3 Mikado	OMI	JPMod	1423	100	80	296	300	230	See Note #264
4-6-2	K-5a Pacific	OMI	Ajin	1473	87	87	407	400		Pre-War
4-6-2	K-5 Pacific	OMI	Ajin	1472	88	87	407	400		Circa-1940
4-6-2	K-5a Pacific	OMI	Ajin	1473.1		87	484	460		Pre-War, fp.
4-6-2	K-5a Pacific	OMI	Ajin	1471.1		87	484	460		Post War, fp.
4-6-2	K-5 Pacific	OMI	Ajin	1472.1		87	484	460		Circa-1940, fp.
4-6-2	K-5a Pacific	OMI	Ajin	1471	100	86	407	400		Post War

Nashville, Chatanooga & St. Louis Railroad

Whyte Class	Owner Class & Type	Model Production					List Price	Resale		Remarks
		Importer	Builder	Cat #	Quan.	Yrs.		Mint	Avg.	
2-8-2	L-2 Mikado	Key	Samh		50	81	335	350		#650 Class, Rect. Tender

New York Central System

Whyte Class	Owner Class & Type	Model Production					List Price	Resale		Remarks
		Importer	Builder	Cat #	Quan.	Yrs.		Mint	Avg.	
0-6-0	B-11L Switcher	Alco	KMT	S-166	450	77	165	160	140	Can Motor
0-6-0	B-11L Switcher	Alco	KMT	S-116S	50	77	279	235	190	See Note #265
0-6-0	B-10 Switcher	LMB	KMT		500	69	55	170	130	
0-8-0	U-2d Switcher	MTSImp	SKI		130	89	634	600		fp.
0-8-0	U-2d Switcher	MTSImp	SKI		20	89	550			
0-8-0	U-3a Switcher	Akane	Akane			63	48	150	120	USRA
0-8-0	U-3 Switcher	PSC	D&D	15872-1		90	557	530		fp.
0-8-0	U-3 Switcher	PSC	D&D	15872		90	470	440		
0-8-0	U-3a Switcher	W&R	Samh		115	87				USRA; #7750-7796
0-10-0	M-1a Switcher	CustB	KSM	ST-236	500	77-78	164	190	150	
2-6-0	E-1A Mogul	Key	Samh		75	87	414	350		fp.
2-6-0	E-1D Mogul	Key	Samh		75	87	414	410		fp.
2-8-0	G-46h Consol	Alco	Rok-Am	S-120	400	77	165	235		
2-8-2	H-5 Mikado	Key				91	850	830		fp., double air pump
2-8-2	H-5 Mikado	Key				91	795	790		double air pump
2-8-2	H-5 Mikado	Key				91	795	790		single air pump
2-8-2	H-5 Mikado	Key				91	850	830		fp., single air pump
2-8-2	H-5t Mikado	OMI	TaeHwa	1418	175	80	266		270	22" min. radius
2-8-2	H-6a Mikado	Key	Samh		250	77	160	350	290	USRA #1800 series
2-8-2	H7e Mikado	OMI	Ajin	1517	100	90	642			w/A1C tender
2-8-2	H7e Mikado	OMI	Ajin	1518	150	90	656			
2-8-2	H7e Mikado	OMI	Ajin	1527	100	90	642			w/4 axle tender
2-8-2	H-10a Mikado	OMI	JPMod	1426	150	80	307		290	See Note #266
2-8-2	H-10a Mikado	OMI	Ajin	1454.1	25	89	593	560		fp.
2-8-2	H-10a Mikado	OMI	Ajin	1454	175	89	500	470		
2-8-2	H-10b Mikado	PFM	SKI	P	200	81	448		350	
2-8-2	H-10b Mikado	LMB	KMT			61-67	50-65	290	235	See Note #1169
2-8-2	H-10b Mikado	OMI	JPMod	1429	150	81	337		320	Big Four Version
2-8-2	H-10b Mikado	LMB	KMT			61-67	50-65	290	235	See Note #1171
2-8-2	H-10b Mikado	PFM	Atlas/Kawai	H	5	60	144	1000	1000	Crown, Handbuilt

New York Central System (cont'd)

In 1922, New York Central decided they needed some new Mikados. The H–10, of which there was only one, was built by Lima and proved to be everything the motive-power department expected. Subsequent orders were placed with Lima for H–10a's and b's. The roster finally numbered 1,000 Mikados. These engines looked like they were designed by a model railroader. With a "Beetle Browed" Elesco feedwater heater, the external dry pipe, and a wealth of modern appliances and external plumbing, they exemplify the look of modern Lima-built steam power. The beautifully detailed model pictured is a H–10a, built by Ajin for Overland Models.

Whyte Class	Owner Class & Type	Model Production				List Price	Resale		Remarks
		Importer	Builder	Cat #	Quan.	Yrs.		Mint	Avg.
2-8-4	A-2a Berkshire	PFM	Atlas/Asahi	CR	95	60	99	1400	1200	See Note #1170
2-6-6-2	NE-2 Articulated	CustB	DaiYng	ST-237	300	78	380	450		See Note #271
4-4-0	American	KenK		3538		65	30	130	100	NYC&HR
4-4-0	American	LMB				65	30	130	100	NYC&HR
4-4-0	#999 American	Aristo				58	43	120	90	See Note #272
4-4-0	#999 American	MBA				59	30	160		fp. black with gold lettering
4-4-0	#999 American	Gem	Katsumi	1000F	100	59	28	180		
4-4-0	#999 American	Gem	Katsumi	1000F	700	60	28	190	140	fp., See Note #272
4-6-0	Ten-Wheeler	Smart	Takara			60-61		260		See Note #1172
4-6-0	Ten-Wheeler	LMB			50	62				
4-6-0	Ten-Wheeler	LMB			600	61	30	160	130	See Note #273
4-6-0	Ten-Wheeler	LMB			500	61	27	120	90	Kit, See Note #273
4-6-0	Ten-Wheeler	Intl	KTM	12-E		62	50	180	150	
4-6-0	Ten-Wheeler	Prec				61	30	150	120	See Note #273
4-6-0	F-12a Ten-Wheeler	PSC	D&D	15366-3		89	527	500		See Note #1173
4-6-0	F-12a Ten-Wheeler	PSC	D&D	15366-1		89	527	500		See Note #1174
4-6-0	F-12a Ten-Wheeler	PSC	D&D	15366		89	467	440		See Note #1175
4-6-0	F-12a Ten-Wheeler	PSC	D&D	15366-2		89	467	440		See Note #1176
4-6-0	F-12e Ten-Wheeler	PSC	D&D	15368		89	467	440		See Note #1177
4-6-0	F-12e Ten-Wheeler	Gem	Tsubomi	KT-107	330	75	124-185	200	180	
4-6-0	F-12e Ten-Wheeler	PSC	D&D	15368-1		89	527	500		fp., See Note #1177
4-6-0	F-51 Ten-Wheeler	KenK		3512		59-68	30-40	190	150	See Note #274
4-6-0	F-51 Ten-Wheeler	KenK		3512K		63	27	130	100	Kit, See Note #274
4-6-2	Pacific	PFM	Atlas		1	58	14			Kit
4-6-2	K-3g Pacific	Alco	Kobra		600	76	135	150	130	See Note #1331
4-6-2	K-5 Pacific	Sun	Samh		50	78	190	260	235	cp.
4-6-2	K-5 Pacific	Sun	Samh		600	77	169	235	200	See Note #275
4-6-2	K-11 Pacific	MTSC	Samh							Mercury
4-6-4	Hudson	PSC		15314		87	495	470		See Note #1179
4-6-4	J-1 Hudson	PFM	Tensh	P	155	56	35	220	190	Kit
4-6-4	J-1 Hudson	Aristo				57	40	150	120	Kit
4-6-4	J-1 Hudson	Cont	Tetsudo			58	35	200	160	
4-6-4	J-1 Hudson	PFM	Tensh	P	25	59	35	235	210	Kit
4-6-4	J-1 Hudson	PFM	Tensh #110	P	250	59	40	260	230	fp., See Note #556
4-6-4	J-1 Hudson	PFM	Tensh #110	P	125	55	40	235	200	fp., See Note #556
4-6-4	J-1 Hudson	PFM	Tensh #110	P	250	58	40	250	220	fp., See Note #556

New York Central System (cont'd)

New York Central had several classes of "Mohawks" (Mountains to non-Central buffs). None capture the Central's "look" better than the L-3 class. With Central's distinctive turret cover that curved gracefully down the side of the firebox, the centered non-visored headlight, disc drivers, huge tenders, and clean lines, these engines looked, at first glance, like stretched Hudsons. Samhongsa built this fine replica of the L-3a class for Key Imports in 1983.

Whyte Class	Owner Class & Type	Model Production					List Price	Resale		Remarks
		Importer	Builder	Cat #	Quan.	Yrs.		Mint	Avg.	
4-6-4	J-1 Hudson	PFM	Tensh #110	P	470	57	40	250	220	fp., See Note #556
4-6-4	J-1 Hudson	PFM	Tensh	P	200	57	35	220	200	Kit
4-6-4	J-1 Hudson	PFM	Tensh	P	125	58	35	230	200	Kit
4-6-4	J-1 Hudson	PFM	Tensh	P	2	54				Kit
4-6-4	J-1 Hudson	PFM	Tensh #110	P	30	60	40	260	235	
4-6-4	J-1 Hudson	PFM	Tensh	P	97	55	35	210	190	See Note #1182
4-6-4	J-1 Hudson	MBA				58	35			
4-6-4	J-1 Hudson	PFM	Tensh #110	P	200	56	45	240	210	See Note #556
4-6-4	J-1 Hudson	PFM	Tensh #110	P	1	54				
4-6-4	J-1b Hudson	Key								
4-6-4	J-1b Hudson	Sun		HO126C		90	229	220		See Note #1180
4-6-4	J-1c Hudson	Key	Samh		75	84	457		430	1940 version
4-6-4	J-1c Hudson	Key	Samh		50	84	529		490	fp., 1940 version
4-6-4	J-1d Hudson	Key	Samh		50	84	529		500	fp., 1940/50 version
4-6-4	J-1e Hudson	WMC	Mizuno	MO83	677	77	270	410	350	See Note #277
4-6-4	J-1e Hudson	Sun		HO126b		90	229	220		Big Four Version
4-6-4	J-1e Hudson	Sun		HO126A		90	229	220		See Note #1181
4-6-4	J-1e Hudson	Key	Mizuno		85	83	527	590	530	fp., See Note #558
4-6-4	J-1e Hudson	Sun		HO126a		90	229	220		See Note#1329
4-6-4	J-1e Hudson	Sun		HO126c		90	229	192		See Note#1184
4-6-4	J-1e Hudson	Sun		HO126B		90	229	192		See Note #1183
4-6-4	J-1e Hudson	Key	Mizuno		80	83	527	570	530	fp., See Note #557
4-6-4	J-2 Hudson	Key	Mizuno							See Note #1185
4-6-4	J-2 Hudson	Key	Mizuno		75					See Note #1186
4-6-4	J-2 Hudson	Key	Mizuno		75					See Note #1187
4-6-4	J-3 Hudson	WMC		M-174		82	540			See Note #1188
4-6-4	J-3a Hudson	Key					1070	1020		fp., See Note #1189
4-6-4	J-3a Hudson	LMB	KMT			66-70	65-100	320	235	See Note #272
4-6-4	J-3a Hudson	Key	Mizuno			85	529		500	See Note #1190
4-6-4	J-3a Hudson	Key	Mizuno			85	529		500	See Note #1191
4-6-4	J-3a Hudson	Intl					54	52	180	150	
4-6-4	J-3a Hudson	Key					1070	1020		See Note #1192
4-6-4	J-3a Hudson	LMB	KMT			78	360			fp. 20th Century
4-6-4	J-3a Hudson	LMB	KMT			78	270			20th Century
4-6-4	J-3a Hudson	LMB	KMT			78	270	340		See Note #272
4-6-4	J-3a Hudson	LMB	KMT			78	360		350	fp., See Note #272
4-6-4	J-3a Hudson	LMB	KMT			71	75	260	210	

New York Central System (cont'd)

Almost every rail fan over the age of 40 can identify the New York Central J–3a Hudson instantly. Lionel made some outstanding O-scale models of this engine in the 1940s. It was every boy's dream to own one. Alco built the prototype J–3a for the Central in 1937. The J–3a's were the culmination of the Hudson wheel arrangement on the Central and were commonly assigned to pull the "20th Century." It wasn't until 1985 that a brass importer decided to produce a high-quality scale model of this famous engine. Westside Models contracted with Micro Cast Mizuno of Japan and imported this model as their "Craftsman Series #4."

Whyte Class	Owner Class & Type	Model Production					List Price	Resale		Remarks
		Importer	Builder	Cat #	Quan.	Yrs.		Mint	Avg.	
4-6-4	J-3a Hudson	LMB	KMT			68	130	350	290	fp. 20th Century #5445
4-6-4	J-3a Hudson	LMB	KMT		200	62	50	235	190	#5405
4-6-4	J-3a Hudson	LMB			800	62-70	100	320	235	20th Century
4-6-4	J-3a Hudson	PFM	Atlas	H	10	57	116	1200		Handbuilt
4-6-4	J-3a Hudson	PFM	Sakura/Takeno	CR	100	64	140	2400		See Note #276
4-6-4	J-3a Hudson	PSC		15470		86	498			fp., See Note #1193
4-6-4	J-3a Hudson	PSC		15478		84				See Note #1093
4-6-4	J-3a Hudson	PSC		15470	75	84	495	540		fp., See Note #1193
4-6-4	J-3a Hudson	WMC	Mizuno	M-174		80	540	590	520	See Note #280
4-6-4	J-3a Hudson	WMC	Mizuno			78	412	470	410	See Note #279
4-6-4	J-3a Hudson	WMC	Mizuno	M-117	400	78	330	790	760	See Note #278
4-6-4	J-3a Hudson Set	PSC		15332		85	1375	1550		See Note #1330
4-8-2	L-2a Mohawk	Key	Samh		100	81	360	450		See Note #287
4-8-2	L-2a Mohawk	PFM	Atlas/Kawai	H	5	60	147	2500		See Note #1094
4-8-2	L-2b Mohawk	Key	Samh		100	81	643	610		fp., See Note #288
4-8-2	L-2b Mohawk	Key	Samh		10	89	579	550		
4-8-2	L-2b Mohawk	Key	Samh		100	81	360	380	330	See Note #288
4-8-2	L-2b Mohawk	Key	Samh		60	89	643	610		fp.
4-8-2	L-2c Mohawk	CustB	KSM	ST-905	100	81	408	340	310	
4-8-2	L-2d Mohawk	Key	Samh				495	490		
4-8-2	L-2d Mohawk	Key	Samh				643	640		fp., See Note #289
4-8-2	L-2d Mohawk	Key	Samh		100	81	360	440	350	See Note #289
4-8-2	L-3a Mohawk	Key	Samh		50	83	414	430	400	See Note #1195
4-8-2	L-3a Mohawk	PFM	Tensh #136	P	600	58	50	190	150	See Note #281
4-8-2	L-3a Mohawk	PFM	Tensh #236	P	25	60	45	160	140	Brass Kit
4-8-2	L-3a Mohawk	PFM	Tensh #136	P	100	61	50	220	190	See Note #282
4-8-2	L-3a Mohawk	PFM	Tensh #236	P	25	61	45	160	140	Brass Kit
4-8-2	L-3a Mohawk	Key	Samh		300	77	160	210	190	See Note #283
4-8-2	L-3a Mohawk	PFM	Tensh #236	P	100	58	45	160	140	Brass Kit
4-8-2	L-3a Mohawk	PFM	Tensh #136	P	100	62	50	235	200	See Note #282
4-8-2	L-3a Mohawk	PFM	Tensh #136	P	100	60	50	210	180	See Note #282
4-8-2	L-3a Mohawk	Key	Samh		50	83	414	470	440	Improved model
4-8-2	L-3a Mohawk	PFM	Tensh #236	P	25	59	45	160	140	Brass Kit

New York Central System (cont'd)

The Central's K–5 Pacifics were built in 1925 and cost $57,000. The K–5 was about as far as the Central could go with the Pacific design. Bigger boilers would have exceeded axle loading. It's not surprising that they bore a strong resemblance to the Hudsons. Sunset imported a Samhongsa-built model of this brutish Pacific in 1978.

The Central's first Hudsons were the J–1 Class, built in 1927. There were eventually bigger and more powerful Hudsons built, but none ever captured the look of speed, power, and purpose that characterized these engines. Mizuno built this exquisite model for Westside Model Company in 1977.

Whyte Class	Owner Class & Type	Model Production					List Price	Resale		Remarks
		Importer	Builder	Cat #	Quan.	Yrs.		Mint	Avg.	
4-8-2	L-3a Mohawk	PFM	Tensh #136	P	200	59	50	200	160	See Note #282
4-8-2	L-3b Mohawk	Key	Samh		200	80	190		200	See Note #286
4-8-2	L-3b Mohawk	Key	Samh		70	85	414	410		
4-8-2	L-3b Mohawk	Key	Samh		200	77	170	210	190	See Note #285
4-8-2	L-4a Mohawk	Key	Samh		300	77	170	210	190	See Note #284
4-8-2	L-4a Mohawk	Key	Samh		129	85	414	410		
4-8-2	L-4b Mohawk	Key	Samh		15	83	414	400		
4-8-2	L-4b Mohawk	LMB	KMT		490	69	85	290	260	See Note #1196
4-8-2	L-4b Mohawk	Key	Samh		300	77	160	220	190	72" Scullin Drivers
4-8-2	L-4b Mohawk	Key	Samh		65	83	486	460		fp.
4-8-4	Niagara	Intl				54	70	185	190	
4-8-4	Niagara	MBA				66	90			
4-8-4	Niagara	PFM				88	1449	1167		
4-8-4	S-1a Niagara	Key				93	1030			#6000
4-8-4	S-1a Niagara	Key				93	1130			fp. #6000

New York Central System (cont'd)

New York Central had streamlined locos prior to the "20th Century" and the "Empire State Express," but the previous styling was definitely "bathtub." Central hired Henry Dreyfus to streamline these two locos, and his efforts came off quite well. Rather than cover everything, he molded the new sheet metal to the contours of the loco and left much of the running gear exposed. The paint scheme for the "Empire State Express" was striking. The lower half of the boiler was black, the top gray, the shroud black with lots of stainless steel trim. In later years, the firebox shrouding was removed. Precision Scale imported this "Empire State" loco in 1983.

The zenith of steam locomotive design on the New York Central was reached with the introduction of the 4-8-4 "Niagara." Built late in the steam era, 1945, Central was already experimenting with diesels. Sleek looking for a big engine, the appearance was more due to clearance limitations than aesthetics. With a main boiler course of 100 inches, there simply wasn't any room for a steam dome. Magnificent as they were, they were no match for the new diesels. They lasted until August of 1953, when the diesel finally displaced them. Key imported this handsome Samhongsa model of the S-1b in 1982.

Whyte Class	Owner Class & Type	Model Production					List Price	Resale		Remarks
		Importer	Builder	Cat #	Quan.	Yrs.		Mint	Avg.	
4-8-4	S-1b Niagara	Key	Samh		150	82	415		390	See Note #1199
4-8-4	S-1b Niagara	Key	Samh		70	85			550	fp., See Note #1199
4-8-4	S-1b Niagara	Key	Samh		29	85			510	
4-8-4	S-1b Niagara	Key				93	1130			fp., See Note #1201
4-8-4	S-1b Niagara	Key				93	1030			See Note #1201
4-8-4	S-1b Niagara	LMB	KMT			66-69	70-85	380	310	One of LMB's best
4-8-4	S-1b Niagara	NPP	KMT		50	77	295	290	260	fp.

New York Central System (cont'd)

Whyte Class	Owner Class & Type	Model Production					List Price	Resale		Remarks
		Importer	Builder	Cat #	Quan.	Yrs.		Mint	Avg.	
4-8-4	S-1b Niagara	NPP	KMT		250	77	230	250	200	
4-8-4	S-1b Niagara	PFM	Atlas/KTM	P	19	54	30	120	100	See Note #290 & 291
4-8-4	S-1b Niagara	PFM	Atlas/KTM	P	4	54		140	120	See Note #1197
4-8-4	S-1b Niagara	PFM	Atlas/KTM	P	20	55	35			See Note #1332
4-8-4	S-1b Niagara	PFM	Atlas/KTM	P	11	55	30	220	190	See Note #291
4-8-4	S-1b Niagara	PFM	Atlas/KTM	P	6	56	30	235	200	See Note #291
4-8-4	S-1b Niagara	PFM	Atlas/KTM	P	1	56	40			See Note #1197
4-8-4	S-1b Niagara	PFM	Atlas/KTM	P	416	57	50	250	210	See Note #290
4-8-4	S-1b Niagara	PFM	Atlas/KTM	P	529	58	50	250	220	See Note #290
4-8-4	S-1b Niagara	PFM	Atlas/KTM	P	190	59	50	260	235	See Note #292
4-8-4	S-1b Niagara	PFM	Atlas/KTM	P	100	60	50	270	250	
4-8-4	S-1b Niagara	PFM	Tensh			85	1200		1110	See Note #1200
4-8-4	S-1b Niagara	PSC								PT-5 tender
4-8-4	S-2a Niagara	Key	Samh		49	82	450	550	530	
4-8-4	S-2a Niagara	Key	Samh		60	85				
4-8-4	S-2a Niagara	Key	Samh		65	86	593		550	fp., #5500
4-8-4	S-2a Niagara	Key				93	1130			fp. #5500 , poppet valve
4-8-4	S-2a Niagara	Key				93	1030			#5500 , poppet valve
4-8-4	S-2a Niagara	PSC								Poppet valve; PT-6 tender

New York, Chicago & St. Louis Rwy. (NKP) (NYC&StL)

Whyte Class	Owner Class & Type	Model Production					List Price	Resale		Remarks
		Importer	Builder	Cat #	Quan.	Yrs.		Mint	Avg.	
0-6-0	B-11b Switcher	LMB				71	55	170	130	
0-8-0	Switcher	W&R				87		360		USRA; #271-295
2-8-2	H-5A Mikado	OMI	TaeHwa	1417	125	79	266			
2-8-2	H-6a Mikado	Key	Samh		50	81	340	350	290	See Note #296
2-8-2	H-6d Mikado	Key	Samh		100	81	336		290	#627 Light USRA
2-8-4	S Berkshire	LMB	KTM			60	48	180	150	Japanese Motor
2-8-4	S Berkshire	LMB	KTM			60	50	190	160	See Note #300
2-8-4	S-1 Berkshire	Key	Samh		50	82	415	440		Solid pilot; #700,726,727
2-8-4	S-1 Berkshire	Key				93	1070			fp.#715, See Note #1204
2-8-4	S-2 Berkshire	Key	Samh		50	84	471		450	fp. #765
2-8-4	S-2 Berkshire	Key				93	1070			fp.#740, See Note #1206
2-8-4	S-2 Berkshire	OMI	JPMod	1449	125	82	360			See Note #1205

The NYC&StL is far better known as the "Nickel Plate," and that name is synonymous with the Berkshire 2–8–4 wheel arrangement. The Nickel Plate Berkshires were the brainchild of the "Advisory Mechanical Committee" of the C&O, NKP, and PM. The design they developed became the standard for several roads. In 1934 the first engines of the S Class were delivered by Alco. NKP's total roster of S–1 through S–3 Class Berkshires totaled 80 engines by 1949. Samhongsa built this model of the S2/3 Class for Key Imports in 1982.

New York, Chicago & St. Louis Rwy. (cont'd)

Whyte Class	Owner Class & Type	Model Production					List Price	Resale		Remarks
		Importer	Builder	Cat #	Quan.	Yrs.		Mint	Avg.	
2-8-4	S-2/3 Berkshire	Key	Samh		120	82	400		380	See Note #1207
2-8-4	S-3 Berkshire	Aristo				66	60	150	100	
2-8-4	S-3 Berkshire	Key				93	1070			fp.#779, See Note #1208
2-8-4	S-3 Berkshire	Key				93	995			See Note #1208
2-8-4	S-3 Berkshire	PFM	Atlas/Asahi	P	780	60	50	210	190	#770-779; Pittman motor.
2-8-4	S-3 Berkshire	PFM	Atlas/Asahi	P	590	61	50	220	190	See Note #297
2-8-4	S-3 Berkshire	PFM	Atlas/Asahi	P	255	63	50	235	200	
2-8-4	S-3 Berkshire	PFM	Atlas/Asahi	S	2	63				See Note #7
2-8-4	S-3 Berkshire	PFM	Atlas/Asahi	P	200	64	50	260	230	Brake Shoes added
2-8-4	S-3 Berkshire	PFM	Atlas/Asahi	P	225	65	60	280	210	
2-8-4	S-3 Berkshire	PFM	Atlas/Asahi	P	240	66	60	290	260	
2-8-4	S-3 Berkshire	PFM	Atlas/Asahi	P	330	68	65	310	280	See Note #299
2-8-4	S-4 Berkshire	Key				93	995			See Note #1209
2-8-4	S-4 Berkshire	Key				93	1070			fp.#801, See Note #1209
2-6-6-2	I-3 Articulated	Key	Samh		50	82	600		570	USRA W&LE
4-6-4	L-1b Hudson	NPP	Kimura/NKP		150	77	172	200	180	See Note #302
4-6-4	L-1b Hudson	NPP	Kimura/NKP		150	77	172	190	180	See Note #301
4-6-4	L-1b Hudson	NPP	Kimura/NKP		150	77	209	230	190	fp., See Note #302
4-6-4	L-1a Hudson	NPP	Kimura/NKP		25	83	190			See Note #1333
4-6-4	L-1b Hudson	NPP	Kimura/NKP		150	77	200	210	190	fp., See Note #301
4-8-2	K-3 Mountain	Sun	Samh			76	142	190		See Note #303

New York, New Haven & Hartford Railroad

Whyte Class	Owner Class & Type	Model Production					List Price	Resale		Remarks
		Importer	Builder	Cat #	Quan.	Yrs.		Mint	Avg.	
0-8-0	Switcher	W&R	Samh		65	88	421	530		#3410-3434
0-8-0	Switcher	W&R	Samh		32	88	492	620		fp., #3410-3434
2-6-0	K-1b Mogul	NERS	Samh			85	330			fp.
2-6-0	K-1d Mogul	NERS	Samh			85	285			See Note #1213
2-6-0	K-1b Mogul	NERS	Samh			85	285			See Note #1214
2-6-0	K-1d Mogul	NERS	Samh			85	330			See Note #1215
2-8-2	J-1 Mikado	Key	Samh		25	81	357	420	350	fp, #3000-3024

After World War I, the NYO&W needed new motive power and opted for a fleet of dual-use 4–8–2's. Weight restrictions on the southern end of the line dictated an engine somewhat lighter than the common USRA light 4–8–2. The NYO&W engines were dimensionally similar to the Southern Railway's TS Class, but the resemblance ended there. Engine #405 was specially streamlined and painted for the ''Mountaineer Special,'' a train for resort service. Painted maroon, orange, and black, with a Russian iron boiler jacket, this engine presented a striking appearance pulling her consist of similarly painted heavyweight coaches. NPP imported this loco in 1983. The model was advertised as a Y–2 but is actually engine #405, a Class Y.

New York, New Haven & Hartford Railroad (cont'd)

Whyte Class	Owner Class & Type	Importer	Builder	Cat #	Quan.	Yrs.	List Price	Mint	Avg.	Remarks
2-8-2	J-1 Mikado	Key	Samh		250	81	300	320	290	3000 class
2-10-2	L-1 Santa Fe	CustB	DaiYng	ST-201B	175	82	460		350	See Note #294
2-10-2	L-1 Santa Fe	CustB	DaiYng	ST-201A	150	82	460		350	See Note #293
4-6-0	#846 Ten-Wheeler	Emp	Kobra?			80	210	230	200	
4-6-2	I-4 Pacific	CustB	KMT	ST-219	530	77	230	270	235	Elesco FWH
4-6-4	I-5 Hudson	CustB	KSM	ST-203	300	79	265	235	210	See Note #295
4-8-2	R-1a Mountain	Key	Samh		50	84	443	420		w/correct tender
4-8-2	R-1a Mountain	Key	Samh		50	84	535	510		fp.#3314, w/correct tender
4-8-2	R-3a Mountain	CustB	KSM	ST-218	250	80	365	350	300	3-cyl, Elesco FWH
4-8-2	R-1b Mountain	Key	Samh		50	84	443	420		See Note #1216
4-8-2	R-1a Mountain	Key	Samh		50	84	443	420		See Note #1217
4-8-2	R-1b Mountain	Key	Samh		50	84	535	510		fp.#3340, w/correct tender

New York, Ontario & Western Railway (NYO&W)

Whyte Class	Owner Class & Type	Importer	Builder	Cat #	Quan.	Yrs.	List Price	Mint	Avg.	Remarks
2-6-0	Mogul	ModX				85	120			Camelback
2-6-0	Mogul	NPP	Kimura/NKP		400	75	170	180		Camelback, fp.
2-6-0	Mogul	NPP	Kimura/NKP		100	75	160	190		Camelback
2-8-0	W Consol	NPP	Daeki		150	84	300	300		
4-6-0	U-1 Ten-Wheeler	ModX				84	119			Camelback, fp.
4-6-0	U-1 Ten-Wheeler	NPP	Kimura/NKP		400	75	170	190		Camelback, fp.
4-6-0	U-1 Ten-Wheeler	NPP	Kimura/NKP		100	75	164	190		Camelback
4-6-0	U-1 Ten-Wheeler	ModX				84	100			Camelback
4-8-2	Y-2 Mountain	NPP	TaeHwa		50	83	360			fp., See Note #1218
4-8-2	Y-2 Mountain	NPP	KMT		650	73	180	220		See Note #560
4-8-2	Y-2 Mountain	NPP	TaeHwa		50	83	300			See Note #1218
4-8-2	Y-2 Mountain	CustB	KSM	ST-229	100	81	408	380		

Norfolk & Western Railway (N&W)

Whyte Class	Owner Class & Type	Importer	Builder	Cat #	Quan.	Yrs.	List Price	Mint	Avg.	Remarks
0-8-0	S-1a Switcher	PSC	D&D	15786-1		90	557	530		fp.,#200-244
0-8-0	S-1 Switcher	PSC	D&D	15784		90	470	440		#255-284
0-8-0	Switcher	PFM	Tensh	H	1	57		2200		See Note #304
0-8-0	S-1 Switcher	PSC	D&D	15784-1		90	557	530		fp.,#255-284
0-8-0	S-1a Switcher	PFM	Samh	P		79	215	250	220	ref. MM 3-4/80
0-8-0	S-1a Switcher	PSC	D&D	15786		90	470			#200-244
2-8-0	W-2 Consol	NWSL	Jonan	7-1		76	190	220	190	See Note #305
2-8-0	G-1 Consol	Alco	Rok-Am	S-132		80	239	235	180	Quality problems
2-6-6-2	Z-1a/L-96 Articulated	CustB	DaiYng	ST-839	300	79	350	450	380	See Note #193
2-6-6-4	Class "A"	Key	Samh		100	82	755	910	760	See Note #306
2-6-6-4	Class "A"	Key	Samh		100	82	755	910	760	See Note #307
2-6-6-4	Class "A"	Key	Samh			91				See Note #949
2-6-6-4	Class "A"	Key	Samh			91	1420	1410		fp. #1235, See Note #306
2-6-6-4	Class "A"	Key	Samh			91				fp., Note #949
2-6-6-4	Class "A"	Key	Samh			91	1420	1200		fp., See Note #307
2-6-6-4	Class "A"	Key	Samh		100	82	685	650		See Note #949
2-6-6-4	Class "A"	Key	Samh			91				See Note #306
2-6-6-4	Class "A"	Key	Samh			91				See Note #307
2-6-6-4	Class "A"	PFM	United		500	79	915	1060		See Note #1219
2-6-6-4	Class "A"	PFM	Atlas/Asahi	S	201	62				
2-6-6-4	Class "A"	PFM	Atlas/Asahi	P	200	62	95	705		
2-6-6-4	Class "A"	PFM	Atlas/Asahi	P	270	60	95	590		
2-6-6-4	Class "A"	PFM	Tensh	H	1	57				See Note #304
2-6-6-4	Class "A"	PFM	Atlas/Asahi	P	350	61	95	650		
2-8-8-2	Y-2 Articulated	CustB	Goto	ST-840	100	80	830	740		CB Royale Series
2-8-8-2	Y-3 Articulated	CustB	Goto	St-288	250	78	768	820		See Note #311
2-8-8-2	Y-4 Articulated	Key	Samh		50	82	715	700		

Norfolk & Western Railway (cont'd)

N&W was no stranger to big articulateds. Some of the most successful designs ever built regularly ran on their heavy grades and across the flat sections of Virginia. The Y–3 Class was basically a USRA design with several improvements. Worthington feedwater heaters and large tenders with six-wheel trucks were added after 1923. Many of these engines were sold off to other roads during World War II. The few engines that remained lasted until 1958–59. In the late 1970s, N.J. Custom Brass contracted with Goto to produce several different roads' 2–8–8–2's. The N&W Y–3 was one of those that was marketed in the "CB Royale" series.

Whyte Class	Owner Class & Type	Model Production					List Price	Resale		Remarks
		Importer	Builder	Cat #	Quan.	Yrs.		Mint	Avg.	
2-8-8-2	Y-5 Articulated	Key	Samh		50	82	715	670		
2-8-8-2	Y-6a Articulated	Key	Samh		50	82	715	780		
2-8-8-2	Y-6 Articulated	Key	Samh		50	82	715	670		
2-8-8-2	Y-6b Articulated	Key	Samh		50	81	685	780		See Note #310
2-8-8-2	Y-6b Articulated	Key	Samh		150	81	685			See Note #309
2-8-8-2	Y-6b Articulated	PFM	Atlas/Asahi	CR	100	62	150	1030		See Note #1948
2-8-8-2	Y-6b Articulated	PFM	Atlas/Asahi	CR	105	58	150	950		Blue United box
2-8-8-2	Y-6b Articulated	PFM	Atlas/Asahi	CR	100	60	150	920		Blue United box
2-8-8-2	Y-6b Articulated	PFM	Atlas/Asahi	CR	189	59	150	920		See Note #308
2-8-8-2	Y-6b Articulated	PFM	Atlas	S	1	58				See Note #7 & #1220
4-6-0	Ten Wheeler	PFM	Atlas		2	55				
4-6-2	E-2a Pacific	NWSL	Toho		500	71	75	210	180	See Note #312
4-6-2	E-2a Pacific	NWSL	Orion		250	72	120	210	160	1912 era
4-6-2	E-2a Pacific	NWSL	Orion		500	72	120	200	170	1920 era
4-6-2	E-3 Pacific	WMC	Samh	MO-113	500	78	170	200	160	See Note #1221
4-8-0	M-2 12 Wheeler	Sun	DongJ	HO61	100	83	342	340		See Note #1222
4-8-0	M-1 12 Wheeler	LMB	KMT	1025		63-67	48-50	260	180	
4-8-0	M-1 12 Wheeler	Sun	Lhee Do	HO62	85	83	340	320		See Note #1223
4-8-0	M-2 12 Wheeler	Sun	DongJ	HO63	100	84	342	340		Worthington FWH
4-8-2	K-1 Mountain	Key	Samh		60	85	529	500		w/16000 gal. tdr., fp.
4-8-2	K-1 Mountain	Key	Samh		40	85	529	500		w/22000 gal. tdr., fp.
4-8-2	K-1 Mountain	Key	Samh		60	85	464	450		w/22000 gal. tdr.
4-8-2	K-2 Mountain	Key	Samh		300	79	300	320		See Note #589
4-8-2	K-2 Mountain	Key	Samh		20	82	357		380	fp., See Note #589
4-8-2	K-2/K-2a Mountain	Key	Samh		200	78	190	260	220	Heavy USRA
4-8-2	K-3 Mountain	Sun	Samh	HNW501	300	76	142	200	170	Water Buffalo
4-8-4	J Northern	Sun	Samh	H009	75	83	450	580	530	See Note #1225
4-8-4	J Northern	Sun	Samh	H008	125	83	450	580	530	See Note #1226
4-8-4	J Northern	Sun	Samh			83			540	fp., Limited Edition; #604
4-8-4	J Northern	Sun	Samh		35	83	450		420	Limited Edition; #604
4-8-4	J Northern	Sun	Samh	H008A	35	83	450			fp., Limited Edition #604
4-8-4	J Northern	Sun	Samh		800	79	239	320	290	RM review 4/79.
4-8-4	J Northern	PFM	Toby	CR	49	60	125	3500		fp. by Tenshodo
4-8-4	J Northern	PFM	Toby	CR	65	61	125	2800		See Note #1947
4-8-4	J Northern	PFM	Tensh	H	1	57				See Note #304
4-8-4	J Northern	Gem	Olympia	EH-123	310	67	110	470	410	

Norfolk & Western Railway (cont'd)

The first of Norfolk & Western's J Class 4–8–4's were constructed in the railroad's own shops at Roanoke, Va., in 1941. Little did they know that an engine of this same class would be running 50 years later. Designed for fast passenger train service, they appeared to have small drivers for that purpose. While big, fast 4–8–4's were being built by other roads with 80-inch drivers, N&W went to 70-inch drivers. It was not a mistake. The excellent balance of the locomotive allowed one engineer to really open one up on a test run and he exceeded 110 mph.

Twelve-wheelers weren't common, but the N&W had a total of 285 of these engines. Used primarily as switchers and branch line power, where the 4–8–0 wheel arrangement allowed for a more powerful locomotive than a 2–8–0 of similar size, they provided good service. The most modern of the N&W 4–8–0's was the Class M–2. N&W began downgrading these engines when they bought thirty 0–8–0 switchers from C&O in 1951. Dong Jin produced this excellent replica for Sunset Models in 1983.

Whyte Class	Owner Class & Type	Model Production					List Price	Resale		Remarks
		Importer	Builder	Cat #	Quan.	Yrs.		Mint	Avg.	
4-8-4	J Northern	Gem	Olympia	EH-123P	170	67	125	530	440	fp.
C-C+C-C	Steam Turbine	Alco	KMT	D-168	175	81	1100	880	670	See Note #313
C-C+C-C	Steam Turbine	Alco	KMT	D-168	175	82	880	670	600	See Note #313

Northern Pacific Railway (NP)

Whyte Class	Owner Class & Type	Model Production					List Price	Resale		Remarks
		Importer	Builder	Cat #	Quan.	Yrs.		Mint	Avg.	
0-6-0	L-9 Switcher	PFM	Fujiyama	P	700	75	180	200	190	#1040-1134
0-8-0	Switcher	W&R	Samh		80	87				#1174-1193

Northern Pacific Railway (cont'd)

Northern Pacific had only eight engines of the A–3 Class. All were built by Baldwin in 1938. These engines were identical to three engines built for the Spokane, Portland and Seattle. Primarily intended as fast passenger power, they occasionally took their turn at freight service. Fujiyama built 590 "Crown" models of the A–3 for PFM between 1971 and 1978.

Whyte Class	Owner Class & Type	Model Production					List Price	Resale		Remarks
		Importer	Builder	Cat #	Quan.	Yrs.		Mint	Avg.	
2-6-2	T-1 Prairie	PFM	Fujiyama	P	490	68	60	200	190	See Note #314
2-6-2	T-1 Prairie	PFM	Fujiyama	P	500	75	205	235	210	See Note #314
2-6-2	T-1 Prairie	PFM	Fujiyama	P	500	71	75	200	190	See Note #314
2-8-0	F-1 Consol	Gem	Olympia	GN-113	16	66	55	290	180	
2-8-0	Y-1 Consol	PFM	Samh	P	535	77	180	210	160	
2-8-0	F-1 Consol	Gem	Olympia	GN-113	13	65	50	350	200	
2-8-0	Y-2 Consol	W&R	Samh		21	90				
2-8-0	Y-2 Consol	W&R	Samh		54	90				fp.
2-8-2	W Mikado	PFM	SKI	P		80	374	340	320	Coal Tender
2-8-2	W Mikado	PFM	SKI	P		80	374	350	300	Oil Tender
2-8-2	W-1 Mikado	PFM	SKI	P		82	431	350	300	See Note #1224
2-8-2	W-1 Mikado	PFM	SKI	P	200	82	431	350	300	See Note #356
2-8-2	W-2 Mikado	PFM				82	432		280	
2-8-2	W-3 Mikado	Key	Samh		50	84	450			
2-8-2	W-3 Mikado	Key	Samh		20	84	486			fp. #1974
2-8-2	W-3 Mikado	NWSL	Toby		200	61-64	60	350	260	See Note #1227
2-8-2	W-5 Mikado	Key	Samh		75	84	450			
2-8-2	W-5 Mikado	Key	Samh		35	84	508			fp. #1846 w/ Elesco FWH
2-8-2	W-5 Mikado	Key	Samh		30	84	486			fp. #1855
2-8-2	W-5 Mikado	Key	Samh		75	84	465			Elesco FWH
2-8-2	W-5 Mikado	NWSL	Toby		150	62-64	60	350	290	See Note #315
2-8-8-2	Z-3 Articulated	PFM				88	642	610		
2-8-8-2	Z-3 Articulated	PFM	SKI	P		85	700		610	22E tender
2-8-8-2	Z-4 Articulated	W&R	Samh			86	800	760		standard version
2-8-8-2	Z-4 Articulated	W&R	Samh			86	857	810		fp. w/booster
2-8-8-2	Z-4 Articulated	W&R	Samh			86	850	800		fp., standard version
2-8-8-2	Z-4 Articulated	W&R	Samh		24	86	807	900		See Note #1229
2-8-8-2	Z-4 Articulated	W&R	Samh		11	86	807	900		#4500-4503 w/o booster
2-8-8-2	Z-4 Articulated	W&R	Samh		12	86	807	900		w/booster
2-8-8-2	Z-4 Articulated	W&R	Samh		32	86				fp., w/booster
2-8-8-4	Yellowstone	Akane	Akane							
2-8-8-4	Z-5 Yellowstone	PFM	Fujiyama	CR	143	69	198	820	780	Crown
2-8-8-4	Z-5 Yellowstone	PFM	Fujiyama	CR	195	66	188	950	875	Crown; #5000
2-8-8-4	Z-5 Yellowstone	PFM	Fujiyama	CR	300	75	495	940	820	See Note #1945
2-8-8-4	Z-5 Yellowstone	PFM	Fujiyama	CR		85		1050		fp., See Note #1946
2-8-8-4	Z-5 Yellowstone	Key	Samh		100	82	729		670	1940 Version
2-8-8-4	Z-5 Yellowstone	Key	Samh		135	83	829			fp.; 1950's version
2-8-8-4	Z-5 Yellowstone	Key	Samh		100	86	729	690		1930's version
2-8-8-4	Z-5 Yellowstone	Key	Samh		100	82	729		670	1930's version
4-6-0	S-4 Ten-Wheeler	PFM	Imai	P	300	64	30	190	160	See Note #318
4-6-0	S-4 Ten-Wheeler	PFM	Samh	P	750	75	155	190	180	See Note #319

Northern Pacific Railway (cont'd)

Whyte Class	Owner Class & Type	Model Production					List Price	Resale		Remarks
		Importer	Builder	Cat #	Quan.	Yrs.		Mint	Avg.	
4-6-2	Q-1 Pacific	W&R	Samh		16	91				fp., black
4-6-2	Q-1 Pacific	W&R	Samh		9	91				w/snow plow
4-6-2	Q-1 Pacific	W&R	Samh		36	91				fp., passenger gray
4-6-2	Q-1 Pacific	W&R	Samh		41	91				See Note #1333
4-6-2	Q-1 Pacific	W&R	Samh		18	91				
4-6-2	Q-1 Pacific	W&R	Samh		20	91				w/snow plow, fp. black
4-6-2	Q-3 Pacific	W&R	Samh		96	85	472	560	530	
4-6-2	Q-4 Pacific	W&R	Samh		96	85	472	560	530	
4-6-2	Q-5 Pacific	W&R	Samh		23	89				
4-6-2	Q-5 Pacific	W&R	Samh		37	89				fp., gray
4-6-2	Q-5 Pacific	W&R	Samh		30	89				fp., black
4-6-2	Q-6 Pacific	W&R	Samh		27	89				Version #1, fp. black
4-6-2	Q-6 Pacific	W&R	Samh		12	89				Version #2
4-6-2	Q-6 Pacific	W&R	Samh		20	89				Version #1, fp. black
4-6-2	Q-6 Pacific	NWSL			500	65	55	380	290	
4-6-2	Q-6 Pacific	W&R	Samh		20	89				Version #1
4-6-2	Q-6 Pacific	W&R	Samh		23	89				Version #1, fp. gray
4-6-2	Q-6 Pacific	W&R	Samh		18	89				Version #1, fp. gray
4-6-2	Q-5,6 Pacific tender	W&R	Samh		25	89				
4-8-0	X Twelve Wheeler	PFM	Samh	P	500	78	213	220	180	
4-8-4	A Northern	CustB	Goto	ST-234	600	77	375	470	410	See Note #320
4-8-4	A-1 Northern	Key	Samh		300	78	257	260	250	See Note #1231
4-8-4	A-2 Northern	W&R	Samhongsa		30	92				See Note#1230
4-8-4	A-2 Northern	W&R	Samhongsa		8	92				w/Worthington FWH
4-8-4	A-2 Northern	W&R	Samhongsa		16	92				w/Worth FWH, fp. black
4-8-4	A-2 Northern	W&R	Samhongsa		5	92				w/Wilson FWH
4-8-4	A-2 Northern	W&R	Samhongsa		46	92				w/Worth FWH, fp. gray
4-8-4	A-2 Northern	OMI	JPMod	1448	200	81	369	390	350	#2650-2659
4-8-4	A-2 Northern	W&R	Samhongsa		25	92				w/Wilson FWH, fp. black
4-8-4	A-3 Northern	PFM	Fujiyama	CR	150	71	200	700	680	Crown; #2660-2667
4-8-4	A-3 Northern	PFM	Fujiyama	CR	150	72	225	700	680	Crown; #2660-2667
4-8-4	A-3 Northern	PFM	Fujiyama	CR	290	78	595	750	720	See Note #263
4-8-4	A-3 Northern	W&R	Samhongsa		27	93				fp., black
4-8-4	A-3 Northern	W&R	Samhongsa		8	93				
4-8-4	A-3 Northern	W&R	Samhongsa		50	93				fp., passenger gray
4-8-4	A-4 Northern	Ortl	DaiYng	0284	125	83	407		440	See Note #1232
4-8-4	A-5 Northern	Ortl	DaiYng	0285	75	83	407		410	See Note #1233
4-8-4	A-5 Northern	PFM	Fujiyama	CR	200	65	140	1200		See Note #1944

Northern Pacific owned 12 Class Z–5 2–8–8–4's, which were built by Alco and Baldwin. Built to haul heavy freight between Glendive, MT, and Mandan, ND, they eliminated the need for pairs of 2–8–2's that had been used in the past. With a tractive effort of 140,000 lbs. and a booster with 13,000 lbs., they pulled whatever was put behind them. They lasted for 20 years, until late June of 1950. Fujiyama built over 700 "Crown" models of this engine for PFM from 1969 through 1975. Fujiyama was one of the premier builders in Japan and discontinued production in 1990. Models carrying the Fujiyama label are now produced by Erie-Limited.

Northern Pacific Railway (cont'd)

Whyte Class	Owner Class & Type	Importer	Builder	Cat #	Quan.	Yrs.	List Price	Mint	Avg.	Remarks
4-8-4	A-5 Northern	PFM	Fujiyama	CR	140	67	140	1100		Crown
4-8-4	A-5 Northern	PFM	Fujiyama	CR	300	73	275	1000		Crown
4-8-4	A-5 Northern	W&R	Samhongsa		12	93				
4-8-4	A-5 Northern	W&R	Samhongsa		51	93				fp., passenger gray
4-8-4	A-5 Northern	W&R	Samhongsa		29	93				fp., black
4-6-6-4	Z-6 Challenger	PFM	Tensh #165	LP	250	75	525	820	760	See Note #316
4-6-6-4	Z-6 Challenger	PFM	Tensh #165	LP	300	71	285	760	670	fp.
4-6-6-4	Z-6 Challenger	PFM	Tensh #165	LP	100	76	525	880	820	See Note #316
4-6-6-4	Z-6 Challenger	PFM	Tensh #165	LP	230	69	245	670	590	#5100-5120, unpainted
4-6-6-4	Z-8 Challenger	PFM	Tensh	H	1	57				See Note #1236
4-6-6-4	Z-8 Challenger	Key	Samh		200	81	685	705	620	See Note #317
4-6-6-4	Z-8 Challenger	PFM	Tensh		150	79	1245	1590		fp. Vestibule Cab
4-6-6-4	Z-8 Challenger	PFM	Tensh			86	1760	1870		fp. Vestibule Cab

Pennsylvania Railroad (PRR)

Whyte Class	Owner Class & Type	Importer	Builder	Cat #	Quan.	Yrs.	List Price	Mint	Avg.	Remarks
0-4-0	A-5 Switcher	Sun	SMI	HO102	500	89	150			
0-4-0	A-5s Switcher	Key	Samh			88	435	510		fp., See Note #1234
0-4-0	A-5s Switcher	Key	Samh			88	435	510		fp., See Note #1235
0-4-0	A-5s Switcher	Key	Samh			88	330	390		See Note #1234
0-4-0	A-5s Switcher	Gem	Olympia	GN-128	750	75	135	220	190	
0-4-0	A-5s Switcher	Key	Samh			88	330	390		See Note #1235
0-4-0	A-5s Switcher	Sunset					180			"Prestige Series"
0-6-0	Switcher	AHM		L-5023		62	24	140	120	Shifter
0-6-0	Switcher	AHM		L-5032		62	24	140	120	Shifter
0-6-0	B-6 Switcher	PSC	D&D	15404			269			original
0-6-0	B-6 Switcher	PSC	D&D	15404.1			310			fp. Green
0-6-0	B-6 Switcher	OMI	Muramatsu	1413	400	79	200		160	
0-6-0	B-6s Switcher	PSC	D&D	15684			269			rebuilt
0-6-0	B-6s Switcher	PSC	D&D	15684.1			310			fp. Green
0-6-0	B-6s Switcher	Key	Samh		45	87	321	380		#8026 w/70F66B Tender
0-6-0	B-6s Switcher	Key	Samh		50	87	371	370		#8026, fp.
0-6-0	B-6sa Switcher	Key	Samh		8	87	321	380		#60
0-6-0	B-6sa Switcher	Gem	Olympia	GN-129	730	69	60	190	160	
0-6-0	B-6sa Switcher	Key	Samh		60	87	371	430		#60, fp.
0-6-0	B-6sb Switcher	PSC	D&D	15726.1			310			fp. Green
0-6-0	B-6sb Switcher	PSC	D&D	15714			269			Standard
0-6-0	B-6sb Switcher	PSC	D&D	15380			269			1916/17 Version
0-6-0	B-6sb Switcher	PSC	D&D	15718.1			310			fp. Green
0-6-0	B-6sb Switcher	PSC	D&D	15724			269			Late Version, 1926
0-6-0	B-6sb Switcher	Sun	SMI	HO103	500	89	150			
0-6-0	B-6sb Switcher	Key	Samh		65	87	371	430		#6380, fp.
0-6-0	B-6sb Switcher	PSC	D&D	15724.1			310			fp. Green
0-6-0	B-6sb Switcher	Key	Samh		10	87	321	380		#6380
0-6-0	B-6sb Switcher	PSC	D&D	15726			269			See Note #1237
0-6-0	B-6sb Switcher	PSC	D&D	15718			269			1923/24 Version
0-6-0	B-6sb Switcher	PSC	D&D	15380.1			310			fp. Green
0-6-0	B-6sb Switcher	PSC	D&D	15714.1			310			fp. Green
0-6-0	B-6sb Switcher	Red	KMT		500	67	53	190	140	
0-6-0	B-8 Switcher	Key				93	543			fp., See Note #1238
0-6-0	B-8 Switcher	Key				93	543			fp., See Note #1239
0-6-0	B-8 Switcher	Key				93	495			See Note #1239
0-6-0	B-8 Switcher	Key				93	495			See Note #1240
0-6-0	B-8 Switcher	Key				93	495			See Note #1238
0-6-0	B-8 Switcher	Key				93	543			fp., See Note #1240
0-6-0T	B-8a Switcher	Key				93	543			fp., See Note #1241
0-6-0T	B-8a Switcher	Key				93	495			See Note #1241
0-6-0T	B-8a Switcher	PSC	D&D	15716			269			Saddle Tank
0-6-0T	B-8a Switcher	PSC	D&D	15716.1			310			fp. Green
0-6-0T	B-8a Switcher	Key				93	543			fp., See Note #1242

Pennsylvania Railroad (cont'd)

Pennsy built two huge K–5 Pacifics in what some think was an attempt to duplicate the performance of a 4–6–4. These two engines did not rewrite the design for 4–6–2's on the PRR, but they did influence the design of the M–1a Mountains, incorporating a cast-steel cylinder saddle with internal steam delivery pipes. They were also the only PRR Pacifics with feedwater heaters. Westside Model Company imported this Katsumi-built model in 1972.

Whyte Class	Owner Class & Type	Model Production					List Price	Resale		Remarks
		Importer	Builder	Cat #	Quan.	Yrs.		Mint	Avg.	
0-6-0T	B-8a Switcher	Key				93	495			See Note#1242
0-6-0T	B-8a Switcher	CustB	KSM	ST-820	500	78	140	160	130	
0-8-0	C-1 Switcher	LMB	KMT		900	61	45	300	210	#6556; 56″ drivers
0-8-0	C-1 Switcher	Key	Samh			88	410	480		w/70F66B Tender
0-8-0	C-1 Switcher	Key	Samh			88	465	550		fp., w/70F66B Tender
0-8-0	C-1 Switcher	Intl				62	43	235	180	2nd & 3rd drivers blind
0-8-0	C-1 Switcher	CustB	KSM	ST-828	400	78	207	260		#6550-6639
0-8-8-0	CC-2 Switcher	CustB	KMT	ST-207	329	77	360	530		See Note #1243
2-6-0	F-3 Mogul	Gem	Olympia	GN-116	150	72	90	200		Blue box
2-6-0	F-3 Mogul	Gem	Olympia	GN-116P	150	72	105-132	250		fp., blue box
2-6-0	F-3 Mogul	Gem	Olympia	GN-116	715	66	40	200		Green box
2-6-0	F-3 Mogul	Gem	Samh	ST-506	370	74		190		
2-6-0	F-3c Mogul	MBA			35	59	30	180	150	See Note #1244
2-8-0	H-1 Consol	Emp	Kobra	DL-102		79	150	235		Congdon Stack
2-8-0	H-1a Consol	Emp	Kobra	DL-104		79	150	180	150	Cap Stack; 1874
2-8-0	H-1a Consol	Emp	Kobra	DL-104		79	150	180	150	Cap Stack
2-8-0	H-3 Consol	Emp	Kobra	DL-101		78	150	160	140	See Note #321
2-8-0	H-3 Consol	Emp	Kobra	DL-101		79	150	180	150	
2-8-0	H-6A Consol	Sun	SMI	HO-152DP	100	91	300			fp.
2-8-0	H-6A Consol	Sun	SMI	HO-152D	100	91	300			
2-8-0	H-6sb Consol	RWks	Samh			92	685	670		fp. #2846
2-8-0	H-6sb Consol	Lam	CAB		900	73	175	280		See Note #1245
2-8-0	H-6sb Consol	RWks	Samh			92	585	570		
2-8-0	H-6sb Consol	Lam	CAB		900	73	165-175	320		
2-8-0	H-6sb Consol	Lam	CAB		900	75	195	320		NMRA Review 4/75
2-8-0	H-8sa Consol	Key	Samh			88	285	330		fp.. See Note #1246
2-8-0	H-8/9 Consol	Sun	Samh	HO-32K	50	79	180	210	190	Kit; See Note #1247
2-8-0	H-8/9 Consol	Sun	Samh	HO-32	300	79	225	320		See Note #1247
2-8-0	H-9 Consol	Key								
2-8-0	H-9 Consol	Key								fp.
2-8-0	H-9 Consol	Sun		HO27	300	79	220	240		
2-8-0	H-10 Consol	Sun	SMI	H10	500	87	172	170		w/High Tender
2-8-0	H-10 Consol	Key								fp.
2-8-0	H-10 Consol	Key								
2-8-0	H-10s Consol	Key	Samh			88	285	330		fp.. See Note #1248
2-8-0	H-10s Consol	Gem	Olympia	GN-110P	125	70	70	210	170	fp., See Note #1249
2-8-0	H-10s Consol	Gem	Olympia	GN-110	475	70	60	190	150	See Note #1249
2-8-0	H-10s Consol	Gem	Olympia	RS-110	50	64	75	570	290	See Note #1250

Pennsylvania Railroad (cont'd)

It's no wonder that the K–4 was often referred to as "America's Most Famous Pacific." In all, Pennsy had 410 and they were everywhere. Although the fleet of engines provided excellent performance, Pennsy was always experimenting with ways to improve efficiency and performance. Custom Brass imported this model of #5399 with Franklin poppet valves in 1988. Pennsy's experience with the test results of this engine convinced them to use poppet valves on the T–1 duplexes, a decision they would learn to regret.

| Whyte Class | Owner Class & Type | Model Production | | | | | List Price | Resale | | Remarks |
		Importer	Builder	Cat #	Quan.	Yrs.		Mint	Avg.	
2-8-0	H-10s Consol	Gem	Olympia	GN-110	263	66	50	200	160	See Note #1249
2-8-0	H-10s Consol	Gem	Olympia	EH-110	500	64	50	200	180	See Note #1249
2-8-0	H-10s Consol Tender	Gem	Olympia	OT-110	100	70		90		
2-8-0	H-51 Consol	MBA				59				Long Island RR
2-8-0	H-51a Consol	Intl	Takara			61	33	180	150	Long Island RR
2-8-2	L-1 Mikado	Sun	Samh	HO-64	300	79	250			
2-8-2	L-1s Mikado	Ortl		0735		87	354	350		
2-8-2	L-1s Mikado	Ortl		P735		87	414	410		
2-8-2	L-1s Mikado	PFM	Atlas/Asahi	S	1	65				See Note #7 & #561
2-8-2	L-1s Mikado	PFM	Atlas/Asahi	P	820	65	50	235	165	See Note #561
2-8-2	L-1s Mikado	PFM	Atlas/Asahi	P	280	66	50	240	200	See Note #561
2-8-2	L-1s Mikado	PFM	Atlas/Asahi	P	280	67	55	250	210	See Note #561
2-8-2	L-1s Mikado	PFM	Atlas/Asahi	P	340	69	70	250		See Note #561
2-8-2	L-1s Mikado	PFM	Atlas/Asahi	P	500	71	90	260		See Note #561
2-8-2	L-1s Mikado	PFM	Atlas/Asahi	P	502	73	140	270		See Note #561
2-8-2	L-1s Mikado	PFM	Atlas/Asahi	P	450	76	245	290		See Note #1251
2-8-2	L-2s Mikado	Key	Samh		200	78	200	320		See Note #1252
2-10-0	I-1 Decapod	Sun		HO119A		89	200	200		See Note #1253
2-10-0	I-1 Decapod	Sun		HO119B		89	210	210		See Note #1254
2-10-0	I-1s Decapod	PFM	Atlas/Asahi	S	1	67				See Note #7
2-10-0	I-1s Decapod	PFM	Atlas/Asahi	P	500	71	100	350	300	See Note #322
2-10-0	I-1s Decapod	Key	Samh		65	84	443			See Note #1255
2-10-0	I-1s Decapod	PFM	Atlas/Asahi	P	600	70	90	320	280	See Note #322
2-10-0	I-1s Decapod	Key	Samh			88	625	730		See Note #1256
2-10-0	I-1s Decapod	Key	Samh			88	675	790		fp., See Note #1256
2-10-0	I-1s Decapod	Key	Samh		300	79	230	260	235	See Note #1257
2-10-0	I-1s Decapod	PFM	Atlas/Asahi	P	490	68	70	260	200	See Note #461
2-10-0	I-1s Decapod	Key	Samh		50	84	443			See Note #1258
2-10-0	I-1s Decapod	Key	Samh			88	625	730		See Note #1259
2-10-0	I-1s Decapod	Key	Samh			88	675	790		fp., See Note #1259
2-10-0	I-1sa Decapod	Key	Samh			88	675	790		fp., See Note #1260
2-10-0	I-1sa Decapod	Key	Samh			88	625	730		See Note #1260
2-10-0	I-1sa Decapod	Key	Samh			88	675	790		fp., See Note #1261
2-10-0	I-1sa Decapod	Key	Samh			88	625	730		See Note #1261

Pennsylvania Railroad (cont'd)

Pennsy had a huge number of 2–8–0 Consolidations—over 3,300. The zenith of the class was the H–10s, and they wound up on all parts of the railroad before the final end of steam. The H10 was not a revolutionary design. It incorporated the same boiler as used on the G–5 ten-wheelers and E–6 Atlantics and was an evolution of earlier classes of 2–8–0's. The H–10's major difference was the incorporation of cylinders 1-inch larger than on the previous class. Gem Models imported more than 1,500 of these Olympia-built models between 1964 and 1970.

Whyte Class	Owner Class & Type	Model Production					List Price	Resale		Remarks
		Importer	Builder	Cat #	Quan.	Yrs.		Mint	Avg.	
2-10-2	N-1s Santa Fe	PSC/WMC		MO-157		81	341	350		See Note #325
2-10-2	N-1s Santa Fe	Gem	Samh	SH-109	630	71	103	260		See Note #1262
2-10-2	N-1s Santa Fe	Gem	Samh	SH-109	400	74	185	260		See Note #1334
2-10-2	N-1s Santa Fe	PSC		15200		83	229			Kit
2-10-2	N-1s Santa Fe Tender	Gem	Samh	T-109	100	74		90		
2-10-2	N-1sa Santa Fe	WMC		MO-157	300	79	284	290	260	See Note #325
2-10-2	N-2 Santa Fe	Akane	Akane			63	70	235	260	
2-10-2	N-2a Santa Fe	WMC	Samh	M-118	400	78	190	235	200	See Note #324
2-10-2	N-2a Santa Fe	Alco	Kobra	S-119	400	77	185	200	180	See Note #323
2-10-2	N-2a Santa Fe	Alpha				84			170	
2-10-4	J-1 Texas	HOT				60-62		260		Frame partly cast Zamac
2-10-4	J-1 Texas	WMC	KTM	MO-88	711	77	230	410		See Note #1263
2-10-4	J-1 Texas	Key	Samh			92	1075	1060		fp.
2-10-4	J-1 Texas	WMC	KTM	MO-88	120	78	357	410		Can motor
2-10-4	J-1 Texas	Key	Samh			92	1000	1000		
2-10-4	J-1 Texas	Key	Samh			95	85		550	
2-10-4	J-1 Texas	MBA				60	80			cataloged
2-10-4	J-1 Texas	AHM	KTM		402	66	90	320	260	See Note #326
2-10-4	J-1a Texas	Key	Samh			92	1000	1000		
2-10-4	J-1a Texas	Key	Samh			92	1075	1060		fp.
2-10-4	J-1a Texas	Key	Samh		109	85		550		
2-8-8-0	HC-1s Articulated	CustB	KMT	ST-808	255	78	497	650	530	See Note #1264
2-8-8-2	HH-1 Articulated	CustB	Goto	ST-836	150	78	768	880	820	See Note #327
4-4-0	D-16sb American	Gem	Olympia	GN-117	653	67	50	180		
4-4-0	D-16sb American	RWks	Samh			89	665	660		fp. #1223
4-4-0	D-16sb American	WMC	Samh	MO-82	801	77	140	180	160	See Note #1265
4-4-0	D-16sb American	RWks	Samh			89	565	560		
4-4-2	E-3sd Atlantic	CustB	KSM	ST-233	125	82	361	410	380	
4-4-2	E-3sd Atlantic	Key	D&D		20	89	629	610		fp., See Note #1266
4-4-2	E-3sd Atlantic	Key	D&D		23	89	629	610		fp., See Note #1267
4-4-2	E-3sd Atlantic	Key	D&D		20	89	557	530		See Note #1268

Pennsylvania Railroad (cont'd)

The Pennsy Q–2 4–4–6–4 was one of the most powerful locomotives ever built—almost 8,000 horsepower. Every indication was that they were a truly successful design—powerful, efficient, and not slippery. Nonetheless, they could not stem the invasion of the diesel. Built in 1945, they were gone by 1949. This striking combination of power and good looks well illustrates steam power at its zenith. Key imported this exquisite Samhongsa-built model. The model appears factory painted and combines the prototype's good looks with excellent performance.

Lima, Baldwin, and Pennsy's own Juniata shops combined to build a total of 574 L–1 2–8–2's between 1914 and 1919. Characterized by a solid, simple design, the L–1's didn't get modern appliances until the late '20s. Hard to mistake, with the rectangular Belpaire firebox and horizontal air tank above the pilot, the L–1's became the symbol of what a steam freight engine should look like. From 1965 through 1976, PFM imported over 3,100 models of this famous engine. Built by Atlas/Asahi in Japan, these models are renowned for their accuracy and durability.

Whyte Class	Owner Class & Type	Model Production					List Price	Resale		Remarks
		Importer	Builder	Cat #	Quan.	Yrs.		Mint	Avg.	
4-4-2	E-3sd Atlantic	Key	D&D		7	89	557	530		
4-4-2	E-3sd Atlantic	Key	D&D		4	89	557	530		See Note #1267
4-4-2	E-3sd Atlantic	Key	D&D		6	89	629	610		fp., See Note #1268
4-4-2	E-5s Atlantic	Key	D&D		24	89	629	610		fp., See Note #1269
4-4-2	E-5s Atlantic	Key	D&D		28	89	629	610		fp., See Note #1270
4-4-2	E-5s Atlantic	Alco	Kobra	S-115		76	125	120	100	
4-4-2	E-5s Atlantic	Key	D&D		6	89	557	530		See Note #1270
4-4-2	E-5s Atlantic	Key	D&D		5	89	557	530		See Note #1269

Pennsylvania Railroad (cont'd)

Pennsy had more engines in any given class than just about anybody else. Atlantics were no exception, with over 690 engines from Class E1 through E29. The culmination of the design was the Class E6s, with 82 engines. Without stokers or power reverse, they were still liked by their crews for their good speed and easy steaming. Designed primarily for fast passenger service between Jersey City and Washington, DC, with an occasional trip as far west as Harrisburg, Pa., these engines compared well in performance with the early Pacifics. Alco Models imported this Rok-Am-built model in 1981.

Whyte Class	Owner Class & Type	Model Production					List Price	Resale		Remarks
		Importer	Builder	Cat #	Quan.	Yrs.		Mint	Avg.	
4-4-2	E-6s Atlantic	Key	D&D		6	89	557	530		See Note #1271
4-4-2	E-6s Atlantic	Key	D&D		18	89	629	610		fp., See Note #1271
4-4-2	E-6s Atlantic	Gem	Olympia	EH-118	209	66	45	230		
4-4-2	E-6s Atlantic	Gem	Olympia	GN-118P	150	71	85	260	220	fp.
4-4-2	E-6s Atlantic	Gem	Olympia	GN-118	450	71		200		
4-4-2	E-6s Atlantic	Gem	Olympia	GN-118	300	64	55	200		
4-4-2	E-6s Atlantic	Alco	Rok-Am	S-122	300	81	330	260	235	
4-4-2	E-6s Atlantic	Key	D&D				629	610		See Note #1272
4-4-2	E-6s Atlantic Tender	Gem	Olympia	OT-110	50	64		60		
4-4-2	E-7s Atlantic	Key	D&D				557	530		w/70P58F Tender
4-4-2	E-7s Atlantic	Key	D&D				629	610		fp., w/70P58F Tender
4-6-0	G-5s Ten-Wheeler	Alco	Samh					330		
4-6-0	G-5s Ten-Wheeler	Gem	Olympia	GN-119	332	69	60	180	150	
4-6-0	G-5s Ten-Wheeler	Gem	Olympia	GN-119	454	66	55	160	140	
4-6-0	G-5s Ten-Wheeler	MGray	KTM		300	63	44	180	150	
4-6-0	G-5s Ten-Wheeler	WMC	KTM	MO-62	984	75	140	160	140	See Note #1273
4-6-2	K-2s Pacific	WMC	Samh	MO-111	400	78	199	200	180	See Note #1274
4-6-2	K-3s Pacific	WMC	Samh	MO-112	400	78	199	200	180	See Note #1275
4-6-2	K-4s Pacific	PSC	D&D	15708-11		88	499	470		See Note #1276
4-6-2	K-4s Pacific	Alco	KMT	S-128		78	330	320	290	See Note #337
4-6-2	K-4s Pacific	Alco	Samh			81	310		330	#1120; 1940 version
4-6-2	K-4s Pacific	Key	Samh			88	635	760		fp., See Note #1277
4-6-2	K-4s Pacific	Alco	Samh		350	81	412	410	350	See Note #336
4-6-2	K-4s Pacific	PSC	D&D	15708-1		88	499	470		slat pilot, fp. Green
4-6-2	K-4s Pacific	Sun	Samh	HO-60	300	80	315	340	300	See Note #331
4-6-2	K-4s Pacific	PFM	Atlas/Asahi	P	600	75	180	250	220	See Note #1278
4-6-2	K-4s Pacific	Key	Samh			88	635	760		fp., See Note #1279
4-6-2	K-4s Pacific	PSC	D&D	15708-10		88	499	470		#5399 w/poppet valves, fp.
4-6-2	K-4s Pacific	PFM	Atlas/Asahi	P	920	60	50	235	200	See Note #329
4-6-2	K-4s Pacific	Key	Samh			88	557	670		fp., See Note #451
4-6-2	K-4s Pacific	PSC	D&D	15708-4		88	499	470		cast pilot, fp. Tuscan/Gold
4-6-2	K-4s Pacific	Red	Toho		500	67	68	180	150	See Note #1281
4-6-2	K-4s Pacific	PSC	D&D	15708-8		88	499	470		See Note #585
4-6-2	K-4s Pacific	PFM	Atlas/Asahi			80	495	470	400	See Note #580

Pennsylvania Railroad (cont'd)

Whyte Class	Owner Class & Type	Importer	Builder	Cat #	Quan.	Yrs.	List Price	Mint	Avg.	Remarks
4-6-2	K-4s Pacific	PFM	Atlas/Asahi	P	503	73	140	220	200	See Note #1284
4-6-2	K-4s Pacific	Key	Samh			88	560			See Note #1285
4-6-2	K-4s Pacific	PSC	D&D	15708-9		88	499	470		#5399 w/poppet valves
4-6-2	K-4s Pacific	Key	Samh			88	635	760		fp., See Note #1286
4-6-2	K-4s Pacific	PFM	Atlas/Asahi	P	450	70	70	200	180	See Note #1278
4-6-2	K-4s Pacific	Key	Samh		80	89	635	610		fp., See Note #1287
4-6-2	K-4s Pacific	PSC	D&D	15708		88	449	420		slat pilot
4-6-2	K-4s Pacific	CustB	DaiYng	ST-823	100	83	465			See Note #336
4-6-2	K-4s Pacific	PFM	Atlas/Asahi	P	200	62	50	260	235	See Note #329
4-6-2	K-4s Pacific	PFM	Atlas/Asahi	S	1	62				See Note #7
4-6-2	K-4s Pacific	PFM	Atlas/Asahi	P	400	68	65	190	160	See Note #1278
4-6-2	K-4s Pacific	Key	Samh			88	635	760		fp., See Note #1280
4-6-2	K-4s Pacific	PSC	D&D	15708-6		88	499	470		See Note #1279
4-6-2	K-4s Pacific	CustB	DaiYng	ST-810	100	85	492	460	440	#3770; Disc Drivers
4-6-2	K-4s Pacific	Key	Samh			88	635	760		See Note #458
4-6-2	K-4s Pacific	Key	Samh			88	557	670		See Note #1282
4-6-2	K-4s Pacific	PSC	D&D	15708-5		88	499	470		streamlined, unpainted
4-6-2	K-4s Pacific	PSC	D&D	15708-12		88	499	470		See Note #1283
4-6-2	K-4s Pacific	Key	Samh		30	89	557			See Note #1284
4-6-2	K-4s Pacific	CustB	DaiYng	ST-866	100		465			See Note #333
4-6-2	K-4s Pacific	PSC	D&D	15808-3		88	499	470		cast pilot, fp. Green/Gold
4-6-2	K-4s Pacific	CustB	DaiYng	ST-856	100	85	492	460	440	See Note #335
4-6-2	K-4s Pacific	Key	Samh			88	635	760		fp., See Note #448
4-6-2	K-4s Pacific	Key	Samh			88	635	760		fp., See Note #449
4-6-2	K-4s Pacific	Key	Samh		70	89	635	610		fp., See Note #447
4-6-2	K-4s Pacific	Sun	Samh	HO-60K	30	80	241			Kit
4-6-2	K-4s Pacific	PSC	D&D	15708-7		88	499	470		w/Disk Drivers, unpainted
4-6-2	K-4s Pacific	PFM	Atlas/Asahi	P	502	71	94	210	190	See Note #1293
4-6-2	K-4s Pacific	PFM	Atlas/Asahi	P	200	64	50	290	270	See Note #329
4-6-2	K-4s Pacific	PSC	D&D	15808-2		88	499	470		slat pilot, fp. Tuscan
4-6-2	K-4s Pacific	Key	Samh			88	635	760		fp., See Note #1288
4-6-2	K-5 Pacific	Key				93	995			fp., See Note #1289
4-6-2	K-5 Pacific	Key				93	815			See Note #1290
4-6-2	K-5 Pacific	Key				93	815			See Note #1291
4-6-2	K-5 Pacific	WMC	KTM	MO-32	1462	72	120	200	180	See Note #1292
4-6-2	K-5 Pacific	Key				93	815			See Note #1293
4-6-2	K-5 Pacific	Key				93	995			fp., See Note #1293
4-6-2	K-5 Pacific	Key				93	995			fp., See Note #1294
4-6-2	K-5 Pacific	Key				93	815			See Note #1295
4-6-2	K-5 Pacific	Key				93	995			fp., See Note #1296
4-6-2	K-5 Pacific	WMC	KTM	MO-32	48	73	140	235	200	See Note #1292
4-8-2	M-1 Mountain	Gem	KTM	DH-101	400	60	60	260	200	See Note #1298
4-8-2	M-1 Mountain	Gem	KTM	DH-101	100	61				See Note #1298
4-8-2	M-1 Mountain	MBA				60	60	235	180	
4-8-2	M-1 Mountain	Ortl	Samh	0583		86	464			See Note #1299
4-8-2	M-1 Mountain	Ortl	Samh	P583		86	514			fp., See Note #1300
4-8-2	M-1 Mountain	Sun	SMI	HO111		89	200	200		See Note #1301
4-8-2	M-1 Mountain	Sun	Samh	HO-26	300	80	270		290	See Note #338
4-8-2	M-1 Mountain	Sun	Samh	HO-26K	10	80	200			Kit
4-8-2	M-1a Mountain	Gem	KTM	DH-103	300	61	60	260	200	See Note #1304
4-8-2	M-1a Mountain	Gem	KTM	DH-103	250	63		310	260	
4-8-2	M-1a Mountain	Ortl	Samh	0584		86	464			See Note #1306
4-8-2	M-1a Mountain	Ortl	Samh	P584		86	514			fp., See Note #1305
4-8-2	M-1a Mountain	Sun				89				low cost series
4-8-2	M-1a Mountain	Sun	SMI	HO112	300	89	200			low cost series
4-8-2	M-1a Mountain	Sun	Samh	HO-26A	300	80	270		290	See Note #1302
4-8-2	M-1a Mountain	WMC	KTM	MO-33	1004	72-73	130	310	260	See Note #1303
4-8-2	M-1a Tender	Gem	KTM	KT-103	100	62				
4-8-2	M-1b Mountain	Gem	Sankyo	SM107B	300	68	65	290	235	See Note #1307
4-8-2	M-1b Mountain	Gem	Sankyo	SM-107A	300	68	68	290	235	See Note #1308
6-8-6	S-2 Turbine	Gem	Olympia	EH-101P	60	68	140	530	440	fp., rare
6-8-6	S-2 Turbine	Alco	KMT	S-125	500	77	370	370	320	See Note #1309
6-8-6	S-2 Turbine	Gem	Olympia	RS-101	51	60	200	1290	1120	See Note #1310
6-8-6	S-2 Turbine	Gem	Olympia	EH-101	247	68	125	450	380	See Note #1311

Pennsylvania Railroad (cont'd)

Whyte Class	Owner Class & Type	Importer	Builder	Cat #	Quan.	Yrs.	List Price	Mint	Avg.	Remarks
6-8-6	S-2 Turbine	CustB	DaiYng	ST-807	485	77-78	250	290	260	See Note #1312
6-8-6	S-2 Turbine	MBA				60	125	350	290	cataloged
6-8-6	S-2 Turbine	Key	Samh					1120		fp.
6-8-6	S-2 Turbine	Key	Samh					1030		
4-4-4-4	T-1 Duplex	Key	Samh					1215	1140	fp.,See Note #1313
4-4-4-4	T-1 Duplex	Key	Samh					1125	1020	See Note #1313
4-4-4-4	T-1 Duplex	Alco	KMT	S-118	180	77	375	660		fp., See Note #1314
4-4-4-4	T-1 Duplex	Key	Samh					1215	1140	fp.,See Note #1315
4-4-4-4	T-1 Duplex	Key	Samh		100	83	630			See Note #1319
4-4-4-4	T-1 Duplex	Key	Samh					1125	1020	See Note #1317
4-4-4-4	T-1 Duplex	Gem	Sankyo	IM-104P	40	68	150	290	235	fp., See Note #1318
4-4-4-4	T-1 Duplex	Key	Samh					1215	1140	fp.,See Note #1317
4-4-4-4	T-1 Duplex	Key	Samh					1215	1140	fp.,See Note #1316
4-4-4-4	T-1 Duplex	Alco	KMT	S-118	500	77	375	620	540	See Note #1314
4-4-4-4	T-1 Duplex	Key	Samh					1125	1020	See Note #1315
4-4-4-4	T-1 Duplex	Gem	Sankyo	IM-104	460	68	100	235	200	See Note #1318
4-4-4-4	T-1 Duplex	Key	Samh		100	83	630			See Note #1320
4-4-4-4	T-1 Duplex	Key	Samh					1125	1020	See Note #1316
4-4-4-4	T-1 Duplex	Sunset				93				
4-4-4-4	T-1 Duplex	Sunset				93				
4-4-4-4	T-1 Duplex	Sunset				93				
4-4-4-4	T-1 Duplex Tender	Gem	Sankyo	SM-007	50	69		90		Long Distance Tender
4-6-4-4	Q-1 Duplex	CustB	DaiYng	ST-809	400	79	315	440		See Note #339
4-6-4-4	Q-1 Duplex	CustB	DaiYng	ST-809S	200	78	325	500		See Note #1321
4-4-6-4	Q-2 Duplex	WMC	KTM	MO-20		70	120	470	350	See Note #1322
4-4-6-4	Q-2 Duplex	PSC/WMC	KTM	15278		82	429	530	470	Kit
4-4-6-4	Q-2 Duplex	Key	Samh					1290		fp., #6131 Original
4-4-6-4	Q-2 Duplex	MBA				60	175	650	560	See Note #1323
4-4-6-4	Q-2 Duplex	Gem	Sankyo	IM-103	497	69	120	260	235	poor runner
4-4-6-4	Q-2 Duplex	PSC/WMC	KTM		200	81	641	660	590	
6-4-4-6	S-1 Duplex	Key	SKI			89	1295	1290		fp., original version
6-4-4-6	S-1 Duplex	Gem	Olympia	EH-106P	72	65	225	705	590	fp.
6-4-4-6	S-1 Duplex	Gem	Olympia	EH-106	203	65	210	650	530	
6-4-4-6	S-1 Duplex	Key	SKI			89	1295	1290		fp, deskirted version
6-4-4-6	S-1 Duplex	CustB	DaiYng	ST-859	250	81	715		560	#6100

The "Standard Railroad of the World" generally stuck with rather conservative designs. Yet the long awaited replacement for the K-4 Pacifics wasn't a stock model 4-8-4, but a rigid frame 4-4-4-4. Essentially a 4-8-4 with duplex cylinders, the T-1 should have been an immediate success, but it wasn't. Initial reports showed them to be efficient and powerful, but as time went by maintenance costs and the continuing incursion of the diesels made the T-1s unnecessary. Key imported this Samhongsa-built version of "as-built" T-1 with full skirting and the long "chisel" nose. This skirting was soon removed from the prototype to gain access to the cylinders and the Franklin poppet valve mechanism, which proved to be a significant maintenance problem. The original Loewy-designed streamlining was simplified, which actually improved the locomotive's appearance. They lasted little more than six years.

Pere Marquette Railroad (PM)

Whyte Class	Owner Class & Type	Model Production					List Price	Resale		Remarks
		Importer	Builder	Cat #	Quan.	Yrs.		Mint	Avg.	
2-8-4	N Berkshire	OMI	JPMod	1450	25	82	360	530	470	bacame C&O
2-8-4	N Berkshire	Key					1070			fp., See Note #1324
2-8-4	N-1/N-2 Berkshire	Key	Samh		50	82	400	620	570	See Note #1325
2-8-4	N-1 Berkshire	Key					1070			fp., See Note #1326
2-8-4	N-1 Berkshire	Key					995			See Note #1335
2-8-4	N-1 Berkshire	LMB				61	60	260	235	See Note #122
2-8-4	N-2 Berkshire	Key					1070			fp., See Note #1327
2-8-4	N-2 Berkshire	Key					995			See Note #1336

Phila. & Reading Railroad (also see RDG)

Whyte Class	Owner Class & Type	Model Production					List Price	Resale		Remarks
		Importer	Builder	Cat #	Quan.	Yrs.		Mint	Avg.	
0-4-0	A-4A Switcher	OMI	MSM	1511	140	89	478			
4-4-0	D-8c Camelback	OMI	MSM	1509	75	89	494	470		#400-409
4-4-2	Atlantic	OMI	MSM	1504	50	89	507	480		#342

The P&LE was a New York Central affiliate that got most of its steam power as hand-me-downs. Not so with the A–2 Berkshires. These seven engines (#9400–9406) were built by Alco and delivered in 1948. With straight running boards, a low stack and domes, these engines looked bigger than they actually were. Alco Models imported this excellent example of late steam in 1975.

Pittsburgh & Lake Erie Railroad (P&LE)

Whyte Class	Owner Class & Type	Model Production					List Price	Resale		Remarks
		Importer	Builder	Cat #	Quan.	Yrs.		Mint	Avg.	
2-8-2	H-10b Mikado	OMI	Ajin	1453	100	89	521	490		Vestibule Cab
2-8-4	A-2a Berkshire	Alco	KMT		700	75	260	320	290	See Note #267
2-8-4	A-2a Berkshire	PFM	Atlas/Asahi	CR	95	60	99	1900		See Note #1170

Reading Railroad

Whyte Class	Owner Class & Type	Model Production					List Price	Resale		Remarks
		Importer	Builder	Cat #	Quan.	Yrs.		Mint	Avg.	
0-4-0	A-5a Switcher	Gem	Tsubomi	KT-104	500	69	70	160	130	Camelback
0-4-0	A-5a Switcher	Gem	Tsubomi	KT-104	400	72	100	190	140	Camelback
0-4-0	A-5a Switcher	Gem	Tsubomi	KT-104P	500	69	80	200	160	Camelback, fp.
0-4-0	Switcher	MBA				60	18			Camelback, cataloged
0-4-0	A-5a Switcher	Gem	Tsubomi	KT-104	550	68	45	150	120	Camelback
0-4-0	A-5a Switcher	Gem	Tsubomi	KT-104P	100	72	125	200	190	Camelback, fp.

Reading Railroad (cont'd)

As far back as 1880, the Reading was building Camelback 2–8–0's. Engines got bigger and more powerful with each successive class. The culmination of the Camelback 2–8–0 was achieved in the class I8–sb., engine #1584 was built by MSM and imported by Overland Models in 1988.

In 1919, Reading departed from the Camelback design and in 1923 received from Baldwin what was to be their final class of 2–8–0's, the I10–sa. Their very wide Wooten fireboxes for burning anthracite coal left little room for the cab. Gem imported this excellent example of engine #2014 from Japan in 1973 and 1980. The model was made by a relatively little-known builder, Mochizuki.

| Whyte Class | Owner Class & Type | Model Production | | | | | List Price | Resale | | Remarks |
		Importer	Builder	Cat #	Quan.	Yrs.		Mint	Avg.	
0-4-0	A-4B Switcher	OMI	MSM	1512	60	89	320			
0-6-0	B-8a Switcher	Gem	Tsubomi	KT-105P	120	70	65	210	160	See Note #340
0-6-0	B-8a Switcher	Gem	Tsubomi	KT-105	600	70	150	235	180	Camelback
2-8-0	I10-sa Consol	Gem	Mochizuki	MO-101	509	73	150	220	180	
2-8-0	I10-sa Consol	Gem	Mochizuki	MO-101	280	80	225	260	235	Improved detail; can motor
2-8-0	I5-c Consol	Gem	Olympia	EH-105	250	61	60	290	200	See Note #1338
2-8-0	I5-c Consol	Gem	Olympia	GN-105	47	64	55	350	290	
2-8-0	I5-c Consol Tender	Gem	Olympia	GN-105A	250	61				
2-8-0	I8-b Consol	CustB	KSM	ST-899	250	81	345	290	250	Camelback
2-8-0	I8-b Consol	CustB	KSM	ST-899K	50	81	215	290	250	Kit, Camelback
2-8-0	I8-sb Consolidation	OMI	MSM	1494	100	88	514	480		w/2 air pumps
2-8-0	I8-sb Consolidation	OMI	MSM	1495	100	88	514	480		w/1 air pump
2-10-0	J-1 Decapod	CustB	DaiYng	ST-927	65	84	515	420	400	
2-10-2	K-1 Santa Fe	CustB	DaiYng	ST-805	250	80	365	350	310	#3011-3020
2-10-2	K-1sde Santa Fe	NPP	Wyang		75	85	393	370		See Note #1339
2-10-2	K-1sd Santa Fe	NPP	Wyang		75	85	393	370		See Note #1340

Reading Railroad (cont'd)

Whyte Class	Owner Class & Type	Model Production					List Price	Resale		Remarks
		Importer	Builder	Cat #	Quan.	Yrs.		Mint	Avg.	
2-8-8-2	N-1sd Articulated	CustB	DaiYng	ST-888	75	82	715	770	620	As Built
2-8-8-0	N Articulated	CustB	DaiYng	ST-888M	75	82	715	790	760	Rebuilt Version
4-4-0	D8sd Camelback	OMI	MSM	1510	125	89	494	470		#400-409
4-4-2	P-5se Camelback	OMI	MSM	1503	150	89	464	440		
4-4-2	P-5 Atlantic	CustB	KSM	ST-922	150	83	388	400	350	Camelback
4-6-0	L-7sb Ten-Wheeler	CustB	KSM	ST-877	350	82	220	320	290	Camelback
4-6-2	G-1 Pacific	CustB	KMT	ST-844S	100		695	670	590	fp., "Crusader"
4-6-2	G-1b Pacific	CustB	KMT	ST-844	100		695	670	590	fp., "Crusader" #117
4-6-2	G-3 Pacific	CustB	KSM	ST-891	250	79	282	350	260	
4-6-2	G-2sa Pacific	Emp	Kobra	DL-108		80	220	235	210	
4-8-4	T-1 Northern	CustB	DaiYng	ST-801	500	77	210	260	235	See Note #341
4-8-4	T-1 Northern	OMI	Ajin	1474	250	88	365			See Note #341 & #1341
4-8-4	T-1 Northern	Gem	Olympia	RS-104	50	63	125	1175	730	See Note #341 & #1342
4-8-4	T-1 Northern	Gem	Olympia	DH-104	225	64		375		
4-8-4	T-1 Northern	Gem	Olympia	DH-104	75	63	100	375	200	See Note #341
4-8-4	T-1 Northern	Gem	Olympia	EH-104	300	63	100	375	190	See Note #341
4-8-4	T-1 Northern	CustB	DaiYng	ST-801X	95	83	448	375		See Note #341

Richmond, Fredericksburg & Potomac RR (RF&P)

Whyte Class	Owner Class & Type	Model Production					List Price	Resale		Remarks
		Importer	Builder	Cat #	Quan.	Yrs.		Mint	Avg.	
2-8-4	Berkshire	Key				93	1070			fp. #571
2-8-4	Berkshire	Key				93	995			unpainted
4-8-2	Mountain	Sun	Samh		200	77	142	190	160	See Note #342
4-8-4	Northern	PFM	Fujiyama	CR	300	76	475	1000	940	See Note #344
4-8-4	Northern	PFM	Fujiyama	CR	245	68	160	880	790	See Note #343
4-8-4	Northern	OMI	Rok-Am	1409	400	78	257	235	200	See Note #345
4-8-4	Northern	OMI	Rok-Am	1421	30	80	315	320	235	See Note #346
4-8-4	Northern	OMI	Rok-Am	1409		78	287	320	290	See Note #1343
2-8-8-2	Articulated	CustB	Goto	ST-838	100	79	768	880	820	See Note #347

RF&P had two classes of modern 4–8–4's: the "Generals" and the "Governors." The Generals were similar to the ACL R–1's and were too large for the clearances into Washington, DC. To alleviate this problem, the Governors were aquired in 1938 and 1945. The first group of Governors was equipped with Vanderbilt or modified Hicken tenders and carried the names of famous Virginia governors on the sand box. The second group of engines, formally designated Governors, bore the names of famous Virginia statesmen and are often referred to as the "Statesman" class. This group of engines was equipped with rectangular tenders. Rok–Am built this handsome engine for Overland Models in 1978.

Rutland Railroad

| Whyte Class | Owner Class & Type | Model Production | | | | | List Price | Resale | | Remarks |
		Importer	Builder	Cat #	Quan.	Yrs.		Mint	Avg.	
2-6-0	E-1d Mogul	Key	Samh		75	89	414	390		fp. #144
2-8-0	G-34 Consol	Key	Samh		75	84	379			with stoker
2-8-0	G-34 Consol	Key	Samh		75	84	379			without stoker
2-8-2	Mikado	Key			40					
4-6-0	F2J Ten Wheeler	OMI	Ajin	1436	200	85	357			#74-76, ex. NYC
4-6-0	F2J Ten Wheeler	OMI	Ajin	1436		86	379			fp., #74-79, ex. NYC
4-6-2	#80 Pacific	NERS					520			
4-6-2	#81-82 Pacific	NERS					525			
4-8-2	L-1 Mountain	PFM	SKI	P	200	83	458	420		can motor; idler gearbox

St. Louis — San Francisco Rwy. (Frisco)

| Whyte Class | Owner Class & Type | Model Production | | | | | List Price | Resale | | Remarks |
		Importer	Builder	Cat #	Quan.	Yrs.		Mint	Avg.	
2-8-0	#1306 Consol	Hall	Goto			82	157			reduced price sale
2-8-0	#1306 Consol	Hall	Goto		700	76-81	199	210	180	
2-8-2	#4000 Mikado	Key	Samh		100	78	160	210	190	Light USRA
2-8-2	#4200 Mikado	Hall	DongJ		500	76	180	200	180	
2-8-2	#4000 Mikado	Key	Samh		100	81	336	320	300	Light USRA
2-10-0	# 1613 Decapod	PFM	Atlas/Asahi	P	200	71	75	410	380	See Note #349 & #562
2-10-0	# 1613 Decapod	PFM	Atlas/Asahi	P	595	66	55	210	180	See Note #562
2-10-0	Decapod	Sun	SMI	HO119DP						
2-10-0	# 1613 Decapod	PFM	Atlas/Asahi	P	400	77	295	350	320	See Note #348
2-10-0	Decapod	Sun	SMI	HO119P						fp.
2-10-0	# 1613 Decapod	PFM	Atlas/Asahi	P	290	67	55	220	190	See Note #562
2-10-0	# 1613 Decapod	PFM	Atlas/Asahi	P	380	69	60	250	220	See Note #562
2-10-0	# 1613 Decapod	PFM	Atlas/Asahi	P	455	65	50	200	170	See Note #562
2-10-0	# 1613 Decapod	PFM	Atlas/Asahi	P	500	73	145	320	290	See Note #562
2-10-0	# 1613 Decapod	PFM	Atlas/Asahi	P	600	70	75	260	235	See Note #562
2-10-0	# 1613 Decapod	PFM	Atlas/Asahi	P	330	68	55	200	200	See Note #562
2-10-0	# 1613 Decapod	PFM	Atlas/Asahi	S	1					See Note #7
4-4-0	#182 American	Hall	KyongD			78	129	140	120	#182-187
4-6-2	Pacific	Sun	SMI	HO13	90	88	384	380		Unstreamlined
4-6-2	Pacific	Sun	SMI	HO13A	90	88	384	380		Streamlined, Firefly
4-8-2	#1500 Mountain	PFM	Toby	P	500	68	75	800	750	

The Frisco owned 30 Baldwin light Mountains, built from 1923 through 1926. The design exemplified good, clean proportions, which were highlighted by the Frisco's penchant for cleanliness, gold striping, and polished steel trim. The high-mounted air tanks were not applied to all engines in the class. Frisco liked long-distance locomotive runs, and the #1500s often went straight through from St. Louis to Memphis, a distance of 305 miles. PFM imported 500 of these Toby-built locos in 1968.

St. Louis — San Francisco Rwy. (cont'd)

Whyte Class	Owner Class & Type	Model Production					List Price	Resale		Remarks
		Importer	Builder	Cat #	Quan.	Yrs.		Mint	Avg.	
4-8-2	#4300 Mountain	OMI	DongJ	1412	100	79	279	280	235	Coal Version
4-8-2	#4400 Mountain	OMI	DongJ	1415	150	79	279	280	235	See Note #350
4-8-2	#4422 Mountain	OMI	DongJ	1416	150	79	279			
4-8-2	#4500 Mountain	AmBr	Fomras		6	82	3500			Handbuilt; oil tender
4-8-2	#4500 Mountain	Hall	DongJ		250	79	279	270	235	See Note #356
4-8-2	#4500 Mountain	PFM	Tsubomi	H	6	59	150	1880	1700	Handbuilt

St. Louis — Southwestern Railway (Cotton Belt)

Whyte Class	Owner Class & Type	Model Production					List Price	Resale		Remarks
		Importer	Builder	Cat #	Quan.	Yrs.		Mint	Avg.	
0-8-0	#500 Switcher	Hall								
2-8-0	#770 Consol	Hall	DongJ		600					
4-4-2	E-1 Atlantic	FED		63-5		76-77	125	150	130	See Note #351
4-4-2	E-1 Atlantic	FED		63-5		76-77	75	120	90	See Note #1344
4-8-2	L-O Mountain	OMI	Ajin	1457	50	85	423			#657-679
4-8-4	L-1 Northern	WMC	Goto	MO-30	875	72	133	330	290	See Note #352

Seaboard Air Line Railroad

Whyte Class	Owner Class & Type	Model Production					List Price	Resale		Remarks
		Importer	Builder	Cat #	Quan.	Yrs.		Mint	Avg.	
2-6-6-4	Articulated	Sun	DongJ	HO37B		82	600			became B&O Kb-1/Kb-1a
4-8-2	M-2 Mountain	PFM								

Soo Line Railroad

Whyte Class	Owner Class & Type	Model Production					List Price	Resale		Remarks
		Importer	Builder	Cat #	Quan.	Yrs.		Mint	Avg.	
2-8-0	F-10/21 Consol tndr	W&R	Samh		15	90				
4-6-2	H-3 Pacific	PFM	SKI	P		84	550	380		See Note #1345
2-8-0	F-21 Consol	W&R	Samh		26	90				fp.
2-8-0	F-10/21 Consol	W&R	Samh		27	90				
4-8-2	N-20 Mountain	PFM				88	550	440		Compound pumps
2-8-0	F-10 Consol	W&R	Samh		27	90				fp.
4-6-2	H-23 Pacific	PFM	SKI	P		84	550	380		See Note #1346
4-8-2	N-20 Mountain	PFM				88	550	440		single pump

Southern Railway

Whyte Class	Owner Class & Type	Model Production					List Price	Resale		Remarks
		Importer	Builder	Cat #	Quan.	Yrs.		Mint	Avg.	
0-8-0	Switcher	W&R	Samh		50	87				#1878–1897
0-8-0	Switcher		Akane						250	USRA w/ clear vision tender
2-8-0	Ks Consol	OMI	Kobra	1404	500	77	155	200	170	See Note #1349
2-8-2	Ms-4 Mikado	PFM	Samh	P	400	78	225	210	190	See Note #354
2-8-2	Ms Mikado	Emp		DL-103		78	185	190	160	See Note #353
2-8-2	Ms-1 Mikado	Key	Samh		150	78	200	220	200	USRA Light
2-8-2	Ms-4 Mikado	PFM	Samh	P	350	78	215	200	180	Worthington FWH
2-8-4	#2716 Kanawha	Key	Samh			83	415	650		See Note #1347
2-8-4	#2716 Kanawha	Key				93	1070			fp. #2716, See Note #1347
2-8-4	#2716 Kanawha	Key				93	995			See Note #1347
2-10-2	Ss-1 Santa Fe	Key	Samh		150	78	210	300	280	See Note #357
2-8-2 + 2-8-0	Ms-2 Mikado Tractor	PSC	Samh	MO-133		81	369	560	530	See Note #355 & #1348
2-8-2 + 2-8-0	Ms-2 Mikado Tractor	WMC	Samh	MO-133		78	328	560	530	See Note #355
4-6-0	F-1 Ten Wheeler	PFM	Atlas/Asahi	P	500	77	299	410	350	Baldwin Version
4-6-2	Ps-4 Pacific	PFM	Atlas/Asahi	P	250	65	55	235	210	

Southern Railway (cont'd)

Mention the Southern Railway and conversation will probably turn to on the famous Southern PS–4 Pacifics. With their beautiful green, gold, red, and black paint scheme, they prove that you don't have to streamline a locomotive to make it appealing. Although the basic paint scheme prevailed over the entire railroad, minor variations of color and trim could be found from division to division. PFM imported over 4,600 models of this Atlas/Asahi built-engine between 1961 and 1976.

Southern management was never very enthusiastic about articulateds, so when they needed greater power to climb the Blue Ridge grades, they tried an easy way out, taking old 2–8–0 mechanisms and mounting them under the tenders of Mikados. This idea failed for several reasons. As the tender fuel supply dwindled, so did the tractive effort. Also mechanical defects in the steam supply system to the rear engine were a constant problem. Samhongsa produced this unusual model for Westside Model Company in 1978.

Whyte Class	Owner Class & Type	Model Production				List Price	Resale		Remarks
		Importer	Builder	Cat #	Quan.	Yrs.		Mint	Avg.	
4-6-2	Ps-4 Pacific	PFM	Atlas/Asahi	P	500	73	150	260	250	
4-6-2	Ps-4 Pacific	PFM	Atlas/Asahi	P	600	76	225	260	260	See Note #358
4-6-2	Ps-4 Pacific	PFM	Atlas/Asahi	P	500	71	90	250	250	
4-6-2	Ps-4 Pacific	PFM	Atlas/Asahi	P	145	64	50	220	200	
4-6-2	Ps-4 Pacific	PFM	Atlas/Asahi	P	265	67	55	240	220	
4-6-2	Ps-4 Pacific	PFM	Atlas/Asahi	P	683	61	50	210	180	Serial #2301-2670
4-6-2	Ps-4 Pacific	PFM	Atlas/Asahi	P	190	63	50	220	190	
4-6-2	Ps-4 Pacific	PFM	Atlas/Asahi	P	390	69	65	250	235	
4-6-2	Ps-4 Pacific	PFM	Atlas/Asahi	P	1112	60	50	200	160	
4-8-2	Ts-1 Mountain	Key	Samh		100	81	336	350	320	See Note #359
4-8-2	Ts Mountain	PFM	Atlas/Nakayama	H	12	62	147	5000	4500	Handbuilt

Southern Pacific Lines (SP)

Whyte Class	Owner Class & Type	Model Production					List Price	Resale		Remarks
		Importer	Builder	Cat #	Quan.	Yrs.		Mint	Avg.	
0-6-0T	S-2 #217 Switcher	WMC	Samh	MO-89		77	145	180	160	See Note #361
0-6-0T	#966 Switcher	WMC	Nish	MO-15	600	69	60	235	210	See Note #360
0-6-0	Switcher	WAS	Kawai			57				Sausage Tender
0-6-0	Switcher	PFM	Atlas		1	56	47			
0-6-0	#1200 Switcher	Prgn				58	28	150	130	
0-6-0	S-?? Switcher	MGray								
0-6-0	S-8 Switcher	Sun	SMI	HO105B	300	77	129			
0-6-0	S-8 Switcher	Sun	Samh	HO16	300	77	150	180	160	See Note #364
0-6-0	S-10 Switcher	Sun	Samh	HO16A	300	77	135	190	160	See Note #365
0-6-0	S-10 Switcher	Sun				89	172			Sausage Tender
0-6-0	S-10 Switcher	Sun	SMI		300	89	172			Sausage Tender
0-6-0	S-12 Switcher	PFM	SKI	P		84	513		380	See Note #1353
0-6-0	S-12 Switcher	Sun				89	172			Vandy Tender
0-6-0	S-12 Switcher	MBA	KTM		400	60	40	160	140	See Note #1350
0-6-0	S-12 Switcher	Bal	KTM			67-68	50	235	210	See Note #362
0-6-0	S-12 Switcher	Sun	SMI		300	89	172			Vanderbilt Tender
0-6-0	S-12 Switcher	PFM	SKI	P		84	513		380	See Note #1354
0-6-0	S-12 Switcher	Bal	KTM			66	40	200	180	See Note #362
0-6-0	S-14 Switcher	PFM	SKI	P		84	513		380	See Note #1351
0-6-0	S-14 Switcher	PFM	SKI	P		84	513		380	See Note #1352
0-8-0	SE-4 Switcher	Bal	KTM			67-71	55-60	235	180	
0-8-0	SE-4 Switcher	CustB	KSM	ST-246	250	80	281	235	200	
2-6-0	Mogul	PFM	Toby		320	63				
2-6-0	Mogul	PFM	Atlas	H	1	55				
2-6-0	M-6 Mogul	Sun	TaeHwa	HO-65	100	81	270		260	See Note #593
2-6-0	M-8 Mogul	Cont				59	32	170	140	See Note #1355
2-6-0	M-9 Mogul	Sun	TaeHwa	HO-65A	100	81	270		260	Two Tender Styles
2-6-0	M-21 Mogul	Key	Samh		1000	75	140	190	170	See Note #363
2-6-0	M-21 Mogul	Intl				61	43	170	140	See Note #563
2-6-0	M-21 Mogul	MBA				58-61	34-44	180	140	See Note #563
2-6-2	PR-1,2 Prairie	WMC	Goto	MO-19	735	70-71	80	200	180	See Note #1356
2-8-0	Consolidation	PFM	Unknown	H	1	57				See Note #1357
2-8-0	#770 Consol	Hall	DongJ		600					See Note #371

The Southern Pacific owned 13 classes of Pacifics totalling 149 in all. Shown above is the P–13 Class, the last and heaviest Pacifics acquired by the Southern Pacific. Engines #631–633 were built by Baldwin in 1928, and served the SP until 1955. Somewhat heavier than the USRA 4–6–2's, these engines generated 45,850 lbs. of tractive effort as compared to the USRA Heavy Pacific's 43,900 lbs. Custom Brass imported 400 of these excellent Goto-built models in 1975.

Southern Pacific Lines (cont'd)

The Southern Pacific owned only ten Berkshires, all of them purchases from the Boston & Maine in 1945. Acquired to help ease the load on the Rio Grande Division during the final days of World War II, they lasted only until 1951, when they were scrapped. Built by Lima in 1928 as coal burners, they were converted to oil in 1950. With their huge eight-sided sand dome and Coffin feedwater heater, they never quite looked like SP locomotives, even when the coal tenders were replaced with the whale-back oil tenders. Balboa imported this highly detailed model in 1968.

Whyte Class	Owner Class & Type	Model Production					List Price	Resale		Remarks
		Importer	Builder	Cat #	Quan.	Yrs.		Mint	Avg.	
2-8-0	C-2 Consol	Ortl		0129	125	83	264	210		#2600-2611
2-8-0	C-9 Consol	Bal	KTM			67-71	55-70	290	235	See Note #368
2-8-0	C-9 Consol	Key	Samh		100	81	280		290	#2830
2-8-0	C-9 Consol	Sun	Samh	HO33	150	87	172			
2-8-0	C-8 Consol	Key	Samh		100	81	280		270	#2733
2-8-0	C-9 Consol	Bal	KTM			71	80	275	260	fp.
2-8-0	C-9 Consol	Key	Samh		100	80	266		250	See Note #369
2-8-0	C-9 Consol	Sun				87	172	170		
2-8-0	C-10 Consol	Sun		HO34	150					
2-8-0	C-10 Consol	Key	Samh		100	81	265	280	250	See Note #409
2-8-0	C-10 Consol	MBA	KMT		500	60	48	200	160	Short Vanderbilt tender
2-8-0	C-15 Consol	Alco	Rok-Am	S-134	300	79	200	200	180	See Note #370
2-8-0	C-19 Consol	Sun	ThaWha	HO70B		87	328	320		Coastline Version
2-8-0	C-19 Consol	Sun	ThaWha	HO70A		87	328	320		El Paso Version
2-8-0	C-24 Consol	Hall	KMT		500	80	167	210	180	See Note #563
2-8-2	MK-2 Mikado	Sun		HO83	90	86	357	350		
2-8-2	MK-2 Mikado	Sun		HO83	200	86	357			
2-8-2	MK-4 Mikado	Sun		HO84	200	86	357			
2-8-2	MK-4 Mikado	Sun		HO84	90	86	357	350		
2-8-2	MK-5 Mikado	Bal	KTM			67-68	65	290	260	Pacific Lines
2-8-2	MK-5 Mikado	Bal	KTM			71	120	350	290	fp.
2-8-2	MK-5 Mikado	Bal	KTM			65	53	410	300	See Note #372; SPT&NO
2-8-2	MK-5 Mikado	Bal	KTM			71	110	330	280	Pacific Lines
2-8-2	MK-6 Mikado	Alco	Rok-Am	S-131	300	80	330	290	235	See Note #374
2-8-2	MK-10 Mikado	WMC	Samh	MO-103	400	77	170	200	180	See Note #1358
2-8-2	MK-11 Mikado	WMC	Samh	MO-104	400	77	170	200	180	See Note #1359
2-8-4	B-1 Berkshire	PSC		15536						ex. B&M; Worthington FWH
2-8-4	B-1 Berkshire	WMC	Nakamura	MO-91	600	77	330	350	320	See Note #82 & 375
2-8-4	B-1 Berkshire	PSC		15514						Coffin FWH
2-8-4	B-1 Berkshire	PSC/WMC	Nakamura	MO-91		82	415			
2-8-4	B-1 Berkshire	Bal				68	70	350	290	ex. B&M; blue box
2-8-4	B-1 Berkshire	WMC	Nakamura	MO-106	100	77	330	390	350	See Note #383
2-6-6-2	MM-3 Articulated	NPP	Daeki		50	83	555	630		fp.
2-6-6-2	MM-3 Articulated	NPP	Daeki		200	83	490	550		
2-10-0	Decapod	Sun	Samh	HO03	800	76	135	180	150	MR Review 8/76

Southern Pacific Lines (cont'd)

Whyte Class	Owner Class & Type	Model Production					List Price	Resale		Remarks
		Importer	Builder	Cat #	Quan.	Yrs.		Mint	Avg.	
2-10-2	F-1 Santa Fe	Sun	DongJ	HO-19A	200	81	345		310	Worthington FWH
2-10-2	F-4 Santa Fe	Sun	DongJ	HO-19	200	81	345			6-wheel tender
2-10-2	F-5 Santa Fe	Bal	KTM			66	60	320	270	See Note #376
2-10-2	F-5 Santa Fe	WMC	KTM	MO-95	505	77	250	275	260	See Note #1576
2-8-8-2	AC-1 Articulated	WMC	Nakamura			80	800	760	720	See Note #378
2-8-8-2	AC-1 Articulated	PSC	Nakamura	15270		84	829	1030	1000	
2-8-8-4	AC-9 Yellowstone	Gem	Akane	650	18	62		500	410	Unsprung
2-8-8-4	AC-9 Yellowstone	Gem	Akane	IM-101	196	64	150	500	440	Unsprung
2-8-8-4	AC-9 Yellowstone	MGray	KTM			63	139	670	650	
	AC-9 Yellowstone	Bal	KTM			68	150	560	470	
2-8-8-4	AC-9 Yellowstone	Gem	Akane	650	19	63	150	500	410	Unsprung
2-8-8-4	AC-9 Yellowstone	Sun	DongJ	HO-28	250	81	500	560	500	
4-2-4T	#1 C.P. Huntington	MBA			50	57-60	21	150	130	"CP Huntington"
4-2-4T	#1 C.P. Huntington	Key			200	86	257			fp., "CP Huntington"
4-2-4T	#1 C.P. Huntington	MBA			600	57-60	23-30	170	130	fp., "CP Huntington"
4-2-4T	#1 C.P. Huntington	Key	Samh		200	82	285	330	280	"CP Huntington"
4-4-0	#1500 American	Cont				58	25	160	130	
4-4-0	American	MBA			1	58	32	100		fp., See Note #382
4-4-0	American	MBA			1	58	32	100		See Note #382
4-4-0	#1500 American	KenK	KMT		225	57		160	130	See Note #1577
4-4-0	#60 American	Bal				70	60	235	200	CP "Jupiter"
4-4-0	#60 American	Bal				71	142	290	260	fp., See Note #384
4-4-0	#60 American	Bal				70	98	235	200	See Note #384
4-4-2	A-3 Atlantic	PFM	Samh	P	750	75	148	180	150	See Note #388
4-4-2	A-3 Atlantic	PFM	Goto	P	285	69	70	220	190	See Note #385
4-4-2	A-3 Atlantic	PFM	Goto	P	480	68	60	210	160	See Note #385
4-4-2	A-3 Atlantic	WMC	Goto	MO-39A	100	76	120	190	170	See Note #411
4-4-2	A-4 Atlantic	WMC	Goto				139	160	140	
4-4-2	A-5 Atlantic	Gem	Olympia	GN-114	310	65	45	180	150	
4-4-2	A-5 Atlantic Tender	Gem	Olympia	OT-114	100	65		60		
4-4-2	A-6 Atlantic	Intl				50	18	100	70	Kit
4-4-2	A-6 Atlantic	MBA			550	60	42	180	140	#3000
4-4-2	A-6 Atlantic	WMC	Mizuno	MO-69	950	76	200	235	210	fp., WMC G-File #69
4-4-2	E-1 Atlantic	FED		63-5		76-77	125	180	130	See Note #386
4-4-2	E-1 Atlantic	FED		63-5		76-77	75	120	90	See Note #387
4-4-2	#3000 Atlantic	PFM	Atlas/Tsubomi	H	5	59	116	2115	1880	Handbuilt
4-6-0	T-1 Ten-Wheeler	PSC	Samh	15438		85	429	470	420	See Note #390
4-6-0	T-1 Ten-Wheeler	WMC	Samh	MO-86		77	200			See Note #390
4-6-0	T-1 Ten-Wheeler	WMC	Samh	MO-85	600	77	140	180	140	See Note #1361
4-6-0	T-23/26 Ten-Wheeler	Sunset		HO68						

When someone mentions the Southern Pacific GS Series, most railfans think of the beautiful "Daylight" engines. Many forget that streamlining was not applied to the GS–1 engines (#4400–4409). SP was evidently happy with their performance, for they eventually owned 96 GS Class 4–8–4's. Fujiyama built 295 of these "Crown" models for PFM in 1967.

Southern Pacific Lines (cont'd)

Whyte Class	Owner Class & Type	Importer	Builder	Cat #	Quan.	Yrs.	List Price	Mint	Avg.	Remarks
4-6-0	T-28 Ten-Wheeler	Sunset		HO71A						
4-6-0	T-28 Ten-Wheeler	PSC		15614		87	349			
4-6-0	T-28 Ten-Wheeler	PSC		15614-1		87	389			fp.
4-6-0	T-28 Ten-Wheeler	WMC	KTM	MO-3	500	64	45	210	180	See Note #389
4-6-0	T-31 Ten Wheeler	PSC		15616		87	349			
4-6-0	T-31 Ten Wheeler	PSC		15616-1		87	389			fp.
4-6-0	T-31 Ten-Wheeler	WMC	KTM	MO-29	1000	71-72	100	300	210	See Note #1360
4-6-2	P-1 Pacific	MBA				59	36			cataloged
4-6-2	P-1 Pacific	WMC	Mizuno	MO-51	690	74	150	190	160	See Note #1362
4-6-2	P-10 Pacific	Bal	KTM			65	55	320	270	
4-6-2	P-10 Pacific	Bal	KTM			65	58	350	290	Sreamlined
4-6-2	P-10 Pacific	WMC	KTM	MO-115	398	78	300	290	280	See Note #1364
4-6-2	P-10 Pacific	WMC	KTM	MO-116	345	78	300	290	260	See Note #1363
4-6-2	P-13 Pacific	CustB	Goto	ST-244	400	75	250	380	350	See Note #391
4-6-2	P-13 Pacific	PFM	Unknown	H	1	57				Vanderbilt tender
4-6-2	P-14 Pacific	Hall	KMT		500	72	135	330	290	T&NO "Sunbeam"
4-6-2	P-3 Pacific	Key	Samh		65	87	493	470		fp.
4-6-2	P-3 Pacific	Key	Samh		10	87	443	420		
4-6-2	P-4 Pacific	Soho	Mizuno	1311	49	77	280	320	290	See Note #393
4-6-2	P-4 Pacific	WMC	Mizuno	MO-64	1180	76	190	220	190	See Note #392
4-6-2	P-5 Pacific	Key	Samh		10	87	430	470		
4-6-2	P-5 Pacific	Key	Samh		65	87	495	530		fp.
4-6-2	P-5 Pacific	LMB				63	35	180	140	
4-6-2	P-5 Pacific	MBA	KMT		550	59	45	210	180	
4-6-2	P-5 Pacific	PFM	Tensh #142	CR	300	61	50	290	260	fp., See Note #565
4-6-2	P-5 Pacific	PFM	Tensh #142	CR	300	62	50	320	290	fp. Crown
4-6-2	P-5 Pacific	PFM	Tensh #142	CR	105	67	60	350	320	fp., See Note #566
4-8-0	TW-8 Twelve Wheeler	MGray				65	50	410	380	
4-8-0	TW-8 Twelve Wheeler	WMC	KTM	MO-16	670	69	60	260	200	WMC G-File #16
4-8-2	MT-1 Mountain	Key	Samh		50	83	421		450	See Note #1367
4-8-2	MT-1 Mountain	Key	Samh		40	83	421		450	See Note #1368
4-8-2	MT-1 Mountain	Key	Samh		75	83	421		450	See Note #1366
4-8-2	MT-1 Mountain	Key	Samh		50	83	421		450	See Note #1365
4-8-2	MT-2 Mountain	Alco	Rok-Am	S-129	300	79	292	260	235	See Note #394
4-8-2	MT-2 Mountain	Alco	Rok-Am	S-130	300	79	292	260	235	See Note #395
4-8-2	MT-2 Mountain	Alpha				84	250		235	
4-8-2	MT-3 Mountain	Bal	KTM			67	70	380	320	
4-8-2	MT-3 Mountain	Key								
4-8-2	MT-3 Mountain	MGray	KTM			62	65	380	300	
4-8-2	MT-3 Mountain	Sun	SMI	HO113A	200		89	270		
4-8-2	MT-4 Mountain	Bal	KTM			67	70	470	410	Skyline Casing
4-8-2	MT-4 Mountain	Sun	SMI	HO113	150		89	270		
4-8-2	MT-4 Mountain	Key	Samh		75	82	400		440	Skyline Casing
4-8-2	MT-4 Mountain	Key	Samh		75	82	400		440	
4-8-2	MT-4 Mountain	MGray	KTM			61-62	60-65	470	380	See Note #567
4-8-2	MT-5 Mountain	Key	Samh		75	82	400		380	Skyline Casing
4-8-2	MT-5 Mountain	Sun	SMI	HO114	150		89		270	
4-8-2	MT-5 Mountain	Soho	KTM	1310		78	350	350	300	Super-detailed WMC #4367
4-8-2	MT-5 Mountain	WMC	KTM	MO-71	1111	76	220	260	235	See Note #396
4-10-2	SP-1 Sou Pac	Key	Samh		75	84	614			fp., See Note #1369
4-10-2	SP-2/3 Sou Pac	WMC	KTM	MO-14	1	76	200+			Interim Model
4-10-2	SP-2/3 Sou Pac	Key	Samh		75	84	600			fp.black, See Note #1370
4-10-2	SP-2/3 Sou Pac	Key	Samh		35	84	529			See Note #1370
4-10-2	#5000 Sou Pac	Sunset	DongJ							
4-10-2	SP-2/3 Sou Pac	WMC	KTM	MO-14	24	71	130	350	290	See Note #404
4-10-2	SP-2/3 Sou Pac	WMC	KTM	MO-14	464	68-69	70	320	280	See Note #564
4-10-2	SP-1 Sou Pac	Key	Samh		25	84	529			fp., See Note #1369
4-10-2	SP-2/3 Sou Pac	WMC	KTM	MO-14	1173	73-74	160	320	280	See Note #405
4-10-2	SP-1 Sou Pac	MGray	KTM			63	75	320	260	See Note #559
4-8-4	Northern	PFM	Atlas	H	1	55				Handbuilt
4-8-4	Northern	PFM	Atlas	H	1	56				Handbuilt
4-8-4	GS-1 Northern	Bal	KTM			70	120	410	340	Master Series
4-8-4	GS-1 Northern	Key	Samh				1150			fp., See Note#1375
4-8-4	GS-1 Northern	Key	Samh				1150			fp., See Note#1376

Southern Pacific Lines (cont'd)

In 1925, the Southern Pacific purchased 16, three-cylinder 4–10–2 engines from Alco and followed this up with an additional order for 33 more in 1926–27. Built to replace 2–10–2's which were not considered fast enough, these engines lived up to the SP's expectations. Three classes—SP–1, 2, and 3—were designated. All engines had the same basic dimensions: 26- and 28- by 32-inch cylinders, 63-inch drivers, and 96,000 lbs. of tractive effort. One engine was saved from the scrappers torch, #5021. The 4–10–2 was a rare breed on American railroads. The only other railroad to use this wheel arrangement was the Union Pacific. Samhongsa produced this beautiful model of the SP–3 class for Key Imports in 1984.

| Whyte Class | Owner Class & Type | Model Production | | | | | List Price | Resale | | Remarks |
		Importer	Builder	Cat #	Quan.	Yrs.		Mint	Avg.	
4-8-4	GS-1 Northern	Key	Samh				1150			fp., See Note#1377
4-8-4	GS-1 Northern	Key	Samh				1150			fp., See Note#1374
4-8-4	GS-1 Northern	Key	Samh				1150			fp., See Note#1373
4-8-4	GS-1 Northern	Key	Samh				1150			fp., See Note#1378
4-8-4	GS-1 Northern	Key	Samh				1150			fp., See Note#1372
4-8-4	GS-1 Northern	PFM	Fujiyama	CR	295	67	135	760	590	rectangular tender
4-8-4	GS-1 Northern	Sun	Samh	HO45	600	78	200	270	235	See Note #1378
4-8-4	GS-2 Northern	WMC		M-182		81	500		440	See Note #403
4-8-4	GS-2 Northern	Bal	KTM			70	120	450	380	Master Series
4-8-4	GS-2 Northern	Sun	SMI	HO127C	100	89	200			
4-8-4	GS-2 Northern	WMC		M-182		82	499	460	420	See Note #403
4-8-4	GS-3 Northern	Key	Samh				775	760		See Note #1381
4-8-4	GS-3 Northern	Sun	SMI	HO127D	100	89	200			
4-8-4	GS-3 Northern	WMC				81	500		440	See Note #402
4-8-4	GS-4 Northern	Bal	KTM			70	120	350		fp., See Note #1380
4-8-4	GS-4 Northern	PFM	Atlas/KTM	P	1	59	58			fp., See Note #397 & 398
4-8-4	GS-4 Northern	Sun	SMI	HO127AP	100	89				fp.
4-8-4	GS-4 Northern	Sun	SMI	HO127A	100	89	200			
4-8-4	GS-4 Northern	Bal	KTM			66-68	63-70	290	260	"Daylight"
4-8-4	GS-4 Northern	PFM	Atlas/KTM	P	340	59	50	200	180	See Note #397 & 398
4-8-4	GS-4 Northern	PSC/WMC	KTM	MO-49		83	513	570	550	
4-8-4	GS-4 Northern	MBA				60	75			cataloged
4-8-4	GS-4 Northern	WMC	KTM			80	500		440	See Note #402
4-8-4	GS-4 Northern	WMC	KTM	MO-49	175	77	220	290	260	fp. "Daylight"
4-8-4	GS-4 Northern	Bal	KTM	MO-49	1073	74		260	260	"Daylight"
4-8-4	GS-4 Northern	PFM	Atlas/KTM	P	656	58	50	200	180	See Note #397
4-8-4	GS-4 Northern	WMC	KTM	MO-49	626	77	200	260	250	See Note #413
4-8-4	GS-4 Northern	MGray	KTM			63	70	290	260	See Note #399
4-8-4	GS-4 Northern	PFM	Atlas/KTM	P	50	60	50	210	190	
4-8-4	GS-4 Northern	Bal	KTM			70	97	320	290	See Note #400
4-8-4	GS-4 Northern	Bal	KTM			67	80	350	320	fp., See Note #1382
4-8-4	GS-4 Northern	Key	Samh		40	91	560	630	ERR	fp., See Note #1383
4-8-4	GS-5 Northern	WMC	KTM	M-176		80	500		375	See Note #402
4-8-4	GS-5 Northern	Sun	SMI	HO127B	100	89	200			
4-8-4	GS-6 Northern	Sun	SMI	HO127E	100	89	200			
4-8-4	GS-6 Northern	WMC	KTM			81	500		440	See Note #1597

Southern Pacific Lines (cont'd)

Whyte Class	Owner Class & Type	Model Production					List Price	Resale		Remarks
		Importer	Builder	Cat #	Quan.	Yrs.		Mint	Avg.	
4-8-4	GS-6 Northern	WMC	KTM	MO-56	1395	75	180	260	235	See Note #401
4-8-4	GS-6 Northern	Intl				58	55	235	180	See Note #412
4-8-4	GS-7/8 Northern	WMC	Goto	MO-30	875	72	133	350	300	See Note #1384
4-6-6-2	AM-2 Cab Forward	Bal				65	140	590	470	See Note #1385
4-6-6-2	AM-2 Cab Forward	WMC	Nakamura	MO-137		79	823	870	760	See Note #1386
4-6-6-2	AM-2 Cab Forward	PSC		10048		80-82	569	890		Kit
4-8-8-2	AC-4 Cab Forward	WMC	KTM	MO-99	303	77	400	470	440	See Note #1387
4-8-8-2	AC-4 Cab Forward	Bal	KTM			71	170	560	500	fp.
4-8-8-2	AC-4 Cab Forward	MGray	KTM			64	135	470	410	See Note #1388
4-8-8-2	AC-4 Cab Forward	Sun	SMI	HO82A	100	86	527	500		late version
4-8-8-2	AC-4 Cab Forward	PSC	KTM	15208						
4-8-8-2	AC-4 Cab Forward	Key	Samh		30	84	857		820	fp., Sacramento Gray
4-8-8-2	AC-4 Cab Forward	Key	Samh		50	84	771		730	
4-8-8-2	AC-4 Cab Forward	Bal	KTM			68	150	530	510	See Note #379
4-8-8-2	AC-4/5/6 Cab Forward	PSC		15037		80	429			See Note #591
4-8-8-2	AC-4 Cab Forward	WMC	KTM	MO-99	303	78	400	500		See Note #1389
4-8-8-2	AC-4 Cab Forward	Key	Samh		35	84	843		800	fp., later standard
4-8-8-2	AC-5 Cab Forward	Sun	SMI	HO82C		86	527	500		late version
4-8-8-2	AC-5 Cab Forward	Key	Samh		50	84	771			
4-8-8-2	AC-5 Cab Forward	Key	Samh		35	84	843			fp.
4-8-8-2	AC-5 Cab Forward	PSC	KTM	15304						
4-8-8-2	AC-5 Cab Forward	Sun	SMI	HO82B		86	527	500		early version
4-8-8-2	AC-6 Cab Forward	WMC	KTM		100	79	628	670	590	See Note #381
4-8-8-2	AC-6 Cab Forward	WMC	KTM	MO-139	100	79	628	670	590	See Note #410
4-8-8-2	AC-6 Cab Forward	Sun	SMI	HO82D		86	527	500		early version
4-8-8-2	AC-6 Cab Forward	Sun	SMI	HO82E		86	527	500		late version
4-8-8-2	AC-6 Cab Forward	Key	Samh		30	84	843			fp.
4-8-8-2	AC-6 Cab Forward	PSC	KTM	15306						
4-8-8-2	AC-6 Cab Forward	WMC	KTM	MO-139	100	79	566	590	530	Improved Drive
4-8-8-2	AC-6 Cab Forward	Key	Samh		20	84	771			
4-8-8-2	AC-7 Cab Forward	WMC	KTM			80	550	590	540	
4-8-8-2	AC-7 Cab Forward	Key	Samh		10	84				fp., #4151

Undoubtedly the locomotive most unique to the Southern Pacific is the Cab-Forward. Designed to alleviate the problem of crew suffocation in the long snow sheds in the Sierra Nevada mountains, these engines evolved from the MC–2 Class 2–6–6–2 into the huge AC–12 Class 4–8–8–2. All of the cab-forwards were oil burners, a necessity considering that coal firing would have required a stoker the length of the engine. These seemingly unorthodox engines numbered over 270 examples in all classes. The 20 engines of the AC–12 class were the culmination of this design concept. PFM imported this limited-production model in 1976.

Southern Pacific Lines (cont'd)

Whyte Class	Owner Class & Type	Model Production					List Price	Resale		Remarks
		Importer	Builder	Cat #	Quan.	Yrs.		Mint	Avg.	
4-8-8-2	AC-7 Cab Forward	Key	Samh		10	84	843			fp., #4151
4-8-8-2	AC-7 Cab Forward	Key	Samh			84	771	920		See Note #1390
4-8-8-2	AC-7 Cab Forward	Key	Samh		10	84				See Note #1391
4-8-8-2	AC-7 Cab Forward	Sun	SMI	HO150		91	400			
4-8-8-2	AC-7 Cab Forward	Sun	SMI	HO150P		91	600			fp.
4-8-8-2	AC-7/8 Cab Forward	PSC	KTM	15308						
4-8-8-2	AC-8 Cab Forward	Key	Samh		10	84	843		770	fp.
4-8-8-2	AC-8 Cab Forward	Key	Samh		10	84				fp., #4177
4-8-8-2	AC-10 Cab Forward	Gem	Akane	AK-106	13	62	90	350	320	
4-8-8-2	AC-10/11/12 Cab Forward	Key	Samh		75	84	843			
4-8-8-2	AC-10/11/12 Cab Forward	PSC	KTM	15038	30	80	439	670		See Note #592
4-8-8-2	AC-10 Cab Forward	Gem	Akane	AK-106	4	64		350	320	
4-8-8-2	AC-10 Cab Forward	Key	Samh		10	84	843	950		fp., #4205
4-8-8-2	AC-10 Cab Forward	Gem	Akane	AK-106	28	63			350	fp., #4294
4-8-8-2	AC-11 Cab Forward	Aristo				59	80	290	175	
4-8-8-2	AC-11 Cab Forward	Prgn				58	80	290	175	#4200 Series
4-8-8-2	AC-11 Cab Forward	Key			10		843	900		fp., #4245
4-8-8-2	AC-11 Cab Forward	Intl	Takara			59	80	300	235	
4-8-8-2	AC-11 Cab Forward	Akane	Akane	600F		59	63	380	320	
4-8-8-2	AC-11 Cab Forward	ACI				55-57		290		
4-8-8-2	AC-12 Cab Forward	Sun	SMI	HO151P	100	91	600			fp.
4-8-8-2	AC-12 Cab Forward	Sun	SMI	HO151		91	400			
4-8-8-2	AC-12 Cab Forward	PFM	Tensh #127	H	5	55	112	2500	2300	See Note #377
4-8-8-2	AC-12 Cab Forward	PFM	Tensh		50	84	1750	1760	1410	fp., handbuilt
4-8-8-2	AC-12 Cab Forward	PFM	Atlas/KTM	H	1	54				
4-8-8-2	AC-12 Cab Forward	PFM	Atlas/KTM	H	1	56	80			
4-8-8-2	AC-12 Cab Forward	PFM	Tensh	H	5	57		3000	2600	See Note #377
4-8-8-2	AC-12 Cab Forward	PFM	Tensh #127	H	5	56	133	3000	2700	See Note #377
4-8-8-2	AC-12 Cab Forward	PFM	Tensh #167	LP	300	74	850	1175	1000	See Note #1046
4-8-8-2	AC-12 Cab Forward	PFM	Tensh #167	LP	200	76	850	1290	1060	See Note #380
4-8-8-2	AC-12 Cab Forward	WMC	KTM			80	660	705	620	30" min. radius
4-8-8-2	AC-12 Cab Forward	WMC	KTM			81	660	920	850	Re-run
4-8-8-2	AC-12 Cab Forward	Gem	Akane	IM-106	100	64	150	410	350	sprung drivers
4-8-8-2	AC-12 Cab Forward	Key	Samh		50	84	843		800	
4-8-8-2	AC-12 Cab Forward	Bal	KTM			68	150	620	530	

Southern Pacific — Texas & New Orleans (SPT&NO)

Whyte Class	Owner Class & Type	Model Production					List Price	Resale		Remarks
		Importer	Builder	Cat #	Quan.	Yrs.		Mint	Avg.	
2-6-0	M-4 Mogul	PFM	Fujiyama	P	470	66	35	190	160	See Note #366
2-6-0	M-4 Mogul	PFM	Fujiyama	P	475	70	60	200	180	See Note #366
2-6-0	M-4 Mogul	PFM	Fujiyama	P	600	77	225	235	200	See Note #367
2-6-0	M-4 Mogul	PFM	Fujiyama	P	315	67	48	190	170	See Note #366
2-6-0	M-4 Mogul	PFM	Fujiyama	P	500	74	110	210	190	See Note #366
4-4-0	E-23 American	PFM	Fujiyama	P	820	66	35	170	150	
4-4-0	E-23 American	PFM	Fujiyama	P	370	69	50	180	160	See Note #1392
4-4-0	E-23 American	PFM	Fujiyama	P	500	74	135	190	180	

Spokane, Portland & Seattle Railway (SP&S)

Whyte Class	Owner Class & Type	Model Production					List Price	Resale		Remarks
		Importer	Builder	Cat #	Quan.	Yrs.		Mint	Avg.	
2-8-0	N-6 Consol	W&R	Samh		44	90				fp.
2-8-0	N-6 Consol	W&R	Samh		21	90				
2-8-0	N-6 Consol tender	W&R	Samh		20	90				
2-8-2	Q-3 Mikado	NWSL								
4-8-4	E-1 Northern	W&R	Samh		9	93				
4-8-4	E-1 Northern	W&R	Samh		52	93				fp. black
4-8-4	E-1 Northern	W&R	Samh	LP	100	76	525	760	705	See Note #236
4-6-6-4	Z-6 Challenger	PFM	Tensh #165	LP	250	75	525	900	850	See Note #236

Spokane, Portland & Seattle Railway (cont'd)

The Great Northern and the Northern Pacific were rival roads in the Pacific Northwest, so it appears strange that they should jointly own the Spokane, Portland and Seattle. When neither railroad could gain an uncontested right-of-way into Portland, they decided to put aside their differences and jointly construct a railroad that served both companies. This joint ownership resulted in the SP&S being stocked with a mixture of NP and GN equipment. The Z–6 Class 4–6–6–4 was an example of a design that was used by all three roads. The SP&S engines were oil burners, whereas the NP predecessors were designed to burn a low-grade bituminous coal. In 1937, six of these fine engines came to the SP&S from Alco. Two of these engines were sold to the Great Northern in 1939. Pacific Fast Mail imported this limited-production Tenshodo built-model between 1969 and 1975.

Whyte Class	Owner Class & Type	Model Production					List Price	Resale		Remarks
		Importer	Builder	Cat #	Quan.	Yrs.		Mint	Avg.	
4-6-6-4	Z-6 Challenger	PFM	Tensh #165	LP	300	71	285	850	800	fp.
4-6-6-4	Z-6 Challenger	PFM	Tensh #165	LP	230	69	245	800	750	unpainted
4-6-6-4	Z-8 Challenger	Key	Samh		50	81	690		705	Oil Fired
4-6-6-4	Z-8 Challenger	Key	Samh		50	83				

Texas & Pacific Railway (T&P)

Whyte Class	Owner Class & Type	Model Production					List Price	Resale		Remarks
		Importer	Builder	Cat #	Quan.	Yrs.		Mint	Avg.	
0-6-0	B-6 Switcher	Hall		HS0294		86-87	242	240		
2-8-0	#401 Consol	Hall		HS0181		86-87	257	250		

Texas & Pacific owned the first true 2–10–4, and little did they know that it would ultimately became the most famous 2–10–4 in America, long after the era of big steam had passed. Engine #610 was revived and in 1976 was one of the engines to pull the "Freedom Train." T&P's 2–10–4 began a trend in design that culminated in the C&O T–1 and the PRR J–1 2–10–4's. Models of the T&P I–1 are not common. LMB imported this KMT-built model in 1958.

Texas & Pacific Railway (cont'd)

Whyte Class	Owner Class & Type	Importer	Builder	Cat #	Quan.	Yrs.	List Price	Mint	Avg.	Remarks
2-8-2	H-2 Mikado	Key	Samh		125	79	200	235	210	Light USRA
2-8-2	H-2r Mikado	Key	Samh		75	81	320	380	350	See Note #406
2-10-2	G-1b Santa Fe	PRB	Gang San	2001	250	86	440			
2-10-4	#600 Texas	Cont	KMT			59	70	325	275	See Note #1393
2-10-4	I Texas	LMB	KMT		100	58	70	325	275	#600 Series
2-10-4	I-1a Texas	Sun	Samh		600	78	235	360	340	See Note #407
4-6-0	D-8 Ten Wheeler	Gem	Olympia	GN-115	428	65	40	180	150	
4-6-2	P-1b Pacific	Hall	DongJ	HSO104		84	349	390	375	See Note #1394
4-8-2	M-1 Mountain	Hall	DongJ		200	81	343	380	330	See Note #408

Union Railroad

Whyte Class	Owner Class & Type	Importer	Builder	Cat #	Quan.	Yrs.	List Price	Mint	Avg.	Remarks
0-10-2	S-7 Switcher	PFM	Atlas/Asahi	P	1	65				See Note #7
0-10-2	S-7 Switcher	PFM	Atlas/Asahi	P	460	65	70	380	320	See Note #1396
0-10-2	S-7 Switcher	PFM	Atlas/Asahi	P	170	67	70	410	350	See Note #1395

What had to be the largest switcher ever built was the Union Railroad's 0–10–2 "Union" type. Nine of these Baldwin-built monsters (#301–309) worked the steel mills around Pittsburgh for several years before being sold to the Duluth, Missabe & Iron Range Railroad, where they replaced aging articulateds. With a tractive effort of 90,900 lbs. without booster, and 108,050 lbs. with the booster, they exceed the biggest 0–10–0's by over 10,000 lbs. Atlas/Asahi produced an excellent model of this interesting prototype for Pacific Fast Mail in 1965 and 1967.

Union Pacific Railroad (UP)

Whyte Class	Owner Class & Type	Importer	Builder	Cat #	Quan.	Yrs.	List Price	Mint	Avg.	Remarks
0-6-0	S Switcher	PFM	KTM/Adachi	S	1	62				See Note #7
0-6-0	S Switcher	Bal	KTM			70	70	210	180	fp.
0-6-0	S-6 Switcher	Orti	WYang	0373	150	84	293	290		#4451-4480
0-6-0	S Switcher	PFM	KTM/Adachi	P	500	65	40	210	190	#4474
0-6-0	S Switcher	PFM	KTM/Adachi	P	700	60	35	160	140	#4474
0-6-0	S Switcher	PFM	KTM/Adachi	P	345	62	35	190	160	#4474
0-6-0	S Switcher	PFM	KTM/Adachi	P	400	61	35	180	150	#4474
0-6-0	S Switcher	PFM	KTM/Adachi	P	250	67	45	235	210	#4474
0-6-0	S Switcher	Bal	KTM			70	60	200	180	
2-8-0	Consol	OMI	JPMod	1443	75	81	280		270	See Note #415
2-8-0	#413 Consol	OMI	JPMod	1444	150	81	280		270	See Note #414
2-8-0	#6200 Consol	PFM	Atlas/Asahi	P	215	63	45	220	190	

Union Pacific Railroad (cont'd)

Union Pacific's locomotives are often described as big, powerful, and brawny, but rarely as beautiful. Performance and durability were more important than good looks. UP #2890 is an example of the "Common Standard Heavy Type." All engines of this type had Walschaerts valve gear, Hodges trailing trucks, and short Vanderbilt tenders. Over the years, modifications were made to cabs, tenders, stacks, drivers, domes, valve gear, and trailing trucks, Even with all these modifications, the engines retained their distinctive UP look. In 1989, Ajin Precision produced this model in the unstreamlined and streamlined versions for Overland Models.

| Whyte Class | Owner Class & Type | Model Production | | | | | List Price | Resale | | Remarks |
		Importer	Builder	Cat #	Quan.	Yrs.		Mint	Avg.	
2-8-0	#6200 Consol	PFM	Atlas/Asahi	P	350	62	45	220	180	
2-8-0	#6200 Consol	PFM	Atlas/Asahi	P	500	72	95	250	220	
2-8-0	#6200 Consol	PFM	Atlas/Asahi	P	700	76	225	260	235	See Note #569
2-8-0	#6200 Consol	PFM	Atlas/Asahi	P	500	70	80	250	210	See Note #568
2-8-0	#6200 Consol	PFM	Atlas/Asahi	P	140	64	45	230	190	
2-8-0	#6200 Consol	PFM	Atlas/Asahi	P	190	65	45	235	200	
2-8-0	#6200 Consol	PFM	Atlas/Asahi	P	475	61	45	210	180	
2-8-2	#2480 Mikado	Key	Samh		125	84	500	470		fp.
2-8-2	#2480 Mikado	Key	Samh		150	86	500	470		fp., #2480
2-8-2	#2480 Mikado	Key	Samh		100	77	160	210	190	Light USRA
2-8-2	MK-1 Mikado	Ortl	DaiYng	0372		84	379	370		w/o number boards
2-8-2	MK-1 Mikado	Ortl	DaiYng	0371		84	379	370		w/number boards
2-8-2	MK-1 Mikado	Ortl	DaiYng	P371		84	457	430		fp.
2-8-2	MK-6 Mikado	Bal	KMT			67-71	100	410	350	See Note #416
2-8-2	MK-7 Mikado	LMB	KMT			67-71	65-80	280	200	#2200 Class
2-8-2	MK-9 Mikado	Ortl	DaiYng	0074	300	81	295			#2295-2310
2-8-2	MK-10 Mikado	Ortl								
2-10-2	#5000 Santa Fe	Bal	KTM		300	66-67	63-70	350	290	
2-10-2	#5003 Santa Fe	Key	SKI		35		619	640		See Note #1399
2-10-2	#5000 Santa Fe	PSC		15296		84	429			
2-10-2	#5000 Santa Fe	WMC		MO-124	435	78	307	350	290	See Note #1400
2-8-8-0	#3500 Articulated	Sun	Samh	HO-79		84	410		410	Compound Articulated
2-8-8-0	#3500 Articulated	Sun	Samh	HO-31	400	79	370	470	410	Simple Articulated
2-8-8-0	#3500 Articulated	W&R	Samh		25	91				See Note #1402
2-8-8-0	#3500 Articulated	W&R	Samh		49	91				Version 2, fp.
2-8-8-0	#3500 Articulated	W&R	Samh		42	91				Version 1, fp.
2-8-8-0	#3500 Articulated	W&R	Samh		8	91				Version 1
2-8-8-0	#3500 Articulated	W&R	Samh		7	91				Version 2
2-8-8-0	#3500 Artic tender	W&R	Samh		15	91				
2-8-8-2	#3570 Articulated	CustB	Goto	ST-295	200	79	768	880	820	See Note #417
4-4-0	#119 American	PFM	United		879	69	90	250	220	See Note #384
4-4-0	#119 American	Bal				70	98/2	235	200	See Note #1403
4-4-0	#119 American	PFM	United		290	68	90	235	200	See Note #384
4-4-0	#119 American	PFM	United		500	71	100	260	235	See Note #384
4-4-0	#119 American	Bal				70	60	235	200	

Union Pacific Railroad (cont'd)

Union Pacific's first Mikes were ordered to handle passenger service in the mountains. These engines (#500–549), bought in 1911, set the stage for later purchases, until the UP had over 370 Mikes on the roster at one time or another. Mike #2001 was part of an order of 35 engines (#2000–2034) built by Baldwin in 1911–12. With 57-inch drivers, she was not designed for speed but for power. The long smoke box, small domes, and large cab provide clear evidence that this was a Harriman road engine. When the 2–10–2's and the 4–10–2's arrived, most of the Mikes were bumped down to local freights. Still, many survived well into the 1940s, performing yeoman service on troop trains and other war-related freight duties. The model pictured was imported by Balboa in 1966 as part of their "Master Series."

| Whyte Class | Owner Class & Type | Model Production | | | | | List Price | Resale | | Remarks |
		Importer	Builder	Cat #	Quan.	Yrs.		Mint	Avg.	
4-4-0	#119 American	Bal				71	142/2	530	480	fp., See Note #1403
4-4-2	A-2 Atlantic	WMC	Goto	MO-39	1576	73-74	120	160	140	
4-6-0	#1242 Ten Wheeler	Sun	Samh	HO-53	500	78	150	180	160	See Note #418
4-6-2	Pacific	WMC				69	70	200	180	#2860-2911
4-6-2	#2906 Pacific	CustB	DaiYng	ST-869	175	84	515	470	450	See Note #419
4-6-2	P77 Pacific	OMI	Rok-Am	1400	550	77	164			Oil Burner
4-6-2	P77 Pacific	OMI	Rok-Am	1400	50	77	193			Coal Burner
4-6-2	P77 Pacific	OMI	Ajin	1481	150	89	500	470		See Note #1413
4-6-2	P77 Pacific	OMI	Ajin	1479	150	89	500	470		See Note #1414
4-6-2	P77 Pacific	OMI	Ajin	1480	100	89	514	490		#2906 Streamlined
4-8-2	#7000 Mountain	WMC	KTM			81	345		235	
4-8-2	#7000 Mountain	PSC	KTM	15135		84	435			Cab Detail
4-8-2	#7000 Mountain	PFM	Atlas/Nakayama	H	12	62	147	5000		See Note #1203
4-8-2	#7000 Mountain	Bal	KTM			66-68	60-70	260	235	Coal Version
4-8-2	#7002 Mountain	Bal	KTM			71	110	560	470	See Note #420
4-8-2	#7002 Mountain	Bal	KTM			71	150	820	705	fp. Streamlined
4-8-2	#7002 Mountain	Key	KTM			86	529	975		fp. Streamlined
4-8-2	#7850 Mountain	WMC	KTM	MO-84A	275	77	220	235	210	Young Valve Gear
4-8-2	#7850 Mountain	WMC	KTM	MO-84	499	77	220	260	235	See Note #421
4-8-4	Northern	PFM	Tensh	CR	28	57	125	1880	1645	
4-8-4	Northern	PFM	Tensh	CR	3	56	97	1880	1645	
4-8-4	FEF-1 Northern	PFM	United		150	81	780	690	490	See Note #423
4-8-4	FEF-1 Northern	PFM	Atlas/Asahi	P	2	75	285	330	320	#800-819
4-8-4	FEF-1 Northern	PFM	Atlas/Asahi	P	600	74	285	320	290	#800-819
4-8-4	FEF-1 Northern	PFM	Atlas/Asahi	P	600	76	285	350	330	#800-819
4-8-4	FEF-1 Northern	PFM	Atlas/Tetsudo	H	4	56	97	2820	2585	See Note #422
4-8-4	FEF-2 Northern	PFM	Toby	CR	100	64	125	1880	1410	See Note #1404
4-8-4	FEF-2 Northern	Key	Samh		50	83	515		490	detailed smokebox interior
4-8-4	FEF-2 Northern	PFM	Toby	CR	35	59	125	820	705	See Note #1950
4-8-4	FEF-2 Northern	PFM	Toby	CR	100	62	125	1880	1410	See Note #1404
4-8-4	FEF-2 Northern	Key				91	965	1000		fp., See Note #1405
4-8-4	FEF-2 Northern	Key				91	965	1000		fp., See Note #1406
4-8-4	FEF-2 Northern	PFM	Toby	CR	50	58	125	1410	1290	See Note #424

Union Pacific Railroad (cont'd)

Some of the most attractive, and certainly well-known, engines of the UP were the FEF-3 Class 4-8-4's. The last series of 4-8-4's built for the UP were 1944 Alco products. Dimensionally identical to the previous FEF-2 series these engines were designed to operate at 90 mph, with a top speed of 110 mph. With a large and roomy cab, elephant ears, and good proportions, these engines were as handsome as they were powerful. Some sported a two-tone gray paint scheme that beautifully complemented the passenger consist. Even in the black paint with silver trim these engines were striking. Engine #844, renumbered #8444, still exists and is occasionally used in fan-trip service. Westside imported this Katsumi, built model in 1976.

Whyte Class	Owner Class & Type	Model Production					List Price	Resale		Remarks
		Importer	Builder	Cat #	Quan.	Yrs.		Mint	Avg.	
4-8-4	FEF-2 Northern	WMC	KTM	MO-46	1007	75	170	290	260	See Note #1412
4-8-4	FEF-3 Northern	Key	Samh		75	83	550			#8444; Super Classic
4-8-4	FEF-3 Northern	Key				91	965	1000		fp., See Note #1407
4-8-4	FEF-3 Northern	WMC	KTM	MO-46	1007	75	170	260	250	See Note #1408
4-8-4	FEF-3 Northern	WMC	KTM	MO-46	800	76	200	280	260	See Note #1409
4-8-4	FEF-3 Northern	Key	Samh		50	83	515			See Note #1410
4-8-4	FEF-3 Northern	MGray				64	80	350	290	w/o Smoke Lifters
4-8-4	FEF-3 Northern	MGray				64	82	390	320	Smoke Lifters
4-8-4	FEF-3 Northern	OMI		1535						w/auxiliary tender
4-8-4	FEF-3 Northern	Key	Samh		75	84	590			fp.; #8444; Super Classic
4-10-2	#5090 Overland	OMI	DongJ	1408	500	78	254	290	235	2-cylinder rebuild
4-10-2	#8000 Overland	LMB				78	300		280	
4-10-2	#8000 Overland	LMB			150	66	100	320	260	3-cylinder
4-10-2	#8000 Overland	WMC	KTM	MO-24	670	71	100	320	290	See Note #425
4-12-2	#9000 Union Pacific	Key	Samh		5	84	529	800		See Note #1411
4-12-2	#9000 Union Pacific	Key	Samh		80	89	788	920		fp., as delivered
4-12-2	#9000 Union Pacific	Key	Samh		80	84	529	675		See Note #1415
4-12-2	#9000 Union Pacific	Key	Samh		75	84				fp., See Note #1416
4-12-2	#9013 Union Pacific	PFM	Atlas	H	1	56	164	3300		
4-12-2	#9013 Union Pacific	Key	Samh		55	89	788	950		fp., "Bald Face"
4-12-2	#9000 Union Pacific	MBA			12	59	150	800	705	fp.
4-12-2	#9000 Union Pacific	Key	Samh		75	84				fp., See Note #1417
4-12-2	#9000 Union Pacific	LMB	KMT			62-67	130	350	235	See Note #1418
4-12-2	#9000 Union Pacific	Key	Samh		75	84	579			fp., See Note #1419
4-12-2	#9000 Union Pacific	Key	Samh		5	84	507			See Note #1419
4-12-2	#9000 Union Pacific	Key	Samh		75	84		740		fp., See Note #1415
4-12-2	#9000 Union Pacific	Sun	Samh	HO-18	600	78	228	380	320	See Note #1420
4-6-6-4	Challenger	Imp						430		fp., wood box
4-6-6-4	Challenger	Key	Samh			93	1630			fp., See Note #1426
4-6-6-4	Challenger	Key	Samh			93	1520			unpainted
4-6-6-4	Challenger	Key	Samh			93	1660			fp., See Note #1421
4-6-6-4	Challenger	Key	Samh			93	1630			fp., See Note #1427
4-6-6-4	Challenger	Key	Samh			93	1520			unpainted
4-6-6-4	Challenger	Key	Samh			93	1630			fp., See Note #1424
4-6-6-4	Challenger	Key	Samh			93	1630			fp., See Note #1423
4-6-6-4	Challenger	LMB				60	95		350	

Union Pacific Railroad (cont'd)

Whyte Class	Owner Class & Type	Model Production					List Price	Resale		Remarks
		Importer	Builder	Cat #	Quan.	Yrs.		Mint	Avg.	
4-6-6-4	Challenger	OLEX				60	72	350	260	See Note #428
4-6-6-4	Challenger	PFM	Atlas	H	1	54				Handbuilt
4-6-6-4	Challenger	Sun	SMI	HO116A	200	90	543			coal
4-6-6-4	Challenger	Imp						380		velvet box
4-6-6-4	Challenger	Key	Samh		40	89	1225			See Note #1432
4-6-6-4	Challenger	Key	Samh			93	1660			fp., See Note #1431
4-6-6-4	Challenger	Sun	SMI	HO116B	200	90	543			oil
4-6-6-4	#3700 Challenger	Key	Samh		10	84	786		750	Coal
4-6-6-4	#3700 Challenger	Key	Samh		20	85	786			Coal
4-6-6-4	#3700 Challenger	Key	Samh		75	80	500	530	470	Coal; modernized
4-6-6-4	#3700 Challenger	Key	Samh		55	84	857		810	fp., Coal
4-6-6-4	#3700 Challenger	Key	Samh		100	80	500	530	470	Oil, modernized
4-6-6-4	#3800 Challenger	Key	Samh		200	80	500	530	470	Oil Version
4-6-6-4	#3800 Challenger	Key	Samh		15	84	786		750	Oil
4-6-6-4	#3800 Challenger	PFM	Tensh #114	CR	7	56	117	1900		See Note #427
4-6-6-4	#3800 Challenger	PFM	Tensh #114	CR	6	57		2000		See Note #1949
4-6-6-4	#3800 Challenger	PFM	Tensh #114	CR	2	55	90	2100		See Note #427
4-6-6-4	#3800 Challenger	PFM	Tensh #114	CR		59	143	2000		See Note #427
4-6-6-4	#3800 Challenger	Sat				60's	85	440	380	All drivers powered
4-6-6-4	#3800 Challenger	Sat				60's	85	440	380	All drivers powered
4-6-6-4	#3800 Challenger	Sat				60's	99	470	410	fp., All drivers powered
4-6-6-4	#3800 Challenger	Key	Samh		65	84	857		810	fp., Oil
4-6-6-4	#3800 Challenger	Key	Samh		200	80	500	530	470	Coal fired
4-6-6-4	#3800 Challenger	Key	Samh		50	87	893	840		Coasting drive
4-6-6-4	#3800 Challenger	MBA		CSA-1	30	58	85	410	350	See Note #1428
4-6-6-4	#3800 Challenger	Sat				60's	99	470	410	fp., All dvrs. pwd.
4-6-6-4	#3900 Challenger	Imp								
4-6-6-4	#3900 Challenger	Key	Samh		100	'82				#3977 Oil Version
4-6-6-4	#3900 Challenger	Key	Samh		25	85	810		780	Oil version
4-6-6-4	#3900 Challenger	Key	Samh		50	82	713		650	#3895 Coal Version
4-6-6-4	#3900 Challenger	Key	Samh		50	82	713	760	650	#3985 coal version
4-6-6-4	#3900 Challenger	PFM	Tensh #114	LP	150	62	180	1050		See Note #429
4-6-6-4	#3900 Challenger	PFM	Tensh #114	LP	300	73	425	950		See Note #430
4-6-6-4	#3900 Challenger	PFM	Tensh			83	1597			fp. two-tone gray
4-6-6-4	#3900 Challenger	PFM	Tensh #114	LP	300	75	585	1175		See Note #431
4-6-6-4	#3900 Challenger	PFM	Tensh #114	LP	305	63	180	1000		See Note #429
4-6-6-4	#3967 Challenger	Key	Samh		40	85	857		850	fp., See Note #1422
4-6-6-4	#3977 Challenger	Key	Samh		25	85	900		870	See Note #1425
4-6-6-4	#3978 Challenger	Key	Samh		25	85	900		870	See Note #1429
4-6-6-4	#3988 Challenger	Key	Samh		25	85	857		850	fp., See Note #1430
4-8-8-4	Big Boy	Sun		HO117A		90	543	520		early version
4-8-8-4	Big Boy	Sun	SMI	HO117A	200	90	543			early version
4-8-8-4	Big Boy	Sun	SMI	HO117B	200	90	543			late version
4-8-8-4	Big Boy	Sun		HO117B		90	543	520		late version
4-8-8-4	#4000 Big Boy	Gem	Olympia	RS-102	10	61		1120		See Note #1440 & 435
4-8-8-4	#4000 Big Boy	Gem	Olympia	RS-102	25	62		1175		See Note #1440 & 435
4-8-8-4	#4000 Big Boy	Gem	Olympia	EH-102	300	63		975		See Note #435
4-8-8-4	#4000 Big Boy	Gem	Olympia	RS-102	13	63		1940		See Note #1440 & 435
4-8-8-4	#4000 Big Boy	Gem	Olympia	RS-102	6	64		1940		See Note #1437 & 435
4-8-8-4	#4000 Big Boy	Gem	Olympia	EH-102	4	65		975		See Note #435
4-8-8-4	#4000 Big Boy	Gem	Olympia	EH-102P	50	67	225	650	590	fp., See Note #435
4-8-8-4	#4000 Big Boy	Key	Samh		100	80	712	700	650	fp., #4020 Class
4-8-8-4	#4000 Big Boy	Key	Samh		100	81	720	700		#4000 as delivered
4-8-8-4	#4000 Big Boy	Key	Samh		100	81	720	730	670	See Note #445
4-8-8-4	#4000 Big Boy	Key	Samh		50	83	830	760		See Note #1441
4-8-8-4	#4000 Big Boy	Key	Samh			92	1680	1600		fp., See Note #1435
4-8-8-4	#4000 Big Boy	Key	Samh			92	1680	1600		fp., See Note #1436
4-8-8-4	#4000 Big Boy	Key	Samh			92	1680	1600		fp., See Note #1438
4-8-8-4	#4000 Big Boy	LMB				61	170	500	440	
4-8-8-4	#4000 Big Boy	MBA			50	61	185	530	470	
4-8-8-4	#4000 Big Boy	PFM	Tensh #126	H	8	55	123	2600		See Note #433
4-8-8-4	#4000 Big Boy	PFM	Tensh #126	H	6	56	154	2470		See Note #433
4-8-8-4	#4000 Big Boy	PFM	Tensh #126	H	11	57	154	2350		See Note #433
4-8-8-4	#4000 Big Boy	PFM	Tensh #126	H	30	58	154	2250		See Note #1433

Union Pacific Railroad (cont'd)

The Union Pacific was the only American railroad to own the 4–12–2 wheel arrangement. These huge engines, known as "9000s" were built to replace aging Mallets between Ogden, Utah, and Cheyenne, Wyoming. Distinctive not only in their unusual wheel arrangement, they also were 3–cylinder engines with Gresley valve gear. The last order of these Alco-built monsters (#9078–9087) was delivered with one-piece integral cast cylinders and frame, Duplex stokers, and Worthington Type SA feedwater heaters. This beautiful Samhongsa-built model of #9081 faithfully captures the correct detail for this version of a truly unique engine. Key imported this and several other versions of the "9000s" in 1984.

The Union Pacific initiated the 4–6–6–4 "Challenger" wheel arrangement. Experiments with large rigid-frame locos (the famous 4–12–2) convinced UP management that the performance they wanted couldn't be gotten without articulation. The first Challengers built by Alco proved to be quite successful. These engines proved to be test beds for many new ideas and modifications that led to several design improvements culminating in the 1942 order for 20 locos (#3950–3969) from Alco. These engines made no compromises and incorporated the state-of-the-art in steam locomotive design. These engines proved so successful that several roads duplicated the design. Pacific Fast Mail imported this Tenshodo-built limited production model in 1962.

Whyte Class	Owner Class & Type	Model Production					List Price	Resale		Remarks
		Importer	Builder	Cat #	Quan.	Yrs.		Mint	Avg.	
4-8-8-4	#4000 Big Boy	PFM	Tensh #126	CR	136	59	178	1400		See Note #437
4-8-8-4	#4000 Big Boy	PFM	Tensh #126	CR	300	61	188	1050		See Note #438
4-8-8-4	#4000 Big Boy	PFM	Tensh #126	CR	156	62	188	760	705	See Note #438
4-8-8-4	#4000 Big Boy	PFM	Tensh #126	CR	150	63	188	790	730	See Note #438
4-8-8-4	#4000 Big Boy	PFM	Tensh #126	CR	50	65	188	820	760	See Note #1434
4-8-8-4	#4000 Big Boy	PFM	Tensh #126	CR	100	66	188	850	790	See Note #1439 & 439
4-8-8-4	#4000 Big Boy	PFM	Tensh #126	CR	100	67	188	910	850	See Note #440
4-8-8-4	#4000 Big Boy	PFM	Tensh #126	CR	150	69	225	940	880	fp.
4-8-8-4	#4000 Big Boy	PFM	Tensh #126	CR	10	70	225	1700	1470	See Note #441
4-8-8-4	#4000 Big Boy	PFM	Tensh #126	CR	300	72	345	1060	940	See Note #442

Union Pacific Railroad (cont'd)

Whyte Class	Owner Class & Type	Model Production					List Price	Resale		Remarks
		Importer	Builder	Cat #	Quan.	Yrs.		Mint	Avg.	
4-8-8-4	#4000 Big Boy	PFM	Tensh #126	CR	190	77	1085	1175	1060	See Note #443
4-8-8-4	#4000 Big Boy	PFM	Tensh			82	1395	1175		
4-8-8-4	#4020 Big Boy	Key	Samh		50	83	830		760	See Note #1441

United States Railroad Administration (USRA)

Whyte Class	Owner Class & Type	Model Production					List Price	Resale		Remarks
		Importer	Builder	Cat #	Quan.	Yrs.		Mint	Avg.	
0-6-0	Switcher	Intl				52	18	130	90	See Note #446
0-6-0	Switcher	MBA				60	30			
0-6-0	Switcher	Gem	Akane	AK-201	26	64		130		
0-6-0	Switcher	NWSL	Rok-Am	54-1		79	150	160	150	See Note #451 & 452
0-6-0	Switcher	Intl				59	35	130	100	
0-6-0	Switcher	NWSL	Rok-Am	55-1		80	190	180	160	See Note #451 & 452
0-6-0	Switcher	Akane	Akane			29-33	130	100		See Note #450
0-6-0	Switcher	Aristo				57	30	120	80	fp.
0-6-0	Switcher	Gem	Akane	AK-201	12	63	20	120	90	See Note #1492
0-6-0	Switcher	Intl				59	25			Kit
0-6-0	Switcher	Alco	Kobra	S-101	500	76	125	140	120	See Note #446
0-6-0	Switcher	NWSL	Rok-Am	54-1	800	76	135-140	160	150	See Note #452
0-8-0	Switcher	Gem	Akane	325	39	63	48	170	120	
0-8-0	Switcher	Gem	Akane	FM-203	200	64				
0-8-0	Switcher	Gem	Akane	FM-203	100	64		220	190	
0-8-0	Switcher	Gem	Akane	FM-203	100	64		200	190	Southern
0-8-0	Switcher	Gem	Akane	325	36	64		170		
0-8-0	Switcher	Gem	Akane	FM-203	100	64		200	180	NYC
0-8-0	Switcher	Gem	Akane	FM-203	1	67	50	220	190	CB&Q Version
0-8-0	Switcher	Gem	Akane	FM-203	10	67	50	220	190	
0-8-0	Switcher	PFM	Tensh	H	1	55				
0-8-0	Switcher	PFM	Tensh #133	P	406	56	40	160	130	fp.
0-8-0	Switcher	PFM	Tensh #233	P	251	56	30	140	120	Kit
0-8-0	Switcher	PFM	Tensh #133	P	285	57	35	150	130	
0-8-0	Switcher	PFM	Tensh #233	P	150	58	30	140	120	Kit
0-8-0	Switcher	PFM	Tensh #133	P	245	58	35	150	130	
0-8-0	Switcher	PFM	Tensh #233	P	125	59	30	150	120	Kit
0-8-0	Switcher	PFM	Tensh #133	P	295	59	35	160	140	
0-8-0	Switcher	PFM	Tensh #133	P	310	60	35	160	140	
0-8-0	Switcher	PFM	Tensh #233	P	100	60	30	150	130	Kit
0-8-0	Switcher	PFM	Tensh #133	P	198	61	35	160	140	
0-8-0	Switcher	PFM	Tensh #133	P	102	62	35	160	150	
0-8-0	Switcher	PFM	Tensh #133	P	225	62	40	180	160	See Note #453
0-8-0	Switcher	PFM	Tensh #233	P	35	62	30	150	130	Kit
0-8-0	Switcher	PFM	Tensh #133	P	200	63	45	180	160	See Note #453
0-8-0	Switcher	Gem	Akane	FM-203	2	67	50	200	180	NYC
0-8-0	Switcher	Alco	Kobra	S-102		77	135	160	150	
0-8-0	Switcher	Gem	Akane	FM-203	1	76	50	210	190	Southern
0-8-0	Switcher	PFM	Tensh #233	P	195	57	30	140	120	Kit
2-8-2	Light Mikado	Akane	Akane			63	52	180	160	See Note #1445
2-8-2	Light Mikado	Akane	Akane			64	55	180	160	See Note #1445
2-8-2	Light Mikado	Gem	Akane	415	50	63		210		See Note #1445
2-8-2	Light Mikado	Gem	Akane	415	44	64		210		See Note #1445
2-8-2	Light Mikado	Gem	Akane	FM-208	25	65		210		See Note #1445
2-8-2	Light Mikado	Key	Samh		100	77	160	210	190	See Note #1443
2-8-2	Light Mikado	Key	Samh		100	77	160	220	200	GTW
2-8-2	Light Mikado	Key	Samh		100	77	160	210	190	NYC
2-8-2	Light Mikado	Key	Samh		100	77	160	210	190	UP
2-8-2	Light Mikado	Key	Samh		100	78	200	220	200	See Note #1444
2-8-2	Light Mikado	Key	Samh		150	78	200	220	200	Southern MS-1
2-8-2	Light Mikado	OLEX				60	30	180	130	fp.
2-8-2	Light Mikado	PFM	Atlas/Kawai	H	1	56				See Note #454
2-8-2	Light Mikado	PFM	Atlas/Kawai	H	1	58	140			See Note #454
2-8-2	Light Mikado	PFM	Atlas/Asahi	P	440	62	50	260	210	See Note #455

United States Railroad Administration (cont'd)

Whyte Class	Owner Class & Type	Model Production					List Price	Resale		Remarks
		Importer	Builder	Cat #	Quan.	Yrs.		Mint	Avg.	
2-8-2	Light Mikado	PFM	Atlas/Asahi	P	500	63	50	280	250	See Note #455 & 570
2-8-2	Light Mikado	PFM	Atlas/Asahi	P	155	64	50	280	250	See Note #455 & 570
2-8-2	Light Mikado	PFM	Atlas/Asahi	P	230	66	55	280	250	See Note #455 & 570
2-8-2	Light Mikado	PFM	Atlas/Asahi	P	600	77	325	350	290	See Note #456
2-8-2	Heavy Mikado	Akane	Akane			64	55	200	160	See Note #1445
2-8-2	Heavy Mikado	Gem	Akane	425	67	64		220		See Note #1445
2-8-2	Heavy Mikado	OMI	JPMod	1425	95	80	296	295	260	
2-8-2	Heavy Mikado	Gem	Akane	FM-209	2	65		210		See Note #1445
2-8-2	Heavy Mikado	Sun	ThaHwa	HO64H	300	87	143	140		
2-10-2	Light Santa Fe	Gem	Akane	FM-212		68	75	290		
2-10-2	Light Santa Fe	Sun	ThaHwa			88	180	180		
2-10-2	Light Santa Fe	Key	Samh		100	78	210	235	200	See Note #1446
2-10-2	Light Santa Fe	Key	Samh		100	78	210	250	220	See Note #457
2-10-2	Light Santa Fe	Key	Samh		100	78	210	235	210	Southern
2-10-2	Heavy Santa Fe	Gem	Akane	FM-213	12	67	60-75	290	260	
2-10-2	Heavy Santa Fe	Gem	Akane	475	24	64		280	260	
2-10-2	Heavy Santa Fe	Key	Samh		250	78	170	210	190	
2-10-2	Heavy Santa Fe	Akane	Akane			63	70	270	260	
2-10-2	Heavy Santa Fe	Gem	Akane	475	58	63		280	260	
2-10-2	Heavy Santa Fe	Gem	Akane	FM-213	150	65			260	
2-10-2	Heavy Santa Fe	Sun	ThaHwa			88	180	180		
2-6-6-2	Articulated	Akane	Akane			63-64	90	380	340	See Note #1447
2-6-6-2	Articulated	Intl	Takara			59	60	350	260	IMP-Takara Label
2-6-6-2	Articulated	Akane	Akane			59	45	260	235	
2-6-6-2	Articulated	Gem	Akane	500	22	64		400		See Note #1447
2-6-6-2	Articulated	Key	Samh		75	81	557	760	730	Canon motor, full cab detail
2-6-6-2	Articulated	Akane	Akane			62	70	260	235	See Note #434
2-6-6-2	Articulated	Intl	Takara			59	55			Kit; IMP-Takara Label
2-6-6-2	Articulated	Gem	Akane	500	60	63		400		See Note #1447
2-6-6-2	Articulated	Gem	Akane	FM-215	96	64				See Note #1447
2-8-8-2	USA Articulated	CustB	Goto	ST-291	125	79	768	820	760	Royale Series; VGN version
2-8-8-2	Articulated	Gem	Akane	FM-216	6	67	120	670	470	See Note #436

The United States Railway Administration was roundly criticized for its operation of the American railroad system during World War I. But one thing it couldn't be criticized for was its excellent steam locomotive designs of that period. Several different wheel arrangements were designed, most in light and heavy versions, which shared a variety of common design elements and parts. This design philosophy provided for easy maintenance and reduced costs of construction and repair. Almost every major railroad in the U.S. had some USRA designed locomotives on the roster. In the mid 1960s, Gem Models began importing Akane-built models of of a variety of USRA steam locomotives. This was the first time any importer/builder had comprehensively covered the USRA roster. The USRA heavy 2–10–2 is an excellent example of the quality models Akane was producing at that time.

United States Railroad Administration (cont'd)

The USRA 0–8–0 became the standard design for heavy steam switchers. This well-balanced design shared many appliances and parts with the other USRA designs, allowing railroads to more efficiently manage parts inventories and service their locomotives quickly. By 1953 over 1,200 0–8–0's of the USRA design had been built for U.S. railroads. In fact, the very last steam locomotive built for U.S. service was built by the N&W and was the USRA 0–8–0. In 1968, Gem Models began importing a series of Akane-built USRA designs. The quality of these models was significantly improved over previous USRA imports.

Whyte Class	Owner Class & Type	Model Production					List Price	Resale		Remarks
		Importer	Builder	Cat #	Quan.	Yrs.		Mint	Avg.	
2-8-8-2	Articulated	Gem	Akane	FM-216	220	64		670	470	See Note #436
4-6-2	Light Pacific	PFM	Atlas/Asahi	P	350	68	60	220	200	
4-6-2	Light Pacific	PFM	Atlas/Asahi	P	455	62	50	200	180	See Note #459
4-6-2	Light Pacific	PFM	Atlas/Asahi	P	165	65	55	220	190	
4-6-2	Light Pacific	PFM	Atlas/Asahi	P	250	63	50	210	180	See Note #570
4-6-2	Light Pacific	PFM	Atlas/Asahi	S	1	63				See Note #7
4-6-2	Light Pacific	Key	Samh		175	79	266	270	235	
4-6-2	Light Pacific	Sun				87	143	140		
4-6-2	Heavy Pacific	MGray	KTM			62	58	290	235	Erie K-5
4-6-2	Heavy Pacific	Akane	Akane			63	52	200	160	4-wheel tender trucks
4-6-2	Heavy Pacific	Akane	Akane			63	52	210	180	4-Wheel Trucks
4-6-2	Heavy Pacific	Gem	Akane	375	64	64		200		See Note#1449
4-6-2	Heavy Pacific	Key	Samh		100	80	315		300	Erie K-5
4-6-2	Heavy Pacific	Key	Samh		250	80		400		fp., Erie K-5
4-6-2	Heavy Pacific	Akane	Akane			64	55	235	190	See Note #460
4-6-2	Heavy Pacific	Akane	Akane			64	55	235	190	See Note #460
4-6-2	Heavy Pacific	Gem	Akane	375	64	63		200		See Note#1449
4-6-2	Heavy Pacific	Sun				87	157	150		
4-8-2	Light Mountain	Gem	Akane	FM-210	36	65		260	220	See Note #1445
4-8-2	Light Mountain	Key	Samh		100	81	335	380	350	
4-8-2	Light Mountain	Gem	Akane	440	50	63		260	220	See Note #1445
4-8-2	Light Mountain	Akane	Akane			64	63	260	220	See Note #1445
4-8-2	Light Mountain	Gem	Akane	440	59	64		260	220	See Note #1445
4-8-2	Light Mountain	Sun	ThaHwa	HO91L	500	87	157	150		
4-8-2	Heavy Mountain	Gem	Akane	450	17	64		280		
4-8-2	Heavy Mountain	Sun	ThaHwa	HO91H		87	157	150		
4-8-2	Heavy Mountain	Gem	Akane	450	32	63		280		
4-8-2	Heavy Mountain	Key·	Samh		200	78	190		200	
4-8-2	Heavy Mountain	Akane	Akane	AK-21		63	60	270	200	

Virginian Railway

Whyte Class	Owner Class & Type	Model Production					List Price	Resale		Remarks
		Importer	Builder	Cat #	Quan.	Yrs.		Mint	Avg.	
0-8-0	C-16 Switcher	W&R	Samh			37	88	492	470		fp. #240-254; also C&O
0-8-0	C-16 Switcher	W&R	Samh			37	88				#240-254; also C&O

Virginian Railway (cont'd)

The Virginian Railway was one of the most interesting coal haulers in the East. With a mixture of big steam, 2–8–8–2, 2–6–6–6's, and modern 2–8–4's, the Virginian was frequently photographed. Even with all this big power, the largest single class of locomotives was the Mb Class 2–8–2. Fairly small when compared to other roads' 2–8–2's of that time period, the Mb's provided coal mine and branch line service. Overland Models imported this fine replica from Ajin Precision in 1988. This model is especially interesting in that the valve rod linkage operates as does the prototype, a detail that is all too frequently omitted on models.

The Virginian's 2–6–6–6's were not identical copies of C&O's engines but used different tenders, small sand domes, and were somewhat lighter than the C&O engines. Ajin Precision of Korea produced the Virginian and C&O versions of this engine in 1992. This is the first model of a Blue Ridge with the correct sand domes.

Whyte Class	Owner Class & Type	Model Production					List Price	Resale		Remarks
		Importer	Builder	Cat #	Quan.	Yrs.		Mint	Avg.	
2-8-2	Mb Mikado	OMI	Ajin	1428	200	88	485	460	390	#420-461
2-8-4	BA Berkshire	Key	Samh		30	85	485	460		fp. #505
2-8-4	BA Berkshire	Key	Samh		50	83	414	410		
2-8-8-0	AF Articulated	WMC	Samh			79	395	500	440	See Note #472
2-8-8-2	USA Articulated	CustB	Goto	ST-291		79	668			see Note #473
2-8-8-2	USE Articulated	CustB	Goto	ST-913	30	82	1100		870	See Note #474
2-8-8-2	USD Articulated	CustB	Goto	ST-948	30	85	998		940	Royale, fp., two motors
2-6-6-6	AG Alleghany	Gem	Akane	IM-109	100	64	150	530	430	See Note #1551
2-6-6-6	AG Alleghany	Akane	Akane					530	430	See Note #1551
2-6-6-6	AG Alleghany	Key	Samh		75	81	685			See Note #1552
2-6-6-6	AG Alleghany	OMI	Ajin	1540.1		92				fp.
2-10-10-2	AE Articulated	CustB	KMT	ST-826	200	79	675	950		#800-809
2-8-8-8-2	Xa Triplex	PSC	Samh	15354			629			
2-8-8-8-4	Xa Triplex	WMC				79	950			See Note #475

Virginia & Truckee Railroad

Whyte Class	Owner Class & Type	Model Production					List Price	Resale		Remarks
		Importer	Builder	Cat #	Quan.	Yrs.		Mint	Avg.	
2-6-0	#20 Mogul	MEW				71	70	235	200	"Tahoe", NMRA rev. 5/70
2-6-0	#20 Mogul	MEW		402		69	63	210	180	See Note #469
2-6-0	#26 Mogul	BCM	Samh					590	640	
4-4-0	#11 American	PFM	Atlas		1	55				"Reno" original
4-4-0	#11 American	PFM	Atlas/Asahi	P	150	63	30	160	140	"Reno" original
4-4-0	#11 American	PFM	Atlas/Asahi	P	200	62	30	160	140	"Reno" original
4-4-0	#11 American	PFM	Atlas/Asahi	S	1	62				"Reno" orig., See Note #7
4-4-0	#11 American	PFM	Atlas/Asahi	P	120	59	30	160	140	See Note # 1553
4-4-0	#11 American	PFM	Atlas/Asahi	P	365	65	35	160	150	"Reno" original
4-4-0	#11 American	PFM	Atlas/Asahi	P	692	59	30	150	130	See Note # 470
4-4-0	#11 American	PFM	Atlas/Asahi	P	385	68	43	180	160	"Reno" original
4-4-0	#11 American	PFM	Atlas/Asahi	P	285	66	35	170	160	"Reno" original
4-4-0	#11 American	PFM	Atlas/Asahi	P	385	68	43	180	160	"Reno" modern
4-4-0	#11 American	PFM	Atlas/Asahi	P	490	60	30	150	140	See Note # 470
4-4-0	#11 American	PFM	Atlas/Asahi	P	190	64	30	160	150	"Reno" original
4-4-0	#12 American	Intl				52	15	130	100	"Genoa"
4-4-0	#12 American	KenK				58	24	160	130	"Genoa"
4-6-0	Ten-Wheeler	Sun	GangSan	HO93	200	87	200	200		#25
4-6-0	Ten-Wheeler	GHB				89	270	210		See Note #1556
4-6-0	Ten-Wheeler	Key	Samh		50	86	429	400		#25, fp.
4-6-0	Ten-Wheeler	Key	Samh		200	86	329	330		#25
4-6-0	#26 Ten Wheeler	PFM	Atlas/KTM	P	230	58	34	180	150	
4-6-0	#26 Ten Wheeler	PFM	Atlas/KTM	P	465	60	38	190	160	
4-6-0	#26 Ten Wheeler	PFM	Atlas/KTM	P	260	59	35	180	160	
4-6-0	#26 Ten Wheeler	WMC	KTM	MO-13	460	68	45	190	160	See Note #1554
4-6-0	#26 Ten Wheeler	PFM	Atlas/KTM	P	1	55				
4-6-0	#26 Ten Wheeler	PFM	Atlas/KTM	P	268	57	34	170	150	

Wabash Railway

Whyte Class	Owner Class & Type	Model Production					List Price	Resale		Remarks
		Importer	Builder	Cat #	Quan.	Yrs.		Mint	Avg.	
0-6-0	B-7 Switcher	Hall	DongJ	HSO109	200	77	205		190	
2-6-0	F-4 Mogul	Intl				60	30	190	130	
2-6-0	F-4 Mogul	AHM		401		65	60	160	130	
2-10-2	L-1 Santa Fe	Sunset	Samh	HO-20	200	77	169	220	190	Worthington BL FWH
4-6-0	Ten Wheeler	OLEX				60	32	160	160	
4-6-2	J-1 Pacific	WMC	Nakamura	MO-70		76	150	190	170	fp. blue; See Note #1555
4-6-2	J-1 Pacific	WMC	Nakamura	MO-70		76	129	170	150	See Note #1555
4-6-2	J-1 Pacific	NPP	Nakamura		250	75	193	190	180	See Note #945
4-6-2	J-1 Pacific	NPP	Nakamura		250	75	193	180	160	See Note #1559
4-6-2	J-1 Pacific	WMC	Nakamura	MO-70		76	129	160	150	See Note #1560
4-6-2	J-1 Pacific	Soho	Nakamura	0640	100	78	120			See Note #1562
4-6-2	J-1 Pacific	WMC	Nakamura	MO-70		77	150	180	150	fp. blue; See Note #1560
4-6-4	P-1 Hudson	Hall	Ajin	HSO110	375	79	279	290	260	See Note #476
4-8-2	M-1 Mountain	PFM	Atlas/Sono	H	10	60	147	1880		See Note #1201
4-8-2	M-1 Mountain	Hall	DongJ		500	77	175	210	180	
4-8-4	O-1 Mountain	PFM	Tetsudo	H	1	56	125	3290	3055	Handbuilt

Western Maryland Railway

Whyte Class	Owner Class & Type	Model Production					List Price	Resale		Remarks
		Importer	Builder	Cat #	Quan.	Yrs.		Mint	Avg.	
2-8-0	H-8 Consol	CustB	KSM	ST-915A	75	82	382	425		As Built
2-8-0	H-8 Consol	CustB	KSM	ST-915B	125	82	382	350		See Note #1566
2-8-0	H-9 Consol	Ortl	Samh	0547		85	379	475		See Note #1563
2-8-0	H-9 Consol	Ortl	Samh	0548		85	379	475		See Note #1564
2-8-0	H-9 Consol	Ortl	Samh	P547		85	427	525		fp., See Note #1563
2-8-0	H-9 Consol	Ortl	Samh	P548		85	427	525		fp., See Note #1564
2-8-0	H-9 Consol	PFM	Atlas	H	1	55				
2-8-0	H-9 Consol	PFM	Samh	P	750	75	165	375		See Note #1565

Western Maryland Railway (cont'd)

The Russian government placed an order for 1,230 2–10–0 Decapods shortly before World War I. By 1918, the Russian revolution had put the country in turmoil and 200 engines remained undelivered. Most of these engines were ultimately purchased by American railroads from all parts of the country. The Western Maryland purchased ten of these engines and classified them as I–1's. Sunset Models imported this model in 1990 using the ''Prestige Series'' mark. Models in this series incorporate excellent mechanisms but have reduced detailing to keep the manufacturing costs down and thus make them affordable to a larger market.

The heaviest Consolidations ever produced were the 50 Western Maryland H–9 and H–9a 2–8–0's constructed by Baldwin in 1921 and 1923. Weighing 309,910 lbs. and exerting a tractive effort of 71.500 lbs., the H–9 was the largest loco, which could negotiate the curvature through the Blackwater Canyon, fighting to move loaded coal hoppers up the three percent Black Fork grade over the Alleghenies. The Pacific Fast Mail model shown was produced by Samhongsa in 1975. It is an excellent example of the quality of models that were beginning to emerge from the Korean builders during that time period.

Whyte Class	Owner Class & Type	Model Production					List Price	Resale		Remarks
		Importer	Builder	Cat #	Quan.	Yrs.		Mint	Avg.	
2-10-0	I-1 Decapod	CustB	DaiYng	ST-917	110	84	515	350		See Note #1567
2-10-0	I-1 Decapod	CustB	DaiYng	ST-898	250		375	575		
2-10-0	I-1 Decapod	Sun	SMI	HO120P	100	90	300	295		fp.
2-10-0	I-1 Decapod	Sun	SMI	HO120	100	90	250	250		
4-6-2	K-2 Pacific	Ortl		0494C		88	379	375		See Note #1568
4-6-2	K-2 Pacific	Ortl		0091	175	83				See Note #1569
4-6-2	K-2 Pacific	Ortl		P4940		88	450	450		fp., See Note #1570
4-6-2	K-2 Pacific	Ortl		04940		88	379	370		See Note #1570
4-6-2	K-2 Pacific	Ortl				83				See Note #1572
4-6-2	K-2 Pacific	Ortl		P494C		88	450	430		fp., See Note #1568

Western Maryland Railway (cont'd)

Whyte Class	Owner Class & Type	Model Production					List Price	Resale		Remarks
		Importer	Builder	Cat #	Quan.	Yrs.		Mint	Avg.	
4-8-4	J-1 Potomac	PCH	Daeki			86		440	350	same as NPP model
4-8-4	J-1 Potomac	NPP	Daeki		150	85	394	440	350	
4-8-4	J-1 Potomac	PFM	SKI	P	200	80	398	400	330	ref. MM 7/80
4-6-6-4	M-2 Challenger	CustB	DaiYng	ST-864	200	80	548	650	620	
4-6-6-4	M-2 Challenger	CustB	DaiYng	ST-864X		80	548	650	620	short rerun
3-Tk Shay	150 Ton Shay	Key	Samh							WM #6
3-Tk Shay	150 Ton Shay	PSC	KTM	15141		84	529	550	530	WM #6
3-Tk Shay	150 Ton Shay	WMC	KTM		[12		350	410	350	WM #6
3-Tk Shay	150 Ton Shay	PSC	KTM	15141.1		84	419			

Western Pacific Railroad (WP)

Whyte Class	Owner Class & Type	Model Production					List Price	Resale		Remarks
		Importer	Builder	Cat #	Quan.	Yrs.		Mint	Avg.	
0-6-0	S-31 Switcher	IHM/PSC	KSM			75	79	240	320	290	See Note #478
2-8-0	C-43 Consol	Sun	TaeHwa	HO66A	100	82	270		260	See Note #480
2-8-0	C-43 Consol	Sun	TaeHwa	HO66	100	82	270		260	See Note #479
2-8-2	MK-60 Mikado	PFM	United	P	401	71	92	260	235	#327-331
2-8-2	MK-60 Mikado	PFM	United	P	200	78	385	350	290	See Note #483
2-8-2	MK-60 Mikado	PFM	United	P	385	68	85	250	220	See Note #482
2-8-2	MK-60 Mikado	PFM	United	P	490	67	65	235	200	See Note #481
2-8-2	MK-60 Mikado	PFM	United	P		81	385	400	330	
2-8-2	MK-60 Mikado	PFM	United	P	505	74	195	290	260	#327-331
2-6-6-2	M-80 Articulated	Key	Samh		65	82	585		560	See Note #572
2-6-6-2	M-80 Articulated	Key	Samh		60	82	585		560	See Note #573
4-6-0	TP-29 Ten Wheeler	PFM	Tensh/Adachi	P	500	70	60	180	140	See Note #484
4-6-0	TP-29 Ten Wheeler	PFM	Tensh/Adachi	P	530	71	75	245	220	See Note #484
4-8-2	MT-44 Mountain	PFM	Atlas/Asahi	P	600	72	130	345	300	See Note #1574
4-8-4	GS-64 Northern	WMC	KTM			75	180	280	235	See Note #486
4-8-4	GS-64 Northern	WMC	KTM	M-183		81	513		440	See Note #485
4-6-6-4	M-100 Challenger	Key	Samh		150	82	607		590	fp. & lettered

In 1938, Western Pacific purchased seven Challengers from Alco that were almost identical to the Union Pacific engines. They spent most of their 12-year life hauling fast freight across the desert between Portola, Ca., and Salt Lake City, Utah. Solidly designed, these Challengers provided excellent service to the Western Pacific. Samhongsa, one of the premier builders in Korea, produced 150 of these excellent engines for Key Imports in 1982.

Wheeling & Lake Erie Railroad (W&LE)

Whyte Class	Owner Class & Type	Model Production					List Price	Resale		Remarks
		Importer	Builder	Cat #	Quan.	Yrs.		Mint	Avg.	
2-8-4	K-1 Berkshire	Key	Samh		40	83	414	440	410	#6400 Class
2-8-4	K-1 Berkshire	Key				93	1070			See Note #1575
2-8-4	K-1 Berkshire	Key				93	995			See Note #1580
4-8-2	J-1 Mountain	Sun	Samh	HO2A	300	76	142	260	235	ex. N&W K-3

Wilmington & Weldon Railway

Whyte Class	Owner Class & Type	Model Production					List Price	Resale		Remarks
		Importer	Builder	Cat #	Quan.	Yrs.		Mint	Avg.	
0-6-0	Switcher	MBA				60	25	170		

Yosemite Valley Railway

Whyte Class	Owner Class & Type	Model Production					List Price	Resale		Remarks
		Importer	Builder	Cat #	Quan.	Yrs.		Mint	Avg.	
2-6-0	#25 Mogul	BCM	Samh					510	470	
2-6-0	#26 Mogul	BCM	Samh					510	470	
2-6-0	#27 Mogul	BCM	Samh					660	590	
2-6-0	#28 Mogul	BCM	Samh					660	590	

Miscellaneous Steam Locomotives

Whyte Class	Owner Class & Type	Model Production					List Price	Resale		Remarks
		Importer	Builder	Cat #	Quan.	Yrs.		Mint	Avg.	
0-4-0T	Switcher	KenK		2101R		58-69	8-11	70	50	Plantation Loco
0-4-0T	Switcher	Prec				61	9	70	50	Plantation Loco
0-4-0T	Switcher	KenK		2114		65	14	90	60	Factory Loco
0-4-0T	Switcher	KenK		2101K		58-69	7-10	60	40	Plantation Loco, Kit
0-4-0T	Switcher	LMB		2101K		58-69	8	60	40	Plantation Loco, Kit
0-4-0T	Switcher	Lam				70	9	80	50	Plantation Loco
0-4-0T	Switcher	VTS			400	73	42			
0-4-0T	Switcher	FZoo				87	300	300	200	"Gypsy"
0-4-0T	Switcher	LMB		2101R	550	58-69	9-11	70	50	Plantation Loco #2
0-4-0	Switcher	LMB				59	70	120	90	
0-4-0	Switcher	Gem	Tsubomi	DH-126	39	76	75	140	120	See Note #489

Very early brass models of steam locomotives imported into this country were hand built by small groups of modelers in Japan. As such, they were often very crude and had little to recommend them except for a low price and the appeal of brass construction as opposed to the die-cast models available at the time. Probably the earliest Japanese brass model advertised in a national modeling magazine was the "Tootsie Roller" from International Models. With sand-cast drivers and no rivet detail, it wasn't much. The model shown above is a later version which has been improved with rivets, better driver centers, and finer turned parts. How far we have come!

Miscellaneous Steam Locomotives (cont'd)

Whyte Class	Owner Class & Type	Importer	Builder	Cat #	Quan.	Yrs.	List Price	Mint	Avg.	Remarks
0-4-0	Switcher	LMB		2102K		65	10	70	60	Kit; See Note #487
0-4-0	Switcher	Intl				58	95	120	90	
0-4-0	Switcher	LMB		2102R		65	11	80	60	See Note #487
0-4-0	Switcher	Intl				55	15	90	80	Camelback
0-4-0	Switcher	KenK		2102R		58	10-13	90	70	See Note #487
0-4-0	Switcher	LMB				58-59	60-70	120	90	
0-4-0	Switcher	KenK		2102K		58-59	9-12	80	60	Kit; See Note #487
0-4-0	Switcher	Intl				50	8	50	30	Kit, Mini-Roller
0-4-0	Switcher	MBA				59	8			See Note #487
0-4-0	Steam Dummy	KenK		3526		65	20	90	80	See Note #1578
0-4-0	Switcher	Key	KTM		200	85	186			See Note #1579
0-4-0	Switcher	LMB	KMT			60	11	70	50	See Note #491 & 0-6-0
0-4-0	Switcher	Prec	KMT			61	8	60	30	See Note #491 & 0-6-0
0-4-0	Switcher	KenK	KMT	2105K		59	11	70	50	See Note #491 & 0-6-0
0-4-2T	Switcher	Gem	Olympia	VL-2	200	60	125	150	130	Saddle Tank
0-4-2T	Switcher	Gem	Olympia	VL-1	150	60	20	120	100	fp., Saddle Tank
0-4-2T	Switcher	LMB				59	20	120	100	Saddle Tank
0-4-4T	Forney	MTSImp				90	285			See Note #1581
0-4-4T	Forney	MTSImp		029A		90	285			See Note #1582
0-6-0T	Switcher	PFM	Tensh			51-56	9	60	50	
0-6-0T	Switcher	F&G		35-RU			11			See Note #493
0-6-0T	Switcher	Intl		T.R.		49-50	11-13	90	60	See Note #1583
0-6-0T	Switcher	HOT							30	Tank Switcher
0-6-0T	Switcher	KenK							60	
0-6-0T	Switcher	MBA				59	13	80		cataloged
0-6-0T	Switcher	LMB				71	21	65	50	Side Tank
0-6-0	Switcher	AHM		L-5016		62	10	50	30	
0-6-2	Switcher	LMB				71	23	70	50	Side Tank
0-8-0T	Switcher	NWSL	Toby	2-1	1000	73	65	120	100	See Note #596
0-8-0T	Switcher	NWSL	Toby	2-1	500	65	17	100	90	See Note #596
0-4-4-0T	Articulated	KenK				64		120	90	Plantation Mallet

Not all favorites were replicas of specific prototype locomotives, some merely represented general types. Shown above is a 2–6–2 which PFM labeled the "Prairie King." It had the general look of turn-of-the-century Baldwin-built engines and is a favorite among modelers and collectors interested in this period of railroading. Atlas-Asahi (United) occasionally made these generic models combining parts from other prototypes into a plausible model. From 1959 through 1962, PFM imported over 1,450 of these interesting models.

Miscellaneous Steam Locomotives (cont'd)

Whyte Class	Owner Class & Type	Importer	Builder	Cat #	Quan.	Yrs.	List Price	Mint	Avg.	Remarks
0-4-4-0T	Articulated	Red	KMT		500	64	20	120	90	MR rev. 9/64
0-6-6-0	Articulated	WMC	KTM			79		330	290	See Note #490
0-6-6-0	Articulated	Aristo	KTM			58	65	290	235	Compound Mallet
2-4-2T	Columbia	Gem	Kumata	1001K	1198	59	7	80	40	See Note #494
2-4-2T	Columbia	Sun					53	110		Baldwin, Kit
2-4-4T	Forney	LMB	KMT		250	64	20	130	100	
2-4-4T	Forney	DiMo				64	25	120	90	MR rev. 7/64
2-4-2	Columbia	KenK		3524R		61	19	80	80	
2-4-2	Columbia	Prec				61	17	80	60	Kit; Baldwin
2-4-2	Columbia	LMB				61	19	120	90	Slope-Back Tender
2-4-2	Columbia	LMB				61	17			Kit
2-6-0T	Mogul	LMB						90	70	
2-6-0	Mogul	LMB				64	23	100	80	1880 Porter
2-6-0	Mogul	FED		2602HO		73	40	80	60	Spartan; Circa 1910
2-6-0	Mogul	Bal				70	30	150	110	Porter, fp.
2-6-0	Mogul	FED		2602HO		74	50	80	70	Spartan; Circa 1910
2-6-0	Mogul	Aristo				58	25	90	60	Old Time
2-6-0	Mogul	Intl	Kawai			58	28	100	70	
2-6-0	Mogul	KenK		3509		59-69	25	120	90	Porter
2-6-0	Mogul	LMB				60	20	90	70	1880 Porter
2-6-0	Mogul	FED		2601HO		75	65	90	80	Spartan; Circa 1880
2-6-0	Mogul	FED ·		2601HO		74	50	80	70	Spartan; Circa 1880
2-6-0	Mogul	FED		2601HO		73	40	80	60	Spartan; Circa 1880
2-6-0	Mogul	LMB				66	25	100	80	Porter
2-6-0	Mogul	FED		2602HO		75	65	90	80	Spartan; Circa 1910
2-6-2T	Prairie	LMB				69		70	50	Side Tank
2-6-2T	Prairie	KenK	KMT	3541	1500	69	23	80	60	Side Tank
2-6-2T	Prairie	LMB				78-84	43-50	80	60	Side Tank
2-6-2T	Prairie	Gem	Kumata	1001K	1198	59	7	60	40	See Note #494
2-6-2	Prairie	PFM	Atlas-Asahi		200	58	38	160	130	See Note #492
2-6-2	Prairie	PFM	Atlas-Asahi		300	61	38	180	150	See Note #492
2-6-2	Prairie	PFM	Atlas-Asahi		330	60	38	180	140	See Note #492
2-6-2	Prairie	PFM	Atlas-Asahi		290	59	38	170	130	See Note #492
2-6-2	Prairie	PFM	Atlas-Asahi		151	57	38	160	120	See Note #492
2-6-2	Prairie	PFM	Atlas-Asahi		190	62	38	190	150	See Note #492
2-8-0	Consol	Intl				59	35	120	80	Camelback
2-8-0	Consol	GW				50				"Brass Betsy" Kit
2-10-0	Decapod	WMC	Samh			79	175	180	150	See Note #495
2-8-2T	Mikado	NWSL		3-01		74	70	100	90	1895 Baldwin
2-8-2T	Mikado	NWSL		3-01		77	80	100	90	1895 Baldwin
2-8-2	Mikado	MBA				59	31			cataloged
2-8-2	Mikado	MGray	KTM			62	38	150	130	1898 Baldwin
2-8-2	Mikado	Intl				56	35	120	80	
4-4-0	American	FED		4402HO		73	40	70	60	Spartan; Circa 1910
4-4-0	American	Akane	Akane			62	25	90	60	Old Time
4-4-0	American	FED		4402HO		75	65	90	70	Spartan; Circa 1910
4-4-0	American	FED		4402HO		74	50	80	60	Spartan; Circa 1910
4-4-0	American	IMPT	Akane			60	23	80	60	
4-4-0	American	Intl				59	24	80	60	
4-4-0	American	FED		4401HO		73	40	70	60	Spartan; Circa 1880
4-4-0	American	Intl				52	15	60	40	Old Time
4-4-0	American	Aristo				58	25	70	50	fp. "Texas"
4-4-0	American	Gem	Akane	100	6	63	18	80	50	
4-4-0	American	FED		4401HO		74	50	80	60	Spartan; Circa 1880
4-4-0	American	Gem	KMT	ST-103	950	74		180		
4-4-0	American	FED		4401HO		75	65	90	70	Spartan; Circa 1880
4-2-4T	Inspection loco	Red	KMT		300	63	30	120	90	See Note #497
4-4-2T	Atlantic	DiMo				64	25	80	50	
4-6-0	Ten Wheeler	MBA				59	30			cataloged
4-6-0	Ten Wheeler	Intl				54-55	18	100	90	Old Time Camelback
4-6-2	Pacific	MBA				59	31			cataloged; Baldwin
4-6-2	Pacific	Intl				54	24	110	90	Kit
4-6-4	Royal Hudson	PFM	Samh			93	1470			fp., See Note #1561
4-8-2	Mountain	Intl				54	50	160	130	Alco-built
4-8-4	Northern	Key	Samh		300	78	257	260	220	Timker #1111

PART II

ROD-TYPE LOGGERS

Logging Locomotives, Rod Type

Whyte Class	Owner Class & Type	Importer	Builder	Cat #	Quan.	Yrs.	List Price	Mint	Avg.	Remarks
0-4-0	Switcher	FED			1000	71	10	60	50	fp.
0-8-0T	Switcher	NWSL	Toby	2-1	1000	73	65	90	80	See Note #596
0-8-0T	Switcher	NWSL	Toby	2-1	500	65	17	70	50	See Note #596
0-4-4-0T	Vulcan Duplex	PFM	United			85	525	530	500	See Note #595
0-4-4-0T	Vulcan Duplex	PFM	United			80	390	440	380	See Note #595
0-4-4-0T	Vulcan Duplex	PFM	United		335	68	70	320	290	50-Ton Duplex
0-4-4-0T	Vulcan Duplex	PFM	United		450	67	65	290	260	50-Ton Duplex
0-4-4-0T	Mallet	Red	KMT		500	64	20	120	90	MR Review 9/64
2-6-0T	Mogul	FED			1000	71	19	80	60	fp.
2-6-2T	#6 Prairie	NWSL			500	71	43	180	150	Saginaw Logging
2-6-2T	#103 Prairie	NWSL	Toby		500	70-72	43	180	150	Peninsula Terminal
2-6-2T	#9 Prairie	NWSL			500	68-70	43	180	150	See Note #599
2-6-2T	#9 Prairie	NWSL			500	68	43	180	150	CD Johnson Lumber
2-6-2T	#6 Prairie	NWSL			500	69	43	160	130	Saginaw Logging
2-6-2T	#103 Prairie	NWSL			300	68	43	150	120	See Note #598
2-6-2T	#22-23 Prairie	Ortl		0153						
2-6-2T	#24-25 Prairie	Ortl		0154						
2-6-2T	#3 Prairie	Ortl	Ajin	0094	200	81	236	280	230	See Note #600
2-6-2T	#3 Prairie	Ortl	Ajin	P094		81	250	290	230	See Note #600
2-6-2	Prairie	PFM	Atlas/Asahi	P	500	71	75	190	160	See Note #597
2-6-2	Prairie	PFM	Atlas/Asahi	P	575	69	65	180	150	See Note #597
2-6-2	Prairie	PFM	Atlas/Asahi	P	400	77	185	250	200	See Note #597
2-6-2	Prairie	PFM	Atlas/Asahi	S	1	69				See Note #7
2-6-2	#45 Prairie	PFM	Samh	P	775	77	145	220	190	Rayonier
2-6-2	Prairie	PFM	Atlas/Asahi	P	501	74	130	210	180	See Note #597
2-6-2	#30 Prairie	PSC		15584						Sierra RR
2-8-0	#18 Consol	NWSL				74	150	230	200	See Note #606
2-8-0	#28 Consol	PSC		15582						Sierra RR
2-8-0	#24 Consol	WMC		MO-79	900	76	120	180	150	Sierra RR; WMC G-File #79
2-10-2T	Santa Fe	Ortl	Jonan	0391		84	250	250		fp., Sugar Pine Logging #5
2-4-4-2	Articulated	Ortl	Samh							fp., See Note#1610
2-4-4-2	Articulated	Gem	Akane	SM-101	500	62	90	300	260	See Note#1609
2-4-4-2	Articulated	Gem	Jonan	IM-105	111	82	375	350	290	See Note#1608

Most rail fans think of geared locos when they consider logging operations, but many logging operations had rod engines on their roster. Most were small tank engines, but as loadings increased, more power was needed . The first 2–6–6–2 tank engine was purchased by the Booth-Kelly Lumber Company of Springfield, Oregon, in 1910. Delivered as a woodburner, she was soon converted to oil. Northwest Short Line imported this excellent Toby-built replica of Booth-Kelly #2 in 1975.

Logging Locomotives, Rod Type (cont'd)

More common to the logging railroads were the rigid-frame tank engines. One of the largest tank engines ever built was delivered to the Sugar Pine Lumber company's subsidiary Minarets & Western Railway in 1923. Northwest Short Line also imported this Toby-built model in 1974.

Whyte Class	Owner Class & Type	Model Production					List Price	Resale		Remarks
		Importer	Builder	Cat #	Quan.	Yrs.		Mint	Avg.	
2-4-4-2	#126 Articulated	Gem	Akane	625	30	63	90	250	190	See Note#1607
2-4-4-2	#126 Articulated	Gem	Akane	625	41	64		250	190	See Note#1607
2-8-2	#34 Mikado	Sunset		HO78						
2-8-2	#45 Mikado	NWSL	Toby		500	71-72	65	220	190	See Note #607
2-8-2	#5 Mikado	NWSL			300	63-66	50	220	190	See Note #1606
2-8-2	#70 Mikado	NWSL	Toby		800	71-72	75	220	190	Rayonier
2-8-2T	Mikado	NWSL		3-1		74	70	100	90	Baldwin Side Tank
2-8-2T	Mikado	NWSL		3-1		77	80	100	90	Baldwin Side Tank
2-8-2T	#11 Mikado	PSC	Kodama	15576		87	255	250	200	See Note #1604
2-8-2T	#11 Mikado	PSC	Kodama	15450		87	255	250	200	See Note #1602
2-8-2T	#16 Mikado	NWSL			500	65-67	45	235	190	See Note #609
2-8-2T	#16 Mikado	NWSL	Toby		500	73	120	260	220	See Note #609
2-8-2T	#2/3 Mikado	PSC	Kodama	15574		87	255	250	200	See Note #1605
2-8-2T	#37 Mikado	PSC	Kodama	15572		87	255	250	200	See Note #1601
2-8-2T	#9,10,12 Mikado	PSC	Kodama	15578		87	255	250	200	See Note #1603
2-6-6-2T	#6 Articulated	CustB	DaiYng	ST-224	170	82	598		490	Hammond Lumber Co.
2-6-6-2T	#8 Articulated	NWSL	Toby		300	64-65		470	350	See Note #604
2-6-6-2T	#12 Articulated	NWSL	Toby		202	59	50	820	650	See Note #603
2-6-6-2T	#108 Articulated	NWSL	Toby		500	69-70	75	410	290	Weyerhauser
2-6-6-2T	#8 Articulated	NWSL	Toby		300	67	64	590	470	See Note #605
2-6-6-2T	#2 Articulated	NWSL	Toby			75	295	470	350	Booth Kelly
2-6-6-2	#11 Articulated	NWSL	Toby		500	68	70	410	350	Kosmos Timber Co.
2-6-6-2	#11 Articulated	NWSL			208	60-61	60	350	290	See Note #602
2-6-6-2	#38 Articulated	PFM	United		500	62	60	240	210	Sierra
2-6-6-2	#38 Articulated	PFM	United		700	68	80	280	250	Sierra
2-6-6-2	#38 Articulated	PFM	United		400	70	90	280	250	Sierra
2-6-6-2	#38 Articulated	PFM	United		410	58	60	220	190	Sierra
2-6-6-2	#38 Articulated	PFM	United		500	72	130	290	260	Sierra
2-6-6-2	#38 Articulated	PFM	United		375	60	60	230	200	Sierra
2-6-6-2	#38 Articulated	PFM	United		175	61	60	235	200	Sierra
2-6-6-2	#38 Articulated	PFM	United		255	66	65	260	235	Sierra
2-6-6-2	#38 Articulated	PFM	United		255	64	65	250	220	Sierra
2-6-6-2	#38 Articulated	PFM	United		290	67	70	270	240	Sierra
2-6-6-2	#38 Articulated	PFM	United		330	65	65	260	230	Sierra
2-6-6-2	#38 Articulated	PFM	United		600	75	240	290	260	Sierra
2-6-6-2	#38 Articulated	PFM	United		470	63	65	250	220	Sierra
2-6-6-2	#120 Articulated	PFM	United		150	81	536	530	450	Rayonier
2-6-6-2	#38 Articulated	PFM	United		882	59	60	220	190	See Note #601

Logging Locomotives, Rod Type (cont'd)

Although logging railroads typically used geared locomotives, there were several lumbering operations in which rod locomotives worked just as well. If the run to the mill was long and relatively flat, rod locomotives were the obvious answer. The Rayonier employed #70, a Baldwin-built 2–8–2 for just such service. Northwest Short Line imported this Toby-built model in 1971.

The Sugar Pine Lumber Co. employed some of the biggest rigid-frame tank engines ever used in logging operations. This fine model of Sugar Pine #5 was built by Jonan Models and imported by Oriental Limited in 1984.

Whyte Class	Owner Class & Type	Model Production					List Price	Resale		Remarks
		Importer	Builder	Cat #	Quan.	Yrs.		Mint	Avg.	
2-6-6-2	Articulated	Sun		HO71	200	87	384	380		CSF&E "Trojan"
2-6-6-2	Articulated	Sun		HO72	200	87	384	380		CSF&E "Sampson"
2-8-8-2	#200 Articulated	NWSL	Toho		250	71-72	129	530	410	See Note #611
2-8-8-2	#201 Articulated	NWSL			500	69	129	470	350	See Note #610

PART III

GEARED LOGGERS

Climax Geared Locomotives

Trucks	Class	Tons	Gauge	Importer	Builder	Cat #	Quan.	Yrs.	List Price	Mint	Avg.	Remarks
					Model Production					Resale		
2	C		HO	PFM	United		1	67				See Note# 7
2	B		HO	FZoo	Sugi			84	190	225		
2	A		HOn3	WMC				74	105	210	190	See Note #1584
3	C		HO	PFM	United			80	431	470	410	See Note #1585
3	C		HO	PFM	United			80	431	500	440	See Note# 618
2	A		HO	WMC				74	90	180	150	Horizontal Boiler
2	A	12		NWSL				80	175			
2	A	12	HOn3	NWSL	Sanko		100	71-72	80	180	150	See Note #1148
2	A	1	HO	NWSL	Sanko		400	71-72	80	160	140	See Note #1148
2	A	15	HO/HOn3	NWSL	Sanko		500	72	85	200	160	See Note #1137
2	B	15	HOn3	NWSL	Sanko		200	72		210	180	See Note #1137
2	B	18	HOn3	FZoo	Sugi			84	190	190		
2	B	18	HOn30	FZoo	Sugi			84	110			Kit
2	B	18	HOn3	FZoo	Sugi			84	110			Kit
2	B	18	HOn30	FZoo	Sugi			84	190	190		
2	B	70	HO	PFM	Atlas-Asahi		1	55	48			See Note# 612
2	A	12	HO	NWSL		3-2		76	140	180	150	Vertical Boiler
2	A	12	HOn30	NWSL				77	140	190	160	Vertical Boiler
2	A	12	HOn3	NWSL		4-2		76-77	140	190		Vertical Boiler
2	A	12	HOn3	WMC	Naka	MO-42	710	73-74	90	200	180	See Note# 617
2	A	12	HO	WMC	Naka	MO-42	710	73-74	90	200	180	See Note# 617
2	B	70	HO	PFM	Atl-Asahi	S-13	250	58	48	280	250	Note# 613 & 615
2	B	70	HO	PFM	Atl-Asahi	S-13	200	59	48	280	260	See Note# 616

The Climax Manufacturing Company of Corry, Pa., produced a geared locomotive for logging operations that was quite popular with eastern loggers. Probably due to low working stresses, early Climaxes had a reputation for dependability and long life. The Class B Climax engines had one cylinder on each side connected to a shaft which was connected by a bevel gear arrangement that drove a drive shaft which connected to the truck axles via a spyroid gear arrangement. This complicated and heavy mechanism, located under the locomotive, was not always popular with the crews when the locomotive broke down in the woods. In contrast, much of the Shay's popularity derived from the fact that the mechanism was exposed on one side of the locomotive. Pacific Fast Mail imported this replica of a Class B woodburner.

Climax Geared Locomotives (cont'd)

Trucks	Class	Tons	Gauge	Importer	Builder	Cat #	Quan.	Yrs.	List Price	Mint	Avg.	Remarks
2	B	70	HO	PFM	Atl-Asahi	S-13	399	56	48	260	235	Note# 613 & 614
2	B	70	HO	PFM	Atl-Asahi	S-13	100	57	48	270	240	Note# 613 & 615
2	B		HO	PFM	Atl-Asahi	S-16	645	64	55	300	270	Note# 1586
2	B		HO	PFM	Atl-Asahi	S-16	290	67	60	320	290	Note# 1586
2	B		HO	PFM	Atl-Asahi	S-16	230	65	60	300	280	Note# 1586
2	B		HO	PFM	Atl-Asahi	S-16	511	74	158	410	380	
2	B		HO	PFM	Atl-Asahi	S-16	380	69	85	330	300	See Note# 613
2	B		HO	PFM	Atl-Asahi	S-16	250	66	60	310	280	See Note# 1586
2	B		HO	PFM	Atl-Asahi	S-16	401	71	100	340	310	See Note#1587
2	B		HO	PFM	Atl-Asahi	S-16	465	63	55	290	260	See Note# 613
2	B		HO	PFM	Atl-Asahi	S-65	500	72	100	320	290	
2	B		HO	PFM	Atl-Asahi	S-65	470	68	60	290	260	See Note# 1588
2	B		HO	PFM	Atl-Asahi	S-65	400	70	65	300	280	
2	B		HO	PFM	Atl-Asahi	S-65	600	76	225	350	320	
2	B		HO	PFM				84	456			Elk River #3
3	B		HO	PFM				87	800			Abernathy-Lougheed
3	B		HO	United				88	500			Abernathy-Lougheed

Dunkirk Geared Locomotives

Trucks	Class	Tons	Gauge	Importer	Builder	Cat #	Quan.	Yrs.	List Price	Mint	Avg.	Remarks
2	B	16	HO	NWSL			150	80	195	235	210	Kulp,Thomas #1
2	B	16	HO/HOn3	NWSL			300	80	188	220	200	Kulp,Thomas #1

Heisler Geared Locomotives

Trucks	Class	Tons	Gauge	Importer	Builder	Cat #	Quan.	Yrs.	List Price	Mint	Avg.	Remarks
2		37	HO/HOn3	WMC	KTM	MO-05	650	65	60	350	320	See Note #1589
3	C	90	HO	KEY	Samh		200	85	525	820		See Note# 1590

The Heisler Locomotive was a popular competitor of the Shay. Meadow River #6 weighed in at 90 tons and was one of the biggest Heislers ever built. Using two double-acting steam pistons in a ''V'' arrangement with the jack-shafts and gearing located under the centerline of the locomotive, it wasn't as easy to work on as a Shay, which has all of its gearing exposed on the right side of the locomotive. Nonetheless, dozens of Heislers were used in the woods with good success. Key imported this Samhongsa-built replica in 1985. The prototype still runs during the summer at the Cass Scenic Railroad in West Virginia.

Heisler Geared Locomotives (cont'd)

Trucks	Class	Tons	Gauge	Importer	Builder	Cat #	Quan.	Yrs.	List Price	Mint	Avg.	Remarks
3	C	90	HO	KEY	Samh			85	514	760		See Note # 1591
3	C	90	HO	KEY	Samh			85	514	670		See Note # 1592
2		65	HO	PFM	Atl-Asahi			79	355	470	410	NMRA Review 5/80
2		65	HO	PFM	Atl-Asahi			77		440	380	
2		65	HO	PFM	Atl-Asahi		700	76	235	410	235	
2			HO	PFM	Atl-Asahi	S-15	54	60	50	310	280	
2			HO	PFM	Atl-Asahi	S-15	450	57	50	290	260	See Note# 619
2			HO	PFM	Atl-Asahi	S-15	620	63	55	320	290	
2			HO	PFM	Atl-Asahi	S-15	125	59	50	300	280	w/Pittman Motor
2			HO	PFM	Atl-Asahi	S-15	155	65	55	330	300	
2			HO	PFM	Atl-Asahi	S-15	25	58	50	300	270	See Note# 620
2			HO	PFM	Atl-Asahi	S-15	500	73	125	350	320	
2			HO	PFM	Atl-Asahi	S-15	545	62	50	320	290	
2			HOn3	PSC		15142		83				WLCo #2
2			HOn3	PSC		15260		83				WLCo #3
2			HO	PSC		15322		83				WLCo #3

Shay Geared Locomotives

Trucks	Class	Tons	Gauge	Importer	Builder	Cat #	Quan.	Yrs.	List Price	Mint	Avg.	Remarks
2	A-2	20	HO/HOn3	Bal	KTM			67-71	55-60	350	230	
2			HOn30	FZoo				87	180	180		Mich-Cal #2
2			HOn3	FZoo				87	180	180		Mich-Cal #2
2			HOn30	FZoo				87	190	190		T-Boiler Baby Shay
2			HOn3	FZoo				87	190	190		T-Boiler Baby Shay
2			HO	Intl	TMS			48	48	410	350	See Note# 621
2			HO	MBA	TMS			54		440	380	Cast Side Frames
2	A-2	13	HOn3	NWSL			200	79	316	350	300	See Note# 628
2	A-2	13	HO	NWSL			300	79	316	350	300	See Note# 628
2	A	18	HO	NWSL	Sanko		700	73	75	260	235	2-Cylinder
2	A	18		NWSL				74	90	290	260	
2	A		HOn3	PSC	KTM	15150		83	285			2-Cylinder; wood
2	A		HOn30	PSC	KTM	15290		83	285			2-Cylinder; wood
2			HOn3/HOn30	Direct	JoeW			84				Baby T-Boiler
2			HOn3/HOn30	Lam	JoeW			83	180			Mich-Cal #2
2			HOn3/HOn30	FZoo				84	190			MR rev. 10/85
2	A	18	HOn3	NWSL	Sanko		300	73	75	290	260	2-Cylinder
2	A-2	13	HO	NWSL				79	316	350	300	See Note# 628
2		13	HO	NWSL	JDL	7-2		81	380		350	See Note# 626
2		13	HOn3	NWSL	JDL	8-2		81	380		350	See Note# 626
2			HO/HOn3	PFM	Atlas-Asahi		200	82	442		410	See Note# 625
2	A-2		HO/HOn3	PFM	Atlas-Asahi			80	448	470	410	See Note# 629
2		24	HOn3	PFM	Atlas-Asahi		175	69	70	310	280	Cowichan
2		24	HOn3	PFM	Atlas-Asahi		240	67	70	290	260	Cowichan
2		24	HOn3	PFM	Atlas-Asahi							See Note #1593
2		24	HOn3	PFM	Atlas-Asahi		250	70	70	320	290	Cowichan
2				PFM	Atlas-Asahi			79	431	500	380	See Note# 631
2		24	HOn3	PFM	Atlas-Asahi		350	74	160	350	320	Cowichan
2				PFM	Atlas-Asahi							See Note# 627
2	B-2	90		PFM	Atlas-Asahi		50	77	300	590	490	Michigan
2	B-2	24	HOn3	PFM	Atlas-Asahi			79	495	500	470	See Note# 630
2	B-2		HO	PFM	Atlas-Asahi		2	62				
2	B-2	24	HO	PFM	Atlas-Asahi			79	495	470	440	See Note# 630
2	B-2	90		PFM	Atl-Asahi	S-31	245	60	50	470	350	See Note# 624
2	B-2	90		PFM	Atl-Asahi	S-31	200	61	50	530	410	See Note# 624
2	B-2		HO	PFM	Atl-Asahi	S-41	280	67	70	390	330	
2	B-2		HO	PFM	Atl-Asahi	S-41	625	64	55	370	320	
	B-2		HO	PFM	Atl-Asahi	S-41	340	68	70	390	340	
2		24	HO	Direct	Atl-Asahi			84			320	Benson
2		24	HO/HOn3	PFM	Atl-Asahi			83	442			See Note #625
2		24	HO	PFM	Atl-Asahi			84	325			Caddo River
2		24	HOn3	PFM	Atl-Asahi			84	325			Caddo River

Shay Geared Locomotives (cont'd)

The Meadow River Lumber Company was one of the largest producers of hardwood products in the world. To keep the mill supplied, a large roster of Shays was used over an extensive logging railroad near Rainelle, West Virginia. Meadow River Shay #7 is an 80 ton, 3-truck locomotive built in 1923. Fairly modern, this Shay incorporates a cast, steel frame, cast trucks, and a Radley-Hunter stack. This engine now resides at the Cass Scenic Railroad in West Virginia. Key Imports produced this excellent model in 1983.

Lima's "ultimate" Shay was the "Pacific Coast" which was built to compete with the Willamette, a Shay copy that was making serious inroads into the West Coast locomotive market. Superheating and lower gear ratios increased performance. PFM imported over 1,800 of these fine engines.

| Trucks | Class | Tons | Model Production | | | | | | List Price | Resale | | Remarks |
			Gauge	Importer	Builder	Cat #	Quan.	Yrs.		Mint	Avg.	
2	B-2		HO	PFM	Atl-Asahi	S-41	500	73	145	420	360	
2	B-2		HO	PFM	Atl-Asahi	S-41	400	66	70	380	330	
2	B-2		HO	PFM	Atl-Asahi	S-41	420	77	250	440	380	
2	B-2		HO	PFM	Atl-Asahi	S-41	170	65	55	380	320	
2	B-2		HO	PFM	Atl-Asahi	S-41	1030	62	55	360	300	

Shay Geared Locomotives (cont'd)

Trucks	Class	Tons	Gauge	Importer	Builder	Cat #	Quan.	Yrs.	List Price	Mint	Avg.	Remarks
2	B-2		HO	PFM	United	S-41	400	70	80	410	350	W/Balloon Stack
2	B-2		HO	PFM	United	S-41	635	63	55	360	310	
2	B-2		HO	PFM	United	S-41	1	74	145			
2	B-2		HO	PFM	United	S-5	200	61	50	350	300	4-Wheel Pickup
2	B-2		HO	PFM	United	S-5	50	58	57	350	300	
2	B-2		HO	PFM	United	S-5	289	57	50	330	280	See Note# 622
2	B-2		HO	PFM	United	S-5	715	55	50	320	260	See Note# 622
2	B-2		HOn3	PFM	United	S-5	51	56	50	340	290	Flywheel
2	B-2		HO	PFM	United	S-5	200	59	50	340	290	See Note# 623
2	B-2		HO	PFM	United	S-5	273	58	50	330	280	4-Wheel Pickup
2	B-2		HO	PFM	United	S-5	405	56	57	320	270	See Note# 622
2	B-2		HO	PFM	United	S-5	100	60	50	350	290	4-Wheel Pickup
2		24	HO	PFM	United	S-64	400	74	160	350	320	Hillcrest-Osborne
2		24	HO	PFM	United	S-64	350	72	100	330	300	Hillcrest-Osborne
2		24	HO	PFM	United	S-64	380	67	70	290	260	Hillcrest-Osborne
2		24	HO	PFM	United	S-64	300	70	70	320	290	Hillcrest-Osborne
2		24	HO	PFM	United	S-64	470	69	70	300	280	Hillcrest-Osborne
2		24	HO	PFM	United	S-78	350	72	100	320	290	Benson
2		24	HO	PFM	United	S-78	425	69	70	290	260	Benson
2		24	HO	PFM	United	S-78	300	70	70	300	280	Benson
2		24	HOn3	PFM	United	S-78	400	74	160	350	320	Benson
2		24	HOn3	PFM	United	S-78	195	69	70	320	290	Benson
2		24	HO	PFM	United	S-78	300	72	100	350	320	Benson
2		24	HOn3	PFM	United	S-78	250	70	70	330	300	Benson
2			HO	Pike	TMS			55	50	410	350	Similar to Intl
2	Bn-1	50	HOn3	WMC				79	400	380	320	Bn-1 3-cylinder
2	A-2	18	HO	WMC	KTM			80	300	290	280	fp., Ali-San
2	A-2	18	HO/HOn3	WMC	KTM			79	279	260	235	Ali-San
2	B-1	50	HO	WMC				79	400	380	320	B-1 3-cylinder
2		24	HOn3	WMC				79	284	330	290	Kelly Island
2	A	20	HO	WMC		MO-148		79-83	250-269	260	235	MKF; 2-cylinder
3			HO	Intl	TMS			52	50			See Note# 621

Diminutive Shays have always been popular with model railroaders and collectors alike. Over the years, Pacific Fast Mail has produced a variety of small shays in the 25- to 40-ton range, both in standard and narrow gauge. Shown above is the Hillcrest #1. Note the outward canted cylinders to accommodate the standard-gauge trucks. The same model was also produced with narrow-gauge trucks and was known as the Cowichan Valley #1. The narrow-gauge model incorporates non-slanted cylinders. These shays incorporated open-frame motors and a diminutive but highly reliable mechanism that provided excellent operation. Between 1967 and 1974, Pacific Fast Mail imported over 2,900 Cowichan and Hillcrest Shays.

Shay Geared Locomotives (cont'd)

The Feather River–Hutchison Lumber Company 3-truck Shay model is noteworthy as it is the first Korean-built model of a Shay locomotive to be imported into this country. Built in 1980 by Samhongsa for Key Imports, the model depicts a late-model oil-burning Shay with girder underframe and superheater. The most unique feature of this model is the large cab which extends forward over the cylinders. The prototype was a 90-ton locomotive. However, the model better represents a prototype of the 65- to 70-ton class. This model represents a significant step forward for Samhongsa. The construction of Shays was thought by many to be beyond the skills of Korean builders. This model and the Samhongsa Shays that followed proved this belief to be incorrect.

The Westside Lumber Company was one of the largest softwood lumbering operations in the United States. To keep this operation running, the roster of 3-foot gauge geared engines included 4 Heislers, 2 small tank locos, and 11 Shays. WSLCo. took good care of their equipment and all of the engines had a pleasant balanced look about them. Pictured above is WSLCo. #14 which has been converted from oil to coal and painted for the fictitious Tioga Lumber Company. In 1984 Nakamura, one of Japan's finest builders, produced several of the WSLCo. Shays for Precision Scale Co. All of these engines were excellent models and established a standard of quality for narrow-gauge Shays that has rarely been exceeded.

| Trucks | Class | Tons | Model Production | | | | | | List Price | Resale | | Remarks |
			Gauge	Importer	Builder	Cat #	Quan.	Yrs.		Mint	Avg.	
3	C	150	HO	KEY	Samh			75	83	496	580		fp., See Note#1594
3		90	HO	KEY	Samh			300	80	310	320	330	See Note# 632
3			HO	MBA					54	55	470	410	Cast Side Frames
3		150	HO	MGray	KTM				64	77	590	470	See Note #1594
3		150	HO	WMC				<12	76-78	350			See Note #1594

Shay Geared Locomotives (cont'd)

Many of the early Shay models were generic and did not attempt to depict a specific prototype—they were more representative of a general class of Lima Shay. The model shown above is occasionally mistaken for the Western Maryland #6 but is instead a generic representation of an unsuperheated oil-burning locomotive in the 150-ton class. Over 500 of these locomotives were imported by Pacific Fast Mail between 1956 and 1960.

Trucks	Class	Tons	Gauge	Importer	Builder	Cat #	Quan.	Yrs.	List Price	Mint	Avg.	Remarks
3		150	HO	PSC	KTM	15141		83	529			See Note #1595
3		150	HO	PSC	KTM	15141-1	25	84	419			Kit, See Note #1595
3			HO	PFM	United			81	431	460	350	See Note# 637
3			HO	PFM	United			79	495	530	470	See Note# 633
3	B-3		HO	PFM	United	S-59	340	68	75	460	430	See Note #634
3	B-3		HO	PFM	United	S-59	500	73	170	490	470	See Note #634
3	B-3		HO	PFM	United	S-59	280	64	60	410	380	See Note #634
3	B-3		HO	PFM	United	S-59	400	70	88	470	450	W/Balloon Stack
3	B-3		HO	PFM	United	S-59	280	65	60	420	390	See Note #634
3	B-3		HO	PFM	United	S-59	570	66	65	430	410	See Note #634
3	B-3		HO	PFM	United	S-59	2	74	170	500	480	See Note #634
3	B-3		HO	PFM	United	S-59	240	67	65	450	420	See Note #634
3	B-3		HO	PFM	United	S-59	420	77	290	530	500	See Note #634
3		70	HO	PFM	United	S-77	500	72	110	570	500	See Note# 639
3		70	HO	PFM	United	S-77	700	75	225	590	530	See Note# 639
3		70	HO	PFM	United	S-77	660	69	80	560	470	NMRA Review 3/70
3		65	HOn3	WMC/PSC		MO-178		82	450			WLCo. #15
3	C-2	80	HOn3	PSC	Nakamura	15151		83	445			WLCo. #10
3		70	HO	Key	Samh			83	414	580	540	Meadow River #7
3		70	HO	Key	Samh			83	414	580	540	See Note #1596
3		150	HO	Key	Samh			84	486			GC&E #12
3			HO	Train	Naka			84	300			WLCo. #12
3			HOn3	PSC	Nakamura	15132		84	515			WLCo. #12
3			HOn3	PSC	Nakamura	15132-1		84	355			Kit; WLCo. #12
3			HOn3	PSC	Nakamura	15124		84	525			WLCo. #14
3			HOn3	PSC	Nakamura	10098		84	355			Kit; WLCo. #14
3		65	HOn3	WMC/PSC		MO-178		84				WLCo. #15
3			HOn3	PSC		15142						WLCo. #2
3			HOn3	PSC		15260						WLCo. #3
3	C-3			PFM	United	S-9	95	59	60	470	410	See Note #624

Shay Geared Locomotives (cont'd)

The largest Shay ever built was used by the the West Virginia Pulp and Paper Company in the vicinity of Cass, West Virginia. This engine began life as a 150 ton 3-truck Shay for the Greenbrier, Cheat & Elk Railroad and was later converted into a 192-ton 4-truck monster. Samhongsa built this outstanding replica for Key Imports in 1984.

Trucks	Class	Tons	Gauge	Importer	Builder	Cat #	Quan.	Yrs.	List Price	Mint	Avg.	Remarks
3	C-3			PFM	United	S-9	344	56	60	410	350	See Note #624, saturated
3	C-3			PFM	United	S-9	100	60	60	530	470	See Note #624, superheated
3	C-1	70	HO/HOn3	PSC	Nakamura			78	200			Note# 640, Kit
3		70		PSC		10021		81	229			
3	C-2	80	HO/HOn3	WMC	Nakamura			80-81	380	410	380	See Note# 638
3	C-1	70	HO	WMC	Nakamura	MO-109	470	77-80	330-365	390	350	See Note# 640
3	C		HO/HOn3	WMC		MO-272		83	400			
4		120	HO	PSC		10026		81	379			
4		120	HO	PSC		10027		81	379			
4	D	120	HO/HOn3	WMC	Nakamura			79				Kit; Hassinger
4			HOn3	WMC	Nakamura	MO-150		79	400	460	410	Westside #16
4	D	120	HO	WMC	Nakamura	MO-250		79	400	500		Hassinger
4	D	120	HOn3	WMC	Nakamura	MO-250		79	400	550		See Note# 641
4	D	150	HO	WMC/PSC	Nakamura	15238		80	545	775		See Note# 642
4	D	192	HO	Key	Samh			84	525	950		See Note #1598

Willamette Geared Locomotives

Trucks	Class	Tons	Gauge	Importer	Builder	Cat #	Quan.	Yrs.	List Price	Mint	Avg.	Remarks
2			HO	BCM	Samh			88	615	700		C/N 30 and C/N 25
3		70	HO	PFM	United		150	81	545	550	430	See Note# 635
3		70	HO	NWSL	FuMod		500	68-69	75	470	440	Saturated Steam
3		70	HO	PFM	United		150	81	548	550	430	See Note# 636
3		70	HO	OMI	MSM	1484	100	89	674	640		See Note #1599
3		70	HO	OMI	MSM	1485	100	89	674	640		Medco #3
3		75	HO	OMI	MSM	1486	75	89	674	640		See Note #1600

PART IV

NARROW-GAUGE STEAM LOCOMOTIVES

Colorado & Southern (C&S)

Whyte Class	Owner Class & Type	Model Production					List Price	Resale		Remarks
		Importer	Builder	Cat #	Quan.	Yrs.		Mint	Avg.	
2-6-0	Mogul	JoeW	Sango			82	55		50	HOn3/HOn30 Kit
2-6-0	#8 Mogul	Key				85	393		380	fp.
2-6-0	#8 Mogul	Key				85	350		330	
2-6-0	#9 Mogul	Key				85	393		380	fp.
2-6-0	#6 Mogul	Key				85	393		380	fp.
2-6-0	#9 Mogul	Key				85	350		330	
2-6-0	#22 Mogul	Key	Samh		300	80	230	250	200	
2-6-0	#6 Mogul	Key				85	350		330	
2-6-0	#9 Mogul	Lam		902	500	74-75	170	210	190	See Note #643
2-6-0	#6 Mogul	Lam		903		76	170	200	190	Straight Stack; low domes
2-6-0	#21 Mogul	PFM	KTM		200	64	38	300	275	
2-6-0	#21 Mogul	PFM	KTM		300	59	38	250	220	See Note #644
2-6-0	#21 Mogul	PFM	KTM		400	60	38	260	235	
2-6-0	#21 Mogul	PFM	KTM		230	62	38	280	260	
2-6-0	Mogul	PFM	United		1	55				Handmade
2-6-0	#21 Mogul	PFM	KTM		235	65	38	320	300	
2-6-0	#21 Mogul	PFM	KTM		200	61	38	270	250	See Note #645
2-6-0	#21 Mogul	PFM	KTM		300	63	38	290	270	
2-8-0	#74 Consol	Bal				68-69	50	220	190	
2-8-0	#71-73 Consol	Key	Samh		400	79	230	270	235	See Note #646
2-8-0	#58 Consol	Key	Samh		50	82	285	310	270	
2-8-0	#60 Consol	Key	Samh		200	82	307	330	290	Snowplow Pilot
2-8-0	#65 Consol	Key	Samh		50	82	285		270	
2-8-0	B-4D Consolidation	OMI	MSM	1522	100	90	536			#69
2-8-0	B-4D Consolidation	OMI	MSM	1523	150	90	543			#70 Oil Burner
2-8-0	#65 Consol	PFM	KTM		480	62	40	260	235	See Note #946
2-8-0	#65 Consol	PFM	KTM		235	65	40	330	300	See Note #946
2-8-0	#65 Consol	PFM	KTM		500	64	40	300	280	See Note #946
2-8-0	#60 Consol	PSC		15032						
2-8-0	#75 Consol	PSC				83	335			
2-8-0	#75 Consol	PSC		15202		83	229			Kit
2-8-0	#63-70 Consol	Sun		HON04						

Colorado & Southern's 2–8–0 #69 exemplifies the look of Rocky Mountain narrow-gauge railroading. Snowplow pilot, slide valves, bear-trap stack, and top-mounted air tanks provided a look that was unique to the Western narrow gauge. Although the C&S engines all had a strong family resemblance, many came from other railroads. Number 60 was built in 1886 for the Utah & Northern. Prior to the late 1970s narrow-gauge steam locomotive models were not known as good runners. The advent of the high-efficiency ''can'' motor alleviated many of the electrical pickup problems that had plagued earlier models and did much to improve the operational reliability of these small engines. Overland Models imported this fine replica of #69 in 1990.

Colorado & Southern (cont'd)

Whyte Class	Owner Class & Type	Model Production					List Price	Resale		Remarks
		Importer	Builder	Cat #	Quan.	Yrs.		Mint	Avg.	
2-8-0	#60 Consol	Sunset		HON03						
2-8-0	#74 Consol	WMC	Mizuno			78	227	270	210	also RGS
2-8-0	#75 Consol	WMC	Mizuno	MO-179		80	355	350	320	
2-8-0	#76 Consol	WMC		MO-07	25	67	145	1290	1060	WMC G-File #7
2-8-0	#75 Consol	WMC	Mizuno	MO-179		81				fp.

Denver, South Park & Pacific (DSP&P)

Whyte Class	Owner Class & Type	Model Production					List Price	Resale		Remarks
		Importer	Builder	Cat #	Quan.	Yrs.		Mint	Avg.	
2-6-6T	#55 Bogie	Bal				65-68	50	235	200	Modernized version
2-6-6T	Mason Bogie	JoeW	Sango			83	50			HOn3/HOn30 Kit
2-6-6T	#15 Mason Bogie	PFM	United		490	66	70	290	235	"Breckenridge"
2-6-6T	#15 Mason Bogie	PFM	United		3	65				See Note #7
2-6-6T	#15 Mason Bogie	PFM	United		474	73	135	320	260	"Breckenridge"
2-6-6T	#15 Mason Bogie	PFM	United		7	74	135	350	290	"Breckenridge"
2-8-6T	#28 Mason Bogie	Bal			100	65-67	90	470	350	See Note #661
2-8-6T	#28 Mason Bogie	CustB	DaiYng	ST-213-3M	125	81	357	350	280	"Denver"; modernized
2-8-6T	#28 Mason Bogie	CustB	DaiYng	ST-213-3O	125	81	357	350	280	See Note #662

The "Mason Bogie" was one of the most unusual locomotive types to run anywhere. What looks like a fairly long rigid-frame locomotive is anything but. The locomotive chassis and the trailing truck were both free to swivel under the locomotive superstructure. This unusual arrangement provided a lovomotive that could negotiate tight turns, but the mechanical trade-offs were hardly worth the effort. Still the DSP&P owned a total of 23 Mason Bogies. PFM imported this model of #15 in 1966.

Denver & Rio Grande Western (D&RGW)

Whyte Class	Owner Class & Type	Model Production					List Price	Resale		Remarks
		Importer	Builder	Cat #	Quan.	Yrs.		Mint	Avg.	
0-6-0T	Switcher	Kem							120	Kit
0-6-0T	Class 48 Switcher	PSC	Samh	15058	250	80	199		200	ex. RGS #14
2-8-0	C-16 Consol	JoeW	Sango			83		60	50	HOn3/HOn30 Kit
2-8-0	C-16 Consol	Kem				57	50			See Note #649
2-8-0	C-16 Consol	Kem				57	50			See Note #648
2-8-0	C-16 Consol	PFM	United		1	55				
2-8-0	C-16 Consol	PSC	Kodama	15123-1			435			fp.,#278
2-8-0	C-16 Consol	PSC	Kodama	15123			395			
2-8-0	C-16 Consol	PSC	Kodama	15146-1			449			fp., #268
2-8-0	C-16 Consol	PSC	Kodama	15146			398			#268
2-8-0	C-16 Consol	Sunset				91	170			#268

Denver & Rio Grande Western (cont'd)

Whyte Class	Owner Class & Type	Model Production					List Price	Resale		Remarks
		Importer	Builder	Cat #	Quan.	Yrs.		Mint	Avg.	
2-8-0	C-16 Consol	Sunset				91	170			#223
2-8-0	C-16 Consol	Sunset				91	170			#278
2-8-0	C-16 Consol	Sunset				91	170			#271
2-8-0	C-16 Consol	Sunset				91	204			fp., #278
2-8-0	C-16 Consol	Sunset				91	220			fp., #268 "Bumblebee"
2-8-0	C-16 Consol	Sunset				91	204			fp., #223
2-8-0	C-16 Consol	Sunset				91	204			fp., #271
2-8-0	C-16 Consol	Sunset				91	204			fp., #268
2-8-0	C-16 Consol	Tomalco						440	290	fp.
2-8-0	C-16 Consol	WMC		MO-77		78	150	200	180	#278
2-8-0	C-16 Consol	WMC	Kodama	MO-22	2079	70-76	130	190	160	See Note #650
2-8-0	C-16 Consol	WMC	KTM	MO-77		77	140	190	160	See Note #647
2-8-0	C-16 Consol	WMC	KTM	MO-77		71	130	200	150	#268
2-8-0	C-16 Consol	WMC				78	220	235	200	See Note #651
2-8-0	C-16 Consol	WMC/PSC	Kodama			82	395	395		#271
2-8-0	C-16 Consol	WMC/PSC	Kodama	MO-77		82	379		320	#268
2-8-0	C-17 Consol	Key	Samh			79	200	235	200	See Note #652
2-8-0	C-18 Consol	Key	Samh		800	77	140	200	180	See Note #653
2-8-0	C-18 Consol	Key	Samh			85	336	330		#319
2-8-0	C-18 Consol	Key	Samh			85	336	330		#316
2-8-0	C-19 Consol	Bal	KTM			70	70	210	180	#340
2-8-0	C-19 Consol	Bal	KTM			66-69	43-50	200	160	#340
2-8-0	C-19 Consol	Key	Samh			85	379			fp., #315
2-8-0	C-19 Consol	Key	Samh			81	300		290	fp., #340
2-8-0	C-19 Consol	Key	Samh			81	270		260	#345
2-8-0	C-19 Consol	Key	Samh			85	379			fp., #318
2-8-0	C-19 Consol	Key	Samh			85	336			#318
2-8-0	C-19 Consol	Key	Samh			85	379			fp., #319
2-8-0	C-19 Consol	Key	Samh			85	336			#315
2-8-0	C-19 Consol	Key	Samh			78	150	220	160	#346 with C-18 tender
2-8-0	C-19 Consol	Key	Samh			85	379			fp., #316
2-8-0	C-21 Consol	Bal				65-69	55	175	180	See Note #1611
2-8-0	C-21 Consol	CustB	KMT	ST-260-3	358	76	195	210	180	#360, poor motor
2-8-0	C-21 Consol	CustB	KMT	ST-261-3	358	76	195	210	180	#361, poor motor
2-8-0	C-21 Consol	PSC		15490						
2-8-0	C-25 Consol	PSC		15492		82	200			fp., #375

For many years, sturdy little Consolidations were the mainstay motive power of the D&RGW narrow gauge. Though a specific tally is difficult to determine because locos were traded around among the railroad's constituent lines, classes ranged up to C–25. The Baldwin C–19 Class Consolidations were constructed at the same time (1881) as the C–16 class but were more than 14,000 lbs. heavier at 74,260 lbs. and exerted a tractive effort of 18,947 lbs. The prototype #345 was wrecked in 1951 and subsequently scrapped. Key Imports produced this Samhongsa-built model in 1981. This model and other narrow-gauge engines built at that time began the use of high-efficiency tape recorder "can" motors. This has led to significant improvement in operating characteristics.

Denver & Rio Grande Western (cont'd)

The D&RGW K–27 Mikes (#450–464) were the first locomotives of this wheel arrangement on the road. Known as "Mud Hens," for their tendency to leave the rails and get in the mud, these 1903 Baldwin engines started life as compounds with slope-back tenders, but from 1907 though 1909 were modified to single expansion engines with Walschaerts valve gear and rectangular tenders. Evidently, the modification program solved the derailment problem and these engines served well into the 1950s. Nakamura of Japan produced this excellent model for Westside Model Company in 1977. The model pictured is the "modern" version of the prototype with piston valves and Walschaerts valve gear. The Nakamura narrow-gauge engines of this period set a new standard for quality and performance in narrow-gauge models.

Whyte Class	Owner Class & Type	Model Production					List Price	Resale		Remarks
		Importer	Builder	Cat #	Quan.	Yrs.		Mint	Avg.	
2-8-0	C-25 Consol	WMC	Nakamura	MO-58	1500	75	170	275		#375; See Note #1612
2-8-2	K-27 Mikado	PFM	United		100	59		235		See Note #654
2-8-2	K-27 Mikado	PFM	United		970	63	60	280		See Note #655
2-8-2	K-27 Mikado	PFM	United		300	64	60	300		See Note #655
2-8-2	K-27 Mikado	PFM	United		280	65	60	320		See Note #655
2-8-2	K-27 Mikado	PFM	United		700	77	365	410		See Note #658
2-8-2	K-27 Mikado	PFM	SKI			81	325			
2-8-2	K-27 Mikado	PSC		15550			295			#460
2-8-2	K-27 Mikado	PSC	Nakamura	M-184		82	429	560		#455
2-8-2	K-27 Mikado	PSC	Nakamura	15098		82	449	590		#461; See Note #1614
2-8-2	K-27 Mikado	PSC	Nakamura	15100		82	362	450		Kit; See Note #1614
2-8-2	K-27 Mikado	PSC	Nakamura	15101		84	319	440		Kit; #453
2-8-2	K-27 Mikado	PSC	Nakamura	15099		84	485	575		#453
2-8-2	K-27 Mikado	WMC	Nakamura	MO-52		74	170	345		See Note #1617
2-8-2	K-27 Mikado	WMC	Nakamura	MO-61	800	75	170	345		See Note #1616
2-8-2	K-27 Mikado	WMC	Nakamura	MO-61A	1000	76	180	360		See Note #656
2-8-2	K-27 Mikado	WMC	Nakamura	MO-67		77	183	390		See Note #657
2-8-2	K-28 Mikado	PFM	United		1	54				See Note #659
2-8-2	K-28 Mikado	PFM	United		18	55	55			Kit
2-8-2	K-28 Mikado	PFM	United		13	55	70			Handmade
2-8-2	K-28 Mikado	PFM	United		17	55	55	880	705	See Note #659
2-8-2	K-28 Mikado	PFM	United		123	56	55			Kit
2-8-2	K-28 Mikado	PFM	United		153	56	55	290	260	See Note #659
2-8-2	K-28 Mikado	PFM	United		450	65	60	290	260	
2-8-2	K-28 Mikado	PFM	United		330	66	60	300	270	
2-8-2	K-28 Mikado	PFM	United		500	70	85	350	320	
2-8-2	K-28 Mikado	PFM	United		500	75	180	410	380	
2-8-2	K-28 Mikado	PSC				81	249			Kit
2-8-2	K-28 Mikado	PSC	Nakamura	15214-1		83	295			1950 era; upgraded kit
2-8-2	K-28 Mikado	PSC	Nakamura	15214		83	449			1950 era
2-8-2	K-28 Mikado	WMC		MO-02	500	64-67	40-60	210	180	
2-8-2	K-28 Mikado	WMC				78	420	460	410	Excellent Model
2-8-2	K-36 Mikado	Bal				65-69	60-65	235	200	
2-8-2	K-36 Mikado	PFM	United		4	58	125			Handmade
2-8-2	K-36 Mikado	PFM	Fujiyama		600	77	375	530	440	See Note #660

Denver & Rio Grande Western (cont'd)

The D&RGW's third class of 2–8–2's were built by Baldwin in 1925 and classified as K–36s (#480–489). Considerably larger than the K–27's and K–28's, they weighed in at 187,000 lbs. and exerted a tractive effort of 36,200 lbs. These were the largest 2–8–2's that were built by Baldwin for the D&RGW. Although the K–37's were heavier, they were converted from standard gauge engines. In 1977, two of the finest model builders, Fujiyama and Nakamura, produced outstanding models for Pacific Fast Mail and Westside, respectively. Rarely has the collector been given the opportunity to choose between two models of the same prototype which are of such high quality. Shown above is the Nakamura version.

Whyte Class	Owner Class & Type	Model Production					List Price	Resale		Remarks
		Importer	Builder	Cat #	Quan.	Yrs.		Mint	Avg.	
2-8-2	K-36 Mikado	WMC	Nakamura	MO-78		77	270	380	330	NMRA Review 9/77
2-8-2	K-37 Mikado	PFM	United		205	60	50	290	260	
2-8-2	K-37 Mikado	PFM	Fujiyama			78	492	470	390	
2-8-2	K-37 Mikado	PSC		15588						Non-shielded pilot
2-8-2	K-37 Mikado	PSC		15494						Shielded pilot
2-8-2	K-37 Mikado	WMC	Nakamura	MO-47		74	174	260	235	
4-6-0	T-12 Ten Wheeler	Bal			600	67-68	50	160	130	
4-6-0	T-12 Ten Wheeler	Bal				69	55	170	140	
4-6-0	T-12 Ten Wheeler	WMC	Mizuno	MO-55	950	75	120	150	130	See Note #1618

East Broad Top

| Whyte Class | Owner Class & Type | Model Production | | | | | List Price | Resale | | Remarks |
		Importer	Builder	Cat #	Quan.	Yrs.		Mint	Avg.	
2-6-2	#11 Prairie	Hall	Samh	HN0027		87	298	290		
2-6-2	#11 Prairie	Hall	Samh	HN0028		87	327	350		fp.
2-8-2	#12 Mikado	Hall	Samh	HN0003		87	298	290		
2-8-2	#12 Mikado	Hall	Samh	HN0003		87	327	350		fp.
2-8-2	#14 Mikado	Hall	Samh	HN0004		87	298	290		
2-8-2	#14 Mikado	Hall	Samh	HN0004		87	327	350		fp.
2-8-2	#15 Mikado	Hall	Samh	HM0005		87	298	290		
2-8-2	#15 Mikado	Hall	Samh	HM0005		87	327	350		fp.
2-8-2	#16 Mikado	Hall	Samh	HN0006		84	298			
2-8-2	#16 Mikado	Gem	Seiko	SM-104	250	64	50	245		
2-8-2	#16 Mikado	Hall	Samh	HN0006		84	327			fp.
2-8-2	#17 Mikado	Hall	Samh	HN0007		84	298	290		
2-8-2	#17 Mikado	Hall	Samh	HN0007		84	327	350		fp.
2-8-2	#18 Mikado	Hall	Samh	HN0008		84	298	290		
2-8-2	#18 Mikado	Hall	Samh	HN0008		84	327	350		fp.

In March of 1918, the East Broad Top took delivery of its next-to-last narrow-gauge steam locomotive, #17. This engine was, at that time the largest locomotive on the railroad weighing in at 133,500 lbs. Number 18, which would be delivered in 1920, would outweigh her by only 1,100 lbs. This stock Baldwin design has served the railroad for over 70 years and can be seen at Orbisonia, Pa., today. Hallmark Models produced this excellent model of #17 in 1984, when they produced a large variety of models of the equipment that is still extant. The locomotive models were state-of-the-art and incorporate some of the finest, most reliable mechanisms that have been built for HO narrow-gauge models.

Miscellaneous

| Whyte Class | Owner Class & Type | Model Production | | | | | List Price | Resale | | Remarks |
		Importer	Builder	Cat #	Quan.	Yrs.		Mint	Avg.	
0-4-0	Switcher	FZoo				87	40	40		Kit, Porter Loco Co.
0-4-0	"Gypsy"	FZoo				87	300	300	200	
0-4-0	Switcher	KenK		2111R		64	12	90	70	See Note #666
0-4-0	Switcher	KenK		2111R		70	13	90	80	Industrial Loco
0-4-0	Steam Dummy	KenK		3554		65	20	90	80	See Note #665
0-4-0	Switcher	Koppel				83	95			
0-4-0	Switcher	LMB		2111R		70	13	90	80	Industrial Loco
0-4-0	Switcher	LMB		2111K		64	11	80	60	Kit; See Note #666
0-4-0	Switcher	LMB		2111R		64	12	90	70	See Note #666
0-4-0T	Switcher	KenK		2103K		59-70	11	90	60	Plantation "Mudhen"
0-4-2	Vulcan	WMC		MO-12	135	68	18	90	110	See Note #1619
0-4-2	Vulcan	WMC		MO-12	142	78	50	100	120	See Note #1619
0-4-2T	Vulcan	Fairf	KMT		1000	65	17	120	90	Baldwin; See Note #1620
0-4-2T	Vulcan	KenK	KMT	3556		65	17	120	90	Baldwin
0-4-2T	Vulcan	LMB	KMT			65	17	120	90	Baldwin
0-4-4-0	"Mallay"	F&G		27-RU		66	23			Logger

Miscellaneous (cont'd)

The H.K. Porter Company was established in Pittsburgh, Pa., in 1866 and specialized in turning out small locomotives for narrow-gauge and industrial railroads. Porter ultimately became the world's largest supplier of locomotives for mining operations, having found their niche in building small engines that operated on compressed air. However, before the turn-of-the-century, Porter built a variety of 4–4–0's and 2–6–0's for many narrow-gauge railroads throughout the country. The model pictured was imported by Ken Kidder and was also available from LMB and Diamond Models. In the early '60s, builders often sold the same model to several different importers. This was a low-cost model and was available in a standard-gauge version as well.

Whyte Class	Owner Class & Type	Model Production					List Price	Resale		Remarks
		Importer	Builder	Cat #	Quan.	Yrs.		Mint	Avg.	
0-4-4-0T	Mallet	Red	KMT		430	65	20	150	140	Plantation Mallet
0-6-0T	Switcher	FZoo	JWorks			89	107			Kit
2-4-2T	Columbia	LMB				84	180			Forney
2-4-2T	Columbia	LMB				69	30	140	120	Forney
2-4-2T	Columbia	Sun					53			Baldwin, Kit
2-4-4T	Forney	DiMo	KMT		150	64	25	120	90	MR rev. 7/64
2-4-4T	Forney	FZoo	JWorks			89	129			Kit
2-4-4T	Forney	F&G	KMT	26-RU	150	66	22			See Note #667
2-4-4T	Forney	LMB	KMT		200	65	20	140	120	See Note #1621
2-4-4T	Forney	LMB				78	150		150	NYC
2-6-0	Mogul	DiMo				65	25			Porter; MR rev. 5/65
2-6-0	Mogul	FZoo				83				Baldwin "dachshund" kit
2-6-0	Mogul	FZoo				83				Screwdriver Kit
2-6-0	Mogul	FZoo	Sango			89	130			Kit
2-6-0	Mogul	KenK		3555		65	28	150	120	Porter
2-6-0	Mogul	LMB		3555		66-69	25-28	150	130	Porter
2-6-0	Mogul	NWSL		2602	1000	73-75	40-65	90	60	Circa 1910; Spartan
2-6-0	Mogul	NWSL		2601	1000	73-75	40-65	90	60	Circa 1880; Spartan
2-6-0	Mogul	PSC		15264		83				Porter
2-6-2	#24 Prairie	PFM	United		1	56				See Note #668
2-6-2	Prairie	PSC		15248						
2-6-2	Prairie	PSC		15246						
2-6-6-2T	Articulated	PFM	United		350	78	495	500	470	See Note #670
2-8-2+ 2-8-2	American Garratt	WMC	Nakamura		100	81	856		730	See Note #673
4-4-0	American	NWSL		4401	1000	73-75	40-65	90	60	Circa 1880 Spartan
4-4-0	American	NWSL		4402	1000	73-75	40-65	90	60	Circa 1910 Spartan

New Berlin & Winfield

Whyte Class	Owner Class & Type	Model Production					List Price	Resale		Remarks
		Importer	Builder	Cat #	Quan.	Yrs.		Mint	Avg.	
2-6-0	Mogul	Gem	Sankyo	ST-102	297	67	35	130	100	See Note #1622

Nevada County

Whyte Class	Owner Class & Type	Model Production					List Price	Resale		Remarks
		Importer	Builder	Cat #	Quan.	Yrs.		Mint	Avg.	
2-8-0	#9 Consol	WMC		MO-23		67-69	43-60	185	155	See Note #671

Rio Grande Southern (RGS)

Whyte Class	Owner Class & Type	Model Production					List Price	Resale		Remarks
		Importer	Builder	Cat #	Quan.	Yrs.		Mint	Avg.	
0-6-0T	#14 Switcher	IHM/PSC		15058	250	80	199		200	Also D&RGW #105
2-8-0	C-17 Consol	Key			150	81	270		260	#41
2-8-0	C-19 Consol	Key			55	81	300		280	#40, fp.
2-8-0	#74 Consol	WMC				75	227	260	200	
2-8-2	K-27 Mikado	PSC				84				#461
2-8-2	K-27 Mikado	PSC		M-165		85				
2-8-2	K-27 Mikado	WMC				81	455		420	#455
4-6-0	#20 Ten Wheeler	PFM	United		250	64	40	250	220	See Note #1623
4-6-0	#20 Ten Wheeler	PFM	United		485	63	40	210	200	Tender Drive
4-6-0	#20 Ten Wheeler	PFM	United		250	65	40	280	260	See Note #664
4-6-0	#20 Ten Wheeler	PSC		15418-1		85	365		350	fp.
4-6-0	Ten Wheeler	PSC	Samh	15081	50	80	220			Combo Kit
4-6-0	#22 Ten Wheeler	PSC	Samh	15079	35	80	269	290	260	
4-6-0	#22 Ten Wheeler	PSC		15420-1		85	365		350	fp.
4-6-0	#20 Ten Wheeler	PSC		15418		85	329		310	
4-6-0	#25 Ten Wheeler	PSC		15422-1		85	365		350	fp.
4-6-0	#25 Ten Wheeler	PSC	Samh	15422-1		84	300			Kit
4-6-0	#20 Ten Wheeler	PSC	Samh	15418-1		84	300			Kit
4-6-0	#22 Ten Wheeler	PSC		15420		85	329		310	
4-6-0	#25 Ten Wheeler	PSC	Samh	15080	60	80	269	290	260	
4-6-0	#25 Ten Wheeler	PSC		15422		85	329		310	
4-6-0	#22 Ten Wheeler	PSC	Samh	15420-1		84	300			Kit
4-6-0	#20 Ten Wheeler	PSC	Samh	15078	85	80	269	290	260	
4-6-0	#20 Ten Wheeler	Sunset				86	360		340	fp.
2-8-0	C-17 Consol	Key	Samh		150	79	200	235	200	See Note #663

Rio Grande Southern #20 came on the line from the Florence and Cripple Creek in 1919, along with two other ten-wheelers. Built by Schenectady in 1899, she was known as the ''Portland'' on the F&CC. Number 20 was also the star of a Hollywood Western of the 1950s ''A Ticket to Tomahawk.'' PFM imported this dainty little locomotive in 1964.

Southern Pacific

Whyte Class	Owner Class & Type	Model Production					List Price	Resale		Remarks
		Importer	Builder	Cat #	Quan.	Yrs.		Mint	Avg.	
2-6-0	Mogul	JoeW	Sango			83			50	HOn3/HOn30 Kit
2-8-0	#1 Consol	WMC	Mizuno	MO-08	300	70	60	190	160	See Note #1624
2-8-0	#1 Consol	WMC	Mizuno	MO-08	300	67	50	180	150	See Note #1625
4-6-0	#9 Ten Wheeler	PFM	United		500	65	40	210	180	
4-6-0	#9 Ten Wheeler	WMC		MO-01	500	65-69	40-45	200	160	
4-6-0	#18 Ten Wheeler	WMC		MO-11		65-69	43-50	200	160	G-File #11
4-6-0	#8 Ten Wheeler	WMC		MO-04	300	65-69	40-45	200	180	See Note #1626

Sandy River & Rangely Lakes

Whyte Class	Owner Class & Type	Model Production					List Price	Resale		Remarks
		Importer	Builder	Cat #	Quan.	Yrs.		Mint	Avg.	
2-4-4T	#10 Forney	FZoo				84	230			
2-6-0	Mogul	FZoo				84	175			

Sumpter Valley

Whyte Class	Owner Class & Type	Model Production					List Price	Resale		Remarks
		Importer	Builder	Cat #	Quan.	Yrs.		Mint	Avg.	
2-6-6-2	#250 Articulated	PFM	United		275	68	80	380	320	See Note #1627
2-6-6-2	#250 Articulated	PFM	United		475	66	65	350	290	See Note #1627
2-6-6-2	#250 Articulated	PFM	United		200	78	495	500	470	See Note #669

Uintah

Whyte Class	Owner Class & Type	Model Production					List Price	Resale		Remarks
		Importer	Builder	Cat #	Quan.	Yrs.		Mint	Avg.	
2-6-6-2T	Articulated	PFM	United		350	78	495	560	500	See Note #670

Locomotives often found their way to several railroads, but few have as interesting a history as Unitah #50 and 51. Originally built as tank engines, they were sold to the Sumpter Valley, after which the side tanks were removed and a tender was added. The Sumpter Valley then sold the engines to a railroad in Guatamala, where they lasted into the mid-'60s. Pacific Fast Mail imported both the Uintah and Sumpter Valley versions of this United-built model in 1978.

White Pass & Yukon

Whyte Class	Owner Class & Type	Model Production					List Price	Resale		Remarks
		Importer	Builder	Cat #	Quan.	Yrs.		Mint	Avg.	
2-8-2	#70 Mikado	PFM	United		500	68	60	225		

The White Pass & Yukon received its first Baldwin built Mikado (#70) in 1938 and later purchased three more engines (#71–73). These engines were basically a Baldwin stock model with inside frames, a straight boiler, and Walschaerts valve gear. Their resemblance to the East Broad Top's Mikados is no coincidence. Both were stock-model Baldwins. Pacific Fast Mail imported this fine little HOn3 Mike in 1968.

PART V

DIESELS

American Locomotive Co., Inc. (Alco)

Road	AAR Code	Class & Phase	Type	Model Production					List Price	Resale		Remarks
				Importer	Builder	Cat #	Quan.	Yrs.		Mint	Avg.	
GN	B-B	100 Ton	Sw	Ortl	FM			86	200			See Note #1629
Erie	B-B	100 Ton	Sw	Ortl	FM			86	200			See Note #1630
	B-B	100 Ton	Sw	Ortl	FM			86	200			See Note #1631
	B-B	1000 RS	Sw	Intl				51	23	75	60	Kit
	B-B	44 Ton	Sw	PFM	United		102	56	20	125	90	
	B-B	S-1	Sw	Alco	KMT	D-116		69	43	100		See Note #674
	B-B	S-1	Sw	Alco	KMT	D-116		77	95	100		660 hp.
AT&SF	B-B	S-1	Sw	Key	Samh			85	221	240		cp. #2304
	B-B	S-1	Sw	Key	Samh			84	186	200		
NYC	B-B	S-1	Sw	Key	Samh			85	221	240		cp. #8560
PRR	B-B	S-1	Sw	Key	Samh			85	221	250		cp. #5661
	B-B	S-2	Sw	Alco	KMT	D-129		76	95	100		Short re-run
	B-B	S-2	Sw	Alco	Samh			81	175	175		See Note #675
	B-B	S-2	Sw	Alco	KMT	D-129		69	43	100		1000 hp.
	B-B	S-2	Sw	Key	Samh			84	186	190		
AT&SF	B-B	S-2	Sw	Key	Samh			84	186	190		
	B-B	S-2	Sw	Trains	KMT		1000	67	35	100		1000 hp.
	B-B	S-3	Sw	Alco	KMT	D-154		76	95	100		See Note #676
	B-B	S-3	Sw	Key	Samh				186	190		
	B-B	S-4	Sw	Alco	KMT	D-165		76	95	100		1000 hp.
	B-B	S-4	Sw	Alco	Samh			81	175	175		See Note #675
PRR	B-B	S-4	Sw	Key	Samh			84	193	200		with antennas
B&O	B-B	S-4	Sw	Key	Samh			86	221	250		fp., B&O #9012
	B-B	S-4	Sw	Key	Samh			84	186	155	100	
	B-B	S-5	Sw	Alco	KMT	D-155		76	97	100		See Note #677
	B-B	S-6	Sw	Alco	KMT	D-155		76	97	100		See Note #678
	B-B	C415	Sw	PSM				67	40	125	100	1500 hp. Center Cab

The Alco S–1 was the first in a series of switchers that numbered over 3,600 units between 1950 and 1958. Sharing the same general squarish hood shape of the RS–1, the units resembled the Alco road switcher with the short hood removed. Built in 1950, the S–1 was Alco's answer to EMD's SW7 switcher. The S–1, 2,3, and 4 switchers all were very similar in appearance. The major distinguishing feature of the S–1 is the Blunt trucks and radiator shutters smaller than those used on the S–2s and S–4s. Alco Models imported the S–1 in 1969 and 1977. The later model was equipped with a much-improved drive mechanism.

American Locomotive Co., Inc. (cont'd)

Road	AAR Code	Class & Phase		Type	Importer	Builder	Cat #	Quan.	Yrs.	List Price	Mint	Avg.	Remarks
	B-B	C420 DL-721A		RSw	Alco	KMT	D-110	700	68	43	140	120	See Note #1632
	B-B	C420 DL-721A		RSw	Alco	KMT	D-115	500	68	43	135	115	See Note #1633
	B-B	C420 DL-721A		RSw	Alco	KMT	D-110	700	75	95			2000 hp., LoH
	B-B	C420 DL-721A		RSw	Alco	KMT	D-115	500	75	95			2000 hp., HiH
Sev	B-B	C420 DL-721A	I	RSw	OMI	Ajin	1857	150	84	214	214		See Note #1634
LI	B-B	C420 DL-721A	II	RSw	OMI	Ajin	5794	50	90	334	281		See Note #1635
LV	B-B	C420 DL-721A	I	RSw	OMI	Ajin	5787	40	90	334	281		See Note #1636
L&N	B-B	C420 DL-721A	I	RSw	OMI	Ajin	5789	13	90	334	281		See Note #1637
L&HR	B-B	C420 DL-721A	II	RSw	OMI	Ajin	5793	25	90	334	281		See Note #1638
NKP	B-B	C420 DL-721A	I	RSw	OMI	Ajin	5790	15	90	334	281		See Note #1639
SAL	B-B	C420 DL-721A	I	RSw	OMI	Ajin	5792	12	90	334	281		See Note #1640
LI	B-B	C420 DL-721A	I	RSw	OMI	Ajin	5788	50	90	334	281		See Note #1641
TC	B-B	C420 DL-721A		Cab	OMI	Ajin	5799	20	89	334	281		#400-401
Sev	B-B	C420 DL-721A	II	RSw	OMI	Ajin	1858	100	84	214	214		See Note #1646
Monon	B-B	C420 DL-721A	II	RSw	OMI	Ajin	5799	15	90	334	281		See Note #1642
L&HR	B-B	C420 DL-721A	I	RSw	OMI	Ajin	5786	15	90	334	281		See Note #1643
L&N	B-B	C420 DL-721A	II	RSw	OMI	Ajin	5795	10	90	334	281		See Note #1644
LI	B-B	C420 DL-721A	I	RSw	OMI	Ajin	1856	50	84	214	214		HiH
N&W	B-B	C420 DL-721A	I	RSw	OMI	Ajin	5791	20	90	334	281		See Note #1645
SP&S		C425 DL-640B											
BN,	B-B	C425 DL-640B	II	RSw	OMI	Ajin	1926.1	N/A	87	307	258		fp.

The RS-1 was Alco's first road switcher, a unit designed to compete with EMD for the market in light road switchers. With a total of 607 units delivered to U.S. roads between 1940 and 1957, Alco was definitely a strong influence in the marketplace. The RS-1 was the immediate predecessor to Alco's very popular RS-2 and RS-3 locomotives. Easily distinguished from its later counterparts by its angular lines and relatively square hoods, the RS-1 had a longer production run than any other diesel locomotive in American history. Samhongsa produced this excellent replica of the PRR version in 1982.

American Locomotive Co., Inc. (cont'd)

Road	AAR Code	Class & Phase		Type	Importer	Builder	Cat #	Quan.	Yrs.	List Price	Mint	Avg.	Remarks
						Model Production					Resale		
PRR	B-B	C425 DL-640B	II	RSw	OMI	Ajin	1925	20	86	236			
NH	B-B	C425 DL-640B	II	RSw	OMI	Ajin	1924.1	N/A	87	307	258		fp.
PRR	B-B	C425 DL-640B	II	RSw	OMI	Ajin	1925	30	85	236	236		w/Dynamic Brake
NH	B-B	C425 DL-640B	II	RSw	OMI	Ajin	1924	35	86	236			
NH	B-B	C425 DL-640B	II	RSw	OMI	Ajin	1924	50	85	236	236		w/o Dynamic Brakes
E-L	B-B	C425 DL-640B	I	RSw	OMI	Ajin	1923	40	85	236	236		w/Dynamic Brake
	B-B	C430		RSw	Alco	KMT	D-144	800	74	73	145	125	See Note #684
RDG	B-B	C430		RSw	OMI	Ajin	1927	25	85	236	236		See Note #1646
NYC	B-B	C430		RSw	OMI	Ajin	1928	60	88	236	198		
NYC	B-B	C430		RSw	OMI	Ajin	1928	50	86	236			See Note #1647
RDG	B-B	C430		RSw	OMI	Ajin	1927	19	86	236			
RDG	B-B	C430		RSw	OMI	Ajin	1927	35	88	236	198		
Susq	B-B	C430		RSw	OMI	Ajin	1928	50	85	236	236		See Note #1647
UP	B-B	DL-640		RSw	OMI	Ajin	1889	125	85	222	222		w/Dynamic Brake
Sev	B-B	DL-640		RSw	OMI	Ajin	1890	50	85	222	222		See Note #1649
PRR	B-B	DL-640		RSw	OMI	Ajin	1891	50	85	222	222		See Note #1650
PRR	B-B	FA-1		Cab	Key	Samh		40	84	221			
	B-B	FA-1		Cab	Key	Samh		40	84	214		174	late, lg numberboards
	B-B	FA-1		Cab	Key	Samh		130	84	214		174	early, sm numberboards
MKT	B-B	FA-1		Cab	OMI	Ajin	1881.4	N/A	87	243	243		fp., See Note #1651
UP	B-B	FA-1		Cab	OMI	Ajin	1881	125	84	207	207		See Note #1651
GN	B-B	FA-1		Cab	OMI	Ajin	1881	125	84	207	207		See Note #1651
PRR	B-B	FA-1		Cab	OMI	Ajin	1882	50	84	207	207		See Note #1653
	B-B	FA-1		Cab	OMI	Ajin	1883	50	84	207	207		See Note #1654
E-L	B-B	FA-1		Cab	OMI	Ajin	1880	75	84	207	207		See Note #1653
	B-B	FA-1		Cab	OMI	Ajin	1884	60	84	207	207		See Note #1656
	B-B	FA-1 A&B		Cab	Alco	KMT	D-109	500	75	165	210	165	See Note #1657
PRR	B-B	RS-1		RSw	Alco	Samh		100	82	206	175		can motor
	B-B	RS-1		RSw	Alco	KMT	D-106	750	71	68	125	110	Freight
	B-B	RS-1		RSw	Alco	KMT	D-106	250	77	130	135	125	
	B-B	RS-1		RSw	Alco	Samh		300	82	206		155	
AT&SF	B-B	RS-1		RSw	Key	Samh		50	84	200	165		dual service

The DL-600b, or RSD-15, depending on who you are talking to, was built from 1956-60 using the Alco #251B engine which developed 2,400 hp. Both low- and high-hood versions were built. The low-hood AT&SF versions were often referred to as "Alligators." On the C&O they were called "Dragon Ladies." In all, 85 units were built for several American roads. Alco Models imported this model in 1973 from Kumata and in 1983 from Samhongsa. The Samhongsa model had the better drive train.

American Locomotive Co., Inc. (cont'd)

Road	AAR Code	Class & Phase		Type	Importer	Builder	Cat #	Quan.	Yrs.	List Price	Mint	Avg.	Remarks
PRR	B-B	RS-1		RSw	Key	Samh			50	84	200	165		with antennas
	B-B	RS-1		RSw	Key	Samh			150	84	200	165		Standard
	B-B	RS-1		RSw	Red					50	25			See Note #679
	B-B	RS-1		RSw	Sunset					85	105	90		
	B-B	RS-11 DL-701		RSw	Alco	Samh		200	81	206		150	HiH; Full Tank
	B-B	RS-11 DL-701		RSw	Alco	Samh		200	81	206		150	See Note #685
	B-B	RS-11 DL-701		RSw	Alco	KMT	D-108	1000	69	43	135	110	1800 hp.
SP	B-B	RS-11 DL-701		RSw	Key	Samh		100	86	221	186		HiH
SP	B-B	RS-11 DL-701		RSw	Key	Samh		75	86	221	186		HiH
NP/BN	B-B	RS-11 DL-701		RSw	Key	Samh		150	86	221	149		HiH
	B-B	RS-2		RSw	Alco	KMT	D-132	1000	72	68	125	105	1500 hp.
	B-B	RS-2		RSw	Alco	KMT	D-132	200	77-78	130-138	138	140	1500 hp.
	B-B	RS-2		RSw	Alco	Samh		200	83	216		150	1500 hp.
	B-B	RS-2		RSw	Intl				51	23			crude
NH	B-B	RS-2		RSw	Key	Samh		50	84			170	
	B-B	RS-2		RSw	Key	Samh		50	84			170	
	B-B	RS-27 DL-640		RSw	Alco	KMT	D-101		67	43	115	90	See Note #1661
PRR	B-B	RS-27 DL-640		RSw	Alco	KMT	D-101P		83	175			2400 hp., PRR
several	B-B	RS-27 DL-640		RSw	Alco	KMT	D-101		83	175			2400 hp., UP, Soo, GBW
	B-B	RS-27 DL-640		RSw	LMB	KMT			20	67			
	B-B	RS-3		RSw	Alco	KMT	D-123	200	77-78	130-138	140	120	See Note #1660
	B-B	RS-3		RSw	Alco	KMT	D-123	1000	72	68	120	110	1600 hp.
PRR	B-B	RS-3		RSw	Alco	Samh		50	82	221	190	175	1600 hp.
	B-B	RS-3		RSw	Alco	Samh		50	82	224	190	155	1600 hp., Canadian
	B-B	RS-3		RSw	Alco			300	82	216		150	1600 hp.
	B-B	RS-3	III	RSw	E&P	KMT			84	250	195		late carbody
Erie	B-B	RS-3	II	RSw	Key	Samh		5	84			185	
NYC	B-B	RS-3		RSw	Key	Samh		5	84			175	
PRR	B-B	RS-3		RSw	Key	Samh		10	84				with antennas
	B-B	RS-3	I	RSw	Key	Samh		20	84			170	Standard
NH	B-B	RS-3		RSw	Key	Samh		10	84				
	B-B	RS-3		RSw	Sunset				85	108	90		
	B-B	RS-32 DL-721		RSw	Alco	Samh	D-118	200	81	206	175	165	See Note #1658
	B-B	RS-32 DL-721		RSw	Alco	KMT	D-118	900	70	43	140	120	See Note #1659
	B-B	RS-36 DL-701A		RSw	Key	Samh		75	86	221	186		
	B-B	S-5/6		Sw	Alco	KMT	D-155	500	76	97	125	100	See Note #677, #678
PRR	B-B	T-6 DL-440		TSw	Alco	KMT	D-112P	800	74	64	115	90	See Note #682
N&W	B-B	T-6 DL-440		TSw	Alco	KMT	D-112N	400	74	64	110	85	See Note #682
	B+B-B+B	FA-2 & FB-2		Cab	OMI	Ajin	1809	100	82	367	375		
	C-C	C628 DL-628		RSw	Alco	KMT	D-139	405	72	70	140	120	See Note #690
	C-C	C628 DL-628		RSw	Alco	KMT	D-138	825	72	70	150	130	See Note #689
	C-C	C628 DL-628		RSw	Ortl	Samh	0363		84	236		190	Standard
SP	C-C	C628 DL-628		RSw	Ortl	Samh	0364		84	236		190	LoH
	C-C	C628 DL-628		RSw	Ortl	Samh	0383	50	84	236		190	HiH
	C-C	C628 DL-628		RSw	Ortl	Samh	0754		91	342			LoH

American Locomotive Co., Inc. (cont'd)

Road	AAR Code	Class & Phase	Type	Importer	Builder	Cat #	Quan.	Yrs.	List Price	Resale Mint	Resale Avg.	Remarks
SCL	C-C	C628 DL-628	RSw	Ortl	Samh	P755		87	300			LoH, fp.
D&H	C-C	C628 DL-628	RSw	Ortl	Samh	P756		87	300			LoH, fp.
LV	C-C	C628 DL-628	RSw	Ortl	Samh	P757		87	300			LoH, fp.
PRR	C-C	C628 DL-628	RSw	Ortl	Samh	P758		87	300			LoH, fp.
CRR	C-C	C628 DL-628	RSw	Ortl	Samh	P759		87	300			LoH, fp.
SP	C-C	C628 DL-628	RSw	Ortl	Samh	P760D		87	300			LoH, fp.
	C-C	C628 DL-628	RSw	Ortl	Samh	0761		88	250			LoH, fp.
Monon	C-C	C628 DL-628	RSw	Ortl	Samh	P960		88	300			LoH, fp.
L&N	C-C	C628 DL-628	RSw	Ortl	Samh	P961		88	300			LoH, fp.
C&NW	C-C	C628 DL-628	RSw	Ortl	Samh	P962		88	300			HiH, fp.
	C-C	C630	RSw	Alco	KMT	D-104	800	68	48	150	125	See Note #691
	C-C	C630	RSw	Alco	KMT	D-117		68	48	145	120	See Note #691
ACL	C-C	C630	RSw	OMI	Ajin	6150	424	356				#2011-2013 1966 era
C&O	C-C	C630	RSw	OMI	Ajin	6151	424	356				#2100-2103 1971-74 era
C&O	C-C	C630	RSw	OMI	Ajin	6151.1	531	446				cp. blue
CR	C-C	C630	RSw	OMI	Ajin	6152	424	356				#6769,6772,6776-77
Conrail	C-C	C630	RSw	OMI	Ajin	6152.1	531	446				cp. blue
L&N	C-C	C630	RSw	OMI	Ajin	6153	424	356				#1425-1432
N&W	C-C	C630	RSw	OMI	Ajin	6154	424	356				#1130-1134; 1968 era
N&W	C-C	C630	RSw	OMI	Ajin	6154.2	531	446				cp. blue
N&W	C-C	C630	RSw	OMI	Ajin	6155	424	356				#1135-39, w/F-M sd frms
N&W	C-C	C630	RSw	OMI	Ajin	6155.1	531	446				cp. black
N&W	C-C	C630	RSw	OMI	Ajin	6155.2	531	446				cp. blue
PRR	C-C	C630	RSw	OMI	Ajin	6156	424	356				#6315-6329
RDG	C-C	C630	RSw	OMI	Ajin	6157	424	356				#5307-5377
SCL	C-C	C630	RSw	OMI	Ajin	6158	424	356				#2211-2213
SCL	C-C	C630	RSw	OMI	Ajin	6158.1	531	446				cp.
SP	C-C	C630	RSw	OMI	Ajin	6159	424	356				#7800-7814; 1967 era
SP	C-C	C630	RSw	OMI	Ajin	6159.1	531	446				cp. gray/red
SP	C-C	C630	RSw	OMI	Ajin	6160	424	356				Slug #1000,1,2
SP	C-C	C630	RSw	OMI	Ajin	6160.1	531	446				cp.
UP	C-C	C630	RSw	OMI	Ajin	6161	424	356				#2900-2909; 1968-70 era
UP	C-C	C630	RSw	OMI	Ajin	6161.1	531	446				cp. yellow/gray
	C-C	C630	RSw	Ortl	Samh	0365		84	236		190	Standard
UP	C-C	C630	RSw	Ortl	Samh	0366		84	236		190	HiH
	C-C	C630	RSw	Ortl	Samh	0384		84	236			See Note #1660
CN	C-C	C630	RSw	Ortl	Samh	0385		84	246			
CP	C-C	C630	RSw	Ortl	Samh	0450		85	246			
	C-C	C630	RSw	Ortl	Samh	0763		87	250			LoH
	C-C	C630	RSw	Ortl	Samh	0763		91	342			LoH
	C-C	C630	RSw	Ortl	Samh	O771		86	250			HiH
UP	C-C	C630	RSw	Ortl	Samh	P766		86	300			fp., LoH
PRR	C-C	C630	RSw	Ortl	Samh	P767		86	300			fp., LoH
CRR	C-C	C630	RSw	Ortl	Samh	P768		86	300			fp., LoH
RDG	C-C	C630	RSw	Ortl	Samh	P769		86	300			fp., LoH, w/Hi-ad Trucks
C&O	C-C	C630	RSw	Ortl	Samh	P770		86	300			fp., LoH, w/Hi-ad Trucks
N&W	C-C	C630	RSw	Ortl	Samh	P771		86	300			fp., HiH
CRR	C-C	C630	RSw	Ortl	Samh	P963		88	300			fp., w/hi-ad trucks
SP	C-C	C630	RSw	Ortl	Samh	P964		88	300			fp.
L&N	C-C	C630	RSw	Ortl	Samh	P965		88	300			fp.
	C-C	C636	RSw	Alco	KMT	D-141	438	80	215	185	165	See Note #1661
	C-C	C636	RSw	Alpha				84	200		165	
Demo	C-C	C636	RSw	OMI	Ajin	6162		92	424	356		#636-1,2,3 (Alco Demo)
BN	C-C	C636	RSw	OMI	Ajin	6163		92	424	356		#4360-4369
BN	C-C	C636	RSw	OMI	Ajin	6163.1		92	531	450		cp. green & black
CR	C-C	C636	RSw	OMI	Ajin	6164		92	424	356		#6780-6794

American Locomotive Co., Inc. (cont'd)

The C–636 was the last new model built by Alco and was intended to compete with the EMD SD–45. Production began in 1967 and lasted only one year, with a total of 34 units being produced. The "Century" car-body design began in 1963 with the introduction of the C–420. The most visible difference from previous models was the shortened nose and the change from side-mounted shutters to a top-mounted radiator arrangement. The same locomotive was built by Montreal Locomotive works in Canada. Overland has captured the compact bulk of this interesting prototype in this model painted for the Alco Demonstrator locomotive.

| Road | AAR Code | Class & Phase | Type | Model Production | | | | | List Price | Resale | | Remarks |
				Importer	Builder	Cat #	Quan.	Yrs.		Mint	Avg.	
Conrail	C-C	C636	RSw	OMI	Ajin	6164.1		92	531	450		cp. blue
IC	C-C	C636	RSw	OMI	Ajin	6165		92	424	356		#1100-1105
PC	C-C	C636	RSw	OMI	Ajin	6166		92	424	356		#6630-6344
SP&S	C-C	C636	RSw	OMI	Ajin	6167		92	424	356		#330-335,340-343
	C-C	C636	RSw	Ortl	Samh	0367		84	236		200	
	C-C	C636	RSw	Ortl	Samh	0772		87	250			LoH
IC	C-C	C636	RSw	Ortl	Samh	P773		86	300			fp., LoH
SP&S	C-C	C636	RSw	Ortl	Samh	P774		86	300			fp., LoH
BN	C-C	C636	RSw	Ortl	Samh	P775		86	300			fp., LoH
CRR	C-C	C636	RSw	Ortl	Samh	P776		86	300			fp., LoH
	C-C	C636	RSw	Ortl	Samh	0772		91	342			LoH
	C-C	C643DH DL-400	RSw	Alco	KMT	D-111	700	70	53	195	175	See Note #1662
SP	C-C	DH-643	RSw	OMI	Ajin	1911	200	90	467	450		See Note #1663
WP&Y	C-C	DL-535 MLW	RSw	PSC	Mizuno	007-1		83	289	250		fp., See Note #1664
WP&Y	C-C	DL-535 MLW	RSw	PSC	Mizuno			79	259	225	210	See Note #1664
	C-C	RSD-15 DL-600B	RSw	Alco	KMT	D-114		68	48	145	125	See Note #1665
	C-C	RSD-15 DL-600B	RSw	Alco	Samh	D-102		83	200		170	HiH
	C-C	RSD-15 DL-600B	RSw	Alco	KMT	D-102		68	48	160	140	See Note #1666
	C-C	RSD-15 DL-600B	RSw	Alco		D-102		80	210		165	HiH
	C-C	RSD-15 DL-600B	RSw	Alco	Samh	D-102		83	200		165	LoH
	C-C	RSD-15 DL-600B	RSw	Alco	KMT	D-102	400	73	73	150	130	See Note #1667
PRR	C-C	RSD12 DL-702	RSw	OMI	Ajin	5147.1	5	89	414	348		See Note #1668
Sev	C-C	RSD12 DL-702	RSw	OMI	Ajin	5148	39	89	327	275		See Note #1669
LS&I	C-C	RSD12 DL-702	RSw	OMI	Ajin	5146	20	89	327	275		#1800-1804
NKP	C-C	RSD12 DL-702	RSw	OMI	Ajin	5145	70	89	327	275		See Note #1670
	C-C	RSD-4/5 I	RSw	Alco	Samh	D-121	200	82	224	220		

American Locomotive Co., Inc. (cont'd)

Alco records refer to this locomotive as a DL–108, but the Southern Railroad referred to them as DL–109s. Otto Kuhler designed the unique car-body that makes these units easily identifiable. Introduced in 1940, a total of 78 units were built by 1945. Designed for passenger service, these units were also quite successful as freight power. The busy side appearance, with several windows, doors, and grilles, of the DL–109s was replaced with a much cleaner design on the PA locomotives that were built to replace the DLs. Overland's model of this early Alco diesel successfully captures the subtle shape of the Kuhler-designed front end and is complete with a myriad of fine detail.

Road	AAR Code	Class & Phase	Type	Importer	Builder	Cat #	Quan.	Yrs.	List Price	Mint	Avg.	Remarks
	C-C	RSD-4/5	RSw	Alco	KMT	D-121	200	77	130	130	130	See Note #681
	C-C	RSD-4/5 III	RSw	Alco	Samh	D-121A	200	82	221	220		See Note #1671
	C-C	RSD-4/5	RSw	Alco	KMT	D-121	500	72	70	130	110	See Note #680
	C-C	RSD-4/5	RSw	Key	Samh		100	84	210	176		
AT&SF	C-C	RSD-4/5	RSw	Key	Samh			86	250			fp.
	C-C	RSD-5	RSw	PSM				72	63	125	100	See Note #680
UP	B+B-B+B	C-855A (DL-855)	RSw	Alco	KMT	D-107	600	71	120	200	175	See Note #1672
UP	B+B-B+B	C-855A (DL-855)	RSw	Ortl	Samh	P263		84	439			fp., UP
UP	B+B-B+B	C-855A (DL-855)	RSw	Ortl	Samh	0263	200	83	400	370	340	
UP	B+B-B+B	C-855B (DL-855)	RSw	Alco	KMT	D-105	300	71	175	160	190	See Note #1672
UP	B+B-B+B	C-855B (DL-855)	RSw	Ortl	Samh	0264	100	83	372	340	320	
CRIP	A1A-A1A	DL-103 A	Cab	OMI	Ajin	1982	40	87	314	264		#624
GM&O	A1A-A1A	DL-105 A	Cab	OMI	Ajin	1985	30	87	271	228		#270-271
GM&O	A1A-A1A	DL-105 A	Cab	OMI	Ajin	1992		92	380	320		#270-271
SRR	A1A-A1A	DL-107 A	Cab	OMI	Ajin	1988	30	87	264	222		DP6400-DP6401
Milw	A1A-A1A	DL-107 A	Cab	OMI	Ajin	1991	30	87	264	222		#14A,14B
CRIP	A1A-A1A	DL-107 A	Cab	OMI	Ajin	1983	30	87	264	222		#621,623
ATSF	A1A-A1A	DL-107 A	Cab	OMI	Ajin	1986	30	87	285	240		#50 Plated
C&NW	A1A-A1A	DL-107 A	Cab	OMI	Ajin	1990	30	87	264	222		#5007A
AT&SF	A1A-A1A A1A-A1A	DL-107 A and DL-108B	Cab	OMI	Ajin	6309		92	795			2-unit Set 50 & 50A
ATSF	A1A-A1A	DL-108 A	Cab	OMI	Ajin	1987	30	87	264	222		#50A Plated
SRR	A1A-A1A	DL-108 A	Cab	OMI	Ajin	1989	30	87	228	192		DP6400A-DP6401A
SRR	A1A-A1A	DL-108 A	Cab	OMI	Ajin	6318		92	380	320		DP6400A/01 Class
SRR	A1A-A1A	DL-108 B	Cab	OMI	Ajin	6319		92	380	320		DP6400A/01 Class
	A1A-A1A	DL-109 A	Cab	Hall	Ajin		300	80	230	200	180	
CRIP	A1A-A1A	DL-109 A	Cab	OMI	Ajin	1984	40	87	314	264		#621 EMD Rebuild
CRIP	A1A-A1A	DL-109 A	Cab	OMI	Ajin	6316		92	380	320		#621-623 as delivered
CRIP	A1A-A1A	DL-109 A	Cab	OMI	Ajin	6317		92	380	320		#621 "Christine" EMD form
NH	A1A-A1A	DL-109 A	Cab	OMI	Ajin	1993	30	87	264	222		DER-1b #0710-0749
NH	A1A-A1A	DL-109 A	Cab	OMI	Ajin	6312		92	380	320		#0700-0709
NH	A1A-A1A	DL-109 A	Cab	OMI	Ajin	6313		92	380	320		Class DER-1a-b-c
NH	A1A-A1A	DL-109 A	Cab	OMI	Ajin	6314		92	380	320		Class DER-1c
NH	A1A-A1A	DL-109 A	Cab	OMI	Ajin	6315		92	380	320		Class DER-1b
NH	A1A-A1A	DL-109 A	Cab	OMI	Ajin	1994	30	87	271	228		Class DER-1b
NH	A1A-A1A	DL-109 A	Cab	OMI	Ajin	1996	30	87	264	222		Class DER-1a-b-c
NH	A1A-A1A	DL-109 A	Cab	OMI	Ajin	1992	30	87	264	222		DER-1-A #0700-0709
NH	A1A-A1A	DL-109 A	Cab	OMI	Ajin	1995	30	87	264	222		Class DER-1c

American Locomotive Co., Inc. (cont'd)

Road	AAR Code	Class & Phase	Type	Importer	Builder	Cat #	Quan.	Yrs.	List Price	Mint	Avg.	Remarks
NH	A1A-A1A	DL-109/110	Cab	Hall	KMT		200	71		225	200	See Note #692, fp.
	A1A-A1A	DL-109/110	Cab	Hall	KMT		500	71	97	200	175	See Note #692
CNR		HR616	Rsw	OMI	Ajin	5293			TBA	TBA		#2100-2129 MF-32a Class
	A1A-A1A+ A1A-A1bA	PA-1/PB-1	Cab	Ortl	Samh	0168	125	82	228			A powered, B dummy
AT&SF	A1A-A1A+ A1A-A1A	PA-1/PB-1	Cab	Ortl	Samh	0169	50	82	228			A powered, B dummy
	A1A-A1A+ A1A-A1A	PA-1/PB-1	Cab	Ortl	Samh	0305		84	450			both powered
	A1A-A1A	PA-1	Cab	Ortl		0166	50	82	228			
	A1A-A1A	PA-1	Cab	Ortl		0167	25	82	228			AT&SF,D&RGW,D&H
PRR	A1A-A1A	PA-1	Cab	Key	Samh			86	205			with antennas
D&H	A1A-A1A	PA-1	Cab	OMI	Ajin	5948	25	89	317	266		ex. AT&SF #16-19
UP	A1A-A1A	PA-1	Cab	OMI	Ajin	5946	20	89	295	248		w/cast pilot
D&RGW	A1A-A1A	PA-1	Cab	OMI	Ajin	5908	10	89	284	239		
Wabash	A1A-A1A	PA-1	Cab	OMI	Ajin	5947	15	89	284	239		#1020 A, 1021 A
D&RGW	A1A-A1A	PA-1	Cab	OMI	Ajin	5907	15	89	284	239		w/Large Side Number Boards
NYC	A1A-A1A	PA-1	Cab	OMI	Ajin	5922	25	89	284	239		#4200-4207
SP	A1A-A1A	PA-1	Cab	OMI	Ajin	5934	20	89	284	239		See Note #1674
ATSF	A1A-A1A	PA-1	Cab	OMI	Ajin	5901	20	89	317	266		Original #51- ,70L-73L
PRR	A1A-A1A	PA-1	Cab	OMI	Ajin	5930	25	89	299	251		See Note #1675
UP	A1A-A1A	PA-1	Cab	OMI	Ajin	5944	10	89	284	239		See Note #1676
GN&O	A1A-A1A	PA-1	Cab	OMI	Ajin	5913	10	89	284	239		#290-292
UP	A1A-A1A	PA-1	Cab	OMI	Ajin	5943.1	10	89	377	317		Original
PRR	A1A-A1A	PA-1	Cab	OMI	Ajin	5929	25	89	299	251		See Note #1677
NH	A1A-A1A	PA-1	Cab	OMI	Ajin	5920	30	89	284	239		#0760-0786
Erie	A1A-A1A	PA-1	Cab	OMI	Ajin	5911	20	89	284	239		#850-861
E-L	A1A-A1A	PA-1	Cab	OMI	Ajin	5912	25	89	284	239		#850-861
MP	A1A-A1A	PA-1	Cab	OMI	Ajin	5917	15	89	284	239		#8001-8008
NKP	A1A-A1A	PA-1	Cab	OMI	Ajin	5928	20	89	284	239		See Note #1678
UP	A1A-A1A	PA-1	Cab	OMI	Ajin	5943	20	89	284	239		See Note #1679
AT&SF	A1A-A1A	PA-1	Cab	OMI	Ajin	5903	29	89	317	266		Modernized, plated
SP	A1A-A1A	PA-1	Cab	OMI	Ajin	5935	25	89	293	246		See Note #1680
T&NO	A1A-A1A	PA-1	Cab	OMI	Ajin	5942	16	89	284	239		#200-201
UP	A1A-A1A	PA-1	Cab	OMI	Ajin	5944.1	10	89	377	317		Modernized
ATSF	A1A-A1A	PA-1	Cab	OMI	Ajin	5905	25	89	339	284		See Note #1681
Sou	A1A-A1A	PA-3	Cab	OMI	Ajin	5933	20	89	284	239		#6900-6905
SP	A1A-A1A	PA-3	Cab	OMI	Ajin	5939	20	89	284	239		Original #6023-6045

In the never ending quest for more horsepower, Alco built three dual-engined diesel-hydraulics for the Southern Pacific, numbered 9018–9020. Identified as Class DH–643 by Alco, these monsters incorporated two type 251C 2,150 hp prime movers and a German-built hydraulic transmission. These unique units are easily identified by their two large radiator shutter areas and very short front hood. Overland Models imported this impressive engine in 1990.

American Locomotive Co., Inc. (cont'd)

Road	AAR Code	Class & Phase	Type	Importer	Builder	Cat #	Quan.	Yrs.	List Price	Mint	Avg.	Remarks
ATSF	A1A-A1A	PB-1	Cab	OMI	Ajin	5904	25	89	284	239		See Note #1688
NH	A1A-A1A	PB-1	Cab	OMI	Ajin	5921	30	89	284	239		#4300-4303
PRR	A1A-A1A	PB-1	Cab	OMI	Ajin	5931	15	89	251	211		See Note #1689
D&RGW	A1A-A1A	PB-1	Cab	OMI	Ajin	5910	25	89	253	212		See Note #1690
SP	A1A-A1A	PB-1	Cab	OMI	Ajin	5936	15	89	251	211		#5910-5915
NYC	A1A-A1A	PB-1	Cab	OMI	Ajin	5923	10	89	284	239		4300-4303
ATSF	A1A-A1A	PB-1	Cab	OMI	Ajin	5902	20	89	284	239		See Note #1686
UP	A1A-A1A	PB-1	Cab	OMI	Ajin	5945	25	89	251	211		#997B,999B
D&RGW	A1A-A1A	PB-1	Cab	OMI	Ajin	5909	10	89	251	211		#600B, 601B
ATSF	A1A-A1A	PB-1	Cab	OMI	Ajin	5906	15	89	306	257		See Note #1687
	A1A-A1A	PB-1		Ortl	KMT	0307		83	197			Powered B
	A1A-A1A	PB-1		Ortl	KMT	0306		84	141			Unpowered B
	A1A-A1A	PA-1 (DL-304)	Cab	Bal	KMT			68	50	110		fp.
	A1A-A1A	PB-1 (DL-305)	Cab	Bal	KMT			68	23	80		fp., See Note #694
	A1A-A1A+ A1A-A1A	PA-1 /PB-1	Cab	Bal	KMT			68	73			fp., See Note #696
	A1A-A1A+ A1A-A1A	PA-1 /PB-1	Cab	WMC	KMT			74	75			fp., See Note #696
	A1A-A1A+ A1A-A1A	PA-1 /PB-1	Cab	WMC	KMT			75	140			fp., See Note #696
	A1A-A1A	PB-1/2		Key	Samh			86	175			powered B unit
NYC	A1A-A1A	PB-2	Cab	OMI	Ajin	5925	10	89	251	211		#4304
SP	A1A-A1A	PB-2	Cab	OMI	Ajin	5938	12	89	251	211		#5920-5924
SP	A1A-A1A	PB-3	Cab	OMI	Ajin	5941	10	89	251	211		#5920-5924
PRR	A1A-A1A+ A1A-A1A	PA- /PB	Cab	Key	Samh			86	430			See Note #1682
UP	A1A-A1A+ A1A-A1A	PA- /PB	Cab	Key	Samh			86	430			fp., A & B powered
SP	A1A-A1A+ A1A-A1A	PA-3/PB-3	Cab	Key	Samh			86	365			See Note #1683
SP	A1A-A1A+ A1A-A1A	PA-3/PB-3	Cab	Key	Samh			86	435			fp., See Note #1684
AT&SF	A1A-A1A+ A1A-A1A+ A1A-A	PA/PB/PA	Cab	Key	Samh			86	635			fp., See Note #1685

Baldwin Locomotive Works

Road	AAR Code	Class & Phase	Type	Importer	Builder	Cat #	Quan.	Yrs.	List Price	Mint	Avg.	Remarks
AT&SF	B-B		Sw	MBA				60	22	110	85	
	B-B		Sw	MBA				60	20	90	70	
MKT	B-B	AS-16	RSw	Hall	Samh	HS0258						
	B-B	AS-16	RSw	Hall	Samh	HS0265						
	B-B	AS-16	RSw	Hall	Samh	HS0028						
	B-B	AS-16 (DS-14)	RSw	Hall	KMT		500	69	50	130	115	
	B-B	AS-16 (DS-14)	RSw	Hall		HS0028		88	199	167		
	B-B	AS-416	RSw	Hall		HS0030		88	203	170		
	B-B	AS-416	RSw	Hall	Samh	HS0030						
	B-B	DRS-4-4-1000	RSw	Hall	Samh	HS0261						
	B-B	DRS-4-4-15 (DS-14)	RSw	PSM				71	55	130	115	See Note #1692
	B-B	DRS-4-4-1500	RSw	Hall		HS0255		88	199	167		
	B-B	DRS-4-4-1500	RSw	Hall	Samh	HS0255						
	B-B	DRS-6-6-1500	RSw	Hall	Samh	HS0260						
	B-B	DRS-6-6-1500	RSw	Hall	Samh	HS0031						
	B-B	DRS-6-6-2000	RSw	Hall	Samh	HS0269						
	B-B	DRS-6-6-2000	RSw	Hall	Samh	HS0270						
	B-B	DR-4-4-15 A&B	RSw	Hall	KMT		500	71	75	175	155	
	B-B	DS-4-4-10	Sw	Hall	Samh	HS0033		82	211		170	See Note#1693
	B-B	DS-4-4-6	Sw	Hall	Samh			82	211		170	See Note#1694
CNR		HR616	Rsw	OMI	Ajin	5293			TBA	TBA		
	B-B	RF-16A	Cab	Alco	KMT	D-119A		74	64	120	100	See Note #1695
	B-B	RF-16A	Cab	Alco	KMT			73-77	32-43	80	65	See Note #1696
	B-B	RF-16A	Cab	Alco	KMT	D-119A	1000	69	43	110	90	See Note #1697

Baldwin Locomotive Works (cont'd)

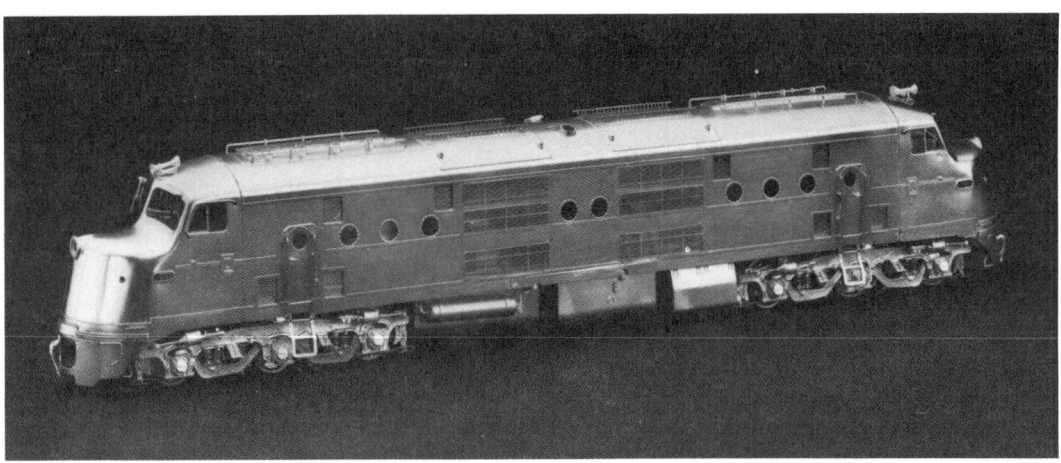

From 1946 through 1948 Baldwin built a total of 26 DR–6–4–20 diesel locomotives. Only four roads—PRR, CNJ, GM&O, and NdeM—were purchasers. All but the NdeM units used the "Babyface" cab design and CNJ had the only double enders. Baldwin's design philosophy was strongly rooted in the practices of the steam era and did not stress standardization, but rather tailored the locomotive to the particular road's desires. Although all 26 locos were classified as DR 6–40–20, they were quite different in appearance. Overland Models imported two CNJ versions in 1989. The early version, engines #2000–2002, is pictured.

Road	AAR Code	Class & Phase	Type	Importer	Builder	Cat #	Quan.	Yrs.	List Price	Mint	Avg.	Remarks
						Model Production			List Price	Resale		
Sev	B-B	RF-16A	Cab	OMI	Ajin	1862	125	84	221	221		
PRR	B-B	RF-16A	Cab	OMI	Ajin	1864	75	84	221	221		
O	B-B	RF-16A	Cab	Ortl	Samh	P1020		89	374			fp., green
	B-B	RF-16A&B	Cab	Alco	KMT	D-119S	200	72	75	180	140	See Note#1698
	B-B	RF-16A&B	Cab	Alco	KMT	D-119S		74	95	200	150	See Note#1698
	B-B	RF-16A-B-A	Cab	Alco	KMT			77		285	250	See Note#1698
	B-B	RF-16B	Cab	Alco	KMT	D-119BD		73	33	75	60	See Note#1699
	B-B	RF-16B	Cab	Alco	KMT	D-119B	600	69	40	100	75	
	B-B	RF-16B	Cab	OMI	Ajin	1863	100	84	193	193		
PRR	B-B	RF-16B	Cab	Ortl	Samh	P1021		89	328	276		fp., Green
	B-B	RS-12	RSw	Hall	Samh	HS0263						
	B-B	RS-6-6-20	RSw	Hall	Samh	HS0228						
	B-B	S-12	Sw	Hall	KMT		500	69	50	125	110	
	B-B	S-12	Sw	Hall	KMT		200	82				
	B-B	VO-1000	Sw	Hall	Samh		200	82	211		170	See Note#1701
	B-B	VO-1000	Sw	Hall	KMT		500	71	50	120	100	
	B-B	VO-1000	Sw	Hall	KMT		500	72	55	130	110	
	B-B	VO-1000	Sw	Hall	Samh		200	82	211		170	See Note#1702
	C-C	AS-616	RSw	Hall	Samh	HS0262						
	C-C	AS-616	RSw	Hall	KMT		500	69	50	135	120	
	C-C	AS-616	RSw	Hall	Samh	HS0032						
	C-C	AS-616	RSw	Hall	Samh	HS0267						
	C-C	AS-616	RSw	Hall		HS0032		88	203	170		
	C-C	AS-616	RSw	Hall	Samh	HS0268						See Note#1703
	C-C	AS-616	RSw	Hall	KMT		500	74	98	145	125	See Note#1704
	C-C	AS-616	RSw	Hall		HS0266		88	199	167		
PRR	C-C	BP20A (DR-6-4-20)	Cab	Ortl	Samh	P1049		88	374	314		fp., Tuscan, Twin HL
PRR	C-C	BP20A (DR-6-4-20)	Cab	Ortl	Samh	0777		89	306	258		Twin Headlight, Original
PRR	C-C	BP20A (DR-6-4-20)	Cab	Ortl	Samh	P777		87	357			fp., Tuscan, Twin HL
PRR	C-C	BP20A (DR-6-4-20)	Cab	Ortl	Samh	0778		87	292			Single Headlight
PRR	C-C	BP20A (DR-6-4-20)	Cab	Ortl	Samh	P778B		89	374	314		See Note#1705

Baldwin Locomotive Works (cont'd)

Probably the best known Baldwin diesels were the "Centipedes." A total of 54 units were built between 1945 and 1948, and only three roads were purchasers. The 2–D + D–2 arrangement put a lot of wheels on the rails and accounted for the nickname. These 3,000-hp units used the same "Babyface" cab design popular on other Baldwin units of that period. The PRR roster of these units numbered 24 and they were normally run in pairs—one unit with antennas, one without. Pictured is the Overland Models PRR version built by Ajin.

Road	AAR Code	Class & Phase	Type	Importer	Builder	Cat #	Quan.	Yrs.	List Price	Mint	Avg.	Remarks
PRR	C-C	BP20A (DR-6-4-20)	Cab	Ortl	Samh	P777B		89	374	314		fp., Green, Twin HL
PRR	C-C	BP20A (DR-6-4-20)	Cab	Ortl	Samh	P1051		89	374	314		See Note#1706
PRR	C-C	BP20A (DR-6-4-20)	Cab	Ortl	Samh	0778		89	306	258		See Note#1707
PRR	C-C	BP20A (DR-6-4-20)	Cab	Ortl	Samh	P778T		89	374			fp. Tuscan 5-stripe
PRR	C-C	BP20B (DR-6-4-20B)	Cab	Ortl	Samh	P1019		89	328	276		fp., Green, Production
PRR	C-C	BP20B (DR-6-4-20B)	Cab	Ortl	Samh	P1050		89	328	276		fp., Tuscan, Original
PRR	C-C	BP20B (DR-6-4-20B)	Cab	Ortl	Samh	01018		89	266	224		
PRR	C-C	BP20B (DR-6-4-20B)	Cab	Ortl	Samh	0779		89	266	224		Original
PRR	C-C	BP20B (DR-6-4-20B)	Cab	Ortl	Samh	P1052		89	328	276		fp., Tuscan 1-Stripe
PRR	C-C	BP20B (DR-6-4-20B)	Cab	Ortl	Samh	P780		89	328	276		fp., Tuscan, 5-Stripe
PRR	C-C	BP20B (DR-6-4-20B)	Cab	Ortl	Samh	P781		89	328	276		fp. green, original
PRR	A1A-A1A	BP20A (DR-6-4-20)	Cab	Alco	KMT	D-120A		73	75	140	120	See Note#1708
PRR	A1A-A1A	BP-20A&B (DR-6-4-20)	Cab	Alco	KMT	D-120S		73	120	180	175	See Note#1709
PRR	A1A-A1A	BP-20B (DR-6-4-20)	Cab	Alco	KMT	D-120B		73	50	80	65	See Note#1710
	C-C	DRS-6-6-1500	RSw	Hall		HS0031		88	203	170		
PRR	C-C	RT-624	TSw	CustB	KMT	DE-136	200	79-80	210	210	175	
	A1A-A1A	DRS-6-4-1500	RSw	Hall		HS0029		88	203	170		
CNJ	A1A-A1A	DR-6-4-20	Cab	OMI	Ajin	5136	125	89	350	294		See Note#1711
CNJ	A1A-A1A	DR-6-4-20	Cab	OMI	Ajin	5137	75	89	350	294		See Note#1712
CNJ	A1A-A1A	DR-6-4-20	Cab	OMI	Ajin	5136.1	50	89	557	468		See Note#1713
CNJ	A1A-A1A	DR-6-4-20	Cab	Red	KMT		500	71	68			"Double-Ender"
PRR	2-D + D-2	DR-12-8-1500	Cab	OMI	Ajin	5258	25	90	525	425		Centipede
PRR	2-D + D-2	DR-12-8-1500	Cab	OMI	Ajin	1929	12	86	360			Centipede
PRR	2-D + D-2	DR-12-8-1500	Cab	OMI	Ajin	5257	40	90	525	425		Centipede
PRR	2-D + D-2	DR-12-8-1500	Cab	OMI	Ajin	5299	50	90	525	425		Centipede
PRR	2-D + D-2	DR-12-8-1500	Cab	OMI	Ajin	1930.1	N/A	87	420	353		Centipede
PRR	2-D + D-2	DR-12-8-1500	Cab	OMI	Ajin	1931	85	86	360			See Note#1714
PRR	2-D + D-2	DR-12-8-1500	Cab	OMI	Ajin	1931	40	86	360			Centipede

Baldwin Locomotive Works (cont'd)

Baldwin's AS–616 Class of diesel road switchers were built from 1950 through 1955. With their very square car body mounted atop Baldwin's unique cast-frame trucks, they exemplified the "brick-on-a-flatcar" school of locomotive design. Hallmark imported this model in 1969.

The PRR BP–20s were the only DR–6–4–20 units with the "Shark" car-body. All of the other units used the "Babyface" car body. Alco Models imported this Kumata-built model in 1973.

Road	AAR Code	Class & Phase	Type	Importer	Builder	Cat #	Quan.	Yrs.	List Price	Mint	Avg.	Remarks
Demo	2-D+D-2	DR-12-8-1500	Cab	OMI	Ajin	5259	35	90	525	425		Centipede
PRR	2-D+D-2	DR-12-8-1500	Cab	OMI	Ajin	5298	75	90	525	425		Centipede
PRR	2-D+D-2	DR-12-8-1500	Cab	OMI	Ajin	1931.1	N/A	87	420	353		Centipede
PRR	2-D+D-2	DR-12-8-1500	Cab	OMI	Ajin	1930	13	86	360			Centipede
PRR	2-D+D-2	DR-12-8-1500	Cab	OMI	Ajin	1929.1	N/A	87	420	353		Centipede
PRR	2-D+D-2	DR-12-8-1500	Cab	OMI	Ajin	1932	35	86	360			Centipede
PRR	2-D+D-2	DR-12-8-1500	Cab	OMI	Ajin	1932	60	86	360			See Note#1715
PRR	2-D+D-2	DR-12-8-1500	Cab	OMI	Ajin	1932.1	N/A	87	420	353		Centipede
SBD	2-D+D-2	DR-12-8-1500	Cab	OMI	Ajin	1943	40	86	367			Centipede
PRR	2-D+D-2	DR-12-8-1500	Cab	OMI	Ajin	1929	50	86	360			Centipede
PRR	2-D+D-2	DR-12-8-1500	Cab	OMI	Ajin	1930	30	86	360			Centipede
	2-D+D-2	DR-12-8-1500 (2)	Cab	Hall	KMT		300	71	100	200	150	See Note#1716
	2-D+D-2	DR-12-8-1500 (2)	Cab	Hall	KMT		200	81	300	265	240	See Note#1717
	2-D+D-2	DR-12-8-1500	Cab	Hall	KMT		300	71	107	250	200	See Note#1718

GM Electro-Motive Division

Road	AAR Code	Class & Phase	Type	Importer	Builder	Cat #	Quan.	Yrs.	List Price	Mint	Avg.	Remarks
						5894		91				
AT&SF	B-B		Sw	Hall				82	105		85	See Note #755
			RSw	OMI	Ajin	5894.1	25	91	427			
			RSw	OMI	Ajin	5895.1	25	91	427			
	B-B		Sw	PFM	Kemt		17	54	24	80	55	See Note #715
	B-B		Sw	PFM	Kemt		38	55	24	85	60	See Note #715
	B-B		Sw	PFM	Kemt		3	56	30	90	65	See Note #716
	B-B		Sw	PFM	Kemt		28	56	29	85	60	See Note #715
	B-B		Sw	PFM	Kemt		5	56	29	60	40	See Note #717
	B-B		Sw	PFM	Kemt			57	30	90	65	See Note #716
	B-B		Sw	PFM	Kemt			57	29	60	40	See Note #717
	B-B		Sw	PFM	Kemt			57	30	95	70	See Note #715
	B-B		Sw	PFM	Tensh		100	58	30	105	75	See Note #718, fp.
	B-B		Sw	PFM	Tensh		79	59	30	115	85	See Note #719, fp.
	B-B	MP15	Sw	OMI	Ajin	5076	30	87	221			
	B-B	MP15	Sw	OMI	Ajin	5076	20	90	295			re-run
	B-B	MP15 A-C	Sw	Alco	KMT		300	81	227	190	165	MR Review 2/82
MKT	B-B	MP15 A-C	Sw	OMI	Ajin	5080	10	87	236			#56-59
LI	B-B	MP15 A-C	Sw	OMI	Ajin	5083	35	87	236			#150-172
Milw	B-B	MP15 A-C	Sw	OMI	Ajin	5081	25	87	236			#434-497
SBD	B-B	MP15 A-C	Sw	OMI	Ajin	5084	10	87	236			#4001-4019
SP	B-B	MP15 A-C	Sw	OMI	Ajin	5082	26	87	236			#2700-2759
Milw	B-B	MP15 A-C	Sw	OMI	Ajin	5081	10	90	304			re-run
LI	B-B	MP15 A-C	Sw	OMI	Ajin	5083	15	90	304			re-run
SP	B-B	MP15 A-C	Sw	OMI	Ajin	5082	30	90	304			re-run
Milw	B-B	MP15 A-C	Sw	OMI	Ajin	8081	25	90	304	255		re-run
LI	B-B	MP15 A-C	Sw	OMI	Ajin	8083	15	90	304	255		re-run
MKT	B-B	MP15 A-C	Sw	OMI	Ajin	5080	10	90	304			re-run
	B-B	MP15 D-C	Sw	Alco	KMT		200	81	224	185	160	
	B-B	MP15 D-C	Sw	OMI	Ajin	5078	20	87	221			
SP	B-B	MP15 D-C	Sw	OMI	Ajin	5077	22	87	221			
SRR	B-B	MP15 D-C	Sw	OMI	Ajin	5079	40	87	221			
SP	B-B	MP15 D-C	Sw	OMI	Ajin	5077	20	90	295			re-run
	B-B	MP15 D-C	Sw	OMI	Ajin	5078	15	90	295			re-run
SRR	B-B	MP15 D-C	Sw	OMI	Ajin	5079	30	90	295			re-run

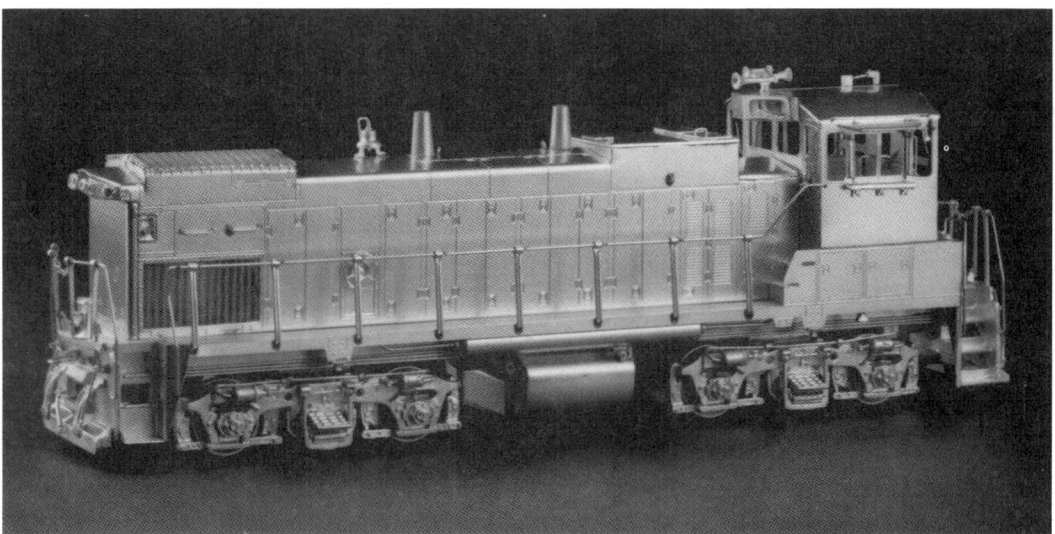

The MP–15 A–C is an MP–15 which uses an alternator and rectifier in place of the DC transmission. This allows these units to use much the same control electronics as used on EMD's bigger power. Built to replace aging GP–7s and 9s, it was only moderately successful, for EMD's GP–15–1 filled a similar market niche. Overland's superb model of the SP version of this unit is pictured.

GM Electro-Motive Division (cont'd)

EMD's NW–2 switcher used the 567 Series 1,000 hp., 12-cylinder engine that seemed to last forever. NW–2s were built from 1939 to 1949 with several variations in equipment and appliances. C&O #5065 shows a later version with the conical stacks and single taper from the cab to hood. These units were quite popular with the roads, for over 1,140 were sold by EMD. Overland's C&O version was imported in 1992.

Road	AAR Code	Class & Phase		Type	Importer	Builder	Cat #	Quan.	Yrs.	List Price	Mint	Avg.	Remarks
											Resale		
					Model Production								
	B-B	NW-2		Sw	Alco	KMT	D-148		75	90	125	100	1000 hp.
B&M	B-B	NW-2		Sw	OMI	Ajin	6188		92	313	265		#1210-1213
C&O	B-B	NW-2		Sw	OMI	Ajin	6190		92	313	265		#5060-5065
C&O	B-B	NW-2		Sw	OMI	Ajin	6190.1		92	406	340		cp. blue
CB&Q	B-B	NW-2		Sw	OMI	Ajin	6191		92	313	265		#9220-9247
GN	B-B	NW-2		Sw	OMI	Ajin	6192		92	313	265		#151-162
Milw	B-B	NW-2		Sw	OMI	Ajin	6193		92	313	265		#670-672
MP	B-B	NW-2		Sw	OMI	Ajin	6194		92	313	265		#1002-1008
NKP	B-B	NW-2		Sw	OMI	Ajin	6195		92	313	265		#11-22
PRR	B-B	NW-2		Sw	OMI	Ajin	6196		92	313	265		#9155-9176
PRR	B-B	NW-2		Sw	OMI	Ajin	6196.1		92	406	340		cp.
UP	B-B	NW-2		Sw	OMI	Ajin	6198		92	313	265		#1076-1095
UP	B-B	NW-2		Sw	OMI	Ajin	6198.1		92	434	365		cp. Yellow/Gray
SP	B-B	NW-2E		Sw	OMI	Ajin	6197		92	313	265		#1312-1331
SP	B-B	NW-2E		Sw	OMI	Ajin	6197.1		92	434	365		cp. Grey/red
WP	B-B	NW-2U		Sw	OMI	Ajin	6199		92	313	265		#607-608
	B-B	NW-2	II	Sw	Ortl	Samh	0556	75	85	182		150	Phase I/II stacks
	B-B	NW-2	II	Sw	Ortl	Samh	0068		81	150	140	120	See Note #725
	B-B	NW-2	III	Sw	Ortl	Samh	0069		81	150	140	120	See Note #726
	B-B	NW-2	III	Sw	Ortl	Samh	0557		85	182		150	6 rows of louvers
SRR	B-B	NW-2	III	Sw	Ortl	Samh	P885		88	218	183		fp., Green
GN	B-B	NW-2	III	Sw	Ortl	Samh	P884		86	217			fp.
PRR	B-B	NW-2	IV	Sw	Ortl	Samh	P883		88	218	183		fp.
UP	B-B	NW-2	IV	Sw	Ortl	Samh	P882		86	217			fp.
	B-B	NW-2	IV	Sw	Ortl	Samh	0558	75	85	182		150	
	B-B	NW-2	V	Sw	Ortl	Samh	0070		81	150	140	120	See Note #727
GN	B-B	NW-3		Sw	OMI	Ajin	1808	100	82	200	200		See Note #720
GN	B-B	NW-3		Sw	OMI	Ajin	1839.1	10	82	264	264		Modern, fp.
GN	B-B	NW-3		Sw	OMI	Ajin	1827.1	10	82	264	264		Original, fp.
GN	B-B	NW-3		Sw	OMI	Ajin	1821	200	82	200	200		See Note #721
GN	B-B	NW-5		Sw	OMI	Ajin	1804	300	81	190	190	155	
GN	B-B	NW-5		Sw	OMI	Ajin	5087	150	90	324			modernized
GN	B-B	NW-5		Sw	OMI	Ajin	5086	75	90	324			Original
CN	A1A-A1A	GMD-1		Sw	CustB	KMT	DE-106	170	73	80	160	130	See Note#1833

GM Electro-Motive Division (cont'd)

Road	AAR Code	Class & Phase		Type	Importer	Builder	Cat #	Quan.	Yrs.	List Price	Mint	Avg.	Remarks
	B-B	GMD-1		Sw	CustB	KMT	DE-107	170	73	80	145	120	See Note#1834
ATSF	B-B	RCE		Sw	OMI	Ajin	5595		90	TBA			See Note #1867
C&IM	B-B	RS-1325		Sw	Trains	KMT	107		67	50	140	120	See Note #724
	B-B	SC		Sw	Alco	Samh	D-182		82	199		140	600 hp., w/cast frame
UP	B-B	SW		Sw	Alco	Samh		400	82	199	180	165	See Note #1550
	B-B	SW-1000		Sw	Alco	KMT		100	81	226	185	160	1000 hp.
	B-B	SW-1000		Sw	OMI	Ajin	5088	15	87	221			
	B-B	SW-1200		Sw	Ortl	Samh	0026	235	80	128	125	110	1200 HP.
	B-B	SW-1200		Sw	Ortl	Samh	0559	25	85	182		150	large fuel tank
	B-B	SW-1500		Sw	Alco	KMT	D-151	1000	71	47	130	115	See Note #722
	B-B	SW-1500		Sw	Alco	KMT		300	76	98	140	125	1500 hp.
	B-B	SW-1500		Sw	Alco	KMT		100	81	223	185	160	1500 hp., re-run
	B-B	SW-1500		Sw	OMI	Ajin	5074	25	87	221			
	B-B	SW-1500		Sw	OMI	Ajin	5071	25	87	221			
	B-B	SW-1500		Sw	OMI	Ajin	5073	10	87	221			Flexi-Coil Trucks
	B-B	SW-1500		Sw	OMI	Ajin	5072	50	87	221			Flexi-Coil Trucks
SP	B-B	SW-1500		Sw	OMI	Ajin	5075	22	87	221			
	B-B	SW-1500		Sw	OMI	Ajin	5074	15	90	295			Full Railing
	B-B	SW-1500		Sw	OMI	Ajin	5070	25	90	295			re-run
SP	B-B	SW-1500		Sw	OMI	Ajin	5075	20	90	295			re-run
	B-B	SW-1500		Sw	OMI	Ajin	5072	40	90	295			re-run
	B-B	SW-1		Sw	Alco	KMT		1500	70	43	125	100	See Note #1549
	B-B	SW-1		Sw	Alco	KMT		300	75	85	130	110	See Note #1549
	B-B	SW-1	II	Sw	Ortl	Samh	0553	75	85	182		150	
NYC	B-B	SW-1	III	Sw	Ortl	Samh	P887		86	217			fp.
	B-B	SW-1	III	Sw	Ortl	Samh	0554		85	182		150	
GN	B-B	SW-1	III	Sw	Ortl	Samh	P886		86	217			fp.
PRR	B-B	SW-1	IV	Sw	Ortl	Samh	P889		86	217			fp.
C&NW	B-B	SW-1	IV	Sw	Ortl	Samh	P888		86	217			fp.
	B-B	SW-1	IV/V	Sw	Ortl	Samh	0555		85	182		150	
	B-B	SW-7	I	Sw	Ortl	Samh	0463		85	182		150	See Note #1547
	B-B	SW-7	II	Sw	Ortl	Samh	0464		85	182		150	See Note #1548
	B-B	SW-8		Sw	Ortl	Samh	0465		85	182		150	See Note #1546
	B-B	SW-9		Sw	Ortl	Samh	0025	235	80	128	125	110	1200 hp.
	B-B	SW-9		Sw	Ortl	Samh	0467		85	182		150	1200 hp.
	B-B	SW-10		Sw	Alco	Samh	D-159	200	82	199	180	165	UP rebuild
	B-B/B-B	TR-2		Sw	Ortl	Samh	0466		85	357			See Note#1545
CB&Q	B-B/B-B	TR-2		Sw	Ortl	Samh	P466		88	414	349		See Note#1544
UP	B-B/B-B	TR-5		Sw	OMI	Ajin	5085	10		364			See Note#1543
UP	B-B/B-B	TR-5A/B		Sw	OMI	Ajin	1854	100	84	354	354		See Note#1542
UP	B-B/B-B	TR-5A/B		Sw	OMI	Ajin	1855	100	84	354	354		See Note#1541
	B-B/B-B	TR-6		Sw	Trains	KMT	101		68	85	175	145	See Note #723
B&O,Milw	B-B/B-B	TR-6		Sw	Trains				66	60	150	125	1600 hp. Cow & Calf
	B-B	TR-6 Calf		Sw	Trains	KMT	103	650	66	30	75	60	1600 hp.
	B-B	TR-6 Cow		Sw	Trains	KMT		745	66	35	85	70	1600 hp.
AT&SF	B-B	115 Class Slug		RSw	Hall	Samh	HS0001		82	105		85	unpowered
	B-B	BL-2		RSw	CustB	Toho	DE-110	435	72	75	110	90	See Note#1210
	B-B	BL-2		RSw	OMI	Ajin	1877	124	84	222	222		See Note #1211
	B-B	BL-2		RSw	OMI	Ajin	1879	50	84	222	222		See Note #1212
	B-B	BL-2		RSw	OMI	Ajin	1878	126	84	222	222		See Note #1918
ATSF	B-B	B39-8		RSw	OMI	Ajin	1938	100	86	272			#7400-7402
ATSF	B-B	B39-8		RSw	OMI	Ajin	1938	50	87	272			re-run
NS	C-C	C39-8		RSw	OMI	Ajin	1939	75	86	279			#8550-8613
AT&SF	B-B	CF-7	III	RSw	Hall	KMT	HS0022	200	81	225		180	F-7 rebuild
AT&SF	B-B	CF-7	V	RSw	Hall	KMT	HS0012	200	81	225		180	F-7 rebuild
AT&SF	B-B	GP-6		RSw					84			180	#2000; round roof
AT&SF	B-B	GP-7		RSw					84			180	See Note #1862
	B-B	GP-7		RSw	Hall	KMT		500	68	50	120	90	
AT&SF	B-B	GP-7		RSw	Key				91	280	240		
NP	B-B	GP-7		RSw	Key				91	380	320		fp., black/yellow
	B-B	GP-7		RSw	Key				91	280	240		
PRR	B-B	GP-7		RSw	Key				91	350	295		See Note#1863
AT&SF	B-B	GP-7		RSw	Key				91	380	320		fp., blue/yellow

GM Electro-Motive Division (cont'd)

Road	AAR Code	Class & Phase	Type	Importer	Builder	Cat #	Quan.	Yrs.	List Price	Mint	Avg.	Remarks
AT&SF	B-B	GP-7	RSw	Key				91	410	345		fp., Zebra Stripe
UP	B-B	GP-7	RSw	OMI	Ajin	6210		92	357	300		See Note #
	B-B	GP-7	RSw	Ortl	Samh	0077	150	81	173	160	140	See Note #756
	B-B	GP-7	RSw	Ortl	Samh	0076	200	81	173	160	140	standard version
	B-B	GP-7	RSw	Ortl	Samh	0290		83	204		165	Standard; improved
	B-B	GP-7	RSw	Ortl	Samh	0291		83	204		165	passenger version
	B-B	GP-7	RSw	Ortl	Samh	0334		84	207		170	chopnose
BN	B-B	GP-7	RSw	Ortl	Samh	P334		85	229			fp., chopnose
	B-B	GP-7	RSw	Sunset			400	84	90	80		freight version
	B-B	GP-7	RSw	Sunset			400	84	90	80		freight version
	B-B	GP-7	RSw	Sunset			200	84	90	80		passenger version
	B-B	GP-7	RSw	Sunset			200	84	90	80		passenger version
PRR	B-B	GP-7	RSw	PFM	Tensh		5	54				fp.
GN	B-B	GP-7	RSw	PFM	Tensh		6	54				fp.
UP	B-B	GP-7	RSw	PFM	Tensh		5	54				fp.
CB&Q	B-B	GP-7	RSw	PFM	Tensh		20	55				fp.
B&O	B-B	GP-7	RSw	PFM	Tensh		25	55				fp.
GN	B-B	GP-7	RSw	PFM	Tensh		40	55				fp.
AT&SF	B-B	GP-7	RSw	PFM	Tensh		50	55				fp.
CRIP	B-B	GP-7	RSw	PFM	Tensh		20	55				fp.
NYC	B-B	GP-7	RSw	PFM	Tensh		66	55				fp.
NP	B-B	GP-7	RSw	PFM	Tensh		20	55				fp.
C&NW	B-B	GP-7	RSw	PFM	Tensh		35	55				fp.
PRR	B-B	GP-7	RSw	PFM	Tensh		20	55				fp.
WP	B-B	GP-7	RSw	PFM	Tensh		10	55				fp.
SP	B-B	GP-7	RSw	PFM	Tensh		20	55				fp.
SOO	B-B	GP-7	RSw	PFM	Tensh		20	55				fp.
UP	B-B	GP-7	RSw	PFM	Tensh		40	55				fp.
KCS	B-B	GP-7	RSw	PFM	Tensh		1	56				fp.
GN	B-B	GP-7	RSw	PFM	Tensh		50	56				fp.
AT&SF	B-B	GP-7	RSw	PFM	Tensh		60	56				fp.
PRR	B-B	GP-7	RSw	PFM	Tensh		20	56				fp.
NYC	B-B	GP-7	RSw	PFM	Tensh		56	56				fp.
CB&Q	B-B	GP-7	RSw	PFM	Tensh		20	56				fp.
SP	B-B	GP-7	RSw	PFM	Tensh		10	56				fp.
UP	B-B	GP-7	RSw	PFM	Tensh		20	56				fp.
B&O	B-B	GP-7	RSw	PFM	Tensh		30	56				fp.
NP	B-B	GP-7	RSw	PFM	Tensh		10	57				fp.
WP	B-B	GP-7	RSw	PFM	Tensh		1	57				fp.
NYC	B-B	GP-7	RSw	PFM	Tensh		50	57				fp.
SOO	B-B	GP-7	RSw	PFM	Tensh		10	57				fp.
AT&SF	B-B	GP-7	RSw	PFM	Tensh		30	57				fp.
B&O	B-B	GP-7	RSw	PFM	Tensh		20	57				fp.
SP	B-B	GP-7	RSw	PFM	Tensh		20	57				fp.
CB&Q	B-B	GP-7	RSw	PFM	Tensh		10	57				fp.
GN	B-B	GP-7	RSw	PFM	Tensh		50	57				fp.
CRIP	B-B	GP-7	RSw	PFM	Tensh		10	57				fp.
UP	B-B	GP-7	RSw	PFM	Tensh		20	57				fp.
PRR	B-B	GP-7	RSw	PFM	Tensh		10	57				fp.
CP	B-B	GP-7	RSw	PFM	Tensh		1	58				fp.
PRR	B-B	GP-7	RSw	PFM	Tensh		10	58				fp.
NYC	B-B	GP-7	RSw	PFM	Tensh		10	58				fp.
WP	B-B	GP-7	RSw	PFM	Tensh		2	58				fp.
CB&Q	B-B	GP-7	RSw	PFM	Tensh		10	58				fp.
B&O	B-B	GP-7	RSw	PFM	Tensh		10	58				fp.
UP	B-B	GP-7	RSw	PFM	Tensh		10	59				fp.
NYC	B-B	GP-7	RSw	PFM	Tensh		30	59				fp.
AT&SF	B-B	GP-7	RSw	PFM	Tensh		10	59				fp.
SP	B-B	GP-7	RSw	PFM	Tensh		10	59				fp.
PRR	B-B	GP-7	RSw	PFM	Tensh		10	59				fp.
WP	B-B	GP-7	RSw	PFM	Tensh		10	59				fp.
B&O	B-B	GP-7	RSw	PFM	Tensh		10	59				fp.
GN	B-B	GP-7	RSw	PFM	Tensh		20	60				fp.
SP	B-B	GP-7	RSw	PFM	Tensh		10	60				fp.

GM Electro-Motive Division (cont'd)

Road	AAR Code	Class & Phase	Type	Importer	Builder	Cat #	Quan.	Yrs.	List Price	Mint	Avg.	Remarks
NP	B-B	GP-7	RSw	PFM	Tensh		25	60				fp.
AT&SF	B-B	GP-7	RSw	PFM	Tensh		20	60				fp.
PRR	B-B	GP-7	RSw	PFM	Tensh		30	60				fp.
CB&Q	B-B	GP-7	RSw	PFM	Tensh		10	60				fp.
NYC	B-B	GP-7	RSw	PFM	Tensh		30	60				fp.
B&O	B-B	GP-7	RSw	PFM	Tensh		20	60				fp.
WP	B-B	GP-7	RSw	PFM	Tensh		1	61				fp.
ACL	B-B	GP-7	RSw	PFM	Tensh		1	63				fp.
	B-B	GP-7B	RSw	Ortl	Samh	0078	100	81	173	160	125	Cabless Booster
AT&SF	B-B	GP-7R	RSw	Hall	Samh	HS0090		82	224		180	See Note #753
AT&SF	B-B	GP-7R	RSw	Hall	Samh	HS0091		82	224		180	See Note #752
AT&SF	B-B/B-B	GP-7R + Slug	RSw	Hall	Samh	HS0089		82	326		260	See Note #754, 2 units
	B-B	GP-9	RSw	Hall	KMT		1500	72	62	110	90	
	B-B	GP-9	RSw	Intl	KMT		500	55	28	80	65	1750 hp.
	B-B	GP-9	RSw	Intl	KMT			55	22			Kit
SP	B-B	GP-9	RSw	Key				91	350	295		fp.
UP	B-B	GP-9	RSw	Key				91	350	295		fp.
	B-B	GP-9	RSw	Olex				60	24	75	65	fp.
	B-B	GP-9	RSw	Olex				60	22	70	60	
	B-B	GP-9	RSw	Ortl	Samh	0087	150	81	173		140	See Note #1864
	B-B	GP-9	RSw	Ortl	Samh	0045	125	80	166		140	See Note #759
	B-B	GP-9	RSw	Ortl	Samh	0044	150	80	166			See Note #1928
	B-B	GP-9	RSw	Ortl	Samh	0293		83	204		185	intermediate - 1957
	B-B	GP-9	RSw	Ortl	Samh	0294		83	204		185	passenger version
	B-B	GP-9	RSw	Ortl	Samh	0292		83	204		185	early version
	B-B	GP-9	RSw	Ortl	Samh	0330		84	207		180	two 48" fans, late
WM	B-B	GP-9	RSw	Ortl	Samh	0333		84	207		180	chopnose
WM	B-B	GP-9	RSw	Ortl	Samh	P333		84	228			chopnose, cp.
CP	B-B	GP-9	RSw	Ortl	Samh	P822		86	300			chopnose
	B-B	GP-9	RSw	Sunset			200	84	90	80		freight version
	B-B	GP-9	RSw	Sunset			200	84	90	80		freight version
UP	B-B	GP-9	RSw	OMI	Ajin	5478	20	91	352			for Gas-Turbine Service
UP	B-B	GP-9	RSw	OMI	Ajin	6211		92	357	300		See Note #1930
UP	B-B	GP-9	RSw	OMI	Ajin	6212		92	357	300		See Note #1931
UP	B-B	GP-9	RSw	OMI	Ajin	6214		92	357	300		See Note #1933
UP	B-B	GP-9	RSw	OMI	Ajin	6215		92	357	300		See Note #1934
UP	B-B	GP-9	RSw	OMI	Ajin	6216		92	357	300		See Note #1935
UP	B-B	GP-9	RSw	OMI	Ajin	6217		92	357	300		See Note #1936
CN	B-B	GP-9	RSw	OMI	Ajin	6219		92	357	300		See Note #1507
CN	B-B	GP-9	RSw	OMI	Ajin	6220		92	357	300		See Note #1488

The EMD E–5 was unique to the CB&Q. Easily distinguished by their stainless steel side panels, lower side windows, and slant nose, there was little chance of confusing them with something else. Only eleven A units and five B units were built which were mechanically similar to the E–6s. Hallmark imported 500 of these Kumata-built models in 1971. All had chrome-plated bodies.

GM Electro-Motive Division (cont'd)

Road	AAR Code	Class & Phase	Type	Importer	Builder	Cat #	Quan.	Yrs.	List Price	Resale Mint	Avg.	Remarks
CN	B-B	GP-9	RSw	OMI	Ajin	6221		92	697	595		See Note #1328
CN	B-B	GP-9	RSw	OMI	Ajin	6222		92	357	300		See Note #1457
C&NW	B-B	GP-9	RSw	PFM	Tensh	#130	1	55				fp.
GN	B-B	GP-9	RSw	PFM	Tensh	#130	1	55				fp.
CB&Q	B-B	GP-9	RSw	PFM	Tensh	#130	50	56				fp.
WP	B-B	GP-9	RSw	PFM	Tensh	#130	50	56				fp.
ACL	B-B	GP-9	RSw	PFM	Tensh	#130	40	56				fp.
C&NW	B-B	GP-9	RSw	PFM	Tensh	#130	50	56				fp.
GN	B-B	GP-9	RSw	PFM	Tensh	#130	53	56				fp.
D&RGW	B-B	GP-9	RSw	PFM	Tensh	#130	40	56				fp.
UP	B-B	GP-9	RSw	PFM	Tensh	#130	50	56				fp.
PRR	B-B	GP-9	RSw	PFM	Tensh	#130	1	56				fp.
N&W	B-B	GP-9	RSw	PFM	Tensh	#130	1	57				fp.
C&NW	B-B	GP-9	RSw	PFM	Tensh	#130	20	57				fp.
UP	B-B	GP-9	RSw	PFM	Tensh	#130	12	57				fp.
D&RGW	B-B	GP-9	RSw	PFM	Tensh	#130	20	57				fp.
GN	B-B	GP-9	RSw	PFM	Tensh	#130	20	57				fp.
CB&Q	B-B	GP-9	RSw	PFM	Tensh	#130	5	57				fp.
C&O	B-B	GP-9	RSw	PFM	Tensh	#130	1	58				fp.
GN	B-B	GP-9	RSw	PFM	Tensh	#130	10	58				fp.
CB&Q	B-B	GP-9	RSw	PFM	Tensh	#130	10	58				fp.
UP	B-B	GP-9	RSw	PFM	Tensh	#130	10	58				fp.
ACL	B-B	GP-9	RSw	PFM	Tensh	#130	10	58				fp.
NdeM	B-B	GP-9	RSw	PFM	Tensh	#130	1	58				fp.
Special	B-B	GP-9	RSw	PFM	Tensh	#130	40	58				See Note #1865
D&RGW	B-B	GP-9	RSw	PFM	Tensh	#130	2	58				fp.
D&RGW	B-B	GP-9	RSw	PFM	Tensh	#130	12	59				fp.
CB&Q	B-B	GP-9	RSw	PFM	Tensh	#130	10	59				fp.
UP	B-B	GP-9	RSw	PFM	Tensh	#130	20	59				fp.
C&NW	B-B	GP-9	RSw	PFM	Tensh	#130	20	59				fp.
GN	B-B	GP-9	RSw	PFM	Tensh	#130	40	59				fp.
ACL	B-B	GP-9	RSw	PFM	Tensh	#130	20	59				fp.
WP	B-B	GP-9	RSw	PFM	Tensh	#130	11	59				fp.
D&RGW	B-B	GP-9	RSw	PFM	Tensh	#130	30	60				fp.
CB&Q	B-B	GP-9	RSw	PFM	Tensh	#130	36	60				fp.
C&NW	B-B	GP-9	RSw	PFM	Tensh	#130	40	60				fp.
WP	B-B	GP-9	RSw	PFM	Tensh	#130	20	60				fp.
ACL	B-B	GP-9	RSw	PFM	Tensh	#130	30	60				fp.
UP	B-B	GP-9	RSw	PFM	Tensh	#130	40	60				fp.
GN	B-B	GP-9	RSw	PFM	Tensh	#130	60	60				fp.
GN	B-B	GP-9	RSw	PFM	Tensh	#130	3	61				fp.
UP	B-B	GP-9B	RSw	OMI	Ajin	6313		92	357	300		See Note #1932
UP	B-B	GP-9B	RSw	OMI	Ajin	6218		92	357	300		See Note #1937
UP	B-B	GP-9B	RSw	OMI	Ajin	6223		92	357	300		See Note #1700
	B-B	GP-9B	RSw	Ortl	Samh	0088	75	81	166	165	140	cabless booster, pwd.
ATSF	B-B	GP-9B	RSw	Ortl	Samh	0046	125	80	173		130	See Note #760
UP	B-B	GP-9MA	RSw	Ortl	Samh	0331		84	207		180	
UP	B-B	GP-9MA	RSw	Ortl	Samh	0332		84	207		180	cabless booster
	B-B	GP-9R	RSw	Hall	Samh	HS0075		82	224		180	See Note #753
UP	B-B	GP-9 "A"		OMI	Ajin	5476	20	91	352			See Note #1866
UP	B-B	GP-9 "B"		OMI	Ajin	5477	20	91	352			See Note #1866
UP	B-B	GP-9MA		OMI	Ajin	5480	40	91	352			See Note #1866
UP	B-B	GP-9MA		OMI	Ajin	5481	40	91	352			See Note #1866
IC	B-B	GP-10		OMI	Ajin	5479	30	91	352			Paducah rebuild
MP,CRR	B-B	GP-15-1	RSw	Hall	KMT	HS0064	200	81	225	200	180	See Note #761
SLSF,CNW	B-B	GP-15-1	RSw	Hall	KMT	HS0063	200	81	225	200	180	See Note #762
SLSF,CNW	B-B	GP-15-1	RSw	Hall				88	140	116		See Note #762
	B-B	GP-15-1	RSw	NPP				83	160		100	See Note #1835
	B-B	GP-18	RSw	Hall	KMT		750	72	64	120	100	See Note #757
	B-B	GP-18	RSw	Hall	KMT		500	72	64	115	95	See Note #758
	B-B	GP-18	RSw	Ortl	Samh	0309		83	207		170	HiH
	B-B	GP-18	RSw	Ortl	Samh	0308		83	207		170	LoH
SRR	B-B	GP-18	RSw	Ortl	Samh	P309		84	229			cp.
L&N	B-B	GP-18	RSw	Ortl	Samh	P308		84	229			cp.

GM Electro-Motive Division (cont'd)

Road	AAR Code	Class & Phase	Type	Importer	Builder	Cat #	Quan.	Yrs.	List Price	Mint	Avg.	Remarks
NYC,PRR	B-B	GP-20	RSw	Ortl	Samh	0030	100	80	150		135	See Note #1836
	B-B	GP-20	RSw	Ortl	Samh	0032	200	80	150	140	120	HiH, w/Dynamic Brakes
	B-B	GP-20	RSw	Ortl	Samh	0031	200	80	150	140	120	LoH, w/Dynamic Brakes
	B-B	GP-20	RSw	Ortl	Samh	0310		83	207		170	LoH
GN	B-B	GP-20	RSw	Ortl	Samh	0311		83	207		170	HiH
UP	B-B	GP-20	RSw	PFM	Tensh		60	61	29			fp.
	B-B	GP-20	RSw	PFM	Tensh		40	61	24			unpainted kit
PRR	B-B	GP-20	RSw	PFM	Tensh		70	61	29			fp.
AT&SF	B-B	GP-20	RSw	PFM	Tensh		190	61	29			fp.
SP	B-B	GP-20	RSw	PFM	Tensh		85	61	29			fp.
CB&Q	B-B	GP-20	RSw	PFM	Tensh		40	61	29			fp.
NYC	B-B	GP-20	RSw	PFM	Tensh		75	61	29			fp.
WP	B-B	GP-20	RSw	PFM	Tensh		20	61	29			fp.
GN	B-B	GP-20	RSw	PFM	Tensh		140	61	29			fp.
B&O	B-B	GP-20	RSw	PFM	Tensh		30	61	29			fp.
	B-B	GP-20	RSw	PFM	Tensh		30	62	24			unpainted kit
GN	B-B	GP-20	RSw	PFM	Tensh		90	62	29			fp.
AT&SF	B-B	GP-20	RSw	PFM	Tensh		100	62	29			fp.
NYC	B-B	GP-20	RSw	PFM	Tensh		50	62	29			fp.
B&O	B-B	GP-20	RSw	PFM	Tensh		30	62	29			fp.
UP	B-B	GP-20	RSw	PFM	Tensh		60	62	29			fp.
WP	B-B	GP-20	RSw	PFM	Tensh		50	62	29			fp.
CB&Q	B-B	GP-20	RSw	PFM	Tensh		70	62	29			fp.
SP	B-B	GP-20	RSw	PFM	Tensh		60	62	29			fp.
PRR	B-B	GP-20	RSw	PFM	Tensh		50	62	29			fp.
	B-B	GP-20	RSw	PFM	Tensh		10	63	24			unpainted kit
PRR	B-B	GP-20	RSw	PFM	Tensh		20	63	29			fp.
CB&Q	B-B	GP-20	RSw	PFM	Tensh		20	63	29			fp.
NYC	B-B	GP-20	RSw	PFM	Tensh		20	63	29			fp.
GN	B-B	GP-20	RSw	PFM	Tensh		20	63	29			fp.
AT&SF	B-B	GP-20	RSw	PFM	Tensh		20	63	29			fp.
UP	B-B	GP-20	RSw	PFM	Tensh		20	63	29			fp.
SP	B-B	GP-20	RSw	PFM	Tensh		10	63	29			fp.
B&O	B-B	GP-20	RSw	PFM	Tensh		30	63	29			fp.
WP	B-B	GP-20	RSw	PFM	Tensh		10	63	29			fp.
AT&SF	B-B	GP-20	RSw	PFM	Tensh		20	64	29			fp.
SP	B-B	GP-20	RSw	PFM	Tensh		40	64	29			fp.
B&O	B-B	GP-20	RSw	PFM	Tensh		40	64	29			fp.
NYC	B-B	GP-20	RSw	PFM	Tensh		20	64	29			fp.
UP	B-B	GP-20	RSw	PFM	Tensh		70	64	29			fp.
WP	B-B	GP-20	RSw	PFM	Tensh		20	64	29			fp.
GN	B-B	GP-20	RSw	PFM	Tensh		60	64	29			fp.
CB&Q	B-B	GP-20	RSw	PFM	Tensh		20	64	29			fp.
PRR	B-B	GP-20	RSw	PFM	Tensh		30	64	29			fp.
SP	B-B	GP-20	RSw	PFM	Tensh		70	65	29			fp.
NYC	B-B	GP-20	RSw	PFM	Tensh		70	65	29			fp.
WP	B-B	GP-20	RSw	PFM	Tensh		10	65	29			fp.
GN	B-B	GP-20	RSw	PFM	Tensh		120	65	29			fp.
PRR	B-B	GP-20	RSw	PFM	Tensh		50	65	29			fp.
B&O	B-B	GP-20	RSw	PFM	Tensh		30	65	29			fp.
AT&SF	B-B	GP-20	RSw	PFM	Tensh		50	65	29			fp.
CB&Q	B-B	GP-20	RSw	PFM	Tensh		40	65	29			fp.
	B-B	GP-28	RSw	Ortl	Samh	O842		88	221	186		LoH
IC	B-B	GP-28	RSw	Ortl	Samh	P843		89	271			LoH, fp. Black Scheme
PRR	B-B	GP-30	RSw	Alco	KMT			80	223	190	175	w/Antennas
N&W, SRR	B-B	GP-30	RSw	Alco	KMT	D-180	200	80	223	Mint	165	HiH
	B-B	GP-30	RSw	Alco	KMT			220	80	223	185	170	LoH
	B-B	GP-30	RSw	CustB	KMT	DE-102	609	73	75	150	125	2250 hp., LoH
PRR	B-B	GP-30	II	RSw	OMI	Ajin	5012	55	87	236	198	LoH #2200-2251
N&W	B-B	GP-30	I	RSw	OMI	Ajin	5004	20	87	236	198	HiH #522-565
	B-B	GP-30	II	RSw	OMI	Ajin	1999	18	87	236	198	See Note#1837
	B-B	GP-30	II	RSw	OMI	Ajin	5010	23	87	236	198	See Note#1838
CPR	B-B	GP-30	II	RSw	OMI	Ajin	5013	20	87	236	198	LoH #8200-8210

GM Electro-Motive Division (cont'd)

Road	AAR Code	Class & Phase		Type	Model Production					List Price	Resale		Remarks
					Importer	Builder	Cat #	Quan.	Yrs.		Mint	Avg.	
	B-B	GP-30	I	RSw	OMI	Ajin	5002	100	87	236	198		LoH AT&SF, B&O
UP	B-B	GP-30		RSw	OMI	Ajin	5001	35	87	236	198		#875 ex. Demo, LoH
SRR	B-B	GP-30	II	RSw	OMI	Ajin	5005	23	87	236	198		HiH #2588-2644
	B-B	GP-30	II	RSw	OMI	Ajin	5009	70	87	236	198		LoH AT&SF, C&O
D&RGW	B-B	GP-30	II	RSw	OMI	Ajin	1997	25	87	236	198		w/HL in Low Nose
SOO	B-B	GP-30	II	RSw	OMI	Ajin	5011	10	87	236	198		See Note#1839
SP	B-B	GP-30	II	RSw	OMI	Ajin	5015	25	87	236	198		LoH #5010-5017
	B-B	GP-30	I	RSw	OMI	Ajin	5003	18	87	236	198		See Note#1839
NKP	B-B	GP-30	II	RSw	OMI	Ajin	1998	18	87	236	198		See Note#1840
UP	B-B	GP-30	II	RSw	OMI	Ajin	5006	70	87	236	198		LoH #800-874, #700-
UP	B-B	GP-30		RSw	OMI	Ajin	5000	42	87	236	198		#808 w/Full Crew Cab
CGW	B-B	GP-30	II	RSw	Ortl	Samh	P815		88	272	228		fp.
SRR	B-B	GP-30	II	RSw	Ortl	Samh	P819		88	272	228		fp.
AT&SF	B-B	GP-30	I	RSw	Ortl	Samh	P786		88	272	228		fp.
	B-B	GP-30	I	RSw	Ortl	Samh	0782		87	221	220		LoH
Road	B-B	GP-30	I	RSw	Ortl	Samh	0792		86	221	220	Avg.	HiH
	B-B	GP-30	II	RSw	Ortl	Samh	0795		86	221	220		LoH
C&O	B-B	GP-30	I	RSw	Ortl	Samh	P790		88	272	228		fp.
RDG	B-B	GP-30	I	RSw	Ortl	Samh	P783		87	272			
UP	B-B	GP-30	II	RSw	Ortl	Samh	P796		88	272	228		fp.
D&RGW	B-B	GP-30	II	RSw	Ortl	Samh	P801		88	272	228	Avg.	fp.
AT&SF	B-B	GP-30	II	RSw	Ortl	Samh	P802		88	272	228		fp.
D&RGW	B-B	GP-30	I	RSw	Ortl	Samh	P784		88	272	228		fp.
CB&Q	B-B	GP-30	II	RSw	Ortl	Samh	P809		88	272	228	Avg.	fp.
CB&Q	B-B	GP-30	I	RSw	Ortl	Samh	P785		88	272	228		fp.
SRR	B-B	GP-30	I	RSw	Ortl	Samh	P794		88	272	228		fp.
UP	B-B	GP-30B		RSw	Ortl	Samh	P821		88	272	228		fp.
UP	B-B	GP-30B		RSw	Ortl	Samh	P820		88	272	228		fp.
UP	B-B	GP-30B	II	RSw	OMI	Ajin	5008	35	87	236	198		Cabless #727B-739B
UP	B-B	GP-30B		RSw	Alco	KMT		220	80	220	180	160	Cabless
UP	B-B	GP-30B	II	RSw	OMI	Ajin	5007	40	87	236	198		Cabless #700B-726B
ATSF	B-B	GP-30u		RSw	OMI	Ajin	5014	40	87	236	198		Rebuild #2700-2785
	B-B	GP-35		RSw	Hall	Hallko		500	75-76	67-90	85	70	Flywheel Drive
AA	B-B	GP-35		RSw	OMI	Ajin	1828	10	82	186	186		See Note #1846
	B-B	GP-35		RSw	OMI	Ajin	1816	150	82	186	186		See Note #1847
	B-B	GP-35		RSw	OMI	Ajin	1815	250	82	186	186		See Note #1843
WM	B-B	GP-35		RSw	OMI	Ajin	1842.1	5	82	229	229		fp.
D&RGW	B-B	GP-35		RSw	OMI	Ajin	1844.1	5	82	229	229		See Note #1842
D&RGW	B-B	GP-35		RSw	OMI	Ajin	1843.1	5	82	229	229		fp.
	B-B	GP-35		RSw	OMI	Ajin	1818	25	82	186	186		See Note #1844
SP	B-B	GP-35		RSw	OMI	Ajin	1845.1	5	82	229	229		fp.
	B-B	GP-35		RSw	OMI	Ajin	1817	40	82	186	186		See Note #1845
ATSF	B-B	GP-35		RSw	OMI	Ajin	1846.1	5	82	229	229		fp.
UP	B-B	GP-35		RSw	OMI	Ajin	1841.1	10	82	229	229		See Note #1848
GN	B-B	GP-35		RSw	OMI	Ajin	1840	5	82	229	229		fp.
	B-B	GP-35		RSw	OMI	Ajin	1866	50	84	221	221		See Note #1850
	B-B	GP-35		RSw	OMI	Ajin	1865	50	84	221	221		See Note #1849
AT&SF	B-B	GP-35		RSw	OMI	Ajin	5069	25	87	236			#1400-1449
RDG	B-B	GP-35		RSw	OMI	Ajin	5050	30	87	236			#6501-6506
NKP	B-B	GP-35		RSw	OMI	Ajin	5058	10	87	236			#910
PRR	B-B	GP-35		RSw	OMI	Ajin	5055	25	87	236			#2250-2320
GN	B-B	GP-35		RSw	OMI	Ajin	5067	15	87	236			#3017-3040
WAB	B-B	GP-35		RSw	OMI	Ajin	5065	15	87	236			#540-547
Frisco	B-B	GP-35		RSw	OMI	Ajin	5061	20	87	236			#700-716
SRR	B-B	GP-35		RSw	OMI	Ajin	5051	15	87	236			HiH
D&RGW	B-B	GP-35		RSw	OMI	Ajin	5064	15	87	236			#3029-3042
C&NW	B-B	GP-35		RSw	OMI	Ajin	5060	20	87	236			#844-866
AA	B-B	GP-35		RSw	OMI	Ajin	5054	30	87	236			#385-394
SP	B-B	GP-35		RSw	OMI	Ajin	5057	25	87	236			#6552-6576
NYC	B-B	GP-35		RSw	OMI	Ajin	5053	25	87	236			#6141-6149
N&W	B-B	GP-35		RSw	OMI	Ajin	5063	15	87	236			HiH, #200-239
UP	B-B	GP-35		RSw	OMI	Ajin	5056	25	87	236			#740-763
GM&O	B-B	GP-35		RSw	OMI	Ajin	5068	15	87	236			#601-613
WM	B-B	GP-35		RSw	OMI	Ajin	5052	25	87	236			#3576-3580

GM Electro-Motive Division (cont'd)

| Road | AAR Code | Class & Phase | Type | Model Production | | | | | List Price | Resale | | Remarks |
				Importer	Builder	Cat #	Quan.	Yrs.		Mint	Avg.	
E-L	B-B	GP-35	RSw	OMI	Ajin	5066	20	87	236			#2562-2586
C&O	B-B	GP-35	RSw	OMI	Ajin	5062	10	87	236			#3520-3529
WP	B-B	GP-35	RSw	OMI	Ajin	5059	20	87	236			#3001-3003
WP	B-B	GP-35 I	RSw	Ortl	Samh	P878		87	272	228		See Note #1851
CB&Q	B-B	GP-35 I	RSw	Ortl	Samh	P826		88	272	228		fp., LoH
PRR	B-B	GP-35 I	RSw	Ortl	Samh	P833		88	272	228		fp., LoH
SSW	B-B	GP-35 I	RSw	Ortl	Samh	P832		88	272	228		fp., LoH
SRR	B-B	GP-35 I	RSw	Ortl	Samh	P841		88	272	228		See Note#1852
CRR	B-B	GP-35 I	RSw	Ortl	Samh	P838		88	272	228		fp., LoH
UP	B-B	GP-35 I	RSw	Ortl	Samh	P830		88	272	228		fp., LoH
D&RGW	B-B	GP-35 I	RSw	Ortl	Samh	P825		88	272	228		fp., LoH
C&O	B-B	GP-35 I	RSw	Ortl	Samh	P828		88	272	228		fp., LoH
AT&SF	B-B	GP-35 I	RSw	Ortl	Samh	P827		88	272	228		fp., LoH
C&NW	B-B	GP-35 I	RSw	Ortl	Samh	P837		89	272			fp., LoH, w/o D.B.
SOO	B-B	GP-35 I	RSw	Ortl	Samh	P835		89	272			fp., LoH
B&O	B-B	GP-35 I	RSw	Ortl	Samh	P829		89	272			fp., LoH
	B-B	GP-35 I	RSw	Ortl	Samh	O840		89	222	180		HiH
BN	B-B	GP-35 I	RSw	Ortl	Samh	P823		89	272			fp., LoH
N&W	B-B	GP-35 I	RSw	Ortl	Samh	P840		89	272	228		fp., HiH
PRR	B-B	GP-35	RSw	PFM	Tensh	159	60	65	35	125		fp.
CB&Q	B-B	GP-35	RSw	PFM	Tensh	159	40	65	35	125		fp.
AT&SF	B-B	GP-35	RSw	PFM	Tensh	159	60	65	35	125		fp.
PRR	B-B	GP-35	RSw	PFM	Tensh	159	140	66	35	125		fp.
GN	B-B	GP-35	RSw	PFM	Tensh	159	210	66	35	125		fp.
SP	B-B	GP-35	RSw	PFM	Tensh	159	110	66	35	125		fp.
NYC	B-B	GP-35	RSw	PFM	Tensh	159	100	66	35	125		fp.
B&O	B-B	GP-35	RSw	PFM	Tensh	159	80	66	35	125		fp.
WP	B-B	GP-35	RSw	PFM	Tensh	159	30	66	35	125		fp.
AT&SF	B-B	GP-35	RSw	PFM	Tensh	159	140	66	35	125		fp.
CB&Q	B-B	GP-35	RSw	PFM	Tensh	159	140	66	35	125		fp.
D&RGW	B-B	GP-35	RSw	PFM	Tensh	159	30	66	35	125		fp.
C&NW	B-B	GP-35	RSw	PFM	Tensh	159	30	66	35	125		fp.
UP	B-B	GP-35	RSw	PFM	Tensh	159	110	66	35	125		fp.
NYC	B-B	GP-35	RSw	PFM	Tensh	159	20	67	48	125		fp.
D&RGW	B-B	GP-35	RSw	PFM	Tensh	159	30	67	48	125		fp.
WP	B-B	GP-35	RSw	PFM	Tensh	159	50	67	48	125		fp.
B&O	B-B	GP-35	RSw	PFM	Tensh	159	20	67	48	125		fp.
C&NW	B-B	GP-35	RSw	PFM	Tensh	159	50	67	48	125		fp.
GN	B-B	GP-35	RSw	PFM	Tensh	159	110	67	48	125		fp. "Big Sky"
UP	B-B	GP-35	RSw	PFM	Tensh	159	20	67	48			fp.
	B-B	GP-38	RSw	Hall			500	75-76	80	90	80	See Note #765
	B-B	GP-38-2	RSw	OMI	Ajin	1867	100	84	221	221		See Note #1855
	B-B	GP-38-2	RSw	Alco	Samh	D-186	200	82	180		150	w/o Dynamic Brakes
	B-B	GP-38-2	RSw	OMI	Ajin	1868	100	84	221	221		See Note #1856
	B-B	GP-38-2	RSw	OMI	Ajin	1868	100	83	271			w/Dynamic Brake
	B-B	GP-38-2	RSw	OMI	Ajin	1869	50	84	221	221		See Note #1854
	B-B	GP-38-2	RSw	OMI	Ajin	1870	75	84	221	221		See Note #1853
	B-B	GP-38-2	RSw	Alco	Samh	D-186B	300	82	180		150	w/Dynamic Brake
	B-B	GP-39	RSw	Hall	Samh							See Note #1857
	B-B	GP-39-2	RSw	Hall	Samh							See Note #1858
	B-B	GP-40	RSw	Hall	Samh							without dynamic brake
	B-B	GP-40	RSw	Alco	KMT	D-143HB	400	71	58	120	100	See Note #1860
	B-B	GP-40	RSw	Alco	KMT	D-143	500	71	58	125	100	See Note #766
	B-B	GP-40	RSw	Alco	KMT	D-143LB	525	71	58	125	105	See Note #1859
	B-B	GP-40	RSw	Gem	Tokaido	TM-102	500	72	50	70	55	See Note#1861
	B-B	GP-40	RSw	Hall	Samh							with dynamic brake
CNR	B-B	GP-40-2	RSw	F&G	KMT	OO-RU	150	78	127	145	125	See Note #768
CNR	B-B	GP-40-2	RSw	F&G	KMT		350	78	127	160	135	See Note #767
NJ Transit	B-B	GP-40P	RSw	OMI	Ajin	5130	40	89	284	239		#4100-4112
SP	B-B	GP-40P-2	RSw	OMI	Ajin	5131	85	89	293	246		#3197-3199
ATSF	B-B	GP-40X	RSw	OMI	Ajin	5120	75	89	284	239		#3800-3809
UP	B-B	GP-40X	RSw	OMI	Ajin	1800	175	81	250	235	215	LoH Demonstrator
SP	B-B	GP-40X	RSw	OMI	Ajin	5122	50	89	284	239		#7200-7201
UP	B-B	GP-40X	RSw	OMI	Ajin	5124	95	89	284	239		#90-95

GM Electro-Motive Division (cont'd)

Road	AAR Code	Class & Phase		Type	Importer	Builder	Cat #	Quan.	Yrs.	List Price	Mint	Avg.	Remarks
								Model Production			Resale		
SP	B-B	GP-40X		RSw	OMI	Ajin	5123	50	89	284	239		#7230-7231
SRR	B-B	GP-40X		RSw	OMI	Ajin	5121	40	89	284	239		HiH, #7000-7002
ATSF	B-B	GP-40X		RSw	OMI	Ajin	1801	100	81	250	235		LoH
SP	B-B	GP-40X		RSw	OMI	Ajin	1802	175	81	260	235	220	LoH w/Tunnel Hoods
SRR	B-B	GP-40X		RSw	OMI	Ajin	1803	50	81	260	240	220	HiH 3500 hp.
MP	B-B	GP-50		RSw	Hall	KMT	HS0073	100	82	240		190	No dynamic brake
C&NW	B-B	GP-50		RSw	Hall	KMT	HS0072	75	82	240		190	
AT&SF	B-B	GP-50		RSw	Hall	KMT	HS0071	200	82	240		190	
SRR	B-B	GP-50		RSw	Hall	KMT	HS0074	50	82	240		190	HiH
AT&SF	B-B	GP-50		RSw	Hall		HS0071		88	142	119		
MP	B-B	GP-50		RSw	Hall		HS0073		88	142	120		
MP	B-B	GP-50		RSw	OMI	Ajin	5128	35	89	277	233		#3500-3529
SRR	B-B	GP-50		RSw	OMI	Ajin	5129	35	89	277	233		#7003-7092
ATSF	B-B	GP-50	I	RSw	OMI	Ajin	5125	35	89	277	233		#3810-3839
BN	B-B	GP-50		RSw	OMI	Ajin	5143	30	89	277	233		#3110-3157
AT&SF	B-B	GP-50	II	RSw	OMI	Ajin	5142	25	89	277	233		#3840-3854
C&NW	B-B	GP-50		RSw	OMI	Ajin	5127	30	89	277	233		#5050-5099
BN	B-B	GP-50	I	RSw	OMI	Ajin	5126	25	89	277	233		#3100-3109
BN	B-B	GP-50	II	RSw	OMI	Ajin	5144	25	89	284	239		Large Cab
NS	B-B	GP-59		Rsw	OMI	Ajin	5952	75	91	357			#4609-4641
D&RGW	B-B	GP-60		Rsw	OMI	Ajin	5951	40	91	357			#3154-3156
SSW	B-B	GP-60		Rsw	OMI	Ajin	5953	60	91	357			#9260-9714
AT&SF	B-B	GP-60		Rsw	OMI	Ajin	5949	50	91	357			#4000-4019
	B-B	F-40	III	Cab	PFM				88	313	265		fp. Chicago RTA
	B-B	F-40	III	Cab	PFM				88	313	265		fp. Caltrain
	B-B	F-40PH		Cab	PFM								
Amtrak	B-B	F-40PH	II	Cab	OMI	Ajin	5893	40	91				
Amtrak	B-B	F-40PH	I	Cab	OMI	Ajin	5889.1	40	91	427			
Amtrak	B-B	F-40PH	III	Cab	OMI	Ajin	5893.1	85	91	427			
MBTA	B-B	F-40PH	II	Cab	OMI	Ajin	5892	25	91	329			
RTA	B-B	F-40PH	I	Cab	OMI	Ajin	5890	25	91	329			
Amtrak	B-B	F-40PH	II	Cab	OMI	Ajin	5891	30	91				
Amtrak	B-B	F-40PH	II	Cab	OMI	Ajin	5891.1	50	91	427			
VIA	B-B	F-40PH-2	III	Cab	OMI	Ajin	5897	15	91	329			
RTA	B-B	F-40PH-2	III	Cab	OMI	Ajin	5896	25	91	329			
VIA	B-B	F-40PH-2	III	Cab	OMI	Ajin	5897.1	200	91	427			
AT&SF	B-B	F-45		Cab	OMI	Ajin	5995	35	91	435			
BN	B-B	F-45		Cab	OMI	Ajin	5996	20	91	435			
BN	B-B	F-45		Cab	OMI	Ajin	5998	20	91	435			
ATSF, BN	B-B	F-45		Cab	CustB	KMT	DE-103	500	72	70	125	100	
	B-B	F-45		Cab	Hall	Goto		525	75-76	70-85	120	105	See Note #772
BN	B-B	F-45		Cab	OMI	Ajin	5999	20	91	435			
BN	B-B	F-45		Cab	OMI	Ajin	5997	20	91	435			
	C-C	FP-45		Cab	Trains	KMT	112	600	69	50	100	80	3600 hp.
CMStP&P	C-C	FP-45		Cab	OMI	Ajin	5993	35	91	435			
	C-C	FP-45		Cab	Trains	KMT	112	600	69	50	100	80	3600 hp.
AT&SF	C-C	FP-45		Cab	OMI	Ajin	5991	50	91	435			
UP	C-C	SD-7		RSw	OMI	Ajin	5166	40	89	324	272		#450-459
	C-C	SD-7		RSw	Ortl	Samh	0114	125	85	236	190		
C&NW	C-C	SD-7		RSw	OMI	Ajin	5162	25	89	324	272		See Note #1913
CB&Q	C-C	SD-7		RSw	OMI	Ajin	5161	25	89	324	272		#300-324
Milw	C-C	SD-7		RSw	OMI	Ajin	5165	20	89	324	272		#504-515
	C-C	SD-7		RSw	Hall	KMT		600	72	70	100		1500 hp.
SP	C-C	SD-7		RSw	OMI	Ajin	5167	30	89	324	272		#5316-5335
GN	C-C	SD-7		RSw	OMI	Ajin	5164	35	89	324	272		#550-572
D&RGW	C-C	SD-7		RSw	OMI	Ajin	5163	30	89	324	272		#5300-5303
B&LE	C-C	SD-7		RSw	OMI	Ajin	5160	10	89	324	272		See Note #1011
	C-C	SD-7		RSw	Hall	KMT		500	74	85	110	85	
	C-C	SD-9		RSw	Hall	KMT		500	73	98	115	90	
	C-C	SD-9		RSw	Hall	KMT		600	74	98	110	85	
Milw	C-C	SD-9	I	RSw	OMI	Ajin	5170	20	89	324	272		#538 w/o Dyn. Bk.
C&G	C-C	SD-9	II	RSw	OMI	Ajin	5173	10	89	324	272		#202-207 w/o Dyn. Bk.
CB&Q	C-C	SD-9	IV	RSw	OMI	Ajin	5186	10	89	324	272		#827-842
NKP	C-C	SD-9	II	RSw	OMI	Ajin	5179	15	89	324	272		#341-359

GM Electro-Motive Division (cont'd)

The EMD FP45 was originally built at the request of Santa Fe to pull the "Super Chief." Basically an SDP45 with a sheet metal shroud, the FP45 was an attempt to provide a unit with a bit more aesthetic appeal and streamlining on the crack passenger trains. The angular nose with a front platform did not compare to the pleasing lines of the E units these locomotives replaced. Only 14 FP45s were sold. Overland's model of Santa Fe #105 accurately captures the "brick-on-a-flatcar" look these units exemplify. EMD later produced over 80 F45s which share the same general car-body design.

Road	AAR Code	Class & Phase		Type	Importer	Builder	Cat #	Quan.	Yrs.	List Price	Mint	Avg.	Remarks
DM&IR	C-C	SD-9	II	RSw	OMI	Ajin	5177	35	89	324	272		#101-130 w/Dyn. Bk.
CB&Q	C-C	SD-9	II	RSw	OMI	Ajin	5175	25	89	324	272		#440-459
SP	C-C	SD-9	I	RSw	OMI	Ajin	5171	40	89	324	272		#5340-5371
C&NW	C-C	SD-9	I	RSw	OMI	Ajin	5168	20	89	324	272		See Note #747
D&RGW	C-C	SD-9	II	RSw	OMI	Ajin	5176	35	89	324	272		See Note#697
C&NW	C-C	SD-9	II	RSw	OMI	Ajin	5174	25	89	324	272		#1721-1724
GN	C-C	SD-9	II	RSw	OMI	Ajin	5178	25	89	324	272		#579-589
GN	C-C	SD-9	I	RSw	OMI	Ajin	5169	30	89	324	272		#573-578
PRR	C-C	SD-9	II	RSw	OMI	Ajin	5180	20	89	324	272		#6900-7600
DM&IR	C-C	SD-9	III	RSw	OMI	Ajin	5183	25	89	324	272		#131-158
GN	C-C	SD-9	III	RSw	OMI	Ajin	5184	20	89	324			#598-599
B&O	C-C	SD-9	II	RSw	OMI	Ajin	5172	15	89	324	272		See Note #818
GN	C-C	SD-9	III	RSw	OMI	Ajin	5184	20	89	324			#509-597
DM&IR	C-C	SD-9	IV	RSw	OMI	Ajin	5187	25	89	324	272		#159-174
SP	C-C	SD-9		RSw	OMI	Ajin	5182	20	89	324	272		#5387-5444
GN	C-C	SD-9	III	RSw	OMI	Ajin	8184	20	89	324	272		#590-597
GN	C-C	SD-9	III	RSw	OMI	Ajin	8185	20	89	324	272		#598-599
	C-C	SD-9	I	RSw	Ortl	Samh	0115	100	85	236	190		Four 36" Fans
	C-C	SD-9	II	RSw	Ortl	Samh	0116	75	85	236	190		Two 48" Fans
B&O	B-B	SD-9		RSw	PFM	Tensh	129	10	55	30	130		fp.
SP	B-B	SD-9		RSw	PFM	Tensh	129	75	55	30	130		fp.
UP	B-B	SD-9		RSw	PFM	Tensh	129	20	55	30	130		fp.
PRR	B-B	SD-9		RSw	PFM	Tensh	129	20	55	30	130		fp.
WP	B-B	SD-9		RSw	PFM	Tensh	129	8	55	30	130		fp.
GN	B-B	SD-9		RSw	PFM	Tensh	129	75	55	30	130		fp.
CB&Q	B-B	SD-9		RSw	PFM	Tensh	129	50	55	30	130		fp.
CMStP&P	B-B	SD-9		RSw	PFM	Tensh	129	10	55	30	130		fp.
C&NW	B-B	SD-9		RSw	PFM	Tensh	129	50	55	30	130		fp.
CMStP&P	B-B	SD-9		RSw	PFM	Tensh	129	60	56	34	130		fp.
WP	B-B	SD-9		RSw	PFM	Tensh	129	50	56	34	130		fp.
GN	B-B	SD-9		RSw	PFM	Tensh	129	106	56	34	130		fp.
PRR	B-B	SD-9		RSw	PFM	Tensh	129	60	56	34	130		fp.
C&NW	B-B	SD-9		RSw	PFM	Tensh	129	50	56	34	130		fp.
KCS	B-B	SD-9		RSw	PFM	Tensh	129	1	56	34	130		fp.
UP	B-B	SD-9		RSw	PFM	Tensh	129	50	56	34	130		fp.
CB&Q	B-B	SD-9		RSw	PFM	Tensh	129	50	56	34	130		fp.
SP	B-B	SD-9		RSw	PFM	Tensh	129	100	56	34	130		fp.
B&O	B-B	SD-9		RSw	PFM	Tensh	129	70	56	34	130		fp.

GM Electro-Motive Division (cont'd)

The SD–18 was one of several variations on the basic SD–7 pattern, which in itself is basically a lengthened GP–7. Six-wheel trucks replaced the GP–7's 4-wheel trucks and horsepower was increased to 1,800 hp in the SD–18 series. EMD had established that a solid, basic design could be modified to serve a variety of needs. The Overland model pictured here shows the C&O version atop Alco RSD–5 trucks. C&O had traded in the RSD–5s in 1963. These engines lasted until the '70s on the C&O, and when they went, they were not missed by the crews, who didn't appreciate the sluggish performance of the unsupercharged engines.

| Road | AAR Code | Class & Phase | Type | Model Production | | | | List Price | Resale | | Remarks |
				Importer	Builder	Cat #	Quan.	Yrs.		Mint	Avg.	
SRR	B-B	SD-9	RSw	PFM	Tensh	129	1	57	30	130		fp.
C&NW	B-B	SD-9	RSw	PFM	Tensh	129	30	57	30	130		fp.
B&O	B-B	SD-9	RSw	PFM	Tensh	129	30	57	30	130		fp.
PRR	B-B	SD-9	RSw	PFM	Tensh	129	1	57	30	130		fp.
WP	B-B	SD-9	RSw	PFM	Tensh	129	10	57	30	130		fp.
AT&SF	B-B	SD-9	RSw	PFM	Tensh	129	10	57	30	130		fp.
GN	B-B	SD-9	RSw	PFM	Tensh	129	50	57	30	130		fp.
CB&Q	B-B	SD-9	RSw	PFM	Tensh	129	10	57	30	130		fp.
SP	B-B	SD-9	RSw	PFM	Tensh	129	30	57	30	130		fp.
CMStP&P	B-B	SD-9	RSw	PFM	Tensh	129	10	57	30	130		fp.
UP	B-B	SD-9	RSw	PFM	Tensh	129	20	57	30	130		fp.
PRR	B-B	SD-9	RSw	PFM	Tensh	129	40	58	30	130		fp.
WP	B-B	SD-9	RSw	PFM	Tensh	129	10	58	30	130		fp.
SP	B-B	SD-9	RSw	PFM	Tensh	129	40	58	30	130		fp.
UP	B-B	SD-9	RSw	PFM	Tensh	129	10	58	30	130		fp.
C&NW	B-B	SD-9	RSw	PFM	Tensh	129	40	58	30	130		fp.
NdeM	B-B	SD-9	RSw	PFM	Tensh	129	12	58	30	130		fp.
GN	B-B	SD-9	RSw	PFM	Tensh	129	50	58	30	130		fp.
B&O	B-B	SD-9	RSw	PFM	Tensh	129	30	58	30	130		fp.
AT&SF	B-B	SD-9	RSw	PFM	Tensh	129	30	58	30	130		fp.
CB&Q	B-B	SD-9	RSw	PFM	Tensh	129	20	59	30	130		fp.
B&O	B-B	SD-9	RSw	PFM	Tensh	129	40	59	30	130		fp.
WP	B-B	SD-9	RSw	PFM	Tensh	129	5	59	30	130		fp.
AT&SF	B-B	SD-9	RSw	PFM	Tensh	129	60	59	30	130		fp.
CMStP&P	B-B	SD-9	RSw	PFM	Tensh	129	20	59	30	130		fp.
SP	B-B	SD-9	RSw	PFM	Tensh	129	50	59	30	130		fp.
UP	B-B	SD-9	RSw	PFM	Tensh	129	10	59	30	130		fp.
PRR	B-B	SD-9	RSw	PFM	Tensh	129	30	59	30	130		fp.
C&NW	B-B	SD-9	RSw	PFM	Tensh	129	30	59	30	130		fp.
DM&IR	B-B	SD-9	RSw	PFM	Tensh	129	20	59	30	130		fp.
GN	B-B	SD-9	RSw	PFM	Tensh	129	60	59	30	130		fp.
CMStP&P	B-B	SD-9	RSw	PFM	Tensh	129	20	60	30	130		fp.

GM Electro-Motive Division (cont'd)

Road	AAR Code	Class & Phase	Type	Importer	Builder	Cat #	Quan.	Yrs.	List Price	Mint	Avg.	Remarks
PRR	B-B	SD-9	RSw	PFM	Tensh	129	80	60	30	130		fp.
GN	B-B	SD-9	RSw	PFM	Tensh	129	80	60	30	130		fp.
B&O	B-B	SD-9	RSw	PFM	Tensh	129	60	60	30	130		fp.
AT&SF	B-B	SD-9	RSw	PFM	Tensh	129	40	60	30	130		fp.
SP	B-B	SD-9	RSw	PFM	Tensh	129	100	60	30	130		fp.
CB&Q	B-B	SD-9	RSw	PFM	Tensh	129	20	60	30	130		fp.
WP	B-B	SD-9	RSw	PFM	Tensh	129	20	60	30	130		fp.
DM&IR	B-B	SD-9	RSw	PFM	Tensh	129	20	60	30	130		fp.
UP	B-B	SD-9	RSw	PFM	Tensh	129	20	60	30	130		fp.
C&NW	B-B	SD-9	RSw	PFM	Tensh	129	40	60	30	130		fp.
	C-C	SD-9	RSw	Trains	KMT		600	68	70	110	85	
	C-C	SD-9	RSw	Trains	KMT		600	68	70	110	85	
SP	C-C	SD-9E	RSw	OMI	Ajin	5181	40	89	324	272		#4300/4400
DM&IR	B-B	SD-18	RSw	OMI	Ajin	6171		92	386			#300 Series rebuilt
C&O	B-B	SD-18	RSw	OMI	Ajin	6169		92	386			w/RSD-5 trucks
C&O	B-B	SD-18	RSw	Ortl	Samh	0440		84	236			LoH, Alco trucks
	B-B	SD-18	RSw	Ortl	Samh	0421		84	236			LoH
	C-C	SD-24	RSw	Hall	KMT		500	74	80	110	95	LoH
	C-C	SD-24	RSw	Hall	KMT		500	74	80	105	90	HiG
UP	C-C	SD-24	RSw	OMI	Ajin	1834	65	83	195	195		See Note #1868
UP,BN	C-C	SD-24	RSw	OMI	Ajin	1835	40	83	195	195		See Note #1869
	C-C	SD-24	RSw	Ortl	Samh	0234	75	84	236			LoH
	C-C	SD-24	RSw	Ortl	Samh	0235	75	84	236			HiH
GN	C-C	SD-24	RSw	PFM	Tensh	141	200	61	30	140		fp.
UP	C-C	SD-24	RSw	PFM	Tensh	141	125	61	30	140		fp.
CB&Q	C-C	SD-24	RSw	PFM	Tensh	141	75	61	30	140		fp.
SP	C-C	SD-24	RSw	PFM	Tensh	141	110	61	30	140		fp.
B&O	C-C	SD-24	RSw	PFM	Tensh	141	65	61	30	140		fp.
AT&SF	C-C	SD-24	RSw	PFM	Tensh	141	190	61	30	140		fp.
PRR	C-C	SD-24	RSw	PFM	Tensh	141	100	61	30	140		fp.
SP	C-C	SD-24	RSw	PFM	Tensh	141	80	62	30	140		fp.
AT&SF	C-C	SD-24	RSw	PFM	Tensh	141	85	62	30	140		fp.
CB&Q	C-C	SD-24	RSw	PFM	Tensh	141	65	62	30	140		fp.
B&O	C-C	SD-24	RSw	PFM	Tensh	141	50	62	30	140		fp.
UP	C-C	SD-24	RSw	PFM	Tensh	141	85	62	30	140		fp.
PRR	C-C	SD-24	RSw	PFM	Tensh	141	80	62	30	140		fp.
GN	C-C	SD-24	RSw	PFM	Tensh	141	80	62	30	140		fp.
SP	C-C	SD-24	RSw	PFM	Tensh	141	40	63	30	140		fp.
UP	C-C	SD-24	RSw	PFM	Tensh	141	40	63	30	140		fp.
GN	C-C	SD-24	RSw	PFM	Tensh	141	60	63	30	140		fp.
CB&Q	C-C	SD-24	RSw	PFM	Tensh	141	30	63	30	140		fp.
AT&SF	C-C	SD-24	RSw	PFM	Tensh	141	6	63	30	140		fp.
B&O	C-C	SD-24	RSw	PFM	Tensh	141	20	63	30	140		fp.
PRR	C-C	SD-24	RSw	PFM	Tensh	141	20	63	30	140		fp.
GN	C-C	SD-24	RSw	PFM	Tensh	141	70	64	30	140		fp.
CB&Q	C-C	SD-24	RSw	PFM	Tensh	141	40	64	30	140		fp.
B&O	C-C	SD-24	RSw	PFM	Tensh	141	30	64	30	140		fp.
SP	C-C	SD-24	RSw	PFM	Tensh	141	70	64	30	140		fp.
AT&SF	C-C	SD-24	RSw	PFM	Tensh	141	70	64	30	140		fp.
UP	C-C	SD-24	RSw	PFM	Tensh	141	45	64	30	140		fp.
PRR	C-C	SD-24	RSw	PFM	Tensh	141	50	64	30	140		fp.
UP	C-C	SD-24	RSw	PFM	Tensh	141	125	65	35	140		fp.
PRR	C-C	SD-24	RSw	PFM	Tensh	141	80	65	35	140		fp.
SP	C-C	SD-24	RSw	PFM	Tensh	141	119	65	35	140		fp.
GN	C-C	SD-24	RSw	PFM	Tensh	141	130	65	35	140		fp.
CB&Q	C-C	SD-24	RSw	PFM	Tensh	141	110	65	35	140		fp.
AT&SF	C-C	SD-24	RSw	PFM	Tensh	141	100	65	35	140		fp.
B&O	C-C	SD-24	RSw	PFM	Tensh	141	50	65	35	140		fp.
GN	C-C	SD-24	RSw	PFM	Tensh	141	130	66	35	140		fp.
B&O	C-C	SD-24	RSw	PFM	Tensh	141	80	66	35	140		fp.
CB&Q	C-C	SD-24	RSw	PFM	Tensh	141	60	66	35	140		fp.
PRR	C-C	SD-24	RSw	PFM	Tensh	141	100	66	35	140		fp.
SP	C-C	SD-24	RSw	PFM	Tensh	141	50	66	35	140		fp.
AT&SF	C-C	SD-24	RSw	PFM	Tensh	141	90	66	35	140		fp.

GM Electro-Motive Division (cont'd)

The SD–40 set the stage for EMD's dominance of the diesel market during the late '60s and early '70s. Over 880 units were sold, and the SD–40–2's that followed became the best-selling diesel road unit in history. Easily recognized with large platforms at either end, these units are still in service on many roads. A large fuel tank completely fills the space between the trucks. Alco Models imported this KMT-built model of the SD–40 in 1971. The model is well made and represents the state-of-the-art for that period; but compared to today's models, it lacks drive-system sophistication and fine detailing.

| Road | AAR Code | Class & Phase | | Type | Model Production | | | | | List Price | Resale | | Remarks |
					Importer	Builder	Cat #	Quan.	Yrs.		Mint	Avg.	
UP	C-C	SD-24		RSw	PFM	Tensh	141	110	66	35	140		fp.
ATSF	C-C	SD-24 slug		RSw	OMI	Ajin	1836	36	83	114	114		See Note #1870
UP	C-C	SD-24 slug		RSw	OMI	Ajin	1832	41	83	114	114		UP Slug
UP	C-C	SD-24B		RSw	OMI	Ajin	1833	75	83	195	195		Cabless
	C-C	SD-24B		RSw	Ortl	Samh	0236	50	84	236			
UP	C-C	SD-24M		RSw	OMI	Ajin	1831	84	83	195	195		See Note #1871
ATSF	C-C	SD-26		RSw	OMI	Ajin	1830	76	83	195	195		See Note #1872
	C-C	SD-35		RSw	Alco				82				
B&O	C-C	SD-35		RSw	OMI	Ajin	5531	10	90	387			
C&O	C-C	SD-35		RSw	OMI	Ajin	5534	15	90	387			#20L,C
N&W	C-C	SD-35		RSw	OMI	Ajin	5538	25	90	387			See Note#1874
L&N	C-C	SD-35		RSw	OMI	Ajin	5537	15	90	387			#9001,4
CNJ	C-C	SD-35		RSw	OMI	Ajin	5533	40	90	387			
WM	C-C	SD-35		RSw	OMI	Ajin	5543	25	90	387			#126B,C-129B,C
SRR	C-C	SD-35		RSw	OMI	Ajin	5541	25	90	387			See Note#1873
C of G	C-C	SD-35		RSw	OMI	Ajin	5532	10	90	387			
CR	C-C	SD-35		RSw	OMI	Ajin	5535	15	90	387			#20B
ACL	C-C	SD-35	II	Cab	OMI	Ajin	5530	10	90	387			#201B-207B
SCL	C-C	SD-35		RSw	OMI	Ajin	5540	20	90	387			#107C-108A,C
SP	C-C	SD-35		RSw	OMI	Ajin	5542	25	90	387			#126A,D-129A,D
PRR	C-C	SD-35		RSw	OMI	Ajin	5539	10	90	387			#1300-1301
CR	C-C	SD-35		RSw	OMI	Ajin	5536	20	90	387			#9000,2,3,5
L&N	C-C	SDP-35		RSw	OMI	Ajin	5544	10	90	387			#430A-D,438A-D
UP	C-C	SDP-35		RSw	OMI	Ajin	5547	50	90	387			#6500A-6506A
UP	C-C	SDP-35		RSw	OMI	Ajin	1899	105	86	279	279		#1400-1409
SCL	C-C	SDP-35		RSw	OMI	Ajin	5545	10	90	387			#9010-9019
SBD	C-C	SDP-35		RSw	OMI	Ajin	5546	10	90	387			#1800-1831
	C-C	SD-38-2		RSw	Alco				82	185		155	w/Dynamic Brakes
	C-C	SD-38-2		RSw	Alco				82	185		155	w/o Dynamic Brakes
Milw	C-C	SDL-39		RSw	OMI	Ajin	5119	185	88	307	258		#582-590
Milw	C-C	SDL-39		RSw	OMI	Ajin	5119	100	91	391			Re-run
	C-C	SD-40		RSw	Alco	KMT	D-142LB		71	59	125	100	See Note #1875
	C-C	SD-40		RSw	Alco	KMT	D-142HB		71	59	115	95	See Note #1876
	C-C	SD-40		RSw	Alco	KMT	D-142		71	59	115	90	See Note #769
	C-C	SD-40		RSw	Alco	KMT			74	59			re-run
	C-C	SD-40		RSw	OMI	Ajin	1941	35	86	236			See Note #1877

GM Electro-Motive Division (cont'd)

Road	AAR Code	Class & Phase	Type	Importer	Builder	Cat #	Quan.	Yrs.	List Price	Mint	Avg.	Remarks
	C-C	SD-40	RSw	OMI	Ajin	1936	80	86	236			See Note #1878
	C-C	SD-40	RSw	OMI	Ajin	1934	10	86	236			See Note #1879
SP	C-C	SD-40	RSw	OMI	Ajin	1935	50	86	243			LoH w/HL in nose
	C-C	SD-40	RSw	OMI	Ajin	1933	90	86	236			See Note #1879
MP	C-C	SD-40	RSw	OMI	Ajin	5110	25	88	264	222		#3000-3089
N&W	C-C	SD-40	RSw	OMI	Ajin	5111	22	88	264	222		HiH, #1580-1624
CNJ	C-C	SD-40	RSw	OMI	Ajin	5104	15	88	264	222		#3061-3069
C&O	C-C	SD-40	RSw	OMI	Ajin	5105	8	88	264	222		#7450-7469
SOO	C-C	SD-40	RSw	OMI	Ajin	5112	14	88	264	222		#737-756
UP	C-C	SD-40	RSw	OMI	Ajin	5115	35	88	264	222		#3000-3039
GTW	C-C	SD-40	RSw	OMI	Ajin	5108	10	88	264	222		#5900-5903
CR	C-C	SD-40	RSw	OMI	Ajin	5107	28	88	264	222		#6240-6284
GTW	C-C	SD-40	RSw	OMI	Ajin	5018	10	88	264	222		#5900-5903
C&NW	C-C	SD-40	RSw	OMI	Ajin	5106	22	88	264	222		#867-895
SRR	C-C	SD-40	RSw	OMI	Ajin	5113	17	88	264	222		#3170-3200
UP	C-C	SD-40	RSw	OMI	Ajin	5116	35	88	264	222		#3083-3122
B&O	C-C	SD-40	RSw	OMI	Ajin	5102	12	88	264	222		#7500
WM	C-C	SD-40	RSw	OMI	Ajin	5118	17	88	364	306		#7445-7449
GM&O	C-C	SD-40	RSw	OMI	Ajin	5109	5	88	264	222		#901-921
CB&Q	C-C	SD-40	RSw	OMI	Ajin	5103	30	88	264	222		#875-879
C&O	C-C	SD-40	RSw	OMI	Ajin	5377	10	90	357			#7527-7536
BN	C-C	SD-40	RSw	OMI	Ajin	5372	15	90	357			#6300-6319
L&N	C-C	SD-40	RSw	OMI	Ajin	5385	10	90	357			#1249-1258
CGW	C-C	SD-40	RSw	OMI	Ajin	5379	10	90	357			#401-409
PC	C-C	SD-40	RSw	OMI	Ajin	5388	10	90	357			#6240-6284
CRR	C-C	SD-40	RSw	OMI	Ajin	5380	10	90	357			#3000-3007
GM&O	C-C	SD-40	RSw	OMI	Ajin	5383	10	90	357			#901-921
KCS	C-C	SD-40	RSw	OMI	Ajin	5384	10	90	357			#630-636
UP	C-C	SD-40	RSw	OMI	Ajin	5397	25	90	357			#3048-3082
CNR	C-C	SD-40	RSw	OMI	Ajin	5374	25	90	357			#5126-5175
SOO	C-C	SD-40	RSw	OMI	Ajin	5389	15	90	357			#737-756
SP	C-C	SD-40	RSw	OMI	Ajin	5391	25	90	357			#7300-7385
UP	C-C	SD-40	RSw	OMI	Ajin	5398	30	90	357			#3083-3122
B&O	C-C	SD-40	RSw	OMI	Ajin	5371	15	90	357			#7591-7594
SRR	C-C	SD-40	RSw	OMI	Ajin	5390	20	90	357			#3170-3185, HiH
UP	C-C	SD-40	RSw	OMI	Ajin	5393	30	90	357			#3000-3007
PRR	C-C	SD-40	RSw	OMI	Ajin	5387	15	90	357			#6040-6104
BN	C-C	SD-40	RSw	OMI	Ajin	5373	15	90	357			#6335-6338
CNJ	C-C	SD-40	RSw	OMI	Ajin	5376	15	90	357			#3061-3069
CNJ	C-C	SD-40	RSw	OMI	Ajin	5378	15	90	357			#867-878
UP	C-C	SD-40	RSw	OMI	Ajin	5394	30	90	357			#3008-3039
WM	C-C	SD-40	RSw	OMI	Ajin	5399	15	90	357			#7445-7449
CPR	C-C	SD-40	RSw	OMI	Ajin	5375	25	90	357			#5532-5564
SP	C-C	SD-40	RSw	OMI	Ajin	5392	10	90	357			#8400-8478
CR	C-C	SD-40	RSw	OMI	Ajin	5381	258	90	357			#6285-6324
N&W	C-C	SD-40	RSw	OMI	Ajin	5386	15	90	357			#1610-1624, HiH
GTW	C-C	SD-40	RSw	OMI	Ajin	5382	10	90	357			#5900-5911
	C-C	SDP-40F	RSw	Gem	KMT	KT-109	500	74	100	100	80	See Note #770
SP	C-C	SD-40E	RSw	OMI	Ajin	5114	40	88	264	222		#7300-7385
SP	C-C	SD-40T-2	RSw	Alco	Samh		200	82	227		195	See Note #777
D&RGW	C-C	SD-40T-2	RSw	Alco	Samh	D-175	200	82	227		195	Tunnel Motor
SP	C-C	SD-40T-2	RSw	Alco	Samh	D-175S	200	82	227		195	See Note #776
D&RGW	C-C	SD-40T-2	RSw	Key	Samh			85	229		185	tunnel Motor
D&RGW	C-C	SD-40T-2	RSw	Key	Samh			85	271		220	fp., tunnel Motor
SP	C-C	SD-40T-2	RSw	Key	Samh			85	271		220	fp., snoot; Cotton Belt
SP	C-C	SD-40T-2	RSw	Key	Samh			85	229		185	long nose
SP	C-C	SD-40T-2	RSw	Key	Samh			85	271		220	fp.
D&RGW	C-C	SD-40T-2	RSw	OMI	Ajin	5340	50	88	313			#5398-5413
D&RGW	C-C	SD-40T-2	RSw	OMI	Ajin	5339	46	88	313			#5386-5397
D&RGW	C-C	SD-40T-2	RSw	OMI	Ajin	5338	46	88	313			#5341-5355
SP	C-C	SD-40T-2	RSw	OMI	Ajin	5337	35	88	313			#8499-8573
SP	C-C	SD-40T-2	RSw	OMI	Ajin	5336	60	88	313			w/116" nose
SP	C-C	SD-40T-2	RSw	OMI	Ajin	5335	30	88	313			w/81" nose
SP	C-C	SD-40T-2	RSw	PSC		15112		83	185		150	long nose tunnel motor

GM Electro-Motive Division (cont'd)

SP and D&RGW needed diesels that would continue to operate properly in their long tunnels. The problem was traced to insufficient clean air for the prime mover. To solve this problem, the air intakes were moved from the top of the engine to running board height. Obviously, it must have worked, for EMD sold 310 such units. This Key Imports model illustrates the excellent level of detail that has come to be expected on today's brass models. Accuracy extends to specific types of horns and brake gear used by the prototype railroads. It is no longer sufficient to paint a generic model for a particular road.

Road	AAR Code	Class & Phase	Type	Importer	Builder	Cat #	Quan.	Yrs.	List Price	Mint	Avg.	Remarks
SP	C-C	SD-40T-2	RSw	PSC		15111-1		83	169		140	See Note#1880
D&RGW	C-C	SD-40T-2	RSw	PSC		15111		83	176			tunnel motor
SP	C-C	SD-40T-2	RSw	PSC		15112		83	185		150	long nose tunnel motor
D&RGW	C-C	SD-40T-2	RSw	PSC		15111		83	176			tunnel motor
SP	C-C	SD-40T-2	RSw	PSC		15111-1		83	169		140	See Note#1880
AT&SF	C-C	SD-40u	RSw	OMI	Ajin	5370	30	90	357			w/smoke defeator
AT&SF	C-C	SD-40u	RSw	OMI	Ajin	5101	50	88	264	222		#5000-5019
UP	C-C	SD-40X	RSw	OMI	Ajin	5396	25	90	357			#3046-3047
UP	C-C	SD-40X	RSw	OMI	Ajin	5395	30	90	357			#3040-3045
UP	C-C	SD-40X	RSw	OMI	Ajin	1937	10	86	236			See Note #1881
UP	C-C	SD-40X	RSw	OMI	Ajin	1937	105	86	279			w/flared radiators
UP	C-C	SD-40X	RSw	OMI	Ajin	5117	30	88	307	258		#3040-3045
AT&SF	C-C	SD-40-2	RSw	Alco	KMT			79	209	200	175	LoH, "Snoot"
	C-C	SD-40-2	RSw	Alco	KMT			79	209	200	175	3000 hp., LoH
UP&KCS	C-C	SD-40-2	RSw	Alco	KMT			79	209	200	175	LoH, "Snoot"
N&W/Sou	C-C	SD-40-2	RSw	Alco	KMT	D-170		80	210	175	150	HiH
ICG	C-C	SD-40-2	RSw	OMI	Ajin	5341.1	4	88	400	336		ICG #6030-6033, fp.
UP	C-C	SD-40-2	RSw	OMI	Ajin	5331	40	88	293			#3498-3658
NS	C-C	SD-40-2	RSw	OMI	Ajin	5320.2	5	88	400	336		High Hood
MKT	C-C	SD-40-2	RSw	OMI	Ajin	5317	25	88	293	246		See Note #1885
SOO	C-C	SD-40-2	RSw	OMI	Ajin	5324	30	88	293	246		See Note #1894
CNR	C-C	SD-40-2	RSw	OMI	Ajin	5306	85	88	293			See Note #1886
RI	C-C	SD-40-2	RSw	OMI	Ajin	5323	20	88	293	246		See Note #1888
BN	C-C	SD-40-2	RSw	OMI	Ajin	5305	25	88	293	246		
Milw	C-C	SD-40-2	RSw	OMI	Ajin	5316	25	88	293	246		See Note #1889
N&W	C-C	SD-40-2	RSw	OMI	Ajin	5320.1	10	88	400	336		High Hood
L&N	C-C	SD-40-2	RSw	OMI	Ajin	5313	25	88	293	246		See Note #1887
BN	C-C	SD-40-2	RSw	OMI	Ajin	5303	20	88	293	246		
C&NW	C-C	SD-40-2	RSw	OMI	Ajin	5309	35	88	293	246		
CNR	C-C	SD-40-2	RSw	OMI	Ajin	5306	100	89	334	281		re-run
L&N	C-C	SD-40-2	RSw	OMI	Ajin	5313.1	5	88	400	336		See Note #1892
SRR	C-C	SD-40-2	RSw	OMI	Ajin	5326	25	88	293			HiH
SOO	C-C	SD-40-2	RSw	OMI	Ajin	5325	35	88	293	246		See Note #1896
UP	C-C	SD-40-2	RSw	OMI	Ajin	5330	60	88	293			#3300-3398
UP	C-C	SD-40-2	RSw	OMI	Ajin	5334	20	88	293			Canadian Pool
N&W	C-C	SD-40-2	RSw	OMI	Ajin	5321.1	10	88	400	336		See Note #1895
BCR	C-C	SD-40-2	RSw	OMI	Ajin	5342	15	88	300			#751-762
L&N	C-C	SD-40-2	RSw	OMI	Ajin	5314.1	5	88	400	336		fp.

GM Electro-Motive Division (cont'd)

Road	AAR Code	Class & Phase	Type	Importer	Builder	Cat #	Quan.	Yrs.	List Price	Mint	Avg.	Remarks
KCS	C-C	SD-40-2	RSw	OMI	Ajin	5311	25	88	293	246		
CPR	C-C	SD-40-2	RSw	OMI	Ajin	5308	35	88	293	246		
L&N	C-C	SD-40-2	RSw	OMI	Ajin	5314	25	88	293			
N&W	C-C	SD-40-2	RSw	OMI	Ajin	5321	10	88	293	246		See Note#1884
MP	C-C	SD-40-2	RSw	OMI	Ajin	5318	25	88	293			
CR	C-C	SD-40-2	RSw	OMI	Ajin	5310	40	88	293	246		See Note #1883
UP	C-C	SD-40-2	RSw	OMI	Ajin	5328	40	88	293			#3123-3242
CPR	C-C	SD-40-2	RSw	OMI	Ajin	5307	35	88	293	246		
CNR	C-C	SD-40-2	RSw	OMI	Ajin	5343	50	89	286			w/o dynamic brakes
ICG	C-C	SD-40-2	RSw	OMI	Ajin	5341	26	88	293	246		ICG #6030-6033
KCS	C-C	SD-40-2	RSw	OMI	Ajin	5312	20	88	293			
N&W	C-C	SD-40-2	RSw	OMI	Ajin	5320		88	293	246		See Note #1882
AT&SF	C-C	SD-40-2	RSw	OMI	Ajin	5300	40	88	293	246		
MP	C-C	SD-40-2	RSw	OMI	Ajin	5319	25	88	293	246		See Note #1890
UP	C-C	SD-40-2	RSw	OMI	Ajin	5333	35	88	293			#3794, porch pot
Milw	C-C	SD-40-2	RSw	OMI	Ajin	5315	35	88	293			
UP	C-C	SD-40-2	RSw	OMI	Ajin	5332	50	88	293			#3659-3808
B&O	C-C	SD-40-2	RSw	OMI	Ajin	5302	25	88	293	246		
AT&SF	C-C	SD-40-2	RSw	OMI	Ajin	5301	30	88	293	246		
NS	C-C	SD-40-2	RSw	OMI	Ajin	5321.2	5	88	400	336		Low Hood, fp.
CR	C-C	SD-40-2	RSw	OMI	Ajin	5310.1	10	88	400	336		See Note #1893
SRR	C-C	SD-40-2	RSw	OMI	Ajin	5327	25	88	293			HiH
ONR	C-C	SD-40-2	RSw	OMI	Ajin	5322	25	88	293			
UP	C-C	SD-40-2	RSw	OMI	Ajin	5329	40	88	293			#3243-3297
CPR	C-C	SD-40-2	RSw	OMI	Ajin	5308	70	89	334	281		re-run
RI	C-C	SD-40-2	RSw	OMI	Ajin	5323.1	5	88	400	336		See Note #1891
BN	C-C	SD-40-2B	RSw	OMI	Ajin	5304	25	88	293	246		
CP	C-C	SD-40-2F	RSw	OMI	Ajin	5155	150	90	353	297		See Note #1897
	C-C	SD-45	RSw	Alco	KMT	D-130	600	69	48	145	110	3600 hp.
	C-C	SD-45	RSw	Hall	KMT	HS0086		83	267		190	standard
UP	C-C	SD-45	RSw	Hall	KMT	HS0087		83	267		190	See Note #1898
SP	C-C	SD-45	RSw	Hall	KMT	HS0085		83	267		190	
GN	C-C	SD-45	RSw	OMI	Ajin	6070	20	90	359	301		#400-407
SRR	C-C	SD-45	RSw	OMI	Ajin	6088	20	90	359	301		See Note#1905
Milw	C-C	SD-45	RSw	OMI	Ajin	6074	15	90	359	301		#4000-4005
NP	C-C	SD-45	RSw	OMI	Ajin	6078	20	90	359	301		#3600-3603
UP	C-C	SD-45	RSw	OMI	Ajin	6096	20	90	359	301		#3624-3649
UP	C-C	SD-45	RSw	OMI	Ajin	6095	20	90	359	301		#3600-3621
SP	C-C	SD-45	RSw	OMI	Ajin	6090	10	90	359	301		#8935-8963
N&W	C-C	SD-45	RSw	OMI	Ajin	6076	20	90	359	301		See Note#1902
SP	C-C	SD-45	RSw	OMI	Ajin	6093	15	90	359	301		See Note #1900
SRR	C-C	SD-45	RSw	OMI	Ajin	6087	15	90	359	301		See Note#1899
ATSF	C-C	SD-45	RSw	OMI	Ajin	6051	15	90	359	301		See Note #1906
SP	C-C	SD-45	RSw	OMI	Ajin	6089	15	90	359	301		#8800-8844
GN	C-C	SD-45	RSw	OMI	Ajin	6072	15	90	359	301		#418-426
BN	C-C	SD-45	RSw	OMI	Ajin	6057	15	90	359	301		#6543-6567
GN	C-C	SD-45	RSw	OMI	Ajin	6071	15	90	359	301		#408-417
Demo	C-C	SD-45	RSw	OMI	Ajin	6099	12	90	359	301		Demo #4351
PRR	C-C	SD-45	RSw	OMI	Ajin	6080	20	90	359	301		#6105-6234
E-L	C-C	SD-45	RSw	OMI	Ajin	6068	20	90	359	301		#3601-3620
C&S	C-C	SD-45	RSw	OMI	Ajin	6062	15	90	359	301		#868-874
BN	C-C	SD-45	RSw	OMI	Ajin	6055	15	90	359	301		See Note#1903
E-L	C-C	SD-45	RSw	OMI	Ajin	6069	20	90	359	301		#3621-3634
CB&Q	C-C	SD-45	RSw	OMI	Ajin	6064	15	90	359	301		#526-530
ATSF	C-C	SD-45	RSw	OMI	Ajin	6054	45	90	359	301		#5501-5502
N&W	C-C	SD-45	RSw	OMI	Ajin	6075	12	90	359	301		See Note#1901
RDG	C-C	SD-45	RSw	OMI	Ajin	6081	20	90	359	301		#7600-7604
D&RGW	C-C	SD-45	RSw	OMI	Ajin	6066	40	90	359	301		#5315-5324
N&W	C-C	SD-45	RSw	OMI	Ajin	6077	15	90	359	301		See Note#1904
UP	C-C	SD-45	RSw	OMI	Ajin	6097	25	90	359	301		#1-50
SP	C-C	SD-45	RSw	OMI	Ajin	6091	10	90	359	301		#9008-9030
NP	C-C	SD-45	RSw	OMI	Ajin	6079	20	90	359	301		#3604-3619
SP	C-C	SD-45	RSw	OMI	Ajin	6092	15	90	359	301		#9069-9103
ATSF	C-C	SD-45	RSw	OMI	Ajin	6053	20	90	359	301		#5426-5477

GM Electro-Motive Division (cont'd)

Road	AAR Code	Class & Phase	Type	Importer	Builder	Cat #	Quan.	Yrs.	List Price	Mint	Avg.	Remarks
D&RGW	C-C	SD-45	RSw	OMI	Ajin	6067	40	90	359	301		#5325-5336
	C-C	SD-45	RSw	Ortl	Samh	0335		84	236		190	LoH; 1966 standard
C&NW	C-C	SD-45	RSw	Ortl	Samh	0337		84	236		190	no dynamic brakes
SP	C-C	SD-45	RSw	Ortl	Samh	0338		84	236		190	L shaped window
UP	C-C	SD-45	RSw	Ortl	Samh	0362		84	236		190	LoH; late standard
	C-C	SD-45	RSw	Ortl	Samh	0389		84	236			LoH, late, SF,D&RGW
NP/BN	C-C	SD-45	RSw	Ortl	Samh	0340		84	236		190	3 window cab
	C-C	SD-45	RSw	PFM	FuMod	D-9	750	71	55	150	125	3600 hp.
ATSF	C-C	SD-45B	RSw	OMI	Ajin	6052	40	90	359	301		See Note #1907
AT&SF	C-C	SDF-45	RSw	OMI	Ajin	5994	30	91	435			
AT&SF	C-C	SDFP-45	RSw	OMI	Ajin	5992	70	91	435			
BN	C-C	SDP-45	RSw	OMI	Ajin	5770	150	92	493			#30L,C-36L,C
BN	C-C	SDP-45	RSw	OMI	Ajin	5770	150	90	368	309		See Note #1557
E-L	C-C	SDP-45	RSw	OMI	Ajin	5781	35	90	368	309		#3635-3653
E-L	C-C	SDP-45	RSw	OMI	Ajin	5782	35	90	368	309		#3654-3668
GN	C-C	SDP-45	RSw	OMI	Ajin	5780	35	90	368	309		#6593-6599
SP	C-C	SDP-45	RSw	OMI	Ajin	5783	55	90	368	309		#3200-3209
Erie	C-C	SDP-45	RSw	Ortl	Samh	0343		84	236		195	Erie, plus short re-run
GN/BN	C-C	SDP-45	RSw	Ortl	Samh	0341		84	236		195	
SP	C-C	SDP-45	RSw	Ortl	Samh	0342		84	236		195	
UP	C-C	SD-45m	RSw	Ortl	Samh	P339		84	264			fp., Sulzer power
UP	C-C	SD-45m	RSw	Ortl	Samh	0339		84	236		190	Sulzer power
UP	C-C	SD-45m	RSw	OMI	Ajin	6098	20	90	359	301		#60-65
SP	C-C	SD-45T-2	RSw	OMI	Ajin	5772	60	90	368			
SP	C-C	SD-45T-2	RSw	PSC		15180		85	180		145	
SP	C-C	SD-45T-2	RSw	PSC		15180		85	180		145	
SP	C-C	SD-45T-2	RSw	OMI	Ajin	5771	75	90	368	309		#9175-9204
SP	C-C	SD-45T-2	RSw	OMI	Ajin	5771	90	92	393			
SP	C-C	SD-45T-2	RSw	Ortl	Samh	0439		85	236			Tunnel Motor
	C-C	SD-45T-2	RSw	Alco	KMT		500	77	142	230	190	See Note #1908
SP	C-C	SD-45T-2	RSw	OMI	Ajin	5772	60	90	368	309		SP/SSW #9371-9378
SP	C-C	SD-45X	RSw	PSC		15464		85	180		145	
SP	C-C	SD-45X	RSw	PSC		15464		85	180		145	
Demo	C-C	SD-45X	RSw	OMI	Ajin	5784	25	90	368	309		#5740 Demo
SP	C-C	SD-45X	RSw	OMI	Ajin	5785	50	90	368	309		#9500-9502
AT&SF	C-C	SD-45-2	RSw	OMI	Ajin	5777	15	90	368			
CCR	C-C	SD-45-2	RSw	OMI	Ajin	5776	25	90	368	309		#3607-3624
E-L	C-C	SD-45-2	RSw	OMI	Ajin	5778	35	90	368	309		#3669-3681
ATSF	C-C	SD-45-2	RSw	OMI	Ajin	5773	50	90	368	309		#5625-5661
AT&SF	C-C	SD-45-2	RSw	OMI	Ajin	5775	55	90	368	309		#5510
AT&SF	C-C	SD-45-2	RSw	OMI	Ajin	5774	50	90	368	309		#5800 series
AT&SF	C-C	SD-45-2	RSw	OMI	Ajin	5777	90	92	393			
SP	C-C	SD-45-2	RSw	Ortl	Samh			85	236		190	
	C-C	SD-45-2	RSw	Ortl	Samh	0422		85	236		190	Standard
E-L	C-C	SD-45-2	RSw	Ortl	Samh	0423		85	236		190	
AT&SF	C-C	SD-45-2	RSw	PSC		15178		85	180		145	
AT&SF	C-C	SD-45-2	RSw	PSC		15178		85	180		145	
CR	* C-C	SD-50	RSw	OMI	Ajin	5040	20	89	334	281		re-run
KCS	C-C	SD-50	RSw	OMI	Ajin	5037	10	90	334	281		re-run
D&RGW	C-C	SD-50	RSw	OMI	Ajin	5039	28	88	257	216		re-run
MP	C-C	SD-50	RSw	OMI	Ajin	5041	10	88	257	216		re-run
Chessie	C-C	SD-50	RSw	OMI	Ajin	5038.1	15	89	441	370		See Note #1455
KCS	C-C	SD-50	RSw	OMI	Ajin	5037	8	88	257	216		
SBD	C-C	SD-50	RSw	OMI	Ajin	1887	50	85	250	250		
MP	C-C	SD-50	RSw	OMI	Ajin	5041	20	88	257	216		re-run
MP	C-C	SD-50	RSw	OMI	Ajin	5041	20	89	334	281		re-run
NS	C-C	SD-50	RSw	OMI	Ajin	5036	11	88	257	216		#6505-6525, re-run
C&NW	C-C	SD-50	RSw	OMI	Ajin	5042	15	87	257	216		#7001-7035
CR	C-C	SD-50	RSw	OMI	Ajin	5040	20	88	257	216		re-run
SBD	C-C	SD-50	RSw	OMI	Ajin	5035	20	89	334	281		re-run
NS	C-C	SD-50	RSw	OMI	Ajin	5036.1	10	89	427	359		See Note #1456
MP	C-C	SD-50	RSw	OMI	Ajin	5041	15	87	257	216		#5000-5059
C&NW	C-C	SD-50	RSw	OMI	Ajin	5042	20	89	334	281		re-run
D&RGW	C-C	SD-50	RSw	OMI	Ajin	5039	42	90	349	293		re-run

GM Electro-Motive Division (cont'd)

The EMD E-7 was the next-to-last step in the evolution of the passenger version of the "Covered Wagon" car-body design. The long slant-nose of the earlier E4-6s gave way to the same general nose appearance as the freight units, although the retention of the rectangular side windows is reminiscent of the E4-6s. From a mechanical standpoint, the E-7 was almost identical to the earlier E-6. Between 1945 and 1949, EMD produced 428 A units and 82 B units. Samhongsa produced these excellent replicas of the PRR E-7 for Oriental Limited in 1989.

| Road | AAR Code | Class & Phase | Type | Model Production | | | | | List Price | Resale | | Remarks |
				Importer	Builder	Cat #	Quan.	Yrs.		Mint	Avg.	
B&O/C&O	C-C	SD-50	RSw	OMI	Ajin	5038	20	89	334	281		re-run
B&O/C&O	C-C	SD-50	RSw	OMI	Ajin	5038	20	88	257	216		re-run
NS	C-C	SD-50	RSw	OMI	Ajin	5036	20	89	334	281		#6505-6525, re-run
D&RGW	C-C	SD-50	RSw	OMI	Ajin	5039	20	89	334	281		re-run
CR	C-C	SD-50	RSw	OMI	Ajin	1895	60	85	250	250		Conrail
KCS	C-C	SD-50	RSw	OMI	Ajin	1898	20	86	250	250		
CR	C-C	SD-50	RSw	OMI	Ajin	5040	45	87	257	216		#6700-6779
C&NW	C-C	SD-50	RSw	OMI	Ajin	5042.1	6	89	427	359		EMD SD50, C&NW
SBD	C-C	SD-50	RSw	OMI	Ajin	5035	10	87	257	216		#8500-8623
D&RGW	C-C	SD-50	RSw	OMI	Ajin	5039	36	88	279	234		re-run
C&NW	C-C	SD-50	RSw	OMI	Ajin	5042	22	88	257	216		re-run
D&RGW	C-C	SD-50	RSw	OMI	Ajin	5039	25	87	257	216		
	C-C	SD-50	RSw	Hall		HS0088						
D&RGW	C-C	SD-50	RSw	OMI	Ajin	1893	75	85	250	250		
NS	C-C	SD-50	RSw	OMI	Ajin	5036	15	87	257	216		#6505-6525
B&O/C&O	C-C	SD-50	RSw	OMI	Ajin	5038	30	87	257	216		See Note #1457
MP,C&NW	C-C	SD-50	RSw	OMI	Ajin	1897	40	86	250	250		See Note#1909
C&O,MP	C-C	SD-50	RSw	OMI	Ajin	1888	75	85	250	250		C&O,MP,UP
CR	C-C	SD-60	RSw	OMI	Ajin	5048.1	10	89	427	359		#6780-6831, fp.
Oakway	C-C	SD-60	RSw	OMI	Ajin	5047	60	88	279	234		re-run
Demo	C-C	SD-60	RSw	OMI	Ajin	5150	70	88	279	234		#1,2,3,4
BN	C-C	SD-60	RSw	OMI	Ajin	5043	30	87	257	216		#8300-8302
NS	C-C	SD-60	RSw	OMI	Ajin	5045	20	89	334	281		re-run
Demo	C-C	SD-60	RSw	OMI	Ajin	5150	20	89	334	281		re-run
C&NW	C-C	SD-60	RSw	OMI	Ajin	5044	15	89	334	281		re-run
BN	C-C	SD-60	RSw	OMI	Ajin	5043	25	88	279	234		re-run
UP	C-C	SD-60	RSw	OMI	Ajin	5046	75	87	257	216		
C&NW	C-C	SD-60	RSw	OMI	Ajin	5044.1	10	89	427	359		#8000-8054, fp.
BN	C-C	SD-60	RSw	OMI	Ajin	5043.1	10	88	339	285		#8300-8302, fp.
NS	C-C	SD-60	RSw	OMI	Ajin	5045	17	88	257	216		re-run
Demo	C-C	SD-60	RSw	OMI	Ajin	5150	43	90	349	293		re-run
C&NW	C-C	SD-60	RSw	OMI	Ajin	5044	40	88	257	216		re-run
UP	C-C	SD-60	RSw	OMI	Ajin	5046	75	88	279	234		re-run
NS	C-C	SD-60	RSw	OMI	Ajin	5045	25	87	257	216		#6550-6603
Oakway	C-C	SD-60	RSw	OMI	Ajin	5047	45	90	349	293		re-run
Oakway	C-C	SD-60	RSw	OMI	Ajin	5047	25	89	334	281		re-run
NS	C-C	SD-60	RSw	OMI	Ajin	5045.1	10	89	427	359		#6550-6603, fp.
UP	C-C	SD-60	RSw	OMI	Ajin	5046	56	88	257	216		re-run
CR	C-C	SD-60	RSw	OMI	Ajin	5048	10	88	279	234		re-run

GM Electro-Motive Division (cont'd)

Road	AAR Code	Class & Phase	Type	Model Production				List Price	Resale			Remarks
				Importer	Builder	Cat #	Quan.	Yrs.		Mint	Avg.	
C&NW	C-C	SD-60	RSw	OMI	Ajin	5044	15	87	259	218		#8000-8054
BN	C-C	SD-60	RSw	OMI	Ajin	5043	20	89	334	281		re-run
C&NW	C-C	SD-60	RSw	OMI	Ajin	5044	47	88	279	234		re-run
BN	C-C	SD-60	RSw	OMI	Ajin	5043	20	88	257	216		re-run
CR	C-C	SD-60	RSw	OMI	Ajin	5048	25	89	334	281		re-run
UP	C-C	SD-60	RSw	OMI	Ajin	5046	30	89	334	281		re-run
Oakway	C-C	SD-60	RSw	OMI	Ajin	5047	40	88	257	216		
SOO	C-C	SD-60	RSw	OMI	Ajin	5151	15	88	279	234		#6000
CR	C-C	SD-60	RSw	OMI	Ajin	5048	38	88	259	218		#6780-6831
UP	C-C	SD-60	RSw	OMI	Ajin	5046	60	90	349	293		re-run
BN	C-C	SD-60M	RSw	OMI	Ajin	5198	60	90	357	300		Wide Nose
UP	C-C	SD-60M	RSw	OMI	Ajin	5159	300	89	353	297		Wide Nose
SOO	C-C	SD-60M	RSw	OMI	Ajin	5199	60	90	357	300		Wide Nose
UP	C-C	SD-60M	RSw	OMI	Ajin	5159	100	90	357	300		re-run
UP	D-D	DD35A	RSw	Alco	KMT	D-176	390	80	337	300	250	5000 hp.
UP	D-D	DD35A	RSw	OMI	Ajin	1914	55	86	371	311		See Note #1919
UP	D-D	DD35A	RSw	OMI	Ajin	1915	70	86	371	311		See Note #1719
UP	D-D	DD35A	RSw	OMI	Ajin	1892	90	86	371	371		See Note #1720
UP	D-D	DD35A	RSw	OMI	Ajin	1892	45	91	520			Re-run
UP	D-D	DD35A	RSw	OMI	Ajin	1915	80	91	520			Re-run
UP	D-D	DD35AX	RSw	OMI	Ajin	1837	225	83	360	302		See Note #1721
UP,SP	D-D	DD35B	RSw	Alco	KMT		340	80	295	300	275	Note #774
UP/SP	D-D	DD35B	RSw	OMI	Ajin	1917	40	86	360	302		See Note #1722
UP	D-D	DD35B	RSw	OMI	Ajin	1918	60	86	371	311		See Note #1723
UP/SP	D-D	DD35B	RSw	OMI	Ajin	1917	45	91	509			Re-run
UP	D-D	DD35B	RSw	OMI	Ajin	1918	80	91	509			Re-run
UP	C-C	DD40AX	RSw	Alco	KMT	D-149		76	225	350	300	See Note #775
UP	D-D	DD40AX	RSw	Key	Samh			83	386		315	See Note #1724
UP	D-D	DD40AX	RSw	Key	Samh			83	386		315	See Note #1725
UP	D-D	DD40AX	RSw	Key	Samh			84	429		350	fp., 6900 class
UP	D-D	DD40AX	RSw	Key	Samh			84	429		350	fp., 6925 class
UP	D-D	DD40AX	RSw	OMI	Ajin	1861.1	25	83	436	436		See Note #1726
UP	D-D	DD40AX	RSw	OMI	Ajin	5407		90	577			w/strobe lights
UP	D-D	DD40AX	RSw	OMI	Ajin	5408		90	577			w/smoke lifters
UP	D-D	DD40AX	RSw	OMI	Ajin	5410		90	577			w/roof mounted horn
UP	D-D	DD40AX	RSw	OMI	Ajin	5406		90	577			w/roof siren
UP	D-D	DD40AX	RSw	OMI	Ajin	5405		90	577			#6925-6946
UP	D-D	DD40AX	RSw	OMI	Ajin	5404		90	577			#6900-6924
UP	D-D	DD40AX	RSw	OMI	Ajin	5409		90	577			w/anti-climber
CB&Q	B-B	FT A	Cab	OMI	Ajin	5208	38	88	207	174		
SRR	B-B	FT A	Cab	OMI	Ajin	5241	24	88	207	174		w/o Dynamic Brakes
DL&W	B-B	FT A	Cab	OMI	Ajin	5214	24	88	207	174		
B&M	B-B	FT A	Cab	OMI	Ajin	5206	45	88	207	174		
D&RGW	B-B	FT A	Cab	OMI	Ajin	5219	30	88	207	174		w/Large Number Bds.
AT&SF	B-B	FT A	Cab	OMI	Ajin	5251	40	88	207	174		Passenger Units
RDG	B-B	FT A	Cab	OMI	Ajin	5239	20	88	207	174		
MP	B-B	FT A	Cab	OMI	Ajin	5231	8	88	207	174		
ACL	B-B	FT A	Cab	OMI	Ajin	5202	8	88	207	174		#300A-323A
NYC	B-B	FT A	Cab	OMI	Ajin	5233	24	88	207	174		
NYO&W	B-B	FT A	Cab	OMI	Ajin	5235	22	88	207	174		
Milw	B-B	FT A	Cab	OMI	Ajin	5229	23	88	207	174		
GN	B-B	FT A	Cab	OMI	Ajin	5226	30	88	207	174		Modernized
SSW	B-B	FT A	Cab	OMI	Ajin	5243	6	88	207	174		Side Number Boards
SAL	B-B	FT A	Cab	OMI	Ajin	5247	7	88	207	174		w/o Dynamic Brakes
	B-B	FT A	Cab	OMI	Ajin	5255	30	88	207	174		w/o Dynamic Brakes
LV	B-B	FT A	Cab	OMI	Ajin	5227	25	88	207	174		
NP	B-B	FT A	Cab	OMI	Ajin	5237	33	88	207	174		
WP	B-B	FT A	Cab	OMI	Ajin	5249	40	88	207	174		#900 Series
AT&SF	B-B	FT A	Cab	OMI	Ajin	5200	75	88	207	174		Side Number Boards
D&RGW	B-B	FT A	Cab	OMI	Ajin	5216	45	88	207	174		Side Number Boards
CRI&P	B-B	FT A	Cab	OMI	Ajin	5212	17	88	207	174		
Erie	B-B	FT A	Cab	OMI	Ajin	5221	18	88	207	174		
LV	B-B	FT A	Cab	OMI	Ajin	5228	18	88	186	156		
GN	B-B	FT A	Cab	OMI	Ajin	5223	55	88	207	174		Side Number Boards

GM Electro-Motive Division (cont'd)

The SD60M represents the state-of-the-art in diesel locomotive design. Standard SD–60s are virtually indistinguishable from their predecessors—the SD–50s. The major difference is an increase in horsepower from 3,500 to 3,800. SD–60s are also the first EMD diesels to use microprocessor controls. The Burlington Northern SD60M shown above incorporates the large "crew cab" and displays the "Desert Storm" paint scheme in commemoration of the war with Iraq. Overland Models has continued to produce models of the latest versions of diesel power.

| Road | AAR Code | Class & Phase | Type | Model Production | | | | | List Price | Resale | | Remarks |
				Importer	Builder	Cat #	Quan.	Yrs.		Mint	Avg.	
SSW	B-B	FT A	Cab	OMI	Ajin	5245	7	88	207	174		w/Large Number Bds.
B&O	B-B	FT A	Cab	OMI	Ajin	5204	12	88	207	174		
Demo	B-B	FT A	Cab	OMI	Ajin	5253	13	88	207	174		w/o Dynamic Brakes
C&NW	B-B	FT A	Cab	OMI	Ajin	5210	12	88	207	174		
D&RGW	B-B	FT A	Cab	OMI	Ajin	5218	40	88	207	174		Modernized
GN	B-B	FT A	Cab	PFM	Tensh		3	55	23	75	65	fp.,Powered A
AT&SF	B-B	FT A	Cab	PFM	Tensh		1	56	11			Dummy, fp. freight
PRR	B-B	FT A	Cab	PFM	Tensh		2	58	11	60		Dummy
GN	B-B	FT A	Cab	PFM	Tensh		2	58	11	60	50	fp., Dummy
AT&SF	B-B	FT A	Cab	PFM	Tensh		2	58	11	60		Dummy, fp. Passenger
AT&SF	B-B	FT A	Cab	PFM	Tensh		2	58	20	85	75	fp., Passenger
GN	B-B	FT A	Cab	PFM	Tensh		2	58	20	85		Powered A
NYC	B-B	FT A	Cab	PFM	Tensh		2	58	11	60		Dummy
C&NW	B-B	FT A	Cab	PFM	Tensh		1	60	11	60		Dummy
AT&SF	B-B	FT A	Cab	PFM	Tensh		1	60	11	60		Dummy, fp. Passenger
GN	B-B	FT A	Cab	PFM	Tensh		1	60	11	60		Dummy
CN	B-B	FT A	Cab	PFM	Tensh		1	60	11	60		Dummy
UP	B-B	FT A	Cab	PFM	Tensh		1	60	11	60	50	Dummy A-Unit, fp.
SSW	B-B	FT B	Cab	OMI	Ajin	5246	5	88	186	156		
NYO&W	B-B	FT B	Cab	OMI	Ajin	5236	22	88	186	156		
MP	B-B	FT B	Cab	OMI	Ajin	5232	8	88	186	156		
D&RGW	B-B	FT B	Cab	OMI	Ajin	5220	50	88	186	156		
Milw	B-B	FT B	Cab	OMI	Ajin	5230	20	88	186	156		
NP	B-B	FT B	Cab	OMI	Ajin	5238	32	88	186	156		
B&O	B-B	FT B	Cab	OMI	Ajin	5205	9	88	186	156		
GN	B-B	FT B	Cab	OMI	Ajin	5224	40	88	186	156		
RDG	B-B	FT B	Cab	OMI	Ajin	5240	20	88	186	156		
AT&SF	B-B	FT B	Cab	OMI	Ajin	5201	70	88	186	156		
CB&Q	B-B	FT B	Cab	OMI	Ajin	5209	35	88	186	156		
Erie	B-B	FT B	Cab	OMI	Ajin	5222	18	88	186	156		
SRR	B-B	FT B	Cab	OMI	Ajin	5242	18	88	186	156		w/o Dynamic Brakes
ACL	B-B	FT B	Cab	OMI	Ajin	5203	8	88	186	156		#300B-323B
CRI&P	B-B	FT B	Cab	OMI	Ajin	5213	17	88	186	156		
AT&SF	B-B	FT B	Cab	OMI	Ajin	5252	40	88	186	156		Passenger Units
NYC	B-B	FT B	Cab	OMI	Ajin	5234	24	88	186	156		
B&M	B-B	FT B	Cab	OMI	Ajin	5207	40	88	186	156		

GM Electro-Motive Division (cont'd)

Road	AAR Code	Class & Phase	Type	Importer	Builder	Cat #	Quan.	Yrs.	List Price	Mint	Avg.	Remarks
Demo	B-B	FT B	Cab	OMI	Ajin	5254	11	88	186	156		w/o Dynamic Brakes
WP	B-B	FT B	Cab	OMI	Ajin	5250	40	88	186	156		#901-912
C&NW	B-B	FT B	Cab	OMI	Ajin	5211	10	88	186	156		
D&RGW	B-B	FT B	Cab	OMI	Ajin	5217	45	88	186	156		
DL&W	B-B	FT B	Cab	OMI	Ajin	5215	21	88	186	156		Short "B" Unit
SSW	B-B	FT B	Cab	OMI	Ajin	5244	6	88	186	156		
SAL	B-B	FT B	Cab	OMI	Ajin	5248	7	88	186	156		w/o Dynamic Brakes
UP	B-B	FT B	Cab	PFM	Tensh		1	56	9			Dummy B-Unit, fp.
UP	B-B	FT B	Cab	PFM	Tensh		1	57	9			Dummy
AT&SF	B-B	FT B	Cab	PFM	Tensh		2	57	9			Dummy, fp. Freight
GN	B-B	FT B	Cab	PFM	Tensh		4	57	9	50	40	Dummy B-Unit, fp.
AT&SF	B-B	FT B	Cab	PFM	Tensh		2	57	9			Dummy, fp. Passenger
	B-B	FT B	Cab	PFM	Tensh		9	58	19			Dummy
AT&SF	B-B	FT B	Cab	PFM	Tensh		2	58	10			Dummy, fp. Passenger
GN	B-B	FT B	Cab	PFM	Tensh		1	58	9			Dummy
UP	B-B	FT B	Cab	PFM	Tensh		3	58	10	50	40	Dummy B-Unit, fp.
AT&SF	B-B	FT B	Cab	PFM	Tensh		2	58	10			Dummy, fp. Freight
	B-B	FT B	Cab	PFM	Tensh		20	60	19			Dummy
SRR	B-B	FTS B	Cab	OMI	Ajin	5256	12	88	186	156		w/o Dynamic Brakes
GN	B-B	FTS B	Cab	OMI	Ajin	5225	45	88	186	156		Short "B" Unit
	B-B/B-B	FT A&B	Cab	Hall	Goto			68	70	190	150	See Note #729
	B-B/B-B	FT A&B	Cab	Hall	Goto			71	75	200	175	Powered A, Dummy B
	B-B/B-B	FT A&B	Cab	Hall	Ajin		50	80	250		250	Powered A & B
	B-B/B-B	FT A&B	Cab	Hall	Ajin		300	80	220		200	Powered A, Dummy B
	B-B/B-B	FT A&B	Cab	Hall	Ajin		250	80	230		210	See Note #730
	B-B/B-B	FT A&B	Cab	Hall	Ajin		50	80	260		260	See Note #731
B&M	B-B/B-B	FT A&B	Cab	Hall		016		88	400	336		fp., Maroon
AT&SF	B-B/B-B	FT A&B	Cab	Hall		001		88	400	336		fp., Passenger
SLSW	B-B/B-B	FT A&B	Cab	Hall		012		88	400	336		fp., Cotton Belt Black
CB&Q	B-B/B-B	FT A&B	Cab	Hall		005		88	400	336		fp., Freight Gray
	B-B/B-B	FT A&B	Cab	Hall		X09		88	372	312		See Note #1748
SAL	B-B/B-B	FT A&B	Cab	Hall		015		88	400	336		See Note #1745
AT&SF	B-B/B-B	FT A&B	Cab	Hall		003		88	400	336		fp., Freight Blue
	B-B/B-B	FT A&B	Cab	Hall		X02		88	403	339		See Note #1747
C&NW	B-B/B-B	FT A&B	Cab	Hall		X07		88	464	375		See Note #1744
NP	B-B/B-B	FT A&B	Cab	Hall		011		88	400	336		fp., Black/Yellow
	B-B/B-B	FT A&B	Cab	Hall		X05		88	403	339		See Note #1746
	B-B/B-B	FT A&B	Cab	Hall		X03		88	403	339		See Note #1749
CRIP	B-B/B-B	FT A&B	Cab	Hall		006		88	400	336		fp., Red/Black
	B-B/B-B	FT A&B	Cab	Hall		X04		88	403	339		See Note #1743
MP	B-B/B-B	FT A&B	Cab	Hall		010		88	400	336		fp., Blue/Gray
B&O	B-B/B-B	FT A&B	Cab	Hall		017		88	400	336		fp., Blue/Black/Gray
AT&SF	B-B/B-B	FT A&B	Cab	Hall		X01		88	403	339		
Demo	B-B/B-B	FT A&B	Cab	Hall		008		88	400	336		fp., #103
	B-B/B-B	FT A&B	Cab	Intl				54	38	100	75	1350 hp., fp.
C&NW	B-B/B-B	FT A&B	Cab	PFM	Tensh	106/07	5	54	28	145		fp., A pwd. B dummy
PRR	B-B/B-B	FT A&B	Cab	PFM	Tensh	106/07	5	54	28	145		See Note #1753
GN	B-B/B-B	FT A&B	Cab	PFM	Tensh	106/07	5	54	28	145		See Note #1751
AT&SF	B-B/B-B	FT A&B	Cab	PFM	Tensh	106/07	11	54	28	145		See Note #1757
AT&SF	B-B/B-B	FT A&B	Cab	PFM	Tensh	106/07	5	54	28	145		See Note #1755
NYC	B-B/B-B	FT A&B	Cab	PFM	Tensh	106/07	5	54	28	145		See Note #1751
UP	B-B/B-B	FT A&B	Cab	PFM	Tensh	106/07	5	54	28	145		See Note #1751
	B-B/B-B	FT A&B	Cab	PFM	Tensh		22	55	25			unptd kit, A pwd, B dum
AT&SF	B-B/B-B	FT A&B	Cab	PFM	Tensh	106/07	5	55	30	145		See Note #1755
AT&SF	B-B/B-B	FT A&B	Cab	PFM	Tensh	106/07	20	55	30	145		See Note #1757
UP	B-B/B-B	FT A&B	Cab	PFM	Tensh	106/07	6	55	30	145		fp., A pwd. B dummy
C&NW	B-B/B-B	FT A&B	Cab	PFM	Tensh	106/07	5	55	30	145		fp., A pwd. B dummy
GN	B-B/B-B	FT A&B	Cab	PFM	Tensh	106/07	12	55	30	145		fp., A pwd. B dummy
PRR	B-B/B-B	FT A&B	Cab	PFM	Tensh	106/07	5	55	30	145		See Note #1753
CN	B-B/B-B	FT A&B	Cab	PFM	Tensh	106/07	1	55	30	145		See Note #1751
NYC	B-B/B-B	FT A&B	Cab	PFM	Tensh	106/07	6	55	30	145		fp., A pwd. B dummy
PRR	B-B/B-B	FT A&B	Cab	PFM	Tensh	106/07	1	56	34	145		See Note #1750
	B-B/B-B	FT A&B	Cab	PFM	Tensh		10	56	25	145		unptd kit, A pwd, B dum
C&NW	B-B/B-B	FT A&B	Cab	PFM	Tensh	106/07	5	56	28	145		fp., A pwd, B dummy

GM Electro-Motive Division (cont'd)

Union Pacific always seemed to have the biggest locomotives, be they steam or diesel. At the time (1969), the DD40AX with a 6000-hp power plant held the honors. Built as a special order for UP, they didn't show significant economies over the standard units available at the time. In all, UP owned 47 of these monsters. Key imported this Samhongsa-built model in 1983. It contained two motors, as did the prototype. Models of engines of this size are too large for most model railroads and are either seen at club layouts, where the curves are broad, or in display cases.

Road	AAR Code	Class & Phase	Type	Importer	Builder	Cat #	Quan.	Yrs.	List Price	Mint	Avg.	Remarks
CN	B-B/B-B	FT A&B	Cab	PFM	Tensh	106/07	6	56	34	145		fp., A pwd. B dummy
GN	B-B/B-B	FT A&B	Cab	PFM	Tensh	106/07	10	56	28	145		fp., A pwd. B dummy
AT&SF	B-B/B-B	FT A&B	Cab	PFM	Tensh	106/07	5	56	28	145		fp., A pwd, B dummy
C&NW	B-B/B-B	FT A&B	Cab	PFM	Tensh	106/07	10	56	34	145		fp., A pwd. B dummy
AT&SF	B-B/B-B	FT A&B	Cab	PFM	Tensh	106/07	25	56	34	145		See Note#1755
CP	B-B/B-B	FT A&B	Cab	PFM	Tensh	106/07	5	56	34	145		See Note#1751
AT&SF	B-B/B-B	FT A&B	Cab	PFM	Tensh	106/07	10	56	34	145		See Note#1757
UP	B-B/B-B	FT A&B	Cab	PFM	Tensh	106/07	10	56	34	145		fp., A pwd. B dummy
NYC	B-B/B-B	FT A&B	Cab	PFM	Tensh	106/07	8	56	34	145		fp., A pwd. B dummy
AT&SF	B-B/B-B	FT A&B	Cab	PFM	Tensh	106/07	2	56	45	145		See Note#
PRR	B-B/B-B	FT A&B	Cab	PFM	Tensh	106/07	10	56	34	145		See Note#1753
NYC	B-B/B-B	FT A&B	Cab	PFM	Tensh	106/07	5	56	28	145		fp., A pwd, B dummy
GN	B-B/B-B	FT A&B	Cab	PFM	Tensh		10	56	28	145		fp., A pwd, B dummy
UP	B-B/B-B	FT A&B	Cab	PFM	Tensh	106/07	10	57	30	145		fp., A pwd. B dummy
	B-B/B-B	FT A&B	Cab	PFM	Tensh		10	57	25	145		unptd kit, A pwd, B dum
NYC	B-B/B-B	FT A&B	Cab	PFM	Tensh	106/07	10	57	30	145		fp., A pwd. B dummy
AT&SF	B-B/B-B	FT A&B	Cab	PFM	Tensh	106/07	10	57	30	145		See Note#1757
PRR	B-B/B-B	FT A&B	Cab	PFM	Tensh	106/07	20	57	30	145		See Note#1753
AT&SF	B-B/B-B	FT A&B	Cab	PFM	Tensh	106/07	10	57	30	145		See Note#1755
GN	B-B/B-B	FT A&B	Cab	PFM	Tensh	106/07	23	57	30	145		fp., A pwd. B dummy
C&NW	B-B/B-B	FT A&B	Cab	PFM	Tensh	106/07	10	57	30	145		fp., A pwd. B dummy
CP	B-B/B-B	FT A&B	Cab	PFM	Tensh	106/07	1	57	30	145		See Note#1751
NYC	B-B/B-B	FT A&B	Cab	PFM	Tensh	106/07	1	58	45	145		fp., A & B powered
C&NW	B-B/B-B	FT A&B	Cab	PFM	Tensh	106/07	10	58	30	145		fp., A pwd. B dummy
NYC	B-B/B-B	FT A&B	Cab	PFM	Tensh	106/07	15	58	30	145		fp., A pwd. B dummy
AT&SF	B-B/B-B	FT A&B	Cab	PFM	Tensh	106/07	4	58	39	145		See Note#1754
UP	B-B/B-B	FT A&B	Cab	PFM	Tensh	106/07	15	58	30	145		fp., A pwd. B dummy
GN	B-B/B-B	FT A&B	Cab	PFM	Tensh	106/07	3	58	29	145		fp., A & B powered
AT&SF	B-B/B-B	FT A&B	Cab	PFM	Tensh	106/07	10	58	30	145		See Note#1755
PRR	B-B/B-B	FT A&B	Cab	PFM	Tensh	106/07	1	58	39	145		See Note#1753
GN	B-B/B-B	FT A&B	Cab	PFM	Tensh	106/07	30	58	30	145		fp., A pwd. B dummy
AT&SF	B-B/B-B	FT A&B	Cab	PFM	Tensh	106/07	1	58	30	145		See Note#1751
UP	B-B/B-B	FT A&B	Cab	PFM	Tensh	106/07	4	58	39	145		fp., A & B powered
AT&SF	B-B/B-B	FT A&B	Cab	PFM	Tensh	106/07	10	58	30	145		See Note#1757
PRR	B-B/B-B	FT A&B	Cab	PFM	Tensh	106/07	20	58	30	145		See Note#1753
CP	B-B/B-B	FT A&B	Cab	PFM	Tensh	106/07	1	58	30	145		See Note#1751
PRR	B-B/B-B	FT A&B	Cab	PFM	Tensh	106/07	30	59	30	145		See Note#1753
UP	B-B/B-B	FT A&B	Cab	PFM	Tensh	106/07	20	59	30	145		fp., A pwd. B dummy

GM Electro-Motive Division (cont'd)

Road	AAR Code	Class & Phase		Type	Importer	Builder	Cat #	Quan.	Yrs.	List Price	Mint	Avg.	Remarks
C&NW	B-B/B-B	FT A&B		Cab	PFM	Tensh	106/07	20	59	30	145		fp., A pwd. B dummy
AT&SF	B-B/B-B	FT A&B		Cab	PFM	Tensh	106/07	40	59	30	145		See Note #1757
AT&SF	B-B/B-B	FT A&B		Cab	PFM	Tensh	106/07	20	59	30	145		See Note #1755
NYC	B-B/B-B	FT A&B		Cab	PFM	Tensh	106/07	20	59	30	145		fp., A pwd. B dummy
	B-B/B-B	FT A&B		Cab	PFM	Tensh		10	59	25			unptd kit, A pwd, B dum
GN	B-B/B-B	FT A&B		Cab	PFM	Tensh	106/07	50	59	30	145		fp., A pwd. B dummy
UP	B-B/B-B	FT A&B		Cab	PFM	Tensh	106/07	20	60	30	145		fp., A pwd. B dummy
AT&SF	B-B/B-B	FT A&B		Cab	PFM	Tensh	106/07	30	60	30	145		See Note #1757
PRR	B-B/B-B	FT A&B		Cab	PFM	Tensh	106/07	1	60	30	145		See Note #1752
GN	B-B/B-B	FT A&B		Cab	PFM	Tensh	106/07	70	60	35	145		fp., A pwd. B dummy
NYC	B-B/B-B	FT A&B		Cab	PFM	Tensh	106/07	20	60	30	145		fp., A pwd. B dummy
C&NW	B-B/B-B	FT A&B		Cab	PFM	Tensh	106/07	20	60	30	145		fp., A pwd. B dummy
AT&SF	B-B/B-B	FT A&B		Cab	PFM	Tensh	106/07	20	60	30	145		See Note #1755
PRR	B-B/B-B	FT A&B		Cab	PFM	Tensh	106/07	30	60	30	145		See Note #1753
CB&Q	B-B/B-B	FT A&B		Cab	PFM	Tensh	106/07	1	60	30	145		See Note #1751
	B-B/B-B	FT A&B		Cab	PFM	Tensh		10	60	25			unptd kit, A pwd, B dum
NYC	B-B/B-B	FT A&B		Cab	PFM	Tensh	106/07	75	68	50	145		fp., A pwd. B dummy
AT&SF	B-B/B-B	FT A&B		Cab	PFM	Tensh	106/07	100	68	50	145		See Note #1757
UP	B-B/B-B	FT A&B		Cab	PFM	Tensh	106/07	25	68	50	145		fp., A pwd. B dummy
PRR	B-B/B-B	FT A&B		Cab	PFM	Tensh	106/07	25	68	50	145		See Note #1753
UP	B-B/B-B	FT A&B		Cab	PFM	Tensh	106/07	25	69	50	145		fp., A pwd. B dummy
PRR	B-B/B-B	FT A&B		Cab	PFM	Tensh	106/07	25	69	50	145		See Note #1753
AT&SF	B-B/B-B	FT A&B		Cab	PFM	Tensh	106/07	50	69	50	145		See Note #1755
GN	B-B/B-B	FT A&B		Cab	PFM	Tensh	106/07	175	69	50	145		fp., A pwd. B dummy
CB&Q	B-B	F-2/3A	I	Cab	Ortl		P902A		89	240	202		fp.
	B-B	F-3A	IV	Cab	NPP				76	118	200	160	
Monon	B-B	F-3A	I	Cab	OMI	Ajin	5437		90	243	204		See Note #1765
MEC	B-B	F-3A	II	Cab	OMI	Ajin	5446	10	90	243	204		#671A, 672A
TP&W	B-B	F-3A	I	Cab	OMI	Ajin	5440		90	221	186		#100
NYC	B-B	F-3A	II	Cab	OMI	Ajin	5488	20	90	243	204		Freight #1606-1635
Monon	B-B	F-3A	I	Cab	OMI	Ajin	5435		90	243	204		See Note #1761
GTW	B-B	F-3A	II	Cab	OMI	Ajin	5472	15	90	243	204		#9006,9027
UP	B-B	F-3A	III	Cab	OMI	Ajin	5554		90	243	204		#1446-1455
NYC	B-B	F-3A	II	Cab	OMI	Ajin	5490	20	90	243	204		#3500-3503
NP	B-B	F-3A	II	Cab	OMI	Ajin	5494	15	90	243	204		#6500-6550
D&RGW	B-B	F-3A	III	Cab	OMI	Ajin	5550		90	243	204		See Note #1762
MP	B-B	F-3A	II	Cab	OMI	Ajin	5484	10	90	243	204		See Note #1767
D&RGW	B-B	F-3A	I	Cab	OMI	Ajin	5429		90	243	204		#551,552,553,554
B&O	B-B	F-3A	II	Cab	OMI	Ajin	5452	20	90	243	204		#82-84, 86-88
WP	B-B	F-3A	II	Cab	OMI	Ajin	5518	15	90	243	204		#801-803A
SL&SF	B-B	F-3A	II	Cab	OMI	Ajin	5470	18	90	243	204		#5000-5047
CB&Q	B-B	F-3A	II	Cab	OMI	Ajin	5464	12	90	243	204		pass. #9961A, 9962C
UP	B-B	F-3A	III	Cab	OMI	Ajin	5556		90	243	204		#517
PRR	B-B	F-3A	II	Cab	OMI	Ajin	5496	25	90	243	204		See Note #1763
UP	B-B	F-3A	II	Cab	OMI	Ajin	5512	30	90	243	204		See Note #1768
SL&SF	B-B	F-3A	III	Cab	OMI	Ajin	5551		90	243	204		#5002-5016
CGW	B-B	F-3A	II	Cab	OMI	Ajin	5458	10	90	243	204		See Note #1766
C&NW	B-B	F-3A	II	Cab	OMI	Ajin	5456	20	90	243	204		See Note #1760
SRR	B-B	F-3A	I	Cab	OMI	Ajin	5438		90	221	186		#4129-4206
GM&O	B-B	F-3A	II	Cab	OMI	Ajin	5474	10	90	243	204		#807,808,884
KCS	B-B	F-3A	I	Cab	OMI	Ajin	5433		90	243	204		#50-53
ATSF	B-B	F-3A	I	Cab	OMI	Ajin	5425		90	243	204		#16L,C-21L,C
DL&W	B-B	F-3A	II	Cab	OMI	Ajin	5466	10	90	243	204		#621A, C, 657
CB&Q	B-B	F-3A	II	Cab	OMI	Ajin	5462	12	90	243	204		freight #163C-166C
CNR	B-B	F-3A	II	Cab	OMI	Ajin	5460	40	90	243	204		#9000,9002,9003,9005
Erie	B-B	F-3A	II	Cab	OMI	Ajin	5468	10	90	243	204		#800A-D-806A
UP	B-B	F-3A	II	Cab	OMI	Ajin	5514	30	90	243	204		#1410A-1445A
ATSF	B-B	F-3A	II	Cab	OMI	Ajin	5450	25	90	243	204		#19
	B-B	F-3A	III	Cab	OMI	Ajin	5553		90	243	204		#4128-4206
UP	B-B	F-3A	II	Cab	OMI	Ajin	5510	30	90	243	204		#1400A-1409A freight
DL&W	B-B	F-3A	I	Cab	OMI	Ajin	5427		90	243	204		#801A, #801C
BAR	B-B	F-3A	II	Cab	OMI	Ajin	5524	10	90	221	185		#600B-603B
CNJ	B-B	F-3A	II	Cab	OMI	Ajin	5454	20	90	243	204		#50-59
GM&O	B-B	F-3A	I	Cab	OMI	Ajin	5431		90	243	204		#800-806

GM Electro-Motive Division (cont'd)

Road	AAR Code	Class & Phase		Type	Importer	Builder	Cat #	Quan.	Yrs.	List Price	Mint	Avg.	Remarks
SAL	B-B	F-3A	II	Cab	OMI	Ajin	5500	10	90	243	204		#4022-4032
MP	B-B	F-3A	III	Cab	OMI	Ajin	5552		90	243	204		See Note #1764
NYO&W	B-B	F-3A	II	Cab	OMI	Ajin	5492	15	90	243	204		#501-503, 821, 822
RI	B-B	F-3A	II	Cab	OMI	Ajin	5449	35	90	257	215		#49 w/o upper hl.
	B-B	F-3A	I	Cab	Ortl	Samh	0430		85	200			sprung trucks
	B-B	F-3A	II	Cab	Ortl	Samh	0432		85	200			sprung trucks
PRR	B-B	F-3A	II	Cab	Ortl	Samh	0433		85	204			spg trucks, w/antenna
	B-B	F-3A	III	Cab	Ortl	Samh	0434		85	200			sprung trucks
	B-B	F-3A	IV	Cab	Ortl	Samh	0436		85	200			sprung trucks
C&EI	B-B	F-3A	IV	Cab	Ortl	Samh	P662		86	207			
D&RGW	B-B	F-3A	III	Cab	Ortl	Samh	P920A		88	240	202		fp., 4-Stripe
WP	B-B	F-3A	II	Cab	Ortl	Samh	P918A		88	240	202		Plated
WM	B-B	F-3A	II	Cab	Ortl	Samh	P917A		88	240	202		fp., Fire Ball Scheme
NP	B-B	F-3A	I	Cab	Ortl	Samh	P903A		88	240	202		fp., Freight Scheme
LV	B-B	F-3A	IV	Cab	Ortl	Samh	P925A		88	240	202		fp., Red
B&O	B-B	F-3A	II	Cab	Ortl	Samh	P906A		88	240	202		fp.
Milw	B-B	F-3A	IV	Cab	Ortl	Samh	P926A		88	240	202		fp.
CB&Q	B-B	F-3A	II	Cab	Ortl	Samh	P957A		88	240	202		fp., Cal. Zephyr
C&NW	B-B	F-3A	II	Cab	Ortl	Samh	P907A		89	240	202		fp., Freight Scheme
Monon	B-B	F-3A	I	Cab	Ortl	Samh	P901A		89	240	202		fp., Black/Gold
NYC	B-B	F-3A	II	Cab	Ortl	Samh	P912A		89	240	202		fp., Lightning Stripe
AT&SF	B-B	F-3A	III	Cab	Ortl	Samh	P924A		89	228			fp., plated
UP	B-B	F-3A	II	Cab	Ortl	Samh	P916A		89	228			fp.
Erie	B-B	F-3A	II	Cab	Ortl	Samh	P910A		89	240	202		fp., as delivered
CB&Q	B-B	F-3A	II	Cab	Ortl	Samh	P908A		89	240	202		fp., Freight Scheme
B&M	B-B	F-3A	I	Cab	Ortl	Samh	P904A		89	240	202		Maroon & Gold
Monon	B-B	F-3A	I	Cab	Ortl	Samh	P956A		89	240	202		fp., Red/Gray
	B-B	F-3A	I	Cab	Ortl	Samh	0161	75	82	194			
	B-B	F-3A	II	Cab	Ortl	Samh	0163	140	82	194			w/rivet detail
	B-B	F-3A	III	Cab	Ortl	Samh	0164	65	82	194			w/rivet detail
	B-B	F-3A		Cab	Sunset								
	B-B	F-3A		Cab	Sunset								
WP	B-B	F-3B	II		OMI	Ajin	5519	10	90	221	186		#801B, C - 803B, C
NP	B-B	F-3B	II		OMI	Ajin	5495	15	90	221	186		#6500B,C-6505B,C
NYC	B-B	F-3B	II		OMI	Ajin	5491	16	90	221	186		#3600-3601
CB&Q	B-B	F-3B	II		OMI	Ajin	5465	12	90	221	186		Pass. #9960B-9962B
C&NW	B-B	F-3B	II		OMI	Ajin	5457	15	90	221	186		See Note #1769
PRR	B-B	F-3B	II		OMI	Ajin	5497	20	90	221	186		#9500B-9528B
ATSF	B-B	F-3B	I		OMI	Ajin	5426		90	221	186		#16A,B-21A,B
DL&W	B-B	F-3B	I		OMI	Ajin	5428		90	221	186		#801B
Erie	B-B	F-3B	II		OMI	Ajin	5469	10	90	221	186		#800B-806B
GM&O	B-B	F-3B	II		OMI	Ajin	5475	8	90	221	186		#B-80-B82
CNR	B-B	F-3B	II		OMI	Ajin	5461	30	90	221	186		#9001, 9004
NYO&W	B-B	F-3B	II		OMI	Ajin	5493	10	90	221	186		#821, 822B
UP	B-B	F-3B	II		OMI	Ajin	5515	30	90	221	186		#1442B,c-1458B,C
KCS	B-B	F-3B	I		OMI	Ajin	5434		90	221	186		#50-53
CGW	B-B	F-3B	II		OMI	Ajin	5459	10	90	221	186		See Note#1756
MEC	B-B	F-3B	II		OMI	Ajin	5447	10	90	221	185		#671B, 672B
DL&W	B-B	F-3B	II		OMI	Ajin	5467	8	90	221	186		#621B
UP	B-B	F-3B	II		OMI	Ajin	5513	30	90	221	186		#969B-978B
SRR	B-B	F-3B	I		OMI	Ajin	5439		90	243	204		#4320-4384
BAR	B-B	F-3B	II		OMI	Ajin	5523	10	90	243	204		#500A-507A
SL&SF	B-B	F-3B	II		OMI	Ajin	5471	10	90	221	186		#5100-5117
NYC	B-B	F-3B	II		OMI	Ajin	5489	16	90	221	186		#2404-2419
B&O	B-B	F-3B	II		OMI	Ajin	5453	18	90	221	186		#82,4,6X,AX,88X
Monon	B-B	F-3B	I		OMI	Ajin	5436		90	221	186		#61C,63C,63C
ATSF	B-B	F-3B	II		OMI	Ajin	5451	25	90	221	186		#19
MP	B-B	F-3B	II		OMI	Ajin	5485	8	90	221	186		See Note#1770
UP	B-B	F-3B	II		OMI	Ajin	5511	30	90	221	186		q
CNJ	B-B	F-3B	II		OMI	Ajin	5455	15	90	221	186		#1A,2B,3C,4D,5E
GM&O	B-B	F-3B	I		OMI	Ajin	5432		90	221	186		#800-806
D&RGW	B-B	F-3B	I		OMI	Ajin	5430		90	221	186		#551,552,553,554
CB&Q	B-B	F-3B	II		OMI	Ajin	5463	10	90	221	186		#66-Bfs
	B-B	F-3B	II		Ortl	Samh	0112	137	82	160	150		Powered B-Unit

GM Electro-Motive Division (cont'd)

More than any other locomotive, the EMD FT spelled the end of steam. Designed to be permanently coupled together in A–B or A–B–A sets, these locomotives could generate 2,700-hp and 4,050 hp, respectively. From 1939 to 1945, almost 1,100 FTs were built. The basic design of the car body with the "Bulldog" nose set the stage for the F–3s and F–7s that followed. The name "EMD" became synonymous with diesel locomotives. A variety of importers have produced these popular locomotives and the number of variations has grown quite large. Overland Models imported this fine A–B set of Burlington FTs in 1988.

Road	AAR Code	Class & Phase		Type	Importer	Builder	Cat #	Quan.	Yrs.	List Price	Mint	Avg.	Remarks
	B-B	F-3B	IV		Ortl	Samh	0113	79	82	160	150		Powered B-Unit
	B-B	F-3B	I		Ortl	Samh	0162	65	82	160	150		Powered B-Unit
	B-B	F-3B	II/III		Ortl	Samh	0165	125	82	160	150		Powered B-Unit
	B-B	F-3B	IV		Ortl	Samh	0437		85	164	150		sprung trucks
	B-B	F-3B	I		Ortl	Samh	0431		85	164	150		sprung trucks
	B-B	F-3B	II/III		Ortl	Samh	0435		85	164	150		sprung trucks
WP	B-B	F-3B	II/III		Ortl	Samh	P918B		89	203	170		Plated
C&NW	B-B	F-3B	II/III		Ortl	Samh	P907B		89	203	170		fp., Freight Scheme
Erie	B-B	F-3B	II/III		Ortl	Samh	P910B		89	203	170		fp., as delivered
LV	B-B	F-3B	IV		Ortl	Samh	P925B		89	203	170		fp., Red
Milw	B-B	F-3B	IV		Ortl	Samh	P926B		89	203	170		fp.
NYC	B-B	F-3B	II/III		Ortl	Samh	P912B		89	203	170		fp., Lightning Stripe
B&O	B-B	F-3B	II/III		Ortl	Samh	P906B		89	203	170		fp.
Monon	B-B	F-3B	I		Ortl	Samh	P901B		89	203	170		fp., Black/Gold
NP	B-B	F-3B	I		Ortl	Samh	P903B		89	203	170		fp., Freight Scheme
SRR	B-B	F-3B	II/III		Ortl	Samh	P915B		89	203	170		fp., Green
B&M	B-B	F-3B	I		Ortl	Samh	P904B		89	203	170		Maroon & Gold
UP	B-B	F-3B	II/III		Ortl	Samh	P916B		89	192			fp.
CB&Q	B-B	F-3B	II/III		Ortl	Samh	P957B		89	203	170		fp., Cal. Zephyr
PRR	B-B	F-3B	IV		Ortl	Samh	P927B		89	152			fp.
CB&Q	B-B	F-3B	II/III		Ortl	Samh	P908B		89	203	170		fp., Freight Scheme
D&RGW	B-B	F-3B	II/III		Ortl	Samh	P920B		89	203	170		fp., 4-Stripe
	B-B	F-3B				Sunset							
	B-B	F-3B				Sunset							
	B-B/B-B	F-3 A&A	II	Cab	NPP			480	74	118	190	150	1500 hp.
	B-B/B-B	F-3 A&B		Cab	Hall	KMT		800	70	70	200	175	See Note #732
	B-B/B-B	F-3 A&B	IV/V	Cab	NPP			200	75	140	210	175	See Note #733
Milw	B-B	F-7A		Cab	OMI	Ajin	5651		90	243	204		See Note #1783
SRR	B-B	F-7A		Cab	OMI	Ajin	5679		90	243	204		#4207-4269
RI	B-B	F-7A		Cab	OMI	Ajin	5671		90	243	204		#100-127 Freight
Erie	B-B	F-7A		Cab	OMI	Ajin	5633		90	243	204		#711A,D - #713A,D
UP	B-B	F-7A		Cab	OMI	Ajin	5686		90	243	204		#1466-1483
DL&W	B-B	F-7A		Cab	OMI	Ajin	5631		90	243	204		#6300 Series
ATSF	B-B	F-7A		Cab	OMI	Ajin	5604		90	243	204		See Note #1776
Rdg	B-B	F-7A		Cab	OMI	Ajin	5667		90	243	204		#266-283
WAB	B-B	F-7A		Cab	OMI	Ajin	5691		90	243	204		#600 Series
T&P	B-B	F-7A		Cab	OMI	Ajin	5657		90	243	204		#1500-1582

GM Electro-Motive Division (cont'd)

Road	AAR Code	Class & Phase		Type	Importer	Builder	Cat #	Quan.	Yrs.	List Price	Mint	Avg.	Remarks
													Model Production / **Resale**
GN	B-B	F-7A		Cab	OMI	Ajin	5639		90	243	204		#400 Series
RI	B-B	F-7A		Cab	OMI	Ajin	5672		90	243	204		#675-677 Passenger
WM	B-B	F-7A		Cab	OMI	Ajin	5692		90	243	204		#53-66
GM&O	B-B	F-7A		Cab	OMI	Ajin	5641		90	243	204		#811B, 812A,B, 813A
UP	B-B	F-7A		Cab	OMI	Ajin	5698		90	250	210		See Note #1779
D&RGW	B-B	F-7A		Cab	OMI	Ajin	5628		90	243	204		#551,4 - #5761,4
SPP/WC	B-B	F-7A		Cab	OMI	Ajin	5676		90	243	204		See Note#1778
ATSF	B-B	F-7A		Cab	OMI	Ajin	5602		90	243	204		See Note #1777
WP	B-B	F-7A		Cab	OMI	Ajin	5695		90	243	204		#913A,D = 924A,D
C&S	B-B	F-7A		Cab	OMI	Ajin	5622		90	243	204		#700A,D - 702A,D
WM	B-B	F-7A		Cab	OMI	Ajin	5693		90	243	204		#231-242
SOO	B-B	F-7A		Cab	OMI	Ajin	5674		90	243	204		#212A,B-#214A,B
MKT	B-B	F-7A		Cab	OMI	Ajin	5653		90	243	204		See Note #1781
PRR	B-B	F-7A		Cab	OMI	Ajin	5666		90	243	204		See Note #1773
PRR	B-B	F-7A		Cab	OMI	Ajin	5665		90	250	210		See Note #1784
SP	B-B	F-7A		Cab	OMI	Ajin	5681		90	243	204		See Note #1772
B&LE	B-B	F-7A		Cab	OMI	Ajin	5610		90	243	204		#701A-728A
B&O	B-B	F-7A		Cab	OMI	Ajin	5608		90	243	204		#4480-4636
NYC	B-B	F-7A		Cab	OMI	Ajin	5660		90	221	186		#2420-2474
RF&P	B-B	F-7A		Cab	OMI	Ajin	5669		90	243	204		#1101-1110
C&O	B-B	F-7A		Cab	OMI	Ajin	5614		90	243	204		7000-7093
ATSF	B-B	F-7A		Cab	OMI	Ajin	5600		90	243	204		See Note #1785
NP	B-B	F-7A		Cab	OMI	Ajin	5661		90	243	204		See Note #1775
T&NO	B-B	F-7A		Cab	OMI	Ajin	5684		90	243	204		See Note #1774
CGW	B-B	F-7A		Cab	OMI	Ajin	5618		90	243	204		#153-156
C&NW	B-B	F-7A		Cab	OMI	Ajin	5616		90	243	204		#4067A,C-#102A,C
ACL	B-B	F-7A		Cab	OMI	Ajin	5606		90	243	204		#348-423
CNR	B-B	F-7A		Cab	OMI	Ajin	5626		90	243	204		#9159
LV	B-B	F-7A		Cab	OMI	Ajin	5645		90	243	204		#560-574 even
KCS	B-B	F-7A		Cab	OMI	Ajin	5643		90	243	204		See Note #1782
CB&Q	B-B	F-7A		Cab	OMI	Ajin	5620		90	243	204		See Note#1780
PRR	B-B	F-7A		Cab	OMI	Ajin	5663		90	243	204		See Note#1786
GTW	B-B	F-7A		Cab	OMI	Ajin	5637		90	243	204		#9020, 9021
WAB	B-B	F-7A		Cab	OMI	Ajin	5689		90	243	204		#1140,A-1189,A
CNR	B-B	F-7A		Cab	OMI	Ajin	5624		90	243	204		#9028-9142 even
MP	B-B	F-7A		Cab	OMI	Ajin	5655		90	243	204		#577-594
SP	B-B	F-7A		Cab	OMI	Ajin	5683		90	243	204		#6180-6445
L&N	B-B	F-7A		Cab	OMI	Ajin	5647		90	243	204		#800,849, 900-918
Milw	B-B	F-7A		Cab	OMI	Ajin	5649		90	243	204		See Note #1771
NYC	B-B	F-7A		Cab	OMI	Ajin	5658		90	243	204		#1636-1699
B&M	B-B	F-7A		Cab	OMI	Ajin	5612		90	243	204		#4265A-4268A
C&NW	B-B	F-7A		Cab	OMI	Ajin	5699		90	243	204		#421 #1975 ERA
D&RGW	B-B	F-7A		Cab	OMI	Ajin	5629		90	243	204		#5701,4 - #5761,4
SL&SF	B-B	F-7A		Cab	OMI	Ajin	5635		90	243	204		#5018-5039
	B-B	F-7A	I	Cab	Ortl	Samh	0350		84	200		185	See Note#1787
PRR	B-B	F-7A	I	Cab	Ortl	Samh	0351		84	203			w/antennas
	B-B	F-7A	II	Cab	Ortl	Samh	0353		84	200			
	B-B	F-7A	II	Cab	Ortl	Samh	0125	100	82	180		150	Powered A-Unit
	B-B	F-7A	I	Cab	Ortl	Samh	0124	125	82	180		150	Powered A-Unit
	B-B	F-7A	II	Cab	Ortl	Samh	0672		86	171			
	B-B	F-7A	I	Cab	Ortl	Samh	0661		86	171			w/o dynamic brakes
RDG	B-B	F-7A	I	Cab	Ortl	Samh	P671		87	207	174		fp.
GN	B-B	F-7A	II	Cab	Ortl	Samh	P673		87	207	174		fp., Empire Builder
	B-B	F-7A	I	Cab	Ortl	Samh	0663	!	86	171			w/dynamic brakes
PRR	B-B	F-7A	I	Cab	Ortl	Samh	P664	!	87	214	180		See Note #1788
SP	B-B	F-7A	I	Cab	Ortl	Samh	P665	!	86	207			fp., Black Widow
UP	B-B	F-7A	I	Cab	Ortl	Samh	P666	!	86	207			fp.
C&O	B-B	F-7A	II	Cab	Ortl	Samh	P675	!	87	207	174		fp.
CGW	B-B	F-7A	I	Cab	Ortl	Samh	P668	!	86	207			fp.
L&N	B-B	F-7A	I	Cab	Ortl	Samh	P669	!	86	207			fp.
CB&Q	B-B	F-7A	I	Cab	Ortl	Samh	P670	!	86	204			
RDG	B-B	F-7A	I	Cab	Ortl	Samh	P671	!	86	207			fp.
	B-B	F-7A	II	Cab	Ortl	Samh	0672		86	171			
GN	B-B	F-7A	II	Cab	Ortl	Samh	P673		86	207			fp., Empire Builder

GM Electro-Motive Division (cont'd)

The EMD F–3 series was introduced in 1949 as the next step in the evolution of the EMD "Covered Wagon" road-type diesel. Horsepower was increased to 1,500, using the same basic prime mover used in the FTs. Several changes were made to the basic car body making it easy to identify the F–3s. Fans now protruded above the roof line, three evenly spaced portholes replaced the four clustered portholes on the FTs, and the large rear overhang common to the FTs was gone. Several importers have produced a large variety of F–3s, each with detailing specific to a particular road. Shown above is Overland's F–3 Phase II A–B–A set, detailed and painted for UP.

Road	AAR Code	Class & Phase		Type	Importer	Builder	Cat #	Quan.	Yrs.	List Price	Mint	Avg.	Remarks
SRR	B-B	F-7A	II	Cab	Ortl	Samh	P674		86	207			fp., Green
C&O	B-B	F-7A	II	Cab	Ortl	Samh	P675		86	207			fp.
AT&SF	B-B	F-7A	II	Cab	Ortl	Samh	P676		86	207			fp., War Bonnet
GN	B-B	F-7A	I	Cab	Ortl	Samh	P667	!	87	207	174		fp., Empire Builder
WM	B-B	F-7A	I	Cab	Ortl	Samh	P717		86	207			fp., w/fireball
B&O	B-B	F-7A	I	Cab	Ortl	Samh	P929A		89	240			fp.
C&NW	B-B	F-7A	I	Cab	Ortl	Samh	P931A		89	240			fp.
WAB	B-B	F-7A	I	Cab	Ortl	Samh	P936A		89	240			fp.
MKT	B-B	F-7B		Cab	OMI	Ajin	5654		90	221	186		See Note#1791
T&NO	B-B	F-7B		Cab	OMI	Ajin	5685		90	221	186		See Note #1794
C&S	B-B	F-7B		Cab	OMI	Ajin	5623		90	221	186		#700B,C - #702B,C
CB&Q	B-B	F-7B		Cab	OMI	Ajin	5621		90	221	186		#167B-169B
RI	B-B	F-7B		Cab	OMI	Ajin	5673		90	221	186		See Note #1790
WP	B-B	F-7B		Cab	OMI	Ajin	5697		90	221	186		See Note#1792
SL&SF	B-B	F-7B		Cab	OMI	Ajin	5636		90	221	186		#5118-5139
Rdg	B-B	F-7B		Cab	OMI	Ajin	5668		90	221	186		#266B-271B
SOO	B-B	F-7B		Cab	OMI	Ajin	5675		90	221	186		#500B-503B
NYC	B-B	F-7B		Cab	OMI	Ajin	5659		90	243	204		#1700-1873
Milw	B-B	F-7B		Cab	OMI	Ajin	5650		90	221	186		#48B-50B, #68B-79B
ACL	B-B	F-7B		Cab	OMI	Ajin	5607		90	221	186		#329B-403B
D&RGW	B-B	F-7B		Cab	OMI	Ajin	5630		90	221	186		#5552,3 - #5742,3
UP	B-B	F-7B		Cab	OMI	Ajin	5687		90	221	186		See Note#1804
C&O	B-B	F-7B		Cab	OMI	Ajin	5615		90	221	186		7500-7546 Freight
L&N	B-B	F-7B		Cab	OMI	Ajin	5648		90	221	186		#700-716
SRR	B-B	F-7B		Cab	OMI	Ajin	5680		90	221	186		#4385-4428
ATSF	B-B	F-7B		Cab	OMI	Ajin	5603		90	221	186		See Note #1798
CNR	B-B	F-7B		Cab	OMI	Ajin	5625		90	221	186		#9029-9063 odd
CGW	B-B	F-7B		Cab	OMI	Ajin	5619		90	221	186		See Note #1800
Milw	B-B	F-7B		Cab	OMI	Ajin	5652		90	221	186		#87B-121B
NP	B-B	F-7B		Cab	OMI	Ajin	5662		90	221	186		See Note#1799
WM	B-B	F-7B		Cab	OMI	Ajin	5694		90	221	186		#401-414
WP	B-B	F-7B		Cab	OMI	Ajin	5696		90	221	186		See Note #1802
ATSF	B-B	F-7B		Cab	OMI	Ajin	5605		90	221	186		See Note #1805
SOO/WC	B-B	F-7B		Cab	OMI	Ajin	5678		90	221	186		See Note#1789

GM Electro-Motive Division (cont'd)

The EMD E–3 through E–6 used the long "shovel nose" car body configuration, which was similar to the EA & E1 locomotives. This step in the EMD evolution of the passenger diesel was marked by an increase from 1,800 to 2,000 hp, facilitated by using two of the new #567 engines. Diesel buffs will note that the car body appearance improved with the replacement of the oval windows with portholes and smaller grilles. EMD produce a total of 87 E6As and 26 E6Bs. Overland Models imported 12 different versions of the E6A. The model shown is the Southern version.

| Road | AAR Code | Class & Phase | Type | Model Production | | | | | List Price | Resale | | Remarks |
				Importer	Builder	Cat #	Quan.	Yrs.		Mint	Avg.	
MP	B-B	F-7B	Cab	OMI	Ajin	5656		90	221	186		#587B-594B
GM&O	B-B	F-7B	Cab	OMI	Ajin	5642		90	221	186		#B65-B74
B&LE	B-B	F-7B	Cab	OMI	Ajin	5611		90	221	186		#701B-726B
RF&P	B-B	F-7B	Cab	OMI	Ajin	5670		90	221	186		#1151-1160
SOO/WC	B-B	F-7B	Cab	OMI	Ajin	5677		90	221	186		See Note#1806
ATSF	B-B	F-7B	Cab	OMI	Ajin	5601		90	221	186		See Note #1801
B&O	B-B	F-7B	Cab	OMI	Ajin	5609		90	221	186		#5420-5519
DL&W	B-B	F-7B	Cab	OMI	Ajin	5632		90	221	186		#6322-6362
PRR	B-B	F-7B	Cab	OMI	Ajin	5664		90	221	186		#9600B
CPR	B-B	F-7B	Cab	OMI	Ajin	5627		90	221	186		See Note#1797
GN	B-B	F-7B	Cab	OMI	Ajin	5638		90	243	204		See Note #1795
Erie	B-B	F-7B	Cab	OMI	Ajin	5634		90	221	186		#711B,C - #713B,C
LV	B-B	F-7B	Cab	OMI	Ajin	5646		90	221	186		#561-571 odd
UP	B-B	F-7B	Cab	OMI	Ajin	5688		90	243	204		#910B,C Passenger
KCS	B-B	F-7B	Cab	OMI	Ajin	5644		90	221	186		See Note#1793
B&M	B-B	F-7B	Cab	OMI	Ajin	5613		90	221	186		265B-4268B
WAB	B-B	F-7B	Cab	OMI	Ajin	5690		90	221	186		#1100B-1108B
C&NW	B-B	F-7B	Cab	OMI	Ajin	5617		90	221	186		See Note #1796
GN	B-B	F-7B	Cab	OMI	Ajin	5640		90	221	186		See Note #1803
SP	B-B	F-7B	Cab	OMI	Ajin	5682		90	221	186		#8080-8303
B&O	B-B	F-7B	I	Ortl	Samh			89	202			fp.
	B-B	F-7B	I	Ortl	Samh	0126	75	82	154		130	Powered B-Unit
	B-B	F-7B	I	Ortl	Samh	0160	50	82	160			w/o dynamic brakes
	B-B	F-7B	I	Ortl	Samh	0223	50	82	160			
	B-B	F-7B	I	Ortl	Samh	0352		84	164			
	B-B	F-7B	I	Ortl	Samh	0692		86	139			w/o dynamic brakes
	B-B	F-7B	I	Ortl	Samh	0693		86	139			w/dynamic brakes
SP	B-B	F-7B	I	Ortl	Samh	P694		86	172			fp., Black Widow
UP	B-B	F-7B	I	Ortl	Samh	P695		86	172			fp.
C&EI	B-B	F-7B	I	Ortl	Samh	P696		86	172			fp.
PRR	B-B	F-7B	I	Ortl	Samh	P697		87	172	144		fp.
GN	B-B	F-7B	I	Ortl	Samh	P698		87	172	144		fp., Empire Builder
CGW	B-B	F-7B	I	Ortl	Samh	P699		86	172			fp., as delivered
L&N	B-B	F-7B	I	Ortl	Samh	P700		86	172			fp.
CB&Q	B-B	F-7B	I	Ortl	Samh	P701		86	172			fp.
RDG	B-B	F-7B	I	Ortl	Samh	P702		87	172	144		fp.
C&NW	B-B	F-7B	I	Ortl	Samh	P931B		89	202			fp.

GM Electro-Motive Division (cont'd)

Road	AAR Code	Class & Phase		Type	Importer	Builder	Cat #	Quan.	Yrs.	List Price	Mint	Avg.	Remarks
WAB	B-B	F-7B	I		Ortl	Samh	P936B		89	202			fp.
WP	B-B	F-7B	I		Ortl	Samh	P937B		89	192			fp., freight
WP	B-B	F-7B	I		Ortl	Samh	P954B		89				fp., plated
SRR	B-B	F-7B	I		Ortl	Samh	P959B		89	152			fp.
	B-B	F-7B	II		Ortl	Samh	0354		84	164			
	B-B	F-7B	II		Ortl	Samh	0703		86	139			
GN	B-B	F-7B	II		Ortl	Samh	P704		87	172	144		fp.
SP	B-B	F-7B	II		Ortl	Samh	P705		87	172	144		fp.
SRR	B-B	F-7B	II		Ortl	Samh	P707		86	172			fp.
PRR	B-B	F-7B	II		Ortl	Samh	P706		87	172	144		fp.
C&O	B-B	F-7B	II		Ortl	Samh	P708		87	172	144		fp.
AT&SF	B-B	F-7B	II		Ortl	Samh	P709		86	172			fp.
UP	B-B	F-7B	II		Ortl	Samh	P710		86	172			fp.
WM	B-B	F-7B	I		Ortl	Samh	P719		86	172			fp. black
WP	B-B	F-7B	I	Ortl	Samh		P720	86	172			fp.	
UP	B-B	F-7B			PFM	Tensh		1	56				Dummy B-Unit, fp.
	B-B	F-7/9B	II		Ortl	Samh	0127	125	82	154		130	Powered B-Unit
	B-B/B-B	F-7 A&B		Cab	PFM	Tensh		9	55	25	90	75	See Note #696, Kit
GN	B-B/B-B	F-7 A&B		Cab	PFM	Tensh	119/20	4	55	30	130	110	See Note #734
AT&SF	B-B/B-B	F-7 A&B		Cab	PFM	Tensh	119/20	2	55	30	130	110	See Note #734
C&NW	B-B/B-B	F-7 A&B		Cab	PFM	Tensh	119/20	1	55	30	130	110	See Note #734
GN	B-B/B-B	F-7 A&B		Cab	PFM	Tensh		2	55	28	110	90	See Note #728
AT&SF	B-B/B-B	F-7 A&B		Cab	PFM	Tensh		3	56	28			Kit, Note #734, pass
CP	B-B/B-B	F-7 A&B		Cab	PFM	Tensh	119/20	1	56	34	140		See Note #696, fp.
GN	B-B/B-B	F-7 A&B		Cab	PFM	Tensh	119/20	3	56	34	140		See Note #696, fp.
GN	B-B/B-B	F-7 A&B		Cab	PFM	Tensh		11	56	28			Kit, See Note #734
KCS	B-B/B-B	F-7 A&B		Cab	PFM	Tensh	119/20	2	56	34	140		See Note #696, fp.
	B-B/B-B	F-7 A&B		Cab	PFM	Tensh		3	56	25	95	80	See Note #696, Kit
AT&SF	B-B/B-B	F-7 A&B		Cab	PFM	Tensh		2	56	28			Kit, Note #734, freight
GN	B-B/B-B	F-7 A&B		Cab	PFM	Tensh	119/20	3	59	30	140		See Note #696, fp.
Milw	B-B	F-9A		Cab	OMI	Ajin	5739		90	243	204		See Note #1818
Milw	B-B	F-9A		Cab	OMI	Ajin	5740		90	243	204		#125A, 126A Freight
L&N	B-B	F-9A		Cab	OMI	Ajin	5737		90	243	204		#919-926
ATSF	B-B	F-9A		Cab	OMI	Ajin	5725		90	243	204		#281,C-289,C
D&RGW	B-B	F-9A		Cab	OMI	Ajin	5732		90	243	204		#5771,5774
NP	B-B	F-9A		Cab	OMI	Ajin	5743		90	243	204		See Note #1819
C&S	B-B	F-9A		Cab	OMI	Ajin	5730		90	243	204		#700D
NP	B-B	F-9A		Cab	OMI	Ajin	5745		90	243	204		See Note #1820
SL&SF	B-B	F-9A		Cab	OMI	Ajin	5734		90	243	204		#5005,5007 Rebuilt
	B-B	F-9A		Cab	Ortl	Samh	0357		84	200		150	Powered A-Unit
	B-B	F-9A		Cab	Ortl	Samh	0128	100	82	180		150	Powered A-Unit
	B-B	F-9A		Cab	Ortl	Samh			84	164			powered
	B-B	F-9A		Cab	Ortl	Samh	0687		86	171			
NP	B-B	F-9A		Cab	Ortl	Samh	P688		86	207			fp.
L&N	B-B	F-9A		Cab	Ortl	Samh	P689		86	207			fp.
D&RGW	B-B	F-9A		Cab	Ortl	Samh	P690		87	207	174		fp.
CB&Q	B-B	F-9A		Cab	Ortl	Samh	P691		87	207	174		fp.
AT&SF	B-B	F-9A		Cab	Ortl	Samh	P958A		89	240	202		fp., Freight Scheme
Milw	B-B	F-9A		Cab	Ortl	Samh	P946A		89	240			fp.
D&RGW	B-B	F-9A		Cab	Ortl	Samh	P945A		89	228			fp., Single Stripe
NP	B-B	F-9A		Cab	Ortl	Samh	947A		89	326			fp. freight
NP	B-B	F-9A		Cab	Ortl	Samh	P947A		89	228			fp., Freight Scheme
C&O	B-B	F-9A		Cab	PFM	Tensh		1	56	11	80		A Dummy, fp.
AT&SF	B-B	F-9A		Cab	PFM	Tensh		1	56	11	80		A Dummy, fp. freight
AT&SF	B-B	F-9A		Cab	PFM	Tensh		1	56	20	80		A Powered, fp.
GN	B-B	F-9A		Cab	PFM	Tensh		4	56	11	80		A Dummy, fp.
NYC	B-B	F-9A		Cab	PFM	Tensh		1	57	11	80		A Dummy, fp.
CMStP&P	B-B	F-9A		Cab	PFM	Tensh		1	58	11			A Dummy, fp. Milw
CP	B-B	F-9A		Cab	PFM	Tensh		3	58	20			A Powered, fp.
CMStP&P	B-B	F-9A		Cab	PFM	Tensh		1	58	11			A Dummy, fp. UP
C&O	B-B	F-9A		Cab	PFM	Tensh		4	58	11			A Dummy, fp.
NYC	B-B	F-9A		Cab	PFM	Tensh		2	58	11			A Dummy, fp.
CP	B-B	F-9A		Cab	PFM	Tensh		1	58	11			A Dummy, fp.
SRR	B-B	F-9A		Cab	PFM	Tensh		1	58	11			A Dummy, fp.

GM Electro-Motive Division (cont'd)

Road	AAR Code	Class & Phase	Type	Importer	Builder	Cat #	Quan.	Yrs.	List Price	Mint	Avg.	Remarks
SP	B-B	F-9A	Cab	PFM	Tensh		1	58	11			A Dummy, fp.
AT&SF	B-B	F-9A	Cab	PFM	Tensh		6	58	11			A Dummy, fp. pass
UNK	B-B	F-9A	Cab	PFM	Tensh		5	58	20			A Powered, fp.
C&O	B-B	F-9A	Cab	PFM	Tensh		1	58	20			A Powered, fp.
D&RGW	B-B	F-9A	Cab	PFM	Tensh		1	58	11			A Dummy, fp.
GN	B-B	F-9A	Cab	PFM	Tensh		9	58	11			A Dummy, fp.
AT&SF	B-B	F-9A	Cab	PFM	Tensh		3	58	11			A Dummy, fp. freight
C&NW	B-B	F-9A	Cab	PFM	Tensh		2	58	11			A Dummy, fp.
GN	B-B	F-9A	Cab	PFM	Tensh		1	58	20			A Powered, fp.
UNK	B-B	F-9A	Cab	PFM	Tensh		4	59	20			A Powered, fp.
NYC	B-B	F-9A	Cab	PFM	Tensh		1	59	11			A Dummy, fp.
C&O	B-B	F-9A	Cab	PFM	Tensh		1	59	11			A Dummy, fp.
NYC	B-B	F-9A	Cab	PFM	Tensh		1	59	20			A Powered, fp.
AT&SF	B-B	F-9A	Cab	PFM	Tensh		1	59	11			A Dummy, fp. pass
GN	B-B	F-9A	Cab	PFM	Tensh		3	59	11			A Dummy, fp.
C&NW	B-B	F-9A	Cab	PFM	Tensh		1	59	11			A Dummy, fp.
GN	B-B	F-9A	Cab	PFM	Tensh		1	60	11			A Dummy, fp.
UNK	B-B	F-9A	Cab	PFM	Tensh		1	60	20			A Powered, fp.
SP	B-B	F-9A	Cab	PFM	Tensh		1	60	11			A Dummy, fp.
AT&SF	B-B	F-9A	Cab	PFM	Tensh		2	60	11			A Dummy, fp. freight
WP	B-B	F-9A	Cab	PFM	Tensh		1	60	11			A Dummy, fp.
B&O	B-B	F-9A	Cab	PFM	Tensh		1	60	11			A Dummy, fp.
UNK	B-B	F-9A	Cab	PFM	Tensh		5	63	11			A Dummy, fp.
SP	B-B	F-9A	Cab	PFM	Tensh		1	63	11			A Dummy, fp.
UNK	B-B	F-9A	Cab	PFM	Tensh		4	65	20			A Powered, fp.
UP	B-B	F-9Am	Cab	OMI	Ajin	5751		90	243	204		See Note #1823
UP	B-B	F-9Am	Cab	OMI	Ajin	5753		90	243	204		See Note #1822
RI	B-B	F-9Am	Cab	OMI	Ajin	5747		90	243	204		See Note #1821
Demo	B-B	F-9Am	Cab	OMI	Ajin	5755		90	243	204		See Note #1820
UP	B-B	F-9Am	Cab	Ortl	Samh	0358		84	200			
	B-B	F-9A	Cab	Gem	Tokaido	TM-101	500	71	40	50	40	
MKT	B-B	F-9B		OMI	Ajin	5742		90	221	186		#75B,D,E,F
CNR	B-B	F-9B		OMI	Ajin	5727		90	221	186		#6600-6637
SL&SF	B-B	F-9B		OMI	Ajin	5735		90	221	186		#5249-5152
L&N	B-B	F-9B		OMI	Ajin	5738		90	221	186		#717-720
ATSF	B-B	F-9B		OMI	Ajin	5726		90	221	186		See Note#1824
NP	B-B	F-9B		OMI	Ajin	5746		90	221	186		See Note #1826
D&RGW	B-B	F-9B		OMI	Ajin	5733		90	221	186		#5752,5763,5772,5773
NP	B-B	F-9B		OMI	Ajin	5744		90	221	186		See Note #1825
CPR	B-B	F-9B		OMI	Ajin	5728		90	221	186		#1900-1907
CPR	B-B	F-9B		OMI	Ajin	5729		90	221	186		#864-868 "B"
Gn	B-B	F-9B		OMI	Ajin	5736		90	221	186		See Note#1827
Milw	B-B	F-9B		OMI	Ajin	5741		90	221	186		#125B,C,D, #126B,C,D
	B-B	F-9B		Ortl	Samh	0711		86	139			
NP	B-B	F-9B		Ortl	Samh	P712		87	172	144		fp.
	B-B	F-9B		Ortl	Samh	0359		84	164			powered
L&N	B-B	F-9B		Ortl	Samh	P713		87	172			fp.
D&RGW	B-B	F-9B		Ortl	Samh	P714		87	172	144		fp.
AT&SF	B-B	F-9B		Ortl	Samh	P958B		88	193	162		fp., Freight Scheme
Milw	B-B	F-9B		Ortl	Samh	P946B		89	202			fp.
NYC	B-B	F-9B		PFM	Tensh		1	57	10			B Dummy, fp.
UNK	B-B	F-9B		PFM	Tensh		18	57	10			B Dummy, fp.
GN	B-B	F-9B		PFM	Tensh		1	57	10			B Dummy, fp.
AT&SF	B-B	F-9B		PFM	Tensh		1	58	19			fp., powered, freight
GN	B-B	F-9B		PFM	Tensh		1	58	10			B Dummy, fp.
UNK	B-B	F-9B		PFM	Tensh		3	58	19	75	65	Powered B-Unit, fp.
CP	B-B	F-9B		PFM	Tensh		1	58	19			fp., powered
AT&SF	B-B	F-9B		PFM	Tensh		1	58	10			B Dummy, fp. pass
NYC	B-B	F-9B		PFM	Tensh		1	58	10			B Dummy, fp.
AT&SF	B-B	F-9B		PFM	Tensh		1	58	10			B Dummy, fp. freight
C&O	B-B	F-9B		PFM	Tensh		1	58	10			B Dummy, fp.
GN	B-B	F-9B		PFM	Tensh		2	59	10			B Dummy, fp.
UNK	B-B	F-9B		PFM	Tensh		3	59	19			Powered B-Unit, fp.
UNK	B-B	F-9B		PFM	Tensh		1	59	19	75	65	B Dummy, fp.

GM Electro-Motive Division (cont'd)

FP7s were built as dual-service locomotives that could handle freight and passenger trains equally well. They are four feet longer than standard F units to accommodate the steam generator and water tanks needed for passenger service. The difference is noticeable in the spacing of the fuel tanks—there is a large space between the front truck and the fuel tank. Ajin Precision has done an excellent job of depicting the C&O FP7. Independently sprung axles and individual gearboxes on each axle, combined with an excellent can motor incorporating two flywheels, provide a model with superior performance.

Road	AAR Code	Class & Phase	Type	Importer	Builder	Cat #	Quan.	Yrs.	List Price	Mint	Avg.	Remarks
AT&SF	B-B	F-9B		PFM	Tensh		1	59	10			B Dummy, fp. pass
AT&SF	B-B	F-9B		PFM	Tensh		1	60	10			B Dummy, fp. freight
UNK	B-B	F-9B		PFM	Tensh		1	60	10			B Dummy, fp.
AT&SF	B-B	F-9B		PFM	Tensh			60	19			fp., powered, passenger
UNK	B-B	F-9B		PFM	Tensh		1	62	19	75	65	Powered B-Unit, fp.
UNK	B-B	F-9B		PFM	Tensh		2	63	10			B Dummy, fp.
UNK	B-B	F-9B		PFM	Tensh		3	64	10			B Dummy, fp.
UNK	B-B	F-9B		PFM	Tensh		1	65	10			B Dummy, fp.
UP	B-B	F-9Bm		OMI	Ajin	5754		90	221	186		See Note #1830
RI	B-B	F-9Bm		OMI	Ajin	5748		90	221	186		See Note #1829
UP	B-B	F-9Bm		OMI	Ajin	5752		90	221	186		See Note #1828
SP	B-B	F-9m "A"		OMI	Ajin	5749		90	243	204		See Note #1831
SP	B-B	F-9m "B"		OMI	Ajin	5750		90	221	186		See Note #1832
	B-B/B-B	F-9 A&B	Cab	Intl				55	28	75	50	1750 hp., Kit
GN	B-B/B-B	F-9 A&B	Cab	PFM	Tensh		24	58	30			fp., A & B powered
C&O	B-B/B-B	F-9 A&B	Cab	PFM	Tensh	131/32	30	56	30			fp. A pwd, B dummy
AT&SF	B-B/B-B	F-9 A&B	Cab	PFM	Tensh	131/32	40	56	30			See Note #1811
GN	B-B/B-B	F-9 A&B	Cab	PFM	Tensh		1	56				fp., A & B powered
CMStP&P	B-B/B-B	F-9 A&B	Cab	PFM	Tensh	131/32	10	56	30			See Note #1809
GN	B-B/B-B	F-9 A&B	Cab	PFM	Tensh	131/32	60	56	30			fp. A pwd, B dummy
AT&SF	B-B/B-B	F-9 A&B	Cab	PFM	Tensh	131/32	20	56	30			See Note #1810
UNK	B-B/B-B	F-9 A&B	Cab	PFM	Tensh		9	56	28			See Note #696, fp.
NYC	B-B/B-B	F-9 A&B	Cab	PFM	Tensh	131/32	30	56	30			fp. A pwd, B dummy
C&NW	B-B/B-B	F-9 A&B	Cab	PFM	Tensh	131/32	10	56	30			fp. A pwd, B dummy
	B-B/B-B	F-9 A&B	Cab	PFM	Tensh		15	56	25	80	70	See Note #696, Kit
CMStP&P	B-B/B-B	F-9 A&B	Cab	PFM	Tensh	131/32	10	56	30			See Note #1808
AT&SF	B-B/B-B	F-9 A&B	Cab	PFM	Tensh	131/32	25	57	30			See Note #1811
SRR	B-B/B-B	F-9 A&B	Cab	PFM	Tensh	131/32	20	57	30			fp. A pwd, B dummy
	B-B/B-B	F-9 A&B	Cab	PFM	Tensh		20	57	25	85	75	See Note #696, Kit
GN	B-B/B-B	F-9 A&B	Cab	PFM	Tensh	131/32	30	57	30			fp. A pwd, B dummy
UNK	B-B/B-B	F-9 A&B	Cab	PFM	Tensh		10	57	28	105	85	See Note #728

GM Electro-Motive Division (cont'd)

In 1954, EMD introduced the F–9, a logical step in the evolution of the successful "Covered Wagon" series of freight engines initiated by the FT series. Appearance differences from the F–7 are small, primarily in the type of grill work and placement of car-body filters. PFM began importing Tenshodo-built EMD diesels in 1955, and Tenshodo-built FT, F–7s and F–9s kept pace with EMD. The early builders of EMD models of the "Covered Wagons" had one thing in common: they couldn't get the nose contour correct. Tenshodo's entire series of F Units looked a little "odd." Still, modelers and collectors loved them for the fine paint work and variety of colorful paint schemes.

Road	AAR Code	Class & Phase	Type	Importer	Builder	Cat #	Quan.	Yrs.	List Price	Mint	Avg.	Remarks
C&NW	B-B/B-B	F-9 A&B	Cab	PFM	Tensh	131/32	10	57	30			fp. A pwd, B dummy
D&RGW	B-B/B-B	F-9 A&B	Cab	PFM	Tensh	131/32	11	57	30			fp. A pwd, B dummy
C&O	B-B/B-B	F-9 A&B	Cab	PFM	Tensh	131/32	10	57	30			fp. A pwd, B dummy
NYC	B-B/B-B	F-9 A&B	Cab	PFM	Tensh	131/32	20	57	30			fp. A pwd, B dummy
SRR	B-B/B-B	F-9 A&B	Cab	PFM	Tensh	131/32	10	58	30			fp. A pwd, B dummy
CMStP&P	B-B/B-B	F-9 A&B	Cab	PFM	Tensh	131/32	10	58	30			See Note#1808
SRR	B-B/B-B	F-9 A&B	Cab	PFM	Tensh		2	58	30			fp., A & B powered
C&O	B-B/B-B	F-9 A&B	Cab	PFM	Tensh	131/32	10	58	30			fp., A pwd. B dummy
NYC	B-B/B-B	F-9 A&B	Cab	PFM	Tensh	131/32	20	58	30			fp., A pwd. B dummy
	B-B/B-B	F-9 A&B	Cab	PFM	Tensh		10	58	25	85	75	See Note #696, Kit
CMStP&P	B-B/B-B	F-9 A&B	Cab	PFM	Tensh		1	58	30			See Note#1812
SP	B-B/B-B	F-9 A&B	Cab	PFM	Tensh		9	58	30			fp., A & B powered
PRR	B-B/B-B	F-9 A&B	Cab	PFM	Tensh		5	58	30			fp., A & B powered
NdeM	B-B/B-B	F-9 A&B	Cab	PFM	Tensh		9	58	30			fp., A & B powered
NYC	B-B/B-B	F-9 A&B	Cab	PFM	Tensh		19	58	30			fp., A & B powered
SP	B-B/B-B	F-9 A&B	Cab	PFM	Tensh	131/32	7	58	30			fp., A pwd. B dummy
C&NW	B-B/B-B	F-9 A&B	Cab	PFM	Tensh		8	58	30			fp., A & B powered
D&RGW	B-B/B-B	F-9 A&B	Cab	PFM	Tensh		5	58	30			fp., A & B powered
AT&SF	B-B/B-B	F-9 A&B	Cab	PFM	Tensh	131/32	20	58	30			See Note#1811
AT&SF	B-B/B-B	F-9 A&B	Cab	PFM	Tensh		11	58	30			See Note #1813
AT&SF	B-B/B-B	F-9 A&B	Cab	PFM	Tensh		2	58	30			See Note #1814
B&O	B-B/B-B	F-9 A&B	Cab	PFM	Tensh		6	58	30			fp., A & B powered
AT&SF	B-B/B-B	F-9 A&B	Cab	PFM	Tensh	131/32	10	58	30			See Note#1810
GN	B-B/B-B	F-9 A&B	Cab	PFM	Tensh	131/32	50	58	30			fp, A pwd. B dummy
UP	B-B/B-B	F-9 A&B	Cab	PFM	Tensh		5	58	30			fp., A & B powered
C&NW	B-B/B-B	F-9 A&B	Cab	PFM	Tensh	131/32	10	58	30			fp., A pwd. B dummy
CN	B-B/B-B	F-9 A&B	Cab	PFM	Tensh		2	58	30			fp., A & B powered
C&O	B-B/B-B	F-9 A&B	Cab	PFM	Tensh		2	58	30			fp., A & B powered
SP	B-B/B-B	F-9 A&B	Cab	PFM	Tensh		2	58	30			See Note #1813
SP	B-B/B-B	F-9 A&B	Cab	PFM	Tensh	131/32	40	59	30			fp., A pwd. B dummy
C&NW	B-B/B-B	F-9 A&B	Cab	PFM	Tensh	131/32	15	59	30			fp., A pwd. B dummy
CN	B-B/B-B	F-9 A&B	Cab	PFM	Tensh	131/32	2	59	30			fp., A pwd. B dummy
CP	B-B/B-B	F-9 A&B	Cab	PFM	Tensh	131/32	2	59	30			fp., A pwd. B dummy
NdeM	B-B/B-B	F-9 A&B	Cab	PFM	Tensh	131/32	3	59	30			fp., A pwd. B dummy
PRR	B-B/B-B	F-9 A&B	Cab	PFM	Tensh	131/32	2	59	30			See Notye #1815
CMStP&P	B-B/B-B	F-9 A&B	Cab	PFM	Tensh	131/32	10	59	30			See Note#1808

GM Electro-Motive Division (cont'd)

The EMD E-2s were a short-lived variation that were built exclusively for the UP. Only two A–B–B sets were produced. Mechanically, they were similar to the E–A and E–1s that preceded them. The original high-mounted number boards on each side of the headlight did little to enhance the appearance. They were later removed and small side-mounted number boards installed. The Overland model depicts this unique engine as delivered. Ajin Precision has done an excellent job of capturing the shape of the nose on this very unusual model.

| | | | | Model Production | | | | | List Price | Resale | | |
Road	AAR Code	Class & Phase	Type	Importer	Builder	Cat #	Quan.	Yrs.		Mint	Avg.	Remarks
B&O	B-B/B-B	F-9 A&B	Cab	PFM	Tensh	131/32	11	59	30			fp., A pwd. B dummy
AT&SF	B-B/B-B	F-9 A&B	Cab	PFM	Tensh	131/32	40	59	30			See Note #1811
	B-B/B-B	F-9 A&B	Cab	PFM	Tensh		10	59	25	85	75	See Note #696, Kit
GN	B-B/B-B	F-9 A&B	Cab	PFM	Tensh	131/32	200	59	30			fp., A pwd. B dummy
C&O	B-B/B-B	F-9 A&B	Cab	PFM	Tensh	131/32	15	59	30			fp., A pwd. B dummy
CMStP&P	B-B/B-B	F-9 A&B	Cab	PFM	Tensh	131/32	10	59	30			See Note#1809
GN	B-B/B-B	F-9 A&B	Cab	PFM	Tensh		10	59	39			fp., A & B powered
NYC	B-B/B-B	F-9 A&B	Cab	PFM	Tensh	131/32	100	59	30			fp., A pwd. B dummy
SRR	B-B/B-B	F-9 A&B	Cab	PFM	Tensh	131/32	10	59	30			fp., A pwd. B dummy
D&RGW	B-B/B-B	F-9 A&B	Cab	PFM	Tensh	131/32	10	59	30			fp., A pwd. B dummy
UP	B-B/B-B	F-9 A&B	Cab	PFM	Tensh	131/32	13	59	30			fp., A pwd. B dummy
WP	B-B/B-B	F-9 A&B	Cab	PFM	Tensh	131/32	20	59	30			fp., A pwd. B dummy
AT&SF	B-B/B-B	F-9 A&B	Cab	PFM	Tensh	131/32	20	59	30			See Note #1810
WP	B-B/B-B	F-9 A&B	Cab	PFM	Tensh	131/32	10	60	30			fp., A pwd. B dummy
D&RGW	B-B/B-B	F-9 A&B	Cab	PFM	Tensh	131/32	52	60	30			fp., A pwd. B dummy
CMStP&P	B-B/B-B	F-9 A&B	Cab	PFM	Tensh	131/32	10	60	30			See Note #1809
B&O	B-B/B-B	F-9 A&B	Cab	PFM	Tensh	131/32	30	60	30			fp., A pwd. B dummy
CB&Q	B-B/B-B	F-9 A&B	Cab	PFM	Tensh	131/32	30	60	30			fp., A pwd. B dummy
AT&SF	B-B/B-B	F-9 A&B	Cab	PFM	Tensh	131/32	40	60	30			See Note#1811
PRR	B-B/B-B	F-9 A&B	Cab	PFM	Tensh	131/32	50	60	30			See Note #1816
SP	B-B/B-B	F-9 A&B	Cab	PFM	Tensh	131/32	110	60	30			fp., A pwd. B dummy
C&O	B-B/B-B	F-9 A&B	Cab	PFM	Tensh	131/32	30	60	30			fp., A pwd. B dummy
GN	B-B/B-B	F-9 A&B	Cab	PFM	Tensh	131/32	150	60	30			fp., A pwd. B dummy
C&NW	B-B/B-B	F-9 A&B	Cab	PFM	Tensh	131/32	40	60	30			fp., A pwd. B dummy
	B-B/B-B	F-9 A&B	Cab	PFM	Tensh		20	60	25	85	75	See Note #696, Kit
CMStP&P	B-B/B-B	F-9 A&B	Cab	PFM	Tensh	131/32	10	60	30			See Note #1808
SRR	B-B/B-B	F-9 A&B	Cab	PFM	Tensh	131/32	50	60	30			fp., A pwd. B dummy
NYC	B-B/B-B	F-9 A&B	Cab	PFM	Tensh	131/32	80	60	30			fp., A pwd. B dummy
UP	B-B/B-B	F-9 A&B	Cab	PFM	Tensh	131/32	12	60	30			fp., A pwd. B dummy
AT&SF	B-B/B-B	F-9 A&B	Cab	PFM	Tensh	131/32	20	60	30			See Note#1810

GM Electro-Motive Division (cont'd)

Road	AAR Code	Class & Phase	Type	Importer	Builder	Cat #	Quan.	Yrs.	List Price	Mint	Avg.	Remarks
B&O	B-B/B-B	F-9 A&B	Cab	PFM	Tensh	131/32	50	61	30			fp., A pwd. B dummy
UP	B-B/B-B	F-9 A&B	Cab	PFM	Tensh	131/32	25	61	30			fp., A pwd. B dummy
C&NW	B-B/B-B	F-9 A&B	Cab	PFM	Tensh	131/32	20	61	30			fp., A pwd. B dummy
CB&Q	B-B/B-B	F-9 A&B	Cab	PFM	Tensh	131/32	20	61	30			fp., A pwd. B dummy
D&RGW	B-B/B-B	F-9 A&B	Cab	PFM	Tensh	131/32	40	61	30			fp., A pwd. B dummy
AT&SF	B-B/B-B	F-9 A&B	Cab	PFM	Tensh	131/32	60	61	30			See Note #1811
NYC	B-B/B-B	F-9 A&B	Cab	PFM	Tensh	131/32	70	61	30			fp., A pwd. B dummy
WP	B-B/B-B	F-9 A&B	Cab	PFM	Tensh	131/32	20	61	30			fp., A pwd. B dummy
SRR	B-B/B-B	F-9 A&B	Cab	PFM	Tensh	131/32	20	61	30			fp., A pwd. B dummy
C&O	B-B/B-B	F-9 A&B	Cab	PFM	Tensh	131/32	20	61	30			fp., A pwd. B dummy
SP	B-B/B-B	F-9 A&B	Cab	PFM	Tensh	131/32	70	61	30			fp., A pwd. B dummy
GN	B-B/B-B	F-9 A&B	Cab	PFM	Tensh	131/32	143	61	30			fp., A pwd. B dummy
PRR	B-B/B-B	F-9 A&B	Cab	PFM	Tensh	131/32	35	61	30			See Note #1816
	B-B/B-B	F-9 A&B	Cab	PFM	Tensh		20	61	26	85	75	See Note #696, Kit
NYC	B-B/B-B	F-9 A&B	Cab	PFM	Tensh	131/32	70	62	30			fp., A pwd. B dummy
D&RGW	B-B/B-B	F-9 A&B	Cab	PFM	Tensh	131/32	20	62	30			fp., A pwd. B dummy
UP	B-B/B-B	F-9 A&B	Cab	PFM	Tensh	131/32	60	62	30			fp., A pwd. B dummy
GN	B-B/B-B	F-9 A&B	Cab	PFM	Tensh	131/32	150	62	30			fp., A pwd. B dummy
C&NW	B-B/B-B	F-9 A&B	Cab	PFM	Tensh	131/32	40	62	30			fp., A pwd. B dummy
CB&Q	B-B/B-B	F-9 A&B	Cab	PFM	Tensh	131/32	20	62	30			fp., A pwd. B dummy
SP	B-B/B-B	F-9 A&B	Cab	PFM	Tensh	131/32	80	62	30			fp., A pwd. B dummy
AT&SF	B-B/B-B	F-9 A&B	Cab	PFM	Tensh	131/32	80	62	30			See Note #1811
PRR	B-B/B-B	F-9 A&B	Cab	PFM	Tensh	131/32	40	62	30			See Note #1816
	B-B/B-B	F-9 A&B	Cab	PFM	Tensh	131/32	6	62	26			Kit. See Note #696
B&O	B-B/B-B	F-9 A&B	Cab	PFM	Tensh	131/32	30	62	30			fp., A pwd. B dummy
SRR	B-B/B-B	F-9 A&B	Cab	PFM	Tensh	131/32	20	62	30			fp., A pwd. B dummy
NYC	B-B/B-B	F-9 A&B	Cab	PFM	Tensh	131/32	20	63	30			fp., A pwd. B dummy
GN	B-B/B-B	F-9 A&B	Cab	PFM	Tensh	131/32	90	63	30			fp., A pwd. B dummy
CB&Q	B-B/B-B	F-9 A&B	Cab	PFM	Tensh	131/32	30	63	30			fp., A pwd. B dummy
C&O	B-B/B-B	F-9 A&B	Cab	PFM	Tensh	131/32	30	63	30			fp., A pwd. B dummy
AT&SF	B-B/B-B	F-9 A&B	Cab	PFM	Tensh	131/32	20	63	30			See Note #1810
PRR	B-B/B-B	F-9 A&B	Cab	PFM	Tensh	131/32	50	63	30			See Note #1816
SP	B-B/B-B	F-9 A&B	Cab	PFM	Tensh	131/32	80	63	30			fp., A pwd. B dummy
AT&SF	B-B/B-B	F-9 A&B	Cab	PFM	Tensh	131/32	20	63	30			See Note #1811
B&O	B-B/B-B	F-9 A&B	Cab	PFM	Tensh	131/32	20	63	30			fp., A pwd. B dummy
SRR	B-B/B-B	F-9 A&B	Cab	PFM	Tensh	131/32	20	63	30			fp., A pwd. B dummy
D&RGW	B-B/B-B	F-9 A&B	Cab	PFM	Tensh	131/32	10	63	30			fp., A pwd. B dummy
	B-B/B-B	F-9 A&B	Cab	PFM	Tensh		9	63	26	85	75	See Note #696, Kit
UP	B-B/B-B	F-9 A&B	Cab	PFM	Tensh	131/32	10	63	30			fp., A pwd. B dummy
SP	B-B/B-B	F-9 A&B	Cab	PFM	Tensh	131/32	100	64	30			fp., A pwd. B dummy
C&NW	B-B/B-B	F-9 A&B	Cab	PFM	Tensh	131/32	30	64	30			fp., A pwd. B dummy
GN	B-B/B-B	F-9 A&B	Cab	PFM	Tensh	131/32	150	64	30			fp., A pwd. B dummy
B&O	B-B/B-B	F-9 A&B	Cab	PFM	Tensh	131/32	50	64	30			fp., A pwd. B dummy
CB&Q	B-B/B-B	F-9 A&B	Cab	PFM	Tensh	131/32	20	64	30			fp., A pwd. B dummy
AT&SF	B-B/B-B	F-9 A&B	Cab	PFM	Tensh	131/32	105	64	30			fp., A pwd. B dummy
D&RGW	B-B/B-B	F-9 A&B	Cab	PFM	Tensh	131/32	20	64	30			fp., A pwd. B dummy
SRR	B-B/B-B	F-9 A&B	Cab	PFM	Tensh	131/32	50	64	30			fp., A pwd. B dummy
NYC	B-B/B-B	F-9 A&B	Cab	PFM	Tensh	131/32	50	64	30			fp., A pwd. B dummy
UP	B-B/B-B	F-9 A&B	Cab	PFM	Tensh	131/32	60	64	30			fp., A pwd. B dummy
PRR	B-B/B-B	F-9 A&B	Cab	PFM	Tensh	131/32	70	64	30			See Note #1816
C&O	B-B/B-B	F-9 A&B	Cab	PFM	Tensh	131/32	20	64	30			fp., A pwd. B dummy
SP	B-B/B-B	F-9 A&B	Cab	PFM	Tensh	131/32	130	65				fp., A pwd. B dummy
NYC	B-B/B-B	F-9 A&B	Cab	PFM	Tensh	131/32	80	65				fp., A pwd. B dummy
AT&SF	B-B/B-B	F-9 A&B	Cab	PFM	Tensh	131/32	80	65				fp., A pwd. B dummy
C&NW	B-B/B-B	F-9 A&B	Cab	PFM	Tensh	131/32	2	65				fp., A pwd. B dummy
GN	B-B/B-B	F-9 A&B	Cab	PFM	Tensh	131/32	200	65				fp., A pwd. B dummy
PRR	B-B/B-B	F-9 A&B	Cab	PFM	Tensh	131/32	50	65				See Note #1816
B&O	B-B/B-B	F-9 A&B	Cab	PFM	Tensh	131/32	10	65				fp., A pwd. B dummy
CB&Q	B-B/B-B	F-9 A&B	Cab	PFM	Tensh	131/32	20	65				fp., A pwd. B dummy
C&O	B-B/B-B	F-9 A&B	Cab	PFM	Tensh	131/32	10	65				fp., A pwd. B dummy
D&RGW	B-B/B-B	F-9 A&B	Cab	PFM	Tensh	131/32	20	65				fp., A pwd. B dummy
UP	B-B/B-B	F-9 A&B	Cab	PFM	Tensh	131/32	60	65				fp., A pwd. B dummy
AT&SF	B-B/B-B	F-9 A&B	Cab	PFM	Tensh	131/32	75	66				fp., A pwd. B dummy
GN	B-B/B-B	F-9 A&B	Cab	PFM	Tensh	131/32	160	66				fp., A pwd. B dummy

GM Electro-Motive Division (cont'd)

Road	AAR Code	Class & Phase		Type	Importer	Builder	Cat #	Quan.	Yrs.	List Price	Mint	Avg.	Remarks
						Model Production					**Resale**		
D&RGW	B-B/B-B	F-9 A&B		Cab	PFM	Tensh	131/32	40	66				fp., A pwd. B dummy
C&NW	B-B/B-B	F-9 A&B		Cab	PFM	Tensh	131/32	30	66				fp., A pwd. B dummy
CB&Q	B-B/B-B	F-9 A&B		Cab	PFM	Tensh	131/32	40	66				fp., A pwd. B dummy
B&O	B-B/B-B	F-9 A&B		Cab	PFM	Tensh	131/32	80	66				fp., A pwd. B dummy
NYC	B-B/B-B	F-9 A&B		Cab	PFM	Tensh	131/32	60	66				fp., A pwd. B dummy
PRR	B-B/B-B	F-9 A&B		Cab	PFM	Tensh	131/32	120	66				See Note #1816
UP	B-B/B-B	F-9 A&B		Cab	PFM	Tensh	131/32	110	66				fp., A pwd. B dummy
CP	B-B/B-B	F-9 A&B		Cab	PFM	Tensh	131/32	4	66				fp., A pwd. B dummy
SP	B-B/B-B	F-9 A&B		Cab	PFM	Tensh	131/32	80	66				fp., A pwd. B dummy
C&O	B-B/B-B	F-9 A&B		Cab	PFM	Tensh	131/32	10	66				fp., A pwd. B dummy
CN	B-B/B-B	F-9 A&B		Cab	PFM	Tensh	131/32	4	66				fp., A pwd. B dummy
SRR	B-B/B-B	F-9 A&B		Cab	PFM	Tensh	131/32	50	66				fp., A pwd. B dummy
AT&SF	B-B/B-B	F-9 A&B		Cab	PFM	Tensh	131/32	75	66				fp., A pwd. B dummy
GN	B-B/B-B	F-9 A&B		Cab	PFM	Tensh	131/32	68	67	38			fp., A pwd. B dummy
C&NW	B-B/B-B	F-9 A&B		Cab	PFM	Tensh	131/32	20	67	38			fp., A pwd. B dummy
GN	B-B/B-B	F-9 A&B		Cab	PFM	Tensh	131/32	210	68	50			See Note #1817
CP	B-B/B-B	F-9 A&B		Cab	PFM	Tensh	131/32	3	69	50			fp., A pwd. B dummy
CN	B-B/B-B	F-9 A&B		Cab	PFM	Tensh	131/32	3	69	50			fp., A pwd. B dummy
NH	B-B	FL-9		Cab	CustB	KMT	DE-117	150		350			
NH	B-B/B-B	FL-9 A-A Set		Cab	CustB	KMT	DE-117S	50		630			one unit powered
CMSTP&P	B-B	FP7 A		Cab	OMI	Ajin	5832	18	90	243	204		
SRR	B-B	FP7 A		Cab	OMI	Ajin	5825	30	90	243	204		#6130-6149
CPR	B-B	FP7 A		Cab	OMI	Ajin	5849	25	90	243	204		
PRR	B-B	FP7 A		Cab	OMI	Ajin	5819	15	90	243	204		#9832-9871
CRIP	B-B	FP7 A		Cab	OMI	Ajin	5811	12	90	243	204		#402-411
C&EI	B-B	FP7 A		Cab	OMI	Ajin	5807	15	90	243	204		#1600-1609
C&O	B-B	FP7 A		Cab	OMI	Ajin	5806	12	90	243	204		#8000-8015
RDG	B-B	FP7 A		Cab	OMI	Ajin	5820	15	90	243	204		#900-905
CMSTP&P	B-B	FP7 A		Cab	OMI	Ajin	5833	18	90	243	204		
SP	B-B	FP7 A		Cab	OMI	Ajin	5826	30	90	243	204		#6446-6461
SOO	B-B	FP7 A		Cab	OMI	Ajin	5824	12	90	243	204		#500A-505A
ACL	B-B	FP7 A		Cab	OMI	Ajin	5801	10	90	243	204		#850-893
UP	B-B	FP7 A		Cab	OMI	Ajin	5829	20	90	243	204		See Note #1740
P&P	B-B	FP7 A		Cab	OMI	Ajin	5810	30	90	243	204		#90A,C-105A,C
RDG	B-B	FP7 A		Cab	OMI	Ajin	5821	15	90	243	204		#906-907
CP	B-B	FP7 A		Cab	OMI	Ajin	5804	60	90	243	204		#4066-4075
Amtrak	B-B	FP7 A		Cab	OMI	Ajin	5800	20	90	243	204		#110-115 (Ex. SP)
WP	B-B	FP7 A		Cab	OMI	Ajin	5831	30	90	243	204		See Note#1738
B&O	B-B	FP7 A		Cab	OMI	Ajin	5802	10	90	243	204		#8300-8013 (Mixed)
CRR	B-B	FP7 A		Cab	OMI	Ajin	5812	20	90	243	204		See Note #1739
ONR	B-B	FP7 A		Cab	OMI	Ajin	5818	25	90	243	204		#1500-1521
	B-B	FP7 A	I	Cab	Ortl	Samh	0159	50	82	194			D.B. not attached
CP	B-B	FP7 A		Cab	Ortl	Samh	VH-1 14		83	200			See Note #1927
	B-B	FP7 A	II	Cab	Ortl	Samh	0355		84	200			
	B-B	FP7 A	I	Cab	Ortl	Samh	382		84	200			w/o dynamic brakes
	B-B	FP7 A	I	Cab	Ortl	Samh	0682		86	171			
	B-B	FP7 A	I	Cab	Ortl	Samh	0678		86	171			w/dynamic brakes
	B-B	FP7 A	I	Cab	Ortl	Samh	0677		86	171			w/o dynamic brakes
L&N	B-B	FP7 A	I	Cab	Ortl	Samh	P679		86	207			fp.
C&EI	B-B	FP7 A	I	Cab	Ortl	Samh	P680		86	207			fp.
RDG	B-B	FP7 A	I	Cab	Ortl	Samh	P681		86	207			fp.
	B-B	FP7 A	II	Cab	Ortl	Samh	0682		86	171			
SP	B-B	FP7 A	II	Cab	Ortl	Samh	P684		86	207			fp.
UP	B-B	FP7 A	II	Cab	Ortl	Samh	P685		86	207			fp.
C&O	B-B	FP7 A	II	Cab	Ortl	Samh	P686		86	207			fp.
PRR	B-B	FP7 A	II	Cab	Ortl	Samh	P683		87	214	180		fp., w/antennas
WP	B-B	FP7 A	I	Cab	Ortl	Samh	P718		86	207			fp.
PRR	B-B	FP7 A	II	Cab	Ortl	Samh	0356		84	203			w/antennas
WP	B-B	FP7 A	I	Cab	Ortl	Samh	P954A		89	240			fp. plated
SF,Milw	B-B	FP7/9 A		Cab	Hall	Goto		750	71	55	110	90	
	B-B	FP9 A		Cab	CustB	KMT	DE-104	200	72	70	100	80	See Note #773
CNR	B-B	FP9 A		Cab	OMI	Ajin	5850	60	90	243	204		See Note#1742
CNR	B-B	FP9 A		Cab	OMI	Ajin	5851	45	90	243	204		See Note#1741
VIA	B-B	FP9 A		Cab	OMI	Ajin	5854	50	90	243	204		#6500 Series

GM Electro-Motive Division (cont'd)

Road	AAR Code	Class & Phase	Type	Importer	Builder	Cat #	Quan.	Yrs.	List Price	Mint	Avg.	Remarks
CPR	B-B	FP9 A	Cab	OMI	Ajin	5852	55	90	243	204		#1405-1415
CNW	B-B	FP9 A	Cab	OMI	Ajin	5853	12	90	243	204		#4551A, 4052A, 4053A
CPR	B-B	FP9 A	Cab	Ortl	Samh	VH-2 10		83	200			See Note #1927
CB&Q	A1A-A1A	EA	Cab	Ortl		0082	75	81	215			Shovel Nose
ATSF	A1A-A1A	E/C1 A&B	Cab	Hall	KMT		50	71		250	175	See Note #738
ATSF	A1A-A1A/ A1A-A1A	E1 A&B	Cab	Hall	KMT		450	71	85	175	140	1800 hp.
ATSF	A1A-A1A/ A1A-A1A	E1 A&B	Cab	Hall	KMT			82	286		225	See Note #737
	A1A-A1A/ A1A-A1A	E1 A&B	Cab	Hall	KMT			82	334		275	Powered A&B
	A1A-A1A/ A1A-A1A	E1 A&B	Cab	Hall	KMT			82	272		215	Powered A, Dummy B
ATSF	A1A-A1A/ A1A-A1A	E1 A&B	Cab	OMI	Ajin	6201		92	715	600		See Note #1667
ATSF	A1A-A1A/ A1A-A1A	E1 A&B	Cab	OMI	Ajin	6201.1		92	937	800		fp., See Note #1667
UP	A1A-A1A	E2A	Cab	OMI	Ajin	5348	50	90	336			See Note #1727
UP/C& NW/SP	A1A-A1A	E2A	Cab	OMI	Ajin	5346	20	90	330			
UP/C& NW/SP	A1A-A1A	E2A	Cab	OMI	Ajin	5344	50	90	330			Original "COSF" 1938
SP	A1A-A1A	E2A	Cab	OMI	Ajin	5350	70	90	336			See Note #1728
UP/C& NW/SP	A1A-A1A	E2A	Cab	OMI	Ajin	5346	50	90	330			"COLA" 1941
UP/C& NW/SP	A1A-A1A	E2A	Cab	OMI	Ajin	5344	20	90	330			
UP/C& NW/SP	A1A-A1A	E2B	Cab	OMI	Ajin	5345	75	90	265			Original "COSF" 1938
UP/C& NW/SP	A1A-A1A	E2B	Cab	OMI	Ajin	5347	75	90	265			"COLA" 1941
UP/C& NW/SP	A1A-A1A	E2B	Cab	OMI	Ajin	5345	50	90	265			
UP	A1A-A1A	E2B	Cab	OMI	Ajin	5349	75	90	266			See Note #1729
UP/C& NW/SP	A1A-A1A	E2B	Cab	OMI	Ajin	5347	50	90	365			
UP	A1A-A1A	E2B	Cab	Ortl	KMT	0019	50	80	151	140	120	Powered B-Unit
	A1A-A1A	E2B	Cab	Ortl	KMT	0020	40	80	115			unpowered
	A1A-A1A/ A1A-A1A	E2 A&B	Cab	Ortl	KMT	0018	150	80	333	300	265	See Note #746
UP	A1A-A1A	E3A	Cab	OMI	Ajin	5863	20	90	300			
AT&SF	A1A-A1A	E3A	Cab	OMI	Ajin	5860	25	90	333			Plated
MP	A1A-A1A	E3A	Cab	OMI	Ajin	5862	20	90	300			
UP	A1A-A1A	E3B	Cab	OMI	Ajin	5864	40	90	261			
	A1A-A1A/ A1A-A1A	E3 A&B	Cab	Ortl	Samh	0226	75	84	400			w/round portholes, both units powered
	A1A-A1A	E3/6 A	Cab	Hall	KMT		50	71-74		250	175	See Note #740
	A1A-A1A/ A1A-A1A	E3/6 A&B	Cab	Hall	KMT		850	71-74	85	175	140	See Note #739
	A1A-A1A/ A1A-A1A	E3/6 A&B	Cab	Hall	KMT			82	272		215	Powered A, Dummy B
	A1A-A1A/ A1A-A1A	E3/6 A&B	Cab	Hall	KMT		100	82	286		225	See Note #737
	A1A-A1A/ A1A-A1A	E3/6 A&B	Cab	Hall	KMT			82	334		275	Powered A&B
	A1A-A1A	E5A I	Cab	Ortl	Samh	0260		83	242			See Note #1923
	A1A-A1A	E5A II	Cab	Ortl	Samh	0262		83	246			See Note #1924
CB&Q	A1A-A1A/ A1A-A1A	E5 A&B	Cab	Hall	KMT		500	71	88	175	150	See Note #741
	A1A-A1A	E5B		Ortl		0261		83	210			nickel plated
CMStP&P	A1A-A1A	E6A	Cab	OMI	Ajin	5872	25	90	300			
MP	A1A-A1A	E6A	Cab	OMI	Ajin	5873	20	90	300			
SRR	A1A-A1A	E6A	Cab	OMI	Ajin	5878	20	90	300			Re-run
L&N	A1A-A1A	E6A	Cab	OMI	Ajin	5871	10	90	300			
UP	A1A-A1A	E6A	Cab	OMI	Ajin	5883	50	90	300			
KCS	A1A-A1A	E6A	Cab	OMI	Ajin	5870	10	90	300			
SAL	A1A-A1A	E6A	Cab	OMI	Ajin	5876	15	90	300			
ACL	A1A-A1A	E6A	Cab	OMI	Ajin	5867	15	90	300			
AT&SF	A1A-A1A	E6A	Cab	OMI	Ajin	5865	25	90	333			Plated

GM Electro-Motive Division (cont'd)

Road	AAR Code	Class & Phase		Type	Importer	Builder	Cat #	Quan.	Yrs.	List Price	Mint	Avg.	Remarks
						Model Production					Resale		
B&O	A1A-A1A	E6A		Cab	OMI	Ajin	5869	20	90	300			
UP	A1A-A1A	E6A		Cab	OMI	Ajin	5881	40	90	300			
UP	A1A-A1A	E6A		Cab	OMI	Ajin	5880	40	90	300			
	A1A-A1A	E6A		Cab	Ortl	Samh	0654		86	223			Standard
	A1A-A1A	E6A		Cab	Ortl		0225	50	83	217			
	A1A-A1A	E6A		Cab	Ortl	Samh	0152		82	217			Powered A-Unit
UP	A1A-A1A	E6B			OMI	Ajin	5884	30	90	261			
MP	A1A-A1A	E6B			OMI	Ajin	5868	10	90	261			
CRIP	A1A-A1A	E6B			OMI	Ajin	5866	15	90	333			Plated
ACL	A1A-A1A	E6B			OMI	Ajin	5868	10	90	261			
SRR	A1A-A1A	E6B			OMI	Ajin	5879	10	90	261			
UP	A1A-A1A	E6B			OMI	Ajin	5882	50	90	261			
SRR	A1A-A1A	E6B			OMI	Ajin	5879	15	91				Re-run
UP	A1A-A1A	E6B			OMI	Ajin	5882	25	91				Re-run
AT&SF	A1A-A1A	E6B			Ortl	Samh	0252	75	83	184			See Note #1925
	A1A-A1A	E6B			Ortl	Samh	0655		86	198			Dummy B-Unit
AT&SF	A1A-A1A/ A1A-A1A	E6 A&B		Cab	Ortl	Samh	P653		86	486			fp. and plated
PRR	A1A-A1A	E7A	II	Cab	Ortl	Samh	0738			234	196		w/Antennas
PRR	A1A-A1A	E7A		Cab	Ortl	Samh	0150		82	227		185	Powered
	A1A-A1A	E7A		Cab	Ortl	Samh	0149		82	217		185	w/large numberboards
	A1A-A1A	E7A		Cab	Ortl	Samh	0224	75	83	217			small nmbrbds, screens
PRR	A1A-A1A	E7A		Cab	Ortl	Samh	0400		84	229			w/antennas
	A1A-A1A	E7A		Cab	Ortl	Samh	0399		84	223			large nmbrbds, screens
	A1A-A1A	E7A		Cab	Ortl	Samh	0398		84	223			small nmbrbds, louvers
	A1A-A1A	E7A		Cab	Ortl	Samh	0659		86	223			w/large numberboards
CB&Q	A1A-A1A	E7A		Cab	Ortl	Samh	0658		86	229	192		Plated
	A1A-A1A	E7A	II	Cab	Ortl	Samh	0736		87	223	187		
	A1A-A1A	E7A	I	Cab	Ortl	Samh	01024		89	292			w/small numberboards
	A1A-A1A	E7A	II	Cab	Ortl	Samh	01034		89	292			
	A1A-A1A	E7A	I	Cab	Ortl	Samh	01025		89	292			w/large numberboards
PRR	A1A-A1A	E7A	II	Cab	Ortl	Samh	P1038		89	365			fp.
	A1A-A1A	E7A		Cab	Sunset					126	105		
	A1A-A1A	E7A		Cab	Sunset					126	105		
	A1A-A1A	E7B	II		Ortl	Samh	0737			193	162		
	A1A-A1A	E7B/E6B			Ortl	Samh	0151			184			
	A1A-A1A	E7B/E6B			Ortl	Samh	151U			141			unpowered
	A1A-A1A	E7B			Ortl	Samh	0660		86	192			Standard
	A1A-A1A	E7B	II		Ortl	Samh	01035		89	265			
UP	A1A-A1A	E7B	I		Ortl	Samh	P1033		89	307			fp.
	A1A-A1A	E7B	I		Ortl	Samh	01026		89	265			
UP	A1A-A1A	E7B	I		Ortl	Samh	P1033		90	440			fp.
	A1A-A1A	E7B			Sunset								
	A1A-A1A	E7B			Sunset								
	A1A-A1A	E/76B		Cab	Ortl	Samh	151U		82	142			Dummy B-Unit
	A1A-A1A	E/76B		Cab	Ortl	Samh	151		82	184			Powered B-Unit
SLSF	A1A-A1A	E7 A&A		Cab	Hall		HS0179		88	463	373		See Note #1731
	A1A-A1A	E7 A&A		Cab	Hall		HS0171		88	463	373		See Note #1730
	A1A-A1A/ A1A-A1A	E7 A&A		Cab	NPP	KMT		200	75	160	165	140	See Note #743
	A1A-A1A/ A1A-A1A	E7 A&A		Cab	NPP	KMT		50	75	148	150	125	See Note #742
SP	A1A-A1A/ A1A-A1A	E7 A&B	I	Cab	Ortl	Samh	P1031		89	665			fp.
PRR	A1A-A1A/ A1A-A1A	E7 A&B	I	Cab	Ortl	Samh	P1030		89	672			fp.
NYC	A1A-A1A/ A1A-A1A	E7 A&B	I	Cab	Ortl	Samh	P1029		89	665			fp.
NYC	A1A-A1A/ A1A-A1A	E7 A&B	I	Cab	Ortl	Samh	P1036		89	665			fp.
UP	A1A-A1A/ A1A-A1A	E7 A&B	I	Cab	Ortl	Samh	P1032		89	665			fp.
PRR	A1A-A1A/ A1A-A1A	E7 A&B	II	Cab	Ortl	Samh	P1037		90	960			fp.
UP	A1A-A1A/ A1A-A1A	E7 A&B	I	Cab	Ortl	Samh	P1032		90	950			fp.

GM Electro-Motive Division (cont'd)

Road	AAR Code	Class & Phase	Type	Importer	Builder	Cat #	Quan.	Yrs.	List Price	Mint	Avg.	Remarks
	A1A-A1A	E8A	Cab	Bal	KMT			68	50	105	80	See Note #744
CPR	A1A-A1A	E8A	Cab	OMI	Ajin	6010	15	89	293	246		#1800-1802
Amtrak	A1A-A1A	E8A	Cab	OMI	Ajin	6001	15	89	293	246		See Note #1734
N&W	A1A-A1A	E8A	Cab	OMI	Ajin	6034	8	89	293	246		#3806, 3808
C&NW	A1A-A1A	E8A	Cab	OMI	Ajin	6015	10	89	293	246		#5023-5031
RI	A1A-A1A	E8A	Cab	OMI	Ajin	6037	8	89	293	246		#644-655
MP/T&P	A1A-A1A	E8A	Cab	OMI	Ajin	6032	8	89	293	246		#2010-2017
UP	A1A-A1A	E8A	Cab	OMI	Ajin	6044	25	89	293	246		#945-962
KCS	A1A-A1A	E8A	Cab	OMI	Ajin	6027	8	89	293	246		#26-29
Erie	A1A-A1A	E8A	Cab	OMI	Ajin	6019	15	89	293	246		#820-833
NYC	A1A-A1A	E8A	Cab	OMI	Ajin	6033	20	89	293	246		#4064-4095
IC	A1A-A1A	E8A	Cab	OMI	Ajin	6024	8	89	293	246		#4018-4033
WAB	A1A-A1A	E8A	Cab	OMI	Ajin	6047	8	89	293	246		#1003-1005
CB&Q	A1A-A1A	E8A	Cab	OMI	Ajin	6013	15	89	293	246		#9938-9948
	A1A-A1A	E8A	Cab	OMI	Ajin	6021	15	89	293	246		
ACI	A1A-A1A	E8A	Cab	OMI	Ajin	6003	10	89	293	246		#544-546
SRR	A1A-A1A	E8A	Cab	OMI	Ajin	6042	30	89				#2923-2929
CRR	A1A-A1A	E8A	Cab	OMI	Ajin	6017	15	89	293	246		#4022 (ex. E-L #833)
E-L	A1A-A1A	E8A	Cab	OMI	Ajin	6020	25	89	293	246		#809-833
Amtrak	A1A-A1A	E8A	Cab	OMI	Ajin	6000	10	89	293	246		See Note #1733
MKT	A1A-A1A	E8A	Cab	OMI	Ajin	6031	8	89	293	246		#131-135
SP	A1A-A1A	E8A	Cab	OMI	Ajin	6041	15	89	293	246		#6046-6054
SLSF	A1A-A1A	E8A	Cab	OMI	Ajin	6040	8	89	293	246		#2010-2013
CofG/Sou	A1A-A1A	E8A	Cab	OMI	Ajin	6014	8	89	293	246		#811-812
RF&P	A1A-A1A	E8A	Cab	OMI	Ajin	6036	12	89	293	246		#1006-1015
GM&O	A1A-A1A	E8A	Cab	OMI	Ajin	6023	10	89	293	246		#100A
VIA	A1A-A1A	E8A	Cab	OMI	Ajin	6048	8	89	293	246		#1802
C&O	A1A-A1A	E8A	Cab	OMI	Ajin	6011	15	89	293	246		#4000-4026
PRR	A1A-A1A	E8A	Cab	OMI	Ajin	6035	35	89	309	259		See Note #1732
L&N	A1A-A1A	E8A	Cab	OMI	Ajin	6028	8	89	293	246		#794-797
SAL	A1A-A1A	E8A	Cab	OMI	Ajin	6038	8	89	293	246		#3049-3054
B&M	A1A-A1A	E8A	Cab	OMI	Ajin	6009	25	89	293	246		#3821
DL&W	A1A-A1A	E8A	Cab	OMI	Ajin	6018	15	89	293	246		#810-820
FEC	A1A-A1A	E8A	Cab	OMI	Ajin	6022	8	89	293	246		#1031-1035
CB&Q	A1A-A1A	E8A	Cab	Ortl	Samh	0402		82	240			Nickel Plated
	A1A-A1A	E8A	Cab	Ortl	Samh	0401		84	236			Horizontal Grilles
	A1A-A1A	E8A	Cab	Ortl	Samh	0227	75	84	236			
C&O	A1A-A1A	E8A	Cab	Ortl	Samh	0228	75	84	236			
PRR	A1A-A1A	E8A	Cab	Ortl	Samh	0229	75	84	241			
UP	A1A-A1A	E8A	Cab	Ortl	Samh	0230	90	83	235			
	A1A-A1A	E8A	Cab	Ortl	Samh	0231	130	83	197			w/dynamic brakes
SRR	A1A-A1A	E8A	Cab	Ortl	Samh	0233	50	84	236			
NYC	A1A-A1A	E8A	Cab	Ortl	Samh	0232	100	84	236			
	A1A-A1A	E8A	Cab	Ortl	Samh	0585	75	86	223	225		See Note #1921
PRR	A1A-A1A	E8A	Cab	Ortl	Samh	0586	125	86	233			w/antennas
	A1A-A1A	E8A	Cab	Ortl	Samh	0656		86	223	225		w/horizontal grilles
	A1A-A1A	E8A	Cab	Ortl	Samh	01039		89	293			
NYC	A1A-A1A	E8A	Cab	Ortl	Samh	P1044		89	364			fp.
PRR	A1A-A1A	E8A	Cab	Ortl	Samh	P1045		89	364			fp.
B&O	A1A-A1A	E8Am	Cab	OMI	Ajin	6007	12	89	293	246		#1433-1437
ATSF	A1A-A1A	E8Am	Cab	OMI	Ajin	6005	25	89	326	274		#81
	A1A-A1A	E8B		Bal	KMT			68	20	40	30	See Note #695
	A1A-A1A	E8B		Bal	KMT			68	23	55	45	Dummy B-Unit, fp.
ACI	A1A-A1A	E8B		OMI	Ajin	6004	10	89	261	220		#765-766
IC	A1A-A1A	E8B		OMI	Ajin	6026	8	89	261	220		#4104-4105
Milw	A1A-A1A	E8B		OMI	Ajin	6030	15	89	261	220		#30B
	A1A-A1A	E8B		Ortl	Samh	01040		89	264			
ATSF	A1A-A1A	E8Bm		OMI	Ajin	6006	21	89	294	247		#80a, 4A
B&O	A1A-A1A	E8Bm		OMI	Ajin	6008	9	89	261	220		#2414-2419
AT&SF	A1A-A1A/ A1A-A1A	E8A&B	Cab	Ortl	Samh	P1041		90	950			fp. and plated
UP	A1A-A1A	E8/9A	Cab	OMI	Ajin	6016	40	89	364	306		See Note #1735
Amtrak	A1A-A1A	E9A	Cab	OMI	Ajin	6002	15	89	293	246		See Note #1736
C&EI/MP	A1A-A1A	E9A	Cab	OMI	Ajin	6012	8	89	293	246		#1102
IC	A1A-A1A	E9A	Cab	OMI	Ajin	6025	8	89	293	246		#4034-4043

GM Electro-Motive Division (cont'd)

The E8 is probably the most recognizable passenger diesel ever built. After experimenting with a variety of front end designs that varied from bulbous (the E–2) to "shovel nosed" (the E3–6), EMD finally settled on the same general body style as used on the "F" units. Introduced in 1949, over 450 E8s were built by 1953. They were followed by the E9, which was almost indistinguishable from the E8. These were the last of the truly handsome passenger diesels. Overland's model depicts the E8 as it appeared with the early Amtrak paint scheme. Overland has produced a wide variety of E8s with details specific to the particular railroad.

Road	AAR Code	Class & Phase	Type	Importer	Builder	Cat #	Quan.	Yrs.	List Price	Mint	Avg.	Remarks
Milw	A1A-A1A	E9A	Cab	OMI	Ajin	6029	15	89	293	246		#30-35
SAL	A1A-A1A	E9A	Cab	OMI	Ajin	6039	8	89	293	246		#3060
BN	A1A-A1A	E9A	Cab	OMI	Ajin	6049	25	89	307	258		#9910-9925
UP	A1A-A1A	E9A	Cab	OMI	Ajin	6045	30	89	293	246		#951
UP	A1A-A1A	E9A	Cab	OMI	Ajin	6043	40	89	293	246		#931-942
Milw	A1A-A1A	E9A	Cab	Ortl	Samh	0589	75	86	223	225		with dynamic brakes
SP	A1A-A1A	E9A	Cab	Ortl	Samh	0587	50	86	223	225		with dynamic brakes
UP	A1A-A1A	E9A	Cab	Ortl	Samh	0588		86	223	225		with dynamic brakes
CB&Q	A1A-A1A	E9A	Cab	Ortl	Samh	0657		86	229	225		Plated
SP	A1A-A1A	E9A	Cab	Ortl	Samh	P1046		89				fp.
	A1A-A1A	E9A	Cab	Trains		105	1000	67	55	100	80	See Note #745
UP	A1A-A1A	E9B		OMI	Ajin	6046	60	89	261	220		#950B-974B
	A1A-A1A	E9B		Ortl	Samh	0590		86	193	200		See Note #1922
Milw	A1A-A1A	E9B		Ortl	Samh	0592		86	193	200		with dynamic brakes
UP	A1A-A1A	E9B		Ortl	Samh	0591		86	193	200		with dynamic brakes
	A1A-A1A	E9B		Trains		106	1000	67	50	90	75	See Note #745
	A1A-A1A	E9B		WMC	Nakamura			75	70	50	40	See Note #695
	A1A-A1A	E9B		WMC	Nakamura			75	70	50	40	See Note #695
	A1A-A1A/ A1A-A1A	E9 A&B	Cab	Trains				68-69	115	175	150	Powered A&B, fp.
	A1A-A1A/ A1A-A1A	E9 A&B	Cab	Trains				68-69	115	175	150	Powered A&B, fp.
	A1A-A1A/ A1A-A1A	E9 A&B	Cab	WMC	Nakamura			75	140	160	140	See Note #696, fp.
	A1A-A1A/ A1A-A1A	E9 A&B	Cab	WMC	Nakamura			75	140	160	140	See Note #696, fp.

Fairbanks–Morse & Company

| Road | AAR Code | Class & Phase | Type | Model Production | | | | | List Price | Resale | | Remarks |
				Importer	Builder	Cat #	Quan.	Yrs.		Mint	Avg.	
	B-B	CFA-16-4	Cab	Red	KMT		650	71-72	59	250	220	See Note #782
	B-B	CFB-16-4	Cab	Red	KMT		500	71-72	36	170	140	Dummy B, "C-Liner"
	B-B	H-10-44	Sw	Hall	Goto		600	74	75	115	90	See Note #778
D&RGW	B-B	H-10-44	Sw	OMI	Ajin	5024	45	88	221	186		#120-123
	B-B	H-10-44	Sw	OMI	Ajin	5025	35	88	221	186		See Note #1538

When Fairbanks–Morse entered the diesel locomotive business in 1944, their first engines were built by General Electric at their Erie, Pa., plant. F–M provided the prime mover and GE the car body and the electrical components. No model number was assigned—they were simply known as "Erie-Builts." Eight roads purchased a total of 111 units—65 freight and 46 passenger. All units were rated at 2,000 hp and rode on six-wheel, A–1–A trucks. These handsome units, with their long rounded nose and clean side detailing, made a striking appearance regardless of what roads' paint scheme they were wearing. Red Ball imported this passenger version in 1971.

The H–24–66 "Trainmaster" road switcher was generally regarded as F–M's "Classic." With 2,400 hp, and quality electrical and mechanical components, these engines established F–M as a serious producer of heavy road switchers. A total of 127 units were built between 1953 and 1966. Ten roads in the U.S. and Canada purchased trainmasters, with the Virginian being the largest purchaser with 25 units (#50–74). F–M ceased production of diesel locomotives for domestic sales in 1958. Red Ball imported this KMT-built model in 1968.

Fairbanks–Morse & Company (cont'd)

Road	AAR Code	Class & Phase	Type	Importer	Builder	Cat #	Quan.	Yrs.	List Price	Mint	Avg.	Remarks
UP	B-B	H-10-44	Sw	OMI	Ajin	5022	50	88	221	186		#1301-1304
	B-B	H-10-44	Sw	OMI	Ajin	5023	90	88	221	186		See Note #1537
	B-B	H-12-44	Sw	Hall	KMT		600	71	50	115	90	1200 hp.
	B-B	H-12-44	Sw	OMI	Ajin	5026	65	88	221	186		See Note #1536
Milw	B-B	H-12-44	Sw	OMI	Ajin	5089	20	88	221			#730-739
Milw	B-B	H-12-44	Sw	OMI	Ajin	5027	50	88	221	186		See Note #1535
Sev	B-B	H-12-44	Sw	OMI	Ajin	5028	40	88	221	186		See Note #1534
B&O	B-B	H-12-44	Sw	OMI	Ajin	5030	20	88	221	186		B&O/Wabash
SP	B-B	H-12-44	Sw	OMI	Ajin	5029	50	88	221	186		See Note #1533
B&O	B-B	H-12-44	Sw	OMI	Ajin	5030.1	5	89	333	280		Original Paint Scheme
	B-B	H-12-44	Sw	PSM				70-71	55	125	90	1200 hp.
	B-B	H-15-44		Key			100	81				
	B-B	H-16-44	RSw	Key	Samh		125	81	210	195	170	See Note #782
	B-B	H-16-44	RSw	Key	Samh		75	81	210		170	Square Window Cab
	B-B	H-16-44	RSw	Red	KMT		1000	69-72	43	140	110	See Note #779
NYC	B-B	H-20-44	RSw	Alco				81	195	175	155	
N&W	B-B	H-20-44	RSw	Alco								
PRR	B-B	H-20-44	RSw	Alco				81	195	175	155	
UP	B-B	H-20-44	RSw	Alco				81	195	175	155	
AC&Y	B-B	H-20-44	RSw	Alco								
	B-A1A	CPA-24-5	Cab	Red	KMT		250	71	60	135	110	2400 hp., Passenger
	B-A1A	CPB-24-5	Cab	Red	KMT		250	71	38	140	115	2400 hp., Passenger
PRR	A1A-A1A	A&B Erie Built	Cab	Alco				82	410		330	w/Antennas
UP	A1A-A1A	A&B Erie Built	Cab	Alco				82	410		330	
	A1A-A1A	A-Unit Erie Built	Cab	Alco				82	185		150	Early Style
	A1A-A1A	A-Unit Erie Built	Cab	Alco				82	225		180	Late Style
	A1A-A1A	A-Unit Erie Built	Cab	Alco				82	225		180	Early Style
	A1A-A1A	A-Unit Erie Built	Cab	Alco				82	185		150	Late Style
	A1A-A1A	A-Unit Erie Built	Cab	Red	KMT		1000	71	62	145	120	See Note #786
	A1A-A1A	B-Unit Erie Built	Cab	Red	KMT		500	71	36	150	125	See Note #786
	C-C	H-24-66 I	RSw	Alco								"Trainmaster"
	C-C	H-24-66 II	RSw	Alco								"Trainmaster"
	C-C	H-24-66	RSw	Red	KMT		1500	68	48	125	110	See Note #780

General Electric Co. (GE)

Road	AAR Code	Class & Phase	Type	Importer	Builder	Cat #	Quan.	Yrs.	List Price	Mint	Avg.	Remarks
	B-B	44-Ton	Sw	CustB	DaiYng	DE-123		82	215		160	See Note #793
	B-B	44-Ton	Sw	WMC				74	105			See Note #797
	B-B	44-Ton	Sw	WMC				71	60	125	90	See Note #796
	B-B	44-Ton Phase Ib	Sw	W&R	Samh		42	86				Style B
	B-B	44-Ton Phase Ib	Sw	W&R	Samh		47	86				Style A
	B-B	44-Ton Phase Ic	Sw	W&R	Samh		75	84				
	B-B	44-Ton Phase Ic	Sw	W&R	Samh		97	86				
	B-B	44-Ton Phase IIa	Sw	W&R	Samh		40	84				
	B-B	44-Ton Phase IIb	Sw	W&R	Samh		35	84				
	B-B	44-Ton Phase III	Sw	W&R	Samh		50	84				
	B-B	44-Ton Phase IV	Sw	W&R	Samh		59	86				
	B-B	44-Ton Phase IV	Sw	W&R	Samh		100	84				
	B-B	45-Ton	Sw	NWSL								See Note #794
	B-B	45-Ton	Sw	OMI	MSM	5032	100	87	221	186		Type I
	B-B	45-Ton	Sw	OMI	MSM	5033	100	87	221	186		Type II
	B-B	45-Ton	Sw	OMI	MSM	5034	100	87	221	186		Type III
	B-B	70-Ton	Sw	Hall	Goto		700	71	50	100	80	
	B-B	B23-7	RSw	OMI	Ajin	5363	1000	90				Drive System Only
BN	B-B	B32-8	RSw	OMI	Ajin	1947	50	87	279	318		#5497-5491
SSW	B-B	Dash 8-39B	RSw	OMI	Ajin	5158	30	89	334	281		#8040-8075
ATSF	B-B	Dash 8-40B	RSw	OMI	Ajin	5152	75	88	284	239		#7410-7429
NYS&W	B-B	Dash 8-40B	RSw	OMI	Ajin	5189	30	89	334	281		#
CR	B-B	Dash 8-40B	RSw	OMI	Ajin	5141	40	88	285	239		re-run
Demo	B-B	Dash 8-40B		OMI	Ajin	5190	100	89	349	293		#809 Wide Cab
CR	B-B	Dash 8-40B	RSw	OMI	Ajin	5141	75	89	334	281		re-run

General Electric Co. (cont'd)

General Electric produced 323 44-ton switchers between 1940 and 1955. The basic car body, with two hoods and centered cab, was also used on locomotives of 65- and 80-ton ratings. Although small, the 44-tonner was a four-motor design which developed all of 380 hp. Westside Models imported this model in 1971 and 1974.

Road	AAR Code	Class & Phase	Type	Importer	Builder	Cat #	Quan.	Yrs.	List Price	Mint	Avg.	Remarks
CR	B-B	Dash 8-40B	RSw	OMI	Ajin	5141	50	88	285	239		#5060-5089
CR	B-B	Dash 8-40B	RSw	OMI	Ajin	5141.1	15	89	441	370		#5060-5089, fp.
UP	B-B	Dash 8-40BW	RSw	OMI	Ajin	5400	210	91				
LMX	B-B	Dash 8-B39	RSw	OMI	Ajin	5132	105	88	285	239		#8500-8599
LMX	B-B	Dash 8-B39	RSw	OMI	Ajin	5132	40	88	285	239		re-run
SP	B-B	Dash 8-B39	RSw	OMI	Ajin	5134	40	88	284	239		re-run
LMX	B-B	Dash 8-B39	RSw	OMI	Ajin	5132	40	89	334	281		re-run
SP	B-B	Dash 8-B39	RSw	OMI	Ajin	5134	125	88	285	239		#8000-8039
SP	B-B	Dash 8-B39	RSw	OMI	Ajin	5134	65	89	334	281		re-run
	B-B	DES-3	Sw	CustB	KMT	DE-100	750	72	67	105	85	See Note #795
SP	B-B	DF-700	Sw	NWSL				75	85	150	100	See Note #1532
SP	B-B	DF-700	Sw	NWSL				74	75	150	100	SP #1, 50-Ton
NYC	B-B	U23B	RSw	Ortl	Samh	104		81	172		145	See Note #790
C&O	B-B	U23B	RSw	Ortl	Samh	P103A		82	194			fp., See Note #788
	B-B	U23B	RSw	Ortl	Samh	103		81	172		140	See Note #788
L&N	B-B	U23B	RSw	Ortl	Samh	P103B		82	194			fp., See Note #788
Sou	B-B	U23B	RSw	Ortl	Samh	P102		81	194			fp.
L&N	B-B	U23B	RSw	Ortl	Samh	P104		82	194			fp., See Note #790
	B-B	U23B	RSw	Ortl	Samh	102		81	172		145	See Note #789
AT&SF	B-B	U23B	RSw	Ortl	Samh	P103		82	194			fp., See Note #788
	B-B	U25B	RSw	Alco	KMT	D-113		69	43	130	110	2500 hp.
	B-B	U25B	RSw	Alco	KMT	D-113		70	45	140	120	2500 hp.
NYC	B-B	U25B	RSw	Ortl	Samh	P505		85	250			fp., LoH
	B-B	U25B	RSw	Ortl	Samh	O503		85	209			LoH, intermediate
	B-B	U25B	RSw	Ortl	Samh	0071	150	81	170		140	HiH
GN	B-B	U25B	RSw	Ortl	Samh	P504		85	250			fp., LoH
UP	B-B	U25B	RSw	Ortl	Samh	P495		85	250			fp., HiH
	B-B	U25B	RSw	Ortl	Samh	0073		81	170		140	See Note #805
SP	B-B	U25B	RSw	Ortl	Samh	P498	25	85	250			fp., LoH

General Electric Co. (cont'd)

General Electric produced a variety of small industrial diesel switchers with similar characteristics but different design approaches. The 45-ton side-rod locomotive, although only slightly heavier than the more common 44-tonner, used two motors and a chain, and rod drive. In addition, the shape of the cab and the hoods is somewhat different. It would be interesting to know why GE took two such different design approaches on such similar locomotives. Overland Models imported this distinctive little locomotive in 1987.

Road	AAR Code	Class & Phase		Type	Importer	Builder	Cat #	Quan.	Yrs.	List Price	Mint	Avg.	Remarks
	B-B	U25B		RSw	Ortl	Samh	O507		85	207			
AT&SF	B-B	U25B		RSw	Ortl	Samh	P595			250			fp., LoH
UP	B-B	U25B		RSw	Ortl	Samh	P502		85	250			fp., LoH
	B-B	U25B		RSw	Ortl	Samh	O497		85	207			LoH
NH	B-B	U25B		RSw	Ortl	Samh	P506		85	250			LoH
GN	B-B	U25B		RSw	Ortl	Samh	P510			250			LoH
CB&Q	B-B	U25B		RSw	Ortl	Samh	P511			250			LoH
	B-B	U25B	II	RSw	Ortl	Samh	0509		85	207			LoH
C&O	B-B	U25B		RSw	Ortl	Samh	P500	25	85	250			
PRR	B-B	U25B		RSw	Ortl	Samh	P501		85	261			fp., LoH, with antenna
	B-B	U25B		RSw	Ortl	Samh	0072	200	81	170		140	See Note #804
	B-B	U25B		RSw	PSM				69	40	125	100	
	B-B	U25B		RSw	Trains		114	1000	69	40	120	100	2500 hp.
GN	B-B	U28B		RSw	Ortl	Samh	P510		85	250			fp.
	B-B	U28B		RSw	Ortl	Samh	O509		85	207			Phase II
	B-B	U30B		RSw	Ortl				81	172		140	See Note #787
	B-B	U30B		RSw	Ortl	Samh			82	172		140	See Note #792
C&O	B-B	U30B		RSw	Ortl	Samh	P107		82	194			fp. Chessie, LoH
	B-B	U30B		RSw	Ortl	Samh	0107	125	81	172		140	See Note #787
BN	B-B	U30B		RSw	Ortl	Samh	B107		82	194			LoH, fp,
N&W	B-B	U30B		RSw	Ortl		0106	75	81	172		140	HiH
	B-B	U36B		RSw	Alco				82				
Erie	B-B	UM12 A&B		Cab	OMI	Ajin	1814	25	82	367	367		See Note #1514
UP	B-B	UM20 A&B		Cab	OMI	Ajin	1813	175	82	367	367		See Note #1513
UP	B-B+B-B	U50		RSw	Alco				82	260		210	See Note #800
SP	B-B+B-B	U50		RSw	Alco				82	260		210	See Note #802

General Electric Co. (cont'd)

The General Electric industrial switchers from 44 ton to 65 ton were center cab designs. With the advent of the 70-ton model, GE went to the more common end-cab configuration. Boxy in appearance, the locos share the same basic hood and cab design as the 44-tonners. The GE 70-tonner used an engine rated at 500–660 hp. In all, 233 units were built. New England Rail Service imported this Samhongsa-built model.

| Road | AAR Code | Class & Phase | Type | Model Production | | | | | List Price | Resale | | Remarks |
				Importer	Builder	Cat #	Quan.	Yrs.		Mint	Avg.	
SP	B-B+B-B	U50	RSw	LMB				71	75	250	200	See Note #801
	B-B+B-B	U50	RSw	Trains			1500	67	65	250	200	See Note #800
UP	B-B+B-B	U50C	Cab	OMI	Ajin	5095	95	87	386	324		#5012-5039
UP	B-B+B-B	U50C	Cab	OMI	Ajin	5094	45	87	386	324		#5005-5011
UP	B-B+B-B	U50C	Cab	OMI	Ajin	5093	35	87	386	324		#5001
UP	B-B+B-B	U50C	Cab	OMI	Ajin	5092	75	87	386	324		#5000
	C-C	C30-7	RSw	OMI	Ajin	1969	45	87	250	210		See Note #1528
	C-C	C30-7	RSw	OMI	Ajin	1968	55	87	250	210		See Note #1526
	C-C	C30-7	RSw	OMI	Ajin	1806	200	81	250	175		4-Window
	C-C	C30-7	RSw	OMI	Ajin	1970	63	87	250	210		See Note #1527
ATSF	C-C	C30-7	RSw	OMI	Ajin	1971	45	87	250	210		See Note #1530
AT&SF	C-C	C30-7	RSw	OMI	Ajin	1824.1	10	81	293	293		
UP	C-C	C30-7	RSw	OMI	Ajin	1829.1	10	81	293	293		See Note #1529
SCL,L&N	C-C	C30-7	RSw	OMI	Ajin	1825.1	5	81	293	293		2-Window, fp.
	C-C	C30-7	RSw	OMI	Ajin	5361	1000	90				Drive System Only
ATSF	C-C	C30-7	RSw	OMI	Ajin	1826.1	10	81	293	293		4-Window
SCL,L&N	C-C	C30-7	RSw	OMI	Ajin	1805	200	81	250	175		2-Window
UP	C-C	C30-7	RSw	OMI	Ajin	1823.1	10	81	293	293		2-Window, fp.
CR	C-C	C30-7A	RSw	OMI	Ajin	1972	65	87	250	210		#6550-6599
CR	C-C	C32-8	RSw	OMI	Ajin	1940	35	87	334	281		#6610-6619, re-run
	C-C	C32-8	RSw	OMI	Ajin	5362	1000	90				Drive System Only
CR	C-C	C32-8	RSw	OMI	Ajin	1940	50	89	334	281		re-run
CR	C-C	C32-8	RSw	OMI	Ajin	1940	120	86	279	195		#6610-6619
MP/UP	C-C	C36-7	RSw	OMI	Ajin	1974	90	89	278	234		#9000-9059
CR	C-C	C36-7	RSw	OMI	Ajin	1975	55	87	250	210		CR #6620-6644, GE
MP/UP	C-C	C36-7	RSw	OMI	Ajin	1974	95	89	334	281		re-run
MP/UP	C-C	C36-7	RSw	OMI	Ajin	1974	75	88	279	234		re-run
N&W	C-C	C36-7	RSw	OMI	Ajin	1973	25	87	250	210		#8500-8542, N de M
CR	C-C	C39-8	RSw	OMI	Ajin	1946	100	87	279	279		#6620-6644
CR	C-C	C39-8	RSw	OMI	Ajin	1946.1	N/A	87	441	355		#6620-6644, fp.
NS	C-C	C39-8	RSw	OMI	Ajin	1945	75	87	279	318		#8614-8638

General Electric Co. (cont'd)

In December of 1987, General Electric delivered the first of the Dash 8–40C, 4,000 hp diesel locomotives to the Union Pacific. These 75 locomotives proved to be the harbinger of GE's ascendency to dominance in the production of new locomotives for domestic use. The GE four-cycle diesel engine combined with microprocessor controls offer good reliable operation and reduced air pollution. UP's first order of these locomotives used the same cab as used on the C39–8 engines. Pictured above is the Overland Models' version with the "crew cab." This fine model incorporates individually sprung axles with independent gearboxes.

The locomotive that started the UP's love affair with the turbine was the #50. Originally numbered GE demonstrator #101, she made test runs on the Nickel Plate and the Pennsy. For 21 months, the #50 was tested on the UP main lines from Los Angeles to Denver to Kansas City. The locomotives that followed maintained the massive front-end treatment, but no more were ever built double ended. Soho imported this Kumata-built model in 1977.

| Road | AAR Code | Class & Phase | Type | Model Production | | | | | List Price | Resale | | Remarks |
				Importer	Builder	Cat #	Quan.	Yrs.		Mint	Avg.	
NS	C-C	C39-8	RSw	OMI	Ajin	5133	15	89	334	281		re-run
CR	C-C	C39-8	RSw	OMI	Ajin	1946	50	89	334	281		re-run
CR	C-C	C39-8	RSw	OMI	Ajin	1940.1	N/A	89	441	370		#6610-6619, fp.
NS	C-C	C39-8	RSw	OMI	Ajin	5133	75	88	285	239		#8664-8688
UP	C-C	Dash 8-40C	RSw	OMI	Ajin	5135	250	88	285	239		#9100-9174
CSX	C-C	Dash 8-40C	RSw	OMI	Ajin	5157.1	15	89	441	370		#7400-7439, fp.
UP	C-C	Dash 8-40C	RSw	OMI	Ajin	5153	75	88	284	239		#9175-9249
C&NW	C-C	Dash 8-40C	RSw	OMI	Ajin	5156	50	89	334	281		#8501-8530
UP	C-C	Dash 8-40C	RSw	OMI	Ajin	5153	125	89	334	281		re-run

General Electric Co. (cont'd)

Road	AAR Code	Class & Phase	Type	Model Production					List Price	Resale		Remarks
				Importer	Builder	Cat #	Quan.	Yrs.		Mint	Avg.	
UP	C-C	Dash 8-40C	RSw	OMI	Ajin	5135	100	88	285	239		re-run
CSX	C-C	Dash 8-40C	RSw	OMI	Ajin	5157	45	89	334	281		#7400-7439
UP	C-C	Dash 8-40C	RSw	OMI	Ajin	5154	250	90	334	281		Wide Cab #6300 series
CR	C-C	Dash 8-40C	RSw	OMI	Ajin	5188	30	89	334	281		#6025-6049
BCR	C-C	Dash 8-40CM	RSw	OMI	Ajin	5354	75	91	523			
CNR	C-C	Dash 8-40CM	RSw	OMI	Ajin	5353	100	91	523			Wide Cab
UP	C-C	Dash 8-40CW	RSw	OMI	Ajin	5154	100	91	TBA			Wide Cab
UP	C-C	Dash 8-40CW	RSw	OMI	Ajin	5154	225	90	334			#9350-9405

UP's first turbine looked more like an EMD E–2 than the turbines that followed. The long passenger-style car body covered a turbine engine that burned fuel oil. Built in 1939, they were plagued with a variety of mechanical problems and were scrapped in 1942. Alco Models imported this unusual model from KMT. UP did not give up on turbines. They needed high-horsepower units, and in 1948, the diesels available weren't up to the task. In 1948, UP received their first turbine, #50, an Alco–GE-built double ender.

By 1952, UP decided to order ten 4,500-hp turbines from GE. These units proved to be just what UP wanted and they ordered 15 more—the "Verandas." UP's final order of gas-turbines was for units 1–30, the three-unit turbines. These engines were the largest locomotives in the world, generating 7,000 hp and a continuous tractive effort of 146,000 lbs. With upgrades, these engines generated 10,000 hp. Overland produced ten different versions of the 1–30 class three-unit turbine in 1990. These are the finest turbine models ever commercially produced.

General Electric Co. (cont'd)

Road	AAR Code	Class & Phase	Type	Importer	Builder	Cat #	Quan.	Yrs.	List Price	Resale Mint	Resale Avg.	Remarks
C&O	C-C	GP35	RSw	OMI	Ajin	5099	30	88	250	210		#3300-3312
D&H	C-C	GP35	RSw	OMI	Ajin	5098	25	88	250	210		#701-706
AT&SF	C-C	SF30C	RSw	OMI	Ajin	1896	40	87	279	279		Rebuild #9500 Series
AT&SF	C-C	U23C		OMI	Ajin	5031	30	87	250	210		
CB&Q	C-C	U25C	RSw	OMI	Ajin	1955	32	87	278	234		CB&Q, NP
PRR	C-C	U25C	RSw	OMI	Ajin	1954	50	87	278	234		#6500-6519
NP	C-C	U25C	RSw	OMI	Ajin	1953	27	87	278	234		ACL, LS&I, NP
CB&Q	C-C	U28C	RSw	OMI	Ajin	1956	18	87	278	234		CB&Q #562-577, BN
	C-C	U28C	RSw	OMI	Ajin	1958	80	87	250	210		See Note #1518
NP	C-C	U28C	RSw	OMI	Ajin	1957	21	87	278	234		NP #2800-2811, BN
ATSF	C-C	U28CG	RSw	OMI	Ajin	1959	53	87	250	210		See Note #1517
BN	C-C	U30C	RSw	OMI	Ajin	1962	10	87	250	210		Late Version
RDG	C-C	U30C	Cab	OMI	Ajin	5097	25	88	250	210		#6300-6304
	C-C	U30C	RSw	OMI	Ajin	1961	90	87	250	210		See Note #1516
	C-C	U30C	RSw	OMI	Ajin	1960	56	87	250	210		See Note #1515
ATSF	C-C	U30CG	RSw	Hall	Kmt		600	73-74	88	130	100	See Note #798
	C-C	U33	RSw	Alco	Kmt	D-137		70	56	150	120	See Note #799
SP	C-C	U33C	RSw	OMI	Ajin	1965	40	87	250	210		#8585-8796
	C-C	U33C	RSw	OMI	Ajin	1963	115	87	250	210		ATSF,BN,D&H,Guilford
SRR	C-C	U33C	RSw	OMI	Ajin	1964	25	87	250	210		#3805-3814
E-L	C-C	U34CH	RSw	OMI	Ajin	1966	35	87	250	210		E-L #3351-3382, NJT
ATSF	C-C	U36C	RSw	OMI	Ajin	1967	35	87	250	210		#8736-8799
	C-C	U50C	RSw	Alco				82	275		225	
UP	C-C	U50C	RSw	Alco	Kmt	D-134		74	146	220	200	See Note #803
UP	D-D	U50D	Cab	OMI	Ajin	5441	100	92	675			#34-53
UP	D-D	U50D	Cab	OMI	Ajin	5440	80	92	675			#31-33
SP	D-D	U50D	Cab	OMI	Ajin	5442	50	92	675			#9950-9952

General Electric Co. Turbines

Road	AAR Code	Class & Phase	Type	Importer	Builder	Cat #	Quan.	Yrs.	List Price	Resale Mint	Resale Avg.	Remarks
UP	2-C+C-2	#1-2 Gas Turbine	Cab	Alco	KMY					700		5000hp.
UP	2-D+D-2	#80 Gas Turbine	Cab	CustB				78	765	700	630	See Note #808
UP	B-B+B-B	50 Gas Turbine	Cab	MBA			60	60	60	225	175	See Note #810
UP	B-B+B-B	50 Gas Turbine	Cab	Soho	KMT	1005	400	77	198	200	175	See Note #809
UP	B-B+B-B	51 Gas Turbine	Cab	Bal				69	90	300	250	4500 hp., fp.
UP	B-B+B-B	51 Gas Turbine	Cab	Soho	KMT	1002	250	77	250	250	200	See Note #812
UP	B-B+B-B	51 Gas Turbine	Cab	Soho	KMT	1001	250	77	250	250	200	See Note #811
UP	B-B+B-B	61 Gas Turbine	Cab	Bal				71	90	350	300	See Note #813
UP	B-B+B-B	61 Gas Turbine	Cab	Soho	KMT	1003	250	77	268	275	250	See Note #814
UP	B-B+B-B	61 Gas Turbine	Cab	Soho	KMT	1004	250	77	268	275	250	See Note #815
UP	B-B+B-B	63 Gas Turbine	Cab	Trains			500	68	100	280	250	See Note #813
UP	B-B+B-B	Standard Turbine	Cab	OMI	Ajin	5501	20	91	633			w/tender
UP	B-B+B-B	Turbine	Cab	OMI	Ajin	1876	70	85	550	550		See Note #1520
UP	B-B+B-B	Turbine	Cab	OMI	Ajin	1873	30	84	532	532		See Note #1523
UP	B-B+B-B	Turbine	Cab	OMI	Ajin	1875	30	85	465	465		See Note #1522
UP	B-B+B-B	Turbine	Cab	OMI	Ajin	1849	100	84	800	900		#1 8500 hp. 3-Unit
UP	B-B+B-B	Turbine	Cab	OMI	Ajin	1850	50	84	800	900		#18 8500 hp. 3-Unit
UP	B-B+B-B	Turbine	Cab	OMI	Ajin	1851	100	84	800	900		#30 8500 hp. 3-Unit
UP	B-B+B-B	Turbine	Cab	OMI	Ajin	1871	70	84	532	532		See Note #1524
UP	B-B+B-B	Turbine	Cab	OMI	Ajin	1872	100	84	532	532		See Note #1521
UP	B-B+B-B	Turbine	Cab	OMI	Ajin	1874	100	85	522	522		See Note #1525
UP	B-B+B-B	Turbine	Cab	OMI	Ajin	5195		91	657			See Note #1477
UP	B-B+B-B	Turbine (Coal)	Cab	OMI	Ajin	5096	100	89	1830	1537		See Note #1519
UP	B-B+B-B	Veranda Turbine	Cab	OMI	Ajin	5858	50	91	TBA			w/tender
UP	B-B+B-B	Veranda Turbine	Cab	OMI	Ajin	5856	40	91	TBA			w/tender
UP	B-B+B-B	Veranda Turbine	Cab	OMI	Ajin	5855	20	91	TBA			w/tender
UP	B-B+B-B	Veranda Turbine	Cab	OMI	Ajin	5857	30	91	TBA			w/tender
UP	C-C+C-C	1-30 Gas Turbine	Cab	Alco	KMT	D-150	280	78	778	850	775	See Note #816
UP	C-C+C-C	Gas-Turbine	Cab	OMI	Ajin	5018	35	87	919	772		#18, 2-motors
UP	C-C+C-C	Gas-Turbine	Cab	OMI	Ajin	5020	35	87	919	772		#30, 2-motors

General Electric Co. Turbines (cont'd)

The turbines that immediately followed the #50 were the—51–60 class, with an additional order for 15 more—61–75. Several significant design changes were made, and the double-ended design was abandoned. The second series also had catwalks on the side and were labeled "Verandas." These massive units, with eight traction motors and 45,000 hp served the UP so well that they continued to develop even larger turbines. Soho imported this Kumata-built model in 1977.

Road	AAR Code	Class & Phase	Type	Importer	Builder	Cat #	Quan.	Yrs.	List Price	Mint	Avg.	Remarks
UP	C-C+C-C	Gas-Turbine	Cab	OMI	Ajin	5017	60	87	919	772		#6, 2-motors
UP	C-C+C-C	Gas-Turbine	Cab	OMI	Ajin	5019	35	87	919	772		#28, 2-motors
UP	C-C+C-C	Gas-Turbine #50	Cab	OMI	Ajin	5195	100	91	657			Double-Ended
UP	C-C/C-C	3-Unit Gas Turbine	Cab	OMI	Ajin	5761	20	90	1200	965		w/flat silencer
UP	C-C/C-C	3-Unit Gas Turbine	Cab	OMI	Ajin	5768	20	90	1200	965		w/flat silencer #2
UP	C-C/C-C	3-Unit Gas Turbine	Cab	OMI	Ajin	5763	20	90	1200	965		w/flat silencer
UP	C-C/C-C	3-Unit Gas Turbine	Cab	OMI	Ajin	5767	20	90	1200	965		w/raised silencer
UP	C-C/C-C	3-Unit Gas Turbine	Cab	OMI	Ajin	5764	20	90	1200	965		w/raised silencer
UP	C-C/C-C	3-Unit Gas Turbine	Cab	OMI	Ajin	5766	20	90	1200	965		w/raised silencer
UP	C-C/C-C	3-Unit Gas Turbine	Cab	OMI	Ajin	5762	20	90	1200	965		w/raised silencer
UP	C-C/C-C	3-Unit Gas Turbine	Cab	OMI	Ajin	5769	20	90	1200	965		w/raised silencer #25
UP	C-C/C-C	3-Unit Gas Turbine	Cab	OMI	Ajin	5760	40	90	1557	1250		See Note #1531
UP	C-C/C-C	3-Unit Gas Turbine	Cab	OMI	Ajin	5765	20	90	1200	965		w/2 raised silencers #6

Krauss–Maffei

Road	AAR Code	Class & Phase	Type	Importer	Builder	Cat #	Quan.	Yrs.	List Price	Mint	Avg.	Remarks
						Model Production				Resale		
SP	C-C	Krauss-Maffei	Cab	OMI	Ajin	1812	50	83	254	275		Camera Car #8799
SP	C-C	Krauss-Maffei	Cab	OMI	Ajin	1811	150	83	254	275		See Note #1512
SP	C-C	Krauss-Maffei	Cab	OMI	Ajin	1910	90	85	284	325		See Note #1511
D&RGW	C-C	Krauss-Maffei	Cab	OMI	Ajin	1909	110	85	284	325		See Note #1510
SP	C-C	Krauss-Maffei	Cab	OMI	Ajin	1910.1	N/A	87	370	390		fp., See Note#1511

The first Krauss-Maffei diesel hydraulics were imported in 1961 for the D&RGW and SP. In all, 21 units were imported and operated in experimental service to test the merits of using a hydraulic transmission under U.S. mainline railroading conditions. These experiments were not successful and all units were retired. One unit of the 1963 order became a camera car for photographing the SP right-of-way—an ignominious end to a noble experiment. Ajin Precision produced these attractive locos for Overland models in 1985.

Montreal Locomotive Works

Road	AAR Code	Class & Phase	Type	Importer	Builder	Cat #	Quan.	Yrs.	List Price	Mint	Avg.	Remarks
						Model Production				Resale		
BCR	B-B	M420B	RSw	OMI	Ajin	5276		92	370			#681-688 Cabless
BCR	B-B	DL718B		OMI	Ajin	5261	35	90	349	293		See Note #1509
CN	B-B	FPA4	RSw	OMI	Ajin	1810	50	82	192	192	150	
P&W	B-B	M420	RSw	OMI	Ajin	5279		92	370			See Note #1508
CNR	B-B	M420W	RSw	OMI	Ajin	5278		92	370			See Note #1507
BCR	B-B	M420W	RSw	OMI	Ajin	5275		92	370			#640-647 Wide Cab
CNR	B-B	M420W	RSw	OMI	Ajin	5277		92	370			See Note #1506
CNR	B-B	RS10 (DL-700)	RSw	OMI	Ajin	5264	25	90	349	293		See Note #1505
ON	B-B	RS10 (DL-700)	RSw	OMI	Ajin	5267	15	90	349	293		See Note #1504
CNR	B-B	RS10 (DL-700)	RSw	OMI	Ajin	5263	20	90	349	293		See Note #1503
CNR	B-B	RS10 (DL-700)	RSw	OMI	Ajin	5262	30	90	349	293		See Note #1502
CPR	B-B	RS10 (DL-700)	RSw	OMI	Ajin	5265	35	90	349	293		See Note #1501
CPR	B-B	RS10S	RSw	OMI	Ajin	5266	35	90	349	293		See Note #1500
CNR	B-B	RS18 (DL-718)	RSw	OMI	Ajin	5268	30	90	349	293		See Note #1499
CNR	B-B	RS18 (DL-718)	RSw	OMI	Ajin	5271	30	90	349	293		See Note #1498
CNR	B-B	RS18 (DL-718)	RSw	OMI	Ajin	5269	40	90	349	293		See Note #1497
BCR	B-B	RS18 (DL-718)	RSw	OMI	Ajin	5260	35	90	349	293		See Note #1496
CNR	B-B	RS18 (DL-718)	RSw	OMI	Ajin	5270	30	90	349	293		See Note #1495
CPR	B-B	RS18 (DL-718)	RSw	OMI	Ajin	5273	40	90	349	293		See Note #1494
CPR	B-B	RS18R	RSw	OMI	Ajin	5274	55	90	349	293		See Note #1493
CNR	B-B	RSC-18	RSw	OMI	Ajin	5272	75	90	363	305		See Note #1491
CNR	C-C	C630	RSw	OMI	Ajin	5284		90	402			See Note #1490
CNR	C-C	C630	RSw	OMI	Ajin	5283		90	402			See Note #1489
BCR	C-C	C630	RSw	OMI	Ajin	5280		90	402			See Note #1488
CPR	C-C	C630	RSw	OMI	Ajin	5285		90	402			See Note #1487

Montreal Locomotive Works (cont'd)

Road	AAR Code	Class & Phase	Type	Importer	Builder	Cat #	Quan.	Yrs.	List Price	Mint	Avg.	Remarks
BCR	C-C	M630	RSw	OMI	Ajin	5282		90	402			#723-730 Wide Cab
CPR	C-C	M630	RSw	OMI	Ajin	5286		90	402			See Note #1486
CPR	C-C	M630	RSw	OMI	Ajin	5287		90	402			See Note #1485
BCR	C-C	M630	RSw	OMI	Ajin	5281		90	402			See Note #1484
CPR	C-C	M636	RSw	OMI	Ajin	5291		90	402			See Note #1483
CPR	C-C	M636	RSw	OMI	Ajin	5288		90	402			See Note #1482
CPR	C-C	M636	RSw	OMI	Ajin	5290		90	402			See Note #1481
CPR	C-C	M636	RSw	OMI	Ajin	5289		90	402			See Note #1480
CPR	C-C	M640	RSw	OMI	Ajin	5292		90	402			See Note #1479

Miscellaneous Diesels

Road	AAR Code	Class & Phase	Type	Importer	Builder	Cat #	Quan.	Yrs.	List Price	Mint	Avg.	Remarks
CRIP	B-B	Whitcomb 44DE18	Sw	OMI	Ajin	1979	35	87	214	270		
Sev	B-B	Whitcomb 44DE18	Sw	OMI	Ajin	1978	25	87	214			re-run
AT&SF	B-B	Whitcomb 44DE18	Sw	OMI	Ajin	1980	50	87	214	TBA		See Note #1479
Sev	B-B	Whitcomb 44DE18	Sw	OMI	Ajin	1981	35	87	214			
Sev	B-B	Whitcomb 44DE22	Sw	OMI	Ajin	1976	15	87	214			
Sev	B-B	Whitcomb 44DE22	Sw	OMI	Ajin	1977	40	87	214	300		
CRIP		AB-6		Sunset				87	444			
ATSF		Super Chief		Ortl								See Note #834
		Box Cab		Intl				62	23			See Note #819
DRGW	A-A	Cat Ind Switcher	Sw	WMC				76	80			See Note #820
	A-A	Cat Ind Switcher	Sw	WMC		MO-10		71	30			See Note #1478
	B-2	EMD Unit Train		AHM			150	78	650	40		Powered Kit
RI	B-B	EMD Unit Train		NPP				75	352	25		Unpowered Kit
B&M		Flying Yankee		CustB	Orion	DE-168	65	85	665	110	100	fp.
	A-A	Ind Switcher		Gem	Olympia	PH-101	750	60	12	175	150	

The Whitcomb Locomotive Works was a subsidiary of Baldwin but produced locomotives under their own name. Whitcomb is best known for their production of ''critters''—small industrial locomotives. The 44DE18 was a 44-ton locomotive built between 1941 and 1945. The engine was identical in appearance to the Davenport locomotive. Powered by a pair of Caterpillar D–17000s producing 360 hp, the engine used the same power plant as used by GE in their 44-tonners. Overland Models produced these six variations with the various arrangements of handrails and appliances as used by the seven railroads that bought them.

Miscellaneous Diesels (cont'd)

Road	AAR Code	Class & Phase	Type	Model Production					List Price	Resale		Remarks
				Importer	Builder	Cat #	Quan.	Yrs.		Mint	Avg.	
	A-A	Ind Switcher		KenK				60	8	70	55	See Note #822
CNR	C-C	SD50F	RSw	OMI	Ajin	5049	70	89	334	120	110	#592 Combine
CNR	C-C	SD50F	RSw	OMI	Ajin	5049	250	88	321	140	125	
ATSF	B-B	Super Chief Box Cabs		Hall	KMT		250	82	540	40	35	See Note #1476
SP	B-B	TE70-4S		OMI	Ajin	1860.1	20	83	271	35	30	Kit
SP	B-B	TE70-4S		OMI	Ajin	1848	50	83	214	130	115	#350
SP	B-B	TE70-4S		OMI	Ajin	1859.1	20	83	271	45	35	w/Dynamic Brake, fp.
SP	B-B	TE70-4S		OMI	Ajin	1838	125	83	214	140	120	
	B-B	Whitcomb Center Cab		Hall	Samh					60	45	See Note #1475
ATSF	B-B	#1 & #10		Hall	KMT					140	120	See Note #1474
ATSF	B-B	#2611		Hall	KMT					110	95	Final rebuild of #10.
D&RGW	B	#50	Sw	Sunset				87	283			
	B-B	Midwest 65 Ton	Sw	Ortl		0390		84	164			
GN	B-B	100 Ton Oil Electric		Ortl		0593			200			
Erie	B-B	100 Ton Oil Electric		Ortl		0594			200			

PART VI

GASOLINE AND GAS-ELECTRIC RAILCARS

Gasoline & Gas–Electric Railcars

Road	AAR Code	Class & Phase	Type	Importer	Builder	Cat #	Quan.	Yrs.	List Price	Mint	Avg.	Remarks
	1-A	1907 Thomas Flyer		Kemt	Kemt			56-60	15	175	150	
	1-A	1907 Thomas Flyer		Kemt	Kemt	910		81	33			
	1-A	1907 Thomas Flyer		Kemt	Kemt			56-60	9	145	125	
	1-A	1907 Thomas Flyer		Kemt	Kemt	900	500	81	50	60	45	
	1-A	1907 Thomas Flyer		Prec	Prec		900	87	49	130	100	
	1-A	1907 Thomas Flyer		Prec	Prec	910		87	33	275	20	
Ma & Pa		Brill Gas-Electric	Gem	Tsubomi	KT-101		200	67				
Ma & Pa		Brill Gas-Electric	Gem	Tsubomi	KT-101		300	72	70	180	155	
Ma & Pa		Brill Gas-Electric	Gem	Tsubomi	KT-101		450	74	105			
Ma & Pa		Brill Gas-Electric	Gem	Tsubomi	KT-101		230	67	45	130	110	
		Brill Gas-Electric	Syd	Goto	350	569	69	44	145	130		
NP		B-14 Gas-Electric	W&R	Samh			80	84				
UP		M-66,67 Gas-Electric	W&R	Samh			120	84				
		Brill Gas-Electric	Syd	Tsub	350	300	62	33	110	95		
		Brill Gas-Electric	Syd	Tsub	350	215	65	38	70	55		
		Brill Gas-Electric	Syd	Tsub	350	402	61	33	150	130		
	A-A	Cat Ind Switcher	WMC		MO-10	520	67-69	20	135	105	See Note #1473	
UP		DC-3 Rail Detector Car	OMI	Ajin	1303	200	81	300	275	200		
UP		DC-3 Rail Detector Car	OMI	Ajin	1303.1	N/A	87	392	50	40		
DRGW		D&RGW Prospector M-1	CustB	KSM	DE-146	25		325	135	100	Plated; two car M-1.	
DRGW		D&RGW Prospector M-2	CustB	KSM	DE-147	25		325	135	100	Plated; two car M-2	
Soo		EMC Gas-Electric	Ortl		0095	200	81	150	140	110	1924 version	
ATSF		EMC Gas-Elect M160	Hall	KyongD			76	99	400	350		
ATSF		EMC Gas-Elect M180	Bal			70-71	70	150	125			
ATSF		EMC Gas-Elect M190	Hall	Rok-Am		350	75	100	80	60		
		EMC Gas-Electric	Ortl			200	81	160	160	130	See Note #1472	
CNR		E-60 Gas-Electric	Van	Samh			82	290	150	135		
NH		Gas-Electric	CustB	KSM	DE-156	150		232		225		
PRR		Gas-Electric	CustB	KSM	DE-143	200	82	248	200	165		
NP		Gas-Electric	Hall	Samh			81	150	180	150		
		Gas-Electric Combine	KenK				60	33	300			
PRR		Gas-Electric #4663	CustB	FM	DE-167			315	200	165		
GN		GE Gas-Electric	Ortl	Jonan	0027	100	80	275	275		See Note #1471	
GN		GE Gas-Electric	Ortl	Jonan	0028	200	80	325	325		See Note #1471, fp.	
CB&Q		Gas-Electric	Ortl		0184	250	82	200			#9814-9818	
		Hall-Scott Car	MEW				66	36	80	65		

Nobody ever said that gas–electrics had to be beautiful. New Haven owned ten of these Brill-built monsters in 1925, and they were used for branch-line passenger service until the motor bus inevitably put them on the scrap track. With the motor hanging cantilevered out over the truck, one can only wonder if the engine ever just fell off. To make matters worse, New Haven often mounted a snowplow on this end. Custom Brass imported this unusual model from KSM in 1983.

Gasoline & Gas–Electric Railcars (cont'd)

The Erie, like most other major railroads, began to use doodle-bugs as the automobile made inroads into the passenger traffic. St. Louis Car Co. order #1523 was delivered to the Erie Railroad in 1930. Basically a standard design of the manufacturer, the Stillwell roof gave these cars a distinctive appearance. Overland Models imported this unique model in 1986.

As gas-electrics evolved into what was to become the modern day diesel, there was a period when the railroads began to develop the streamlined train. The diesel motorcar was integrated into a short streamlined passenger train. One of the first was the UP M–10000, the "City of Salina." Built in 1935 with a modest 600-hp. Winton diesel engine, the train spawned a total of six streamliners. With the advent of the EMD E–2 the streamliner era was over. Overland Models produced both of these excellent models.

| Road | AAR Code | Class & Phase | Type | Model Production | | | | | List Price | Resale | | Remarks |
				Importer	Builder	Cat #	Quan.	Yrs.		Mint	Avg.	
		Mack ACX Rail Bus		MEW				63	30	45	40	
		Mack Rail Bus		NPP			500	72	29	130	115	
		Mack Rail Truck		FZoo				87	60		125	
		Mack Rail Truck		FZoo				87	60	300		
		Mack-Brill Rail Bus		Red	KMT		550	67	20	393		

Gasoline & Gas–Electric Railcars (cont'd)

One of the most unusual gas railcars that can still be seen on virtually every major Class I railroad is the Sperry. A highly specialized device, this car is operated by the Sperry Rail Service to analyze the condition of the rails. Faulty welds, cracks, and other defects in the rail can be detected by the car's sensitive electronic equipment as it slowly cruises down the track. Hallmark's model depicts car #136. The prototype was modified from NYC gas-electric M–11 by Sperry in 1948.

Road	AAR Code	Class & Phase	Type	Model Production					List Price	Resale		Remarks
				Importer	Builder	Cat #	Quan.	Yrs.		Mint	Avg.	
		Mack-Brill Rail Bus		Red	KMT		900	65-67	18		170	
UP		McKeen M24 & Trailer		OMI	Ajin	1819	10	82	393	393		fp., Wine Color
UP		McKeen M24 & Trailer		OMI	Ajin	1847	N/A	82	393	393		
UP		McKeen M24 & Trailer		OMI	Ajin	1820	10	82	393		140	fp., Yellow & Leaf Brown
UP		McKeen M24 & Trailer		OMI	Ajin	1807	230	82	303		440	
		McKeen Rail Car		KenK				71	40	150		
		McKeen Rail Car		KenK				56	30	150		
		McKeen Rail Car		LMB				68-70	40	150		
		McKeen Rail Car		LMB				78	75	150		
Erie		Motor Car		OMI	MSM	1944	200	86	315	350		
DRGW		Motor Car		PFM				87	142	170		
		Rail Auto Car		F&G		20RU		67	28	150		
DRGW		Rail Car		PFM	SKI			80	119	150		poor runner
		Rail Car 3-Truck		Bal				69	50	214		
		Rail Car 3-Truck		Bal				67-68	46	180		
NYC		Rail Car & Trailer		CustB	Orion	DE-152	100	84	465	180		See Note #1470
		Rail Truck w/trailer		Red	KMT		1000	63	6	180		
		Sperry Rail Car		Hall	Mizuno		700	69	53-54	180		
		Sperry Rail Car		Hall	DongJ		250	81	150	180		
		Tiny Rail Bus		Red	KMT		1000	63	6	180		
UP		M-10000 Unit train		OMI	Ajin							
UP		EMD Unit Train		NPP			150	78	450	500	450	See Note #1469
CB&Q		Twin Cities Zephyr		Ortl		01009		89	850			
CB&Q		Nebraska Zephyr		Ortl		01010		89	607			
UP		Forty-Niner		Ortl						450	400	

Gas–Electric Cars – Narrow Gauge

Road	AAR Code	Class & Phase	Type	Model Production					List Price	Resale		Remarks
				Importer	Builder	Cat #	Quan.	Yrs.		Mint	Avg.	
RGS		Pierce Arrow Goose		Lam			500	81	218	330		See Note #1468
RGS		Rail Car 2-Truck		Bal				67-68	43	271		
RGS		Rail Car 2-Truck		Lam			500	80	180	214		See Note #1466
RGS		Rail Car 3-Truck		Bal				67-68	46	271		
RGS		Wayne Bus Goose		Lam	Sugiyama		500	79	150	358		See Note #1467
RGS		Work Goose		Lam			300	82	180	238		See Note #1465
EBT		M-1 Gas-Electric		Hallmark				83	150	225		

Gas–Electric Cars – Narrow Gauge (cont'd)

There is a saying that if you've seen one narrow gauge gas–electric, you've seen 'em all. Its true, the East Broad Top had the only one. The M–1 makes occasional trips for tourists on the historic East Broad Top Railroad in Orbisonia, Pa. Hallmark imported this excellent replica from Samhongsa in 1983. Unpainted and beautifully factory-painted models were available. Early models of gas-electrics typically did not run well. The EBT M–1 with a can motor and excellent drive mechanism showed that new technology successfully solved an old problem.

Road	AAR Code	Class & Phase	Type	Importer	Builder	Cat #	Quan.	Yrs.	List Price	Mint	Avg.	Remarks
EBT		M-1 Gas-Electric		Hallmark				84	178	270		fp.
EBT		M-1 Gas-Electric		Hallmark				84	150	225		

Budd Manufacturing Co.

Road	AAR Code	Class & Phase	Type	Importer	Builder	Cat #	Quan.	Yrs.	List Price	Mint	Avg.	Remarks
NH	1A-A1	4-Car Set		Hall	Samh	HS0198		85				See Note #1464
CB&Q	B-2	Budd Unit Train		NPP			750	72	130	425		See Note #833
CB&Q	B-2	Budd Unit Train		PacT				67	90	400		See Note #832
NH	1A-A1	Coach		Hall	Samh	HS0199		85				See Note #1463
AT&SF	1A-A1	DC-191 & 192		Hall	Samh	HS0034		85	354	375		See Note #1462
	1A-A1	RDC-1		Hbtn				57-60				See Note #830
	1A-A1	RDC-1 Coach		CustB	KMT	DE-111	615	73	70	135	100	90-passenger coach
	1A-A1	RDC-1 Combine		CustB	KMT	DE-112	300	74	70	145	130	See Note #1461
	1A-A1	RDC-1 Modernized		Hall	Samh	HS0036		85	185	185	160	See Note #1460
CP	1A-A1	RDC-1 Modernized		Hall	Samh	HS0211		85	185	185	160	Corrugated Front
C&O	1A-A1	RDC-1 Original		Hall	Samh	HS0202		85	185	185	160	
	1A-A1	RDC-1 Original		Hall	Samh	HS0035		85	185		160	See Note #1459
SP	1A-A1	RDC-1 Original		Hall	Samh	HS0212		85	185	185	160	SP version
SP,NWP	1A-A1	RDC-1 Original		Hall	Samh	HS0176		85	185	185	160	See Note #1458
C&NW	1A-A1	RDC-1 Original		Hall	Samh	HS0203		85	185	185	160	
B&O	1A-A1	RDC-2 Modernized		Hall	Samh	HS0177		85	185	185	160	Baggage/Diner/Chair
	1A-A1	RDC-2 Modernized		Hall	Samh	HS0038		85	185	185	160	See Note #1454
WP,NP	1A-A1	RDC-2 Original		Hall	Samh	HS0194		85	185	185	160	Zepphyrette version
C&O	1A-A1	RDC-2 Original		Hall	Samh	HS0200		85	185	185	160	
C&NW	1A-A1	RDC-2 Original		Hall	Samh	HS0193		85	185	185	160	
	1A-A1	RDC-2 Original		Hall	Samh	HS0037		85	185	185	160	See Note #1453
MKT	1A-A1	RDC-3 Modernized		Hall	Samh	HS0196		85	185	185	160	

Budd Manufacturing Co. (cont'd)

The Budd-built Rail Diesel Cars (RDC's) were intended to be the salvation of the railroad commuter business. Although it was not to be, they did delay the inevitable for quite some time. In August of 1949, Budd introduced their first RDC and sold over 400 units before they ended production of the RDC in 1962. In 1985, Hallmark Models imported an extensive variety of the RDC models. Each of the basic types—RDC-1 through RDC-4—and the unpowered trailer RDC-9 were produced. These Samhongsa models are the state-of-the-art for RDC fans. The modernized RDC-4 is shown.

| Road | AAR Code | Class & Phase | Type | Model Production | | | | | List Price | Resale | | Remarks |
				Importer	Builder	Cat #	Quan.	Yrs.		Mint	Avg.	
C&O	1A-A1	RDC-3 Modernized		Hall	Samh	HS0201		85	185	185	160	
	1A-A1	RDC-3 Modernized		Hall	Samh	HS0040		85	185	185	160	See Note #1452
CRIP	1A-A1	RDC-3 Original		Hall	Samh	HS0195		85	185	185	160	
	1A-A1	RDC-3 Original		Hall	Samh	HS0039		85	185	185	160	See Note #1451
	1A-A1	RDC-3 RPO		CustB	KMT	DE-113	300	74	70	175	150	See Note #1450
	1A-A1	RDC-4 Modernized		Hall	Samh	HS0197		85	185	185	160	See Note #1448
	1A-A1	RDC-4 Modernized		Hall	Samh	HS0178		85	185	185	160	See Note #1442
	1A-A1	RDC-4 Original		Hall	Samh	HS0041		85	185	185	160	See Note #1401
	1A-A1	RDC-9		Hall	Samh	HS0042		85	185	185	160	B&M,CN,VIA

PART VII

ELECTRICS

Heavy Electric Locomotives

Road	AAR Code	Class & Type	Importer	Builder	Cat #	Quan.	Yrs.	List Price	Mint	Avg.	Remarks
Amtrak	B-B	Electric Loco	GHB	Orion		100	84				
Amtrak	B-B	Electric Loco	GHB	Orion		40	84				See Note #1194
Amtrak	B-B	AEM-7	GHB				87	465			See Note #1178
BA&P	B-B	Box Cab	KenK		3601		57	28	125		
BA&P	B-B	Box Cab	KenK		2056K		57		100		Kit
BA&P	B-B	Box Cab	Syd	Tsub	165	360	57	28	125		4-Wheel Drive
BA&P	B-B	Box Cab	Syd	Tsub	165-A	120	63	30	140		8-Wheel Drive
BA&P	B-B	Box Cab	Syd	Tsub	165	100	58	28	130		4-Wheel Drive
B&M	1-B+B-1		CustB	TAMAC	100	100	85	490			Hoosic Tunnel Electric
CMStP&P	1-B+D+D+B-1	EP-2 Bi-Polar	CustB	KMT	N/A	300	75	N/A			
CMStP&P	1-B+D+D+B-1	EP-2 Bi-Polar	CustB	KMT	300A	N/A	73	216	150		
CMStP&P	1-B+D+D+B-1	EP-2 Bi-Polar	CustB	KMT	300	535	73	190			
CMStP&P	1-B+D+D+B-1	EP-2 Bi-Polar	CustB	KMT	300S	150	83	582			streamlined
CMStP&P	2-B-B	EF-1 A Box Cab	NPP			250	75	150	150		fp., orange & black, 1500 hp.
CMStP&P	2-B-B	EF-1 A Box Cab	NPP	KMT	353	100	85	632			
CMStP&P	2-B-B	Harlowton Switcher	OMI	Ajin	1908	50	85	248	175		#E-57-B
CMStP&P	2-B-B	EF-1 Box Cab	OMI	Ajin	1919	60	86	248			See Note #999
CMStP&P	2-B-B	EP-1A	OMI	Ajin	1916	30	85	296			Streamlined B Unit
CMStP&P	2-B-B	EP-1A Box Cab	OMI	Ajin	1907	50	85	296			#E-22-a Streamlined
CMStP&P	2-B-B	EF-1 Box Cab	OMI	Ajin	1904	100	85	248			#E-25-A
CMStP&P	2-B-B	EF A&B	OMI	Ajin	1942	10	86	493			See Note #998
CMStP&P	2-B-B	EF-2 Box Cab	OMI	Ajin	1905	75	85	248			#E-36-C
CMStP&P	2-B-B	EF-1 A Box Cab	Syd		EF-1	250	63	50	150	125	See Note #997
CMStP&P	2-B-B	EF-1 A Box Cab	Syd			220	64	50	150	125	See Note #997
CMStP&P	2-B-B/B-B	EF-1 A&B Box Cab	NPP	Toho		500	75	213	250	200	fp., See Note #975
CMStP&P	2-B-B/B-B/2-B-B	EF-3 ABA Box Cab	NPP				75	170	150	130	fp., See Note #941

Sixty-five Amtrak AEM-7 locomotives were built by EMD under license from Universal Swedish Electric Co. Ltd. These engines can be seen in regular service between Washington, DC, and New York City. Commonly known as ''Toasters,'' because of their boxy shape and electric power, they regularly reach 125 mph on the Metroliner trains. They have proven to be reliable replacements for the aging GG1s which commanded Amtrak's Northeast corridor for over 50 years. This fine model of the AEM-7 was built by Orion for GHB. The model incorporates working pantographs and fully directional lighting.

Heavy Electric Locomotives (cont'd)

The Virginian owned some of the heaviest electrics ever built. Class EL–2B consisted of four locomotives of two units each. Generating 6,800 hp with a continuous tractive effort of 162,000 lbs., they were excellent at moving heavy coal trains over the stiff grades. They lasted until June of 1962, when the overhead was taken down and electrification ended in favor of diesels. Alco imported these Samhongsa-built monsters in 1980.

Milwaukee Road's "Little Joes" were originally intended for export to the USSR, but cold-war politics cancelled the order. Of the twenty not sent to the USSR, Milwaukee got 12. They were a good solid design, capable of hitting 80mph in passenger service, and also displayed excellent performance in freight service. Overland's beautiful model of the E–79 series locomotive was built by Ajin Precision of Korea in 1986. Overland imported four variations, each with detail differences unique to a particular prototype.

| Road | AAR Code | Class & Type | Model Production | | | | | List Price | Resale | | Remarks |
			Importer	Builder	Cat #	Quan.	Yrs.		Mint	Avg.	
CMStP&P	2-C-1 + 1-C-2	EP-3 Box Cab	CustB	Orion	N/A	10	83				fp.
CMStP&P	2-C-1 + 1-C-2	EP-3 Box Cab	CustB	Orion	N/A	100	81	30	165	140	fp. Passenger Version
CMStP&P	2-D+D-2	EF-4 Little Joe	Alco	KMT	E103M	800	73	125	150	125	
CMStP&P	2-D+D-2	EF-4 Little Joe	NWSL	Toho		1000	72	120	225	175	See Note #848
CMStP&P	2-D+D-2	EF-4 Little Joe	NWSL	Toho		800	73	125	150	125	See Note #848
CMStP&P	2-D+D-2	EF-4 Little Joe	OMI	Ajin	1948	50	86	379			E-21 Passenger
CMStP&P	2-D+D-2	EF-4 Little Joe	OMI	Ajin	1949	50	86	379			E-70
CMStP&P	2-D+D-2	EF-4 Little Joe	OMI	Ajin	1950	40	86	379			E-71

Heavy Electric Locomotives (cont'd)

Road	AAR Code	Class & Type	Importer	Builder	Cat #	Quan.	Yrs.	List Price	Mint	Avg.	Remarks
CMStP&P	2-D+D-2	EF-4 Little Joe	OMI	Ajin	1951	30	86	379			E-79
CMStP&P	B-B	Es-2 Steeple Cab	NPP	KMT		193	80	152			See Note #846
CMStP&P	B-B	Es-2 Steeple Cab	NPP	KMT		100	70				built by GE
CMStP&P	B-B	Es-2 Steeple Cab	OMI	MSM	1894	200	85	214	196		
CMStP&P	B-B	EF-3 Box Cab B	OMI	Ajin	1906	50	85	181	185	170	See Note #893
CMStP&P	B-B	EF Box Cab Booster	Syd		EF-3	144		28	100	80	Dummy booster
CMStP&P	B-B	EF Box Cab Booster	Syd		EF-3	150		28	100	80	Dummy booster
CMStP&P	B-B	EF Box Cab Booster	Syd		EF-2	12		43	150	130	See Note #847
CNS&M	2-C-1+1-C-2	4-Tk Freight Motor	MCW	KMT		150	80	225	200	175	Ex-Oregon Electric #50
CNS&M	2-C-1+1-C-2	4-Tk Freight Motor	MCW	KMT		180	80	225	200	175	Ex-Oregon Electric #51
CNS&M	B-B	Steeple Cab	Soho	KMT	0801	200	75	98	140	125	GE Steeple Cab
CSS&SB	2-D+D-2	Little Joe	Alco	KMT	E-103S	76	73	125	150	125	5500 hp., 4-axles powered
CSS&SB	2-D+D-2	EF-4	OMI	Ajin	1952	30	86	379			#800
CSS&SB	B-B	80-Ton Steeple Cab	Intl							50	See Note #846
CSS&SB	B-B	80-Ton Steeple Cab	KenK	KMT	2056		64-65		100	85	
CSS&SB	B-B	80-Ton Steeple Cab	KenK	KMT	2056K	250	64-65		85	70	See Note #845
CSS&SB	B-B	80-Ton Steeple Cab	NPP	KMT		200	81	170	150	100	#1011-1013
CSS&SB	B-B	B-W 97 Ton	OMI	Ajin	1902	125	85	207			#900-903
CSS&SB	B-B	80-Ton Steeple Cab	WAS				57	25			
CSS&SB	C-C	700 Box Cab	JMS				75	76	125	100	Balance of NPP run
CSS&SB	C-C	700 Box Cab	NPP			500	73	115	120	110	See Note# 850, fp.
CSS&SB	C-C	700 Box Cab	NPP			500	73	100	105	100	See Note# 850
C.U.T.	2-C+C-2	P-1a Box Motor	MEW		703.7		69	60	250	200	See Note #50
C.U.T.	2-C+C-2	P-1a Box Motor	OMI	Ajin	1912	175	87	350			
GN	1-C+C-1	Y-1a Electric	CustB	KMT	342	100	84	632	675	100	fp., FT cabs
GN	1-C+C-1	Y-1 Box Cab	MGray				63	55	250	200	See Note# 854
GN	1-C+C-1	Y-1 Box Cab	PFM	Tensh	168	50	74	225	325	275	fp. Green
GN	1-C+C-1	Y-1 Box Cab	PFM	Tensh			78	366	425	395	fp. "Empire Builder"
GN	1-C+C-1	Y-1 Box Cab	PFM	Tensh			84				fp., See Note #844
GN	1-D-1	Z-1 Box Cab, pair	NPP	KMT	0152	100	76	280	300	250	See Note #856, fp.
GN	1-D-1	Z-1 Box Cab, pair	NPP	KMT		200	79				
GN	1-D-1	Z-1 Box Cab, pair	NPP	KMT		150	76	250	250	200	See Note# 856
GN	1-D-1	Z-1 Box Cab	Ortl	Samh	P392		84	298		240	fp., sprung wheels
GN	1-D-1	Z-1 Box Cab	Ortl	Samh	P879		88	307			fp.
GN	1-D-1	Z-1 Box Cab	Ortl	Samh	0392		84	264		215	sprung wheels
GN	1-D-1	Z-1 Box Cab, pair	Syd	KTM			76	194	200	180	one unit powered
GN	1-D-1	Z-1 Box Cab	Syd	KTM	5000T	50	61	30	175	150	Unpowered
GN	1-D-1	Z-1 Box Cab	Syd	KTM	5000	100	61	43	200	175	See Note# 855
GN	1-D-1	Z-1 Box Cab	Syd	KTM	5000	400	59	43	200	175	See Note# 855
GN	1-D-1	Z-1 Box Cab	Syd	KTM	5000	150	65	50	195	175	See Note# 855
GN	B-B	Box Cab	CustB	KSM	304	500	74	75	80	70	See Note# 851, #5000
GN	B-B	Box Cab	Emp	Kobra	EL205	67	78	80	70	50	See Note# 852
GN	B-D+D-B	W-1 Box Cab	CustB	KMT	323	500	76	215	280	230	See Note# 853
IC	B-B	B-W 97 Ton	OMI	MSM	1903	75	85	207	100	80	#10000-10003
Inland Empire	B-B	Box Cab	KenK				57-60	15-20	100	110	Freight Motor
ITR	B-B	Class B Box Cab	GHB		109		83	275	225		Std, 2-motors
ITR	B-B-B-B	Class C Locomotive	Syd	Tsub	1579	284	59	33	200	150	See Note# 874
ITR	B-B-B-B	Class C Locomotive	Syd	Tsub	1579A	100	62	40	225	175	See Note# 875
ITR	B-B-B-B	Class C Locomotive	Syd	Tsub	1579A	200	66	43	225	175	See Note# 876
ITR	B-B-B-B	Class C Locomotive	Syd	Tsub	1579	600	76	150	250	200	See Note# 876
ITR	B-B	Class B Box Cab	Syd	KMT	1561	100	66	30	175	150	See Note# 873
ITR	B-B	Class B Box Cab	Syd	KMT	1561	120	63	30	150	130	See Note# 873
ITR	B-B	Class B Box Cab	Syd	KMT	1561	80	59	28	130	110	See Note# 873
ITS	B-B-B-B	Class D Motor	CustB	Orion	339	150	83	382	135	120	4-truck
ITS	B-B-B-B	Class C Electric	Syd	Orion		600	76				
LIRR	2-B+B-2	DD-1 Box Motor	Soho	KMT	1251		78	350	275	250	#338; 2 Units
LIRR	2-B+B-2	DD-1 Box Motor	Soho	Nakamura	1251	50	78	350	275	250	#338; 2-units
MISC		Industrial Switcher	Gem	Olympia	PH-102	750	61	12	65	55	one pantograph
MISC		4 Wheel Steeple Cab	Intl							50	See Note #843
MISC		4 Wheel Street Car	Intl				50-55	9-11				See Note #988
MISC		Box Cab Switcher	Intl	Takada	BB-1		50	11	150	125	See Note# 987
MISC		4 Wheel Steeple Cab	Intl							50	17' long, w/pantograph

Heavy Electric Locomotives (cont'd)

In 1915 The Milwaukee Road took delivery of the largest electric locomotive in the world. This 288-ton locomotive developed 3,440 hp and was the pride of the road. Built as a cab and booster arrangement, these units lasted into the 1970s. In 1949, various combinations of cab units and boosters were given different designations. Shown above is one half of an EF5 set. Built by Alco-GE, these units were the first to employ regenerative braking. Nickel Plate products imported this Toho-built model in 1975.

Road	AAR Code	Class & Type	Importer	Builder	Cat #	Quan.	Yrs.	List Price	Mint	Avg.	Remarks
MISC		4 Wheel Ind Switcher	Intl				50	9	60	50	See Note# 986
MISC		Ind. Switcher	KenK	Tsub	1032	50	56-60	8	140	120	4-Wheel Steeple Cab
MISC		Box Cab Frt Motor	KenK	KMT			57-60	15-20			
MISC		Ind. Switcher	KenK				56-60	7			Steeple Cab Kit
MISC	2-C+C-2	Box Motor	MEW	KMT	0151	300	69	60	250	200	See Note# 50
MISC	B	16 Ton Loco	FZoo				87	99	83		
MISC	B	16 Ton Loco	FZoo		350	50	87	99	83		
MISC	B-B	Class D steeple Cab	KenK	KMT			57	20	100	90	See Note# 989
MISC	B-B	D Box Cab	MBA				60	20	75	60	
MISC	B-B	Steeple Cab	MEW	KMT	LES600		59	20		90	See Note# 992
MISC	B-B	Steeple Cab	MEW	KMT	LES601		63	20		90	See Note# 992
MISC	B-B	B-1 Steeple Cab	MTSImp	Kumata	002	200	85	230	210		See Note #842
NYC		P-2	OMI	Ajin	1913	175	87	350			
NYC	1-D-1	S-1 Box Motor	Kaw				65	43	180	160	
NYC	2-C+C-2	P-2a Box Motor	CustB	Mizuno	307	588	74	200	225	200	See Note# 858
NYC	2-D-2	S-2 Box Motor	CustB	Orion	306	500	76	140	210		
NYC	2-D-2	S-2 Box Motor	OMI	Ajin	5139			350	294		
NYC	B-B	S-3	OMI	Ajin	5140	500	71	350	294	145	
NYC	B-B+B-B	T-3a Box Motor	Alco	KMT	E-111	500	74	140	170	155	
NYC	B-B+B-B	T-1 Box Motor	MEW				60	45	160	130	#700
NYC	C-C	R-2 Box Motor	Alco	Samh	E-112	300	82	273		200	
NYC&HR	B-B	S-1	OMI	Ajin	5138		68	350	294	100	
NYNH&H	1-B+B-1	EF-1 Box Cab	MEW				66	53	270	240	
NYNH&H	1-B+B-1	EF-2 Electric	CustB	TAMAC	337	200	83	457	300		
NYNH&H	2-C+C-2	EF-3 Electric	CustB	TAMAC	353	100		632			
NYNH&H	2-C+C-2	EF-3a Electric	CustB	KMT	353	100	85	632	509		fp., streamlined
NYNH&H	1-B+B-1	EP-1 Box Cab	CustB	TAMAC	315	200	81	332		235	
NYNH&H	1-B+B-1	EP-2 Box Cab	CustB	Orion		200	83				
NYNH&H	2-C+C-2	EP-3 Box Cab	MEW	KMT	0098	100	64	60	200	150	
NYNH&H	2-C+C-2	EP-3b Electric	CustB	KMT	313	100	85	598	342		fp.
NYNH&H	2-C+C-2	EP-4 Cab	Alco	KMT	E-115	100	76	180	180	150	
NYNH&H	C-C	EP-5	OMI	Ajin	5295		91	445			w/side vents, modified
NYNH&H	C-C	EP-5	OMI	Ajin	5294		91	445			w/o side vents, original
NYNH&H	C-C	EP-5 Rectifier	Alco	KMT	E-114	500	74	98	220	150	NH, PC
NYNH&H	B-B	Ey-2	OMI	Ajin	5016	200	87	215			#200-214
NYNH&H	C-C	E-33 Rectifier	Alco	KMT	E-102	850	73	85	125	100	See Note #841

Heavy Electric Locomotives (cont'd)

Samuel Insull's revitalization of the South Shore Line continued into the Depression years with the 1930 purchase of three 80-ton, 1600-hp General Electric steeple-cab freight locomotives, #1011–1013. These locomotives were fitted with both pantograph and pole, enabling them to operate on any of the three Insull-owned Chicago-area suburban lines, which included the North Shore and the Chicago, Aurora and Elgin. Nickel Plate Products imported this fine model in 1973.

The Pennsy's P–5 class electrics were of the 2–C–2 designation and were originally built as box cabs in 1931. In 1935, the Pennsy received its first P5a from Westinghouse. Looking for all the world like miniaturized GG–1s, they were, in fact, the precursor of that car body design. Originally intended as fast passenger power, they were soon bumped down to secondary service with the advent of the GG–1s. Regearing them down from 90 mph to 70 mph produced an excellent freight engine. Alco Models imported this Rok-Am-built model in 1980.

Heavy Electric Locomotives (cont'd)

The Pennsy's R–1d 2–D–2 was a one-of-a-kind experiment which evidently didn't work out. With the same general car body design as the early GG–1s and the P–5as, it appeared better proportioned than the P–5a. Little is known of this prototype, and photos are not plentiful. Alpha Models imported this superb Samhongsa replica.

Road	AAR Code	Class & Type	Model Production					List Price	Resale		Remarks
			Importer	Builder	Cat #	Quan.	Yrs.		Mint	Avg.	
N&W		LC-1 Electrics	CustB	Orion	324	70	84	948	850	654	fp., 2-units
OregElect	B-B-B-B	16-wh BoxCab	MCW	KMT	51	50	80	225	195	175	4-Truck
OregElect	B-B-B-B	16-wh Steeple Cab	MCW	KMT	50	50	80	225	195	175	4-Truck
PacElect	B-B	Steeple Cab	Syd	Orion	1624	800	75	78	160	145	
PacElect	B-B	Class D Baldwin	Syd	KenK			60	28	130	115	One Truck Powered
PacElect	B-B	Steeple Cab	Syd	Tsub	1624	200	64	30	140	125	See Note# 940
PacElect	B-B	"Electra" Steeple Cab	Syd	Takada	1544	440	69	35	175	150	See Note #840
PacElect	B-B	Steeple Cab	Syd	Tsub	1624	420	70	38	150	135	See Note# 940
PacElect	B-B	Steeple Cab	Syd	Tsub	1624	295	67	30	145	130	See Note# 940
PacElect	B-B	Steeple Cab	Syd	Tsub	1624	150	60	28	140	125	See Note# 940
Portland Rwy.	B-B	Steeple Cab	Soho	KMT	0802	200	75	98	140	125	#1400
PRR	2-B-2	O1a	OMI	Ajin	5191	100	90	424			
PRR	1-C+C-1	FF-2 Electric	CustB	KMT	344	100	84	632	350	300	fp.
PRR	1-C+C-1	FF-1 Box Motor	CustB	KMT	328	280	78	320	270	225	"Big Liz;" 4800 hp.
PRR	1-C+C-1	FF-2 Box Motor	MGray	KMT	344	100	63	55	200	175	ex. GN Y-1
PRR	1-D-1	L-6 Box Motor	Alco	KMT	E-110	750	73	90	140	100	
PRR	1-D-1	L-6 Box Motor	Alpha				85	260		220	fully sprung
PRR	1-D-1	L-6A Box Motor	Alpha				85	260		220	fully sprung
PRR	1-D-1	L-5 Cab	CustB	KMT	302	545	73	115	130	110	3070 hp., 88" drivers
PRR	2-B+B-2	DD-1 Box Motor	Alco	KMT	E-107	500	70	100	200	150	See Note# 951
PRR	2-B+B-2	DD-1 Box Motor	Soho	Tsub	1211	50	78	350	125	250	See Note# 951
PRR	2-B-2	O-1c Box Motor	Alco	KMT	E-106	750	71	88	165	140	
PRR	2-B-2	O-1b Box Motor	Intl				59	18	135	100	fp.
PRR	2-B-2	O-1a Box Motor	Intl				50	14	120	75	Kit
PRR	2-B-2	O-1a Box Motor	PFM	United		500	54	60		60	
PRR	2-B-2	O-1a Box Cab	TrSp			20	66	58	175	160	
PRR	2-C+C-2	GG-1 Cab	Key	Micro			85	407	342	170	fp., See Note #839
PRR	2-C+C-2	GG-1 Cab	Key	Micro		10	86	407	342		fp., See Note #838
PRR	2-C+C-2	GG-1 Cab	Key	Micro			85	407	342		fp., See Note #837
PRR	2-C+C-2	GG-1 Cab	Key	Micro		60	86	407	342		fp., See Note #835
PRR	2-C+C-2	GG-1 Cab	Key	Micro		200	86	407	342		fp., See Note #834
PRR	2-C+C-2	GG-1 Cab	Lam	Cab		8	76	225	250	200	See Note# 952
PRR	2-C+C-2	GG-1 Cab	Lam	Cab		500	72	130	180	160	3-piece body
PRR	2-C+C-2	GG-1 Cab	Lam	Cab	R980	500	73	198	200	190	See Note #831

Heavy Electric Locomotives (cont'd)

In 1930, the Cleveland Union Terminal opened with much fanfare. The motive power was a new electric of the 2 + C–C + 2 type, which would become the model for the later PRR GG–1s. Built by Alco and GE, these engines operated on 3,000 volts DC, supplied from an overhead catenary system. When the Union terminal was dieselized in the '50s, these engines were converted to 600-volt third rail operation and moved to the New York City area, where they operated in passenger service between Harmon and New York. The small pantograph was used in underground areas in place of the third rail. The Overland models shown above represent the original CUT version and the NYC's P–2b class.

Road	AAR Code	Class & Type	Importer	Builder	Cat #	Quan.	Yrs.	List Price	Mint	Avg.	Remarks
PRR	2-C+C-2	GG-1 Cab	PSC	Nakamura	15061		79-81	130	160	145	Brass Kit, 1-piece body
PRR	2-C-2	P-5b Box Motor	Alco	Rok-Am	E-118	300	80	225	200	180	
PRR	2-C-2	P-5a Modified	Alco	Rok-Am	E-105M	50	80	245	210	180	See Note# 954
PRR	2-C-2	P-5a Box Motor	Alco	Rok-Am	E-105A	300	80	225	200	175	
PRR	2-C-2	P-5a Box Motor	Alco	KMT	E-105	750	71	90	170	140	See Note #829
PRR	2-C-2	P-5a Box Motor	Intl	IMP	2402	50	59-60	35	140	125	Streamlined, fp.
PRR	2-C-2	P-5a Box Motor	LMB				60	33	135	110	
PRR	2-C-2	P5b	OMI	Ajin	5192	75	90	402			
PRR	2-C-2	P5a	OMI	Ajin	5193	75	90	402			
PRR	2-C-2	P5a	OMI	Ajin	5194	125	90	424			
PRR	2-D-2	R-1d	Alpha								
PRR	B-B	E-2b Cab	Alco	KMT	E-119	500	74	115	120	100	2500 hp.
PRR	B-B	E-2b Cab	Alpha				84			240	
PRR	B-B	E-2c Cab	Alpha				84			245	experimental rectifier
PRR	B-B-B	E-3b Cab	Alpha	Samh			85	255		350	rectifier
PRR	C	B-1 Box Cab	Alpha	Samh		200	84	220		185	
PRR	C	B-1 Box Cab	TrSp				68	45	75		
PRR	C-C	EP-5 Rectifier	Alco	KMT	E-114	500	74	98	200	150	NH, PC
PRR	C-C	E-33 Rectifier	Alco	KMT	E-102	850	73	85	125	100	See Note# 687
PRR	C-C	E-44 Rectifier	Alco	KMT	E-101	500	70	58	150	100	4400 hp.
PRR	C-C	E-44 Rectifier	Alco	KMT	E-101	500	68	58	150	100	4400 hp.
PRR	C-C	E-44A Rectifier	Alpha		E-101A		85			240	modified details, new drive
PRR	C/C	B-1 Box Cab	Alco	KMT	E-109	1300	73	63-68	150	110	NMRA Rev.'73, 2-units
SacNorth	B-B	Baldwin Steeple Cab	KenK				59	13	130	115	Freight Motor
SacNorth	B-B	Alco Steeple Cab	MEW	KTM			68	43	250	200	See Note# 983
SacNorth	B-B	Box Cab	Syd	Goto	1010	510	71	50	155	130	See Note# 967
Virginian	1-D-1	EL-1a Jack Shaft	Alco	Rok-Am		100	78	135	135	125	2735 hp.
Virginian	1-D-1	EL-1a Jack Shaft	OMI	Ajin	1853	60	90	378			
Virginian	1-D-1 *3	EL-3a Jack Shaft	Alco	Rok-Am	E-125	250	78	375	375	350	3-Unit Set
Virginian	2-C+C-2	EL-3a Jack Shaft	OMI	Ajin	1900	80	90	365			
Virginian	B-B+B-B	EL-2b; 2-units	Alco	Samh	E-104	150	80	596	675	600	See Note# 957
Virginian	C-C	EL-C Rectifier	Alco	KMT	E-102	850	73	85	160	130	3300 hp.
Virginian	C-C	EL-3a Jack Shaft	OMI	Ajin	1852	160	90	364			
Visalia	B-B	Box Cab	KenK			40	56				1-pantograph, 1-pole
Visalia	B-B	Box Cab	MEW	Tsub	LEB650		60	25	155	90	See Note# 980

Interurbans

Road	Car #	Class & Type	Model Production					List Price	Resale		Remarks
			Importer	Builder	Cat #	Quan.	Yrs.		Mint	Avg.	
CA&E	451-460	Int. Coach	Hank's/GHB	KMT		200	82	185	200		See Note #749
CA&E	311	Kuhlman Wood Interurban	MTM	KMT		200	77	94	200		Dummy, 53 ft., fp.
CA&E	311	Kuhlman Wood Interurban	MTM	KMT	1905	75	77	100	200		#311-315; 53 ft.
CA&E	311T	Kuhlman Wood Interurban	MTM	KMT	1451	640	77	88	150		Unpowered; 53 ft.
CA&E	311	Kuhlman Wood Interurban	MTM	KMT	0506	100	77	105	200		See Note# 867
CA&E	12	Niles Wood Coach	Soho	KMT	0202	400	72	48	160		See Note# 865
CA&E	10	Niles Wood Combine	Soho	KMT	0201	240	72	48	160		See Note# 865
CA&E	300	Niles Wood Combine	MTM	KMT	0155	200	77	105	150		See Note #867
CA&E	300T	Niles Wood Interurban	MTM	KMT			77	94	130		Dummy, 53 ft., fp.
CA&E	450	Riveted Steel Coach	MTL	KMT							
CA&E	109	Wood Funeral Car	Soho	KMT	0204	145	72	48	160		See Note# 865
CA&E	101	Wood Trailer Coach	Soho	KMT	0203	200	72	40	130		See Note# 866
CD&M Electric	62	Interurban, Coach	MTSys	Orion	301	520	55	17			Kit, wood roof
CD&M Electric	500-501	Interurban, Parlor	GSB	KMT	108	200	83	235	250		Red Bird

The Cincinnati & Lake Erie's ''Red Devil'' interurbans looked more like city cars than the typical interurbans of the time. They sat lower than most interurbans and were smaller in size. Constructed of steel and aluminum, they were some of the fastest interurbans ever built. Not only were they fast, but they were also elegant. With interiors trimmed in aluminum, imitation walnut, and ivory, even the coach passengers had leather seats. It must have made commuting rather enjoyable. Hallmark Models imported this interesting model in 1975.

Interurbans (cont'd)

Among the heaviest and most powerful interurbans of the day were the 60-foot multiple-unit combines built by Pullman in 1926 and delivered to the Chicago, South Shore and South Bend as #100-109. Shown is the 100-series combine in its modernized and lengthened post-1940's version. Nickel Plate Products imported this model in 1977.

Road	Car #	Class & Type	Importer	Builder	Cat #	Quan.	Yrs.	List Price	Mint	Avg.	Remarks
CD&M Electric	500-501	Interurban, Parlor	MTL	KMT	500		64	35	150		
CL&A	1920	Light Interurban	MTSys	KMT	300	300	66				
CL&AE		Light Interurban	PacT	Orion	404	500	66	30			See Note# 970
CNS&M	420	Coach	MCW	KMT	420	150	78	127			can motor
CNS&M		Electroliner	MTSys	KMT	300A	210	65				4-car set
CNS&M		Electroliner	NPP	KMT	N/A	250	75	170	175		4-car set
CNS&M			BCreek	Lone Star					495		
CNS&M		Interurban	Intl	KMT	0507	250	57	15	150		See Note# 868
CNS&M	410	Observation	MCW	KMT	410	150	78	110	150		trailer
CNS&M	420	Observation	MCW	KMT	420	150	78	110	150		trailer
CNS&M	410	Parlor/Coach	MCW	KMT	410	150	78	127			can motor
CNS&M	240-244	Refrigerator Trailer	MTSImp	Woo Jung	64	200	87	115	145		unpowered
CNS&M	251	Steel Comb. Coach	Syd	Tsub	251	50	64	30	165		Jewett-built 1917
CNS&M	251	Steel Comb. Coach	Syd	Tsub	251	175	65	30	165		Jewett-built 1917
CNS&M	251	Steel Comb. Coach	Syd	Tsub	251	115	63	30	155	130	Jewett-built 1917
CNS&M	251	Steel Comb. Coach	Syd	Tsub	251	450	69	38	165	140	Jewett-built 1917
CNS&M	700	Steel Shore Trailer	Syd	Toho	700	700	69	38	150	130	Powered; #700-733
CNS&M	700	Steel Shore Coach	Syd	Tsub	700	400	65	30	140	120	Powered; #700-733
CNS&M	700T	Steel Shore Trailer	Syd	Toho	700T	200	69	30	125	110	Dummy; #700-733
CNS&M	700T	Steel Shore Trailer	Syd	Tsub	700T	200	65	22	120	100	Dummy; #700-733
CNS&M	250-256	Steel Combine	MTSImp	HanIn		50	92	260			flywheel drive
CNS&M	150-185	Steel Coach	MTSImp	HanIn		115	92	260			flywheel drive
CNS&M	404-406	Steel Diner	MTSImp	HanIn		50	92	260			flywheel drive
CNS&M	737	Steel "Skokie"	Syd	Tsub	737T	25	58	22	120	100	Unpowered Coach
CNS&M	737	Steel "Skokie"	Syd	Toho	737	500	69	38	150	130	Powered Coach
CNS&M	737	Steel "Skokie"	Syd	Toho	737T	200	69	30	125	110	Unpowered coach
CNS&M	737	Steel "Skokie"	Syd	Tsub	737	200	58	30	140	120	Powered Coach
CNS&M	737	Steel "Skokie"	Syd	Tsub	737T	125	63	22	120	105	Unpowered coach
CNS&M	737	Steel "Skokie"	Syd	Tsub	737	250	63	30	145	125	Powered Coach

Table header (spanning): Model Production — Importer, Builder, Cat #, Quan., Yrs. | List Price | Resale — Mint, Avg.

Interurbans (cont'd)

Road	Car #	Class & Type	Importer	Builder	Cat #	Quan.	Yrs.	List Price	Mint	Avg.	Remarks
CNS&M	203	"MD" Box Motor	Syd	Toho	203T	150	69	30	150	125	See Note# 868
CNS&M	215	"MD" Box Motor	Syd	Toho	215	400	69	38	125	110	See Note# 869
CSS&SB		Motorized Coach	NPP				86	260			Stainless Steel
CSS&SB	30-40	#1 Coach Set	NPP	KMT	N/A	50	73	93	125	95	w/Dummy Trailer
CSS&SB	1601-1618	#100 Combine	NPP				77	79	130	115	
CSS&SB		#1-9 COACH	NPP				84	183	300		Motorized shorty
CSS&SB		Combine Set	NPP	MSM		75	73	93			w/Dummy Trailer
CSS&SB		#23 Coach	NPP	KTM			77	79	225		
CSS&SB		#504 Bagg-Exp.	NPP				84	85	200		
C&LE	120-129	Red Devil	Hall	Rok-Am		500	75	60	90		
C&LE	120-129	Red Devil	MTSys				62	17			
C&LE	635-644	Steel Exp Motor	KenK				65	35	160		See Note# 714
Gal/Hous Electric	IT330	Bluebird	GSB	KMT	0508	100	79	139	250		See Note# 871
IC		Coach & trailer	NPP				76	136	200		See Note #872
Inland Empire		3-Car Wood Brill Set	Ortl	KMT			82	615			
Inland Empire	71,73,74	Brill	Ortl	KMT	0173	125	82	186	260		See Note# 974
Inland Empire	82-84	Brill Wood Combine	Ortl	KMT	0174	125	82	186	200		See Note# 973
Inland Empire	327	Brill Wood Observation	Ortl	KMT	0175	125	82	142	160		
IRR		Combination	KenK				59				See Note #713
IRR	375-377	Combination	Ortl	KMT	0570	86		224			Coach, RPO
IRR	375-377	Combination	Ortl	KMT	P570			281			custom painted
IRR		Wood Freight Motor	Ortl	KMT	0622		87	164			#727
ITR	IT330	Coach	Soho	KMT	0507	250	75	60	70		See Note# 879
ITR	IT330	Coach	Soho	KMT	0508	100	75	60	65		See Note# 880
ITR	IT300	Combine	Soho	KMT	0506	100	75	65	75		See Note# 878
ITR	IT300	Combine	Soho	KMT	0505	250	75	65	80		See Note# 877
ITR	IT350	Observation	Soho	KMT	0509	250	75	63	75		See Note# 881
ITR		System Sleeper	GHB				83	175	145		
ITR	IT350	"City of Decatur"	Soho	KMT	0502		75	125	140		See Note# 884
ITR	IT350	"City of Decatur"	Soho	KMT	0501		75	125	150		
ITR	IT350	"Mound City"	Soho	KMT	0504		75	180	210		
ITR	IT350	"Mound City"	Soho	KMT	0503		75	180	225		See Note# 885
ITS	516-527	Coach	GHB	KMT	103	200	80	165	150		Powered
ITS	260	Combine	GHB	KMT	105	200	81	175	190		Denville local
ITS		Owl Sleeper	GHB	KMT	104	200	81	155	135		Trailer
ITS	510-514	Parlor-Observation	GHB	KMT	102	200	80	160	135		Trailer
Key System	124-189	Bridge Units	KenK	KMT	2054		64	55	350		See Note #968
Key System		Bridge Units	KenK	KMT	2055		64	45	300		See Note #969
MISC		CERA Box Trailer	Soho	KMT	1005	500	69	14	30		See Note #995
MISC		Flat Bed Work Motor	Syd	Takada	000		69	33	150		
MISC		Flat Bed Work Motor	Syd	Takada	000	430	68	33	150		See Note #996
MISC	375	Ind Rwy RPO Pass	KenK		2052		63	30			
MISC		Pole Car	Intl	Tsub	737	250	59	18	195		
MISC		S.T. Freight Motor	MTSys	KMT	234	1000	64	12	100		See Note #711
M&SCR	620	Coach, light interurban	MTSys		320		61	25	160		
NStC&T		#620	Suydam	KMT			200	64				from KMT book
Oregon Elect Ry	1001-1002	Niles Parlor Obs	Syd	Tsub	1001	245	66	35	250		62 foot; Powered
Oregon Elect Ry	1001-1002	Niles Parlor Obs	Syd	Tsub	1001T	100	58	25	195		62 Foot; Unpowered

Interurbans (cont'd)

In 1927, the Chicago, South Shore & South Bend received ten 61-foot steel powered MU coaches, #201-210, from Pullman. The Standard Steel Car Company delivered similar MU powered coaches #30-40 in 1929. Deluxe for their time, these coaches were complete with rotating pairs of bucket seats upholstered in gray Byzantine plush. The smoking section was the enclosed Pullman type with side-aisle, so non-smoking passengers would not have to pass through the smoking compartment. Nickel Plate Products imported the #1 Set in 1973.

To augment its mass suburban electrification program started in 1921, the Illinois Central purchased 280 steel MU cars between 1921 and 1929. These Pullman Standard Steel Car Company powered coaches were designed to be paired with unpowered trailers and could MU with each other to form longer trains of as many as ten cars. These excellent factory-painted cars were imported by Nickel Plate Products in 1976.

| Road | Car # | Class & Type | Model Production | | | | | List Price | Resale | | Remarks |
			Importer	Builder	Cat #	Quan.	Yrs.		Mint	Avg.	
Oregon Elect Ry	1001-1002	Niles Parlor Obs	Syd	Tsub	1001	273	58	33	195		62 foot; Powered
Oregon Elect Ry	1001-1002	Niles Parlor Obs	Syd	Tsub	1001	235	61	33	195		62 foot; Powered
Oregon Elect Ry	1010-1011	Niles Sleeper	Syd	Tsub	1010	75	58	23	400		54 Foot; Dummy Sled
Oregon Elect Ry		Niles WB&A Coach	Syd	Tsub	1907	130	57	30	195		See Note# 905
Oregon Elect Ry	106-109	Niles WB&A Coach	Syd	Tsub	1907T	50	57	23	180		See Note# 906
Oregon Elect Ry		Niles WB&A Coach	Syd	Tsub	1907	70	59	30	195		See Note# 905
Oregon Elect Ry	106-109	Niles WB&A Coach	Syd	Tsub	1907T	50	62	23	160		See Note# 906
Oregon Elect Ry		Niles WB&A Coach	Syd	Tsub	1907	156	62	30	195		See Note# 905
Oregon Elect Ry	106-109	Niles WB&A Coach	Syd	Tsub	1907T	75	59	23	160		See Note# 906
Oregon Elect Ry	900-907	Niles Wood Box Motor	Syd	Tsub	900	109	62	30	185		57 Foot; Baggage/Express

Interurbans (cont'd)

Road	Car #	Class & Type	Importer	Builder	Cat #	Quan.	Yrs.	List Price	Mint	Avg.	Remarks
					Model Production				Resale		
Oregon Elect Ry	900-907	Niles Wood Box Motor	Syd	Tsub	900	83	58	30	180		57 Foot; Baggage/Express
Oregon Elect Ry	900-907	Niles Wood Box Motor	Syd	Tsub	900	50	49	30	180		57 Foot; Baggage/Express
Oregon Elect Ry	103-105	Niles Wood Coach	Syd	Tsub	100	133	58	30	180		57 Foot
Oregon Elect Ry	103-105	Niles Wood Coach	Syd	Tsub	100	88	59	30	200	165	57 Foot
Oregon Elect Ry	100-102	Niles Wood Coach	Syd	Tsub	100T	400	61		175	150	57 Foot; Trailer
Oregon Elect Ry	100-102	Niles Wood Coach	Syd	Tsub	100T	90	59	23	175	145	57 Foot; Trailer
Oregon Elect Ry	50-57	Niles Wood Coach	Syd	Tsub	64	105	62	30	185	170	See Note# 904
Oregon Elect Ry	100-102	Niles Wood Coach	Syd	Tsub	100T	70	58	23	175	140	57 Foot; Trailer
Oregon Elect Ry	58-63	Niles Wood Combine	Syd	Tsub	58	72	58	30	195	160	See Note# 903
Oregon Elect Ry	50-57	Niles Wood Combine	Syd	Tsub	64	170	59	30	195	165	See Note# 904
Oregon Elect Ry	58-63	Niles Wood Combine	Syd	Tsub	58	105	61	30	195	170	See Note# 903
Oregon Elect Ry	58-63	Niles Wood Combine	Syd	Tsub	58	165	59	30	195	165	See Note# 903
Oregon Elect Ry	50-57	Niles Wood Combine	Syd	Tsub	64	72	58	30	195	160	See Note# 904
PacElect	257	1902 Interurban	Syd	Tsub	257	200	63	30	375	125	See Note# 907
PacElect		800 Class	Key	Samh				214	180		Single Pole
PacElect	950	950 Trolley	HiCB	Orion		200	81		180		
PacElect	1446	Baggage-Express	Syd	Tsub	1446	76	58	30	160	130	55' Steel Car
PacElect	1446	Baggage-Express	Syd	Tsub	1446	50	59	30	160	135	55' Steel Car
PacElect	1459	Baggage-Express	Syd	Orion	1459	520	72	45	160		Made from Coaches
PacElect	1446	Baggage-Express	Syd	Tsub	1446	76	61	30	160		55' Steel Car
PacElect	1446	Baggage-Express	Syd	Tsub	1446	126	57	30	150		55' Steel Car
PacElect	400T	Blimp Coach Trailer	Syd	Tsub	400T	110	63	28	125		Dummy, 71' Coach
PacElect	400T	Blimp Coach Trailer	Syd	Orion	400T	420	73	60	125		Dummy, 71' Coach
PacElect	200	California Type	Ortl		0543		86	207	200		
PacElect	1256	Coach	CustB	Orion		50	83		160		fp.
PacElect		Huntington "Alabama"	Whsl	KMT		150	82	180	180		See Note# 944
PacElect	291	Huntington Standard	Syd	Takada	291	617	69	35	160		See Note# 908
PacElect		Long Baggage-Combine	Key	Samh			60	214	180		#1357
PacElect	530	Medium "Five" Coach	Syd	Orion	530	630	74	60	160		40' Wood Coach
PacElect	414-419	Niles Wood Coach	Syd	Takada	414	503	70	38	165		See Note# 911
PacElect	1300	Niles Wood Combine	Syd	Takada	1300	400	70	38	165		See Note# 936
PacElect	5001	PCC Suburban Car	Syd	Toho	5001	600	72	45	100		See Note# 942
PacElect	5001T	PCC Suburban Trailer	Syd	Toho	5001T	200	72	38	85		Unpowered PCC
PacElect	1372	Portland Steel Combine	CustB	Orion	417	100	85	262	160		fp. See Note #708
PacElect	1372	Portland Steel Combine	CustB	Orion	417	50	83	224	160		fp. See Note #708
PacElect	1406	RPO Car	Syd	Tsub	1406	75	61	30	160		55' Steel RPO
PacElect	1407	RPO Car	Syd	Orion	1407	520	72	45	175		Made from a 1252
PacElect	1406	RPO Car	Syd	Tsub	1406/1408	100	59	30	160		55' Steel RPO
PacElect		Short Bag-Combine	Key	Samh	1902	125	85	214	180		#1358-59
PacElect	400	Blimp Steel Coach	Syd	Tsub	400	170	62	35	160		See Note# 909

Interurbans (cont'd)

In 1948–49, the St. Louis Car Company delivered three streamlined blue and aluminum electric interurban trains to the Illinois Terminal System. These were the two-car "City of Decatur," the "Fort Creve Coeur," and the three-car "Mound City." The two-car trains consisted of a combine plus observation, while the three-car "Mound City" was composed of a combine, coach, and observation. This million dollar bid to recapture the waning passenger market was not successful, and the trains were withdrawn from service by 1956. S. Soho & Company imported the "Mound City" in 1975.

The "Tens" (because they were all numbered in the 10xx series) were the last wooden cars purchased by the Pacific Electric. These cars were painted red with tan roofs and were about as big and fast as wooden-bodied interurbans ever got. In 1933, four of these cars were rebuilt into "combos" and renumbered 1360–1363, only to be reconverted back into coaches ten years later, due to the pressure of wartime traffic. E. Suydam & Company was the pioneer in importing high-quality interurbans of American prototypes. Suydam imported over 1,200 of these models between 1959 and 1972.

| Road | Car # | Class & Type | Model Production | | | | | List Price | Resale | | Remarks |
			Importer	Builder	Cat #	Quan.	Yrs.		Mint	Avg.	
PacElect	400	Blimp Steel Coach	Syd	Orion	400	600	73	68	160		See Note# 910
PacElect	400	Blimp Steel Coach	Syd	Tsub	400	423	63	35	160		See Note# 909
PacElect	1299	Steel Business Car	Syd	Tsub	1299	300	67	38	250		
PacElect	1370	Steel Combine	Syd	Tsub	1370	75	64	33	160		57' Steel Combine
PacElect	1370	Steel Combine	Syd	Tsub	1370	125	58	30	160		57' Steel Combine
PacElect	1370	Steel Combine	Syd	Orion	1370	500	73	55	160		57' Steel Combine
PacElect	1370	Steel Combine	Syd	Tsub	1370	150	61	30	160		57' Steel Combine
PacElect	1370	Steel Combine	Syd	Tsub	1370	100	67	33	160		57' Steel Combine
PacElect	1370	Steel Combine	Syd	Tsub	1370	130	56	30	160		57' Steel Combine
PacElect	00157	Tower Car	Syd	Orion	00157	650	74	70	180		wood line Car
PacElect	00150	Wire Greaser	Syd	Takada	00150	307	68	33	180		Wood Tower Car
PacElect	00150	Wire Greaser	Syd	Takada	00150	308	67	33	180		Wood Tower Car

Interurbans (cont'd)

Pacific Electric's business car #1000, the "Commodore," was rebuilt in 1914 from a "Ten" coach, as they were the only cars capable of system- wide operation. After years of service carrying VIPs, #100 served as the "Commodore Limited," an extra-fare deluxe service to Newport Beach and Balboa. Number 1000 was finally retired in 1947 and is now owned by the Orange Empire Railway Museum in Perris, California. This fine model was built by Orion and imported by Suydam in 1972.

| Road | Car # | Class & Type | Model Production | | | | | List Price | Resale | | Remarks |
			Importer	Builder	Cat #	Quan.	Yrs.		Mint	Avg.	
PacElect	1451	Wood Box Motor	Syd	Orion	1451	640	74	68	160		With Foot Boards
PacElect	1451	Wood Box Motor	Syd	Tsub	1451	495	66	33	160		With Pilots
PacElect	999	Wood Coach	HiCB					189			announced
PacElect	994	Wood Coach	HiCB		994		82	169	180		
PacElect	994	Wood Coach	Whsl	KMT		100	84	170	180		See Note# 707
PacElect	1362	Wood Combine	CustB	Orion	414	150	80	224	160		fp. See Note# 923
PacElect	1362-1363	Wood Combine	Syd	Tsub	1362	110	61	30	160		55', 4-Window
PacElect	1362-1363	Wood Combine	Syd	Tsub	1362	100	64	30	160		55', 4-Window
PacElect	1360-1361	Wood Combine	Syd	Orion	1360	640	72	50	160		55', 3-Window
PacElect	1362-1363	Wood Combine	Syd	Tsub	1362	175	69	33	160		55', 4-Window
PacElect	1465	"Blimp" Bagg-Exp.	Syd	Orion	1465	630	73	68	160		See Note# 939
PacElect	498	"Blimp" Combine	Syd	Tsub	498	155	63	35	160		67' Steel Car
PacElect	498	"Blimp" Combine	Syd	Orion	498	630	73	68	160		67' Steel Car
PacElect	1000	"Commodore" Parlor	Syd	Orion	1000	730	72	53	160		See Note# 920
PacElect	801	"Eight" Coach	Syd	Tsub	801	200	68	33	160		See Note# 706
PacElect	800T	"Eight" Trailer	Syd	Tsub	800T	100	68	25	130		See Note# 917
PacElect	800T	"Eight" Trailer	Syd	Tsub	800T	50	63	25	130		See Note# 917
PacElect	800	"Eight" Wood Coach	Syd	Tsub	800	100	63	33	160		See Note# 915
PacElect	800	"Eight" Wood Coach	Syd	Tsub	800	200	68	33	160		See Note# 916
PacElect	1544	"Electra" Steeple Cab	Syd	Takada	1544	455	68	35	175		See Note #705
PacElect	1100	"Eleven"	Syd	Tsub	1100	275	58	30	155		57' Interurban
PacElect	1100	"Eleven"	Syd	Orion	1100	550	71	43	165		See Note# 925
PacElect	1100	"Eleven"	Syd	Tsub	1100	75	57	30	160		57' Interurban
PacElect	1100T	"Eleven" St Trailer	Syd	Tsub	1100T	50	58	22	140		57' Dummy

Interurbans (cont'd)

Originally built in 1910 by the Niles Car Company and acquired by the Pacific Electric in 1918, the 414–419 coaches were the "California Type open-end cars. Number 419 was eventually rebuilt into an attractive #1300 combine. Strictly a one-of-a-kind, it stayed in service in the San Bernadino area until 1941. This beautiful model was imported by Suydam.

Built in 1899 by the Los Angeles Pacific Company, the wire-greaser tower car #00150 is on display at the Orange Empire Railway Museum. Suydam imported this interesting model in 1967 and 1968.

Road	Car #	Class & Type	Model Production					List Price	Resale		Remarks
			Importer	Builder	Cat #	Quan.	Yrs.		Mint	Avg.	
PacElect	1401	"Golden Gate" RPO	Syd	Jonan	1401	600	77	75	160		See Note# 938
PacElect	600	"Hollywood"	MTSys	KMT	308		57	19	160		Suburban
PacElect	650-759	"Hollywood"	Ortl	KMT	0460		85	193	180		Rounded door
PacElect	600-649	"Hollywood"	Ortl	KMT	0461		85	164	180		See Note# 704
PacElect	650	"Hollywood"	Ortl	KMT	0462		85	193	180		See Note# 703
PacElect	5050	"Hollywood"	Soho	Kumata	0290	250	78	100	180		Modernized 600
PacElect	5050	"Hollywood"			KT106S		57	15	180		See Note# 943
PacElect	600	"Hollywood"	Syd	Goto	600	273	6	30	180		See Note# 913
PacElect	5050	"Hollywood"	Syd	Goto	5050	379	66	30	140		Modernized 600
PacElect	600	"Hollywood"	Whsl				85	175			gear drive

Interurbans (cont'd)

Road	Car #	Class & Type	Model Production						List Price	Resale		Remarks
			Importer	Builder	Cat #	Quan.	Yrs.			Mint	Avg.	
PacElect	600T	"Hollywood" Trailer	Ortl				85	145				
PacElect	5050T	"Hollywood" Trailer	Soho	Kumata	0291	100	78	80	140			Unpowered
PacElect	600T	"Hollywood" Trailer	Syd	Goto	600T	70	66	22	140			See Note# 914
PacElect	5050T	"Hollywood" Trailer	Syd	Goto	5050T	100	66	22	140			Unpowered
PacElect	1222	"Long Beach Twelve"	Syd	Tsub	1222	200	61	30	160			See Note# 928
PacElect	1222	"Long Beach Twelve"	Syd	Tsub	1222	100	67	33	160			See Note# 928
PacElect	1222	"Long Beach Twelve"	Syd	Orion	1222	600	73	53	160			See Note# 928
PacElect	1222	"Long Beach Twelve"	Syd	Tsub	1222	200	64	33	160			See Note# 928
PacElect	1222T	"Long Beach Twelve"	Syd	Tsub	1222T	100	64	22	140			See Note# 932
PacElect	1222T	"Long Beach Twelve"	Syd	Tsub	1222T	75	61	22	140			See Note# 932
PacElect	1222T	"Long Beach Twelve"	Syd	Orion	1222T	200	73	43	140			See Note# 932
PacElect	450	"Mount Lowe" Car	Syd	Tsub	456	603	68	33	175			See Note# 912
PacElect	1252	"Portland Twelve"	CustB	Orion	416	50	83	224	180			fp. See Note #702
PacElect	1252	"Portland Twelve"	Syd	Tsub	1252	98	57	30	160			See Note# 934
PacElect	1252	"Portland Twelve"	Syd	Tsub	1252	250	56	30	160			See Note# 933
PacElect	1252T	"Portland Twelve"	Syd	Tsub	1252T	62	57	22	140			Unpowered
PacElect	1252T	"Portland Twelve"	Syd	Tsub	1252T	130	56	22	140			Unpowered
PacElect	1252	"Portland Twelve"	Syd	Orion	1252	500	70	40	160			See Note# 935
PacElect	1372-1376	"Portland" St. Combine	Syd	Tsub	1372	116	58	30	160			See Note# 937
PacElect	1372-1376	"Portland" St. Combine	Syd	Orion	1372	500	71	40	160			
PacElect	1200T	"S. Berdo Twelve"	Syd	Tsub	1200T	60	58	22	160			See Note# 929
PacElect	1200	"S. Berdo Twelve"	Syd	Tsub	1200	50	64	30	180			See Note# 927
PacElect	1200	"S. Berdo Twelve"	Syd	Orion	1200	620	73	55	160			See Note# 927
PacElect	1200	"S. Berdo Twelve"	Syd	Tsub	1200	322	58	30	180			See Note# 927
PacElect	1200	"S. Berdo Twelve"	Syd	Tsub	1200	150	67	33	180			See Note# 927
PacElect	1200	"S. Berdo Twelve"	Syd	Tsub	1200	125	57	30	160			See Note# 926
PacElect	1032	"Ten" Wood Coach	CustB	Orion	413	150	80	224	160			See Note# 923
PacElect	1032T	"Ten" Wood Coach	Syd	Tsub	1032T	75	68	28	140			See Note# 924
PacElect	1032T	"Ten" Wood Coach	Syd	Tsub	1032T	100	64	23	140			See Note# 924
PacElect	1032T	"Ten" Wood Coach	Syd	Tsub	1032T	50	61	23	140			See Note# 924
PacElect	1032	"Ten" Wood Coach	Syd	Tsub	1032	135	61	30	180			55' Interurban
PacElect	1032	"Ten" Wood Coach	Syd	Tsub	1032	200	64	30	180			55' Interurban
PacElect	1032	"Ten" Wood Coach	Syd	Orion	1032	630	72	50	160			See Note# 922
PacElect	1032T	"Ten" Wood Coach	Syd	Tsub	1032T	50	59	23	140			See Note# 924
PacElect	1032	"Ten" Wood Coach	Syd	Tsub	1032	250	68	33	180			See Note# 921
PacElect	1032	"Ten" Wood Coach	Syd	Tsub	1032	50	59	30	140			55' Interurban

Interurbans (cont'd)

Designed as a result of a nationwide search by Pacific Electric officials to find an interurban best suited to the needs of Los Angeles, the #600 series "Hollywood" cars came into being. Easily distinguished by their low, wide center doors, a total of 160 of these cars were delivered from Brill and the St. Louis Car Company between 1924 and 1928. This beautifully proportioned model was built by Goto, one of the premier Japanese builders, and imported by Suydam in 1966.

| Road | Car # | Class & Type | Model Production | | | | | | List Price | Resale | | Remarks |
			Importer	Builder	Cat #	Quan.	Yrs.			Mint	Avg.	
PacElect	735-749	"Valley Sevens"	Whsl				85	175				
PacElect	950	"Venice" Wood Coach	HiCB	KSM	749	100	82	159	190			3-Car Set
PacElect	950	"Venice" Wood Coach	Syd	Tsub	950	500	68	30	160			See Note# 919
PacElect	950	"Venice" Wood Coach	Syd	Tsub	950	220	57	28	160			See Note# 918
PacElect	950	"Venice" Wood Coach	Whsl	KMT		100	84	170	185			See Note# 701
PacElect	950T	"Venice" Wood Coach	Syd	Tsub	950T	120	57	20	140			Unpowered Trailer
PE&E E Rwy	200-220	Steel Coach	Syd	Tsub	200T	50	56	22	300			See Note# 959
PE&E E Rwy	200-220	Steel Coach	Syd	Tsub	200	120	56	30	375			See Note# 958
PE&E E Rwy	502-514	Steel Combine	Syd	Tsub	502	50	56	30	400			Powered, 55 ft.
PE&E E Rwy	750-754	Steel Express	Syd	Tsub	750	50	57	30	400			See Note# 960
PE&E E Rwy	770-772	Steel RPO	Syd		770		57	30	400			Powered, 55 ft.
Phila & Western		Libertyliner	NPP	KMT		250	75	170	170			4-Car Set
PhilaSub Transit		Libertyliner	NPP				75	170	170			
PST		65-76 Interurban	MTSimp	FM		200	87	215	275			See Note# 700
PST		80 Series Interurban	MTSimp	Samh	022A	200	88	265				
PST		80 Series Interurban	MTSimp	Samh	022B	50	88	265				car #80
Sac Northern	82 & 84	Bidwell Parlor Car	Syd	Goto	SNB	304	70	30	150			See Note# 966
Sac Northern		Bidwell Parlor Car	Syd	Goto	SNB	313	67	35	150			See Note# 966
Sac Northern	1003-1006	Holman Wood Coach	MEW				67	33	250			Sold to Key System
Sac Northern	1018-1025	Interurban Coach "Hall-Scott"	MTSimp	FM		60	87	225	245			See Note #699

Interurbans (cont'd)

The Pacific Electric purchased 15 wooden cars from the Golden Gate & Ocean Railroad shortly after the turn of the century. Some, including #1401, were eventually converted to baggage/mail cars. The Suydam model "Golden Gate," shown above, constructed in Japan by Jonan in 1977, features #1401 in the RPO configuration. Subsequently, in 1936, the mail facilities were removed from the car and it became a freight box motor. Before being scrapped in 1947, it had earned the distinction of being the oldest operating electric car in the United States. Suydam imported 600 of these unique models in 1977.

Road	Car #	Class & Type	Model Production					List Price	Resale		Remarks
			Importer	Builder	Cat #	Quan.	Yrs.		Mint	Avg.	
Sac Northern	1018-1025	Interurban Set "Hall-Scott"	MTSimp	FM		60	87	365	395		See Note #698
Sac Northern	1018-1025	Interurban Trlr "Hall-Scott"	MTSimp	FM		10	87	145	160		See Note #699
Sac Northern	125	Niles 3-Window Combine	Syd	Goto	125	435	70	38	170		See Note# 961
Sac Northern	125	Niles 3-Window Combine	Syd	Goto	125	146	67	33	170		See Note# 961
Sac Northern	126	Niles 5-Window Combine	Syd	Goto	126	194	67	33	170		Powered
Sac Northern	126	Niles 5-Window Combine	Syd	Goto	126	430	70	38	170		Powered
Sac Northern	200	Niles Pass Coach	Syd	Goto	200	438	70	38	180		See Note# 962
Sac Northern	200	Niles Pass Coach	Syd	Goto	200	250	67	33	180		See Note# 962
Sac Northern	200	Niles Pass Coach	Syd	Goto	200T		70	30	150		See Note# 963
Sac Northern	220	Niles Wood Coach	Syd	Goto	220	384	70	30	150		See Note# 965
Sac Northern	220	Niles Wood Coach	Syd	Goto	220	93	67	25	150		See Note# 965
Sac Northern	201	Wood Bagg Coach	Syd	Goto	201	6	67				See Note# 964
SP Lines	700	Baggage	HiCB	KMT	2405	100	81	140	175		
SP Lines	300	Coach	HiCB	KMT	2401	100	81	140	175		
SP Lines	300	Coach	HiCB	KMT	2402	50	81	125	150		unpowered
SP Lines	600	Combine	HiCB	KMT	2404	100	81	140	175		powered
SP Lines	428	Trailer Coach	HiCB	KMT	2403	50	81	120	140		unpwd, w/Panto
St. Louis Car. Co.		St. Louis Palace Car	MTSys		318	300	64	29	175		100 w/spoked wheels
St. Louis Car. Co.		St. Louis Palace Car	PacT		319		64	30	175		See Note# 971
St. Louis Car. Co.		St. Louis Palace Car	PacT		318		64	29	175		See Note# 970
Texas Electric		Motorized Coach	GHB				87	230	175		

Interurbans (cont'd)

The Sacramento Northern #125 combine was built in the company's Chico shops and patterned after the arched-window Niles passenger cars. Number 125 was unique in having only three pairs of passenger windows, as it was built to rush fresh berries to market in Sacramento and Oakland, thus becoming known as the "Berry Car." This beautiful model was built by Goto for Suydam in 1967 and 1970.

| Road | Car # | Class & Type | Model Production | | | | | List Price | Resale | | Remarks |
			Importer	Builder	Cat #	Quan.	Yrs.		Mint	Avg.	
Texas Electric	301-321	Steel Combine	GHB	KMT	107	200	82	229	175		Dallas Express
TMER&T		Articulated Interurban	GustB	Orion?	415	75	84	498	410		See Note #688
WB&A		Brill Articulated	GHB	KMT		110	82-87	390	350		See Note #686
WB&A		Niles Wood Coach	Syd	Tsub	1907	190	66	33	195		See Note# 981
WB&A		Niles Wood Coach	Syd	Tsub	1907	70	59	30	195		See Note# 981
WB&A		Niles Wood Coach	Syd	Tsub	1907T	100	66	25	165		See Note# 982
WB&A		Niles Wood Coach	Syd	Tsub	1907T	50	62	23	165		See Note# 982
WB&A		Niles Wood Coach	Syd	Tsub	1907T	75	59	23	165		See Note# 982
WB&A		Niles Wood Coach	Syd	Tsub	1907	130	57	30	195		See Note# 981
WB&A		Niles Wood Coach	Syd	Tsub	1907T	50	57	23	165		See Note# 982
WB&A		Niles Wood Coach	Syd	Tsub	1907	156	62	30	195		See Note# 981

MU & Subway Cars

| Road | Car # | Class & Type | Model Production | | | | | List Price | Resale | | Remarks |
			Importer	Builder	Cat #	Quan.	Yrs.		Mint	Avg.	
NYW&B		MU Car	Metro	Orion		90	86		200		See Note #828
Amtrak/PC		Metroliner	Gem	KMT	KT106S	500	72	80-100	150		See Note# 956
BMT/BRT	1200	El Car Set	WPC	Samh	0203	200	81	245	350		See Note# 863
BMT/BRT	650	El Car Set	WPC	Samh			81	245	350		See Note# 863
BMT		D-Type Articulated	MTSImp	Samh	013	100	87	475	600		2-motors
BMT		Std. Subway Cars	WPC	Samh			81	295	450		3 Car Set
BMT		Std. Subway Car	WPC	Samh	1561		81	155	200		See Note# 864
BMT		Std. Subway Car	SLRT	KMT		167	65	28	150		Unpowered 67 ft.
BMT		Std. Subway Car	SLRT	KMT		135	65	35	200		Powered 67 ft.
CTA	2201-2350	EL Car Set	MTSImp	KMT	004	150	85	325	375		See Note #827
CTA	6001-6130	EL Car Set	MTSImp	Han In	041	50	92	395			2-Car Set
CTA	6201-6470	EL Car Set	MTSImp	Han In	042	50	92	395			2-Car Set
IND		R-4 Subway Cars	CustB	Lhee Do	506	100	81	295	350		See Note# 902
IND		4-Car Work Train	CustB	Lhee Do	350	50	85	377	325		
IRT/Manhattan Elevated		EL Car Set	MTSImp	Han In	024	150	89	375			2-Car Set

MU & Subway Cars (cont'd)

New Haven's Steel open-platform MU cars were built by Standard Steel Car and delivered in 1909. They were unique in many respects. They operated on 11,000 volts AC or 650 Volts DC and had automatic operation of pantographs and third rail shoes for operating on the New York Central's third rail at Woodlawn. A total of 26 cars provided trouble-free performance for over 40 years. N.J. Custom Brass imported these interesting Kumata-built models in 1982.

A total of 122 "D-Type" articulated subway cars were built for the BMT System by the Pressed Steel Car Company. Cars #6001–6003 were built in 1925, cars #6004–6070 were built in 1927, and cars #6071–6121 were built in 1928. Also known as "Triplexes," these cars were used primarily on the Brighton and Sea Beach lines but occasionally appeared on other parts of the system. This excellent set was imported by WPC in 1981.

| Road | Car # | Class & Type | Model Production | | | | | List Price | Resale | | Remarks |
			Importer	Builder	Cat #	Quan.	Yrs.		Mint	Avg.	
IRT	3650-3699	HI-V Subway Car	MTSImp	Han In	027B		89	240			Deck Roof
IRT	3650-3699	HI-V Subway Set	MTSImp	Han In	027A		89	385			See Note #825
IRT		Low-V Subway Car	WPC	Samh			84		175		Single Unit
IRT		Low-V Subway Set	WPC	Samh			84	375	400		3-Car Set
IRT		R-15 Subway Car	MTSImp	Samh	046	100	92	429			2-Car Set
IRT	6500-6899	R-17 Subway Car	MTSImp	Samh	009A	50	86	210	225		See Note #826
IRT	6500-6899	R-17 Subway Set	MTSImp	Samh	009B	25	86	375	400		See Note #822
IRT	7300-7749	R-22 Subway Car	MTSImp	Samh	008A	50	86	210	225		See Note #826

MU & Subway Cars (cont'd)

From 1956 through 1958, the St. Louis Car Company built the R–21 and R–22 series subway cars for the Interborough Rapid Transit division of the New York Subway System. These cars were built as single units, whereas later cars of this type were built in semi-permanently coupled pairs. The model shown above depicts the R–22 series car and was imported by Model Traction Supply Company in 1986.

Road	Car #	Class & Type	Model Production Importer	Builder	Cat #	Quan.	Yrs.	List Price	Resale Mint	Avg.	Remarks
IRT	8570-8805	R-29 Subway Set	MTSImp	Samh	008B	75	86	375	400		See Note #822
IRT	9306-9345	R-33 Subway Car	MTSImp	Samh		5	88				See Note #824
IRT	9306-9345	R-33 Subway Car	MTSImp	Samh		50	88	270	325		See Note #823
IRT	9306-9345	R-33 Subway Car	MTSImp	Samh		25	88	215	270		See Note #824
IRT	9306-9345	R-33 Subway Set	MTSImp	Samh	020A	25	88	475	550		fp., See Note #826
IRT	9346-9523	R-36 Subway Set	MTSImp	Samh		50	88	475	550		See Note #826
IRT/CTA		El Car Trailer	MTSImp	Han In	028	250	89	145			
CRT/CTA	5001-5002	Articulated El Car	MTSImp	Samh	006	100	85	425			2-motors
LIRR		Babylon Express	Soho	KMT	1250	150	79	280	365		See Note# 887
LIRR		Budd M-1	GHB	Orion			80	85		350	fp., 2-Car Set
LIRR		MP54C Coach	Soho	KMT			150	78		175	
LIRR		MP54C Coach	Soho	KMT			150	78		125	unpowered
LIRR		MP-54	WPC	KMT				83	340		See Note #821
LIRR		MP-70 Dbl Deck MU	CustB	Lhee Do	703	250	79	145	250		2-Car Set
LIRR		Ping-Pong	CustB	Orion	701S	100	79	283	395		3-Car Set
LIRR		T54C Trailer	Soho	KMT			150	78			
MISC		Subway car	KenK	KMT	2050			62	17	140	
MISC		Subway car	KenK	KMT	2051			62	13	100	
NYC		3-Car MU Set	CustB	Lhee Do	735	67	83	445	460		See Note# 861
NYNH&H		3 Car Electric MU Set	CustB	KSM	340	100	81	382	425		round roof
NYNH&H		3 Car Electric MU Set	CustB	KMT	N/A	50	80	343	390		See Note #817
NYNH&H		3 Car Electric MU Set	CustB	KMT	734A	50	82	430	440		See Note #807
NYNH&H		3 Car Electric MU Set	CustB	KMT	734A	50	82	430	440		See Note #806
NYNH&H		3 Car Electric MU Set	CustB	KMT	N/A	50	80	343	450		See Note #785
NYNH&H		Open Plat MU Set	CustB	Orion	775S	50	85	715			fp., 3-Car Set
PRR		MP-54 3-Car Set	WPC	KMT	X-116P		83	340	400		See Note #784
PRR		MP-54 Coach	Alco	KMT		750	72		125		See Note #783
PRR		MP-54 Coach	Alco	KMT	X-114	1250	72	53	175		Powered
PRR		MP-54 Coach	Alco	KMT	X-115	1000	72	43	125		See Note #774
PRR		MP-54 Coach	TrSp				63	29			Powered
PRR		MP-54 Coach Set	Alco	KMT	X-116S	125	72	147	340		Three Car Set
PRR		MP-54 Combine	Alco	KMT	X-116	750	72	53	175		Powered
PRR		MP-54 MU Trailer	TrSp				63	19			Unpowered
PRR		Silverliner	Gem	KMT	KT102D	50	68	35	50	40	Dummy Trailer
PRR/RDG		Silverliner	Gem	KMT	KT102S	500	72	80-100	115	100	See Note #771
RDG		MU Car Set	CustB	KSM	749	100	82	356	130	105	3-Car Set

City Cars

Company	Car #	Class & Type	Model Production				List Price	Resale		Remarks
			Importer	Builder	Cat #	Quan.	Yrs.		Mint	Avg.	
		Brill Master Unit	Fair	KMT	379	300	72				
		Open Bench Double Truck Trolley	MTSys	KMT	390	200	61				
		Single Truck Birney	Fair	KMT	321	600	68				
		Single Truck Birney	MTSys	KMT	317	500	66				See Note #985
		Single Truck Birney	MTSys	KMT	316	300	60				See Note #984
Boston		Boston Type "5"	MTSys	KMT	377	200	60				
Boston	6000	City Car	Fair	KMT	380	225	67				See Note #977
Boston	6000	City Car	Fair	KMT	379	125	67				See Note #978
Boston El.		City Car	MTSys	KMT	341	100	61	19-23			See Note #763
Boston El.	341	City Car	MTSys	KMT	341A	100	61	28			single end
Boston El.	2850	City Car	MTSys								double end
Boston El.		Articulated Trolley	CustB	Orion	420	100	85	382	255		
Boston El.		Type 5,5A	MTSImp	Samh	018A	60	88	219			as built
Boston El.		Type 5,5A	MTSImp	Samh	018B	160	88	219			See Note# 709
Boston El.	109	Type 5	MTSys	KMT	0204	150	61	23	125		See Note# 862
Boston El.		Type 5	MTSys				79	235			as built
Boston El.		Type 5	MTSys			300	79	235	195		1929 Modification
Brooklyn	8000	Peter Witt	Fair	KMT	333	500	70		180		
Brooklyn Man. Tr.	2570	City Car	MTSys	KMT	345a	50	62		175		max-min trucks
BRT		Laconia Car	MTSys	KMT	345	50	62	25	175		See Note #750
BRT		Freight Motor	MTSImp	Han In	035A	75	90	255			8-wheel drive 2 doors
BRT		Freight Motor	MTSImp	Han In	035B	75	90	255			8-wheel drive 4 doors
BRT/RDG St Rwy		Crane Car	MTSImp	Kumata/FM	011	80	87	210	250		See Note# 748
CA&E	450	Riveted Stl Coach	SPH	KMT		200	82				
Cinn Car Co.		Double End, Curved Side	MTSys		356	200	63	25	150		
Cinn Car Co.		Single End, Curved Side	MTSys		355	100	63	25	170		
CSL		"Nearside" Trolley	MTSImp	Kumata	005	175	85	215			See Note# 748
CSL	5201-5600	Big Brill	Fair	KMT	346	275	79	98	160		
CSL	169	One Man Car	Fair	KMT	344-1	300	76	80	130		
CSL	101-700	Pullman	Fair	KMT	600	600	73	59			
CSL		M-U Trolley	WPC	Samh				195	160		
CSL	5001-5200	Short Brill	Fair	KMT	347	275	80	128	120		

The Chicago Surface Line's (CSL) "Nearside" trolley was a car designed to make fare collection easier for the conductor. The conductor was placed directly behind the motorman and collected the fares as the passengers entered. Exit was normally through the rear set of front doors. The rear doors were primarily an emergency exit but were often used as an exit in terminals. Model Traction Supply Company imported this Kumata-built car in 1985.

City Cars (cont'd)

Company	Car #	Class & Type	Importer	Builder	Cat #	Quan.	Yrs.	List Price	Mint	Avg.	Remarks
CSL		Street Sweeper	Fair	KMT	235	600	74		175		See Note #735
CSL	2700 Ser.	St. Louis Palace Car	MTSys	KMT	318	300	64	29	175		
CSL	169	Two Man Car	Fair	KMT	345-2	300	76	70	160		
LaRY		Birney Streetcar	Soho	KMT	308		69	22	90		See Note #751
LaRY		Birney Streetcar	Soho	KMT		50	69	22	100		Note# 901 & 751
LaRY		B-1 Open Ends	Soho	KMT	0151	300	70	45	105		Note# 888,889,751
LaRY		B-1 Open Ends	Soho	KMT	0101		70	40	95		Note# 889 & 751
LaRY		B-8 Standard	Soho	KMT	0102		70	40	100		Note# 889 & 751
LaRY		B-8 Standard	Soho	KMT	0152	100	70	43	110		Note# 889,890,751
LaRY		C Sowbellies	Soho	KMT	0153	200	71	45	110		Note# 888,891,751
LaRY		C Sowbellies	Soho	KMT	0103	100	71	40	100		Note# 891 & 751
LaRY		CE Center-Entrance	Soho	KMT	0104		71	40	95		Note# 891 & 751
LaRY		CE Center-Entrance	Soho	KMT	0154	200	71	45	105		Note# 888,891,751
LaRY		F	Soho	KMT	0105	100	71	40	100		Note# 892 & 751
LaRY		F	Soho	KMT	0155	200	71	43	110		Note# 890,892,751
LaRY		F-4	Soho	KMT	0106	200	71	43	110		Note# 893 & 751
LaRY		G	Soho	KMT	0098	100	69	26	90		HOn3, Note #751
LaRY		G	Soho	KMT	0099	100	69	26	90		HO, See Note #751
LaRY		H-1	Soho	KMT	0157	110	71	45	110		Note# 894,888,751
LaRY		H-1	Soho	KMT	0107	60	71	40	100		Note# 894 & 751
LaRY		H-2	Soho	KMT	0108	75	71	40	100		Note# 895 & 751
LaRY		H-3	Soho	KMT	0109	50	71	40	100		Note# 896 & 751
LaRY		K	Soho	KMT	0110	100	71	40	100		Note# 892 & 751
LaRY		K	Soho	KMT	0160	50	71	45	110		Note# 892,888,751
LaRY		L Double-End	Soho	KMT	0111	100	71	40	110		Note# 897 & 751
LaRY		L Double-End	Soho	KMT	0161	100	71	43	120		Note# 897,890,751
LaRY		M Coach	Soho	KMT	0162	200	72	43	110		Note# 898,890,751
LaRY		P-1 Pre-War PCC	Soho	KMT	0114	400	74	43	100		Note# 899 & 751
LaRY		P-2 Mid-War PCC	Soho	KMT	0115	200	74	43	100		Note# 900 & 751
Met St Rwy		Single Truck Trolly	CustB	Orion	404	500	75	60	180		See Note# 976
MISC		1-Truck Birney	Prec				61	10	90		open end trolley
MISC	737	1-Truck Little Guy	MTSys	Toho	314	200	55	12	125		Work Car
MISC		2-Tk Old Timer	MTSys		341		61	23	150		
MISC	Brill	2-Truck Open Bench	MTSImp	Kumata	313	175	84	245	375		
MISC		2-Truck Open Bench	MTSys		350		56	15			Kit
MISC		4 Wheel Coach	BIM	KTM	5000	400	49	15	100		Kit, See Note# 984
MISC		4 Wheel Coach	BIM	KTM	415	75	49	6	75		See Note #
MISC		4 Wheel Mail Car	BIM	KTM	5000	150	49	15	100		See Note# 984, Kit
MISC		4 Wheel Mail Car	BIM		383		49	6	75		Dummy Mail Car Kit
MISC		4 Wheel Street Car	Intl	KMT	0801	200	49	11	75		See Note #712
MISC		4-Wh Open End Car	Prec		3601		61	15	125		
MISC		4-Wheel Birney	Fomras	Fomras			84	98	125		
MISC		4-Wheel Birney	Gem				61	10	90		
MISC	Brill	4-Wheel Sprinkler	MTSys		111		65	20	130		Brill built
MISC		Birney Trolley	LMB	Tsub	1362	110	61	10-13	80		4-Wheel
MISC	2580	Brill, Peter Witt	MTSys	KMT	332	300	65	26	160		TTC #2580
MISC		Brill Master Unit	NWSL	KMT			73	40	125		See Note# 994
MISC		Brill Sprinkler Car	Fomras				85	99	150		
MISC	301-303	CM&B Street Car	PT	KMT		300	66				from Kumata's book
MISC		Dbl Truck Birney	KenK	KTM	2053	100	63	20	200		See Note# 990
MISC		Dbl Truck Birney	LMB				63	20	140		
MISC		Double end PCC	GHB				86				
MISC		Flat Bed Work Motor	MTSImp	Kumata		70	85	124	160		
MISC		IRR Trolley	Intl	KMT	101		56	18	150		Powered
MISC		IRR Trolley Trailer	Intl	KTM	5000T	50	56	15			Unpowered
MISC		Mail Car Kit	MTSys		60		55	6			
MISC		Open Bench Trolley	MTSys		390		61	40-48			
MISC		Open Coney Isl Trolley	Intl				55	12	100		Kit
MISC		Open Coney Isl Trolley	Intl	Orion	701S	100	55	15	125		
MISC		Ten Bench Open Trolley	Ortl		1777			200			
MISC		Open End Trolley	LMB				61	15			
MISC		Open Trolley Trailer	BIM				50	7			See Note# 985
MISC		PCC Trolley	Intl	Tsub	737	200	56	15	140		Powered
MISC		Single Truck Birney	Fomras				84	120	140		

City Cars (cont'd)

| Company | Car # | Class & Type | Model Production | | | | | List Price | Resale | | Remarks |
			Importer	Builder	Cat #	Quan.	Yrs.		Mint	Avg.	
MISC	00150	Sngl Truck Birney	KenK	Takada	2061	307	66	16	80		Vert Shaft Motor
MISC		Sngl Truck Birney	KenK	Takada	1544	455	61	10	75		Slant Shaft Motor
MISC		Sprinkler Car	Fomras	Orion		270	85				
MISC		Toonerville Trolley	Kemt			62	54	12	230		Unpowered
MISC		Toonerville Trolley	Kemt			700	54	25	350		Powered
MISC		Trolley Sprinkler	Fomras			84	126				fp., green; single tk.
MISC		Trolley Sweeper	Hunt	KMT	123	300	66	38	250		
MISC		Work Car	MTSys		100		55	13			2-Car Set, Dk Roof
MISC		PCC 1936-F	WPC	Samh			83	160	200		folding doors
MISC		PCC 1936-B	WPC	Samh			83	160	200		blinker doors
MISC		PCC 1946-F	WPC	Samh			83	160	200		folding doors
MISC		PCC 1946-B	WPC	Samh			83	160	200		blinker doors
MWP&W		Curved Side, Bbl End	MTSys		356	200	63	25	125		
New York		TARS Convertible	Fair	KMT	361	300	73				
NOPS	800	Streetcar "Desire"	MTS/LMB	KMT	378	500	65	27	120		
NStC&T		Car #620	MTSys	KMT	325	200	60				
NStC&T	300-311	Double End, Curved Side	MTSys		356	200	63	25	125		
NStC&T		#620	MTSys		320		60	15			Brass Body Kit
PacElect	100-117	Dbl Truck City Car	HiCB	KMT			81	149	135		
PacElect	320-364	Sngl Tk Birney	KenK	Orion?	2061	650	66-68	12-16	80		Vertical Shaft Motor
Pgh Rwy		1912 Jones Car	Fair	KMT	335	270	76				
Pgh Rwy		1912 Jones Car	Fair	KMT	336	510	76		165		
PRT/PTC		"Nearside" Trolley	MTSImp	Han In	034	125	87	255			
PRT/PTC		"Nearside" Trolley	MTSImp	Kumata	64	25	85	215	280		See Note# 711
PRT/PTC		"Nearside" Trolley	MTSImp	Kumata	64	50	85	215	275		See Note# 710
PTC		Brill Double Truck Snowsweeper	MTSImp	Han In	036	150	90	325			operating brushes 2 motors
PTC		Brill Double Truck Snowsweeper	MTSImp	Han In	036	50	92	325			operating brushes 3 motors
Rdg St Rwy	800-811	800 Series Trolley	MTSImp	Samh	018B-P	40	88	219	250		
San Diego	400-449	Class 5	PacT/Fair	KMT			69	90			
San Diego	400-449	Class 5 Street Car	PacT/Fair	KMT	366	250	69	33-37	125		#400-449, Powered
San Diego	400-449	Class 5 Street Car	PacT/Fair	KMT	366A	150	69	28-33	100		#400-449, Unpwd
San Diego		U-2 LRV	MTSImp	Samh	042	100	92	425			fp. flywheel drive
San Diego		U-2 LRV	MTSImp	Samh	042A	50	92	350			flywheel drive
TARS	1201-1225	1200 Series	CustB	Orion	408	500	73		150		See Note# 978
TARS	401-525	400 Series	CustB	Orion	402	500	75	70	165		See Note# 977
TARS		Brill Convertible	MTSys		382	50	54	17	145		See Note# 979
TARS		Brill Convertible	MTSys		381		54	17	150		Kit; Closed

The flat-bed work motor pictured above has no specific prototype but is a combination of various typical characteristics derived from several prototypes. As such, it may be painted for a variety of street railways and/or modified to better suit your particular tastes. With under-the-floor drive to both trucks, this Suydam import can also be useful as a light transfer locomotive. Built in 1969 by Takada of Japan, this model was a significant step forward in making small, easily hidden, under floor drive mechanisms.

City Cars (cont'd)

| Company | Car # | Class & Type | Model Production | | | | | List Price | Resale | | Remarks |
			Importer	Builder	Cat #	Quan.	Yrs.		Mint	Avg.	
TARS		Dbl Tk Huffliner	MTSys		384		65	25	150		
TARS	556-600	Dbl Tk Huffliner	MTSys	Orion	383	70	65	25	120		Fluted Sides
TARS		Huffliner w/riveted sides	MTSys	KMT	384	150	65				
TARS		TARS 625-685 (body only)	MTSys		375	200	59	200			
TTC	2580	Brill Peter Witt	MTSys	KMT	332	200	60	15			
TTC	2580	Brill Peter Witt	MTSys		332	300	65	27			
Twin Cities	1300	Street Car	NWSL				74	55	130		
Twin Cities	1300	Street Car	NWSL				74	65	180		
VE&PCo.	400-414	2-truck Birney	MTSys	KMT	367A		62	20			
VE&PCo.	400-414	2-truck Birney	MTSys	KMT	367		62	20			
VE&PCo.	400-414	2-truck Birney	MTSys		368		64	24			2-axle drive

Abbreviations

General

AAR	Assocation of American Railroads
Bk	brakes
CB	custom brass
COHS	Chesapeake & Ohio Historical Society
COLA	City of Los Angeles
COSF	City of San Francisco
CP/cp	custom painted
cyl	cylinder
DB	dynamic brakes
Dbl	double
dvrs pwd	driver powered
dyn	dynamic
EL/el	elevated
ex	example
Exp	express
f/p	factory painted
FWH	feedwater heater
Hi-ad	high adhesion
HiH	high hood (diesels)
HL/hl	headlight
LoH	low hood (diesels)
Mikes	Mikado
MM	Mainline Modeler
mod	model
MR	Model Railroader
MU	multiple unit
N de M	Nationales de Mexico
nmbrbds	numberboards
NMRA	National Model Railroad Association
orig	original
pass	passenger
pwd	powered
RDC	rail diesel car
rect	rectangular
rev	review
RM	Railroad Modeler
RMC	Railroad Model Craftsman
RPO	Railway Post Office
RSw	road switcher (diesels)
Sd frms	side frames
SH	superheater cover
sngl	single
st/std	standard
Sw	switcher (diesels)
tdr	tender
tk	truck
TSw	transfer switcher (diesels)
unptd	unpainted
unpwd	unpowered
vers	version

Importers

AHM	Associated Hobby Manufacturers
Akn	Akane Model Railroad Company
Alco	Alco Models
Alpha	Alpha Brass
AmBr	American Brass
Aris	Aristo-Craft Distinctive Miniatures
Austin	M.B. Austin
Bal	Balboa Scale Models
BCre	Beaver Creek
BIM	Beach Island Manufacturing Company
CAB	Cab; Japan
Cont	Continental Models
CustB	Custom Brass (N.J. International)
DiMo	Diamond Models
ESCM	ESCMRA Company
Emp	Empire Midland Model Company
Fair	Fairfield Traction Models
FED	Far East Distributors (NWSL)
F&G	Frew & Gordon, Ltd. (Pike)
FZoo	Flying Zoo

Gem	Gem Models	PSC	Precision Scale Company
GHB	G.H.B. International	PSM	Perfect Scale Models
GHC	G.H.C. Company	Red	Red Ball
GSB	G.S.B. Rail Ltd.	RWks	Railworks
GW	Great Western Locomotive Works	Sat	Sattler's HO Depot
Hall	Hallmark Models, Inc.	SLRT	Silver Leaf Rapid Transit
Hbtn	Hobbytown of Boston	Soho	S. Soho & Company (Precision Brass)
HiCB	High Country Brass	SSSM	South Shore Scale Models
H4W	House of Four Winds	Sun	Sunset Models
Hitt	David Hitt	SunDanc	Sun Dancer
HOT	HO Train Company	Syd	E. Suydam & Company
Hunt	Huntington Model Works	Tak	Takara
IHM	Iron Horse Models	TMS	Tetsudo Mokei Sha
IMP	International Model Products-Takara	Trns	Trains, Inc.
Intl	International Models, Inc.	TrSp	Trackside Specialties
JMS	J.M.S. Industries	Van	Van Hobbies
Kaw	Kaw Valley Scale Models	WAS	Western Aero Supply
Kem	Kemtron	Whsl	Original Whistle Stop, Inc.
KenK	Ken Kidder Railroad Models	WMC	Westside Model Company
Key	Key Imports, Ltd.	WPC	W.P. Car Corporation
Lam	Lambert Associates	WSM	Westside Model Company
LMB	L.M. Blum Models		
MBA	M.B. Austin		

Builders

MCW	Milwaukee Car Works		
MEW	Model Engineering Works	Ajin	Ajin Precision
MGray	Max Gray	Akane	Akane Model Railroad Company
ModW	Models West	DaiYng	Dai Young Models Company
MTL	Model Traction Lines	DongJ	Dong Jin Model Works
MTM	Midwest Trolley Museum, Inc.	Fomras	Fomras Company
MTSys	Model Tramway Systems	FuMod	Fuji Models
NERS	North Eastern Rail Service	Goto	G.O. Model Works Company, Ltd.
NPP	Nickel Plate Products	Hallko	Hallmark Korea Models
Nthn	Northern Imports	Imai	Imai Models Company, Ltd.
NWSL	Northwest Short Line	IMP	International Model Products
OLEX	Olympic Express	Jonan	Jonan Models
OMI	Overland Models Inc.	JPMod	J.P. Models
Ortl	Oriental Limited	JWorks	Joe Works
Over	Overland Models Inc.	Kawai	Kawai Model
PacT	Pacific Traction	Kemt	Kemtron
PCH	Pro Custom Hobbies	KMT	Kumata Models
PFM	Pacific Fast Mail	Kobra	Kobra Models
Pike	Pacific Pike (F&G)	Kodam	T. Kodama
Prec	Precision Miniatures	KookJ	Kook Jea Models
Prgn	Paragon Models	KTM/Kats	Katsumi Mokeiten Company, Ltd.

KoSh	Kodama Shisakusho	Samh	Samhongsa Company, Ltd.
KSM	Korea Scale Models	Sato	Sato Models
KyongD	Kyong Dong	SKI	S.K. International
Miya	Miyazawa Mokei	Seiko	Seiko Models
Mizuno	Micro Cast Mizuno	TaeHwa	Tae Hwa Precision
Naka	Nakamura Seimitsu Company, Ltd.	Takara	IMP/Takara
NAP	N.A.P. Company	Tensh	Tenshodo Model Company
NKP/Park	Park Model Products	TMS/TetsMo	Tetsudo Mokeisha
Olymp	Olympia Precision Models	Toby	Toby Model Company, Ltd.
Orion	Orion Models	Toho	Toho Models
Park/NKP	Park Model Products	Totem	Totem Models
RokAm	Republic of Korea/American	Tsub	Tsubomi Model Company
Sakura	Sakura	United	Atlas Industries, Inc.

Whyte Wheel Arrangement Classification

0-4-0	4-coupled Switcher	
0-4-2	Shifter	
0-6-0	6-coupled Switcher	
0-8-0	8-coupled Switcher	
0-10-0	10-coupled Switcher	
0-10-2	Union	
2-4-2	Columbia	
2-6-0	Mogul	
2-6-2	Prairie	
2-6-6	Bogie	
2-8-0	Consolidation	
2-8-2	Mikado	
2-8-4	Berkshire	
2-8-6	Bogie	
2-10-0	Decapod	
2-10-2	Santa Fe	
2-10-4	Texas	
4-4	Geared 2-truck	
4-4-0	American	
4-4-2	Atlantic	
4-4-4	Jubilee	

4-4-4-4	Duplex	oo◯◯ ◯◯oo
4-4-6-4	Duplex	oo◯◯ ◯◯◯oo
4-6-0	10-Wheeler	oo◯◯◯
4-6-2	Pacific	oo◯◯◯o
4-6-4	Hudson	oo◯◯◯oo
4-8-0	Mastodon	oo◯◯◯◯
4-8-2	Mountain	oo◯◯◯◯o
4-8-4	Northern	oo◯◯◯◯oo
4-10-0	El Gobernador	oo◯◯◯◯◯
4-10-2	Southern Pacific	oo◯◯◯◯◯o
4-12-2	Union Pacific	oo◯◯◯◯◯◯o
0-6-6-0	Articulated	◯◯◯ ◯◯◯
0-8-8-0	Articulated	◯◯◯◯ ◯◯◯◯
2-4-4-2	Articulated	o◯◯ ◯◯o
2-6-6-0	Articulated	o◯◯◯ ◯◯◯
2-6-6-2	Articulated	o◯◯◯ ◯◯◯o
2-6-6-4	Articulated	o◯◯◯ ◯◯◯oo
2-6-6-6	Alleghany	o◯◯◯ ◯◯◯ooo
2-8-8-0	Articulated	o◯◯◯◯ ◯◯◯◯
2-8-8-2	Articulated	o◯◯◯◯ ◯◯◯◯o
2-8-8-4	Yellowstone	o◯◯◯◯ ◯◯◯◯oo
2-8-8-8-2	Triplex	o◯◯◯◯ ◯◯◯◯ ◯◯◯◯o
2-10-10-2	Articulated	o◯◯◯◯◯ ◯◯◯◯◯o
4-6-6-2	Articulated	oo◯◯◯ ◯◯◯o
4-6-6-4	Challenger	oo◯◯◯ ◯◯◯oo

4-8-8-2 Cab Forward

4-8-8-4 Big Boy

The type names are those generally used to designate the various wheel arrangements. In instances where an individual railroad has adopted an alternative designation of its own, such as New York Central's "Niagara" for its 4-8-4 "Northerns," the alternative designation will be referred to either in a caption or in the "Remarks" column accompanying that road's listing.

Tank-type locomotives, i.e., those not requiring a separate tender for fuel and water supply, are designated by the letter "T" immediately following the wheel arrangement code, but the code numerals themselves are the same.

Some very early types, such as a few 4-2-2s built in the 1840s, and the one-of-a-kind experimentals, such as Pennsy's 6-8-6 Turbine and 6-4-4-6 Duplex, have been omitted to keep the list concise.

Notes to the Tables

In the "Remarks" column throughout the tables, readers are referred here to the appropriate numbered note.

1 Ex-NKP H-6a #607.

2 73-inch diameter drivers: Prototype on display at Atlanta, Georgia.

3 Baldwin-built in 1906-07: locomotive identical to Balboa model except for added minor detail; tender same as Balboa 4-4-2.

4 890 built with Pittman motors, 300 made with lost-wax cast headlight.

5 Lost-wax cast headlight on all 1960 and subsequent editions.

6 #0-80 crankpin screws.

7 Silver plated for display/advertising.

8 Cal-Scale lost-wax castings.

9 1964 United AT&SF 1950 series 28-0; RP-25 wheel contours; Plated retainer plate; turned wash-out plugs: spring detail: no brake shoes; Pittman motor; brass conducting drawbar; Cal-Scale air compressor; lost-wax cast headlight.

10 Chem milled wash-out plug detail.

11 Improved spring detail.

12 Tender drilled for sound.

13 Scale tender rivets; new gearbox.

14 Ex-Kansas City, Mexico & Orient locomotives; 10,000 gallon water capacity tender; NMRA Review '74.

15 Single sand dome; no feedwater heater; unsprung drivers; poor runner; coal tender with 12,000 gallon water capacity; #3283 etched on tender side and number boards; pilot projects too far forward; cab vents are open; red box.

16 Extra sand dome included; convertible tender with removable oil bunker; 12,000 gallon water capacity.

17 57-inch drivers; single sand dome; oil tender with 8500 gallon water capacity.

18 57-inch drivers; larger tender.

19 Available from S. Soho; single sand dome: no feedwater heater; unsprung drivers; partly of zamac construction: Poor construction and operation; coal tender with 12,000 gallon water capacity.

20 270 built with Pittman motors; 170 had lost-wax cast headlights.

21 PFM ad in December 1961 MR lists the following improvements over earlier runs; added lost-wax sander valves & dome outlets, grate shakers, blow down, electrical conduit, rivet & ventilator detail on cab, Santa Fe style inspection covers, globe valves and other cylinder block detail, ladders to valve gear hangers, redesigned piping, new feedwater heater,

pop turret, number boards, valve gear hanger, boiler and Pittman DC-70X motor. Brake shoes were added in the mid-60's.

22 NMRA Review 1/74.

23 Sport cab with single ventilator on roof center line; later model feedwater pump: Delta trailing truck; RP-25 wheel contours; oil tender with 15,000 gallon water capacity; correct for #3891-3999.

24 Rectangular cab; convertible tender with 15,000 gallon water capacity and removable oil tank; Delta trailing truck; early style feedwater pump; MR Review 10/79.

25 Factory painted, no lettering; 56 foot tender with 24,500 gallon water capacity; separate boxes for locomotive and tender.

26 Improved model; hinged stack; hex crank pins; sprung and articulated tender trucks; plastic locomotive brake shoes; well detailed with castings.

27 Round smoke box front; all drivers flanged; 56 foot tender; 24,500 gallon water capacity.

28 Notched smoke box front to clear compressors; all drivers flanged; 56 foot tender; 24,500 gallon water capacity.

29 "Madame Queen"; long tender with 20,000 gallon water capacity: needs wide curves unless frame is modified; NMRA Review 5/77.

30 Balboa's first import; MR Review 10/64.

31 Model identical to Balboa; tender identical to Balboa 2-6-2 built in 1910; 74-inch drivers.

32 73-inch spoked drivers; as built.

33 79-inch disc drivers as modernized; tender with 20,000 gallon water capacity; Hodges trailing truck; early style Elesco feedwater pump.

34 Semi-streamlined "Valley Flyer" RM review 8/79.

35 Factory painted, Crown; "Blue Goose"; locomotive and tender too tall; with skirting as delivered.

36 75-inch spoked drivers as built; two sand domes; convertible tender with 15,000 gallon water capacity.

37 79-inch drivers as modernized; two sand domes; convertible tender with 15,000 gallon water capacity.

38 #3462 embossed on tender; early, crude model; unsprung drivers; model drivers measure 78-inch diameter, should be 84-inch. Model has a single dry steam pipe between steam dome and turret, should have two. Poorly detailed with detail either etched into the boiler and cab or crude metal parts and sheet metal formed into crude parts. Box is purplish-red color 3" wide by 15" long. "Akane" on locomotive builders plates on sides of smokebox.

39 Spoked 63-inch diameter drivers, should be 69-inch; later style feedwater pump; Delta trailing truck with

46 1/4″ diameter spoked wheels; oil tender with 15,000 gallon water capacity.

40 Correct 69-inch spoked drivers; later style feedwater pump; Delta trailing truck with 46″ diameter spoked wheels; convertible tender with 15,000 gallon water capacity and removable oil tank; bleeding red foam packing.

41 #3784,3785, thin roller bearing rods.

42 Tapered rods; NMRA Review 1/70.

43 Thin roller bearing rods.

44 1927 original with 73-inch spoked drivers; oil tender with 20,000 gallon water capacity.

45 First rebuild with high Elesco feedwater heater and 80-inch disc drivers; rectangular tender with 20,000 gallon water capacity.

46 Tapered rods; raised stack; can motor.

47 Roller bearing rods; raised stack; 56-foot tender with 24,500 gallon water capacity and 7,000 gallon oil capacity; can motor.

48 Smallest of USRA locomotives built during World War I; rectangular tender with 8,000 gallon water capacity and 16-tons coal capacity or 2,800 gallons of oil.

49 #2200-2399; MR Review 1/78.

50 2635 Horsepower; 204-Ton box motor built by Alco/GE.

51 Super-Mike;70-inch drivers; Westside G-File #110.

52 Simple articulated; Vanderbilt tender.

53 Refer to Mainline Modeler Jan/Feb '81 for plans and photo.

54 ''Lady Baltimore''; 84-inch drivers.

55 ''Cincinnatian'', spoked drivers.

56 Unsprung drivers; President class.

57 Built at B&O Mount Clare shops using boiler shells from old Mikados and Pacifics in 1942-46; 64′7″ long Vanderbilt tender, carrying 23 Tons of coal and 22,000 gallons of water; tenders assigned to locomotives #5560,5569,5570.

58 ''George Emerson'', 4-cylinder rigid frame.

59 Built by Alco in 1928.

60 B&M T-la #4000-4019; external Coffin feedwater heater; Baker valve gear; structure too high and too far forward on frame; unsprung; rear 74-inch drivers are in firebox; Hodges trailing truck; 8-wheel coal tender carries 18 tons, with 12,000 gallon water capacity.

61 B&M T-la #4000-4019; external Coffin feedwater heater; long welded tender; large sand domes; flat shields on air pumps. exported through KMT.

62 #3660-3679 Elesco feedwater heater.

63 Of 496 CNR Moguls,378 were inherited from the Grand Trunk; and 36 from the Grand Trunk Pacific.

64 #470-504;57-inch drivers; model has cam on driver for modification to Stephenson valve gear.

65 #902-926; no cam on driver.

66 63-inch diameter drivers; MR 8/62.

67 Vestibule cab: oil burning; Walschaerts valve gear; 63-inch spoked drivers.

68 #3525-3599; vestibule cab, Belpaire firebox, Walschaerts valve gear; #3525-3546 had Vanderbilt tender, others had rectangular tender; MR 11/80, RMC 11/81.

69 Vanderbilt tender as on #3525-3546; RMC Review 11/81.

70 Light USRA; Grand Trunk Western #3700-3739.

71 #4100-4104; largest in British Empire when built in 1924; Elesco feedwater heater; first CNR locomotives with Vanderbilt tender; can motor; accurate model.

72 #1354-1409; built in 1912-1913; 63-inch drivers; Walschaerts valve gear.

73 #5125-5144; almost identical to J-4a,b,c engines built in 1914-1918; 69-inch drivers; vestibule cab; Walschaerts valve gear; single dome with Elesco feedwater heaters.

74 #5700-5704; 80-inch diameter drivers; 14,000 Imperial gallon tender is largest of all CNR Vanderbilts.

75 #6042-6046; built in 1929;73-inch diameter drivers; vestibule cab.

76 #6060-6097; ''Bullet-nose Betty''; 73-inch Box-Pok drivers; vestibule cab; Vanderbilt tender.

77 #6200,6218 and 6233; Elesco feedwater heater; vestibule cab; Vanderbilt tender; MR Review 2/73.

78 #6200-6234; 73-inch diameter Box-Pok drivers; Walschaerts valve gear; Elesco feedwater heater, vestibule cab; Vanderbilt tender.

79 #6300-6311; Grand Trunk Western locomotive; spoked drivers; main frame outside trailing truck; Baker valve gear; vestibule cab; Vanderbilt tender.

80 #6312-6336; Alco built Grand Trunk Western locomotive; straight running board; conventional main frame; Walschaerts valve gear; vestibule cab; Vanderbilt tender.

81 #6400-6404; streamlined cowl over boiler and domes;77-inch diameter Box-Pok drivers; Baker valve gear; good model; can motor.

82 Westside G-File #106,114; RM Review 6/78.

83 #6405-6410; Lima built Grand Trunk Western streamlined version; 77-inch diameter Box-Pok drivers; Baker valve gear.

84 Grand Trunk Western; NMRA Review 2/79.

85 Plastic locomotive brake shoes.

86 #3000-3004; streamlined speedsters delivered in 1936 with 80-inch diameter drivers.

87 Open cab; rectangular tender with 5,000 gallon water capacity; excellent model.

88 Vestibule cab; rectangular convertible tender with removable oil tank and 8,000 gallon water capacity.

89 #5300-5349; last unstreamlined.

90 #5437-5461; internal dry-pipe steam collection; 63-inch diameter drivers; Walschaerts valve gear; tender has 10,000 gallon water capacity, 18-ton coal capacity; excellent model.

91 #5437-5461; built by Montreal Locomotive Works in 1944; same prototype as in Note #90; workmanship and operation not equal to the Toby model; excessive copper content produces a pink hue in the Samhongsa model.

92 #5100-5194; rebuilt from P-1b; vestibule cab; Elesco feedwater heater.

93 #5787; built in 1917; Walschaerts valve gear; 58-inch diameter drivers.

94 #5800-5814; Walschaerts valve gear; no feedwater heater; well-made model with can motor; 24-inch radius curves; "Canadian Pacific" in white instead of correct gold on tender.

95 #5930-5935; Semi-streamlined; no steam dome.

96 Correct 63-inch diameter drivers; sprung trailing truck journals; ample detail but much of it is mis-aligned.

97 #5930-5935; correct 63-inch diameter drivers; workmanship improved over T-la; vestibule cab detail; movable smoke hood; sprung trailing truck journals.

98 #8000; 3-cylinder, multi-pressure.

99 2900 series; 75-inch drivers; type E superheater, Elesco feedwater heater, no steam dome, semi-streamlined; vestibule.

100 63-inch diameter spoked drivers.

101 #2378-2417; excellent model; Pittman DC-70 motor.

102 #2500-2665;70-inch diameter spoked drivers.

103 #2300-2303; Samhongsa version inferior to the Toby model in workmanship and operation.

104 Last unstreamlined Pacific.

105 Factory painted, Crown; #2860 "Royal Hudson"; Elesco feedwater heater, type E superheater, booster, Buckeye tender trucks.

106 "Royal Hudson", limited edition; excellent model.

107 Correct 75-inch drivers; can motor in firebox; vestibule cab detail; air brake stand; good workmanship.

108 #2820-2849; semi-streamlined; Commonwealth tender trucks.

109 75-inch diameter drivers; Elesco feedwater heater; elephant-ear smoke deflectors added after 1933.

110 Camelback; NMRA Review 10/71.

111 Largest locomotive in New England.

112 Factory painted, model appears as N&W version.

113 Gift from Tenshodo.

114 Silver Series; MR Review 2/77; RM Review 4/77.

115 Last 100 of Lambert silver series; red box.

116 7RB rectangular tender.

117 12VC Vanderbilt tender.

118 12VC Vanderbilt tender; boiler too high; boiler contour incorrect; piping too small.

119 Elesco K-40 feedwater heater; 21 RA rectangular tender; 21,000 gallon tender.

120 Elesco K-40 feedwater heater; 16VC Vanderbilt tender.

121 One gold plated for Bill Ryan.

122 Sprung drivers; incorrect boiler contour.

123 Movable deck apron; movable cab roof ventilators; improved booster piping; box marked "Hy-Grade".

124 #2952; Elesco feedwater heater; flying pumps; Vanderbilt tender.

125 #2956; flying pumps; Vanderbilt tender.

126 #2959; air pumps on pilot deck.

127 21RA rectangular tender; ex-Wabash locomotive via C&EI.

128 #3000-3039; well detailed; maximum boiler diameter correct but placed too far back; wrong sand box.

129 Good workmanship; sparse detail; boiler and driver diameter too small; good sand dome.

130 Actually a USRA with Vanderbilt tender. No specific C&O detail

131 USRA version.

132 With outboard trailing truck and clear vision tender.

133 1300 series; equipped with plastic locomotive brake shoes, NMRA review 2/75.

134 Unsprung.

135 Handbuilt pilot for Akane Models.

136 #1600-1644; 24-inch minimum radius; NMRA Review 1/81.

137 Poor runner; unpainted

138 #1645-1659; late version, single motor.

139 "CB Royale" series; l6VB Vanderbilt tender.

140 Worthington feedwater heater; brass disc driver centers, stainless tires; runs too slowly. PFM supplied faster motors upon request. There was an improvement but the locomotives were still slow for passenger engines. NWSL makes a motor specifically to solve this problem.

141 Elesco feedwater heater; "Sportsman" and "George Washington" locomotives; brass driver centers stainless tires; runs too slowly. PFM supplied faster motors upon request. There was an improvement but the locomotives were still slow for passenger engines. NWSL makes a motor specifically to solve this problem.

142 Streamlined; rebuilt from F-19.

143 Handbuilt by Atlas-Nakayama; operating poppet valve gear, Box is 10 1/2″ by 5″ by 3″, Denim textured. No label. Typed note explains the delicate poppet mechanism.

144 Dimensions and detail in error; rivet detail on a welded cab incorrect; tender does not resemble any known C&O prototype.

145 Handbuilt Custom Series.

146 #300-307 Baker valve gear.

147 "Ruby Signature" model; extra detail; red velvet box.

148 #610-614;63-inch drivers.

149 Built by Atlas/Toby. #610-614.

150 Built by Atlas/Toby; #600-604. Serial number can be found on left rear of frame.

151 Factory painted, incorrect shade of orange; #500-502; 2-motors; poor runner; NMRA Review 2/81.

152 #4942; Vanderbilt tender.

153 #4960; beveled tender.

154 #4941; straight-side tender.

155 Worthington feedwater heater; original tender.

156 Elesco feedwater heater; original tender.

157 Heavy USRA; Worthington feedwater heater.

158 Heavy USRA; C&S #909; Elesco feedwater heater; RM Review 7/78.

159 Blue Toby box. Models came with and without bumpers on tender front.

160 Green United box. United plate mounted on boiler backhead.

161 Window sashes all in closed position. United plate on bottom of frame near drawbar.

162 #5600-5607; Elesco feedwater heater; Box-Pok main driver.

163 Added piping and back-up light.

164 Added detail and wireless draw bar.

165 5000 class; pre-1940 version. MR Review 6/77.

166 5000 class; pre-1940 version.

167 900 class; post 1940 version; MR Review 6/77.

168 Early handbuilt model; heavy USRA.

169 #314-399; heavy USRA.

170 ''Hiawatha''; NMRA Review '72.

171 Box marked F-6; #405.

172 Upgraded model includes lost-wax compressor, whistle and generator, spoked lead truck wheels, tool box and tender piping.

173 Drivers are 79-inch diameter, should be 84-inch.

174 Small Mars light; bell at 12 o'clock position. Two-part red box.

175 Large Mars light; bell at 9 o'clock position, purple velveteen box.

176 Spoked drivers; main frame outside trailing truck.

177 Disc drivers; inside frame.

178 Warren & Ouachita Valley #1; Mid-Continent Railway Museum.

179 5100 class; VIP version.

180 #201-205. Vulclain compound.

181 #1151-1155; original version.

182 VIP; original version.

183 Modern version; larger capacity sand domes than original version.

184 Factory painted, modern version.

185 Original version; lacks hot water pump.

186 Modern version.

187 Second modernization

188 U.S. kit made by ACI. Long Beach, California.

189 ''Old Timer'' assembled from ACI kit.

190 #583; RM Review 5/77.

191 Original version; Vanderbilt tender.

192 Modern version; rectangular tender.

193 Became D&RGW #1453 &1457; ex- N&W

194 Early 1961 production serial numbered 2001-2290; late 1961 version serial numbered 3701-3990; box marked ''L-125''.

195 Sheet steel pilot; box marked ''L-125''.

196 Lost-wax cast boiler-tube pilot.

197 Original version; slide valves; factory painted #3404 &3407

198 Rebuilt version. piston valves.

199 Detailed by Back Shop from UP Challengers.

200 #760-793; Gould Lines; similar to UP 4-6-0; NMRA Review 73.

201 Factory painted, #1600-1609;3-cylinder; double Walschaerts valve gear on right side; brakeman's shack on tender; rectangular cab sides; single dome; tenders had ''Royal Gorge/Moffat Tunnel'' insignia, with pre-1942 ''Denver & Rio Grande Western'' lettering; other tenders had post-1942 windswept style ''Rio Grande'' lettering.

202 Worthington feedwater heater; 3-cylinder; ''sport'' cab; brakeman's shack on tender.

203 Factory painted, #1602; early herald. Elesco feedwater heater; ''sport'' cab.

204 Factory painted, #1609; late herald; Elesco feedwater heater; ''sport'' cab.

205 #1550-1553; ex-N&W K-3 ''Water Buffalo.''

206 #1700-1713: Blue Toby box. Access door on both sides of tender. Coined rear tender step.

207 Coffin feedwater heater; became D&RGW.

208 Ex-Union RR large transfer switcher; packed in gray foam with rubberized horsehair top pad, in dark blue denim-textured cardboard box with silver printing on top and gold printing on end of box.

209 Ex-Union RR Large transfer switcher. packed in gray foam in medium blue cardboard box with gold printing on end; no printing on top of box; printing on box end includes; ''MFG. BY ATLAS INDUSTRIES, INC. KAWAGUCHI,JAPAN, EXCLUSIVELY FOR PACIFIC FAST MAIL'' with PFM winged logo.

210 Air tanks on top of boiler.

211 15 made with Pittman motors. Hand scribed serial number on cab apron.

212 Elesco feedwater heater; caboose included.

213 One motor in firebox; second motor in tender; front drivers unpowered.

214 One motor in firebox driving two mechanisms; drivers under tender unpowered.

215 Original version; heavy USRA.

216 Modernized version; Elesco feedwater heater; disc drivers; Delta trailing truck.

217 Factory painted, modernized version; Elesco feedwater heater; disc drivers; Delta trailing truck.

218 1940 version; Elesco feedwater heater; disc main drivers; spoked front and rear drivers.

219 #401-452. Worthington BL feedwater heater.

220 #388; single pump; convertible coal/oil tender; Westside G-File #73; RM Review 3/77.

221 Factory painted, Glacier Park simplified.

222 Factory painted Glacier Park; models serial numbered on bottom of driver retainer plate.

223 #500-561; RM Review 10/77.

224 Factory painted, unsprung drivers; 34-inch minimum radius.

225 50 built with Pittman motors.

226 Lost-wax cast pumps.

227 Open cab; Vanderbilt tender.

228 Vestibule cab; Vanderbilt tender.

229 #3000-3144; Vanderbilt tender; NMRA Review 1/76.

230 #3210-3254; Vanderbilt tender.

231 Factory painted, Glacier Park. Heavy USRA.

232 Flat bottom Worthington BL feedwater heater and two air pumps on left side.

233 Factory painted, #2106,2119,2127 with 60″ Goat Herald on tender; tender is convertible for coal or oil.

234 Can motor; well-made model; RM Review 7/79.

235 Factory painted, #2003,2007, &2023; models serial numbered on rear of cab.

236 Factory painted, models serial numbered.

237 St. Paul & Pacific ''William Crooks''. Gem obtained models from ''Universal Model Products''.

238 Hinged cab deck apron; offset forward sand dome to clear dry pipe; can motor with enclosed idler gearbox.

239 6-Wheel Vanderbilt tender; Westside G-File #93.

240 Factory painted, slope-front cab. 248 painted black with silver smokebox, 2 unpainted.

241 Painted black with silver smokebox; #2514,2524,2527; with earlier style 60″ Goat Herald on tender

242 Original Version; rectangular cab.

243 Unsprung drivers.

244   Factory painted, Glacier Park; working power reverse.

245   Factory painted, Glacier Park; models serial numbered.

246   3-cylinder transfer switcher; Indiana Harbor Belt.

247   Models serial numbered 1-12.

248   Model #13 has working reverse gear.

249   Camelback; ''Mother Hubbard''.

250   #1750-1890; Heavy USRA; drivers 2-inch undersize; MR Review 7/81.

251   Wood cab, single air pump; Stephenson valve gear; Westside G-File #100.

252   Steel cab; twin air pumps; Walschaerts valve gear; Westside G-File #101.

253   #23-26; built by Baldwin in 1912.

254   Factory painted,16-inch minimum radius.

255   Factory painted, modernized USRA.

256   Factory painted, #101-110; sparsely detailed model with shiny plated drivers and red fiber draw bar; offset forward sand dome to clear external steam pipe.

257   377 series; NMRA Review 3/71.

258   Factory painted, and lettered; light USRA.

259   #1715-1719; ex-Wabash.

260   VIP l5th anniversary set of individually numbered locomotives and caboose numbered 953.

261   5300 series; light USRA; Worthington Type S feedwater heater.

262   Streamlined #151; ''Chippewa''.

263   Serial number and year stamped on retainer plate.

264   #560-565; heavy USRA.

265   With Modeltronics sound system.

266   Michigan Central version.

267   P&LE; incorrect boiler contour, a conical taper from smokebox to firebox; NMRA Review '76.

268   Boston & Albany; MR Review 1/77.

269   Factory painted, Boston & Albany.

270   #11OO-1109; Boston & Albany.

271   #1375-1399; built by Alco in 1912.

272   ''Empire State Express.''

273   Lake Shore & Michigan Southern.

274   #604; Lake Shore & Michigan Southern.

275   MR Review 8/78

276   Centipede tender, two-part red boxes have blackened out C&NW H labels..

277   #5344; spoked drivers; Westside G-File #83; MR Review 8/78.

278   #5405-5454; ''Craftsman Series #4'' on gold label on top of box lid; black label on end of box; Box-Pok drivers; Elesco feedwater heater; rectangular tender with 6-wheel trucks; Westside G-File #117; MR Review 8/78.

279   #5450; ''Craftsman Series #6'' on silver label on end of box; Scullin drivers. PT4 centipede tender; RM Review 3/79.

280   Streamlined ''2Oth Century'', PT4 tender.

281   fp,3 variations; all drivers flanged; one center driver pair blind; two driver pairs blind.

282   Factory painted, actually an L-3c.

283   69-inch Box-Pok drivers; red foam packing.

284   72-inch Scullin drivers.

285   69-inch Box-Pok drivers.

286   Foot boards, long tender.

287   Elesco feedwater heater (eyebrow); RMC Review 3/82.

288   Worthington SA feedwater heater; RMC Review 3/82.

289   Sunken Elesco feedwater heater. RMC Review 3/82.

290   Blind unsprung drivers.

291   Locomotive only, less motor and tender.

292   100 built with Pittman motors.

293   Elesco feedwater heater; pilot mounted pumps; inside bearing trailing truck; model driver diameter of 61 inches should be 63 inches.

294   Pumps on boiler front.

295   Streamlined ''Shore Line''.

296   #586; pre-1930; ex-LE&W light USRA.

297   Serial numbered 2701-2990 on early 1961 production.

298   Brass body, 2-axle drive.

299   Improved boiler contour.

300   Built with Pittman DC-71 B motor.

301   Without smoke deflectors.

302   With smoke deflectors.

303   #841-850; ex-N&W K-3; ''Water Buffalo.''

304   Factory painted, handbuilt for N&W.

305   1930's version; 9,000 gallon tender.

306   1937 version; slab side rods with multiple bearing crossheads; modern tender with 'as-built' version of #1200-1209 with original tender but no auxiliary tender.

307   1950 version; roller bearing rods and alligator crossheads; auxiliary water tender.

308   Pittman motor.

309   #2195-2200; round smokebox door; Key imported N&W Y-5, Y-6 and Y-6a in 1982.

310   #2171-2194; oblong smokebox door.

311   USRA, ''CB Royale'' series; NMRA Review 6/80.

312   1940 era; NMRA Review '72.

313   Two motors drive 12 axles; ''Jawn Henry'', 4500 horsepower.

314   Spoked lead and trailing wheels.

315   Air pumps on smokebox front.

316   Factory painted, serial number plate on back of cab.

317   Last new NP steam locomotives.

318   3-window cab side; back-up light.

319   2-window cab side; without back-up light; NMRA Review 3/76., model includes tender slope sheet and ashpan details for oil to coal conversion.

320   ''CB Royale'' series; first Northern.

321   Late 1880s; RM Review 12/78.

322   Pictured with 90-F-82 tender.

323   USRA with Belpaire Firebox.

324   USRA with Belpaire Firebox; N4b caboose included; Westside G-File #118.

325   Cab interior; can motor.

326   Rare; outside sanders.

327   ''CB Royale'' series; ex-N&W Y-3.

328   Diamond stack and wood beam pilot available separately.

329   Post World War II era; solid pilot, 4 steps at front of tender.

330 Early model; sheet and turnings.

331 Two pilots; two smokebox fronts; long distance tender with brakeman's shack; NMRA Review 6/81.

332 #200-229; as delivered in 1938-39. Piping and detail not as refined an on later PFM version. Brass driver centers.

333 #1188; skyline casing.

334 Open platforms, curved sides.

335 #5399; equipped with operating Franklin OC poppet valves and running board skirts.

336 #3038; elephant ear and stack casing deflectors.

337 #1140;1940 era streamlined version.

338 Well-built model; blind main drivers.

339 Semi-streamlined; brakeman's shack on tender.

340 Camelback; NMRA Review '71.

341 Rebuilt from I-lOsa 2-8-0.

342 #515-520; ex-N&W K-3.

343 #601-606; "Governor" class.

344 #601-606; "Governor" class; year and serial number stamped on retainer plate.

345 #613-622; "Statesman" class; 73-inch drivers, should be 77-inch; rectangular tender. Conversion chassis with new frame, drivers and valve gear was available separately at cost. (approx. $30.00)

346 Factory painted, two-tone gray; #607-612. Hicken's tender.

347 "CB Royale" series; ex. C&O H-7, RF&P #1,2,3.

348 Originally built for USSR as 5′ gauge, converted to 4′ 8 1/2″ gauge and sold to several American RR's due to Russian revolution; with can motor and removable cab.

349 Factory painted with gold PFM logo on tender, 160 pieces were equipped with PFM sound and sold to dealers as demonstrators.

350 #4400-4410. Scullin drivers.

351 Kit #167-4 $19.95; #600-605 Sagami motor.

352 #800-819, later SP GS-7/8.

353 #4501; wrong tender; MR Review 1/79.

354 Elesco feedwater heater; MR Review 1/82.

355 #4535-4539 &4576;2-8-0 booster under tender; NMRA Review 6/89.

356 Convertible coal/oil tender, steel pilot.

357 #5200-5249; light USRA.

358 Hinged apron to tender.

359 Hodges trailing truck.

360 Shop locomotive; NMRA Review '70; Westside G-File #15.

361 Shop locomotive; Westside G-File #89; NMRA Review 9/70.

362 1966 imports had the "water bottle," or "sausage" tender. 1967 import had the clear vision Vanderbilt tender; both in red box.

363 Texas & New Orleans; NMRA Review '76.

364 Slope-back tender; slide valves.

365 Round tender; piston valves.

366 Texas & New Orleans; Vanderbilt tender, high headlight, no number boards.

367 SP T&NO #1645; West Coast version rectangular tender, low headlight, number boards.

368 Available with either a Vanderbilt or whale-back tender; both in blue box.

369 #2819 Northwestern Pacific; NMRA Review 12/80.

370 Built by Baldwin in 1900 for EL Paso & Northwestern; became SF #2505-2508; RM Review 5/79.

371 St. Louis & Southwestern.

372 Texas & New Orleans; brakeman's shack on tender.

373 Small drivers for logging; Westside G-Files # 103 & 104.

374 Elesco feedwater heater; Vanderbilt tender; sport cab.

375 Coffin feedwater heater; ex-Boston & Maine; Westside G-Files #91 & 106.

376 Clamshell stack; in blue box.

377 Only rear mechanism powered.

378 Equalized drivers; tender booster; "Craftsman Series" #9.

379 Better drive than Max Gray engine.

380 Factory painted, individually numbered: cab lighting: drive improved from '74 run, lettered #4278 or #4282.

381 Flat front; super-detailed.

382 Pilot models; Central Pacific "Governor Stanford".

383 WMC G-File #106; 3500 series with 8 wheel coal tender, disc main drivers, Walschaerts valve gear, multiple bearing crossheads, Coffin feedwater heater, 20mm Canon motor.

384 Centennial set; Central Pacific "Jupiter" and Union Pacific #119.

385 Unsprung drivers; Delta trailing truck with booster engine.

386 St. Louis & Southwestern; Sagami motor.

387 St. Louis & Southwestern; Tyco motor.

388 Inside frame trailing truck with 51″ spoked wheels.

389 Unsprung drivers; extra cylinder block for conversion to Walschaerts valve gear; Westside G-File #3.

390 Complete SP fire train; loco equipped with fire apparatus; two water cars with fire apparatus; WMC G-File #85; RM review 8/77.

391 First of "CB Royale" series; Texas & New Orleans #631-633.

392 Long Vanderbilt tender, NMRA Review '76.

393 #2414; shorter 9,000 gallon Vanderbilt tender.

394 Elesco feedwater heater; built in 1924 for El Paso & Southwestern; NMRA Review 1/80.

395 Skyline casing; RM Review 9/79. El Paso and Southwestern, built in 1924.

396 External dry-steam pipe; Westside G-File #71.

397 "Daylight"; blind unsprung drivers.

398 100 made with Pittman motors.

399 "Daylight"; separate skirts; two turbo generators.

400 "Daylight"; idler gearbox; three turbo generators.

401 Both SP and WP decals included.

402 Factory painted, "Daylight"; can motor.

403 Factory painted, "Daylight"; can motor; a few available unpainted;73″ Box-Pok drivers; detailed open cab; #4410-4415.

404 Factory painted, two sand domes; Westside G-file #14.

405 Two sand domes; Westside G-File #14; NMRA Review '74.

406 800 series Elesco feedwater heater.

407 #610; RM Review 11/78; MM article 5/82.

408 #900-904; MR Review 3/82.

409 Northwestern Pacific #2842.

410 Bow front; super detailed.

411 WMC G-File #39-A, KTM DH-13 motor.

412 "Daylight"; model made of copper.

413 "Daylight"; NMRA Review '77.

414 C-57 short Vanderbilt tender.

415 #402-419; C-57 long Vanderbilt tender.

416 Master series; snow plow.

417 "CB Royale" series; ex-C&O H-7 with 24RA tender.

418 RM Review 5/78; MR Review 9/78.

419 Streamlined "bathtubs"; removable smoke deflectors.

420 Master series, streamlined.

421 Oil burner. Walschaerts valve gear; Westside G-File #84.

422 800 series; handbuilt model.

423 Smoke lifters; mars light.

424 820 series; Kemtron swing coupler. Turned headlight. Serial number on frame. Green box with silver letters.

425 3-cylinder; Westside G-File #24; MR Review 10/71.

426 Extra tender included.

427 Headlight on smokebox front; semi-Vanderbilt tender with 6-wheel buckeye trucks; Alco 1936-37.

428 Factory painted, 1936 version; all drivers powered.

429 Factory painted; flat smokebox bottom; rubber tube drive; 14-wheel pedestal tender; Alco 1942-44

430 Factory painted; round smokebox; gear drive.

431 Factory painted; round smokebox; improved drive; serial numbered on rear of cab.

432 All drivers powered.

433 Factory painted, only rear drivers powered.

434 Unsprung drivers, only rear drivers powered.

435 Full round smokebox; all drivers powered.

436 Brake shoes, open frame motor, open gearbox, lighted headlight, no backhead.

437 Factory painted, superdetailed; all drivers powered.

438 Factory painted, all drivers powered by rubber tube drive; flat bottom on smokebox.

439 Factory painted; rivets on cab roof.

440 Factory painted, exhaust pipe from front cylinders.

441 Factory painted, exhaust pipe from forward cylinders; riveted cab roof; all drivers powered.

442 Factory painted, round smokebox; cab interior detail; 48.1 gearing, all drivers powered.

443 Factory painted, serial number plate on back of cab; new quiet gear drive.

444 Later version; coal boards; excellent model; NMRA Review 3/81.

445 As built; cooling pipes on pilot deck.

446 Smallest of the USRA locomotives. Rectangular tender carries 8,000 gallons of water and 16 tons of coal.

447 Factory painted, Brunswick Green, Streamlined #3768 with skirts.

448 1940's version as built, #1120; streamlined.

449 1940's version as built, #3768; streamlined, factory painted Bronze.

450 B&O D-30.

451 1940's postwar version, streamlined, #1120.

452 Can motor with idler gear box; good detail and workmanship; MR Review 11/76.

453 Upgraded model with Cal-Scale castings.

454 Handbuilt, sprung floor plate between engine and tender.

455 #4500; USRA B&O Q-3; standard USRA design with B&O cab.

456 Revised model; sagging cab.

457 DM&IR; air tanks on top of boiler; Elesco feedwater heater

458 1940's version as built, streamlined.

459 Southern style cab (close to B&O P-5).

460 Modernized; 6-wheel tender trucks.

461 Undersize boiler diameter.

462 Rushton stack; Michigan II.

463 Operating poppet valve gear; wrong tender.

464 Cab too high; tender is 6 feet too short; piping incorrect; green felt box.

465 Feather River Shay-Hutchison Lumber Company; 1922.

466 Heavy USRA; Elesco feedwater heater; RM Review 7/78.

467 Diamond stack; Cherry River.

468 Excessive cab roof overhang. Westside G-File #25.

469 Arch bar trucks; wood cab. "Tahoe"; NMRA Review '70.

470 Reno "Original", Motor in tender.

471 Quite, well-made model,24-inch minimum radius.

472 #610; two motors; rebuild of the triplex.

473 "CB Royale" series; #700-720.

474 "CB Royale" series; #736-742; ex-N&W Y-3s.

475 #700; three Canon motors; rebuilt to 2-8-8-0.

476 700 series; streamlined.

477 Pacific Coast three-cylinder.

478 #151-162; similar to D&RGW S-33.

479 #1-20; Stephenson valve gear.

480 #21-63; Walschaerts valve gear.

481 #327-331; no rivets on smokebox; built-up pilot.

482 #327-331; rivets on smokebox; lost-wax cast pilot.

483 #327-331. improved model.

484 #86-106: Gould lines ten wheeler; similar to Rio Grande.

485 #171-180; smoke lifters; NMRA Review '73.

486 SP & WP decals included; same as SP GS-6; MR Review 10/81.

487 Individual locomotive; 4-wheel tender.

488 Kit; locomotive with slope-back tender.

489 "Birdie"; freelance logger; outside frame; runs on HO track but looks more like S Scale narrow gauge.

490 Baldwin-built compound Mallet.

491 Kit; convertible tank locomotive could be built as an 0-4-0 or 0-6-0.

492 "Prairie King"; both straight and diamond stacks included.

493 Tank switcher; two different old-time stacks included.

494 Kit; 2-6-2T or 2-4-2T.

495 Reworked B&0 O-10-0, sold as "The Brute" freelance locomotive; RM Review 12/79.

496 Lehigh Valley inspection locomotive #1.

497 PA&NY Canal & RR inspection locomotive.

498 ''Standard;'' AT&SF #3462.

499 Baldwin #60,000 3-cylinder high-pressure compound with water tube firebox.

500 Drivers unsprung; clear vision tender.

501 2000 series renumbered to 9000 series in 1946.

502 Slope-back tender; SF Modeler Review 11/77.

503 Rebuilt from 2-8-0; clear vision tender.

504 Experimental ''black-plate'' finish.

505 Constructed by Atlas-Asahi; mostly turned details; a few poor castings.

506 Single sand dome; no feedwater heater; unsprung drivers; coal tender has 12,000 gallon water capacity; blue box 2 1/4″ sq. × 15″ long); model is an improvement over International AT&SF 2-8-2 model; MR Review 1/60.

507 Handbuilt by Atlas-Nakayama; coal tender has 12,000 gallon water capacity.

508 Worthington feedwater heater; coal tender with 12,000 gallon water capacity; also represents locomotive #3189.

509 #4060-4085; no brake shoes; late model Elesco feedwater pump; Delta trailing truck; 12,000 gallon tender; accurately scaled model, not highly detailed, green box, cardboard wrapper.

510 #4086-4100; late model Elesco feedwater pump; Delta trailing truck; convertible tender to 15,000 gallon water capacity; NMRA Review 8/77.

511 #4103, 08,09, 10, 14 & 15 had oil tenders with 15,000 gallon water capacity; few castings; model lacks cab rivet detail, valve gear ladders, and brake shoes.

512 #4193-4196; 8-wheel tender carries 18 tons of coal and 12,000 gallons of water; Baker valve gear; Coffin feedwater heater; ex-B&M locomotive. 2Omm Canon coreless motor; Westside G-File #114.

513 8-wheel coal tender; Walschaerts valve gear; Coffin feedwater heater; ex-B&M locomotive.

514 Excellent 8-wheel tender with 9,000 gallon water capacity; also correct for 1600,3010 & 3020 classes.

515 Turtle-back tender with 12,000 gallon water capacity.

516 Westside Lumber #8; three-cylinder; Westside G-File #109; RM Review 10/78.

517 Rectangular cab; Delta trailing truck; old-style feedwater pump; no brake shoes; tender with 15,000 gallon water capacity.

518 Convertible coal/oil tender.

519 Sport cab with single ventilator on roof center line; RP-25 wheel contour; Delta trailing truck; later model feedwater pump, brake shoes; oil tender with 15,000 gallon water capacity, correct for #3891-3899.

520 Fleetwood set of three. Oil tender with 20,000 gallon water capacity; correct for #5006-5010.

521 Whitetop; three-cylinder.

522 #268; modernized; RM Review 3/77.

523 #278; NMRA Review 7/71.

524 #278; with coreless motor.

525 Twin sealed-beam Mars light with extra conventional headlight in box.

526 Whaleback tender with 12,000 gallon water capac-ity; drive modification required to negotiate 30-inch radius curves; NMRA Review 12/76.

527 #1398 &1399; rectangular tender with 12,000 gallon water capacity.

528 #1235 & 1239 received low-mounted feedwater heater, #1256 & 1258 received high-mounted feedwater heater.

529 Excellent model; round-head crank pin screws; 12,000 gallon water capacity.

530 Excellent model; hex-head crank pin screws; 12,000 gallon water capacity tender.

531 Non-streamlined; #1342 received a high-mounted feedwater heater; tender has 12,000 gallon water capacity.

532 Handbuilt by Nakayama; 74-inch drivers; Delta trailing truck; coal tender with 12,000 gallon water capacity.

533 Model comes in blue box with yellow label; 79-inch drivers; turned headlight. Delta trailing truck; later model feedwater pump; tender with 20,000 gallon water capacity; MR Review 5/62.

534 79-inch diameter Baldwin disc drivers, hinged stack.

535 Some factory painted; partly Zamac construction; poor runner; superstructure too high and too far forward on frame; unsprung; rear 74-inch drivers are in firebox; Hodges trailing truck; coal tender with 12,000 gallon water capacity.

536 Oil tender with 10,000 gallon water capacity.

537 Second modernization; 79-inch disc drivers; single large sand dome; rectangular oil tender with 20,000 gallon water capacity.

538 Sprung drivers; poor castings; mostly turnings; firebox too wide; two dry-steam pipes between turret and steam dome; folding stack; handbuilt 84-inch drivers.

539 Handbuilt by Atlas-Kawai; sprung drivers.

540 Factory painted, #3463; model 82-inch drivers, should be 84-inch diameter; no brake shoes; locomotive and tender too tall; rectangular tender with 20,000 gallon water capacity.

541 Factory painted, #3463; brake hangers; rivet detail on tender deck; locomotive and tender too tall. Single box labeled ''Crown''; rectangular oil tender with 20,000 gallon water capacity.

542 Date and serial number on plate on rear of cab.

543 Fleetwood set of three models in one box; correctly proportioned locomotive and tender.

544 Mostly turnings; sprung drivers, no brake shoes; boiler contour and cab incorrect; tender has 24,500 gallon water capacity.

545 Fleetwood set of three models in one box; 56-foot tender with 24,300 gallon water capacity and 7,000 gallon oil capacity.

546 First rebuild with Elesco feedwater heater, 80-inch drivers; rectangular tender with 22,000 gallon water capacity; a few custom painted #3757 by importer.

547 900 horsepower; RM Review 7/77.

548 Tapered rods; sprung drivers; 56-foot tender.

549 Tapered rods; plastic brake shoes; 56-foot tender with 24,500 gallon water capacity, 7,000 gallon oil capacity; built by Atlas-Asahi.

550 Factory painted, with Worthington feedwater heater.

551 Elesco feedwater heater; poor workmanship; wrong valve gear.

552 Locomotive fitted with plastic brake shoes; 250 factory painted black; 250 factory painted black with silver smokebox front.

553 Powered B-unit; 1600 horsepower; "Sharknose".

554 Worthington type SA feedwater heater; two air pumps on side.

555 Very early model patterned after GC&E #12 sans 3rd truck. All turnings and sheet brass, very simplified drive mechanism that runs surprisingly well.

556 Spoked drivers with 36:1 worm and gear, or Box-Pok drivers with 48:1 worm and gear.

557 Streamlined "Commodore Vanderbilt" #5344 with spoked drivers and conventional rods.

558 Streamlined "Commodore Vanderbilt" #5344 with Scullin disc drivers and roller bearing rods.

559 Single sand dome; boiler tube pilot.

560 Importer labeled this engine a Y-2, it is a class Y #405.

561 With Pittman DC-7OX motor and plastic locomotive brake shoes.

562 Originally built for USSR as 5′ gauge, converted to 4′ 8 1/2″ gauge and sold to several American RR's due to Russian revolution; with Pittman DC-62B motor.

563 Texas & New Orleans.

564 Two sand domes; corrugated sheet metal pilot; WMC G-File #14.

565 Factory painted,Crown''; with Tenshodo MH-5 motor.

566 "Crown''; 100 painted, lettered and numbered; 2 painted and numbered but not lettered; 2 unpainted; 1 painted but not lettered and numbered.

567 First HO production locomotive to have brake shoes; skyline casing; in 1982 Key imported well-detailed models of the MT4, both with and without skyline casing.

568 Plastic locomotive brake shoes; Cal-Scale air compressor.

569 Revised model with hex-head crank pin screws, marker conduit, bell cord and coined tender frame.

570 Pittman DC-7OX motor. Locomotive brake shoes fitted.

571 GN original version; #5400-5406.

572 201 class; with optional snowplow.

573 206 class; with optional snowplow.

574 Footboard pilot; two air pumps; auxiliary water-bottle tender; Westside G-File #66, motor is undersize.

575 Road pilot; one air pump; brakeman's seat and window in cab, auxiliary water-bottle tender; l6mm can motor; Westside G-File #66-A.

576 Platinum series; cab details, mechanical lubricator, sound system; coal load in tender.

577 1300 series; equipped with plastic locomotive brake shoes.

578 Worthington BL feedwater heater; rectangular tender.

579 Operating poppet valve shafting.

580 Modern WWII era with solid cast pilot; drop coupler; cab interior detail; modern smokebox front; enclosed gearbox; radio antenna and 4-wheel trucks on tender.

581 #600-604; pilot too high.

582 Boiler diameter undersize; cab was welded, should not show rivet detail; incorrect dome, drivers and tender.

583 Tapered rods. plastic brake shoes. 56-foot tender with 24,500 gallon water capacity, 7,000 gallon capacity; plated retainer plate; brass conducting drawbar. closed gear box; built by Atlas-Asahi; "Santa Fe" in red lettering on box, packed in blue-green foam.

584 Powered A-Unit; PRR version.

585 With disk drivers, factory painted.

586 3-motors; original version; all drivers powered.

587 3-motors; rebuilt version; all drivers powered.

588 Belpaire firebox too narrow (narrower than boiler).

589 Streamlined shroud.

590 Sprung drivers; added valves and piping on smokebox; sander detail.

591 Kit; can be built as AC-4,5 or 6.

592 Kit; can be built as an AC-10,11,12.

593 Two tender styles; pilot too high; lead truck wheels oversized.

594 #1; NMRA Review 4/78.

595 Flat can motor; 18-inch minimum radius.

596 1890 era Baldwin side-tank switcher.

597 Baldwin-built; Oregon-American; ex-Long-Bell #105; no rivet detail on smokebox.

598 Peninsula Terminal, Silver Falls Timber.

599 Georgia Pacific; ex-CD Johnson Lumber.

600 WA Woodward Lumber Company

601 Sierra; 132 made with Pittman motors.

602 Kosmos Timber: Compound Mallet; early models spring belt drive. Conversion chassis available.

603 Crown Willamette Paper; first NWSL loco import; open worm gears; unbraced footboards; turned details.

604 Open gear box; Rayonier.

605 Closed gear box; Rayonier.

606 Sierra RR. NMRA Review '74.

607 California Western "Super Skunk;" ex-Medco #3.

608 Hammond Lumber Company #16; Minarets.

609 Hammond Lumber Company #16 &17; Minarets.

610 Weyerhauser Timber; NMRA Review '70.

611 Improved Drive; Weyerhauser Timber.

612 Pilot model; Eagle Gorge Logging Co.

613 Separate tender available.

614 Solid wheels.

615 Spoked wheels.

616 Separate tender available; spoked wheels; 64 models made with Pittman motor.

617 Vertical boiler; NMRA Review '73; Westside G-File #42.

618 Hillcrest Modern #10.

619 Balloon stack and wood beam pilot available separately.

620 Diamond stack and wood beam pilot available separately.

621 Early model; sheet and turnings.

622 8-wheel pickup and flywheel

623 4-wheel pickup; 100 with Pittman motors.

624 Long frame; steel cab.

625 Benson T-Boiler; 2-cylinder.

626 Michigan California Lumber #2; construction #122; as built in 1883 (Canadian).

627 Michigan III; diamond stack.

628 Construction #60; vertical boiler.

629 T-boiler; Michigan-California Lumber #2.

630 Harrington Lumber; NMRA Review 4/79; Namiki instrument motor.

631 Rushton stack; Michigan II.

632 Feather River Shay-Hutchison Lumber Company; 1922.

633 Diamond stack; Cherry River.

634 Arch bar trucks; wood cab.

635 Construction #1; Coos Bay Lumber #10; MR Review 1/82.

636 Construction #22; Sauk River Lumber #23; MR Review 1/82.

637 Old cab; straight stack; San Joaquin.

638 Three-cylinder; Westside Lumber Company #10.

639 Pacific Coast three-cylinder.

640 Westside Lumber #8; three-cylinder; Westside G-File #109; RM Review 10/78.

641 Whitetop; three-cylinder.

642 C&O C-9, N&W #56, Red River, El Paso & Southwestern; three-cylinder; wood and steel cab; balloon and straight stack supplied, beautifully made, poor runner.

643 ''Beartrap'' spark arrester and high domes.

644 200 built with Romford 3-pole motor.

645 Detachable cinder trap.

646 #71-73 class B4e; NMRA Review 4/80.

647 #268; modernized.

648 Original Montezuma kit.

649 Modernized Montezuma kit.

650 #278; NMRA Review 7/71; DV-130 open frame motor.

651 #278; with coreless motor.

652 #420; Baldwin built in 1887; became RGS #42; RM Review 6/79.

653 #318; MR Review 5/79.

654 #463; round number plate on smokebox front; tool kit and instruction manual included.

655 #463; rectangular number plate on smokebox front.

656 Slide valve; modern.

657 #464; piston valve; NMRA Review 3/77.

658 #463; piston valve; tool kit and instruction manual included; cab interior detail; can motor; MR Review 9/77; NMRA Review 1/78.

659 Lindsay motor; no rivet heads on sideframe.

660 Interior detail; cab roof removable; can motor with idler gearbox.

661 ''Master Series''; ''Denver''.

662 ''Limited Edition''; as built.

663 #42 ex-D&RGW #420; Baldwin-built in 1887; RM Review 6/79.

664 Ex. Florence and Cripple Creek locomotive.

665 Built at National Iron Works in 1882.

666 Industrial locomotive with 4-Wheel tender.

667 Outside frame counter balances.

668 Surrey, Sussex & Southampton.

669 Upgraded model with detailed backhead; ex-Uintah locomotive.

670 Baldwin-built Uintah tank locomotive; RM Review 2/79.

671 Nevada County #9; MR Review 4/71; Westside G-File #23.

672 5579,5582,5583 and 5589. Westside G-File #119: RM Review 9/78.

673 Freelance; two motors; both slide and piston valve cylinders included.

674 660 horsepower; S-3 truck sideframes.

675 Lost-wax cast truck sideframes.

676 660 horsepower; NMRA Review 11/78.

677 800 horsepower; RM Review 7/77.

678 900 horsepower; RM Review 7/77.

679 Kit: ass body and frame.

680 1600 horsepower; six traction motors.

681 1600 horsepower; six traction motors; RM Review 1/78.

682 1000 horsepower; RM Review 7/77.

683 2500 horsepower; low hood; model lacks exhaust stack; RM Review 10/79.

684 3000 horsepower; low hood; RM Review 4/74.

685 1800 horsepower; Eastern version.

686 2 Unit Articulated; 2 motors; MR rev 5/83.

687 E-33 Rectifier Electric; 3300 Horsepower; built by GE; PC, NH, N&W, VGN.

688 Factory painted, Milwaukee 2-car electric articulated interurban,

689 2750 horsepower; six traction motors; low hood; NMRA Review '73.

690 2750 horsepower; six traction motors; high hood.

691 C-630; 3000 horsepower; six traction motors. C-636: Alco RSw; 3600 horsepower; six motors; RM Review 5/80.

692 Powered A-unit, dummy B-unit; 2000 horsepower; MR Review 7/71.

693 Powered A-unit; 2000 horsepower.

694 Dummy B-Unit; 2000 horsepower.

695 Power conversion kit for dummy unit.

696 Powered A-unit, dummy B-unit; Westside G-Files #48 &53.

697 #5305-5314 with dynamic brakes.

698 2-car set, powered coach, dummy trailer; sprung buffers, sprung trucks.

699 Sprung buffers, sprung trucks.

700 Eight wheel underfloor drive.

701 Reviewed MR 7/84; RMC 9/84.

702 Actually a San Bernadino ''Twelve'' car.

703 Modernized, powered.

704 Modernized, unpowered.

705 Steeple cab switcher; NMRA review 7/72.

706 Open end wood car.

707 Review MR 7/84, RMC 9/84.

708 Actually a San Bernadino 1370 combine.

709 Factory painted, 1929 Mod., eight wheel semi-underfloor drive, 2 rail overhead switch.

710 With center door, eight wheel underfloor drive.

711 Without center door, eight wheel underfloor drive.

712 Semi-finished Kit; Birney.

713 #375,376 &378, from Kumata's book.

714 Taylor MCB trucks; became Central California Traction Co. motor.

715 US-made; Lindsay L-140 power truck; 1000 horsepower.

716 US-made; Baker eight wheel drive; 1000 horsepower.

717 US-made; kit.

718 GN, PRR, UP version; Lindsay L-140 drive; 1000 horsepower.

719 GN, PRR, UP version; Baker 8-wheel drive; 1000 horsepower.

720 Original version #5400-5406.

721 Modern version; #175-181.

722 1500 horsepower; MR Review 1/72.

723 Factory painted; cow & calf; B&O, Milwaukee versions; 1600 horsepower.

724 Factory painted, C&IM version; 1325 horsepower; only two built, #30 &31.

725 Stepped hood taper; no door louvers.

726 Stepped hood taper; unbroken door louvers.

727 Straight hood taper; letter board space.

728 Factory painted, kit; powered A-unit, dummy B-unit.

729 Powered A-unit, dummy B-unit; NMRA Review '69.

730 Powered A-Unit, dummy B-unit; with lighted side panels.

731 Powered A&B, with lighted side panels.

732 Powered A-unit, dummy B-unit; 1500 horsepower.

733 Factory painted, NYC, B&O, PRR; 1500 horsepower.

734 Factory painted, powered A-unit, dummy B-unit; 1500 horsepower.

735 McGuire-Cummings single truck sweeper.

736 Powered A-Unit; plated for the CB&Q.

737 Chrome plated; powered A-Unit, dummy B-unit.

738 AT&SF version; 1800 horsepower; Powered A&B units.

739 Powered A-unit, dummy B-unit; 2000 horsepower.

740 Powered A&B-units; 2000 horsepower.

741 Nickel plated for CB&Q.

742 One A-Unit powered, other A-unit unpowered; 2000 horsepower.

743 Factory painted,50 each GN, NYC, IC, C&NW; one A-unit powered, other A-unit unpowered.

744 Factory painted, all wheels powered; 2250 horsepower.

745 Twin powered; 2400 horsepower.

746 Powered A-Unit, dummy B-Unit; UP Version; NMRA Review 4/81.

747 #1701-1710 with steam generator, commuter version.

748 Factory painted, eight wheel underfloor drive.

749 St. Louis curved side interurban coach.

750 1910 vintage curved sides.

751 LARwy was a 3'6" narrow gauge system. The Soho models were built on standard gauge trucks that had to be positioned closer to the center of the car than the prototype to clear the V platform steps. This resulted in excessive overhang.

752 AT&SF 250; rebuild; square cab roof; chopped nose.

753 AT&SF 2244; rebuild; square cab roof; chopped nose; covered dynamic brakes.

754 AT&SF 1310; rebuild; chopped nose; control and slug units; 115 class.

755 Unpowered 115 class slug.

756 Passenger version with optional winterization hatch castings.

757 Add-on dynamic brake; low hood; 1800 horsepower.

758 Add-on dynamic brake; high hood; 1800 horsepower.

759 With dynamic brake; 48-inch fans.

760 Cabless booster with dynamic brake.

761 MoPac, Conrail versions; internal filter.

762 Frisco, C&NW version; body filter.

763 "2 Rooms & a Bath" (Snake cars).

764 Brass body kit #15; prototype used later in Vienna, Austria & Bombay, India.

765 Flywheel drive; 2000 horsepower.

766 Low hood; without dynamic brake; 3000 horsepower; plastic gearboxes on axles are prone to splitting

767 CN wide nose cab; MR Review 11/78.

768 CN conventional cab; MR Review 10/74.

769 Without dynamic brake; low hood; 3000 horsepower.

770 Amtrak version;3000 horsepower; MR Review 10/74.

771 Powered unit with trailer; PRR-RDG.

772 Flywheel drive; 3600 horsepower.

773 AT&SF, Milwaukee version; 3600 horsepower.

774 Unpowered, with pantographs.

775 6600 horsepower; two-engine "Centennial", NMRA Review 7/77.

776 SP tunnel motor; short nose.

777 SP tunnel motor; long nose.

778 Flywheel drive; 1000 horsepower.

779 1600 horsepower;'Baby Trainmaster''.

780 2400 horsepower; "Trainmaster"; straight handrails.

781 No gift wrapping available.

782 Raymond Loewy oval window.

783 Unpowered, without pantographs.

784 3-car Set, both trucks powered in one unit by enclosed gearboxes; modernized version with aluminum window sashes, high speed trucks and new pantographs.

785 "Washboard", factory painted McGinnis color scheme.

786 Powered A-unit; 2000 horsepower passenger version.

787 Low hood; ACL,CB&Q,IC,L&N,Milwaukee,PC.

788 AAR type B trucks; low hood.

789 AAR Type B trucks, high hood.

790 GE FB-2 trucks with optional Blomberg frames, low hood.

791 GE FB-2 trucks; low hood.

792 Blomberg trucks; low hood.

793 Early version with side louvers.

794 HO and HOn3; Korean superstructure; US-made mechanism.

795 NYC; oil electric; MR Review 6/72.

796 Center cab; painted gold.

797 Center cab; no finish.

798 3000 horsepower; covered body; AT&SF.

799 3300 horsepower; NMRA Review 5/71.

800 5000 horsepower; two engines; UP #34.

801 5000 horsepower; two engines; SP version.

802 Nose door; low tail; SP version.

803 5000 horsepower; two engines; UP version.

804 Low hood; early version; single windshield.

805 Low hood; intermediate version; two windshields.

806 ''Washboard'', factory painted McGinnis; coach, combine, parlor.

807 ''Washboard'', factory painted green; coach, combine, parlor.

808 Factory painted, UP-built coal gas turbines.

809 4500 horsepower; two-cab prototype.

810 #51 gas turbine; factory painted; copper bodies; 4500 horsepower; UP.

811 4500 horsepower; original tender.

812 4500 horsepower; round tender.

813 Factory painted, 4500 horsepower; ''Veranda''.

814 4500 horsepower; ''Veranda''; original tender.

815 4500 horsepower; ''Veranda''; round tender.

816 8500 horsepower; two units powered; round tender.

817 ''Washboard'', factory painted green.

818 #1770/1830 Series without dynamic brakes.

819 Blinker doors; (Newark Subway); RMC review 12/83.

820 Folding doors,; RMC review 12/83.

821 Long Island style trucks; all wheels powered on one car; door has porthole windows.

822 2-car Set, Flywheel Drive.

823 Factory painted, powered car, flywheel drive.

824 Factory painted, unpowered car, flywheel drive.

825 2-car Set, Deck Roof.

826 Flywheel Drive.

827 2-car Set, eight wheel underfloor drive, nickel plated bodies, blackened underframe.

828 NY Westchester and Boston.

829 Westinghouse/GE built, early models had poor drives which were replaced.

830 Brass bodies; Hobbytown drive and dummy.

831 Improved Model, single piece body with louvers added, new side frames, better pantographs.

832 Burlington ''Zephyr''; three-car ''Pioneer''.

833 Burlington ''Zephyr''; three-car ''Pioneer''; MR Review 10/72.

834 Single stripe/Tuscan Red #4916.

835 Single stripe/Brunswick Green #4926.

836 #6300-6311; spoked drivers; vestibule cab; Vanderbilt tender.

837 Multi-stripe/Tuscan.

838 Single stripe/silver #4880.

839 Multi-stripe/Brunswick green: gold leaf.

840 Steeple cab switcher; NMRA review 7/72.

841 NH,PC,N&W,VGN.

842 Baldwin-Westinghouse, eight wheel drive.

843 27' long, with single pole and siderods.

844 MU Bus bars; can motor.

845 Kit; Freight Motor; rivet detail on body.

846 Baldwin-Westinghouse; screwdriver assembly kit, no rivet detail on body.

847 Powered B; 1500 hp.

848 5500 horsepower; eight axles powered; replacement spoked wheels available; NMRA Review '73; MR Review 6/73.

849 Factory painted, 3400 horsepower; Baldwin-Westinghouse built.

850 Ex-Cleveland Union Terminal R-2 class; 3000 horsepower; #701-707; MR Review 5/74.

851 GE-built three-phase electric for Cascade Tunnel.

852 Can motor; poor four-wheel drive; Cascade Tunnel motor.

853 Model requires large radius curves.

854 3300 horsepower per unit; became PRR FF-2.

855 2160 horsepower per unit; eight-wheel drive.

856 One unit powered; one dummy.

857 2-D-2 NYC S-3 Electric Box Motor built by GE in 1906 as a 1-D-1.

858 Ex-Cleveland Union Terminal locomotive; 204-ton, Alco-built, 2635 horsepower box cab; NMRA Review '75.

859 Three-car set; one powered.

860 Factory painted, green; car set #2 ''Washboard;'' powered coach, combine, parlor.

861 Factory painted, McGinnis; car set #2 ''Washboard'' powered coach, combine, parlor; model powered by 2-PFM SPUD underfloor trucks.

862 45-foot double-end trolley.

863 Brooklyn Union elevated with poles.

864 67-foot powered subway unit.

865 45-foot; spring belt drive.

866 Unpowered; 48-foot double-ended coach.

867 Factory painted,53-foot; MR Review 11/77.

868 #203-214 merchandise dispatch, road name etched on letterboard

869 #215-239 merchandise dispatch.

870 Sand Springs Railway, Oklahoma.

871 Can motor; gear drive.

872 Factory painted, coach and trailer set; one powered, one sled.

873 Two truck; eight-wheel drive locomotive.

874 Four-truck; eight-wheel drive locomotive; two poles.

875 Four-truck; sixteen-wheel drive locomotive.

876 Four-truck; sixteen wheel drive locomotive; three poles; cast gearbox.

877 Powered; nickel silver construction; #300-302.

878 Powered; brass construction; #300-302.

879 Unpowered trailer; nickel silver construction; #33-331.

880 Unpowered trailer; brass construction; #330-331.

881 Unpowered trailer; nickel silver construction; #350-352.

882 Unpowered trailer; brass construction; #350-352.

883 Two-car train; combine and observation; nickel silver construction.

884 Two-car train; combine and observation; brass construction.

885 Three-car train; combine, coach and observation; nickel silver construction.

886 Three-car train; combine, coach and observation; brass construction.

887 Three-car MU set; one powered, one dummy, one sled; Long Island Railroad MP-54C & T-54C.

888 Includes seats and eclipse fenders.

889	44-1/2 foot coach; low floor drive.
890	Includes eclipse fenders.
891	46-1/2 foot wood coach; California style; center doors; low floor drive.
892	48-foot wood multiple unit; California style; low floor drive.
893	#E-34-C Bobtail, unpowered.
894	48-foot steel multiple unit; California style; Hunter signs.
895	48-foot steel multiple unit; California style; low floor drive.
896	48-foot steel unit; multiple unit; all enclosed car; Hunter signs.
897	48-foot steel all enclosed car; Hunter signs; low floor drive.
898	49-foot steel all enclosed car; spring belt drive.
899	46-foot single-ended pre-War PC car; spring belt drive.
900	46-foot single-ended mid-War PC car; wrap-around anti-climbers.
901	Built on HOn3 trucks.
902	3-car set; 1932 design; Eighth Avenue subway cars.
903	57-foot; long baggage section.
904	57-foot; short baggage section.
905	62-foot wood interurban "Electric Pullman".
906	Unpowered; 62-foot wood interurban.
907	Open end; first interurban in Southern California.
908	Two open ends; Huntington "Old PE" suburban.
909	71-foot coach; two-spring poles; raised conduits on roof.
910	71-foot coach; four-spring poles; conduits flush with roof.
911	Ex. San Diego Southern & Pt. Loma.
912	Arch-window wood interurban.
913	Steel coach; 650 type suburban.
914	Dummy suburban steel coach.
915	47-foot coach; single trolley pole.
916	Two Poles for subway use.
917	Unpowered; 47-foot open end wood interurban.
918	LAP 48-foot interurban; belt drive.
919	LAP 48-foot interurban; gear drive.
920	Business car rebuilt from a "Ten".
921	55-foot wood interurban; open gear box.
922	55-foot wood interurban; closed gear box.
923	Factory painted; lacks vestibule partitions.
924	Unpowered;55-foot wood interurban.
925	57-foot interurban; etched double row rivets.
926	"San Bernardino Twelve"; oval window "Butterfly Twelve"; long wheel base trucks.
927	"San Bernardino Twelve"; 57-foot oval window steel interurban.
928	57-foot steel interurban.
929	Unpowered; "San Bernardino Twelve"; 57-foot steel interurban with oval window.
930	#23-25; long driver fenders.
931	#39-48; RM Review 9/77.
932	1242 class control trailer "sled".
933	"Portland Twelve"; #1252-1263 steel interurban; inaccuracies on first run.
934	"Portland Twelve"; from Portland, Eugene & Eastern.
935	"Portland Twelve"; etched double row of rivets.

936	Rebuilt from San Diego Southern & Pt. Loma #419.
937	Mates to all "Twelves".
938	Ex-Golden Gate & Ocean Railroad; RM Review 11/77.
939	63-foot steel box motor.
940	Eight-wheel rubber tube drive.
941	4500 hp., factory painted, orange & black.
942	#5000-5029 PC double-end car.
943	Unpowered: modernized; poor quality.
944	Private car used on Sacramento Northern.
945	Elesco feedwater heater; S. Soho & Company marketed the last 100 of the NPP production run in 1978.
946	C&S #65 actual never had the fluted domes featured on the PFM model, but #59 did.
947	#6 had a straight stack with low domes and LH piping.
948	Balboa C-21 is not accurate, combines features of both #360 and #361.
949	#1200-1209 as delivered; no auxiliary tender.
950	Two versions, one with Elesco feedwater heater, one without.
951	#10; built by Westinghouse; MR Review 4/71.
952	Factory painted, four maroon, four black.
953	Powered coach, dummy trailer; NMRA Review 5/81.
954	Streamlined modernized version.
955	Powered unit with trailer; PRR-RDG.
956	Powered coach, dummy trailer; Amtrak.
957	6800 horsepower; two units; all axles powered.
958	57-foot "Owl Cars"; portholes and pantographs.
959	57-foot unpowered trailer.
960	55-foot powered baggage.
961	"The Berry Car"; powered.
962	57-foot wood coach; powered.
963	57-foot wood coach; unpowered.
964	57-foot; special order with baggage door.
965	True trailer; unpowered.
966	Unpowered sled observation.
967	Acquired from Northern Electric.
968	Powered; articulated 2-car unit.
969	Unpowered; articulated 2-car unit.
970	Kit; used in cities of Chicago, St. Louis and New Orleans.
971	Kit; used in cities of Chicago, St. Louis and New Orleans; 33-inch nickel silver spoked wheels.
972	Powered commuter cars.
973	Powered; one pantograph, one pole.
974	Powered; one pantograph, two poles.
975	Listed as an EF-1 the model is actually 1/2 of an EF-5 set. 3000 hp., factory painted, orange & black.
976	Ex-Metropolitan Street Railway 8-window; built in 1894.
977	Built by Brill-Jewett in 1908; used later in San Diego as #1031-1050.
978	Built by Osgood-Bradley in 1924.
979	Kit; open summer car.
980	Visala Electric Railway 49-ton Baldwin-Westinghouse.
981	62-foot interurban; sold to Oregon Electric Railway.
982	62-foot unpowered interurban; sold to Oregon Electric Railway.
983	#602; 1000 horsepower; GE/Alco-built.

984   Old-Timer powered car kit.

985   Unpowered open trailer kit.

986   Trolley pole industrial switcher.

987   GE switcher kit; two pantographs.

988   Screw driver assembly kit; two pantographs.

989   Baldwin/Westinghouse-built; 60-ton.

990   Plastic body; Stone & Webster design.

991   57-foot rapid transit; unpowered.

992   GE 50-60-ton; rectangular windows.

993   GE 40-50-ton; arch windows.

994   Brill built in 1930; Yakima Valley #20-22; sold to Portland Traction #4008-4010; also used by Lynchburg, Roanoke, Norfolk and others.

995   Central Electric Railway Association box trailer.

996   Closest to Sacramento Northern Prototype.

997   1500 hp., 8-wheels powered.

998   Both Powered.

999   Original front end, 1940's-50's.

1000   #2526-2534, ex. KCM&O #1010 ''Death Valley Scottie'' loco.

1001   NMRA Review 2/76, 1st Model Imported by Key.

1002   Extended cab, top feed, Delta trailing truck.

1003   Standard cab, top feed, Delta trailing truck .

1004   Standard cab, side feed, Hodges trailing truck.

1005   Extended cab, side feed, Hodges trailing truck.

1006   Standard cab, Coal.

1007   Extended cab side feed, Hodges trailing truck.

1008   Extended cab, top feed, Delta trailing truck.

1009   Standard cab, side feed, Hodges trailing truck.

1010   Extended cab, side feed, Hodges trailing truck.

1011   #801-803 with Steam generator, dynamic brakes.

1012   Extended cab, side feed, Hodges trailing truck.

1013   Extra sand dome included convertible tender with removable oil bunker; 12,000 gallon water capacity.

1014   Modernized, Disk Driver, 22,000 gallon tender, oil.

1015   Modernized, Disk Driver, 22,000 gallon tender, coal.

1016   Modernized, Disk Driver, 15,000 gallon tender, oil.

1017   Modernized, Disk Driver, 15,000 gallon tender, coal.

1018   Minneapolis, standard car #1300 as rebuilt about 1931; fp.yellow, brown, green and black.

1019   2 dome, spoked drivers, Hodges trailing truck 2 dome, disc main driver, Delta trailing truck.

1020   Custom Painted by Pro Custom Hobbies.

1021   USRA, G-File #90; enclosed gearbox; brakeman's seat & window on left side; single air pump; footboard pilot.

1022   Sprung, good detail, poor motor.

1023   Overfire jets on right side only.

1024   6100 class, cab roof is too flat.

1025   Ex. SAL, Elesco feedwater heater, Baker valve gear.

1026   Ex. SAL, Worthington feedwater heater, Walschaerts valve gear.

1027   Unsprung, flat bottom on boiler.

1028   Original as delivered.

1029   1935 version, green/gold.

1030   1935 Version.

1031   ''Cincinnatian'', #5304, factory painted, spoke drivers.

1032   Converted from OMI Monon K-5.

1033   Converted from OMI Monon K-5, upgraded castings, rolled tender coal boards.

1034   Removable cab, high running boards, arch window cab, low side tender with Baker trucks.

1035   Factory painted, removable cab, high running boards, arch window cab, low side tender with Baker trucks.

1036   Factory painted, removable cab, low running boards, rectangular cab windows, high side tender with Fox trucks.

1037   Removable cab, low running boards, rectangular cab windows, high side tender with Fox trucks.

1038   Baker valve gear; short tender; catalogued but not produced.

1039   Walschaerts valve gear, long tender; catalogued but not produced.

1040   Catalogued but not produced.

1041   Elesco feedwater heater; model has 57" drivers; prototype has 61" dia.

1042   Coffin feedwater heater; model has 57" drivers; prototype has 61" dia.

1043   #3620-3659 Worthington feedwater heater.

1044   Streamlined shroud; production uncertain.

1045   Open frame motor; Box-Pok drivers; cab interior partly detailed.

1046   Factory painted, individually numbered, cab lighting, noisy drive.

1047   Model developed by VH models.

1048   Improved detailing, no driver cam.

1049   Model developed by VH models; late 1940's version.

1050   Model developed by VH models; model comes with decals and fact sheet.

1051   #6060; model developed by VH models; model comes with decals and fact sheet.

1052   All weather cab, 8000 gal. tender, interchangeable oil/coal bunkers; developed by VH models.

1053   Factory painted ''Canadian Pacific'' with white lettering on tender sides.

1054   Two engines; Centennial set; Central Pacific ''Jupiter'' and Union Pacific #119.

1055   With Elesco feedwater heater & class V tender.

1056   With Elesco feedwater heater & class V-2 tender, air tank on pilot.

1057   With Elesco feedwater heater & class V-2 tender.

1058   With Elesco feedwater heater & class W tender.

1059   Huntington inventory sold to Models West.

1060   Same model as produced by Huntington.

1061   Model appears as N&W version.

1062   Early handbuilt model with white metal castings, sprung, good runner.

1063   Model is a composite of several locos; details are incorrect for any one version.

1064   ''Sport cab'' and 7RB tender.

1065   ''Sport cab'' and 16VC tender.

1066   ''Sport cab'' and 9RE tender.

1067   ''New-Grade'' Alco Version with superheater cover; backhead; can motor; new open idler gearbox similar to system used on C&O 4-8-4's.

1068   ''New-Grade'' Lima Version; backhead; can motor; new open idler gearbox similar to system used on C&O 4-8-4's.

1069   #2700-2739 Alco version with external air tanks.

1070   #2750 Lima version with internal air tanks.

1071   #2716 Southern version with boiler tube pilot and centered headlight.

1072   Same as #2716 Southern version with pilot and boiler front from late version.

1073   Late version #2760

1074   #2700 Alco version with external air tanks.

1075   #2740 Lima version with internal air tanks.

1076   #2685, ex-PM class N #1201-1215.

1077   #2785 Lima version with internal air tanks.

1078   #2760 Lima version with internal air tanks.

1079   "CB Royal" series; 21RC tender; 2-motors.

1080   Japanese prototype.

1081   Painted by Tenshodo for sale through Tenshodo Hobby Shop in Japan. Model has small brass plaque on loco frame with "Painted by Tenshodo" in raised letters. Only twelve are known to be so labeled.

1082   Factory painted "George Washington".

1083   With rectangular tender.

1084   Factory painted, with different numbers; one version with flying number boards.

1085   Factory painted, with different numbers, working poppet valve shafting.

1086   #605-606, tender has curved coal bunker top side sheets; prototype had angled top side sheets.

1087   #600-604, tender has curved coal bunker top side sheets; prototype had angled top side sheets.

1088   #610-614, picture in Kumata's book, "The Art of Brass", Vol #2, possibly a pilot model.

1089   #610-614, brass driver centers with stainless steel tires, can motor, open idler gearbox.

1090   With cross compound air pump, factory painted.

1091   With single air pump, factory painted.

1092   With cross compound air pump.

1093   USRA with clear vision tender.

1094   #4942 with straight coal boards.

1095   #4960 with sloping coal boards.

1096   Worthington BL feedwater heater, Oriental's first steam loco.

1097   Standard Hudson #3000-3012 with can motor.

1098   #5600-07, with Elesco feedwater heater, factory painted.

1099   #5608-20, with Worthington feedwater heater, factory painted.

1100   Green United box, United plate on driver retainer plate.

1101   CStPM&O "Omaha".

1102   MR Review 11/83; can motor.

1103   Available with link and pin pilot.

1104   Factory painted "Hiawatha", poor paint.

1105   Full skirts or modified skirting; Hiawatha North Woods Section #10-11 streamlined.

1106   79″ drivers, should be 84″,; open frame motor.

1107   Some models painted black without lettering; painted quantities unknown.

1108   Lindsay motor, Zamac tender side frames, unique headlight switch.

1109   Modernized; 73″ drivers, partial streamlining.

1110   #1144, freight version.

1111   #1151 passenger version, lettered Rio Grande.

1112   #1151 passenger version.

1113   Factory painted, #3504, with exhaust steam injector, "Limited Edition" series, Serially Numbered 1-20.

1114   #800-805: can motor; 67″ drivers.

1115   Elesco feedwater heater, 3-cylinder; #1605-1609; sport cab, brakeman's shack on tender.

1116   #1800-1804; open frame motor; 72″ dia. drivers. Early models have brass drivers and green Toby box.

1117   #1700-1713; green box with typewritten label; 19 with Pittman motors; serial number on frame.

1118   Factory painted, #3801, directional lights.

1119   #3700-3708; narrow tender; 67″ dia drivers, should be 70″; open frame motor.

1120   Ex. B&LE, running boards not level.

1121   Ex. B&LE, running boards not level; incorrect boiler contour, some models corrected.

1122   Worthington feedwater heater; caboose included.

1123   #3040-3145 with Elesco feedwater heater on boiler front.

1124   #3152 (ref. MR 4/84 pg.45) available custom painted for $65 additional.

1125   #3007 with Elesco feedwater heater on top of smokebox.

1126   #3024 with Elesco feedwater heater on boiler front; high pilot ladders.

1127   High or mid headlight, Walschaerts valve gear.

1128   High or mid headlight, Baker valve gear.

1129   Handbuilt, painted and hand lettered, serial #'s 1,2,&3, Perkins and Ryan collection.

1130   Factory painted, can motor, steel tires, full equalization.

1131   250 painted,250 unpainted.

1132   oil tender version.

1133   Heavy USRA.

1134   #3100 class; sport cab, rectangular tender.

1135   Handbuilt, painted and hand lettered, serial #'s 1,2,&3, Perkins collection.

1136   #3000 class; Vanderbilt tender.

1137   T-boiler, single truck drive.

1138   With open cab, Vanderbilt tender, 69″ drivers.

1139   With vestibule cab, Vanderbilt tender, 69″ drivers.

1140   Models #1,2,3 unpainted; balance painted black with cab and dome lettering applied; tender herald supplied separately.

1141   Shiny blue two part box with gold band. Sides of box extend halfway down over bottom portion of box. Gold band is at edge where the top and bottom sections of box meet.

1142   Coal version, rectangular tender.

1143   Oil version, sport cab.

1144   Coal version, rectangular tender.

1145   #2506, Closed cab, factory painted black.

1146   Closed cab, factory painted Glacier Park.

1147   Factory painted, Glacier Park, original cab.

1148   Vertical boiler, single truck drive.

1149   Two painted in Glacier Park colors

1150   Huge sandbox on pilot deck, non-vestibule cab, Delta trailing truck, front drivers not powered.

1151   Factory painted with silver smokebox.

1152   295 unpainted; 3 black; 1 in S-1 paint; 1 Glacier Park paint.

1153   100 locos ordered; only pilot model was received.

1154   Westside G-File #34; #1441-1485, 73″ dia. drivers, KTM DH-15 open frame motor.

1155 #410, oil headlight, slide valves, no brake shoes, blue box, silver & gold letters.

1156 Vestibule cab, factory painted Glacier Park.

1157 Model has all turned parts except for die cast air pump.

1158 Handbuilt, painted and hand lettered #2577 with hand painted goat herald on tender, Perkins collection.

1159 Crude, #9 embossed on tender sides.

1160 #1950-1969 Baldwin.

1161 #1970-1991 Baldwin, factory painted #1970.

1162 #1950-1969 Baldwin, factory painted #1950.

1163 #1970-1991 Baldwin.

1164 Not accurate, doesn't resemble Ma & Pa prototype.

1165 Experimental black plate finish to simulate painted locomotive; finish was dull and judged to be unrealistic.

1166 Modern version; NMRA review 7/74.

1167 Modern version with Elesco feedwater heater.

1168 #1121-1125, International Great Northern a MP subsidiary.

1169 Actually an H-10a with large 6-wheel tender.

1170 No brake shoes, blue box silver and gold lettering., Actually a P&LE engine but listed as NYC on the PFM box. Two variations, flat-faced with overfire jets and, ''buttoned jets''.

1171 Actually an H-10a with 4-wheel tender.

1172 Silver box with silver-blue label ''Takara Prototype Plans Line.'' Crude model.

1173 Factory painted,with inclined cylinders 12 ton tender.

1174 Factory painted,with inclined cylinders 10 ton coal tender.

1175 With inclined cylinders 10 ton coal tender.

1176 With inclined cylinders 12 ton coal tender.

1177 With 12 ton coal tender.

1178 Mashima can motor, flywheel.

1179 ''Empire State Express'', streamlined.

1180 Original, with Walschaerts valve gear.

1181 Coffin feedwater heater.

1182 Kit in 2″ × 5″ × 13 1/4″ wood box with hinged cover. Black printing on white label at end of box.

1183 Big Four version.

1184 With Spoked drivers & 6-wheel tender.

1185 Factory painted, square sand domes, 75″ drivers.

1186 Round sand domes, 75″ drivers.

1187 Square sand domes, 75″ drivers.

1188 Streamlined with centipede tender.

1189 Limited Run; factory painted #5426, directional constant lighting, lockable coasting drive.

1190 Factory painted #5445; 20th Century, Scullin drivers; RMC review 10/85.

1191 Factory painted #5445; 20th Century, Box-Pok drivers; RMC review 10/85.

1192 Limited Run; factory painted #5429, directional constant lighting, lockable coasting drive.

1193 De-streamlined; Scullin and Box-Pok drivers; regular and roller bearing rods; standard and Selkirk smokeboxes.

1194 Factory painted; four different road numbers.

1195 ''Roll Over'' Elesco feedwater heater; Lima built.

1196 Scullin drivers and Box-Pok drivers.

1197 Locomotive only, with motor and less tender.

1198 fp., model appears as N&W version. Model had brake hangers.

1199 #6001-6025; RMC review 4/83; 78″ drivers should be 79″.

1200 Factory painted, #6601,6020,6024.

1201 Hand scribed serial number inside smokebox front, on valve gear hanger and on frame.

1202 #6001 class.

1203 Blue box with typewritten label.

1204 #715-739.

1205 Well detailed; sprung and equalized tender trucks; fair runner.

1206 #740-769.

1207 Good running qualities; extra parts for conversion between classes.

1208 #770-779.

1209 #801-832, from W&LE #6401-6432.

1210 1500 hp., rivets are indented.

1211 Type A Pilot, B&M,C&EI,Monon,MP,C&O.

1212 With Solid end Railings, B&M, C&EI.

1213 Baker valve gear.

1214 Stephenson valve gear; RMC review 1/86.

1215 Factory painted, Baker valve gear.

1216 Vanderbilt tender; Elesco feedwater heater; Baker valve gear.

1217 Vanderbilt tender; Elesco feedwater heater; Southern valve gear.

1218 With or without Flory step; two sand domes; large tender.

1219 Improved Detail, RM review 1/80.

1220 Pilot model; pictured in 5th Edition catalog.

1221 Belpaire Firebox; #500-504 ex. PRR; 80″ drivers; Westside G-File #113.

1222 Large tender with 6-wheel trucks; Canon motor.

1223 Small tender with 4-wheel trucks; Canon motor.

1224 Convertible coal/oil tender, wood pilot.

1225 ''Limited Edition''; #605-610 unstreamlined; can motor with torque arm; excellent runner.

1226 Limited Edition; #611 tour version.

1227 Blackened frame; open frame motor; two air pumps on left side; brakeman's shack on rectangular coal tender with 4-wheel trucks.

1228 No evidence that this was made.

1229 Factory painted,#4500-4503 without booster.

1230 Limited Edition #3; serially numbered 1-30, factory painted Passenger Gray.

1231 #2626; ex-Timken ''4-Aces''.

1232 #2670-2677; vestibule cab; centipede tender; solid pilot.

1233 #2680-2689; vestibule cab; centipede tender; General Steel cast pilot.

1234 #3893, with outsloping cylinders & 55S66A tender.

1235 Factory painted, #94 with insloping cylinders.

1236 Model is Z-7,8, sprung drivers; unusual working springs on centipede tender.

1237 Late version, 1926, slope back tender.

1238 #9562 with slope back tender, steel cab, compound air pump.

1239 #2504 with slope back tender, wood cab, single phase air pump, Hose reel box.

1240   #2974 with slope back tender, wood cab, compound air pump.

1241   #2796 saddle tanker, steel cab, slide valves, air pump on side of boiler.

1242   #3130 saddle tanker, air pump on smokebox, backup light on cab roof.

1243   Footboard pilot; detailed cab; interior; enclosed gearboxes; can motor.

1244   Slatted pilot; oil headlight; Belpaire firebox; rectangular tender.

1245   Footboard pilot.

1246   With 70F70E tender.

1247   Good runner; built as an H-8 with additional parts to convert to H-9; footboard pilot; cab interior partly detailed; closed gearbox; can motor.

1248   With 80F81A tender.

1249   Footboard pilot, cab interior partially detailed; open gearbox; open frame motor; drawbar attached to Lines West tender.

1250   Red flocked box with red foam; EH-110 label crossed out, RS-110 hand written; crude hand punched rivet detail on cab, models bear serial number.

1251   With Pittmam DC-7OX motor and plastic locomotive brake shoes; cab apron and hex-head crank pin screws.

1252   Light USRA; footboard pilot; interior partly detailed; open gearbox; can motor.

1253   Low cost series; with 1 air pump and short tender.

1254   Low cost series; with 2 air pumps and long tender.

1255   210-F-82a long range tender; double air pumps; Canon flat can motor.

1256   #4305 with Worthington feedwater heater, double pumps, 90F82 tender.

1257   130-F-82 tender; footboard pilot; detailed cab interior; enclosed gearbox; can motor; brass driver centers.

1258   210-F-82a long range tender; single air pump.

1259   #4293 with Worth. feedwater heater, single pump, 210F82A tender.

1260   Juniata built #1126, single air pump, 210F82A tender.

1261   Juniata built #3720, Double pumps, 90F-82A tender.

1262   Footboard pilot; partly detailed cab interior; open gearbox; one air compressor; KTM open frame motor; Lines West tender with 4-wheel trucks; 63 1/2" drivers with Zamac centers.

1263   WMC G-File #88; solid cast pilot with drop coupler; no cab interior detail; enclosed gearbox; 210-F-84 tender with doghouse and 8-wheel trucks; KTM DH-15 open frame motor; 66 1/2" drivers with Zamac centers, should be 69" dia.

1264   #3700; slatted pilot; detailed cab interior; closed gearboxes; can motor.

1265   #1223; WMC G-File #82: 68" spoked drivers; 12mm Micro-motor.

1266   Double pumps, original cylinders.

1267   Compound pump, 70P58A tender.

1268   Double pumps, modified cylinders.

1269   Original cylinders, compound pump.

1270   Modified cylinders, 2 pumps, 70P58A tender.

1271   1930's with 70P66 tender.

1272   Factory painted, #460 "Lindberg Special", late 20's.

1273   WMC G-File #62; #5700-5749; 68" spoked drivers; heaviest and most powerful ten-wheeler built.

1274   WMC G-File #111; 80" spoked drivers; 20mm Canon motor; slatted pilot located too far ahead of cylinders.

1275   WMC G-File #112; 80" spoked drivers; 20mm Canon motor; slatted pilot located too far ahead of cylinders.

1276   #1188, with skyline casing.

1277   1940's version as Built, #5338; streamlined.

1278   1927-28 version; slatted pilot; no cab interior; closed gearbox; open frame motor; rectangular tender with 4-wheel trucks and 3-steps at front of tender.

1279   1940's postwar version, streamlined, #3678, skirts removed, Factory painted Brunswick green.

1280   1940's version as built, #2665; streamlined.

1281   Early smokebox front detailing; stoker equipped; short tender with 3-step front.

1282   1940's postwar version, streamlined.

1283   #1188, with skyline casing, factory painted.

1284   Streamlined #3768.

1285   1940's version as built, #3768; streamlined.

1286   1940's postwar version, streamlined, #5338.

1287   Factory painted, bronze, streamlined #3768, as delivered.

1288   1940's postwar version, streamlined, #2665.

1289   Factory painted #5698 prewar version, Walschaerts valve gear, 130P75 tender.

1290   Prewar version, Capriotti rotary poppet valve gear, 130P70 tender.

1291   #5698 modernized/130P75 tender.

1292   WMC G-File #32; slatted and cast pilots; cab interior partly detailed; enclosed gearbox; open frame DH-15 motor; rectangular tender with 4-wheel trucks; driver diameter is 78" should be 80".

1293   #5699 modernized, 130P75 tender.

1294   Factory painted #5699 prewar version, Capriotti rotary poppet valve gear, 130P70 tender.

1295   Prewar version, Walschaerts valve gear, 130P75 tender.

1296   Factory painted #5699 modernized, 130P75 tender.

1297   Serial number on rear of frame. Nickel silver driver centers.

1298   Original; slatted pilot; outside steam delivery pipes; one air compressor; no feedwater heater; cab interior partly detailed; enclosed gearboxes; open frame motor; 110-P-75 tender.

1299   Welded coast-to-coast tender.

1300   Welded coast-to-coast tender; lighting installed.

1301   With 11,000 gallon tender; low cost series.

1302   Long Distance tender with doghouse and 6-wheel trucks; footboard and cast steel pilots; original and modernized smokebox fronts; two air pumps; brass driver centers; enclosed gearbox; can motor.

1303   WMC G-File #33; footboard pilot and solid cast pilot with drop coupler; two air compressors; Worthington type S feedwater heater; modern smokebox front; 72" spoked drivers; cab interior partially detailed; enclosed gearboxes; open frame motor; 210-F-75.

1304   Modernized smokebox front; solid cast pilot; two air

compressors; Worthington type S feedwater heater; footboard pilot;210-F-75 tender with 6-wheel trucks.

1305 Riveted coast-to-coast tender; lighting installed.

1306 Riveted coast-to-coast tender.

1307 Modernized smokebox front; solid cast pilot with drop coupler; two air pumps; cab interior partially detailed; enclosed gearbox, open frame motor; 210-F-75 tender with doghouse, antenna and 6-wheel trucks.

1308 Original smokebox front; footboard pilot; two air pumps; cab interior partially detailed; enclosed gearbox; open frame motor; 210-F-75 tender with antenna, doghouse and 6-wheel trucks.

1309 RM review 4/78; drop coupler pilot; separate smoke lifters; cab interior partly detailed; enclosed gearbox; can motor; 8-wheel tender trucks.

1310 Brass driver centers; no smoke lifters; working back up lights; red velvet covered wood presentation box marked RS-101.

1311 Zamac driver centers; smoke lifters; complete cab detail; sprung lead and trailing truck; enclosed gearbox; open frame motor; drawbar on tender with 8-wheel trucks; green flocked box marked RS-101.

1312 #6200; can motor; 180-P-85 tender.

1313 #5500 class, as built.

1314 #5511; Incorrect articulated frame; Altoona version; drop coupler; no cab detail; enclosed gearboxes and can motor;180-P-84 tender with radio antenna and 8-wheel trucks.

1315 #6611; original.

1316 #5545 Modified, deskirted.

1317 #6610; original.

1318 Baldwin version; open frame motor; open gearboxes; no cab detail; 8-wheel tender trucks.

1319 #5500 class as rebuilt in late 1940's; correct rigid frame.

1320 #6610 class; original streamline design by Raymond Loewy; correct rigid frame.

1321 Streamlined; solid cast pilot; detailed cab interior; enclosed gearboxes; can motor; brass driver centers; doghouse and 8-wheel trucks on tender.

1322 WMC G-File #20; solid cast pilot; partly detailed cab interior; enclosed gearboxes; open frame motor; long haul tender with doghouse and 8-wheel trucks; 69″ drivers with zamac centers.

1323 All drivers have same size counterweights; enclosed gearboxes.

1324 #1201-1215; factory painted #1201.

1325 Includes parts to convert classes.

1326 #1216-1227; factory painted #1216.

1327 #1228-1239, sandbox behind steam dome, factory painted #1229.

1328 GY-418c #7200-7232, chop nose, 36″ fans, winterization, non-dynamic brakes; MU'ed to CN GP9 booster "GY-00s" #200-232.

1329 With Coffin feedwater heater & 6-wheel tender.

1330 "Empire State Express"; Locomotive and six cars.

1331 Early attempt by KSM/Kobra to make powered steam. Poor quality.

1332 Locomotive only, with motor and less tender.

1333 With smoke deflectors; backhead; can motor.

1334 With snow plow, factory painted passenger gray.

1335 MR Review 5/75; footboard pilot; partly detailed cab

interior; open gearbox; open frame motor; Lines West tender with 4-wheel trucks.

1336 #1216-1227.

1337 #1228-1239, sandbox behind steam dome.

1338 Tender canopy available separately, EH-105A.

1339 Baldwin built; single sand dome.

1340 Reading built; double sand dome.

1341 Original model had mechanism problems; corrected by importer.

1342 "Ruby Signature" models, handbuilt, serialized.

1343 #613-622; Statesman class; correct 77-inch drivers; rectangular tender.

1344 Tyco motor, poor workmanship; poor runner.

1345 #727-736; Box-Pok main driver; RMC review 2/85.

1346 #2718-2723; RMC review 2/85.

1347 ex-C&O #2716 Alco K-4 Kanawha with external tanks; Southern version has centered headlight and boiler tube pilot, used only in fan trip/public relations service.

1348 Two Canon motors, one in engine and one in tender.

1349 #566-583; NMRA Review 12/78.

1350 Clear vision Vanderbilt tender; operating headlight.

1351 52-C-1 sausage tender.

1352 70-C-10 Vanderbilt tender.

1353 #1269 with 70-C-10 Vanderbilt tender; Sacramento museum.

1354 #1276 with 52-C-1 sausage tender; Sacramento depot switcher.

1355 Walschaerts valve gear; closer to M-10 class.

1356 WMC G-File #19; 70″ drivers; DH-13 open frame motor.

1357 Horizontal spoked pilot, double cam operated valve gear, vertically mounted motor, slope back tender.

1358 Small drivers for logging; Westside G-Files #103; #3935 & 3926; ex. Minarets & Western .

1359 Small drivers for logging; Westside G-Files #104. ex. Newaukum Valley Railroad.

1360 NMRA review 4/72; WMC G-File #29; KTM DH-13 open frame motor; 63″ drivers.

1361 Standard SP T-1 with short Vanderbilt tender.

1362 Harriman; WMC G-File #51; RMC review 12/75; 77″ drivers; KTM DH-13 open frame motor.

1363 WMC G-File #116; KTM RH-2330-S can motor; 73″ drivers.

1364 Streamlined; WMC G-File #115; KTM RH-2330-S can motor.

1365 #4300-4309 as delivered in 1923 with 120-C-2 tender with 4-wheel trucks.

1366 "49er"; streamlined #4315; with skyline casing and C-160 tender.

1367 #4310 as delivered in 1924 with square cab and 120-C-2 tender with 6-wheel trucks.

1368 "Shasta Division"; with snow plow pilot; clam shell stack; C-160 tender.

1369 1930's version; boiler tube pilot; Sunbeam headlight; clamshell stack; one sand dome; "Super Classic"; opening smokebox front with detailed interior; MR review 6/84; factory painted Sacramento gray.

1370 1950's version; sheet metal pilot; Pyle National headlight; two sand domes; "Super Classic"; opening smokebox front with detailed interior; MR review 6/84.

1371   1930's version; boiler tube pilot; Sunbeam headlight; clamshell stack; one sand dome; ''Super Classic''; opening smokebox front with detailed interior; MR review 6/84; unpainted.

1372   Factory painted #4405; gray boiler, Vanderbilt tender.

1373   #4407, Postwar 1953 era, modern features include: blowdown spreaders, sand pipe shields, drip shields on trailing truck, front deck radiator, alligator crossheads, rectangular tender

1374   #4409; ''Shasta'', black & graphite with tunnel clamshell smokestack; snowplow; Vanderbilt tender.

1375   #4406; ''Shasta'', black & graphite with tunnel clamshell smokestack; snowplow; rectangular tender.

1376   #4402, postwar era, modern features include: blowdown spreaders, sand pipe shields, drip shields on trailing truck, pressed steel pilot, alligator crossheads, rectangular tender.

1377   #4408; blue boiler, Vanderbilt tender.

1378   #4471, postwar era, modern features include: blowdown spreaders, sand pipe shields, drip shields on trailing truck, rectangular tender

1379   NMRA review 10/78; RM review 8/78

1380   ''Daylight''; idler gearbox; KTM open frame motor; 79″ drivers (1″ undersize)

1381   Factory painted, #4423 black & graphite

1382   ''Daylight''; KTM open frame motor; enclosed gearbox; 79″ drivers (undersize)

1383   ''Daylight'', available numbers; #4430,4444,4457

1384   ex. St.L&SW; WMC G-File #30 6/78.

1385   ''Master Series''; open frame motor boiler contour.

1386   NMRA Review 10/79; Namiki 16mm coreless motor, inadequate to power loco; 63″ drivers; ''Craftsman Series'' #7″; NMRA Review 2/81.

1387   35″ min. radius; idler gearbox on #6 driver.

1388   Poor spur gear design, can be modified.

1389   28″ min. radius; idler gearbox on #5 driving axle allows tighter turning radius

1390   #4176; 63″ Box-Pok drivers; can motor; sprung Buckeye tender trucks

1391   #4166, 63″ Box-Pok drivers, can motor, sprung Buckeye tender trucks.

1392   Texas & New Orleans, factory painted black with silver smokebox, tender convertible from coal to oil.

1393   #600 Series, same as LMB model.

1394   Elesco feedwater heater; #714-721; 71 1/2″ drivers with 2 extra pair of Box-Pok drivers; can motor.

1395   Large transfer switcher. packed in gray foam in medium blue cardboard box with gold printing on end; no printing on top of box; printing on box end includes; ''MFG. BY ATLAS INDUSTRIES, INC. KAWAGUCHI,JAPAN, EXCLUSIVELY FOR PACIFIC FAST MAIL.''

1396   Large transfer switcher; packed in gray foam with rubberized horsehair top pad.

1397   Texas & New Orleans, factory painted black with silver smokebox, tender convertible from coal to oil.

1398   #600 series, same as LMB model.

1399   Factory painted, Coffin feedwater heater, Walschaerts valve gear, oil tender.

1400   Worthington BL feedwater heater.

1401   CN,CP,NH,VIA.

1402   ''Limited Edition #2''; serially numbered 1-25; factory painted #3548.

1403   Centennial set; Central Pacific ''Jupiter'' and Union Pacific #119; motors totally hidden; mediocre runners.

1404   820 series; Cal-Scale drop coupler pilot. green United box with gold letters.

1405   #820 Oil; two-tone gray with yellow stripe.

1406   #824 Oil; two-tone gray with yellow stripe.

1407   #836 Oil; two-tone gray with yellow stripe.

1408   #835-844; dual exhaust stack; WMC G-File #46,46A; KTM GH-15 open frame motor; Box-Pok drivers.

1409   #844; WMC G-File #46,46A.

1410   Coal, detailed smokebox interior.

1411   ''Super Classic'' #9000 as delivered with Worthington BL feedwater heater.

1412   #820-834; single exhaust stack; WMC G-File #46; coal version

1413   #3218-3225 with 6 axle tender.

1414   #2880-2899 with 9000 gallon tender.

1415   ''Super Classic''; original version, with working Gresley valve gear.

1416   ''Super Classic'' #9000 as delivered with Worthington BL feedwater heater.

1417   ''Super Classic''; double Walschaerts valve gear; bald smokebox front.

1418   NMRA Review 9/71; open frame motor;65″ drivers should be 67″

1419   ''Super Classic''; double Walschaerts valve gear; bald smokebox front.

1420   Includes 2 extra blind driver sets.

1421   Factory painted #3975 two-tone gray/silver, oil version.

1422   Factory painted, #3967 black/graphite; freight coal version with smoke lifters.

1423   Factory painted, #3710 black/graphite, oil version.

1424   Factory painted, #3985 black/graphite, oil version.

1425   #3977 Oil version; smoke deflectors; two-tone gray; silver striping.

1426   Factory painted, #3985 black/graphite, coal version.

1427   Factory painted, #3943 black/graphite, coal version.

1428   Sprung drivers all powered; universal joints on drive shafts; working headlight.

1429   ''Portland Rose'', oil burner with smoke deflectors; two-tone gray, yellow striping.

1430   Factory painted black; freight oil version.

1431   Factory painted #3982 two-tone Gray/Silver, oil version.

1432   Factory painted, #3978 gray with yellow stripe, oil version.

1433   Factory painted, only rear drivers powered; signature model.

1434   3 unpainted; factory painted, all drivers powered by rubber tube drive; flat bottom on smokebox.

1435   ''Super Classic'', late 4000 class, modified; available in three road numbers, #4005,4010,4017.

1436   ''Super Classic'', late 4020 class, modified; available in four road numbers, #4020,4021,4023,4024.

1437 Ruby Signature models, handbuilt, serialized.

1438 "Super Classic", original 4000 class; available in four road numbers, #4000,4002,4014,4018.

1439 4 unpainted; factory painted, all drivers powered by rubber tube drive; flat bottom on smokebox.

1440 Ruby Signature models, handbuilt, serialized.

1441 Improved drive and detail; milled through running boards.

1442 M&StL,C&O,Krautkramer version.

1443 MR Review 12/77; boiler tube pilot; partially detailed cab interior; enclosed gearbox; can motor.

1444 PRR L-2s, footboard pilot; partially detailed cab interior; open gearbox; can motor.

1445 Sprung, good detail, poor motor.

1446 Boiler tube pilot; partially detailed cab interior; enclosed gearbox; can motor; brass driver centers.

1447 Sprung Drivers; both sets of drivers powered; brake shoes.

1448 CN,CP,VIA.

1449 Model is listed as Erie K-5, is actually more generic USRA.

1450 49-passenger coach-RPO-baggage.

1451 Amtrak,CN,CP,DM&IR,NYC,NH,PC.
Am-trak,B&M,CP,VIA,DW&P,GN,NP,PGE,BCR,RDG.

1453 Amtrak,B&M,CN,CP,VIA,LV,LI,NYC,NH,PC.

1454 B&M,CN,CP,VIA,RDG,NP.

1455 CSX ex. B&O/C&O.

1456 Japanese prototype, unpowered trailer. Very thin brass.

1457 GY-418c #4000-4035, chop nose, 36″ fans, non-dynamics, winterization, spark arresters, anti-climber, Blomberg trucks.

1458 SP, NWP as rebuilt with baggage end.

1459 AT&SF,B&O,B&M,CN,CP,VIA,CNJ,DSS&A, LV,NYC,PC,NH,NYS&W,PRSL,RDG,OC&E, C&EI, Amtrak.

1460 Smooth front, B&O, B&M, CP, VIA, CNJ, PGE, BCR, RDG.

1461 71-Passenger coach-baggage.

1462 AT&SF DC-191 &192 set, rebuilt from RDC-1 originals.

1463 Cataloged, Roger Williams powered coach.

1464 Cataloged, Roger Williams 4-car set.

1465 RGS #6; work "Goose" plus trailer.

1466 Factory painted, RGS #5; three-truck passenger "Goose".

1467 Factory painted, RGS #20; Wayne bus bodied freight "Goose".

1468 Factory painted, RGS #4; three-truck "Galloping Goose".

1469 Factory painted, UP M-10000; four-car set.

1470 Factory painted; Baggage-mail combine with trailer.

1471 GN #2302 and coach #600; GE-built.

1472 Circa 1924; sold to GN,NP,B&M.

1473 HOn3 D&RGW #50; ex-Sumpter Valley #101.

1474 Bulldog rebuild of 1A &1B.

1475 Industrial switcher; siderod drive; 65-ton.

1476 Factory painted, original version; MR Review 6/82.

1477 Double ended #50 gas turbine.

1478 HO and H0n3: MR Review 12/71.

1479 #4744 DRF-36d class, AC, continuous clutch.

1480 #4700-4704 DRF-36a class, with high engine water tank.

1481 #4705-4728 DRF-36a class, air start.

1482 #2305-2339 MF36a&b class, with late body filters.

1483 #4729-4743 DRF-36c class, electric start.

1484 #705-722 as delivered.

1485 #4576-4581 DRF-30f class, smooth top.

1486 #4518-4553 DRF-30d class, with high engine water tanks.

1487 #4500-4507 DRF-30c class, with dynamic brakes.

1488 GR-17u #4271-4339,48″ fans, (round mesh top), small crosswise fuel tank, spark arresters, Flexicoil trucks.

1489 #2000-2001 MF30a class, with dynamic brakes.

1490 #2002-2043 MF30b class, with late filters.

1491 #1757-1787 MR14c class, A-I-A trucks, short hood.

1492 Kit; may never have been imported.

1493 #1800-1849, specifically unit #1845.

1494 #8749-8800 DRS-18b class, heavy trucks, dynamic brakes.

1495 #3701-3703 MR18g class, light trucks, early body.

1496 #609-611, chop nose heavy trucks.

1497 #3615-3670 MR18b class, heavy trucks, dynamic brakes.

1498 #3850-3893 MR18g class, light trucks, early body.

1499 #3100-3129 MR18e class, light trucks, short hood.

1500 #8582-8600 DRS-16g class, heavy trucks, dynamic brakes.

1501 #8463-8482 DRS-16c class, steam Boiler, light trucks.

1502 #3074-3093 MR16k class, heavy trucks, dynamic brakes.

1503 #3800-3806 MR16e class, light trucks, without dynamic brakes.

1504 #1400-1401, with steam Boiler. roof; chopped nose.

1505 #3807-3814 MR16f class, light trucks, short hood.

1506 #2500-2559 MR20a&b wide cab.

1507 GR-17q #4228-4244,36″ fans, small longitudinal tank, spark arresters, plow, MU, winterization, dynamic brakes, Flexicoil trucks.

1508 #2001-2005 wide cab.

1509 #619-627 chop nose heavy trucks.

1510 Diesel-hydraulic #4001-4003.

1511 Diesel-hydraulic #9000-9002.

1512 Diesel-hydraulic #9110-9116.

1513 #620-621,620B-621B.

1514 #750 A,B,C,D, Erie Built.

1515 Early BN, C&O,C&NW,C&S (BN).

1516 Late BN,D&H,D.E.,L&N,N&W.

1517 #350-359, #7900-7909.

1518 Late version, UP, SP.

1519 Union Pacific #8080 (ex. #80) coal turbine.

1520 #57 with propane tender.

1521 #61 Veranda with special tender.

1522 Standard turbine without tender.

1523 #65 Veranda with special intake.

1524 #61-75 Veranda with round tender.

1525 #51-60 with round tender.

1526 2-Window, without anti-climber.

1527 4-Window, without anti-climber.

1528 2-Window, with anti-climber.

1529   4-Window, factory painted.
1530   4-Window, with anti-climber, ATSF,BN.
1531   #1 with -6 cab & 2 tenders.
1532   SP #1,50-Ton, HO; HOn3.
1533   #1486-1491 (#2350-2355).
1534   Soo #316-319, AT&SF #544-549.
1535   #6740-6744 (#2310-2314).
1536   With cab Overhang, ATSF, NYC.
1537   With cab Overhang, NYC,NKP, PRR.
1538   With cab Overhang, B&O, CNJ.
1539   Low Hood with dynamic brake & low brake cylinders.
1540   #57 with Propane tender.
1541   Cow & calf, with exterior air coil & tank.
1542   Cow & calf, without dynamic brakes.
1543   Cow & calf, with dynamic brake.
1544   Factory painted, black & gray, cow & calf; both powered.
1545   Cow & lb, both powered.
1546   Single stack; full length handrails.
1547   Arched cab windshield; full length handrails.
1548   Straight top cab windshield.
1549   600 hp., with welded frame.
1550   600 hp. Winton 201-A engine; welded frame.
1551   #900-907; sprung; incorrect sand domes; same loco as C&O. version with the exception of no open covers on cylinder sides. and different over-fire jets.
1552   Incorrect sand domes.
1553   Reno "Modern", motor in tender.
1554   WMC G-File #13; DV-130 motor; 56″ drivers.
1555   WMC G-File #70; #660-675;72″ drivers; DH-13 open frame motor; Elesco feedwater heater.
1556   Same as Sunset model.
1557   #6599 with experimental trucks.
1558   "Royal Hudson" same as Van Hobbies model.
1559   MR Review 4/76; Worthington feedwater heater.
1560   WMC G-File #70; #660-675;72″ drivers; DH-13 open frame motor; Worthington feedwater heater.
1561   CPR "Royal Hudson", painted for BC Rail excursion service
1562   Elesco feedwater heater, same as NPP.
1563   Worthington type SA feedwater heater; brass driver centers.
1564   Sellers exhaust steam injector; brass driver centers.
1565   #801-840 as they appeared in later years; Worthington feedwater heater, twin air pumps; stoker, snowplow pilot.
1566   As rebuilt with pumps on front.
1567   Lacks footboards on tender.
1568   Coal burner, smokebox shortened to proper length.
1569   Coal burner; smokebox is 12″ too long.
1570   Oil burner, smokebox shortened to proper length.
1571   Oil burner, smokebox shortened to proper length.
1572   Oil burner, smokebox is 12″ too long.
1573   Minneapolis; standard car #1300 as rebuilt about 1931, fp. yellow, brown, green and black.
1574   Ex-FEC; NMRA review 6/73; #171-180; open frame motor; enclosed gearbox.
1575   Factory painted #6401, #6401-643.
1576   WMC G-File #95; #3718-3769;63″ drivers; disc main driver; KTM DH-15 open frame motor.
1577   Modern version with short Vanderbilt tender.

1578   Baldwin; coach style body.
1579   "Trevithick", English prototype; first successful steam locomotive.
1580   #6401-6432.
1581   Wood cab, Manhattan, Brooklyn, Chicago.
1582   Steel cab, Manhattan, Brooklyn, Chicago.
1583   "Tootsie Roller", Quite possibly the first "mass produced" Japanese brass model for export. Box is dull yellow with "Tootsie Roller" on end with "S.D.A" labeled in the handle portion of a drawing of a screwdriver.
1584   Horizontal Boiler, can motor.
1585   San Joaquin, early.
1586   Coos Bay, Separate tender available.
1587   NMRA review 3/72; Pittman DC-66 motor; separate tender available.
1588   Pittman DC-66 motor.
1589   Westside Lumber #3; WMC G-File #5; DH-13 motor.
1590   Factory painted, Meadow River #6.
1591   Cass/Meadow River; model is as run on Meadow River.
1592   Mt. Rainier/Pickering.
1593   Cowichan with backhead detail.
1594   Western Maryland #6.
1595   WM #6; MR review 9/84.
1596   Cass #4, RMC review 3/84.
1597   Skyline casing has correct contour; detailed cab interior; can motor.
1598   West Virginia Pulp and Paper Co. #12, rebuilt from GC&E 3-truck.
1599   Medco #4, closed cab.
1600   Rayonier #2, open cab.
1601   Pacific Lumber Co., ex. SPL #4.
1602   Coos Bay, as built.
1603   Coos Bay as used on SP.
1604   Coos Bay, as used.
1605   Ex. SPL #2,3.
1606   Georgia Pacific; incorrect #6 on front of smokebox.
1607   Baldwin Mallet, conventionally sprung.
1608   Baldwin Mallet, external wire spring bears on driver journals; prone to jamming mechanism.
1609   Baldwin Mallet, dark red presentation style box, conventionally sprung, Mantua motor.
1610   Cast boiler, cylinders, frame; conventional springing, enclosed gearbox, brass built-up cab and tender.
1611   Composite model combining features of both #360 and #361.
1612   #375;38″ drivers; KTM DH-15 open frame motor; WMC G-File #58.
1613   Standard Gate cars.
1614   #461; both wood and steel cab provided.
1616   Slide valve; "Mudhen" early version; single phase air pumps; straight running boards; 40″ drivers; WMC G-file #61.
1617   Vauclain Compound; "Mudhen"; DH-13 open frame motor; WMC G-File #52.
1618   WMC G-File #55; 45″ drivers; DV-130 open frame motor.
1619   Baldwin Logger; Kiso Lumber Co.; DV-130 motor; WMC G-File #12
1620   Fairfield imported 1000 in 1965 from Kumata.

1621 Trains and Track Distributors imported 500 2-4-4-T from KMT in 1964; models were available from LMB, DiMo, and F&G.

1622 New Berlin & Winfield,400 units imported, all returned to Japan for repair, only 297 returned.

1623 Tender Drive; no sand dome lever.

1624 WMC G-File #8; motor in cab; DV-130 motor.

1625 WMC G-File #8; tender drive; DH-13 open frame motor.

1626 WMC G-File #4; DV-130 motor; 44″ drivers.

1627 Ex. Uintah with added tender.

1628 ''New Grade'' sold direct from Japan, #2700 with external air tanks. Never advertised.

1629 #5100 oil-electric; built 1926.

1630 #21 oil-electric; built 1927.

1631 Red River Lumber; oil-electric; built 1926.

1632 2400 hp., low hood.

1633 2400 hp., high hood.

1634 Low hood , L&HR,NKP, L&N, LV, SBD.

1635 #222-229 high hood with Hi-Ad trucks.

1636 #404-415 (later CR #2060-71, D&H #405-15).

1637 #1300-1305.

1638 #23-29 (CR#2073-77, BCR #631,632).

1639 #578 (later N&W #2578).

1640 #110-135 (SCL, later L&N #1351-1375).

1641 #200-214 high hood (misc. owners).

1642 #400-401 (L&N #1316,1317/Apache #82).

1643 #21-22 (later CR #2072, ET #106).

1644 #1206-1315.

1645 #413-420, high hood.

1646 With dynamic brake, AAR trucks; low hood ,E-M,L&HR,L&N, Monon,P&N,SBD.

1647 With dynamic brake, Hi-Ad trucks.

1648 With dynamic brake, Hi-Ad trucks.

1649 With dynamic brake, Soo, GBW, C&NW, Alco.

1650 With dynamic brake, antennas.

1651 With dynamic brake, large numberboards.

1652 With dynamic brake, large numberboards.

1653 With dynamic brake, small numberboards.

1654 Without dynamic brake, small numberboards.

1655 With dynamic brake, small numberboards.

1656 Without dynamic brake, large numberboards.

1657 1500 hp., freight.

1658 NYC, D&H, SP, TP&W version.

1659 2000 hp., NYC, SP, TP&W, D&H version.

1660 Standard; with hi-speed trucks.

1661 3600 hp.,6 motor; RM review 5/80; poor rubber 3-prong universals.

1662 4300 hp.2 engines.

1663 Southern Pacific DH-643 #9018-9020.

1664 White Pass & Yukon #101-110.

1665 2400 hp.;6 motors, high hood.

1666 2400 hp.;6 motors, low hood ''Alligator''.

1667 #2-9/#2A,3A,4A 1950's - 1962, (plated).

1668 Factory painted, with bold numbers on cab.

1669 C&O #6700-6709/ B&O #2007-2017, Utah Rwy.

1670 NKP #325-333/ N&W #250-258.

1671 SP; AT&SF; C&O; C&NW; CNJ; CMStP&P; Soo.

1672 5500 hp.8 motors.

1673 5500 hp.8 motors.

1674 Original #6005-6016,6055-6066,6067,6068.

1675 With large numberboards #5750A-5759A.

1676 Modernized #600-603,604-607.

1677 With small numberboards #5750A-5759A.

1678 #180-190, with bell in nose.

1679 Original #944A,997A,600-603,604-607.

1680 Modernized #6005-6016,6055-6066,6067,6068.

1681 Repowered EMD #51LA.

1682 Factory painted, A & B powered; with antennas.

1683 Snowplow; icebreakers; radio antennas; A & B powered.

1684 SP Daylight paint scheme; snowplow; icebreakers; radio antennas; A & B powered.

1685 Warbonnet paint scheme; later version with radio antenna; A unit powered.

1686 Original #51A-62A,70A-73A.

1687 Repowered EMD #51LB.

1688 Modernized #51-62.

1689 #5750B-5758B even numbers.

1690 Steam Generator r #252,253.

1691 900 horsepower; RM Review 7/77.

1692 1500 horsepower; four traction motors; NMRA Review '73.

1693 1000 horsepower; boxy hood and cab; AT&SF 2000 class.

1694 660 horsepower; boxy hood and cab.

1695 Powered A-unit;1600 horsepower; ''Sharknose''.

1696 Dummy A-unit;1600 horsepower; ''Sharknose''.

1697 Powered unit;1600 horsepower; ''Sharknose''; NMRA Review '69.

1698 Powered A&B-units;1600 horsepower; ''Sharknose''.

1699 Dummy B-unit;1600 horsepower; ''Sharknose''.

1700 With see-thru walkways.

1701 1000 horsepower; four stack version; Batz trucks.

1702 1000 horsepower; oval radiator;1939 model.

1703 Late version; Trimount trucks; dynamic brakes.

1704 1600 horsepower; six traction motors; MR Review 10/75.

1705 Factory painted, green, single headlight.

1706 Factory painted, Tuscan 1-stripe, single headlight.

1707 Single headlight, production.

1708 Powered A-unit;2000 horsepower; ''Sharknose''; passenger version.

1709 Powered A-unit, dummy B-unit;2000 horsepower; ''Sharknose''; passenger version.

1710 Dummy B-unit;2000 horsepower; ''Sharknose''; passenger version.

1711 ''Double-Ender'' #2000-2002.

1712 ''Double-Ender'' #2003-2005.

1713 ''Double-Ender'' #2000-2002, factory painted, orange-blue.

1714 Type II, with antennas, long roof vents.

1715 Type II, without antennas, long roof vents.

1716 3000 horsepower, ''Centipede'' four axles powered.

1717 Two motors; eight axles powered; PRR, SAL, NdeM.

1718 3000 horsepower, ''Centipede'' eight axles powered.

1719 Modernized with sand boxes.

1720 Modernized without sand boxes, #70-84.

1721 Without anti-climber #6925-6946.

1722 Original version, #72B-98B.

1723 Modernized with sand boxes.

1724   Factory painted,6900 class; MR review 5/84; two Canon flat can motors.

1725   Factory painted,6925 class; MR review 5/84; two Canon flat can motors.

1726   Without anti-climber #6925-6946, factory painted.

1727   #983/984J SP #6011A1948.

1728   #6017 "Queen Mary'1949.

1729   1948 extended exhaust stacks.

1730   Both Powered, Texas Special, factory painted.

1731   Both Powered, Meteor, factory painted.

1732   #5788A-5799A with twin antennas.

1733   #226-227 (ex. L&N #787-788).

1734   #327-329 (ex. UP #931-933).

1735   #501-506 Crandal cab.

1736   #463-465 (ex. UP #963B-965B).

1737   Slug #123 (ex. F-7B #272B).

1738   #804A,D-805A,D Plated.

1739   #4332,33,35-37,4340,41,44-46.

1740   #911,912, re #1498-1499.

1741   #6500-6542 with ditch lights.

1742   #6500-6542 early version.

1743   Without dynamic brakes ;SG; 1 headlight.

1744   Factory painted, green/yellowish black.

1745   Factory painted, green/yellowish orange.

1746   Without dynamic brakes ;without SG; 1 headlight.

1747   Standard, 2 headlights.

1748   Factory painted, C&NW wrong paint scheme.

1749   Standard,1 headlight.

1750   Factory painted red, A powered B dummy.

1751   Factory painted, A powered B dummy.

1752   Factory painted red, A powered B dummy.

1753   Factory painted green, A & B powered.

1754   Factory painted, passenger scheme, A & B powered.

1755   Factory painted, freight scheme, A powered B dummy.

1756   #101B-112B,101D-104B.

1757   Factory painted, passenger scheme, A powered B dummy.

1758   #150A-154A,155C-159C.

1759   #4224A-4226A,4250-4264.

1760   #4051-54,4055A-C,4066A,C.

1761   #61A,61B,62A,62B,63A,63B,64A.

1762   #5521,5524,5531,5534.

1763   #9500-9561, #9563-9567.

1764   #529-552 with side numberboards.

1765   #81A,81B,82A,82B,83A,83B,84A,84.

1766   #101A-C,115A-C,150-2.

1767   With side numberboards #525-8.

1768   #964A-968A passenger.

1769   #4055B-4063B,4065B,4066B.

1770   #513B-518B,561B-570B.

1771   #48A,C-50A,C #68A,C-79A,C.

1772   #6180-6445 with snowplow pilot.

1773   #1532-1538 with large numberboards, no antenna.

1774   #354-357 'DF-9' passenger.

1775   #6007A-6020A,D;6500C-6502C.

1776   #29L,C-36L,C passenger.

1777   #202C-280,C freight.

1778   #2201A,B-2203A,B #2224A,B.

1779   #913,921 with snowplow pilot.

1780   #163A-169A, #167C-169C.

1781   #208A,C-211A,C;226A,C-119A,C.

1782   #59D,70,71A,C,72,73A,D,74A.

1783   #87A,C-89A,C;106A,C-121A,C.

1784   #9700 Series with large numberboards, with antenna.

1785   #37L,C-47L,C passenger.

1786   #9600 series with small numberboards.

1787   Powered A-Unit; PRR version.

1788   Factory painted, with antennas.

1789   #2201C-2204C freight.

1790   #100B-109B,120B-123B,675B-677B.

1791   #121B-124B, #208B-211B.

1792   #804B,805B, passenger.

1793   #33B,C,70B,71B,72B,C,75B,C.

1794   3542-545 'DF-10' passenger.

1795   #300 Series, with snowplow pilot.

1796   #4067B-#4084B,4091B,4094B.

1797   #4427-4448,4459-4462.

1798   #202A,B-280A,B freight.

1799   #6007B,C-6020B,C #6050B.

1800   #105D-116D, #113B-116B,116E,F,G.

1801   #37A,B-47A,B passenger.

1802   #913B,C = 924B,C with steam headight.

1803   #200 Series #300 series.

1804   #1466B,C-1496B,C freight.

1805   #292A,B-36A,B passenger.

1806   #2500B-2501B passenger.

1807   Factory painted, A powered B dummy.

1808   Factory painted Milwaukee colors, A powered B dummy.

1809   Factory painted UP colors, A powered B dummy.

1810   Factory painted freight scheme, A powered B dummy.

1811   Factory painted passenger scheme, A powered B dummy.

1812   Factory painted UP colors, A & B powered.

1813   Factory painted passenger colors, A & B powered.

1814   Factory painted freight scheme, A & B powered.

1815   Factory painted green, A powered B dummy.

1816   Factory painted red, A powered B dummy.

1817   Factory painted "Big Sky", A powered B dummy.

1818   #93A,C-94A,C passenger.

1819   #6700A,C, #6701A,C, #6702A passenger.

1820   #7051A, #7052A freight.

1821   #4150-4168 ex. UP unit.

1822   #503-540 mixed series (Farr).

1823   #503-540 mixed series.

1824   #281,A,B-289A,B freight.

1825   #6700B,6701B passenger

1826   #7000B,C-#7014B,C Frt.

1827   #470B,C, #472B,C,474B,C.

1828   #501B-542B mixed series.

1829   #4100-4110 ex. UP unit.

1830   #501B-542B mixed series (Farr).

1831   #600-628 mixed series.

1832   #705-721 mixed series.

1833   1000 series; 1200 hp., Canadian.

1834   1900 series, 1200 hp., Canadian.

1835   BN; C&NW; COHS review 5/84.

1836   Low hood ; without dynamic brakes; NYC, PRR.

1837   With headlight in low nose, L&N, ACL.

1838   Low hood with GSC (Alco) trucks.

1839   Low hood without dynamic brakes.

1840 With headlight & bell in low nose.

1841 Repower kit; enclosed drive.

1842 Low hood with dynamic brakes & headlight in nose, factory painted.

1843 Low Hood with dynamic brakes & high headlight.

1844 High hood with dynamic brakes.

1845 Low hood without dynamic brakes.

1846 Low hood with bell in nose & AAR trucks.

1847 Low hood with dynamic brakes & headlight in nose.

1848 Low hood with dynamic brakes & high headlight, factory painted.

1849 Low hood with extended range dynamic brake and anti-climber.

1850 Low hood without dynamic brakes with anti-climber.

1851 Factory painted, high hood, orange & aluminum.

1852 Factory painted, high hood, with AAR B trucks.

1853 Low hood with anti-climber with small dynamic brakes.

1854 Low hood without anti-climber with small dynamic brakes.

1855 Low hood without anti-climber without dynamic brakes.

1856 Low hood without anti-climber with dynamic brakes.

1857 2300 hp., C&O, Kennecott Copper, Atlanta & St. Andrews Bay.

1858 2300 hp., AT&SF, D&H, B&N.

1859 Low hood, with brake; plastic gearboxes on axles are prone to splitting.

1860 High hood, with brake; plastic gearboxes on axles are prone to splitting.

1861 Brass body; Bachmann drive; MR review 12/72.

1862 #2050-2243; low nose; square cab.

1863 Factory painted Brunswick green, with antennas.

1864 1954 version; with winterization hatch and dynamic brakes.

1865 Factory painted, special with display case.

1866 For gas-turbine service.

1867 RCE car #10-13 (ex. passenger F-7B).

1868 Low hood, UP, Kennecott Copper.

1869 High hood, BN, SRR, UP.

1870 Slug #129 (ex. UP SD24).

1871 Low hood, UP #99 (ex. #3999,3100,3200,3399).

1872 Low hood, #4600 class.

1873 #103B,5B,6B, high hood.

1874 #1200-1203; high hood.

1875 Low hood with dynamic brakes.

1876 High hood with dynamic brakes.

1877 Low hood without dynamic brake & high brake cylinders.

1878 Low hood with dynamic brake & high brake cylinders.

1879 Low hood without dynamic brake & low brake cylinders.

1880 Medium nose tunnel motor.

1881 Without flared radiators, special model.

1882 #1625-1639, with extended range dynamic brakes, with early screens.

1883 #6371-6440, with extended range dynamic brakes, with anti climber.

1884 #6139-6207, with low hood.

1885 #600-628, with extended range dynamic brakes, with late screens.

1886 Wide cab, extended range dynamic brakes, anti-climber.

1887 #3554-3583, with extended range dynamic brakes, with early screens.

1888 #4790-4799, without dynamic brakes, with early radiator screens.

1889 #130, with extended range dynamic brakes, with late radiator screens.

1890 #6000-6073, with extended range dynamic brakes ,Now UP #390 series.

1891 #4790-4799, without dynamic brakes, with early radiator screens, factory painted.

1892 #3554-3583, with extended range dynamic brakes , with early screens.

1893 #6371-6440, with extended range dynamic brakes ,with anti climber.

1894 #757-789, without dynamic brakes, with early screens.

1895 #6139-6207, with low hood, factory painted.

1896 #6601-6623, without dynamic brakes, with late screens.

1897 #9000-9024 wide cab & body.

1898 Sulzer power; MR review 4/85; Canon motor, widened hood; UP #60.

1899 #3105-3121 high hood.

1900 #9104-9123 with smoke deflectors.

1901 #1705-1730 high hood.

1902 #1739-1764 high hood.

1903 #6472-6491 4-window cab.

1904 #1765-1789 high hood.

1905 #3122-3159 high hood.

1906 #1800-1849,5500-5529.

1907 #5304-5380 with smoke deflectors.

1908 Tunnel Motor, RM review 12/77.

1909 C&NW, CRR #7000-7034.

1910 Eight wheel underfloor drive.

1911 Folding doors; (Newark Subway); RMC review 12/83.

1912 1600 hp.; rubber-prong universals, poor design.

1913 #1660-1664, without dynamic brakes.

1914 2400 hp.; Alco models first import.

1915 #975 Demo, with Flexi-Coil trucks.

1916 2635 horsepower; 204-ton box motor built by Alco/GE.

1917 Sprung Drivers, USRA, advertised as C&O H-5 but box is labeled USRA.

1918 Type B Pilot, BAR, C&O, FEC, MP, RI, WM.

1919 Original version, with closed off right front railing.

1920 Horizontal bar pilot; cam operated valve gear; vertically mounted motor; slope back tender.

1921 Standard version with vertical grilles and without dynamic brakes.

1922 With vertical grilles and without dynamic brakes.

1923 Nickel plated with removable truck skirts.

1924 Nickel plated with removable truck skirts and interchangeable pilot.

1925 Powered; with three sets of paired windows.

1926 Standard vent grilles, without dynamic brakes.

1927 Built by Samhongsa for Van Hobbies of Canada, no cab interior, smooth sand blast finish.

1928   Early version with 36″ fans, add on dynamic brakes and winterization hatch included.

1929   #100-129, with extended exhaust stacks, winterization (originally #700-729).

1930   #263-294,Narrow fuel tank, flat plate pilot, 36″ fans, winterization, late 70's.

1931   #130-204,early handrail posts, narrow fuel tank, winterization, large snowplow.

1932   #130-204B, spark arresters, narrow fuel tank, early handrail posts, winterization,60's and 70's.

1933   #283, extra vents cut in side, test unit to compare turbocharged units, 36″ fans, winterization, 60's to 80's

1934   #261 with AiResearch turbocharger, 48″ fans, winterization, large fuel tank, early 60's.

1935   #303B,317B,330B,348B, with AiResearch turbocharger, 48″ fans, winterization, large fuel tank, early 60's.

1936   #306,314,315,324 with 2 Elliott turbochargers, 48″ fans, winterization, large fuel tank, early 60's.

1937   #307B,323B,345B, with Elliott turbochargers, 48″ fans, winterization, large fuel tank. early 60's.

1938   No window sashes, serial number on left rear of frame. Green United box with silver letters.

1939   Small Mars light; bell at 12 o'clock position. Purple velveteen box.

1940   Built by Atlas/Toby; #600-604; Pittman motors. Serial number on left rear of frame.

1941   #1700-1713: Blue Toby box. Access door on left side of tender only. Cast rear tender step.

1942   Green United box. Loco has overfire jets.

1943   Blue Toby box. Blackended Baldwin disc drivers.

1944   Brake hangers screwed to retainer plate. Purple velveteen box.

1945   More firebox detail than '66 and '69 models.

1946   Sandbox on pilot deck.

1947   Green United box.

1948   Blue United box.

1949   Hand scribed serial numbers on top of rear frame and/or under pilot.

1950   Serial number on left rear of frame. Swing-coupler pilot. Cast headlight.

1951   fp., no lettering; 56 foot tender with 24,500 gallon water capacity. Serial number on frame. Wooden box.

1952   Serial number on side of frame behind last driver. Separate silver boxes for loco and tender.

1953   Open platform, curved sides.

1954   Can motor, enclosed gearbox, backhead, identification plate on frame labeled ''EM, Seoul Korea, Kobra''

Bibliography

Abdill, George B., *Civil War Railroads.* Bonanza Books, 1961.

———, *Rails West.* Bonanza Books, 1960.

Adams, Kramer, *Logging Railroads of the West.* Bonanza Books, 1961.

All-Time Index, Revised Second Edition. Wayner Publications, 1978.

Allen, Alice B., *Simon Benson: Northwest Lumber King.* Binford & Mort, 1971.

Archer, Robert F., *Lehigh Valley Railroad.* Howell-North Books, 1978.

Baldwin Locomotive Works, *Baldwin Locomotive Works Illustrated Catalog.* Howell-North Books, 1960.

———, *History of the Baldwin Locomotive Works.* Baldwin Locomotive Works, 1923.

———, *The Baldwin Locomotive Works Record No. 76: Logging Locomotives.* Specialty Press, Inc., 1973.

Beaver, Roy C., *Bessemer and Lake Erie Railroad 1869-1969.* Golden West Books, 1969.

Beebe, Lucius, *The Central Pacific and Southern Pacific Railroads.* Howell-North Books, 1966.

Beebe and Clegg, *Rio Grande: Mainline of the Rockies.* Howell-North Books, 1962.

Bender, H.E., Jr., *Uintah Railway.* Howell-North Books, 1970.

Brown, R.A., *The Brown Book.* Darwin Publications, 1980.

Cafky, Morris, *Rails Around Gold Hill.* World Press, Inc., 1955.

Cavanaugh, H.F., *New York Central System.* N.J. International Inc., 1983.

Church, Robert J., *Cab-Forward.* Kratville Publications, 1958.

Clegg and Corley, *Canadian National Steam Power.* Trains & Trolleys, 1969.

Cline, Taber, Casler, *Logging Railroad Era of Lumbering in Pa.,* Vol. 1. Cline, Taber, Casler, 1971.

———, *Logging Railroad Era of Lumbering in Pa.,* Vol. 2. Cline, Taber, Casler, 1971.

———, *Logging Railroad Era of Lumbering in Pa.,* Vol. 3. Cline, Taber, Casler, 1971.

Collias, Joe G., *Frisco Power.* MM Books, 1984.

Combs, *Westward to Promontory.* Garland Books, 1969.

Cook, Richard J., *Famous Steam Locomotives.* Richard J. Book, 1974.

———, *Super Power Steam Locomotives.* Golden West Books, 1969.

Crossen, Forest, *The Switzerland Trail in America.* Pruett Publications, 1962.

Crump, Spencer, *Henry Huntington and the Pacific Electric.* Trans-Anglo Books, 1978.

Development of the Locomotive. Central Steel Company, 1925.

Diesel. General Motors Corp., 1936.

Digerness, *The Mineral Belt,* Vol. #1. Sundance Ltd., 1977.

———, *The Mineral Belt,* Vol. #2. Sundance Ltd., 1978.

Dixon, Thomas W., Jr., *Chesapeake & Ohio Early Diesels.* Andower Junction Publications, 1988.

Dixon and Hundman, *Chesapeake & Ohio K-2, K-3 and K-3a 2-8-2's.* Pacific Fast Mail, 1978.

Dorin, Patrick C., *The Canadian National Railway's Story.* Superior Pub., 1975.

———, *The Lake Superior Iron Ore Railroads.* Superior Pub., 1969.

———, *The Milwaukee Road East.* Superior Pub., 1978.

Duke, Donald, *Southern Pacific Steam Locomotives.* Golden West Books, 1971.

Dunscomb, Guy L., *A Century of Southern Pacific Steam Locomotives.* Dunscomb, 1972.

Ehrenberger & Gschwin, *Smoke Across the Prairie.* National Railway Historical Society, 1975.

———, *Smoke Along the Columbia.* National Railway Historical Society, 1975.

Farrell, Jack W., *The Berkshire and Texas Types.* Pacific Fast Mail, 1988.

Farrell, Pearsall, *The Mountains.* Pacific Fast Mail, 1977.

———, *The Northerns.* Pacific Fast Mail, 1975.

Ferrell, M.H., *Silver San Juan.* Pruett Publications, 1973.

———, *Southern Pacific Narrow Gauge.* Pacific Fast Mail, 1982.

———, *West Side.* Pacific Fast Mail, 1979.

Frey and Schrenk, *Northern Pacific Supersteam Era, 1925-1945.* Golden West, 1985.

Garmany, J.B., *Southern Pacific Dieselization.* Pacific Fast Mail, 1985.

Green, Richard, *The Northern Pacific Railway.* NWSL, 1985.

Harwood, Herbert H., Jr., *Blue Ridge Trolley.* Golden West Books, 1972.

Hauck, *The Collected Colorado Rail Annual.* Colorado Railway Historical Society, 1970.

Hauff and Gertz, *The Willamette Locomotive.* Binford & Mort, 1977.

Hayden, Bob, *Diesel Builders Cyclopedia,* Volume II. Kalmbach Publishing Co., 1980.

Herr, Kincaid, *The Louisville and Nashville Railroad 1850-1942.* L&N Magazine, 1943.

Hilton, George W., *American Narrow Gauge Railroads.* Stanford University Press, 1990.

———, *The Ma & Pa.* Howell-North Books, 1963.

Hirsimaki, Eric, *Lima: The History.* Hundman Publishing, 1986.

Holley, Noel T., *The Milwaukee Electrics.* N.J. International Inc., 1987.

Hollis and Roberts, *East End.* Barnard, Roberts and Co., 1992.

Huddleston, Dixon, *The Allegheny: Lima's Finest.* Hundman Publishing, 1984.

Huddleston, Eugene L., *The Van Sweringen Berkshires.* N.J. International, Inc., 1986.

Hungerford, John B., *Cab-In-Front.* Hungerford Press, 1959.

Jahn and Johnson, *Western Maryland Diesels.* Crusader Press, 1979.

Jeffries, L.E., *N&W: Giant of Steam.* Pruett Publications, 1980.

Johnson, *The Steam Locomotive.* Simmons-Boardman, 1981.

Kaplan and Mellander, *Richmond, Fredericksburg & Potomac Railroad.* Old Line Graphics, 1990.

Keenan, Jack, *Cincinnati & Lake Erie Railroad.* Golden West Books, 1974.

Keilty, Edmund, *Doodlebug Country.* Interurban Press, 1982.

———, *Interurbans without Wires.* Interurban Press, 1979.

———, *The Short Line Doodlebug.* Interurban Press, 1988.

Killoran, John P., *The Cass Collection* Volume I. Trackage Rights, Inc., 1982.

Kindig, Hally, and Poor, *Denver South Park & Pacific,* Picture Supplement. World Press, Inc., 1959.

King, Frank A., *Locomotives of DM&IR.* Pacific Fast Mail, 1984.

———, *Minnesota Logging Railroads.* Golden West Books, 1981.

———, *The Missabe Road.* Golden West Books, 1976.

Kirkland, John F., *Dawn of the Diesel Age.* Interurban Press, 1983.

———, *Diesel Builders,* Volume I. Interurban Press, 1990.

———, *Diesel Builders,* Volume II. Interurban Press, 1989.

Klein, Aaron E., *The History of the New York Central System.* Bonanza, 1985.

Kline, Benjamin, Jr., *Heisler Locomotive 1891-1941.* Kline,.

Knudsen, C.T., *Chicago and North Western Steam Power.* Knudsen, 1965.

Koch, Michael, *Steam & Thunder in the Timber.* World Press, Inc., 1979.

———, *The Shay Locomotive.* World Press, Inc., 1971.

Kohl, D. and R., *Twenty-five Years of Fine Models.* Pacific Fast Mail, 1979.

Kratville, W.W., *The Challenger Locomotives.* Kratville Publications, 1980.

———, *The Mighty 800.* Kratville Publications, 1967.

Kratville and Ranks, *Motive Power of the Union Pacific.* Kratville Publications, 1966.

———, *Union Pacific Locomotives.* Barnhart Press, 1960.

Krause and Crist, *Baltimore & Ohio Heritage 1945-1955.* Railroad Heritage Press,.

Krieg, A., *Last of the Three Foot Loggers.* Golden West Books, 1962.

Labbe and Goe, *Railroads in the Woods.* Howell-North Books, 1970.

Lavallee, Omer, *Van Horne's Road.* Railfare, 1974.

Lee, Thomas R., *Turbines Westward.* T. Lee Publications, 1975.

LeMassena, R.A., *Articulated Steam Locomotives.* Sundance Books, 1979 and 1991.

———, *Rio Grande...to the Pacific!.* Sundance Books, 1974.

Lewis, Lloyd D., *The Virginian Era.* TLC Publishing, 1992.

MacGregor, B., *South Pacific Coast.* Howell-North Books, 1968.

Marre, Pinkepank, *The Contemporary Diesel Spotter's Guide.* Kalmbach Books, 1989.

McCoy and Collman, *The Rio Grande Pictorial.* Sundance Books, 1971.

McFarland, E.M., *The Cripple Creek Road.* Pruett Publications, 1984.

———, *The Midland Route.* Pruett Publications, 1980.

McLean, Harold H., *Pittsburgh and Lake Erie R.R..* Golden West Books, 1980.

Mellander, Deane E., *B&O: Thunder in the Alleghenies.* Carstens Publications, 1983.

Mellander and Kaplan, *The Western Maryland Steam Album.* National Railway Historical Society, 1985.

Middleton, William D., *The Interurban Era.* Kalmbach Publishing Co., 1975.

———, *Traction Classics,* Volume 1. Golden West Books, 1983.

———, *Traction Classics,* Volume 2. Golden West Books, 1985.

———, *When the Steam Railroads Electrified.* Kalmbach Publishing Co., 1974.

Morgan, David P., *Steam's Finest Hour*. Kalmbach Publishing Co., 1971.

―――, *The Mohawk that Refused to Abdicate*. Kalmbach Publishing Co., 1975.

Pennypacker, Bert, *Eastern Steam Pictorial: The Anthracite Roads*. D. Carleton Rail Books, 1975.

―――, *Reading Power Pictorial*. D. Carleton Rail Books, 1973.

Pinkepank, Jerry A., *Diesel Spotter's Guide*. Kalmbach Publishing Co., 1968.

―――, *The Second Diesel Spotter's Guide*. Kalmbach Publishing Co., 1973.

Pinkepank and Marre, *Diesel Spotter's Guide UPDATE*. Kalmbach Publishing Co., 1979.

Poor, M.C., *Denver South Park & Pacific, 1st Edition*. World Press, Inc., 1949.

―――, *Denver South Park & Pacific*, Memorial Edition. World Press, Inc., 1976.

Prince, Richard E., *Atlantic Coast Line Railroad*. R.E. Prince, 1966.

―――, *Louisville and Nashville Steam Locomotives*. R.E. Prince, 1968.

―――, *Norfolk & Western Railway*. R.E. Prince, 1980.

―――, *Norfolk Southern*. R.E. Prince, 1972.

―――, *Richmond Washington Line*. R.E. Prince, 1973.

―――, *Southern Railway System*. R.E. Prince, 1970.

Rainey, Kyper, *East Broad Top*. Golden West Books, 1982.

Ranger, Dan, Jr., *Pacific Coast Shay*. Pacific Railroad Publications, 1973.

Ranks and Lowe, *Southern Steam Power*. Barnhart Press, 1966.

Rehor and Horning, *Berkshire Era*. Rehor, 1967.

Reid, H., *The Virginian Railway*. Kalmbach Publishing Co., 1973.

Reigger, H., *The Kettle Valley and Its Railways*. Pacific Fast Mail,.

Roberts, Charles S., *West End*. Barnard, Roberts and Co., 1991.

Rogers Locomotive Company. George G. Peck, 1893.

Rosenberg and Archer, *Norfolk & Western Steam (The Last 25 Years)*. Quadrant Press, Inc., 1973.

Roster of Union Pacific Locomotives, 1867-1964. Barnhart Press, 1964.

Sagle and Staufer, *B&O Power*. Staufer, 1964.

Shaughnessy, Jim, *Delaware & Hudson*. Howell-North Books, 1967.

Shuster, Huddleston, and Staufer, *C&O Power*. Staufer, 1965.

Sinclair, Angus, *Development of the Locomotive Engine*. M.I.T. Press, 1970.

Sloan and Skowronski, *The Rainbow Route*. Sundance Ltd., 1975.

Staufer, Alvin F., *New York Central's Early Power, Vol. I: 1831-1916*. Staufer, 1967.

―――, *New York Central's Early Power, Vol. II: 1831-1916*. Staufer, 1967.

―――, *Pennsy Power*. Staufer, 1962.

―――, *Thoroughbreds*. Staufer, 1974.

Staufer and May, *New York Central Later Power 1910-1968*. Staufer, 1981.

Staufer and Pennypacker, *Pennsy Power II*. Staufer, 1968.

Swanberg, J.W., *New Haven Power 1838-1968*. Staufer, 1988.

Swengel, Frank M., *American Steam Locomotive: Vol. 1 Evolution*. Midwest Rail Publications, 1967.

Taber, T., and Casler, W., *Climax: An Unusual Steam Locomotive*. Railroadians of America, Inc., 1960.

Trostel, Scott D., *The Detroit, Toledo and Ironton Railroad*. Cam-Tech Publishing, 1988.

Turner, Dixon, and Huddleston, *Chessie's Road*. C&O Historical Society, 1986.

Wagner, F. Hol, Jr., *Colorado Road*. National Railway Historical Society, 1970.

Wakefield, Manville, *To the Mountains by Rail*. Wakefair Press, 1970.

Watson and Brown, *Texas & Pacific*. Boston Mills Press, 1978.

Webb, William, *The Southern Railway System*. The Boston Mills Press, 1986.

Westcott, Linn H., *Steam Locomotives, Cyclopedia Volume I*. Kalmbach Publishing Co., 1960.

Westing, F., *The Locomotives that Baldwin Built*. Bonanza Books, 1966.

Westing and Staufer, *Erie Power*. Staufer, 1970.

White, John H., Jr., *Cincinnati Locomotive Builders 1945-1968*. Smithsonian Institution Press, 1965.

―――, *Early American Locomotives*. Dover Publications, 1972.

Wiener, Lionel, *Articulated Locomotives*. Kalmbach Publishing Co., 1970.

Williams, Harold A., *The Western Maryland Railroad Story*. Western Maryland Railway Co., 1952.

Wood, Charles R., *Lines West*. Bonanza Books, 1967.

Wood, Charles and Dorothy, *Milwaukee Road West*. Superior Pub., 1972.

―――, *The Great Northern Railway*. Pacific Fast Mail, 1979.

Worley, E.D., *Iron Horses of the Santa Fe Trail*. Southwest Railroad Historical Society, 1965.

Wright, Richard K., *America's Bicentennial Queen Engine 449*. Wright Enterprises, 1975.

Young, Andrew D., *St. Louis Car Company Album, A Photographic Record*. Interurban Press, 1984.

Index

Page references in **bold** indicate photographs